T0181099

Lecture Notes in Computer Science 13338

Founding Editors

Gerhard Goos
Karlsruhe Institute of Technology, Karlsruhe, Germany

Juris Hartmanis
Cornell University, Ithaca, NY, USA

Editorial Board Members

Elisa Bertino
Purdue University, West Lafayette, IN, USA

Wen Gao
Peking University, Beijing, China

Bernhard Steffen
TU Dortmund University, Dortmund, Germany

Moti Yung
Columbia University, New York, NY, USA

More information about this series at https://link.springer.com/bookseries/558

Xingming Sun · Xiaorui Zhang · Zhihua Xia ·
Elisa Bertino (Eds.)

Artificial Intelligence and Security

8th International Conference, ICAIS 2022
Qinghai, China, July 15–20, 2022
Proceedings, Part I

 Springer

Editors
Xingming Sun (ID)
Nanjing University of Information Science
and Technology
Nanjing, China

Zhihua Xia (ID)
Jinan University
Guangzhou, China

Xiaorui Zhang (ID)
Nanjing University of Information Science
and Technology
Nanjing, China

Elisa Bertino
Purdue University
West Lafayette, IN, USA

ISSN 0302-9743   ISSN 1611-3349 (electronic)
Lecture Notes in Computer Science
ISBN 978-3-031-06793-8   ISBN 978-3-031-06794-5 (eBook)
https://doi.org/10.1007/978-3-031-06794-5

© The Editor(s) (if applicable) and The Author(s), under exclusive license
to Springer Nature Switzerland AG 2022
This work is subject to copyright. All rights are reserved by the Publisher, whether the whole or part of the
material is concerned, specifically the rights of translation, reprinting, reuse of illustrations, recitation,
broadcasting, reproduction on microfilms or in any other physical way, and transmission or information
storage and retrieval, electronic adaptation, computer software, or by similar or dissimilar methodology now
known or hereafter developed.
The use of general descriptive names, registered names, trademarks, service marks, etc. in this publication
does not imply, even in the absence of a specific statement, that such names are exempt from the relevant
protective laws and regulations and therefore free for general use.
The publisher, the authors, and the editors are safe to assume that the advice and information in this book are
believed to be true and accurate at the date of publication. Neither the publisher nor the authors or the editors
give a warranty, expressed or implied, with respect to the material contained herein or for any errors or
omissions that may have been made. The publisher remains neutral with regard to jurisdictional claims in
published maps and institutional affiliations.

This Springer imprint is published by the registered company Springer Nature Switzerland AG
The registered company address is: Gewerbestrasse 11, 6330 Cham, Switzerland

Preface

The 8th International Conference on Artificial Intelligence and Security (ICAIS 2022), formerly called the International Conference on Cloud Computing and Security (ICCCS), was held during July 15–20, 2022, in Qinghai, China. Over the past seven years, ICAIS has become a leading conference for researchers and engineers to share their latest results of research, development, and applications in the fields of artificial intelligence and information security.

We used the Microsoft Conference Management Toolkit (CMT) system to manage the submission and review processes of ICAIS 2022. We received 1124 submissions from authors in 20 countries and regions, including the USA, Canada, the UK, Italy, Ireland, Japan, Russia, France, Australia, South Korea, South Africa, Iraq, Kazakhstan, Indonesia, Vietnam, Ghana, China, Taiwan, Macao, etc. The submissions cover the areas of artificial intelligence, big data, cloud computing and security, information hiding, IoT security, multimedia forensics, encryption and cybersecurity, and so on. We thank our Technical Program Committee (TPC) members and external reviewers for their efforts in reviewing papers and providing valuable comments to the authors. From the total of 1124 submissions, and based on at least three reviews per submission, the Program Chairs decided to accept 166 papers to be published in three LNCS volumes and 168 papers to be published in three CCIS volumes, yielding an acceptance rate of 30%. This volume of the conference proceedings contains all the regular, poster, and workshop papers.

The conference program was enriched by a series of keynote presentations, and the keynote speakers included Q.M. Jonathan Wu and Brij B. Gupta, amongst others. We thank them for their wonderful speeches.

There were 68 workshops organized in ICAIS 2022 which covered all the hot topics in artificial intelligence and security. We would like to take this moment to express our sincere appreciation for the contribution of all the workshop chairs and participants. We would like to extend our sincere thanks to all authors who submitted papers to ICAIS 2022 and to all TPC members. It was a truly great experience to work with such talented and hard-working researchers. We also appreciate the external reviewers for assisting the TPC members in their particular areas of expertise. Moreover, we want to thank our sponsors: ACM, ACM SIGWEB China, the University of Electronic Science and Technology of China, Qinghai Minzu University, Yuchi Blockchain Research Institute, Nanjing Normal University, Northeastern State University, New York University, Michigan State University, the University of Central Arkansas, Dublin City University,

Université Bretagne Sud, the National Nature Science Foundation of China, and Tech Science Press.

April 2022

Xingming Sun
Xiaorui Zhang
Zhihua Xia
Elisa Bertino

Organization

General Chairs

Yun Q. Shi   New Jersey Institute of Technology, USA
Weisheng Ma   Qinghai Minzu University, China
Mauro Barni   University of Siena, Italy
Ping Jiang   Southeast University, China
Elisa Bertino   Purdue University, USA
Xingming Sun   Nanjing University of Information Science and
                              Technology, China

Technical Program Chairs

Aniello Castiglione   University of Salerno, Italy
Yunbiao Guo   China Information Technology Security
                              Evaluation Center, China
Xiaorui Zhang   Engineering Research Center of Digital
                              Forensics, Ministry of Education, China
Q. M. Jonathan Wu   University of Windsor, Canada
Shijie Zhou   University of Electronic Science and Technology
                              of China, China

Publication Chair

Zhihua Xia   Jinan University, China

Publication Vice Chair

Ruohan Meng   Nanjing University of Information Science and
                              Technology, China

Publicity Chair

Zhaoxia Yin   Anhui University, China

Workshop Chairs

Baowei Wang   Nanjing University of Information Science and
                              Technology, China
Lingyun Xiang   Changsha University of Science and Technology,
                              China

Organization Chairs

Genlin Ji   Nanjing Normal University, China
Jianguo Wei   Qinghai Minzu University and Tianjin University,
                              China
Xiaoyu Li   University of Electronic Science and Technology
                              of China, China
Zhangjie Fu   Nanjing University of Information Science and
                              Technology, China
Qilong Sun   Qinghai Minzu University, China

Technical Program Committee

Saeed Arif   University of Algeria, Algeria
Anthony Ayodele   University of Maryland Global Campus, USA
Zhifeng Bao   Royal Melbourne Institute of Technology,
                              Australia
Zhiping Cai   National University of Defense Technology,
                              China
Ning Cao   Qingdao Binhai University, China
Paolina Centonze   Iona College, USA
Chin-chen Chang   Feng Chia University, Taiwan, Republic of China
Han-Chieh Chao   National Dong Hwa University, Taiwan, Republic
                              of China
Bing Chen   Nanjing University of Aeronautics and
                              Astronautics, China
Hanhua Chen   Huazhong University of Science and Technology,
                              China
Xiaofeng Chen   Xidian University, China
Jieren Cheng   Hainan University, China
Lianhua Chi   IBM Research Center, Australia
Kim-Kwang Raymond Choo   University of Texas at San Antonio, USA
Ilyong Chung   Chosun University, South Korea
Martin Collier   Dublin City University, Ireland
Robert H. Deng   Singapore Management University, Singapore
Jintai Ding   University of Cincinnati, USA
Xinwen Fu   University of Central Florida, USA

Zhangjie Fu	Nanjing University of Information Science and Technology, China
Moncef Gabbouj	Tampere University of Technology, Finland
Ruili Geng	Spectral MD, USA
Song Guo	Hong Kong Polytechnic University, Hong Kong, China
Mohammad Mehedi Hassan	King Saud University, Saudi Arabia
Russell Higgs	University College Dublin, Ireland
Dinh Thai Hoang	University of Technology Sydney, Australia
Wien Hong	Nanfang College of Sun Yat-Sen University, China
Chih-Hsien Hsia	National Ilan University, Taiwan, Republic of China
Robert Hsu	Chung Hua University, Taiwan, Republic of China
Xinyi Huang	Fujian Normal University, China
Yongfeng Huang	Tsinghua University, China
Zhiqiu Huang	Nanjing University of Aeronautics and Astronautics, China
Patrick C. K. Hung	University of Ontario Institute of Technology, Canada
Farookh Hussain	University of Technology Sydney, Australia
Genlin Ji	Nanjing Normal University, China
Hai Jin	Huazhong University of Science and Technology, China
Sam Tak Wu Kwong	City University of Hong Kong, China
Chin-Feng Lai	Taiwan Cheng Kung University, Taiwan, Republic of China
Loukas Lazos	University of Arizona, USA
Sungyoung Lee	Kyung Hee University, South Korea
Hang Lei	University of Electronic Science and Technology of China, China
Chengcheng Li	University of Cincinnati, USA
Xiaoyu Li	University of Electronic Science and Technology of China, China
Feifei Li	Utah State University, USA
Jin Li	Guangzhou University, China
Jing Li	Rutgers University, USA
Kuan-Ching Li	Providence University, Taiwan, Republic of China
Peng Li	University of Aizu, Japan
Yangming Li	University of Washington, USA
Luming Liang	Uber Technology, USA
Haixiang Lin	Leiden University, The Netherlands

Xiaodong Lin	University of Ontario Institute of Technology, Canada
Zhenyi Lin	Verizon Wireless, USA
Alex Liu	Michigan State University, USA
Guangchi Liu	Stratifyd Inc., USA
Guohua Liu	Donghua University, China
Joseph Liu	Monash University, Australia
Quansheng Liu	University of South Brittany, France
Xiaodong Liu	Edinburgh Napier University, UK
Yuling Liu	Hunan University, China
Zhe Liu	Nanjing University of Aeronautics and Astronautics, China
Daniel Xiapu Luo	Hong Kong Polytechnic University, Hong Kong, China
Xiangyang Luo	Zhengzhou Science and Technology Institute, China
Tom Masino	TradeWeb LLC, USA
Nasir Memon	New York University, USA
Noel Murphy	Dublin City University, Ireland
Sangman Moh	Chosun University, South Korea
Yi Mu	University of Wollongong, Australia
Elie Naufal	Applied Deep Learning LLC, USA
Jiangqun Ni	Sun Yat-sen University, China
Rafal Niemiec	University of Information Technology and Management, Poland
Zemin Ning	Wellcome Trust Sanger Institute, UK
Shaozhang Niu	Beijing University of Posts and Telecommunications, China
Srikant Ojha	Sharda University, India
Jeff Z. Pan	University of Aberdeen, UK
Wei Pang	University of Aberdeen, UK
Chen Qian	University of California, Santa Cruz, USA
Zhenxing Qian	Fudan University, China
Chuan Qin	University of Shanghai for Science and Technology, China
Jiaohua Qin	Central South University of Forestry and Technology, China
Yanzhen Qu	Colorado Technical University, USA
Zhiguo Qu	Nanjing University of Information Science and Technology, China
Yongjun Ren	Nanjing University of Information Science and Technology, China
Arun Kumar Sangaiah	VIT University, India

Di Shang	Long Island University, USA
Victor S. Sheng	Texas Tech University, USA
Zheng-guo Sheng	University of Sussex, UK
Robert Simon Sherratt	University of Reading, UK
Yun Q. Shi	New Jersey Institute of Technology, USA
Frank Y. Shih	New Jersey Institute of Technology, USA
Guang Sun	Hunan University of Finance and Economics, China
Jianguo Sun	Harbin University of Engineering, China
Krzysztof Szczypiorski	Warsaw University of Technology, Poland
Tsuyoshi Takagi	Kyushu University, Japan
Shanyu Tang	University of West London, UK
Jing Tian	National University of Singapore, Singapore
Yoshito Tobe	Aoyang University, Japan
Cezhong Tong	Washington University in St. Louis, USA
Pengjun Wan	Illinois Institute of Technology, USA
Cai-Zhuang Wang	Ames Laboratory, USA
Ding Wang	Peking University, China
Guiling Wang	New Jersey Institute of Technology, USA
Honggang Wang	University of Massachusetts-Dartmouth, USA
Jian Wang	Nanjing University of Aeronautics and Astronautics, China
Jie Wang	University of Massachusetts Lowell, USA
Jin Wang	Changsha University of Science and Technology, China
Liangmin Wang	Jiangsu University, China
Ruili Wang	Massey University, New Zealand
Xiaojun Wang	Dublin City University, Ireland
Xiaokang Wang	St. Francis Xavier University, Canada
Zhaoxia Wang	Singapore Management University, Singapore
Jianguo Wei	Qinghai Minzu University and Tianjin University, China
Sheng Wen	Swinburne University of Technology, Australia
Jian Weng	Jinan University, China
Edward Wong	New York University, USA
Eric Wong	University of Texas at Dallas, USA
Shaoen Wu	Ball State University, USA
Shuangkui Xia	Beijing Institute of Electronics Technology and Application, China
Lingyun Xiang	Changsha University of Science and Technology, China
Yang Xiang	Deakin University, Australia

Yang Xiao	The University of Alabama, USA
Haoran Xie	The Education University of Hong Kong, China
Naixue Xiong	Northeastern State University, USA
Wei Qi Yan	Auckland University of Technology, New Zealand
Aimin Yang	Guangdong University of Technology, China
Ching-Nung Yang	National Dong Hwa University, Taiwan, Republic of China
Chunfang Yang	Zhengzhou Science and Technology Institute, China
Fan Yang	University of Maryland, USA
Guomin Yang	University of Wollongong, Australia
Qing Yang	University of North Texas, USA
Yimin Yang	Lakehead University, Canada
Ming Yin	Purdue University, USA
Shaodi You	Australian National University, Australia
Kun-Ming Yu	Chung Hua University, Taiwan, Republic of China
Shibin Zhang	Chengdu University of Information Technology, China
Weiming Zhang	University of Science and Technology of China, China
Xinpeng Zhang	Fudan University, China
Yan Zhang	Simula Research Laboratory, Norway
Yanchun Zhang	Victoria University, Australia
Yao Zhao	Beijing Jiaotong University, China
Desheng Zheng	Southwest Petroleum University, China
Qi Cui	Nanjing University of Information Science and Technology, China

Organization Committee

Tao Ye	Qinghai Minzu University, China
Xianyi Chen	Nanjing University of Information Science and Technology, China
Zilong Jin	Nanjing University of Information Science and Technology, China
Yiwei Li	Columbia University, USA
Yuling Liu	Hunan University, China
Zhiguo Qu	Nanjing University of Information Science and Technology, China
Huiyu Sun	New York University, USA
Le Sun	Nanjing University of Information Science and Technology, China
Jian Su	Nanjing University of Information Science and Technology, China

Qing Tian	Nanjing University of Information Science and Technology, China
Qi Wang	Nanjing University of Information Science and Technology, China
Lingyun Xiang	Changsha University of Science and Technology, China
Zhihua Xia	Nanjing University of Information Science and Technology, China
Lizhi Xiong	Nanjing University of Information Science and Technology, China
Leiming Yan	Nanjing University of Information Science and Technology, China
Li Yu	Nanjing University of Information Science and Technology, China
Zhili Zhou	Nanjing University of Information Science and Technology, China
Qi Cui	Nanjing University of Information Science and Technology, China

Contents – Part I

xx   Contents – Part I

Contents – Part II

Big Data

Cloud Computing and Security

Multimedia Forensics

Contents – Part III

Information Hiding

IoT Security

Artificial Intelligence

DDG-Based Optimization Metrics for Defect Prediction

Yong Chen[1(✉)], Chao Xu[1], Jing Selena He[2], Sheng Xiao[3], and Fanfan Shen[1]

[1] School of Information Engineering, Nanjing Audit University, Nanjing 211815, China
chenyong@nau.edu.cn
[2] Department of Computer Science, Kennesaw State University, Kennesaw 30144-5588, USA
[3] Information Science and Engineering Department, Hunan First Normal University, Changsha 410205, China

Abstract. Software defect prediction helps improve software quality and allocate software test resources reasonably. Many defect prediction models based on software metrics have been proposed. However, the existing software metrics are mainly focused on structure information of source code, and the semantic information is lacking. Compilation optimization is the result of deep analysis of program semantics, and intuitively we believe that it should reflect the semantic information of the program in some ways to help defect prediction. Based on the optimization options widely used in the current compiler, this paper extracts 40 compilation optimization metrics based on DDG of program, and proposes seven types of metrics models that designed by different metrics sets. The relationship between compilation optimization metrics and software defect predictions was evaluated by 10 commonly used classifiers. Experimental results show: a) Compilation optimization metrics have a significant impact on the recall rate of software defect prediction. b) Static code metrics combined with compilation optimization metrics can improve the performance of software defect prediction in most classifiers. c) Code size optimization metrics and performance optimization metrics have their characteristics, combined both of them can get better performance in software defect prediction.

Keywords: Compilation optimization · DDG · Software metrics · Software defect prediction

1 Introduction

In all aspects of people's lives, the proportion of software is increasing, and the problems caused by software defects are becoming more and more serious. However, with the improvement of software scale and complexity, it is more and more difficult to detect software defects. Substantial researches have gone into developing predictive models and tools which help software engineers and testers to quickly narrow down the most likely defective parts of a software code [1–4].

© The Author(s), under exclusive license to Springer Nature Switzerland AG 2022
X. Sun et al. (Eds.): ICAIS 2022, LNCS 13338, pp. 3–16, 2022.
https://doi.org/10.1007/978-3-031-06794-5_1

Defect prediction models often derive a number of metrics and feed into statistical or machine learning classifiers. Substantial researches are based on source code level features such as Halstead features based on the number of operators and operands, McCabe features based on dependencies, CK features for object-oriented programs, etc. However, those features are the shallow representation of the program in source code level. And the deep syntax information of the program is lack. To acquire the semantic information of program to assist software defect prediction, many researchers use deep learning technology to automatically extract software semantic features based on the Abstract Syntax Tree (AST) of source code [5–8]. However, defect characteristics are deeply hidden in programs' semantics and they only cause unexpected output in specific conditions [9]. Meanwhile, ASTs do not show the execution process of programs; instead, they simply represent the abstract syntactic structure of source code.

Compiler is an important tool for program transformation, and it is also the most thorough system for program grammar and semantics analysis. Many defects of program semantics are notified to users by compiling warnings, such as "warning: unused variable x", "warning: variable x is used uninitialized whenever *if* condition is false", et al. However, the compiler does not prevent users from writing redundant and invalid code, because it can be removed by compilation optimization. Compilation optimization is an important part of compiler, which is based on program semantics analysis. As we all know, if a program has more redundant code, its quality will be worse. Therefore, in some situation, software defect is more sensitive in compilation optimization. For example, Fig. 1 shows two code snippets for time delay function that is often used in the embedded system.

```
1 void delay10()          1 void delay10()
2 {                       2 {
3       int i;            3       volatile int i;
4       for(i=0;i<10;i++); 4       for(i=0;i<10;i++);
5 }                       5 }

    (a) buggy code              (b) clean code
```

Fig. 1. Motivation example

In the example, both code snippets define a function of "*delay10*" that is to take up 10 integers add cycles by loops. It is often used in embedded system to satisfy the timing constraints. The only difference of both is that the type definition of the variable "*i*". In the left code, the type of "*i*" is modified with "volatile" to indicate that the variable needs to be read from the memory every time it is used to plays a role of delay, but the right code does not which will be seen as the buggy. However, the defect cannot be detected not only in the traditional model, but also in the ASTs based model. Because the number of lines, operators, operands and even the ASTs of the right code are the same as those of the left code. But from the perspective of redundant code, the variable "*i*" is a local self-increasing variable with no other side effect. Without the "volatile", the code associated with it can be seen as the redundant code and will be deleted by compilation optimization, which make the "*delay10*" function become empty and the defect was revealed.

Therefore, we think that if the features related to compilation optimization are added, the software defects will be better predicted. In this paper, we proposed the Data Dependency Graph (DDG) based optimization metrics to investigate the relationship between compilation optimization options and software defect. Firstly, we propose a set of DDG-based optimization metrics, that is derived of different optimization option of compiler, such as "O0" for no optimization, "O2" for general optimization, "Os" for code size optimization, et al. Within a compiler, the source code is usually converted to the intermediate representation (IR) of the compiler. IR is the normalized representation of source code semantics, and compilation optimization is usually performed on it. Therefore, for acquiring the direct and normalized information of the optimization feature, the DDG is constructed over the compiler IR. Specifically, LLVM is used as our experimental compiler and LLVM IR were used to measure the compilation optimization metrics. Then, to measure our proposed optimization metrics, two open source projects from GitHub is analyzed and the file-level defect flag of them is extracted by manual according to the committing lists. Finally, based on the two open source projects, we empirically evaluate the relationship between defect prediction and compilation optimization metrics by 10 commonly used classifiers with different metrics combinations.

The main contributions of this paper are as following:

- Based on compilation optimization, 40 new software defect metrics are construct-ed. The new metrics can enhance the ability of software defect prediction at the semantic level.
- Seven metrics models are constructed from seven aspects: pure static code metrics (CM), pure compilation optimization metrics (GAM), pure performance optimiza-tion metrics (GO12M), pure code size optimization metrics (GOsM), mixed static code metrics and compilation optimization metrics (CGAM), mixed static code metrics and performance optimization metrics (CGO12M), mixed static code met-rics and code size optimization metrics (CGOsM). And 10 different commonly used classifiers were used to evaluate their influence on software defect prediction.
- Experiments show that the quality of software defect prediction can be improved in many classifiers by combining the 40 new compilation optimization metrics proposed by this paper, especially in recall rate.

The outline of this paper is as follows. In the next section, we briefly introduce the related work. Section 3 describes our proposed Compilation Optimization Metrics, and the experimental are setup and evaluated in Sect. 4. We conclude the paper and highlights future directions in Sect. 5.

2 Related Work

Defect prediction metrics provide objective, reproducible and quantifiable measurements about a software product, and researches have studied it for a long time. Daskalantonakis categorize software metrics based on their intended use as product, process and project metrics [10]. Zhou Yuming et al. [11] conducted an in-depth analysis of the correlation between metrics based on object-oriented programs and program module defects. Fur-thermore, they found that class size metrics have potential mixed effects in analysis and will influence the performance of defect prediction model [12–14]. Therefore, they proposed a method based on linear regression to try to remove this mixed effect. Finally, they conducted an in-depth analysis of the correlation between the package-modularization metrics proposed by Sarkar et al. [15] and the cohesive metrics based on program slices and program module defects [16]. Jiang et al. [17] measure software defects based on the number of developers that touched a code unit, the experience of the developer, and interaction and cognitive behaviors of developers.

Recently, with the rapid development of deep learning technology and the increasing demand for semantic-based software defect prediction, many researchers explore the application of deep learning methods in software defect prediction. They use deep learning technology to automatically extract the semantic features of programs for building the defect prediction model. Wang et al. [5] leveraged DBN for software defect prediction. They used selected AST sequences taken from source code as input to the DBN model, which generate new expressive features, and used machine learning models for classification. Li et al. [6] proposed a CNN based defect prediction model, which leveraged word embedding and a CNN model for defect prediction. Their experimental results show that the defect prediction performance of the CNN model is better than [5]. Zain et al. [7] proposed the 1D-CNN, a deep learning architecture to extract useful knowledge, for identifying and modelling the knowledge in the data sequence, reducing overfitting, and finally, predicting whether the units of code are defects prone. There is also research on deep defect prediction targeting assembly code [8]. It leveraged a CNN model to learn from assembly instructions.

3   Compilation Optimization Metrics

In this section, we will explain the compilation optimization metrics that were developed for the purpose of our study.

For the most popular compilers (such as GCC, LLVM, etc.), they have a lot of optimization options for different optimization goals. But for ease of use, the compiler usually encapsulates multiple optimization options with similar goals into a simple one (such as O2, Os, etc.). Since our paper explores the impact of different compiler optimizations on software defect prediction, the Compilation Optimization Metrics are built primarily based on these simplified optimization options. Specifically, different compilation optimization options will produce different optimization codes. In order to analyze the impact of different compilation optimization options on the code, we build the data dependency graph (DDG) of the program based on LLVM IR.

A DDG of program is a directed graph, $G = (V, E)$ where v is the set of vertices $\{v_1, v_2 \ldots v_n\}$ and E is the set of directed edges $\{\langle v_i, v_j \rangle, \langle v_k, v_l \rangle \ldots\}$. However, in the DDG, each vertex rsepresents an IR, and the directed edges show the data dependencies. If IR v_i must execute before IR v_j, there is one directed edge from v_i to v_j.

In order to better extract program structure and semantic information, we divide DDG nodes into three categories according to the IR instructions. One is the control node, such as "br", "b", "call", "cmp", etc. One is computing nodes, such as "add", "sub", "mul", etc. The third type is memory operation nodes including "load" and "store". Accordingly, we construct 9 types of edges to represent the relationship between different types of nodes.

Based on the DDG of the program, we extracted the following metrics (shown in Table 1) as the compilation optimization metrics, which contain 48 metrics. In the table, the "i" and "j" represent one of above three DDG type.

Table 1. Compilation optimization metrics list.

Metrics name	Definition
$Node_i$	The number of nodes with type i under optimization option '-$O0$'
$Edge_{i,j}$	The number of edges from node with type i to node with type j under optimization option '-$O0$'
$O1\_Nodechange_i$	The increased number of nodes with type i under optimization option '-$O1$' compared to the optimization option '-$O0$'
$O1\_Edgechange_{i,j}$	The increased number of edges from node with type i to node with type j under optimization option '-$O1$' compared to the optimization option '-$O0$'
$O2\_Nodechange_i$	The increased number of nodes with type i under optimization option '-$O2$' compared to the optimization option '-$O0$'
$O2\_Edgechange_{i,j}$	The increased number of edges from node with type i to node with type j under optimization option '-$O2$' compared to the optimization option '-$O0$'
$Os\_Nodechange_i$	The increased number of nodes with type i under optimization option '-Os' compared to the optimization option '-$O0$'
$Os\_Edgechange_{i,j}$	The increased number of edges from node with type i to node with type j under optimization option '-Os' compared to the optimization option '-$O0$'

4 Dataset and Experimental Setup

4.1 Dataset

In our experiments, we use Tesseract-OCR and bitcoin project as our study datasets.

- Bitcoin is an experimental digital currency that enables instant payments to anyone, anywhere in the world. Bitcoin uses peer-to-peer technology to operate with no central authority: managing transactions and issuing money are carried out collectively by the network. It is known as the first implementation of the blockchain.
- Tesseract-OCR is a free and open source OCR engine for image recognition. By 1995, it had become one of the three most accurate recognition engines in the OCR industry. It can read images in various formats and convert them into text in more than 60 languages.

To collect the defects of the datasets, we use the git command to get the right version source code of the two projects. Then, the shell command shown in Fig. 2 is executed, and the fixing information are acquired by time. Finally, we manually flag the defect files combined with the issue information and fixing information in GitHub. The defect information of the two projects is shown in Table 2.

```
for f in $(find ~/benchmark/<PROJECTNAME> -maxdepth 3 -name "*.[cpp|c]" ) ; do
    echo -n $f >> ../fixNum.txt
    echo -n ":" >> ../fixNum.txt
    git log --grep='[F|f][i|I][X|x]' --after="<ReleaseTime>"
        --pretty=oneline $f|sed -n '$=' >>../fixNum.txt
    echo "" >>../fixNum.txt
done
```

Fig. 2. Shell command for extracting fixing information in GitHub.

Table 2. Summary of the datasets used in the experiments.

Project	Release version	Release time	Clean	Buggy
Bitcoin	v0.16.0	2018.2.23	172	74
Tesseract-ocr	3.05.00	2017.2.17	121	112

4.2 Metrics Models

To Evaluate the Relationship Between Optimization Metrics and Defect Prediction, Our Experiments Evaluate Seven Types of Metrics Models as Following.

- **CM:** it includes the static code metrics from the SourceMonitor, which is shown in Table 3. It is baseline of our experiments;
- **GAM:** it includes all of our proposed compilation optimization metrics, which evaluates the influence of the all compilation optimization to defect prediction;
- **GO12M:** it includes the metrics of Nodei, Edgei,j, O1_Nodechangei, O1_Edgechangei,j, O2_Nodechangei, O2_Edgechangei,j, refer to the performance optimization. It evaluates the influence of the performance optimization to defect prediction;
- **GOsM:** it includes the metrics of Nodei, Edgei,j, Os_Nodechangei, Os_Edgechangei,j, which refer to the code size optimization. It evaluates the influence of the code size optimization to defect prediction;
- **CGO12M:** it includes metrics both in CM and GO12M, which evaluates whether the performance optimization metrics can improve the performance of code static metrics in defect prediction;
- **CGOsM:** it includes metrics both in CM and GOsM, which evaluates whether the code size optimization metrics can improve the performance of code static metrics in defect prediction;
- **CGM:** it includes metrics both in CM and GAM, which evaluates whether the compilation optimization metrics can improve the performance of code static metrics in defect prediction.

Table 3. Static code metrics by SourceMonitor.

Metrics name	Definition
Lines	The number of lines in whole file
Statements	The code lines of executable code for a module (not blank or comment)
%Branch	The percent branch statement
%Comments	The percent lines with comments
ClassesDefs	The number of classed defined
Methods/Class	Average methods implemented per Class
Avg Stmts/Method	Average statements per Method
Max Complexity	Line number of most complex method
Max Depth	Line number of deepest block
Avg Depth	Average block depth
Avg Complexity	Average complexity
Functions	The number of functions

4.3 Performance Metrics

To evaluate the performance of our approach, we computed Precision, Recall, and F-measure. These metrics are widely used in machine learning and data mining to assess the effectiveness of classification algorithms. We estimated the values of Precision, Recall, and F-measure based on four statistics: True Positives *(TP)*, False Positives *(FP)*, False Negatives *(FN)*, True Negatives *(TN)*. Their definitions are as follows: if a file is classified as defective when it is truly defective, the classification is a *TP*. If the file is classified as defective when it is actually clean, then the classification is a *FP*. If the file is classified as clean when it is in fact defective, then the classification is a *FN*. Finally, if the issue is classified as clean and it is in fact clean, then the classification is *TN*.

We use the above statistics to estimate Precision, Recall, and F1 score by Eq. (1), Eq. (2) and Eq. (3), respectively.

$$precision = \frac{TP}{TP + FP} \qquad (1)$$

$$Recall = \frac{TP}{TP + FN} \qquad (2)$$

$$F_1 = \frac{2*Precision*Recall}{Precision + Recall} \qquad (3)$$

In order to better evaluate the impact of different compilation optimization options on software defect prediction, we use the relative improvement rate to CM as the actual evaluation value, which are calculated by Eq. (4). In Eq. (4), mtr represents one of the three metrics above, mod presents one of the 7 metrics models in this paper. V_{mtr}^{mod} represents the mtr performance value on the mod metrics model. And Ipr_{mtr}^{mod} represents the improvement rate by the mtr performance metric on the mod metrics model.

$$Ipr_{mtr}^{mod} = \frac{V_{mtr}^{mod} - V_{mtr}^{CM}}{V_{mtr}^{CM}} \tag{4}$$

4.4 Experimental Methodology

In the experimental, we compare the performance of the purely metrics (which contain only 12 static code metrics) and hybrid metrics (which combined 12 source code metrics with our proposed 9 optimization metrics). The classifiers used in this study are selected for their common use in the software engineering defect prediction literature, which is shown in Table 4. These classifiers are using the default settings as specified in Weka. All classifications are carried out on the Weka experimenter with ten-fold cross-validation, which is a standard way of estimating the accuracy of a prediction engine in data mining. The outline of the experimental flow is shown in Fig. 3.

Table 4. Classifiers used in the study.

Name in Weka	Description
BayesNet	Bayes Network classifier
NaiveBayes	Naive Bayes classifier using estimator classes
NaiveBayesUpdateable	An updateable multinomial Naive Bayes classifier
MultilayerPerceptron	A classifier that uses backpropagation to learn a multi-layer perceptron to classify instances
IBk	K-nearest neighbor classifier
KStar	K* is an instance-based classifier, that is the class of a test instance is based upon the class of those training instances similar to it, as determined by some similarity function
AdaBoostM1	Boosting a nominal class classifier using the Adaboost M1 method
J48	A classifier based on a pruned or unpruned C4.5 decision tree
RandomForest	A classifier based on a forest of random trees
RandomTree	A classifier based on a tree that considers K randomly chosen attributes at each node

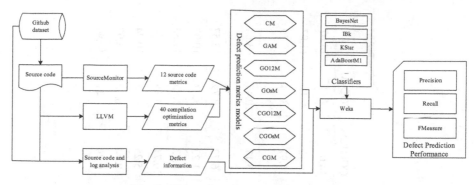

Fig. 3. The outline of the experimental flow.

4.5 Results and Analysis

Table 5 and Table 6 show the Recall improvement and Precision improvement on the two projects of dataset by the Eq. (4), respectively. They are evaluated by 10 different classifiers with default setting in Weka. All values are average values for each single 10-fold cross-validation. We repeated 10-fold cross-validation 10 times to make sure that results are not biased by the data distribution of one specific 10-fold cross-validation.

Table 5 shows that for all classifiers, the recall rate of all other six compilation optimization added metrics modes are better than that of CM model. Comparing GO12M, GOsM and GAM, we can see that GO12M and GOsM have their own characteristics for different classifies. For example, by the NaiveBayesUpdateable classifier, GO12M get the highest improvement rate and GOsM get the lowest value. But by the Multi-layerPerceptron classifier, the situation is just the opposite. On average, GAM which combined GO12M and GOsM get the better results. It achieves 11.95% to Tesseract-OCR and 9.16% to Bitcoin. by Comparing the metrics models with CM metrics and no CM metrics, we can see that the recall rate has not been greatly improved by CM metrics added. Some classifies, such as BayesNet, get no better results. These show that compiler optimization metrics plays an important role in finding more software defects.

In the prediction precision, it can be seen from Table 6 that, without the source code static metrics, GO12M, GOsM and GAM get a lower precision for some classifies. Furthermore, in RandomForest, all six metrics models are not better than CM in precision evaluation. From the previous motivation example, we can see that the addition of optimization factors is mainly to help us find more defects. In fact, we have not found a very intuitive example to improve the precision of defect detection. However, combined with the source code static metrics, the compilation optimization metrics all get better precision performance. The average improvement of CGAM also achieved 5.91% to Tesseract-OCR and 6.39% to Bitcoin. Therefore, to obtain the higher prediction precision, we recommend combining static code features when using compilation optimization metrics.

In order to comprehensively evaluate the impact of compilation optimization options on software defect prediction, we further evaluated the improvement rate of F1 scores. Figure 4 and Fig. 5 show the improvement by F1 score on the two projects of dataset. They are evaluated by the Eq. with mtr = F1.

Table 5. Recall improvement to CM by Different Models.

Models	Tesseract-OCR (%)						Bitcoin (%)					
	GO12M	GOsM	GAM	CGO12M	CGOsM	CGAM	GO12M	GOsM	GAM	CGO12M	CGOsM	CGAM
BayesNet	2.08	2.08	3.80	2.08	2.08	3.80	14.07	4.61	14.07	14.07	4.61	14.07
NaiveBayes	11.60	8.84	13.24	12.98	8.84	22.74	9.12	9.12	9.12	9.12	9.12	11.07
NaiveBayes Updateable	24.10	10.44	17.07	24.10	16.56	20.02	16.97	3.34	10.79	16.97	3.34	10.79
Multilayer Perceptron	0.83	5.83	1.92	3.29	5.83	10.20	3.17	10.45	3.64	3.17	10.45	3.64
IBk	6.13	12.49	18.92	6.13	14.35	20.79	5.32	9.79	13.57	6.72	9.79	13.57
KStar	12.68	19.97	14.27	14.24	19.97	19.78	1.23	7.32	10.33	1.23	7.32	10.33
AdaBoostM1	21.61	13.96	21.61	21.61	16.51	21.61	7.73	11.85	11.33	7.73	11.85	11.33
J48	10.89	12.52	12.52	12.41	12.52	12.98	10.71	4.35	4.52	10.71	4.35	9.54
RandomForest	2.77	7.85	7.86	4.56	7.85	7.86	1.67	6.92	4.77	5.25	6.92	10.74
RandomTree	4.72	7.61	8.29	6.25	7.61	8.29	11.10	4.64	9.45	9.94	6.30	13.92
Average	**9.74**	**10.16**	**11.95**	**10.76**	**11.21**	**14.81**	**8.11**	**7.24**	**9.16**	**8.49**	**7.41**	**10.90**

Table 6. Precision improvement to CM by Different Models.

Models	Tesseract-OCR (%)						Bitcoin (%)					
	GO12M	GOsM	GAM	CGO12M	CGOsM	CGAM	GO12M	GOsM	GAM	CGO12M	CGOsM	CGAM
BayesNet	6.81	1.18	6.81	7.95	1.64	8.17	1.73	0.00	2.15	2.40	1.07	4.63
NaiveBayes	0.76	-4.08	1.53	2.02	-3.01	3.23	3.24	-2.49	4.47	4.42	-1.61	5.44
NaiveBayes Updateable	0.76	-6.99	1.53	1.62	-6.62	2.94	0.98	0.98	2.95	1.02	1.79	17.44
Multilayer Perceptron	1.66	4.10	6.83	2.24	5.64	8.24	2.95	0.00	4.96	4.51	1.30	8.76
IBk	0.00	7.00	9.01	1.80	7.29	10.99	1.36	2.57	3.93	1.92	3.16	3.98
KStar	-6.90	6.75	16.69	-5.35	8.16	16.88	0.00	9.17	9.17	1.38	9.75	11.02
AdaBoostM1	-3.48	-9.07	-3.48	1.18	-0.11	1.19	2.49	-2.49	-0.26	3.71	-1.63	5.19
J48	0.25	-9.66	0.32	1.10	0.01	1.70	0.17	-3.71	3.26	1.18	-3.48	3.90
RandomForest	-4.49	-4.35	-3.17	-3.75	-2.88	-1.51	-1.39	-2.65	-0.60	-0.14	-2.63	2.07
RandomTree	4.13	-4.33	5.87	4.94	-2.69	7.25	0.00	-2.96	0.08	0.23	-2.83	1.48
Average	-0.05	-1.94	4.19	1.38	0.74	5.91	1.15	-0.16	3.01	2.06	0.49	6.39

From the Fig. 4 and Fig. 5, we can see that the F1 score of GAM is better than CM for all classifiers on the dataset. For most classifiers, GO12M and GOsM can also get better F1 score than CN. The results show that the compilation optimization metrics can get better defect features than the traditional metrics. However, GO12M and GOsM are biased towards some classifiers. In Bayes-based classifiers and J48 classifier, GO12M can obtain better F1 score, even higher than GAM, such as NaiveBayesUpdateable and J48. But for the KStar and RandomForest classifiers, the F1 score of GO12M is low. On the contrary, GOsM has relatively smaller F1 score in Bayes-based classifier and J48 classifier, but can obtain higher F1 score in KStar and RandomForest classifiers. In addition, for most classifiers, the F1 scores of GO12M and GOsM are lower than GAM. Therefore, GO12M and GOsM have complementary roles. When using multiple classifiers for ensemble machine learning methods, the GAM is recommended.

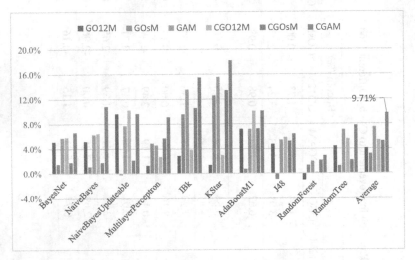

Fig. 4. F1 score improvements to CM in tesseract-OCR.

By comparing CGO12M with GO12M, CGOsM with GOsM, and CGAM with GAM, we find that after combining CM metrics, compilation optimization metrics can get better software defect prediction performance. On average, CGAM can achieve 9.10% performance improvement compared with CM, including 9.71% for tesseract-OCR project and 8.48% for Bitcoin project.

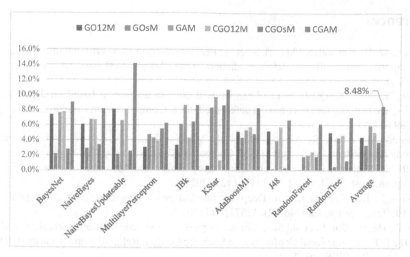

Fig. 5. F1 score improvements to CM in Bitcoin.

5 Conclusion

In this paper, in order to explore the relationship between compilation optimization and software defect prediction, first we propose a set of software defect metrics based on compilation optimization, which is measured by DDG-based IR of compiler. Then, we construct seven kinds of metrics models based on different combination of metrics, and use 10 common classifiers to measure the relationship between each metrics models and software defect prediction. From the experimental results, we can see that:

- Compilation optimization metrics is a better choice to express the software defects features. Static code metrics combined with compilation optimization metrics can improve the performance of software defect prediction.
- Compilation optimization metrics have a significant impact on the recall rate of software defect prediction. For most classifiers, compilation optimization metrics can significantly improve the recall rate of software defect prediction.
- Code size optimization metrics and performance optimization metrics have their own characteristics, we can combine both of them to get better performance in software defect prediction.

Acknowledgement. This work was supported by the Universities Natural Science Research Project of Jiangsu Province under Grant 20KJB520026; the Foundation for Young Teachers of Nanjing Auditing University under Grant 19QNPY018; the National Nature Science Foundation of China under Grant 71972102 and 61902189.

References

1. Mumtaz, B., Kanwal, S., Alamri, S., et al.: Feature selection using artificial immune network: an approach for software defect prediction. Intell. Autom. Soft Comput. **29**(3), 669–684 (2021)
2. Sun, Y., Sun, Y., Qi, J., et al.: Unsupervised domain adaptation based on discriminative subspace learning for cross-project defect prediction. Comput. Mater. Continua. **68**(3), 3373–3389 (2021)
3. Daoud, M., Aftab, S., Ahmad, M., et al.: Machine learning empowered software defect prediction system. Intell. Autom. Soft Comput. **31**(2), 1287–1300 (2022)
4. Albahli, S., Nabi, G.: Defect prediction using akaike and bayesian information criterion. Comput. Syst. Sci. Eng. **41**(3), 1117–1127 (2022)
5. Wang, S., Liu, T., Nam, J., et al.: Deep semantic feature learning for software defect prediction. IEEE Trans. Softw. Eng. **46**(12), 1267–1293 (2020)
6. Li, J., He, P., Zhu, J., et al.: Software defect prediction via convolutional neural network. In: 2017 IEEE International Conference on Software Quality, Reliability and Security (QRS-C), pp. 318–328. IEEE (2017)
7. Zain, Z., Sakri, S., Halimatul, N., et al.: Software defect prediction harnessing on multi 1-dimensional convolutional neural network structure. Comput. Mater. Continua. **71**(1), 1521–1546 (2022)
8. Phan, A., Nguyen, M., Bui, L.: Convolutional neural networks over control flow graphs for software defect prediction. In: IEEE 29th International Conference on Tools with Artificial Intelligence (ICTAI), Boston, MA, USA, pp. 45–52 (2017)
9. Martin, W., Christopher, V., Mario, L.: Toward deep learning software repositories. In: Mining Software Repositories (MSR), Florence, Italy, pp. 334–345 (2015)
10. Daskalantonakis, M.: A practical view of software measurement and implementation experiences within motorola. IEEE Trans. Softw. Eng. **18**(11), 998–1010 (1992)
11. Zhou, Y., Xu, B., Leung, H.: On the ability of complexity metrics to predict fault-prone classes in object-oriented systems. J. Syst. Softw. **83**(4), 660–674 (2010)
12. Zhou, Y., Leung, H., Leung, K., et al.: Examining the potentially confounding effect of class size on the associations between object-oriented metrics and change-proneness. IEEE Trans. Softw. Eng. **35**(5), 607–623 (2009)
13. Zhou, Y., Xu, B., Leung, H., et al.: An in-depth study of the potentially confounding effect of class size in fault prediction. ACM Trans. Softw. Eng. Methodol. **23**(1), 1–51 (2014)
14. Zhao, Y., Yang, Y., Lu, H., et al.: An empirical analysis of package-modularization metrics: Implications for software fault-proneness. Inf. Softw. Technol. **57**(1), 186–203 (2015)
15. Santonu, S., Avinash, C., Girish, M.: Metrics for measuring the quality of modularization of large-scale object-oriented software. IEEE Trans. Softw. Eng. **34**(5), 700–720 (2008)
16. Yang, Y., Zhou, Y., Lu, H., et al.: Are slice-based cohesion metrics actually useful in effort-aware post-release fault-proneness prediction? an empirical study. IEEE Trans. Softw. Eng. **41**(4), 331–357 (2015)
17. Eken, B.: Assessing personalized software defect predictors. In: IEEE/ACM 40th International Conference on Software Engineering: Companion (ICSE-Companion), Gothenburg, Sweden, pp. 488–491. IEEE (2018)

Link Prediction Based on Sampled Single Vertices

Wenxin Jiang[1], Bolun Chen[1,2]([✉]), Zifan Qi[1], and Yongtao Yu[1]

[1] College of Computer Engineering, Huaiyin Institute of Technology, Huaian 223003, China
chenbolun1986@163.com
[2] Institute of Informatics, University of Zurich, C8050 Zurich, Switzerland

Abstract. Link prediction is an important issue in the field of data mining. It has been deeply researched in the computer field. With the rapid development of complex networks, the link prediction method has been continuously developed and improved. In practice, we do not need to score each pair of vertex pairs, but only predict a part of the information that the user is interested in. Therefore, we propose a method of link prediction based on sampling single vertex. Finally, we verify the prediction effect of our algorithm through several real network experiments.

Keywords: Local random walk · Complex network · Link prediction

1 Introduction

In the real world, from the nervous system to the ecosystem, from road traffic to the Internet, from the ant colony structure to the human social relationship, can be described as a complex network system. Within these network systems, nodes are numerous individuals, and the interrelationship between them is represented as a link between nodes. Complex networks are a kind of topology approximation of complex systems. In the process of construction, due to time and space or experimental conditions, there are inevitably errors or redundant links, and many potential links are not detected. Furthermore, complex networks tend to evolve dynamically over time, and their links are constantly added or removed. Therefore, it is necessary to predict missing links and future links based on known network information, which is the problem of network link prediction [1–3].

In social network analysis, link prediction can also be used as a powerful auxiliary tool for accurately analyzing the structure of social networks. For example, online social networks have developed very rapidly in recent years, and link prediction can reveal potential users' recommendations to users [4]. In the analysis of social relations, potential connections between people can be found [5, 6]. The idea and method of link prediction can also be used to judge the type of an academic paper and collaborators in the academic network [7]. The link prediction method can also be directly used for information recommendation, which can be used for recommending customers' products in e-commerce [8], and can also be used for e-mail prediction [9], judging a mobile

© The Author(s), under exclusive license to Springer Nature Switzerland AG 2022
X. Sun et al. (Eds.): ICAIS 2022, LNCS 13338, pp. 17–27, 2022.
https://doi.org/10.1007/978-3-031-06794-5_2

phone in a wireless communication network. Whether the user has a tendency to switch operators. In the monitoring of the network of criminals, link predictions are needed to discover hidden connections between criminals to prevent crime or terrorist activity. It can be used to analyze mixed-types of data by predicting possible links [10]. Links in the Internet of Things affect the routing performance and node reachability in the network, and link prediction can find possible links between nodes in the network to help optimize routing algorithms [11]. Link prediction can also be used to discover hidden links in the Tor dark web, and provide assistance to the government in combating illegal and immoral criminal activities [12]. By studying the link relationship between the data, the electronic network record data can be archived and managed, and it can be converted and stored in common databases using international standards [13]. Link prediction can discover the possible contact between people suffering from infectious diseases in real life and other people, thereby reducing the spread of the virus and protecting susceptible people [14].

Link prediction research not only has a wide range of practical applications, but also has important theoretical research significance. For example, the study of link prediction can also theoretically help people understand the mechanism of complex network evolution [15]. Due to the large number of statistics describing the characteristics of the network structure, it is difficult to compare different mechanisms. Link prediction can provide a simple and fair comparison platform for evolutionary network mechanisms, thus promoting theoretical research on complex network evolution models.

In the link prediction, the most important method is the similarity-based method. The similarity index includes the local similarity index and the global similarity index. The local similarity index includes the common neighbor index [16], the jaccard index [17], AA index [18], PA index [19], the local similarity index is simple to calculate, but due to the limited amount of information used, the prediction accuracy is low, and the global indicator is based on the global path or global random walk, considering the global topology between the vertices. Information has high prediction accuracy, such as Katz index [20], ACT index [21], cos+ index [22], RWR index [23], SimRank index [24], but the global indicator is usually calculated.

For the vertex link prediction query problem mentioned above, if the global indicator is used, it is impossible to calculate a certain class because of the globality of its calculation. It still needs the overall prediction to calculate, and the calculation is very large. For this reason, we adopt appropriate reduction. The idea of precision, which reduces the amount of calculation of the indicator, completes the link prediction query about the vertex in a shorter time.

This paper mainly predicts the possible connected edges of the vertices of interest in the network. After expansion, it can also be used in the link prediction of the whole network. The sampling method is used to design the method.

2 Local Random Walk and Evaluation Index

Global-based random walk indicators tend to be computationally complex and therefore difficult to apply on large-scale networks. Liu Weiping and Lu Linyuan [25] proposed a similarity index based on network local random walk, LRW (local random walk), which only considers the random walk process of finite steps.

2.1 LRW

A particle t starts from the node v_x and $\pi_{xy}(t)$ is defined as the probability that the particle just reaches the node v_y at time $t + 1$, then the system evolution equation can be obtained.

$$\pi_x(t + 1) = P^T \pi_x(t), t \geq 0 \tag{1}$$

where $\pi_x(0)$ is a vector of $N \times 1$, in which only the first element is 1 and 0 otherwise, i.e., $\pi_x(0) = e_x$. Matrix $P = [p_{xy}]$, $p_{xy} = a_{xy}/k_x$. a_{xy} is the element of adjacent matrix A, k_x is the degree of x. Set the initial resource distribution of each node to q_x, then the similarity of the t-step random walk is:

$$s_{xy}^{LRW}(t) = q_x \cdot \pi_{xy}(t) + q_y \cdot \pi_{yx}(t) \tag{2}$$

1. Superposed random walk

   On the basis of LRW, adding the t step and the previous results to get the value of SRW, i.e.:

$$s_{xy}^{SRW}(t) = \sum_{l=1}^{t} s_{xy}^{LRW}(l) = q_x \sum_{l=1}^{t} \pi_{xy}(l) + q_y \sum_{l=1}^{t} \pi_{yx}(l) \tag{3}$$

   The above formulas (1), (2), and (3) calculate that SRW involves the multiplication of $n \times n$-order matrices, and the calculation amount of each iteration is $O(n^3)$. For large-scale networks, the amount of calculation is obviously large, and for related link predictions that only query one or several vertices, it is obviously a waste of time to use these formulas.

   Currently, there are three commonly used indicators to measure the accuracy of link prediction algorithms: AUC [26, 27], Precision [28], and Ranking Score [26].

   The main evaluation indicators of link prediction are as follows:

2.2 AUC

ACU is short for area under the receiver operating characteristic curve, which measures the accuracy of the algorithm as a whole. It refers to the probability that the score of an edge in the test set is higher than the score of a randomly selected edge that does not exist.

The AUC value is the area within the range of the ROC curve. Generally speaking, the more accurate the prediction, the higher the AUC value. We assume that there are n_1 existing edges and n_2 non-existent edges in the network graph. Then there are a total of $n = n_1 + n_2$ edges in the network. We assume that $\{e_1, e_2, \cdots, e_{n1}\}$ and $\{e_{n1+1}, e_{n1+2}, \cdots, e_n\}$ are the set of known and unknown edges, respectively, and s_i is the score of edge e_i. Then for link prediction, the steps to draw the ROC curve are as follows:

- Calculate the score values of all unknown edges and arrange them in descending order. Let the sequence of the sorted edges be: $\left\{e_1', e_2', \cdots, e_n'\right\}$.

- Plot the coordinate axis of the ROC curve. The ordinate is the proportion of known edges in the test set, and the abscissa is the proportion of non-existent links.
- Finally, plot the ROC curve. Starting from the origin of the coordinates, if the unknown link belongs to an edge in the test set, then draw a step along the ordinate direction. If the unknown link belongs to a non-existent link, then draw a step along the abscissa.

Figure 1 shows an example of drawing an ROC curve. We assume that there are 7 connections in the network, namely: a, b, c, d, e, f, and g. Among them, a, b, c, and d, are edges that exist, and e, f, and g are edges that do not exist. We assume that after prediction, the corresponding scores of each edge are: $\{s_a, s_b, s_c, s_d, s_e, s_f, s_g\}$, where: $s_a > s_e = s_b > s_f > s_c > s_d > s_g$.

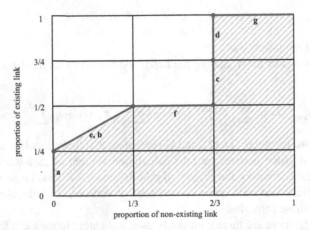

Fig. 1. Schematic diagram of ROC curve drawing.

We sort all edges according to the score, from largest to smallest. First, start from the origin of the coordinate system, because edge a has the largest score and is an existing edge, so the curve moves up one step. Next, edge e and edge b are the existing link and the non-existing link respectively, and $s_e = s_b$, so the curve moves one step along the diagonal. For edge f, since it is a non-existent edge, the curve moves one step to the right. Repeat this process until all edges have been traversed to the end. The area of the shaded part under the ROC curve is the value of AUC, namely: $7.5/12 = 0.625$.

In fact, when calculating the AUC value, we do not need to draw the ROC curve graph. Divide the known connection E into two parts: training set E^T and test set E^P. The AUC value can be expressed in a simpler way as follows: each time an edge randomly selected from the test set E^P is compared with an edge randomly selected from the set $U - E$ of non-existent edges, if the score value of the edge in the test set is higher than the score value of the non-existent edge, 1 points are added; if the two points are equal in value, 0.5 points are added. Independently compare n times. If there are n' times in the test set that the score value of an edge is higher than the score value of an edge that does not exist, there are n'' times that the two points are equal, so AUC is defined as:

$$AUC = \frac{n' + n''}{n} \tag{4}$$

Obviously, if all scores are randomly generated, then the value of AUC is 0.5. Therefore, the larger the AUC value, the higher the accuracy of the prediction algorithm.

We use the above formula to calculate the AUC value of the legend. There are 4 known edges and 3 non-existent edges, so a total of $3 \times 4 = 12$ comparisons are required. In 12 comparisons, the number of scores of edges in the test set greater than that of edges in the non-test set is 7, which are: $S_a > S_e, S_a > S_f, S_a > S_g, S_b > S_f, S_b > S_g, S_c > S_g, S_d > S_g$. And, so $n' = 7$, $n'' = 1$, so $AUC = (7 + 0.5)/12 = 0.625$, the result is consistent with Fig. 1.

Obviously, the higher the Precision value, the higher the accuracy of the link prediction algorithm.

2.3 Precision

Precision only considers whether the top L edges in the target user rating list are predicted accurately. If there are m predictions that are accurate, that is, there are m of the top L edges in the test set, then Precision is defined as:

$$precision = \frac{m}{L} \tag{5}$$

Obviously, the higher the Precision value, the higher the accuracy of the link prediction algorithm.

2.4 Ranking Score

Ranking Score mainly considers the position of the edges in the test set in the final ranking. Let $H = U - E^T$ be the set of unknown edges, and r_i represents the ranking of unknown edges $i \in E^P$ in the ranking. Then the Ranking Score of this unknown edge is $RS_i = r_i/|H|$, Where $|H|$ represents the number of elements in the set H, traverse all the edges in the test set, and get the Ranking Score value:

$$RS = \frac{1}{|E^P|} \sum_{i \in E^P} RS_i = \frac{1}{|E^P|} \sum_{i \in E^P} \frac{r_i}{|H|} \tag{6}$$

Obviously, the smaller the value of RS, the higher the accuracy of the link prediction algorithm.

3   The Idea of Sampling

Our idea is to limit the link query of vertex x to several paths starting from x and not exceeding t. Since such a path may be many, it takes a lot of time to exhaust these paths. We use the sampling method.

For the calculation of formula (3), the key lies in the calculation of the pair. We use the sampling method to calculate the approximation so that the error from the true value is less than the given value ε.

If assume $P_t(x)$ is A set of paths starting from x that do not exceed t in length. If $p \in P_t(X)$, we define $d(p)$ to be the distance from the vertex x to y in p. Then $\pi_{xy}(t)$ can be rewritten:

$$\pi_{xy}(t) = \frac{1}{|P_t(x)|} \sum_{p \in P_t(x)} I(d(p) = t) \tag{7}$$

Here the function

$$I(d(p) = \ell) = \begin{cases} 1 & d(p) = \ell \\ 0 & else \end{cases} \tag{8}$$

If assume $Q_t(x)$ is the k-sampling set of paths starting from x does not exceed t, we use the following $\hat{\pi}_{xy}(\ell)$ to approximate $\pi_{xy}(\ell)$:

$$\hat{\pi}_{xy}(\ell) = \frac{1}{k} \sum_{p \in Q_t(x)} I(d(p) = \ell) \tag{9}$$

Since $P_t(x)$ and $Q_t(x)$ are different (actually $Q_t(x) \subseteq P_t(x)$, $\hat{\pi}_{xy}(\ell)$ as the approximation of $\pi_{xy}(\ell)$, but the larger k, that is, the more samples, the smaller the error, the next step is to choose the appropriate k value, so that the error $|\hat{\pi}_{xy}(\ell) - \pi_{xy}(\ell)|$ is within the given range ε.

We use the Hoeffding bound to determine the k value under the error threshold ε, which is Eq. 10:

$$k \geq \frac{ln(\frac{\delta}{2})}{-2\varepsilon^2} \tag{10}$$

If k is satisfied (10), the probability of $1 - \delta$ is such that the error is less than ε.

4 Methods

We use a random walk method to generate a set of random walk paths of length t $Q_t(x)$. All paths start from vertex x and form a path of length t by random walk. On each node, the path is selected according to the transition probability.

If it is a non-weighted graph, let the adjacency matrix be $A = [a_{ij}]$, if it is a weighted graph, or if the vertex has a graph of attributes, the weight on the edge or the attribute similarity matrix is $W = [w_{ij}]$, we define the random transition probability from vertex v_i to v_j as:

$$t_{ij} = \frac{w_{ij}}{\sum_{v_k \in \Gamma(v_i)} w_{ik}} \tag{11}$$

Here $\Gamma(v_i)$ is a set of direct neighbor nodes of v_i.
Random walks generate the algorithm of set a:

Algorithm 1. GeneratePath(x, L, R)

Input: x: target vertex;

R: Number of sample paths;

L: Length of path;

W: Adjacency matrix or weight matrix;

Output: $Q_L(x)$:Sample path set

1: Calculate transition matrix $T = [t_{ij}]$ based on Eq. (8); $Q_L(x) = \emptyset$;

2: **for** $k = 1$ to R **do**

3:      $P_k = \emptyset$;   (P_k is the k-th path)

4:      Starting from x, Select a vertex in the transfer matrix, denoted as x_1

5:      x_1 joins P_k;

6:      **for** $j = 1$ to L **do**

7:          Starting from x_1, select the next vertex in $\Gamma(x_1)$ according to the transition

            probability, denoted as x_2

8:          x_2 joins P_k

9:          $x_1 = x_2$;

10:     **end for** j

11:     $Q_L(x) = Q_L(x) \cup \{P_k\}$;

12: **end for** k

return $Q_L(x)$

The basic idea of the algorithm is as follows:

Algorithm 2. Node_LP(x)

Input: x: target vertex;

ε: error boundary;

δ: probability;

t : length of path;

Output: the ratings of x and $\hat{\pi}_{xy}(\ell)$,$\ell = 1,2,\dots,t$;

1: Calculate the k value according to formula (9) ;

2: GeneratePaths(x, t, k); (Generate k paths starting from x and having a length of t, stored in $Q_t(x)$)

3: **For** each P in $Q_t(x)$ **do**

4:      **For** $i = 1$ to t **do**

5:          $\hat{\pi}_{xv_i}(i) = \hat{\pi}_{xv_i}(i) + \frac{1}{k}$

6:      **End for** i

7: **End for**

return the ratings of x and $\hat{\pi}_{xy}(\ell)$,$\ell = 1,2,\dots,t$;

5   Experimental Results and Analysis

This paper uses six representative networks [29]: Protein Interaction Network (PPI), Scientist Cooperation Network (NS), US Power Network (Grid), Political Blog Network (PB), Router Network (INT). And the American Airlines Network (USAir), their statistical properties are shown in Table 1.

Table 1 shows the characteristics of each network. Among them, N and M respectively represent the number of nodes and edges in the network. Nc is the number of connected groups in the network and the number of nodes in the largest connected group. For example, in the USAir network, 332/1 means that there is 1 connected group in the network, and the largest connected set contains 332 nodes. e is the efficiency of the network, C is the clustering coefficient of the network, r is the assortativity of the network, and K is the average degree of the network.

Table 1. Topological properties of 6 experimental networks.

Networks	N	M	Nc	e	C	r	K
USAir	332	2126	332/1	0.440	0.749	−0.228	12.807
PB	1224	19090	1222/2	0.397	0.361	−0.079	31.193
NS	1461	2742	379/268	0.016	0.878	0.462	3.754
PPI	2617	11855	2375/92	0.180	0.387	0.454	9.060
Grid	4941	6594	4941/1	0.056	0.107	0.004	2.669
INT	5022	6258	5022/1	0.167	0.033	−0.138	2.492

We use ten algorithms such as: CN, Salton, Jaccard, Sorenson, HPI, HDI, LHN-I, PA, LP and Katz to experiment in six real networks. Next, compare the accuracy with the Node_LP algorithm of this article. Each of the experimental results is the average of the predictions and evaluations obtained by performing 100 random divisions of the original data set (including 90% of the number of links) and the test set (including 10% of the number of links). In Node_LP, we perform AUC calculation on the subgraph calculated for each vertex. We test the set of edges and select the vertices corresponding to the subgraphs and the edges of the remaining vertices. We use the AUC evaluation method as the evaluation index of the algorithm.

Regarding the AUC evaluation methods, the experimental results are shown in Table 2.

From Table 2, we can see that our Node_LP algorithm has the largest AUC value in the three real data sets of USAir, PB, and NS. In the PPI, Grid, and INT data sets, our algorithm can obtain and the rest of the algorithms. Almost the same effect. This shows that the algorithm of this paper is very robust.

Table 2. Comparison of prediction accuracy of 11 algorithms when measured by AUC.

	USAir	PB	NS	PPI	Grid	INT
CN	0.9366	0.9218	0.9404	0.8987	0.5896	0.5451
Salton	0.9230	0.8739	0.9377	0.8980	0.5896	0.5552
Jaccard	0.8854	0.8714	0.4903	0.7691	0.4926	0.7770
Sorensen	0.8876	0.8720	0.9267	0.8980	0.5987	0.5640
HPI	0.8602	0.8502	0.9504	0.8969	0.5957	0.5512
HDI	0.8698	0.8681	0.9248	0.8979	0.5896	0.5569
LHN_I	0.7194	0.7541	0.9391	0.8941	0.5896	0.5631
PA	0.8233	0.8179	0.6147	0.7817	0.4677	0.6183
LP	0.9329	0.9267	0.9312	0.9395	0.6205	0.6230
Katz	0.9110	0.9232	0.9272	0.9196	0.6375	0.3732
Node_LP	**0.9780**	**0.9691**	**0.9723**	**0.9897**	**0.8965**	**0.9120**

6 Conclusion

Link prediction is an important issue in the field of data mining. It has been deeply researched in the computer field. With the rapid development of complex networks, the link prediction method has been continuously developed and improved. In practice, we do not need to score each pair of vertex pairs, but only predict a part of the information that the user is interested in. Therefore, we propose a sample-based single-vertex link prediction method. Our method can effectively reduce the prediction time without changing the topological features of the data set, and achieve better prediction result.

Acknowledgement. This research was supported in part by the National Natural Science Foundation of China under grant No. 61602202, Natural Science Foundation of Jiangsu Province under contract No. BK20160428 and Natural Science Foundation of Education Department of Jiangsu Province under contract No. 20KJA520008. Six talent peaks project in Jiangsu Province (Grant No. XYDXX-034) and China Scholarship Council also supported this work.

References:

1. Lichtenwalter, R.N.: New precepts and method in link prediction. In: Proceedings of ACM KDD 2010, pp. 243–252 (2010)
2. Lv, L., Zhou, T.: Link prediction in complex networks: a survey. Physica A **390**(6), 1150–1170 (2011)
3. Lv, L.: Complex network link prediction. J. Univ. Electron. Sci. Technol. **39**(5), 651–661 (2010). (In Chinese)
4. Papadimitriou, A., Symeonidis, P., Manolopoulos, Y.: Fast and accurate link prediction in social networking systems. J. Syst. Softw. **85**(9), 2119–2132 (2012)

5. Hossmann, T., Nomikos, G., Spyropoulos, T., Legendre, F.: Collection and analysis of multi-dimensional network data for opportunistic networking research. Comput. Commun. **35**(13), 1613–1625 (2012)

6. Jahanbakhsh, K., King, V., Shoja, G.C.: Predicting missing contacts in mobile social networks. Pervasive Mob. Comput. **8**(5), 698–716 (2012)

7. Sun, Y., Barber, R., Gupta, M., Aggarwal, C.C., Han, J.: Co-author relationship prediction in heterogeneous bibliographic networks. In: 2011 International Conference on Advances in Social Networks Analysis and Mining, pp. 121–128. IEEE (2011)

8. Li, X., Chen, H.: Recommendation as link prediction in bipartite graphs: a graph kernel-based machine learning approach. Decis. Support Syst. **54**(2), 880–890 (2013)

9. Huang, Z., Lin, D.K.: The time-series link prediction problem with applications in communication surveillance. INFORMS J. Comput. **21**(2), 286–303 (2009)

10. Boongoen, T., Iam-On, N.: Using link-based consensus clustering for mixed-type data analysis. Comput. Mater. Continua **70**(1), 1993–2011 (2022)

11. Kothandaraman, D., et al.: Energy and bandwidth based link stability routing algorithm for IoT. Comput. Mater. Continua **70**(2), 3875–3890 (2021)

12. Khan, S.A., Alharbi, A., Faizan, M., Alosaimi, W.: A link analysis algorithm for identification of key hidden services. Comput. Mater. Continua **68**(1), 877–886 (2021)

13. Qi, J., Ren, Y., Wang, Q.: Network electronic record management based on linked data. J. Big Data **1**(1), 9 (2019)

14. Al-Tarawneh, H., Al-Kaabneh, K., Alhroob, A., Migdady, H., Alhadid, I.: A hybrid heuristic algorithm for solving covid-19's social distancing at universities campus. Comput. Syst. Sci. Eng. **41**(3), 933–944 (2022)

15. Liu, H.: Using link prediction to infer network evolution mechanism. Chin. Sci. Phys. Mech. Astronomy **41**(7), 816–823 (2011)

16. Newman, M.E.: Clustering and preferential attachment in growing networks. Phys. Rev. E **64**(2), 025102 (2001)

17. Jaccard, P.: Etude comparative de la distribution florale dans une portion des alpes et des jura. Bull. Soc. Vaudoise Sci. Nat. **37**, 547–579 (1901)

18. Adamic, L.A., Adar, E.: Friends and neighbors on the web. Social Netw. **25**(3), 211–230 (2003)

19. Barabási, A.L., Albert, R.: Emergence of scaling in random networks. Science **286**(5439), 509–512 (1999)

20. Katz, L.: A new status index derived from sociometric analysis. Psychometrika **18**(1), 39–43 (1953)

21. Klein, D.J., Randi, C.M.: Resistance distance. J. Math. Chem. **12**(1), 81–95 (1993)

22. Fouss, F., Pirotte, A., Renders, J.M., Saerens, M.: Random-walk computation of similarities between nodes of a graph with application to collaborative recommendation. IEEE Trans. Knowl. Data Eng. **19**(3), 355–369 (2007)

23. Brin, S., Page, L.: The anatomy of a large-scale hypertextual web search engine. Comput. Netw. ISDN Syst. **30**(1), 107–117 (1998)

24. Jeh, G., Widom, J.: SimRank: a measure of structural-context similarity. In: Proceedings of the Eighth ACM SIGKDD International Conference on Knowledge Discovery and Data Mining, pp. 538–543 (2002)

25. Liu, W., Lv, L.: Link prediction based on local random walk. EPL (Europhys. Lett.) **89**(5), 58007 (2010)

26. Zhou, T., Ren, J., Medo, M., Zhang, Y.C.: Bipartite network projection and personal recommendation. Phys. Rev. E **76**(4), 046115 (2007)

27. Hanley, J.A., McNeil, B.J.: The meaning and use of the area under a receiver operating characteristic (ROC) curve. Radiology **143**(1), 29–36 (1982)

28. Herlocker, J.L., Konstan, J.A., Terveen, L.G., Riedl, J.T.: Evaluating collaborative filtering recommender systems. ACM Trans. Inform. Syst. (TOIS) 22(1), 5–53 (2004)
29. http://www.linkprediction.org/index.php/link/resource/data

Operation Configuration Optimization of Power Gas Energy Hub System Considering NOx Emission

Xueqin Zhang[1], Xudong Wang[2(✉)], Jing Duan[3], Wei Chen[2], Xiaojun Sun[2], and Jinyue Xia[4]

[1] State Grid of Shanxi Branch, Taiyuan 030021, China
[2] Shanxi Yitong Gird Protection Co. Ltd., Taiyuan 030021, China
1928879373@qq.com
[3] State Grid Shanxi Electric Power Company Information and Communication Branch, Taiyuan 030021, China
[4] International Business Machines Corporation (IBM), New York 10041NY212, USA

Abstract. Since industrialization, people's demand for energy has reached an unprecedented level, and is increasing with the development of the times. In the 21st century, countless environmental and energy problems are in front of us. The shortage of resources, environmental degradation and global warming all remind us that we need to make changes to deal with the coming energy disaster. In the process of energy supply, it will not only consume energy, but also emit a large number of polluting gases, such as carbon dioxide and nitrogen oxides. In order to improve the efficiency of energy utilization and reduce the emission of polluting gases, energy hub (EH) is proposed. Energy hub is an important model to analyze the coupling effect of multiple energy sources. It can improve the utilization efficiency of multiple energy systems and reduce the emission of polluting gases. However, in the related research of many energy hubs, few optimization schemes take into account the emission of nitrogen oxide n0x. In this paper, particle swarm optimization (PSO) will be used to construct a method considering nitrogen oxide. The optimization model of x emission electric gas energy hub is used to solve this problem.

Keywords: Energy hub · Integrated energy · Particle swarm optimization · Cogeneration · Nox emission

1 Introduction

Most of the existing research on optimal dispatching of integrated power and gas energy system takes the optimal economy as the goal, and is fully launched from the perspectives of dispatching mode, equipment and technical means to improve operation performance, coping with prediction error, taking into account environmental impact and so on. Literature [1] established a CCHP microgrid including renewable energy and energy storage. Considering the conversion efficiency between different energy sources,

© The Author(s), under exclusive license to Springer Nature Switzerland AG 2022
X. Sun et al. (Eds.): ICAIS 2022, LNCS 13338, pp. 28–40, 2022.
https://doi.org/10.1007/978-3-031-06794-5_3

taking the operation cost as the objective function, it cooperatively optimized the multi energy flow in the system to meet the needs of users with multiple loads. Reference [2] discussed the influence of natural gas system equipment and gas price on power system unit combination earlier. Reference [3] discussed the influence of natural gas system equipment and gas price on power system unit combination earlier. Considering the gas transmission constraints of fuel conversion units and natural gas network, literature [4] analyzes the interaction between power system and natural gas system with the goal of minimizing the operation cost of power system. In reference [5], the author will CO2 emissions are considered in the energy hub system, and the energy hub is optimized by genetic algorithm. P2g proposed in document [6] considers the two-stage energy flow of electricity to hydrogen and electricity to natural gas, and combines the hybrid energy storage system with microgrid to ensure the economy and environmental protection of the system when wind power is connected to the grid. According to the literature [7], air pollution control technology is mainly used to reduce the emissions of nitrogen oxides, sulfur dioxide, particulate matter and other air pollutants produced by fossil fuel power plants. Moreover, according to the literature [8], nearly 1/2 of the nitrogen oxides and more than 1/3 of the sulfur dioxide emissions in China come from the power industry. Therefore, this paper will design an optimization model considering NOx emission to solve this problem.

2 Energy Hub

According to reference [9], energy hub is an input-output port model that describes the exchange and coupling relationship between source load network in integrated energy system. According to the literature [10], the combination of different energy carriers in the energy hub has many advantages, such as increasing system stability, power generation flexibility and optimizing operation potential. The energy hub is equivalent to a multi energy conversion center, with multiple input and output interfaces for various types of energy, connecting the supply side and load side. All kinds of energy can be converted, regulated and stored in the energy hub. The energy hub can also connect various current energy networks, such as power network, natural gas network, cooling and heating network and transportation network, so as to realize energy exchange between different energy networks. The coupling matrix of the energy hub is shown in formula (1). Assuming that the input energy flow of the energy hub is p = [P1, P2, ..., PN], and the output energy flow is L = [L1, L2, ..., LN], the coupling matrix C is determined by the scheduling factor v And energy conversion efficiency η Composition, characterizing the distribution and conversion relationship of energy flow. It is generally determined by the type of internal conversion device, conversion efficiency, input energy distribution coefficient and internal topology of the energy hub. In the process of energy hub operation, energy conversion efficiency η. The scheduling factor V is learned by the algorithm of artificial intelligence, so that the optimal solution of energy distribution can be planned.

$$\begin{bmatrix} L_1 \\ L_2 \\ \vdots \\ L_n \end{bmatrix} = \begin{bmatrix} C_{11} & C_{12} & \cdots & C_{1m} \\ C_{21} & C_{22} & \cdots & C_{2m} \\ \vdots & \vdots & \ddots & \vdots \\ C_{n1} & C_{n2} & \cdots & C_{nm} \end{bmatrix} \begin{bmatrix} P_1 \\ P_2 \\ \vdots \\ P_m \end{bmatrix} = \begin{bmatrix} v_{11}\eta_{11} & v_{12}\eta_{12} & \cdots & v_{1m}\eta_{1m} \\ v_{21}\eta_{21} & v_{22}\eta_{22} & \cdots & v_{2m}\eta_{2m} \\ \vdots & \vdots & \ddots & \vdots \\ v_{n1}\eta_{n1} & v_{n2}\eta_{n2} & \cdots & v_{nm}\eta_{nm} \end{bmatrix} \begin{bmatrix} P_1 \\ P_2 \\ \vdots \\ P_m \end{bmatrix} \quad (1)$$

The electricity gas integrated energy system is shown in Fig. 1. The energy transmission part of the system is composed of power network and natural gas network, which are coupled with each other through gas-fired power plant and energy hub.

The energy hub can be regarded as the connecting link between the power network and the natural gas network and the users. It contains a variety of equipment such as energy transmission, energy conversion and energy storage. The electric energy Pe and natural gas Pg at the input port of the energy hub come from the superior power network and natural gas network respectively. After coordination and cooperation of connecting elements (transformer and gas transmission pipeline), energy conversion elements (electric to gas equipment based on carbon capture, cogeneration unit, gas-fired boiler and heat pump) and energy storage elements (heat storage equipment and gas storage equipment), Meet the user's electrical load Le, thermal load Lh and gas load Lg through the output port. According to literature [11], electric energy can be converted into natural gas through electric gas conversion equipment. According to the literature [12], the electric gas conversion equipment absorbs carbon dioxide and releases oxygen in the reaction process, so the device can be regarded as a green energy production equipment. In addition to providing the absorption path of new energy, it also plays an important role in low-carbon environmental protection and energy conservation.

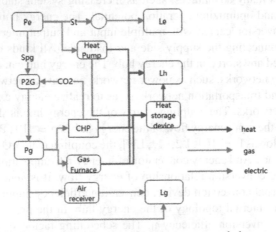

Fig. 1. Operation diagram of power gas energy hub system.

3   Particle Swarm Optimization (PSO)

Particle swarm optimization algorithm is one of heuristic algorithms, which was first proposed in literature [13] by American psychologist Kendy and electrical engineer Eberhart. This algorithm imitates the process of birds, fish and other swarm organisms in nature to cooperate in the process of looking for food. It can mainly solve practical problems such as multi-objective optimization, nonlinear integer and mixed integer constrained optimization, signal processing, neural network training and so on. PSO algorithm corresponds the feasible solution of the optimization problem to a particle in the search space. Particles find the individual optimal particle and global optimal particle under the current number of iterations at a certain speed. Through continuous iteration, full competition and cooperation, the search for the optimal solution in the search space is finally realized.

Particle swarm optimization (PSO) firstly initializes particle swarm randomly in feasible solution space and velocity space, that is, determines the initial position and velocity of particles. There are m particles in d-dimensional space, in which the position and velocity of the ith particle are expressed as Xi = [Xi, 1, Xi, 2, ... Xi, D], and VI = [vi, 1, VI, 2, ... VI, D], respectively. In each iteration, the optimal position PI, D and population extreme value experienced by each particle at each time are determined according to the fitness of each particle. By tracking these two best positions, swarm particles continuously update their own speed and position according to formula (2) and formula (3).

$$V_{i,d}(t+1) = W \times \mathbf{v}_{i,d}(t) + c_1 \times r_1 \left(P_{i,d}(t) - x_{i,d}(t)\right) + c_2 \times r_2 \left(G_{i,d}(t) - x_{i,d}(t)\right) \tag{2}$$

$$x_{i,d}(t+1) = x_{i,d}(t) + v_{i,d}(t+1) \tag{3}$$

where: $I = 1, 2,..., m, d = 1, 2,..., D$. ω Is the inertia weight factor, t is the number of current iterations, C1 and C2 are learning factors, which are generally taken as 2, and R1 and R2 are random numbers evenly distributed between 0 and 1. In addition, in order to prevent particles from flying out of the search range in the iterative process, the particles can be limited by setting the velocity interval Vmin, Vmax and position interval Xmin, Xmax of particles.

Particle swarm optimization (PSO) can effectively solve the problem of scheduling factor V in the coupling matrix of energy hub. After several iterations, the optimal solution of the scheduling factor V is obtained.

4   Objective Function

4.1   Emission Cost

NOx is a polluting gas produced by both coal-fired units and gas-fired units. At present, power plants are generally equipped with low NOx combustion equipment and selective catalytic reduction equipment to reduce NOx emissions. Among them, the operation state of selective catalytic reduction equipment is related to the output power of coal-fired units and gas-fired units. Only when the output power of coal-fired unit and gas-fired unit is greater than the critical threshold, the selective catalytic reduction equipment can be started. In addition, the NOx emission characteristics of coal-fired units can be described by quadratic function, and the NOx emission characteristics of combined cycle gas units are related to output power.

According to reference [14], when the output power of the combined cycle gas unit is lower than the critical threshold, the lean premixed combustion mode with low NOx emission intensity is switched to the diffusion combustion mode with high NOx emission intensity. Therefore, when the gas units are combined cycle gas units, and the coal-fired units and gas units are equipped with low NOx combustion equipment and selective catalytic reduction equipment, the NOx emission models of coal-fired units and gas units can be described as different piecewise functions, as shown in formula (4) and formula (5).

$$Q_i^{NO_x} = \begin{cases} \kappa_i^{NO_x} \delta_i^{NO_x} \left(\alpha_i^{NO_x} P_i^2 + \beta_i^{NO_x} P_i + \gamma_i^{NO_x} \right), \lambda_i^{NO_x} P_{i,max} \le P_i \le P_{i,max} \\ \delta_i^{NO_x} \left(\alpha_i^{NO_x} P_i^2 + \beta_i^{NO_x} P_i + \gamma_i^{NO_x} \right), P_{i,min} \le P_i \le \lambda_i^{NO_x} P_{i,max} \end{cases} \tag{4}$$

$$Q_i^{NO_x} = \begin{cases} \kappa_i^{NO_x} \delta_i^{NO_x} \left(\mu_{L,i}^{NO_x} P_i \right), \chi_i^{NO_x} P_{i,max} \le P_i \le P_{i,max} \\ \kappa_i^{NO_x} \delta_i^{NO_x} \left(\mu_{D,i}^{NO_i} P_i \right), \lambda_i^{NO_x} P_{i,max} \le P_i \le \chi_i^{NO_x} P_{i,max}, i \in \Omega_{GU} \\ \delta_i^{NO_x} \left(\mu_{D,i}^{NO_x} P_i \right), P_{i,min} \le P_i \le \lambda_i^{NO_x} P_{i,max} \end{cases} \tag{5}$$

At the same time, the second formula above is also applicable to the combined thermal power unit in the energy hub. The NOx emission of the gas-fired boiler is directly proportional to its heating capacity, as shown in formula (6).

$$Q_j^{NO_x} = Q_{CHP_j}^{NO_x} + \mu_{GF_j^N}^{NO_f} S_{GF} \eta_{GFj}, j \in \Omega_{EH} \tag{6}$$

This paper uses penalty price transforms the multi-objective optimization problem into a single objective optimization problem. The product of penalty factor and emission is the emission cost of the system, as shown in Formula (7).

$$F_{pc} = \sum_{t \in \Omega_T} \rho^{NO_x} Q_t^{NO_x} \tag{7}$$

4.2 System Operation Cost

The operation cost of environmental economic dispatching of the electricity gas integrated energy system includes the fuel cost of coal-fired units, the gas production cost of natural gas wells and the operation cost of energy hubs, as shown in formula (8).

$$F_{oc} = \sum_{t \in \Omega_T} \left[\sum_{i \in \Omega_{cu}} \rho_i \psi(P_{it}) + \sum_{\omega \in \Omega_{cw}} \rho_\omega Q_{\omega t} + \sum_{j \in \Omega_{zt}} C_{jt} \right] \tag{8}$$

where Cjt represents the operation cost of energy hub J in period T, which is composed of the operation cost of electric to gas equipment, the operation cost of heat storage equipment and the operation cost of gas storage equipment, Represents the operation cost of power to gas equipment in energy hub J.

4.3 Objective Function

The ultimate goal of the power gas energy hub system considering NOx emissions is to maximize the total system revenue and reduce NOx emissions, so as to achieve a balance between system revenue and NOx emissions. Therefore, when the sum of emission cost and system operation cost of the system tends to be the minimum, it is the objective function of the system, as shown in Eq. (9).

$$minF = F_{oc} + F_{pc} \tag{9}$$

5   Constraint Condition

5.1   Power System Constraints

Active power balance constraint See Eq. (10)

$$\sum_{i=1}^{N_G} P_{G_{i,t}} + \sum_{i=1}^{N_{gf}} P_{gf_{i,t}} + \sum_{i=1}^{N_w} P_{w_{i,t}} + \sum_{i=1}^{N_{pv}} pv_{it} + \sum_{i=1}^{N_{CHP}} P_{CHP_{i,t}} + \sum_{i=1}^{N_B} P_{Pb_{i,t}} = \sum_{i=1}^{N_{P2G}} P_{P2G_{i,t}} + P_{Dt} + P_{loss} \tag{10}$$

Bus voltage and branch power flow constraints See Eq. (11). Vmin, Vmax represents the maximum and minimum voltage of the i-th bus, Si represents the power flow distribution on the i-th branch, and S represents the maximum power flow distribution on the i-th branch

$$\left. \begin{array}{c} V \\ |S_{\text{fow},i}| \le S_{\text{fow},j}^{max} \\ i_{min_i^{max}} \end{array} \right\} \tag{11}$$

Climbing power constraint See Eq. (12). Uri, Dri respectively represent the rising rate constraint and falling rate constraint of the ith unit, Pit represents the power of the ith unit at time t, P represents the power of the ith unit at time $t-1$

$$\left. \begin{array}{c} P_{i,t} - P_{i,t-1} < UR_i \\ P_{i,t-1} - P_{i,t} < DR_i \end{array} \right\} \tag{12}$$

Output power constraint See Eq. (13).

$$\left. \begin{array}{c} P \\ gfi \\ min_{gfi, zfi}^{max} \\ P \\ {}_{0 \le P_{P2G_i,} \le P_{P2G_i}^{max}} \\ 0 \le P_{wi,} \le P_{wr} \, {}_{0 \le pv_{i,s} \le pv(K_{tmax}())} \\ CHP_{i\,min_{CHP_{ij}}\,CHP_{ij}^{max}} \end{array} \right\} \tag{13}$$

5.2 Energy Hub Constraints

Thermal node equilibrium constraint See Eq. (14). Where Qhij represents the heat storage capacity at time t, Hdt represents the heat demand at time t, and H_loss represents the heat loss.

$$\sum_{i=1}^{N_{c\|p}} Q_{CHP_{i,t}} + \sum_{i=1}^{N_{Hou}} Q_{HOU_{i,t}} + i = 1NHS \, QHi, t = HD.t + H_{loss} \qquad (14)$$

Thermal constraints of cogeneration and heating units See Eq. (15). Where Q represents the maximum and minimum values of the heat generated by the ith cogeneration generator, and Qmin represents the maximum and minimum values of the heat generated by the ith heating unit.

$$\left. \begin{array}{c} Q \\ min_{HOU_{t,v}} {}^{max}_{HOU_{i,j}} \\ Q_{HOU_i} \\ CHP_{i\,min_{CHP_{id}} {}^{max}_{CHP_{i,\rho}}} \end{array} \right\} \qquad (15)$$

5.3 Natural Gas System Constraints

Gas node equilibrium constraint See Eq. (16). Where Q represents the gas output of the ith equipment at time t, Q represents the gas storage at time t, Q represents the gas demand at time t, and Q represents the gas loss.

$$\sum_{i=1}^{N_M} Q_{S_{i,t}} + \sum_{i=1}^{N_M} Q_{P2G_{i,t}} + \sum_{i=1}^{N_M} Q_{g_{i,t}} = \sum_{i=1}^{N_{c?p}} L_{CHP_{l,t}} + \sum_{i=1}^{N_{gf}} L_{gf_{i,t}} + Q_{D.t} + Q_{loss} \quad (16)$$

Pressure and airflow constraints See Eq. (17). Where: P represents the maximum and minimum pressure between node m and node n

$$\left. \begin{array}{c} P \\ mri\,_{min_{mrn_i}}{}^{,0 \le Q_{mn} \le k_{mn}\sqrt{(P_m^2 - P_n^2)}}_{m-n_i} \end{array} \right\} \qquad (17)$$

5.4 Energy Storage Equipment Constraints

Charge discharge power constraint See Eq. (18) Where: Emax represents the maximum energy storage equipment capacity of different storage types.

$$\left. \begin{array}{c} -ESDC_{i,max} \\ 0 \le P_{SDD_i,} \le E_{max} \end{array} \right\} \qquad (18)$$

6 Example Analysis

6.1 Example Description

In order to verify the feasibility and applicability of the energy hub, it is applied to IEEE-30 node standard test system [15] and Belgium 20 node natural gas system [16]. The system node wiring diagram is shown in Fig. 2 and Fig. 3.

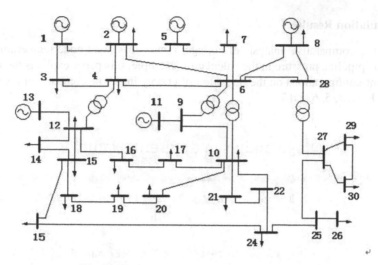

Fig. 2. IEEE-30 node system wiring diagram.

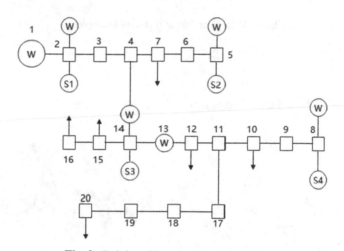

Fig. 3. Belgium 20 node natural gas system.

This paper will illustrate the operation of energy hub under different configuration environments through 5 examples. The configuration is as follows.

Example 1: study the original energy hub configuration without including any renewable energy or energy storage equipment.

Example 2: add energy storage equipment on the basis of example 1 for research.

Example 3: the energy hub includes renewable energy and p2g devices, but does not include energy storage equipment.

Example 4: the energy hub contains only renewable energy.

Example 5: all energy output is included in the energy hub. All energy in the energy hub operates.

6.2 Simulation Results

Through the comparative analysis of voltage, power loss, load node temperature and natural gas pipeline pressure in the calculation example, this paper explains the impact of different configurations on the operation of energy hub. The comparison results are shown in Figs. 4, 5, 6 and 7.

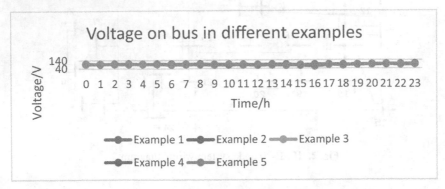

Fig. 4. Voltage on bus in different examples.

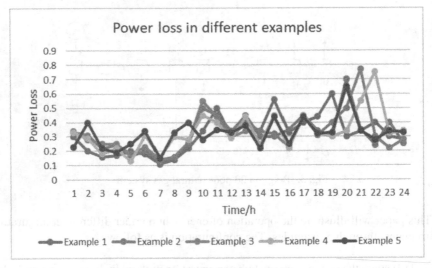

Fig. 5. Power loss in different examples.

The daily variation of voltage in the five examples is shown in Fig. 4. From 1 a.m. to 4 p.m., the load demand is small and the voltage change is small. During the period from 4 pm to 24 PM, the load demand is large. At this time, the power loss will increase with the increase of load demand and decrease with the decrease of load demand, as shown in Fig. 5. Without the support of renewable energy and energy storage equipment, the

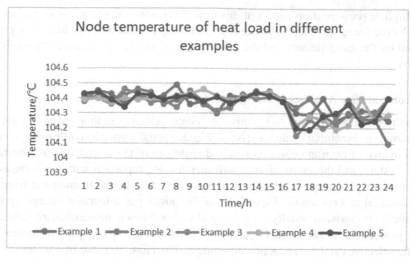

Fig. 6. Node temperature of heat load in different examples.

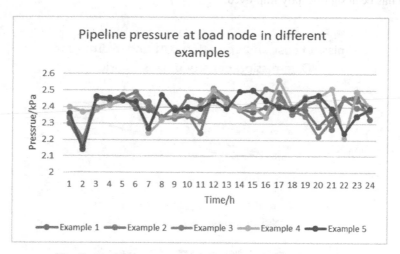

Fig. 7. Pipeline pressure at load node in different examples.

voltage change and power loss change most in example 1. In example 5, since the energy hub includes all energy output, the voltage change and power loss change are the smallest. Figure 6 compares and analyzes the impact of different energy hub configurations on the temperature of the heating system at the heat load node. Since the heat load demand is relatively small from 1 a.m. to 3 p.m., the temperature change in the five examples is small in this time period. The temperature change in example 1 is the largest, and the temperature change in example 5 is the smallest. The pressure variation in the natural gas pipeline in the five examples is shown in Fig. 7. As can be seen from the figure, the pressure of natural gas pipeline will change with the change of load and available energy. Due to the lack of renewable energy and energy storage equipment in example

1, the highest pressure drop occurs at this time. Therefore, the gas generator generates more electric energy to meet the power load. In example 5, due to the reduction of power required by the gas generator and the existence of p2g unit, the pressure change is the smallest.

6.3   Comparative Analysis of Numerical Examples

As shown in Fig. 8, when the NOx emission penalty price is less than 5 times or greater than 8 times the benchmark value, the NOx emission penalty price has little impact on the operation cost of environmental economic dispatching of the electricity gas integrated energy system, and the emission cost will increase in proportion with the increase of NOx emission penalty price. However, in order to reduce the NOx emission from the environmental and economic dispatching of the power gas integrated energy system, when the NOx emission penalty price is equal to 6 or 7 times the benchmark value, the output power of coal-fired unit G1 and cogeneration unit chp1–chp2 will increase to start the selective catalytic reduction equipment, Therefore, in these two scenarios, the operation cost of environmental economic dispatching of electric gas integrated energy system has been significantly improved.

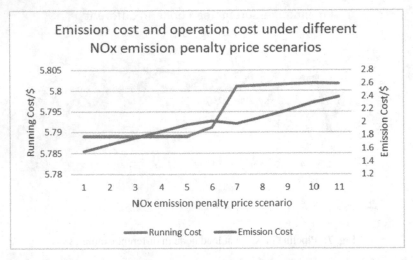

Fig. 8. Emission cost and operation cost under different NOx emission penalty price scenarios.

In each example, the total operating cost, CO2 emission and system loss are calculated respectively. Taking the power on, heat and gas costs of bus 2 as the reference, the power, heat and gas costs of each node as the index, and considering the loss, the power, heat and gas costs of each node are calculated, as shown in Table 1.

In example 1, due to the low price of natural gas, CHP unit is the main source of power supply and heating during the day. In addition, due to the increase of the feed path of the gas system, the natural gas loss also increases. However, with the increase of daytime load, CHP can not meet these loads and can only be purchased from Hou, which increases the operation cost and carbon emission.

Table 1. Operation results under different Energy Hub configurations.

Numerical example	1	2	3	4	5
Social results/$	38790	39150	68580	55620	70560
NOx emissions/Kg	65.1	58.1	48.8	47.8	46.1
Power loss/MWh	18.1	18.1	18	17.9	17.8
Heat loss/Kj/h	99.2	94.1	97.3	97.2	93.9
Gas loss/m^3/h	2.115	1.998	2.016	2.034	1.989
Power load/MWh	151	152	157	141	160

Compared with example 1 and example 2, example 3 has been significantly improved in terms of social benefits, carbon emissions and energy consumption due to the addition of renewable energy, but the loss also increases due to the lack of energy storage equipment in the energy hub. Compared with example 3, the absence of p2g device in example 4 reduces its social benefits, carbon emissions and energy loss.

The example shows that considering the penalty cost of NOx emission and carbon trading mechanism, the NOx emission of electricity gas integrated energy system will be reduced. In addition, according to the sensitivity analysis of different scenarios, with the increase of various influencing parameters, the total cost of environmental economic scheduling of electric gas integrated energy system will increase or decrease monotonically. However, in different scenarios, due to various factors such as shutdown of selective catalytic reduction equipment or startup of electric to gas equipment, the changes of operation cost and emission cost of environmental economic dispatching of electric to gas integrated energy system will be more complex.

References

1. Shahidehpour, M., Yong, F.U., Wiedman, T.: Impact of natural gas infrastructure on electric power systems. Proc. IEEE **93**(5), 1042–1056 (2021)
2. Tao, L., Eremia, M., Shahidehpour, M.: Interdependency of natural gas network and power system security. IEEE Trans. Power Syst. **23**(4), 1817–1824 (2008)
3. Alrajhi, H.: A generalized state space average model for parallel DC-to-DC converters. Comput. Syst. Sci. Eng. **41**(2), 717–734 (2022)
4. Zheng, J.H., Wu, Q.H., Jing, Z.X.: Coordinated scheduling strategy to optimize conflicting benefits for daily operation of integrated electricity and gas networks. Appl. Energy **192**, 370–381 (2017)
5. Zheng, H., Shi, D.: A multi-agent system for environmental monitoring using boolean networks and reinforcement learning. J. Cyber Secur. **2**(2), 85–96 (2020)
6. Nidup, Y.: Awareness about the online security threat and ways to secure the youths. J. Cyber Secur. **3**(3), 133–148 (2021)
7. Chen, T., Fang, Y., Pei, S.: Development and deployment of integrated air pollution control, CO2 capture and product utilization via a high-gravity process: comprehensive performance evaluation. Environ. Pollut. **252**, 1464–1475 (2019)
8. Wen, J.W.: China Energy Statistics Yearbook 2013. China Statistics Press, pp. 44–46 (2013)

9. Wang, Y., Zhang, L., Kang, C.Q.: Summary and prospect of research on optimal planning and operation of energy hub in energy Internet. Chin. J. Electr. Eng. **35**(22), 5669–5681 (2015)

10. Shao, C., Wang, X., Shahidehpour, M., Wang, X., Wang, B.: An MILP-based optimal power flow in multicarrier energy systems. IEEE Trans. Sustain. Energy **8**(1), 239–287 (2017)

11. Cheng, C., Lin, D.: Based on compressed sensing of orthogonal matching pursuit algorithm image recovery. J. Internet Things **2**(1), 37–45 (2020)

12. Liu, C., Fu, Y., Li, Z.Y.: Security-constrained unit commitment with natural gas trans- mission constraints. IEEE Trans. Power Syst. TEMS **24**(03), 1523–1536 (2009)

13. Zhou, Z., Wang, J., Zhu, Z.: Tangent navigated robot path planning strategy using particle swarm optimized artificial potential field. Optik – Int. J. Light Electron Opt. **158**, 639–651 (2017)

14. Saraereh, O.A., Ali, A.: Beamforming performance analysis of millimeter-wave 5g wireless networks. Comput. Mater. Continua **70**(3), 5383–5397 (2022)

15. Wang, C., Nehrir, M.H.: Analytical approaches for optimal placement of distributed generation sources in power systems. IEEE Trans. Power Syst. **19**(4), 2068–2076 (2004)

16. Correa-Posada, C.M., Sanchez-Martin, P.: Integrated power and natural gas model for energy adequacy in short-term operation. IEEE Trans. Power Syst. **30**(6), 3347–3355 (2014)

Fire Detection Approach Based on Vision Transformer

Otabek Khudayberdiev[✉] [iD], Jiashu Zhang, Ahmed Elkhalil,
and Lansana Balde

School of Computing and Artificial Intelligence, Southwest Jiaotong University,
Chengdu, China
khudayberdievotabek@my.swjtu.edu.cn

Abstract. Considering the rapid development of embedding surveillance video systems for fire monitoring, we need to distribute systems with high accuracy and detection speed. Recent progress in vision-based fire detection techniques achieved remarkable success by the powerful ability of deep convolutional neural networks. CNN's have long been the architecture of choice for computer vision tasks. However, current CNN-based methods consider fire classification entire image pixels as equal, ignoring regardless of information. Thus, this can cause a low accuracy rate and delay detection. To increase detection speed and achieve high accuracy, we propose a fire detection approach based on Vision Transformer as a viable alternative to CNN. Different from convolutional networks, transformers operate with images as a sequence of patches, selectively attending to different image parts based on context. In addition, the attention mechanism in the transformer solves the problem with a small flame, thereby provide detection fire in the early stage. Since transformers using global self-attention, which conducts complex computing, we utilize fine-tuned Swin Transformer as our backbone architecture that computes self-attention with local windows. Thus, solving the classification problems with high-resolution images. Experimental results conducted on the image fire dataset demonstrate the promising capability of the model compared to state-of-the-art methods. Specifically, Vision Transformer obtains a classification accuracy of 98.54% on the publicly available dataset.

Keywords: Vision transformer · Self-attention · Convolutional neural networks · Fire detection · Image classification

1 Introduction

The rapid development of digital camera technologies and video/image processing techniques, increasingly involved in different spheres of our modern era. Thereby, there is a significant benefit to utilizing fire detection systems with a computer vision-based approach, then traditional techniques [1]. Fire occurs suddenly and spreads in a short time, causing ecological and financial losses.

© The Author(s), under exclusive license to Springer Nature Switzerland AG 2022
X. Sun et al. (Eds.): ICAIS 2022, LNCS 13338, pp. 41–53, 2022.
https://doi.org/10.1007/978-3-031-06794-5_4

By developing the latest fire detection systems, we can prevent and reduce large-scale fire disasters.

Utilizing video-based fire detection techniques, we can get several advantages such as; monitoring open, wide-range areas in 24 h, availability information of size and location, and quick response by analyzing incidents in real-time [2]. Moreover, nowadays, closed-circuit television systems are installed in many spaces. In connection with this, promote the development of a video-based fire detection system is advisable [3].

Plenty of innovative methods have been proposed, build in accurate and timely fire detection systems. Among them, computer vision and image processing techniques constitute a multitude. In [6] the state-of-the-art fire detection methods are compared and evaluated.

There are three main phases in process of image fire detection algorithm, which are image processing, feature extraction and fire detection [7]. Due to a specific characteristic of flame and consider the complex condition of scenes where fire occurs, such as deference environment, unfavourable weather conditions, shadows, fire-like objects, make detection fire on images challenging task. Image recognition algorithms based on convolutional neural network models demonstrate better performance than traditional methods by automatically learn and extract complex fire-image features [4].

Though the newest fire detection algorithms based on computer vision techniques have high detection accuracy and sufficient speed, the applications based on these approaches still have some limitations [5]. Current fire detection algorithms mostly considered image fire detection as a classification task. The algorithms classify the entire image into one class. However, not all pixels useful. In image classification tasks, target foreground objects should have preference over the background. But convolution operations apply for all pixels, leading to extra computation cost and redundant information.

CNN automatically learns and extracts low-level features such as edges and corners by applying convolutional filters for the whole image. However, due to specific characteristics of fire, high-level features can exist in different scene images. For example, at the beginning of the fire, a small flame can occur in buildings, in cars, and dense environments. But applying high-level filters to all images leads to more computational costs.

Another limitation of convolutions is related spatial-distance concepts. To avoid extensive calculation, convolutional filters are constrained to operate with small regions. But, the long-term interaction between semantic concepts is essential. Previous approaches consider increase kernel size, expand depth of the model or apply other operations such as dilated convolutions, non-local attention layers and global pooling. But these methods lead to insolvencies such as additional modules and computational costs.

To address to aforementioned issues we propose Vision Transformer approach for fire detection on images. Summarizing our work we can express as follows:

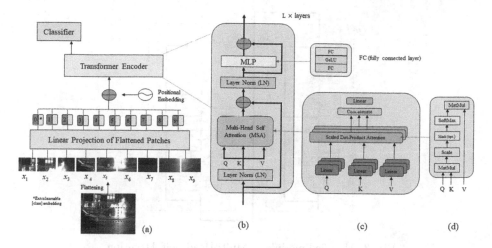

Fig. 1. An overview of standart Vision Transformer architecture

1) We avoid the pixel-convolutional operation on images, and propose spatial attention method converting the feature map into set a sequence of patches by exploring transformer architecture for fire detection.
2) We train and fine-tune model using Swin Transformer [24] as our backbone architecture for fire detection on images.
3) Finally, we evaluate proposed model with other state-of-the-art methods with publicly available dataset. Comparison results show that proposed method outperforms fire detection methods based on CNN archived by 98.54% accuracy.

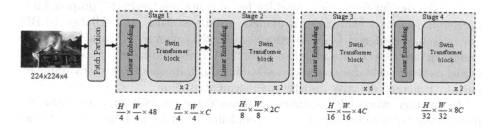

Fig. 2. An overview of Swin Transformer Structure

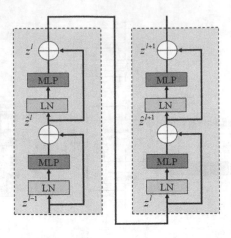

Fig. 3. Modified module of Multi-Head Self Attention

2   Related Work

2.1   CNNs Based Fire Detection

There has been a lot of research into the development of systems that could detect fire with high accuracy indoor and outdoor environment. With the development of CNN in the field of computer vision, many researchers have invested in improving systems for detecting fire in images.

Pionering study in this research appliying CNN [19] propose two different models based on Deep CNN, VGG16 and ResNet50. Modifying Resnet50 by adding extra fully connected layers the authors achieved high accuracy, and showed effectiveness Resnet50 over VGG16 on detection fire on images.

Considering involving more machine learning approaches in [15] proposed fire prevention method utilizing two models, Adaboost-MLP and Adaboost-LBP under similar designed CNN as AlexNet. AlexNet shows his excellent performance in fire detection and other authors [17] also utilize modified AlexNet model as their backbone architecture. Minimizing damage of fire to environment authors proposed effective disaster management system.

In another work [20], authors achieved detection efficiency by reducing parameters SqueezeNet under target problems. In order to minimize cost and flexible installation on CCTV cameras, the size of model was reduced by using small convolution with no dense. Case studies were investigated in [16] with four object detection CNN models such as SSD, R-FCN, Faster-RCNN and YOLO v3. The authors focused their module mainly on region proposal functions. By implementation their proposed method for each models, authors achieved higher performance with YOLO v3 than other models. In [23] authors offered an accurate fire detection approach consists of combination of three modules under AlexNet backbone. Utilizing efficiently multiscale feature extraction, implicit deep supervision and channel attention mechanism, model demonstrates significant results in size and accuracy.

2.2 Vision Transformer

In [13], Vision transformer (ViT) demonstrated how transformers could replace standard convolutional in deep learning networks on large-scale computer vision dataset. The Transformer follows the encoder-decoder architecture, with the ability to process sequential data in parallel without relying on any recurrent network.

Given an image X, it is divided into a sequence of non-overlapping patches p as an individual token, and the dimension d of each patch equals to $p \times p \times c$, where c is a number of channels. The length n of sequence patches $(x_1, x_2, ..., x_n)$ define as $n = hw/p^2$. In standard ViT size of patches equal 16×16 or 32×32. Overview of standard ViT architecture illustrated in Fig. 1.

2.3 Linear Embedding

In the linear embedding layer, the sequence of patches is linearly projected to a 1D vector by a learned embedding matrix E. In the next stage, embedding representation with the additional classification token (CLS) are concatenated, here (CLS) token used for classification purpose. To maintain the spatial arrange of the patches as the same as input image, the positional information E_{pos} is encoded and add to the patch representations. In summary, the output of linearly embedding layer z_0 can express as in Eq. 1.

$$z_0 = [cls; x_1E; x_2E; ...x_nE] + E_{\text{pos}} ,$$
$$E \in \mathbb{R}^{(p^2c) \times d},$$
$$E_{\text{pos}} \in \mathbb{R}^{(n+1) \times d} \tag{1}$$

2.4 Vision Transformer Encoder

The next stage summary of linearly embedding layer z_0 pass to the Transformer Encoder module, as shown in Fig. 1(b). The encoder consists L identical layers, and each layer contains two main subcomponents, a multi-head self-attention block (MSA) and a fully connected feed-forward dense block (MLP). MLP consists of two dense layers with GeLU activation between them. Both components of the encoder use residual skip connection, among with a normalization layer (LN). The output of each component express as:

$$z'_\ell = \text{MSA}\left(\text{LN}\left(z_{\ell-1}\right)\right) + z_{\ell-1}, \quad \ell = 1 \ldots L \tag{2}$$

$$z_\ell = \text{MLP}\left(\text{LN}\left(z'_\ell\right)\right) + z'_\ell, \quad \ell = 1 \ldots L \tag{3}$$

As can be seen in Fig. 2 the first element of sequence z_l^0 passed throw classification block for prediction class can be expressed as function;

$$y = \text{LN}\left(z_L^0\right) \tag{4}$$

2.5 Multi-head Self-Attention Layer (MSA)

A self-attention mechanism is a central component of transformers, which determine the interactions between all sequence entities for the build prediction task. The primary role of self-attention is to capture the interaction amongst all z sequences by encoding each entity in terms of global contextual information. The self-attention head learns attention weights by computing three learnable metrics weights. As shown in Fig. 1 (c), three weights matrices are generated for each input sequence as **Query** $\left(W^Q \in \mathbb{R}^{n \times d_q}\right)$, **Key** $\left(W^K \in \mathbb{R}^{n \times d_k}\right)$, and **Value** $\left(W^V \in \mathbb{R}^{n \times d_v}\right)$, where n is the sequence of entities and d is the embedding dimension. The input sequence X first projected onto these weight matrices as $Q = XW^Q$, $K = XW^K$ and $V = XW^V$. The output $A \in \mathbb{R}^{n \times d_n}$ of self-attention layers expressed as

$$A = soft \max \left(\frac{QK^T}{\sqrt{d_q}}\right) V \tag{5}$$

Next, the value of each patch embeddings vector is multiplied by A and find the patch with high attention scores

$$SA(z) = V \cdot A \tag{6}$$

After that, all the attention heads concatenated and projected through a feed-forward layer with learnable weight W, the output of MSA expressed in equation ()

$$\text{MSA}(z) \, \text{concat}\left(SA_1(z); SA_2(z) \ldots SA_n(z)\right) W \tag{7}$$

In our work, we follow a recent trend of attention based neural networks in Computer vision and extensively evaluated Vision Transformer models. Inspired by high accuracy, a hierarchical feature representation and achievement state of the art result in many image classification task we build upon our fire detection methon under [24] model. In order to reduce training time we utilized pretraied model from timm library [25]

3 Proposed Method

As shown in Fig. 2, architecture consists of four stages. In the first step, an image of size $224 \times 224 \times 3$ passes through a patch splitting module and is subdivided into non-overlapping patches. Each patch (p) is viewed as an individual token, and its feature is a set of a concatenated raw pixels of the RGB image.

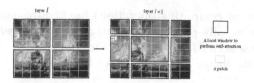

Fig. 4. Shifted windows method of Swin-T for computing self-attention

To generate a hierarchical form, with increasing depth of the network, patch merging layers decrease the number of tokens. Thereby, the first patch merging layer concatenated with the features of each neighboring group patches with 2×2, and a linear layer receive concatenated features as the dimension of 4C. This operation decrease the number of tokens and output dimension by a multiple of $2 \times 2 = 4$, and 2C respectively. In the next 2nd stage, tokens with size $\frac{H}{8} \times \frac{W}{8}$ pass-through patch merging module. The same operation continues in stage 3 and stage 4, with the output resolution of $\frac{H}{16} \times \frac{W}{16}$ and $\frac{H}{32} \times \frac{W}{32}$ respectively.

In the next stage, produced patch tokens path through several Swin Transformer blocks with modified self-attention computation. The Transformer blocks keep the number of tokens with size $\left(\frac{H}{4} \times \frac{W}{4}\right)$ and together with the linear embedding are referred to as stage 1.

Table 1. Architecture of Swin Transformer (Swin-T)

Stage	Output size	Swin-T
Stage 1	4 × (56 × 56)	con 4 × 4, 96-d, LN, [(win.size 7 × 7, dim 96, head 3)×2]
Stage 2	8 × (28 × 28)	con 2 × 2, 192-d, LN [(win.size 7 × 7, dim 192, head 6)×2]
Stage 3	16 × (14 × 14)	con 2 × 2, 384-d, LN [(win.size 7 × 7, dim 384, head 12)×6]
Stage 4	32 × (7 × 7)	con 2 × 2, 768-d, LN [(win.size 7 × 7, dim 768, head 24)×2]

3.1 Swin Transformer Block

Swin Transformer is created by modified the normal multi-head self-attention module (MSA) (as described above) in a Transformer block with a window-shifted module, with the rest of the layers remaining the same. Module illustrated in Fig. 3. Swin Transformer blocks are made up of a shifted window-based MSA module followed by a 2-layer MLP with GELU non-linearity in between. Each MSA module and MLP is preceded by a LayerNorm (LN) layer, and each module is followed by a residual connection.

3.2 Shifted-Window Based Self-Attention

Transformer architecture applied for image classification conducts global self-attention as computation tokens with each other to find interrelation between them. By computing self-attention within the local window, the modified module reduces the number of computing operations for high-resolution images. The windows are set by equally partition the image in a non-overlapping way. Let suppose each window keep $M \times M$ patches, the computation of a window based MSA's patches on the image are $h \times w$ shown in equation:

$$\Omega(\text{W} - \text{MSA}) = 4\,hwC^2 + 2M^2 hwC \tag{8}$$

Computation process with softmax function is the same as mentioned in Sect. 2.

3.3 Shifted Window Partitioning in Successive Blocks

As shown in Fig. 4, the first module employs a standard window partitioning method that begins with the pixel in the top-left corner, and the 8×8 feature map is equally divided into 2×2 windows of size 4×4 (M = 4). After that, the next module takes over a window configuration that is shifted from that of the preceding layer by mapping the windows by $\left(\lfloor \frac{M}{2} \rfloor, \lfloor \frac{M}{2} \rfloor\right)$ pixels from the regularly divided windows. Swin Transformer block with shifted window divided method, computed as:

$$\begin{aligned}
\hat{\mathbf{z}}^l &= \text{W} - \text{MSA}\left(\text{LN}\left(\mathbf{z}^{l-1}\right)\right) + \mathbf{z}^{l-1} \\
\mathbf{z}^l &= \text{MLP}\left(\text{LN}\left(\hat{\mathbf{z}}^l\right)\right) + \hat{\mathbf{z}}^l \\
\hat{\mathbf{z}}^{l+1} &= \text{SW} - \text{MSA}\left(\text{LN}\left(\mathbf{z}^l\right)\right) + \mathbf{z}^l \\
\mathbf{z}^{l+1} &= \text{MLP}\left(\text{LN}\left(\hat{\mathbf{z}}^{l+1}\right)\right) + \hat{\mathbf{z}}^{l+1}
\end{aligned} \tag{9}$$

The shifted window partitioning approach introduces connections between neighboring non-overlapping windows in the previous layer and is found to be effective in connections between neighboring non-overlapping windows in the previous layer and is found to be effective in the image classification task-other parts of the proposed method similar as standard Vision Transformer as we mentioned above in section II, detailed structure illustrated in Table 1.

4   Experimental Results and Discussion

In this section, we first provide the details about the datasets, data augmentation techniques, implementation details, and evaluation metrics. Then, fire detection performance of the proposed method is compared and analyzed with other existing CNN-based methods.

4.1 Dataset

Dataset: To evaluate the proposed method, we chose "FD-dataset" [6] for its large size and image frames captured in challenge scenes on the video. The base of this dataset consists of two well-known benchmark dataset [7,8] and additional images collected by authors. The dataset includes 25 000 images for training, 10 000 for validation, and 5000 for testing. Table 2 describe detailed information of dataset.

Table 2. Fire detection dataset description

Class	Training set	Validation set	Testing set	Total
Fire	17 500	5 000	2 500	25 000
No Fire	17 500	5 000	2 500	25 000

Table 3. Precision, Recall, F_{score} and accuracy between our method and other techniques

Method	Precision (%)	Recall (%)	F1-score (%)	Accuracy (%)
[19]	84.8	97.6	0.90	90.0
[20]	84.6	91.3	0.87	87.3
[17]	83.3	93.2	0.87	87.2
[22]	88.0	98.0	0.92	92.3
[23]	93.5	97.4	0.95	95.3
Ours	95.6	98.7	0.97	98.5

In addition, authors tried to create dataset with more realistic characteristic fire accident scenes with different circumstances such as forest fire, burning buildings, accidents with cars, boat fires, etc. Figure 5 demonstrates some examples of images from "FD-dataset". Moreover, the non-fire folder in the dataset contains challenging images such as night lighting, glare lights, burning clouds, sunset, red colour elements, and fire-like objects.

4.2 Data Augmentation

To the best of my knowledge, in fire and smoke detection, compared with other image classification fields, there are not many publicly available dataset, which can increase the performance of proposed models. Since Transformers do not inherently encode inductive biases to deal with visual data, the model needs a large amount of data, to figure out image-specific properties. To obtain and train with the same size of images, we use an extensive data augmentation technique. Data augmentation generate new images from the existing dataset by applying various manipulation techniques. Standard methods include geometric transformation and colour augmentation strategies.

Because of the specific characteristics of the fire scene, vision-based fire monitoring systems can transmit low-quality captured images, the consequence of unfavourable weather conditions, obstruction by other objects, random noise, etc. Considering these factors, we utilize more sophisticated data augmentation techniques, such as Cutout [9], Mixup [10], and CutMix [11]. These novel methods solved the aforementioned issues in fire detection, with challenging scenes, occluded objects, random noise, etc. We use the same strategies in our model as [12], which increase accuracy and robustness for different kinds of attacks.

Fig. 5. Some example of dataset.

4.3 Implementation Details

We used a model pretrained on ImageNet-1K [26], and fine-tuned it for fire detection purpose on FD-dataset. The model was trained and evaluated with Pytorch framework on PC with Intel Core i7 CPU and NVIDIA GeForce GTX 1080 TI. Specifically, the AdamW optimizer was selected with 100 epochs for training. The initial learning rate was 0.001, weight decay equals 0.05, and batch size is 64.

$$\text{Recall} = \frac{TP}{TP + FN} \tag{10}$$

$$\text{Precision} = \frac{TP}{TP + FP} \tag{11}$$

$$F_{\text{scare}} = \frac{\text{recall} \times \text{precision}}{\text{recall} + \text{precision}} \tag{12}$$

$$\text{Accuracy} = \frac{TP + TN}{TP + FN + FP + TN} \tag{13}$$

4.4 Compared with CNN-Based Fire Detection Methods

Inspired by recent progress achieved models with data augmentation techniques, we trained our model on benchmark dataset with standard augmentation and with aforementioned more sophisticated techniques. Evaluating results on test data show better results with Cutout, Mixup and CutMix techniques, as illustrated in Table 1.

To demonstrate the advantage of our approach, we compare Transformer based fire detection with other existing CNN based methods. We conduct experiments on publicly available dataset named "FD-dataset" [20] and analyze performance models with the same technique as mentioned in [20] such as precision, recall, F1-score and accuracy, detailed comparison models illustrated in Table 3. The most important aspect of fire detection is accuracy; therefore the experimental results are addressed mostly in terms of accuracy.

Our approach achieved 98.54% accuracy with "FD-dataset" without augmentation and 99.4% accuracy with sophisticated augmentation techniques. Vision Transformer based fire detection method outperformed other CNN based fire detection techniques such as Alexnet, VGG16 and ResNet50. The experimental results are shown

$$C_t = f'_t \circ C_{t-1} + i_t \circ \tanh\left(W_c^X * X_t + W_c^H * H_{t-1} + b_c\right)$$

in $L_{/\mathrm{sum}} = L_{\mathrm{cls}} + \alpha$ Table 2.

5 Conclusion

Consider the complex condition of scenes where fire occurs, we need to distribute fire monitoring systems with high accuracy and detection speed. In this study, we show a viable alternative to CNN and propose a fire detection approach based on Vision Transformer. We follow a recent trend of attention based neural networks and avoid the pixel-convolutional operation. To increase detection speed and achieve high accuracy, we propose a fire detection approach based on Vision Transformer. Specifically, the attention mechanism in the transformer provide detection small flames in early stage. Since transformers using global self-attention, which lead computational costs, we utilize Swin Transformer architecture that computes self-attention with local windows. Providing the classification with high-resolution images. Comparison results over state-of-the-art and proposed fire detection models demonstrate superiority over the rest of the latter.

References

1. Zhang, Y., Zhang, S., Zhang, J., Guo, K., Cai, Z.: Key frame extraction of surveillance video based on frequency domain analysis. Intel. Autom. Soft Comput. **29**(1), 259–272 (2021)
2. Zheng, H., Shi, D.: A multi-agent system for environmental monitoring using boolean networks and reinforcement learning. J. Cybersecurity **2**(2), 85 (2020)
3. Wang, J., Zhang, T., Cheng, Y., Al-Nabhan, N.: Deep learning for object detection: a survey. Comput. Syst. Sci. Eng. **38**(2), 65–82 (2021)
4. Liu, Q., Lu, S., Lan, L.: Yolov3 attention face detector with high accuracy and efficiency. Comput. Syst. Sci. Eng. **37**(2), 83–95 (2021)

5. Zhou, J., et al.: Mixed attention densely residual network for single image super-resolution. Comput. Syst. Sci. Eng. **39**(1), 133–46 (2021)
6. Bu, F., Gharajeh, M.S.: Intelligent and vision-based fire detection systems: a survey. Image Vis. Comput. **91** (2019). https://doi.org/10.1016/j.imavis.2019.08.007
7. Li, P., Zhao, W.: Image fire detection algorithms based on convolutional neural networks. Case Stud. Therm. Eng. **19** (2020). https://doi.org/10.1016/j.csite.2020.100625
8. Wu, B., et al.: Visual transformers: token-based image representation and processing for computer vision. arXiv:2006.03677 (2020)
9. Beal, J., Kim, E., Tzeng, E., Park, D.H., Zhai, A., Kislyuk, D.: Toward transformer-based object detection. arXiv:2012.09958 (2020)
10. Chen, C.F.R., Fan, Q. and Panda, R.: CrossViT: cross-attention multi-scale vision transformer for image classification. In: Proceedings of the IEEE/CVF International Conference on Computer Vision, pp. 357–366 (2021)
11. Chen, J., et al.: TransuNet: transformers make strong encoders for medical image segmentation. arXiv:2102.04306 (2021)
12. Khan, S., Naseer, M., Hayat, M., Zamir, S.W., Khan, F.S., Shah, M.: Transformers in Vision: a survey. arXiv:2101.01169 (2021)
13. Dosovitskiy, A., et al.: An image is worth 16×16 words: transformers for image recognition at scale. arXiv:2010.11929 (2020)
14. Faswani, A., et al.: Attention is all you need. arXiv:1706.03762 (2017)
15. Saeed, F., Paul, A., Karthigaikumar, P., Nayyar, A.: Convolutional neural network based early fire detection. Multimedia Tools Appl. 9083–9099 (2019). https://doi.org/10.1007/s11042-019-07785-w
16. Li, P., Zhao, W.: Image fire detection algorithms based on convolutional neural networks. Case Stud. Thermal Eng. **19**, 100625 (2020)
17. Muhammad, K., Ahmad, J., Baik, S.W.: Early fire detection using convolutional neural networks during surveillance for effective disaster management. Neurocomputing **288**, 30–42 (2018)
18. Frizzi, S., Kaabi, R., Bouchouicha, M., Ginoux, J.M., Moreau, E., Fnaiech, F.: Convolutional neural network for video fire and smoke detection. In: IECON 2016–42nd Annual Conference of the IEEE Industrial Electronics Society, pp. 877–882. IEEE (2016)
19. Sharma, J., Granmo, O.-C., Goodwin, M., Fidje, J.T.: Deep convolutional neural networks for fire detection in images. In: Boracchi, G., Iliadis, L., Jayne, C., Likas, A. (eds.) EANN 2017. CCIS, vol. 744, pp. 183–193. Springer, Cham (2017). https://doi.org/10.1007/978-3-319-65172-9_16
20. Muhammad, K., Ahmad, J., Lv, Z., Bellavista, P., Yang, P., Baik, S.W.: Efficient deep CNN-based fire detection and localization in video surveillance applications. IEEE Trans. Syst. Man Cybern. Syst. **49**(7), 1419–1434 (2018)
21. Wu, B. et al.: Visual transformers: token-based image representation and processing for computer vision. arXiv:2006.03677v2 (2020)
22. Muhammad, K., Ahmad, J., Mehmood, I., Rho, S., Baik, S.W.: Convolutional neural networks based fire detection in surveillance videos. IEEE Access **6**, 18174–18183 (2018)
23. Li, S., Yan, Q., Liu, P.: An efficient fire detection method based on multiscale feature extraction, implicit deep supervision and channel attention mechanism. IEEE Trans. Image Process. **29**, 8467–8475 (2020)
24. Liu, Z., et al.: Swin transformer: hierarchical vision transformer using shifted windows. In: Proceedings of the IEEE/CVF International Conference on Computer Vision, pp. 10012–10022 (2021)

25. https://github.com/rwightman/pytorch-image-models
26. Deng, J., Dong, W., Socher, R., Li, L.J., Li, K., Li, F.F.: ImageNet: a large-scale hierarchical image database. In: 2009 IEEE Conference on Computer Vision and Pattern Recognition, pp. 248–255. IEEE (2009)

Construction and Application of Air Pollutant Concentration Prediction Model Based on Multivariate

Li Xin, Pengrui Li[✉], Shuai Zeng, and Yujie Liang

Chengdu University of Information Technology, Chengdu 610225, China
925189684@qq.com

Abstract. For many years, as humans wreak havoc on nature, there are fewer and fewer vegetation on the earth, natural disasters have become more frequent, and air pollution has become more and more serious. However, because air pollution is a global problem, its influencing factors and development trends are very complicated. Therefore, finding the factors that affect the changes in the concentration of pollutants and explaining the relationship between the concentration of air pollutants and the influencing factors is of great significance for humans to understand the trend of changes in the concentration of air pollutants. This paper designs a grey prediction model based on fractional order to predict the pollutant concentration of three non-interfering monitoring points at the same time, and compares the calculated deviation with the measured value to judge whether it is used in the prediction of atmospheric pollutant concentration. With regard to the problem of regional coordinated forecasting, in this paper, a Bayesian network model is constructed to conduct coordinated forecasting of atmospheric pollutant concentration in four interfering regions. The experimental results on the data set show that the algorithm in this paper is suitable for predicting the concentration of air pollutants.

Keywords: Pollutant concentration · Fractional order · Grey model · Bayesian network · Collaborative forecast

1 Introduction

Air Pollution is one of the serious and major environmental problem worldwide [1]. The release of air quality forecast can provide scientific basis for the environmental protection departments timely. The establishment of air quality forecast model of city environmental governance is very necessary [2]. The pollution affects the society, and endangers the survival of life on earth leading to several health hazards such as asthma, lung cancer etc. and environmental hazards such as global warming, acid rains, eutrophication and many more [3]. Air pollutants include sulfur dioxide (SO2), nitrogen dioxide (NO2), carbon monoxide (CO), ozone (O3), PM2.5 and PM10, etc., and their hazards are serious [4]. The three major pollution causing components of environmental air are SO_2 concentration, NO_2 concentration and the particulate matter (PM)[5].

© The Author(s), under exclusive license to Springer Nature Switzerland AG 2022
X. Sun et al. (Eds.): ICAIS 2022, LNCS 13338, pp. 54–68, 2022.
https://doi.org/10.1007/978-3-031-06794-5_5

The prediction of air pollutants is a key research field in the meteorological community. Precise predictions of the concentration of air pollutants can prompt people to go out and protect themselves and reduce the harm to the body caused by air pollution. With the vigorous development of computer technology and the continuous updating of information technology, machine learning and deep learning have become important tools to promote people's detection and prediction methods. The data processing and analysis of deep learning are used to achieve the purpose of predicting the concentration of air pollutants. At present, it is an issue that urgently needs research by scientific researchers. There are few obstacles to air computing; however as the associated data have spatial characteristics. The first problem faced was the insufficient air quality monitoring station because of the higher cost of building and maintaining a station, it is costly to get labeled fine grain air quality training data [6]. The traditional air quality prediction method is to install specific sensors in the residential area, collect air in the community, get basic air monitoring index data and meteorological data, then use some algorithms to process the data, and finally predict the air quality[7].

Although the methods adopted by the above-mentioned researchers have shown good results, there are still some shortcomings. First of all, the previous research on atmospheric prediction was limited to the study of a certain region. With different regions, most of the established models will be inapplicable. On the other hand, in the past, scientific researchers' research on collaborative prediction models was basically applied to the prediction of natural disasters such as earthquakes and landslides, but not to the prediction of atmospheric pollutant concentrations.

In response to the above problems, this paper first proposes a grey model method based on fractional order. The data in the data set from May 10th to May 18th, 2021 are selected as a set of continuous time series and input into the model after preprocessing, then make predictions. After comparing the predicted values with the actual measured values, the pollutant concentration values of the three monitoring points A, B, and C from July 13 to July 15, 2021 are predicted. Then, a Bayesian network model is proposed to coordinate the forecast of atmospheric pollutant concentration at four monitoring points A, A1, A2, and A3, so as to improve the forecasting effect of atmospheric pollutant concentration. The position distribution of the four monitoring points in the coordinate system is shown in Fig. 1.

The main contributions of this paper are as follows:

1) On the basis of the gray prediction model, a fractional-level gray prediction model is proposed, which can be applied to the air pollutant concentration prediction at the three monitoring points of A, B, and C at the same time.
2) Based on the problem that the pollutant concentration in adjacent areas has a certain correlation, a Bayesian network model is proposed for regional collaborative forecasting.
3) The experimental results prove that the grey prediction model based on fractional order and the Bayesian network model have good accuracy in predicting the concentration of regional air pollutants.

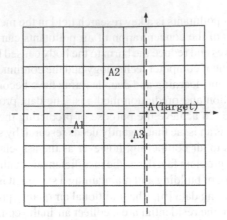

Fig. 1. Schematic diagram of the relative position of each monitoring station. A (0, 0) A1 (−14.4846, −1.9699) A2 (−6.6716, 7.5953) A3 (−3.3543, −5.0138)

2 Related Work

Air quality is closely related to people's daily life because of fast industrialization and urbanization, and it also plays an important role in the comprehensive evaluation of environment [8].

The weather forecasts we know now include short-term, medium-term and long-term. The short term is the forecast of the weather in the next three days, the medium term is the forecast of the weather in 10 days, and the long term is the forecast of more than 10 days, even a month or even a year. Short-term weather conditions are easy to predict, mainly because the influence of interfering factors and uncertain factors are relatively small. And with longer time, interfering factors and uncertain factors will be more and more, which lead to the serious uncertainty of the climate change. At this time, the deviation between the predicted result and the actual result may be large, so the predicted result is difficult to be used as a basis.

2.1 Forecast Based on Grey Model

There are already many models that can be used for atmospheric prediction. Fang Wei et al. proposed that the air quality prediction model based on time-space similarity LSTM selects more effective data for training at the time and space level, and the effect of prediction error is increased by 8% [9]. Huang Chuntao and others proposed a study on the prediction of PM2.5 and PM10 concentrations in Guangzhou based on deep learning. Based on air quality monitoring data and meteorological monitoring data, they constructed random forest models, XGBoost models, long and short-term memory networks, and gated loop units, respectively. The network model predicts the average daily concentration value [10].

2.2 Forecast Based on Bayesian Network Model

Over the years, in the research of collaborative forecasting models, a large number of scientific researchers have tried to build various models to improve the accuracy of collaborative forecasting. Guo Chaozhen and others researched the general model of collaborative comprehensive forecasting IGDSS, using the intelligent decision-making method of comprehensive earthquake forecasting IGDSS-Bayesian network design and implementation, and established a Bayesian network analyzer for comprehensive earthquake forecasting. The system has been applied in Fujian Province. Earthquake Bureau Prediction Center [11]. Liu Shijun and others used the method of correlation analysis to focus on the correlation between the monthly average concentration of the same air pollutants in the Beijing area and the closer Shijiazhuang area. The impact of air quality [12].

3 Related Work

This section first introduces the design process of the gray prediction model based on fractional order, and then introduces the Bayesian network model.

3.1 Grey Prediction Model Based on Fractional Order

The data of consecutive days in a year is a time series. When a single time series is used for forecasting, the sample size of a single time series may be too small to meet the predicted demand, or some data may have anomalies, causing large fluctuations in the series. It can be obtained that the gray modeling method can be used to predict the time series with the unit of day. For example, use the data from May 10 to 18, 2021 as a set of time series for GM(1,1) prediction. Then process the result to get the original time series forecast value. This is the basic idea of the GM(1,1) model (GM(1,1)Model, referred to as GM(1,1)). The GM(1,1) model is different from the traditional gray forecasting method. Its data is not limited to smooth data, which broadens the application range of gray forecasting. Based on the GM(1,1) model, coupled with the fractional accumulation operator, a fractional GM(1.1) model (referred to as FGM(1,1)) is constructed to effectively improve the prediction accuracy. The modeling steps of the FGM(1,1) model are as follows:

1. The data sequence of consecutive days in a year is shown in Eq. (1):

$$x_{(t)}^{(0)} = \left\{ x^{(0)}(1), x^{(0)}(2), \cdots, x^{(0)}(m) \right\}, (t = 1, 2, \cdots, n) \qquad (1)$$

   where t represents the specific pollution factor, $x^{(0)}(k)$ represents the actual average measured concentration of the pollution factor in one day on the corresponding date.

2. Data inspection Before making grey prediction, it is necessary to inspect the original data landline ratio. Among them, the grade ratio inspection formula is shown in Eq. (2). The grade ratio inspection formula was proposed when the gray model was created, so the gray model based on fractional order can make the test effects better.

$$\sigma(k) = x^{(0)}(k-1) \Big/ x^{(0)}(k) \qquad (2)$$

If the level ratio is verified to meet $\sigma(k) \in \left(e^{-2/(n+1)}, e^{2/(n+1)}\right)$, then the data sequence can be considered suitable for GM (1,1) modeling. If the level ratio does not meet the above conditions, you need to do some special processing on the data so that it meets the above conditions. Data processing methods often used include translation and transformation.

3. To construct the generated data sequence, it is necessary to accumulate the original data sequence once, which is recorded as shown in Eq. (3):

$$x_{(t)}^{(1)} = \left\{x^{(1)}(1), x^{(1)}(2), \cdots, x^{(1)}(m)\right\}$$ (3)

where $x^{(1)}(k) = \sum_{i=1}^{k} x^{(0)}(i)$, $(k = 1, 2, \cdots m)$.

Generate a sequence of equal weights $Z_{(t)}^{(1)}$ adjacent to the mean value of $x_{(t)}^{(1)}$, which is shown in Eq. (4):

$$Z_{(t)}^{(1)} = \left\{z^{(1)}(1), z^{(1)}(2), \cdots, z^{(1)}(m)\right\}$$ (4)

where $z^{(1)}(1) = x^{(1)}(1)$, $z^{(1)}(k) = 0.5x^{(1)}(k) + 0.5x^{(1)}(k-1)(k = 2, \cdots, m)$

4. Build the model: use the first-order univariate differential equation to fit the generated data sequence $X_{(t)}^{(1)}$ to obtain the gray prediction model. Its whitening form is shown in Eq. (5):

$$\frac{dx^{(1)}}{dt} + ax^{(1)} = b$$ (5)

where a is the development parameter and b is the gray effect.

The parameter list is denoted as $\hat{a} = (a, b)^T$, Eq. (6) is obtained by the least square method:

$$\hat{a} = (B^T B)^{-1} B^T Y$$ (6)

Where

$$B = \begin{pmatrix} -z^{(1)}(2) & 1 \\ -z^{(1)}(3) & 1 \\ \vdots & \vdots \\ -z^{(1)}(m) & 1 \end{pmatrix} \quad Y = \begin{pmatrix} x^{(0)}(2) \\ x^{(0)}(3) \\ \vdots \\ x^{(0)}(m) \end{pmatrix}$$ (7)

5. Solution and reduction: Find the solution of the whitening equation. the event response sequence is shown in Eq. (8):

$$\hat{x}^{(1)}(k+1) = \left(x^{(0)}(1) - \frac{b}{a}\right)e^{-ak} + \frac{b}{a}k = 1, 2, \cdots, m-1$$ (8)

Accumulate and subtract according to $\hat{x}^{(1)}(k+1) = \hat{x}^{(1)}(k+1) - \hat{x}^{(1)}(k)$ to generate a sequence of restored values:

$$\hat{x}^{(0)} = \left\{\hat{x}^{(0)}(1), \hat{x}^{(0)}(1), \cdots, \hat{x}^{(0)}(m)\right\}$$ (9)

3.2   Forecasting Model Based on Bayesian Network

Bayesian network is a decision-making method that inputs the data of four observation points into the established network model so that they can do prediction work in a more reasonable ratio. Bayesian network is a very effective model for expressing uncertain knowledge and reasoning about the domain. The Bayesian network network has the ability to deal with uncertain knowledge problems and the ability to calibrate and fuse multiple types of information. It has a lot of application space in the prediction of atmospheric pollutant concentration. These are mainly reflected in: First, climate change is fickle, pollutant concentration changes are complex, and there are too many influencing factors; second, the concentration of air pollutants in adjacent areas will affect each other, which requires further research and discussion, and there is still a long way to go. The road needs to be walked, and this idea can be used for reference by scientific researchers. If the data of the four observation points can be fused and expressed through the model, not only can the accuracy of predicting the concentration of atmospheric pollutants be improved to a large extent, but also pave the way for more complex problems in the future.

The Bayesian network can be represented by a 3-tuple $N = \{X, G, P\}$, which consists of the following [11]:

1) A directed acyclic graph $G = \{V, E\}$. $V = \{v1, v2, \cdots, v\|v\|\}$ is the node set of the directed acyclic graph, $E = \{(vi, vj)\}(i = 1, 2, \cdots, \|v\|, j = 1, 2, \cdots, \|v\|)$ is the set of directed edges between nodes.
2) A set of random variables represented by a set of vertices in a directed acyclic graph $G = \{V, E\}$. $X = \{Xv1, Xv2, \cdots, Xv\|v\|\}$, where, $Xvi(i = 1, 2, \cdots, \|v\|)$ indicates the variable corresponding to the node.
3) A table P of conditional probabilities related to a set of nodes V. Conditional probability tables can be subjective beliefs or objective probabilities. The conditional probability table can be described by $P(Xvi|Xparent(vi))$, $Xparent(vi)$ represents the variable set of all parent nodes of the node. It expresses the conditional probability relationship between a node and its parent node. The conditional probability of a node without any parent node is its prior probability.

This paper establishes a Bayesian network for the coordinated forecast of air pollutants between regions, and proposes to input the pollutant concentration data of four observation points into the Bayesian network for calibration and fusion processing. An effective system to optimize and modify the Bayesian network in a concise way.

4   Experimental Result and Analysis

This section first introduces the data set and evaluation indicators used in the experiment, then analyzes the results of the evaluation indicators, and finally explains the applicability of the model.

4.1 Dataset

The data set in this article is selected from the data provided by the organizer of Problem B of the Huawei Cup Graduate Mathematical Modeling Contest in 2021. The data set is about the basic long-term air quality forecast data of monitoring points, including primary pollutant concentration forecast data, primary meteorological forecast data, meteorological measured data and pollutant concentration measured data. The time span of all primary forecast data is 2020-7- 23-2021-7-13, the time span of all measured data is 2019-4-16-2021-7-13, and the total amount of data is in the order of 100,000. The daily forecast time is fixed at 7 o'clock in the morning. At this time, the measured data at 7 o'clock of the day and the time before, as well as the one-time forecast data of the operation date on the current day and the previous day (the forecast time range is as of 23:00 on the third day). The hourly measured data with the monitoring time after 7 o'clock of the day and the forecast data of the operation date on the next day and later are not available. Due to the limitation of the monitoring data authority and the functions of the corresponding monitoring equipment, the measured data of some meteorological indicators cannot be obtained. For the test of the gray model based on the fractional order, this paper selects the data input from May 10, 2021 to May 18, 2021 to build the model to determine whether the model is applicable. For the test based on the Bayesian network model, this article selects the data input from May 14, 2021 to May 18, 2021 to build the model to determine whether the model is applicable.

4.2 Evaluation Index

This paper uses relative error and level ratio deviation to evaluate the applicability and robustness of the model.

4.3 The Experimental Results and Analysis

(1) Based on the fractional order grey model prediction.

Table 1. Model test results.

Date	The original value	Predictive value	Residual	The relative error	Level ratio deviation
2021/5/10	75.000	75.000	0.000	0.000%	–
2021/5/11	67.000	64.537	2.463	3.676%	−0.096
2021/5/12	62.000	63.185	−1.185	1.911%	−0.058
2021/5/13	60.000	61.861	−1.861	3.101%	−0.012
2021/5/14	59.000	60.564	−1.564	2.652%	0.004
2021/5/15	59.000	59.295	−0.295	0.501%	0.021

(continued)

Table 1. (*continued*)

Date	The original value	Predictive value	Residual	The relative error	Level ratio deviation
2021/5/16	60.000	58.053	1.947	3.245%	0.037
2021/5/17	59.000	56.836	2.164	3.667%	0.004
2021/5/18	54.000	55.645	−1.645	3.047%	−0.070

(i)   A prediction and monitoring data contrast is shown below.

As can be seen from Table 1, we have observed and analyzed the level deviation and relative error after the model is established, and the results show that the maximum value is 0.037 < 0.1 in terms of relative error and 0.037 < 0.1 in terms of level deviation, which shows that our model fits well.

(ii)   The forecast and comparison of B monitoring point data are shown below:

Table 2. Model test results.

Date	The original value	Predictive value	Residual	The relative error	Level ratio deviation
2021/5/10	69.000	69.000	0.000	0.000%	–
2021/5/11	65.000	60.717	4.283	6.590%	−0.087
2021/5/12	64.000	62.154	1.846	2.884%	−0.040
2021/5/13	56.000	63.626	−7.626	13.618%	−0.170
2021/5/14	60.000	65.133	−5.133	8.554%	0.045
2021/5/15	68.000	66.675	1.325	1.949%	0.097
2021/5/16	76.000	68.254	7.746	10.193%	0.084
2021/5/17	69.000	69.870	−0.870	1.260%	−0.128
2021/5/18	70.000	71.524	−1.524	2.177%	−0.009

As can be seen from Table 2, we have observed and analyzed the level deviation and relative error after the model is established, and the results show that the maximum value is 0.136 < 0.2 in terms of relative error and 0.097 < 0.1 in terms of level deviation, which indicates that our model fits better.

(iii)   The forecast and comparison of C monitoring point data are shown below:

Table 3. Model test results.

Date	The original value	Predictive value	Residual	The relative error	Level ratio deviation
2021/5/10	107.000	107.000	0.000	0.000%	–
2021/5/11	80.000	78.606	1.394	1.742%	−0.359
2021/5/12	73.000	81.584	−8.584	11.759%	−0.113
2021/5/13	90.000	84.610	5.390	5.989%	0.176
2021/5/14	100.000	87.685	12.315	12.315%	0.086
2021/5/15	80.000	90.809	−10.809	13.511%	−0.270
2021/5/16	90.000	93.983	3.983	4.425%	0.097
2021/5/17	103.000	97.208	5.792	5.624%	0.112
2021/5/18	99.000	100.484	−1.484	1.499%	−0.057

As can be seen from Table 3, we have observed and analyzed the level deviation and relative error after the model is established, and the results show that the maximum value is $0.135 < 0.2$ in terms of relative error and $0.176 < 0.2$ in terms of level deviation, which indicates that our model fits the requirements.

(iv) As can be seen above, we have proved that the model meets the requirements of this data forecast.As a result, the concentration of pollutants at the A monitoring point and the AQI projections are shown in Table 4:

Table 4. Concentration of pollutants at observation points A and AQI forecast results.

The forecast date	Place	Day value prediction							
		SO2 ($\mu g/m^3$)	NO2 ($\mu g/m^3$)	PM10 ($\mu g/m^3$)	PM2.5 ($\mu g/m^3$)	O3 max eight-hour sliding average ($\mu g/m^3$)	CO (mg/m^3)	AQI	Primary pollutant
2021/7/13	Monitoring point A	7	9	19	6	98	0.4	50	O3
2021/7/14	Monitoring point A	7	8	20	6	104	0.4	54	O3
2021/7/15	Monitoring point A	7	7	18	6	110	0.4	59	O3

The concentration of pollutants at observation points B and the AQI projections are shown in Table 5:

Table 5. Observations of Pollutant Concentrations and AQI Predictions.

The forecast date	Place	Day value prediction							
		SO2 ($\mu g/m^3$)	NO2 ($\mu g/m^3$)	PM10 ($\mu g/m^3$)	PM2.5 ($\mu g/m^3$)	O3 max eight-hour sliding average ($\mu g/m^3$)	CO (mg/m^3)	AQI	Primary pollutant
2021/7/13	Monitoring point B	5	9	20	5	50	0.7	25	O3
2021/7/14	Monitoring point B	4	9	20	5	49	0.7	25	O3
2021/7/15	Monitoring point B	4	9	21	4	48	0.8	24	O3

C observation point dye concentration and AQI prediction as shown in Table 6:

Table 6. C Observation Point Pollutant Concentration and AQI Prediction Results.

The forecast date	Place	Day value prediction							
		SO2 ($\mu g/m^3$)	NO2 ($\mu g/m^3$)	PM10 ($\mu g/m^3$)	PM2.5 ($\mu g/m^3$)	O3 max eight-hour sliding average ($\mu g/m^3$)	CO (mg/m^3)	AQI	Primary pollutant
2021/7/13	Monitoring point C	9	22	46	21	170	0.5	110	O3
2021/7/14	Monitoring point C	10	23	50	22	182	0.5	120	O3
2021/7/15	Monitoring point C	10	24	55	23	194	0.5	131	O3

(2) Prediction based on Bayesian network model.

(i) The correlation coefficients for pollutant concentrations at each observation point are shown in Table 7:

64   L. Xin et al.

Table 7. Correlation coefficients for pollutant concentrations.

	A1	A2	A3	A
A1	1	0.791654647	0.709303391	0.667466422
A2	0.791654647	1	0.899704653	0.918209905
A3	0.709303391	0.899704653	1	0.965342304
A	0.667466422	0.918209905	0.965342304	1
	A1	A2	A3	A

(ii) The forecast and comparison of A monitoring point data are shown below:

Table 8. Model test results.

Date	The original value	Predictive value	Residual	The relative error	Level ratio deviation
2021/5/14	59.000	60.564	−1.564	2.652%	0.004
2021/5/15	59.000	59.295	−0.295	0.501%	0.021
2021/5/16	60.000	58.053	1.947	3.245%	0.037
2021/5/17	59.000	56.836	2.164	3.667%	0.004
2021/5/18	54.000	55.645	−1.645	3.047%	−0.070

Table 8 shows that after the model is established, we observe and analyze the level deviation and relative error, and the results show that the maximum value is 0.037 < 0.1 in terms of relative error and 0.037 < 0.1 in terms of level deviation, which shows that our model fits well.

(iii) The forecast and comparison of A1 monitoring point data are shown below:

Table 9. Model test results.

Date	The original value	Predictive value	Residual	The relative error	Level ratio deviation
2021/5/14	58.000	58.000	0.000	0.000%	–
2021/5/15	65.000	68.392	−3.392	5.218%	0.147
2021/5/16	70.000	65.373	4.627	6.610%	0.112
2021/5/17	64.000	62.488	1.512	2.362%	−0.045
2021/5/18	57.000	59.730	−2.730	4.790%	−0.073

As can be seen from Table 9, we have observed and analyzed the level deviation and relative error after the model is established, and the results show that the maximum value is 0.066 < 0.1 in terms of relative error and 0.1 in terms < of level deviation, which indicates that our model fits better.

(iv) The forecast and comparison of A2 monitoring point data are shown below:

Table 10. Model test results.

Date	The original value	Predictive value	Residual	The relative error	Level ratio deviation
2021/5/14	70.000	70.000	0.000	0.000%	–
2021/5/15	94.000	94.358	−0.358	0.380%	0.339
2021/5/16	84.000	83.813	0.187	0.223%	0.006
2021/5/17	76.000	74.446	1.554	2.044%	0.018
2021/5/18	65.000	66.127	−1.127	1.734%	−0.038

As can be seen from Table 10, we have observed and analyzed the level deviation and relative error after the model is established, and the results show that the maximum value is 0.02 < 0.1 in terms of relative error and 0.34 > 0.2 in terms of level deviation, which shows that our model fit effect is general.

(v) The prediction and comparison of A3 monitoring point data are as follows:

Table 11. Model test results.

Date	The original value	Predictive value	Residual	The relative error	Level ratio deviation
2021/5/14	58.000	58.000	0.000	0.000%	–
2021/5/15	66.000	67.992	−1.992	3.018%	0.168
2021/5/16	68.000	64.363	3.637	5.349%	0.081
2021/5/17	60.000	60.928	−0.928	1.546%	−0.073
2021/5/18	57.000	57.676	−0.676	1.186%	0.004

From Table 11, we can observe and analyze the level deviation and relative error after the model is established. The results show that the maximum value of the relative error is 0.053 < 0.1, and the maximum value of the level deviation is 0.168 < 0.2, which shows that our model fits well.

(vi) From the above analysis, we can see that our Bayesian network model can be used as a collaborative forecast for four monitoring points, and the modeling is successful.

From this, the pollutant concentration and AQI prediction results at observation point A are shown in Table 12.:

Table 12. Concentrations of pollutants at monitoring point A and AQI prediction results.

The forecast date	place	Day value prediction							
		SO2 (μg/m^3)	NO2 (μg/m^3)	PM10 (μg/m^3)	PM2.5 (μg/m^3)	O3 max eight-hour sliding average (μg/m^3)	CO (mg/m^3)	AQI	Primary pollutant
2021/7/13	Monitoring point A	7	9	19	6	98	0.4	50	O3
2021/7/14	Monitoring point A	7	8	20	6	104	0.4	54	O3
2021/7/15	Monitoring point A	7	7	18	6	110	0.4	59	O3

The pollutant concentration and AQI prediction results at the observation point A1 are shown in Table 13:

Table 13. Concentrations of pollutants at A1 monitoring points and AQI prediction results.

The forecast date	place	Day value prediction							
		SO2 (μg/m^3)	NO2 (μg/m^3)	PM10 (μg/m^3)	PM2.5 (μg/m^3)	O3 max eight-hour sliding average (μg/m^3)	CO (mg/m^3)	AQI	Primary pollutant
2021/7/13	Monitoring point A1	7	12	24	7	91	0.4	46	O3
2021/7/14	Monitoring point A1	7	11	23	5	80	0.4	40	O3
2021/7/15	Monitoring point A1	7	10	21	4	68	0.4	34	O3

The pollutant concentration and AQI prediction results at the observation point A2 are shown in Table 14.

Table 14. Concentrations of pollutants at A2 monitoring points and AQI prediction results.

The forecast date	place	Day value prediction							
		$SO2$ ($\mu g/m^3$)	$NO2$ ($\mu g/m^3$)	$PM10$ ($\mu g/m^3$)	$PM2.5$ ($\mu g/m^3$)	O3 max eight-hour sliding average ($\mu g/m^3$)	CO (mg/m^3)	AQI	Primary pollutant
2021/7/13	Monitoring point A2	5	16	22	6	61	0.5	31	O3
2021/7/14	Monitoring point A2	5	16	21	5	42	0.5	21	O3
2021/7/15	Monitoring point A2	5	15	19	4	25	0.5	19	PM10

The pollutant concentration at A3 monitoring point and the prediction result of AQI are shown in Table 15:

Table 15. Pollutant concentration and AQI prediction results at A3 observation point.

The forecast date	place	Day value prediction							
		$SO2$ ($\mu g/m^3$)	$NO2$ ($\mu g/m^3$)	$PM10$ ($\mu g/m^3$)	$PM2.5$ ($\mu g/m^3$)	O3 max eight-hour sliding average ($\mu g/m^3$)	CO (mg/m^3)	AQI	Primary pollutant
2021/7/13	Monitoring point A3	4	8	11	5	57	0.3	28	O3
2021/7/14	Monitoring point A3	4	7	10	4	43	0.3	22	O3
2021/7/15	Monitoring point A3	3	6	8	3	30	0.3	15	O3

4.4 Experimental Analysis Summary

Through the above experimental data analysis and results, it is known that the gray prediction model based on fractional order can be well applied to predict the concentration of pollutants at three monitoring points at the same time, and the model based on Bayesian network can be well applied to four Cooperative forecasting of monitoring points and forecast errors are better than other algorithms. In conclusion, our proposed models are good predictors of atmospheric pollutant concentrations.

5 Conclusion

This paper improves the gray model and proposes a gray prediction model based on fractional order, which is applied to predict the concentration of pollutants at three monitoring points at the same time. A Bayesian network model is also proposed to make coordinated forecasting of the pollutant concentration at four monitoring points. This experiment judges the applicability and robustness of the model by analyzing the relative error value and the level ratio deviation value, and confirms that the two models have a high accuracy rate for data prediction, which is better than the existing algorithms.

There is still some room for improvement in the accuracy of air pollutant concentration prediction, and more factors can be introduced when considering influencing factors, such as whether there are factories nearby, whether it is in the city center, etc. These are all directions that can be studied in the future.

References

1. Kalaivani, G., Mayilvahanan, P.: Air quality prediction and monitoring using machine learning algorithm based iot sensor- a researcher's perspective. In: 2021 6th International Conference on Communication and Electronics Systems (ICCES) (2021)
2. Zheng, W., Zhi, T.: Prediction of air quality index based on improved neural network. In: 2017 International Conference on Computer Systems, Electronics and Control (ICCSEC), pp. 200–204 (2017)
3. Dua, R.D., Madaan, D.M., Mukherjee, P.M., Lall, B.L.: Real time attention based bidirectional long short-term memory networks for air pollution forecasting. In: 2019 IEEE Fifth International Conference on Big Data Computing Service and Applications (BigDataService), pp. 151–158 (2019)
4. Li, J., Shao, X., Zhao, H.: An online method based on random forest for air pollutant concentration forecasting. In: Proceedings of the 37th Chinese Control Conference (2018)
5. Sandeep, K.S., Pushpa, B.N.: Developing soft computing based models for prediction of pollutant pm10 of air. In: 2021 5th International Conference on Trends in Electronics and Informatics (ICOEI) (2021)
6. Aruna Kumari, N.S., Ananda Kumar, K.S., Hitesh Vardhan Raju, S., Vasuki, H.R., Nikesh, M.P.: Prediction of air quality in industrial area. In: 2020 International Conference on Recent Trends on Electronics, Information, Communication & Technology (RTEICT), pp. 193–198 (2020)
7. Yang, R., Zhou, H., Ding, D.: Air quality prediction method in urban residential area. In: 2018 11th International Symposium on Computational Intelligence and Design (ISCID), vol. 1, pp. 16–20. IEEE (2018)
8. Zhu, H., Hu, J.: Air quality forecasting using SVR with quasi-linear kernel. In: 2019 International Conference on Computer, Information and Telecommunication Systems (CITS), pp. 1–5. IEEE (2019)
9. Fang, W., Zhu, R.: Air quality prediction model based on time-space similarity LSTM. Comput. Appl. Res. **09**, 014 (2021)
10. Chen, Y., Yang, S., Wang, Q.: Prediction of PM2. 5 concentration in Guangzhou based on LSTM neural network. In: 2021 2nd International Conference on Intelligent Computing and Human-Computer Interaction (ICHCI), pp. 8–12. IEEE (2021)
11. Guo, C., Lin, Z., Guo, K.: Research and application of the general model of collaborative comprehensive forecasting IGDSS. J. Communications (2006)
12. Liu, S., Li, T., Lin, J., Yu, H.: The impact of air pollutants in cities around Beijing on air quality. Natural Science 284–291 (2016)

Research on Management Optimization of College Student Apartment Based on MCR Model

Longruidi Shang[1], Yao Tang[1], Wenzheng Yu[1], Xin Yao[1(✉)], and Hanxiaoya Zhang[2]

[1] School of Geographical Sciences, Nanjing University of Information Science and Technology, Nanjing 210044, China
yaoxin@nuist.edu.cn

[2] Faculty of Science, The University of Auckland, Auckland 1010, New Zealand

Abstract. The gust In recent years, MCR model analysis method has been widely used in geography. It is an attempt and innovation to combine geographical theory and management practice to add MCR model to university apartment management to assist decision making. In NUIST, for example, this study research resistance surface model in university dormitory management optimization under the guidance of the campus road system adjustment and improvement, optimization of campus dormitory management and road traffic modification plan put forward the scientific guidance, based on MCR resistance model of school teaching, scientific research, sports, life four big area resistance situation analysis, Then, the management of campus dormitories is optimized to form visual results through accuracy and provide more possibilities and innovations for future university management and planning.

Keywords: MCR model · Plane of resistance · Optimize the spatial pattern · Optimize dormitory management · Layout of campus

1 Preface

In recent years, MCR model analysis method has been increasingly widely used in geography, such as the analysis of the economic activity in a certain area, ecological analysis and interpretation of the regional influence produced by the interaction of capital flow, traffic flow, information flow and other factors between two different regions, has achieved certain result [1–12].

However, the current mainstream research ideas are often comprehensive analysis of all source points [13–18], and rarely consider the classification of source points and specific analysis of different functions when they are very different [19–24, 31–37]. At the same time, its application is also concentrated in urban and rural planning [25–30], ecological protection and other macro fields [38–44], with little combination with practical management, which still needs further exploration and practice [45–48].

© The Author(s), under exclusive license to Springer Nature Switzerland AG 2022
X. Sun et al. (Eds.): ICAIS 2022, LNCS 13338, pp. 69–79, 2022.
https://doi.org/10.1007/978-3-031-06794-5_6

2021 is the opening year of the 14th five year plan. The 14th five year plan for national economic and social development of the people's Republic of China and the outline of long-term objectives for 2035 put forward higher requirements for the construction and development of "double first-class" colleges and universities, emphasizing the leading role of innovation, advocating innovation in the construction of colleges and universities and realizing the high-quality development of colleges and universities. Under the background of this era, adding MCR model to assist decision-making in university apartment management will be an attempt and innovation of the organic combination of geography theory and management practice; At the same time, the diversity of campus learning and life makes it difficult to avoid the key problem of how to classify the source points and quantify their role in the construction of MCR model.

Taking NUIST as an example, this study combined the resistance surface model with the content of college student dormitory management planning, which has positive theoretical and practice significance for the future innovative college planning.

2 Study Area and Research Method

2.1 Brief Introduction of the Study Area

Nanjing University of Information Engineering was founded in 1960, formerly known as the College of Meteorology of Nanjing University, under the Central (Military Commission) Meteorological Bureau. In 2000, it was under the supervision of the People's Government of Jiangsu Province. In 2004, it was renamed Nanjing University of Information Engineering. It is a national "double first-class" construction university and a key support university for the construction of high-level universities in Jiangsu. It was born to serve the national strategy of New China and the needs of national economic construction. It is now a central and local co-construction university mainly managed by Jiangsu Province.

The main campus of the school is located in Jiangbei New District of Nanjing, covering an area of more than 2000 mu, with geographical coordinates of 32. 202 degrees north latitude and 118. 717 degrees east longitude. In addition, there are university science parks and cultural tourism parks in Jiangbei New District, Liuhe District and Yuhuatai District of Nanjing. There are about 33000 full-time students, including about 27000 ordinary undergraduates, about 5000 postgraduates and about 1000 foreign students (academic students). This study takes the main campus of Nanjing University of Information Engineering as the study area, as shown in the following figure (Fig. 1):

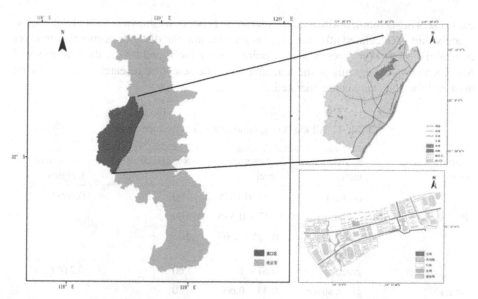

Fig. 1. The location map of Nanjing University of Information Science & Technology.

2.2 Methods of Study

Minimum cumulative resistance model [1]. It is derived from the weighted distance model based on spatial distance. The model takes into account three factors: source, spatial distance and surface resistance characteristics. The formula is expressed as follows:

$$MCR = fmin \sum_{j=n}^{i=m} D_{ij}R_j \qquad (1)$$

where, MCR refers to the minimum cumulative resistance of all source points in a certain area to diffuse to a certain point in space; D_{ij} refers to the outer radiation radius from the center of the source point I to the point J in space; R_j refers to the resistance of the source point I as the support point to the space point J in the transfer process; I is the number of sources as support points; J is a point in space.

Source screening and classification: The main building areas of Nanjing University. of Information Engineering are divided into four parts, namely, living area, sports area, scientific research area and teaching area. It is determined that the sources affecting the circulation of personnel in the area are dormitories, canteens, libraries, teaching buildings, etc. After investigation, a total of 19 source points in four categories were identified on campus.

Selection of resistance factors: The flow of personnel within the school mainly depends on the road within the school. Considering the availability and quantifiable degree of data, the road density in unit grid area is selected as the resistance factor restricting the flow of people on the road. There are 7 types of surface features in this area. The resistance is determined according to the flow of people in unit time of various road personnel flow modes, Resistance classification and weight are calculated by expert scoring combined with analytic hierarchy process, as shown in Table 1. The resistance value is calculated after the layer is grating, and the distance accumulation layer is established by four types of source points respectively, and finally the four types of MCR schematic diagrams of the teaching area, the scientific research area, the living area and the sports area are generated.

Table 1. All kinds of ground features resistance grade.

Geographical objects	Resistance factor	Resistance level	Resistance value	Numerical weights
	canteen	0.1 ~ 0.1675	60	0.5604
Buildings (hm^2)	dormitory	0.17 ~ 0.335	80	
	teaching building	0.335 ~ 0.67	100	
	greenbelt	0.67 ~ 1	60	0.2149
Grass coverage (%)	green space	0.33 ~ 0.66	80	
	space	0 ~ 0.33	100	
	sidewalk	1 ~ 3	5	0.1469
Width of roads(m)	one-way street	3 ~ 5	15	
	dual carriageway	6 ~ 10	25	
	Scrap barriers	1	100	0.0779
Rests	water area	1	100	
	parking lots	1	80	

The importance of four types of source points to different grades was investigated by means of questionnaire statistics, and the questionnaire data were processed by entropy weight method to obtain the weights of four types of source points in different grades (Table 2). The resistance surface layers of the four sources were accumulated according to the weights of different grades to obtain the comprehensive MCR map of the four grades.

Each student apartment has different scores in different grade layers, so the problem of university dormitory management can be transformed into the problem of allocating student apartments to four different grade layers with the smallest comprehensive resistance value. The solution of this problem adopts the idea of NMDS analysis and exhaustive verification. The NMDS analysis method is implemented in R language, and the exhaustive method is implemented in Matlab.

Table 2. Four grades resistance value weight.

Grade	District			
	Experimental region	Teaching region	Sports region	Living region
First grade	0.3247	0.1128	0.1981	0.3644
Second grade	0.251	0.1476	0.264	0.3374
Third grade	0.254	0.1175	0.2558	0.3727
Fourth grade	0.3156	0.1575	0.2711	0.2558

3　Research Results

3.1　MCR Maps for Four Different Types of Sources

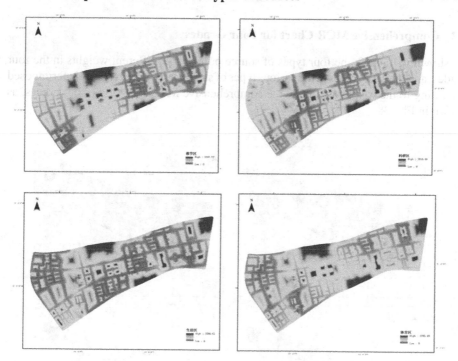

Fig. 2. The schematic diagram of four regional resistance surfaces.

The teaching points in the campus are concentrated in the center of the campus and extend to the east and west along the two main roads in the campus(see Fig. 2). The teaching points in East Quarters Group, Central Quarters Group and Western Quarters Group are evenly distributed and located on both sides of the main roads in the school. The traffic resistance is small, which can basically meet the needs of teachers and students for daily teaching activities. The resistance of the scientific research area is between the teaching area and the living area, mainly concentrated in the vicinity of Central Quarters Group. At the same time, there is a clear strip of east-west low resistance area, indicating that the scientific research area is distributed along two main campus roads, extending to the east and west sides of the campus, with low traffic resistance. Compared with the other three layers, the distribution of facilities in the living area is more uniform and comprehensive. From the resistance surface diagram, it can be clearly observed that there is a wide range of low resistance value surface in the three areas of East Quarters Group, Central Quarters Group and Western Quarters Group, as well as a strip of east-west low resistance belt. The traffic resistance to the living facilities on campus is small, so it can be judged that the distribution of living facilities on campus is reasonable. Sports venues are mainly distributed on both sides of the campus. In the center of the campus, the distribution area is small, which takes into account the East Garden area and the West Garden area well, but there is no obvious low resistance surface in the Middle Garden area, and the traffic resistance in the campus is slightly higher than that in the other three areas, which is not conducive to the circulation of people between the stadiums.

3.2   Comprehensive MCR Chart for Four Grades

As shown in Table 2, the four types of source points have different weights in the four grades, and the MCR maps of the various types of source points in Fig. 2 are superimposed according to the weights to obtain the comprehensive MCR map of the four grades, as shown in Fig. 3:

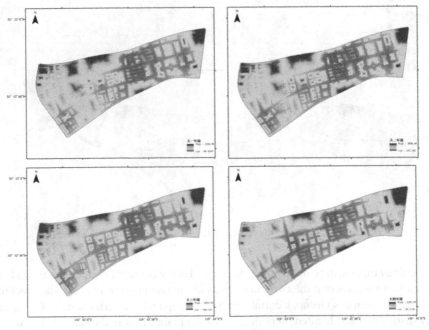

Fig. 3. The schematic diagram of resistance surface of four grades.

As shown in the Fig. 3, the daily activities of freshmen are mainly in the teaching area, and the areas covered by low resistance values are mainly in the teaching buildings of East Quarters Group, Central Quarters Group and Western Quarters Group campuses. The use of the stadium is lower than that of the teaching area, and the resistance values of the scientific research and canteen areas are higher. It shows that freshmen campus life in Nanjing University of Information Engineering is mainly about study and physical exercise, so the dormitory arrangement for freshmen should be as close as possible to these two areas. Sophomore students pay more attention to the use of professional software on the computer after the primary subject study of freshman year. The change of the focus of study and research makes the research area representing the computer laboratory have a lower resistance value, followed by the teaching area, and the sports and living areas have the highest resistance value. The use of campus space by junior students has not changed much compared with that of sophomore students, and the range of low resistance value in the teaching area has further shrunk, accompanied by an increase in the number of times used in the living area. The area of low resistance value of campus canteen expands, and the area of sports and teaching has little change, but it also maintains a high level of use. Compared with the other three grades, the use of campus buildings by senior students is the highest in the living area. At the same time, because of the reduction of schoolwork, the main activities of senior students on campus are no longer to attend classes in the teaching building. Therefore, in the group shape map of the senior grade, not only the range of low resistance value in the teaching area is greatly reduced, but also the overall use of school buildings is further reduced, and the range of low resistance value is the smallest among the four grades.

4 Discussion

At present, there are some contradictions in the arrangement of student dormitories and apartments, and it is found that some dormitory arrangements will increase the travel resistance of teachers and students in school. Therefore, it is considered to adjust the management of road traffic between apartments. A grid diagram of resistance values is established, the area formed by the closing of the resistance lines is a resistance surface, and the resistance surface in the area which is most difficult to reach presents a peak bulge, In the area with lower resistance, the resistance surface is a valley, the concave part of the low resistance line forms a trough line, and the convex part of the high resistance line forms a ridge line. The resistance surface shape calculated by the model objectively reflects the resistance situation of personnel flow in Nanjing University of Information Engineering. As shown in the figure, the two main roads in the campus form a clear area of low resistance. Most of the source points are also located on the low resistance line, and a small number of source points are located near the low resistance area. The resistance surface shape calculated by the model (see Fig. 4) objectively reflects the resistance situation in the campus. Near the two main roads of the campus, two fast lanes have been formed. One is based on Mingde Building and Changwang Building. A fast track in the center of the campus connected by a slot line with a low resistance value; The other is the southwest channel with Wende Building as the base point (valley) and the trough line with lower resistance value. At the same time, a belt-shaped low-resistance area running from east to west is formed around the two main roads. In addition, two strategic points, saddle-shaped areas of resistance contours, are formed on the two main roads (Fig. 4).

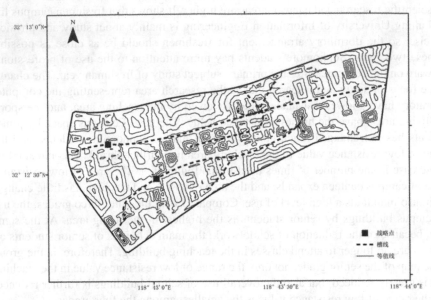

Fig. 4. The Schematic diagram of resistance surface of NUIST.

It can be seen from the figure that the current campus road configuration is relatively perfect, forming a divergent road system with teaching buildings as the center, but the more it expands to the north and south of the campus, the greater the resistance in unit distance, the greater the axial traffic pressure, and the more difficult the traffic organization, especially in the north and south of the campus, where a large number of student dormitories are distributed. And the distance resistance between some dormitories and teaching buildings, canteens and libraries also shows a greater trend, such as students who often need to attend classes in East Quarters Group Teaching Building, but their dormitories are arranged in Central Quarters Group or even Western Quarters Group, the distance between teaching buildings and dormitories is too long, resulting in travel costs and reducing the traffic efficiency of campus roads. From the point of view of housing and transportation, such a road structure also causes inconvenience to daily traffic. To sum up, two suggestions are put forward for the current inter-apartment traffic management: 1) It is suggested to strengthen the campus traffic construction at the two saddles of the South and North districts of Western Quarters Group, and the specific measures can be to add bus stops and adjust bus routes. 2) Supplement on-campus vehicles such as bicycles and electric vehicles, adjust the structure of on-campus traffic roads, and improve on-campus traffic service facilities.

5 Conclusion

In this paper, the area enclosed by the resistance line is the resistance surface, which is a space-time continuum reflecting the movement of transport elements in the process of logistics, similar to the topographic surface. In the most inaccessible area, the resistance surface appears as a peak, and in the area with lower resistance, the resistance surface appears as a valley. The concave part of the low resistance line forms a trough line, and the convex part of the high resistance line forms a ridge line. According to the spatial analysis of the minimum cumulative resistance surface, the connection route between the source points and the radiation range can be determined.

The example of Nanjing University of Information Engineering shows that the application pattern of resistance surface can be inter-provincial or small-scale, such as university campuses. The special nature of the resistance surface is used to provide scientific guidance for the optimization of campus dormitory management and the proposal of road traffic modification scheme, and the visualization results are formed through the precise digitization of geographic objects. The feasibility of the data is high, and the feasibility of the scheme provided by the experimental results is good, which provides more possibilities and innovations for future university planning.

Funding Statement. This work was supported by the National Natural Science Foundation of China "Study on the dynamic mechanism of grassland ecosystem response to climate change in Qinghai Plateau" under grant number U20A2098, and the Second Tibet Plateau Scientific Expedition and Research Program (STEP) under grant number 2019QZKK0804.

References

1. Liang, X., Xu, M.Z., Lv, L.Q., Cui, Y.F., Zhang, F.B.: Classification of debris flow gullies in the margin of Qinghai-Tibet Plateau based on geomorphological features. Journal **75**(7), 1373–1385 (2020)
2. Huang, M.Y., Yue, W.Z., Feng, S.R., Cai, J.J.: Heterogeneity and optimization of ecological security pattern in the core area of Dabie Mountains based on MCR model. J. Natural **34**(4), 771–784 (2019)
3. Sadeghi, M.S.H., Zabihi, M., Vafakhah, Z.: Hazbavi: Spatiotemporal mapping of rainfall erosivity index for different return periods in Iran. Nat. Hazards **87**(1), 35–56 (2017)
4. Zhen, Y., He, R.M., Wu, X.G., Wang, K.: Study on the pattern optimization of production-living-ecological space in villages based on MCR model. Res. Soil Water **28**(5), 362–367 (2021)
5. Chen, N.N., Kang, S.Z., Zhao, Y.H., Zhou, Y.J., Yan, J.: Mountain ecological network construction in Qinling Mountains based on MSPA and MCR models. Chinese J. Applied **32**(5), 545–1553 (2021)
6. Dai, L., Lin, Y.S., Huang, K.Z.: Ecological security network construction of Jiujiang Waterfront city based on MCR model and DO index. Journal **75**(11), 2459–2474 (2020)
7. Li, H.K., Liu, Y.T., Li, Q., Wang, X.L.: Ecological security pattern analysis of rare earth mining area in South China based on MCR model. J. Geographical **40**(6), 989–998 (2020)
8. Hamed, A.Y., Alkinani, M.H., Hassan, M.R.: A genetic algorithm optimization for multi-objective multicast routing. Intell. Autom. Soft **26**(6), 1201–1216 (2020)
9. Zhu, H.: Research on maximum return evaluation of human resource allocation based on multi-objective optimization. Intell. Autom. Soft Comput. **26**(4), 741–748 (2020)

10. Xue, F.C.: Hierarchical geographically weighted regression model. J. Quantum **1**(1), 9–20 (2019)
11. Zhang, X., Zhou, S., Fang, J., Ni, Y.: Pattern recognition of construction bidding system based on image processing **35**, 247–256 (2020)
12. Han, J., Jiang, W., Shi, J., Xin, S., Peng, J.: A method for assessing the fairness of health resource allocation based on geographical grid. Comput., Mater. Continua **64**(2), 1171–1184 (2020)
13. Wu, X., Luo, C., Zhang, Q., Zhou, J., Yang, H.: Text detection and recognition for natural scene images using deep convolutional neural networks. Comput., Mater. Continua **61**(1), 289–300 (2019)
14. Abdullah, B., Daowd, H., Mallappa, S.: Semantic analysis techniques using twitter datasets on big data: comparative analysis study. Comput. Syst. Sci. Eng. **35**(6), 495–512 (2020)
15. Xu, H., Yang, H., Shen, Q., Yang, J., Liang, H.: Automatic terrain debris recognition network based on 3d remote sensing data. Comput., Mater. Continua **65**(1), 579–596 (2020)
16. Liu, Y., Qing, R., Liu, J., Liao, Z., Zhao, Y.: Extracting campus' road network from walking gps trajectories. J. Cyber Secur. **2**(3), 131–140 (2020)
17. Fremier, A.K., et al.: A riparian conservation network for ecological resilience. Biological **19**(1), 29–37 (2015)
18. Liu, D., Chang, Q.: Ecological security research progress in China. Acta Ecologica **35**(5), 111–121 (2015)
19. Loro, M., Ortega, E., Arce, R.M., Geneletti, D.: Ecological connectivity analysis to reduce the barrier effect of roads. An innovative graph-theory approach to define wildlife corridors with multiple paths and without bottlenecks. Landscape and Urban **13**(9), 149–162 (2015)
20. Zhao, X.Q., Xu, X.H.: Research on landscape ecological security pattern in a Eucalyptus introduced region based on biodiversity conservation. Russ. J. Ecol. **46**(1), 59–70 (2015)
21. Wu, J.: Urban ecology and sustainability: The state-of-the-science and future directions. Landscape and Urban **12**(5), 209–221 (2014)
22. David, M.: Theobald: A general model to quantify ecological integrity for landscape assessments and US application. Landscape **28**(10), 1859–1874 (2013)
23. Kukkala, A.S., Moilanen, A.: Core concepts of spatial prioritisation in systematic conservation planning. Biological **88**(2), 443–464 (2012)
24. Su, S., et al.: Assessing land eco- logical security in Shanghai (China) based on catastrophe theory. Stochastic Environ. Res. Risk **25**(6), 737–746 (2011)
25. Esbah, H., Cook, E.A., Ewan, J.: Effects of increasing urbanization on the ecological integrity of open space preserves. Environ. Manage. **43**(5), 846–862 (2009)
26. Heather, T., Peter, K., Michelle, M., Amy, C.: An ecosystem services framework to sup- port both practical conservation and economic development. Proc. Natl. Acad. Sci. U.S.A. **105**, 9457–9464 (2008)
27. Carlorondinini, R.L.: special section: systematic conservation planning in the european landscape: conflicts, environmental changes, and the challenge of countdown. Conservation **21**(6), 1404–1409 (2007)
28. Armsworth, P.R., et al.: Ecosystem-service science and the way forward for conservation. Conservation **21**(6), 1383–1387 (2007)
29. Sun, D., Dawson, R., Li, H., Wei, R., Li, B.: A landscape connectivity index for assessing desertification: a case study of Minqin County. China. Landscape **22**(4), 531–543 (2007)
30. Pascual-Hortal, L., Saura, S.: Comparison and development of new graph-based landscape connectivity indices: towards the priorization of habitat patches and corridors for conservation. Landscape **21**(7), 959–967 (2006)
31. Peter, M., et al.: Ecological thresholds: the key to successful environmental management or an important concept with no practical application? Ecosystems **9**(1), 1–13 (2006)

32. Houlahan, J.E., Findlay, C.S.: Estimating the 'critical' distance at which adjacent land-use degrades wetland water and sediment quality. Landscape Ecol. **19**(6), 677–690 (2004)

33. Verbeylen, G., Bruyn, F.L.D., Adriaensen, F., Matthysen, E.: Does matrix resistance influence red squirrel (sciurus vulgaris l. 1758) distribution in an urban landscape. Landscape Ecology **18**(8), 791–805 (2003)

34. Naveh, Z.: From biodiversity to ecodiversity: a landscape-ecology approach to conservation and restoration. Restoration **2**(3), 180–189 (1994)

35. Richard, H.: The role of corridors in conservation: solution or bandwagon. Trends Ecol. Evol. **7**, 389–392 (1992)

36. Dennis, C.: Social evolution and ecological security. Security **22**(3), 329–334 (1991)

37. Kalantar, B., Pradhan, B., Naghibi, S.A., Motevalli, A., Mansor, S.: Assessment of the effects of training data selection on the landslide susceptibility mapping: a comparison between support vector machine (SVM), logistic regression (LR) and artificial neural networks (ANN). Geomat. Nat. Haz. Risk **9**(1), 49–69 (2018)

38. Huang, F., Yao, C., Liu, W., Li, Y., Liu, X.: Landslide susceptibility assessment in the Nantian area of China: a comparison of frequency ratio model and support vector machine. Geomat. Nat. Haz. Risk **9**(1), 919–938 (2018)

39. Wang, Y., Liu, J., Yan, S., Yu, L., Yin, K.: Estimation of probability distribution of shear strength of slip zone soils in Middle Jurassic red beds in Wanzhou of China. Landslides **14**(6), 2165–2174 (2017)

40. Zhang, L., Peng, J., Liu, Y., Wu, J.: Coupling ecosystem services supply and human ecological demand to identify landscape ecological security pattern: a case study in Beijing-Tianjin-Hebei region. China. Urban **20**(3), 701–714 (2017)

41. Zhuang, J., et al.: Prediction of rainfall-induced shallow landslides in the Loess Plateau, Yan'an, China, using the TRIGRS model. Earth Surf. Proc. Land. **42**, 915–927 (2017)

42. Yu, H., Yin, L., Zhang, H., Zhan, D., Qu, J.: Road distance computation using homomorphic encryption in road networks. Comput., Mater. Continua **69**(3), 3445–3458 (2021)

43. Liu, Y., Qing, R., Liu, J., Liao, Z., Zhao, Y., Ouyang, H.: Extracting campus' road network from walking gps trajectories. J. Cyber Secur. **2**(3), 131–140 (2020)

44. Gill, S.H., Razzaq, M.A., Ahmad, M., Almansour, F.M., Haq, I.U.: Security and privacy aspects of cloud computing: a smart campus case study. Intell. Autom. Soft Comput. **31**(1), 117–128 (2022)

45. Tang, Y., Liu, W., Zhang, C., He, Y., Ji, N., Chen, X.: Research on the traveling characteristics and comparison of bike sharing in college campus-a case study in Hangzhou. J. Internet **2**(3), 89–99 (2020)

46. Tariq, M.U., Babar, M., Jan, M.A., Khattak, A.S., Alshehri, M.D.: Security requirement man- agement for cloud-assisted and internet of things-enabled smart city. Comput., Mater. Continua **67**(1), 625–639 (2021)

47. Xue, Y., Jiao, X., Wang, C., Chen, H., Aloqaily, M.: Analysis and design of university teaching equipment management information system. J. Cyber **3**(3), 177–185 (2021)

48. Munir, R., Wei, Y.F., Ullah, R., Hussain, I., Arshid, K., Tariq, U.: Big data of home energy management in cloud computing. J. Quantum **2**(4), 193–202 (2020)

Sub-base Station Power Optimization Based on QoS and Interference Temperature Constraints for Multi-user Input and Output

Hongwei Li[1], Xiaoli He[1](✉), Yu Song[2], Weijian Yang[1], Haimin Yi[1], Xiaodong Yin[1], and Zhen Zeng[1]

[1] School of Computer Science, Sichuan University of Science and Engineering, Zigong 643000, China
hexiaoli_suse@hotmail.com
[2] Department of Network Information Management Center, Sichuan University of Science and Engineering, Zigong 643000, China

Abstract. In this paper, we study the transmission power allocation of the secondary base station to the secondary user in cognitive radio networks when multiple primary users (PU) and multiple secondary users (SU) adopt NOMA. In the proposed Underlay communication scheme, the communication quality of the primary user should be greater than the preset threshold, otherwise the secondary user communication will be interrupted. The signal-to-noise ratio of the secondary user should be greater than the preset threshold and meet the minimum communication quality requirements of the secondary user. Otherwise, the communication of the secondary user is interrupted. Finally, on the premise of ensuring the quality of service (QoS) of primary and secondary users, the cumulative total interference of secondary users to primary users should not exceed the Interference temperature threshold. Therefore, the convex optimization algorithm is used to maximize the power coefficient of downlink allocation of radio cognitive network, considering the constraints of mutual interference between secondary users, interference between secondary users and primary users, signal-to-noise ratio of secondary users, and interference temperature. This power distribution method is easy to be implemented in practical systems because of its low implementation complexity. Simulation results show that compared with the traditional orthogonal multiple access (OFDMA) scheme and the cooperative OMA scheme, the proposed scheme can better allocate the power coefficients in the downlink, better allocate the system spectrum resources, and lower the probability of secondary user outage.

Keywords: Cognitive radio networks (CRN) · Non-orthogonal multiple access (NOMA) · Spectrum resource allocation · Power allocation · Convex optimization · Machine learning

1 Introduction

In recent ten years, with the continuous vigorous development of science and technology around the world, wireless communication plays an increasingly important role in

© The Author(s), under exclusive license to Springer Nature Switzerland AG 2022
X. Sun et al. (Eds.): ICAIS 2022, LNCS 13338, pp. 80–93, 2022.
https://doi.org/10.1007/978-3-031-06794-5_7

the whole communication industry. The rapid development of wireless communication has led to extensive research on 5G cellular network and other fields. In the previous research, a large part of the research has focused on the technology development of multiple access. Each generation of communication system has its own unique multiple access technology, which can be distinguished by multiple access technology when using multi-user system [1]. For example: Frequency division multiple access (FDMA), time division multiple access (TDMA), code division multiple access (CDMA), orthogonal frequency division multiplexing multiple access (OFDMA). Non-orthogonal multiple Access (NOMA) is a popular technology in the 5th generation mobile communication system (5G), and it is widely regarded as a very promising multiple access method by industry people.

In NOMA, users are multiplexed based on power or code domain and they share the frequency and time sources in the same spatial layer [3]. When NOMA is used for transmission, users with poor channels are assigned more transmission power. NOMA technology differs from traditional multiple access technology in that NOMA uses a non-orthogonal power domain to distinguish users. The so-called non-orthogonal means that data between users can be transmitted in the same time slot, the same frequency point, and only rely on the difference of power to distinguish users.

Two key technologies, serial interference elimination (SIC) and power multiplexing, are used in NOMA [5]. Serial Interference deletion (SIC) is at the sender, similar to CDMA systems, where introducing interference information can achieve higher spectral efficiency, but also suffers from multiple access interference (MAI) problems. NOMA uses a SIC receiver at the receiving end for multi-user detection. The basic idea is to use of serial interference elimination technology step by step strategy, to eliminate interference in the received signal to judgment of users one by one, after amplitude recovery, multiple access interference of the user signal minus from the received signal, and carries on the judgment again for the rest of the user, so operation, until all of the multiple access interference elimination [7]. Power multiplexing technology refers to the SIC at the receiving end to eliminate multiple access interference (MAI), the need to receive the signal on the user to eliminate the order of the user, and the decision is based on the user signal power size. The base station will allocate different signal power to different users at the transmitting end, so as to obtain the maximum performance gain of the system and achieve the purpose of distinguishing users. Of course, NOMA technology still faces some challenges. First of all, the non-orthogonal transmission receiver is very complex, and the design of SIC receiver that meets the requirements also depends on the improvement of signal processing chip technology. Second, power reuse technology is not very mature, there is still a lot of work to do.

Cognitive radio network (CRN) makes full use of the spectrum of wireless network due to its excellent spectrum sensing characteristics. Cognitive radio networks (CRN) are a promising key technology in 5G [9]. Wireless spectrum is the lifeblood of mobile communication systems, and all net-work construction and mobile application services are indispensable. Therefore, the scientific allocation of spectrum resources is a prerequisite for the success of mobile communication systems, and it is related to global roaming and the scale effect of the industrial chain [12]. However, both CRN and NOMA are technologies that address the scarcity of spectrum resources when spectrum is used.

Therefore, we consider that the combination of CRN and NOMA can effectively solve the problems of insufficient spectrum resources and low total channel capacity of the system in recent years. To date, most studies have looked at CRN or NOMA technologies alone [13]. Researchers are also trying to combine these two important technologies, mainly focusing on the maximization of the number of secondary user access and resource allocation [14]. Although there are some studies on power distribution of sub-base stations, the consideration is not perfect. Therefore, there are still many problems in power allocation of the sub-base station in CRN-NOMA, which is also the focus of this paper.

1.1 Related Work

In recent years, cognitive radio networks have developed rapidly, especially in the downlink of Underlay mode. Researchers have carried out extensive research on NOMA technology. At the same time, CRN-NOMA is the main research object of the researchers. Literature [2] presents a long-term resource allocation problem for satellite Iot downlink system with non-orthogonal multiple access to achieve optimal decoding sequence and power allocation. Deep learning is used to obtain the optimal decoding order, which improves the long-term network utilization, average arrival rate and queuing delay performance of NOMA downlink system. Literature [4] this paper proposes a new NOMA downlink link scheme based on IM, the base station according to the concept of IM service for each user to select one or more channel, and according to the concept of NOMA distribution corresponding power level, studied their error rate, interrupt probability and computational complexity, verified the superiority of the proposed IM - NOMA scheme. Literature [6] considers multi-user power domain non-orthogonal multiple access (NOMA) down (DL) and up (UL) communication systems with different fading links. Probability density function (PDF) based on approximate channel gain, as the sum of gamma distribution, is general enough and suitable for multiple NOMA scenarios. The similar expressions of interrupt probability and interrupt floor of NOMA UL system are derived. Literature [8] studied the performance of NOMA in two-layer heterogeneous network with non-uniform small cell deployment, analyzed key performance indicators such as coverage probability and accessibility rate, and analyzed and demonstrated the influence of various network parameters on coverage probability and accessibility rate of NOMA users by considering the channel quality of NOMA users to the service base station. The literature [10] considered the power allocation in the CRN-NOMA hybrid network model and maximized the number of sub-users in the access system. The literature [11] studied in the CRN-NOMA hybrid network, under the premise of ensuring normal communication between *PU* and *SU*, with the goal of maximizing the number of access sub-users, a power allocation algorithm was proposed.

1.2 Related Work

In this study, constraints on power, power factor, interference temperature and QoS guarantee are used to optimize the power distribution factor under multi-user condition, so as to maximize the throughput of multi-user communication.

1.3 Organization of the Paper

The rest of this paper is organized as follows. Section2 establishes system and network model, including system model and mathematical modeling. In Sect. 3, the solution of the problem is proposed and the pseudo-code of the algorithm is given. The parameter values and simulation results are given in Sect. 4. Finally, Sect. 5 concludes this paper.

2 System and Network Model

2.1 System Model

The CRN-NOMA downlink model is studied in this paper. The system adopts Underlay spectrum sharing mode. In this system, primary and secondary users can communicate at the same time to improve spectrum utilization in cognitive radio network. In addition, the sub-base station and the sub-user communicate with each other through NOMA protocol.

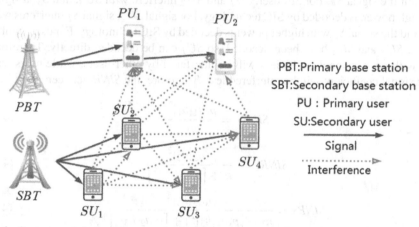

Fig. 1. System model of multi-user communication: primary and secondary users share downlink.

In Fig. 1, the system model consists of a primary base station (PBT) and two primary users (PU), a NOMA-based secondary base station (SBT) and four secondary users (SU). The above base stations and users are modeled and analyzed without considering the interference from primary users to secondary users. In the downlink, the channel gain coefficient from SBT to SU_i ($i = 1,2,3,4$) is expressed as h_i ($i = 1,2,3,4$). Assuming that SU_4 is far from SBT, SU_1 is close to SBT, SU_2 is between SU_1 and SU_3, and SU_3 is between SU_2 and SU_4, then:

$$|h_1|^2 \geq |h_2|^2 \geq |h_3|^2 \geq |h_4|^2 \tag{1}$$

According to the principle of NOMA, SBT allocates more power to SU_4 with poor channel conditions and less power to SU_1 with good channel, and linearly superimposes multiple secondary signals to form a composite signal, which is then transmitted to the target user (SU_1, SU_2, SU_3 and SU_4). The signal X sent by the sender can be expressed as:

$$X = \sqrt{a_1 P_s} s_1 + \sqrt{a_2 P_s} s_2 + \sqrt{a_3 P_s} s_3 + \sqrt{a_4 P_s} s_4 \tag{2}$$

a_i is the power allocation factor of SU_i, $0 < a_1 < a_2 < a_3 < a_4$ and $a_1 + a_2 + a_3 + a_4 = 1$, s_i is the information sent by SBT to secondary users, Ps is the transmission power of SBT. The signal received at SU_i ($i = 1,2,3,4$) can be expressed as:

$$y_i = h_i X + n_i, i = 1, 2, 3, 4 \tag{3}$$

In the downlink of the communication between the secondary base station and the secondary user, the NOMA method is used to send superposition information between the SBT and the SU. To avoid interference between the SU and the SBT, the Successful Interference cancelling (SIC) technology is used to eliminate multiple access interference when the SU receives signals. For user number 4, SU_1, SU_2 and SU_3 interfere with SU_4. Due to the large power obtained by themselves, the mixed signal can be directly decoded to obtain the signal S_4. For 3rd user, SU_1 and SU_2 interfere with SU_3, and S_3, a signal with high power, is decoded by SIC technology. For signal SU_2, signal S_1 interferes with SU_2, and the signal S_2 with higher power is decoded by SIC technology. For user number 1, SU_4, SU_3 and SU_2 have been decoded, so SU_1 can be decoded directly. Therefore, users with poor channel coefficient will be interfered by other users, while users with better signal coefficient will be interfered less. Therefore, the $SINR$ between users is:

$$SINR_1 = \frac{p_s a_1 |h_1|^2}{n_1} \tag{4-a}$$

$$SINR_2 = \frac{p_s a_2 |h_2|^2}{n_2 + \left[p_s a_1 |h_2|^2 \right]} \tag{4-b}$$

$$SINR_3 = \frac{p_s a_3 |h_3|^2}{n_3 + \left[p_s a_1 |h_3|^2 \right] + \left[p_s a_2 |h_3|^2 \right]} \tag{4-c}$$

$$SINR_4 = \frac{p_s a_4 |h_4|^2}{n_4 + \left[p_s a_1 |h_4|^2 \right] + \left[p_s a_2 |h_4|^2 \right] + \left[p_s a_3 |h_4|^2 \right]} \tag{4-d}$$

$SINR_i$ represents the ratio of the signal of the i-th user to the interference noise. To ensure normal communication between sub-users, the following requirements must be met:

$$SINR_i \geq SINR_i^{th}, i = 1, 2, 3, 4 \tag{5}$$

$SINR_i^{th}$ indicates the threshold of $SINR$ that the i-th user must meet to communicate properly. At the same time, the power allocated by each secondary user cannot exceed its threshold:

$$a_i p_s \leq p_i^{th} \tag{6}$$

P_i^{th} represents the maximum available power threshold of the i-th user. For the primary user, since the secondary user uses NOMA mode to transmit the superimposed encoded signals, we treat the superimposed signals of the secondary user and the power integral allocated between them as interference. The received signal can be expressed as:

$$y^{PU} = h_i^{PBT-PU} \sqrt{P_{PBT}}x + h_i^{SBT-PU} \sqrt{P_{PBT}}s + \sigma^2 \tag{7}$$

where h_i^{PBT-PU} and h_i^{SBT-PU} are the channel gain coefficients from PBT and SBT to PU, respectively. x is the useful signal sent by the base station to the primary user, and s is the interference signal from the secondary base station. Assuming that the distance between the primary base station and the secondary base station to the primary user is the same, the power distribution factor is 0.5. Considering the noise generated by the sub-base station to the primary user, the $SINR$ of the primary user can be expressed as:

$$\gamma_1 = \frac{0.5\left|h_1^{PBT-PU}\right|^2 P_{PBT}}{0.5\left|h_1^{SBT-PU}\right|^2 P_{SBT} + \sigma^2} \tag{8-a}$$

$$\gamma_2 = \frac{0.5\left|h_2^{PBT-PU}\right|^2 P_{PBT}}{0.5\left|h_1^{SBT-PU}\right|^2 P_{SBT} + \sigma^2} \tag{8-b}$$

To ensure that the primary user's QoS is not affected, the following conditions are limited:

$$\gamma_i \geq \gamma_i^{th}, i = 1, 2 \tag{9}$$

Interference temperature is a model for quantifying and managing interference sources recommended by FCC at the end of 2003. At the same time, an interference temperature threshold is set to ensure the normal operation of the authorized user system, which is determined by the worst $SINR$ of the authorized user system. Once the accumulated interference of unauthorized users exceeds the interference temperature threshold, the system of authorized users cannot work normally. Otherwise, both authorized and unauthorized users can work properly. The expression is as follows:

$$T_I(f_c, B) = \frac{P_I(f_c, B)}{kB} \tag{10}$$

where k is Boltzmann's constant with a value of 1.38×10^{-23} J/k. And $P_I(f_c, B)$ is the average interference power with frequency f_c and bandwidth B. Due to interference from primary and secondary users, the cumulative interference cannot exceed the interference temperature threshold of the primary user. Otherwise, secondary users cannot share spectrum resources. Where $B = 1$ Hz, the interference temperature constraint is expressed as:

$$\frac{\sum_{i=1}^{4} a_i p_s |h_i|^2}{k} \leq \Gamma^{th} \tag{11}$$

2.2 Mathematical Modeling

Based on the above discussion, in multi-user communication, the power distribution coefficient of the secondary user is optimized to maximize the throughput of the secondary user in NOMA mode. The optimization objective expression is as follows:

$$\max_{a_1,a_2,a_3,a_4} R = \sum_{i=1}^{4} \log_2(1 + SINR_i) \tag{12}$$

$$s.t. \, SINR_i \geq SINR_i^{th}, \, i = 1, 2, 3, 4 \tag{13-a}$$

$$a_i p_s \leq p_i^{th} \tag{13-b}$$

$$\Gamma \leq \Gamma^{th} \tag{13-c}$$

$$a_1 + a_2 + a_3 + a_4 = 1 \tag{13-d}$$

$$0 < a_1 < a_2 < a_3 < a_4 \tag{13-e}$$

Among them, (13-a) represent the QoS requirements that the primary and secondary users must meet. (13-b) indicates that the power of the secondary user cannot exceed the upper limit of the maximum power threshold of the secondary user. (13-c) indicates that the cumulative interference of the secondary user to the primary user cannot exceed the interference temperature threshold of the primary user. (13-d) and (13-e) represent the constraints of the power allocation factor.

3 Problem Solution Method

To solve the model optimization problem, convex optimization method was used to solve the maximum throughput. Convex optimization method needs to meet the following conditions: First, minimize or maximize the objective function. Second, the objective function is either convex or concave. Finally, the feasible domain set formed by constraints is convex.

3.1 Mathematical Modeling

For the convenience of representation, let $G_i = P_s|h_i|^2$, $i = 1, 2, 3, 4$, From (4-a), (4-b), (4-c), (4-d):

$$SINR_1 = \frac{a_1 G_1}{n_1} \tag{14-a}$$

$$SINR_2 = \frac{a_2 G_2}{n_2 + a_1 G_2} \tag{14-b}$$

$$SINR_3 = \frac{a_3 G_3}{n_3 + a_1 G_3 + a_2 G_3} \qquad (14\text{-}c)$$

$$SINR_4 = \frac{a_4 G_4}{n_4 + a_1 G_4 + a_2 G_4 + a_3 G_4} \qquad (14\text{-}d)$$

In order to facilitate calculation and strictly in accordance with NOMA's definition of resource allocation, the farther the secondary user is from the base station, the greater the power allocation factor is (13-d), (13-e), let $a_1 = 0.1$, $a_2 = 0.2$, $a_3 = 0.7\text{-}a_4$, $a_4 = a_4$. According to the constraint condition (12), the following objective function can be obtained:

$$
\begin{aligned}
R &= \sum_{1}^{4} \log_2(1 + SINR_i) = \log_2(\frac{a_1 G_1 + n_1}{n_1}) \\
&+ \log_2(\frac{(a_1 + a_2)G_2 + n_2}{n_2 + a_1 G_2}) + \log_2(\frac{n_3 + (a_1 + a_2 + a_3)G_3}{n_3 + (a_1 + a_2)G_3}) \\
&+ \log_2(\frac{n_4 + (a_1 + a_2 + a_3 + a_4)G_4}{n_4 + (a_1 + a_2 + a_3)G_4}) \\
&= \log_2(0.1G_1 + n_1) - \log_2(n_1) + \log_2(0.3G_2 + n_2) \\
&- \log_2(n_2 + 0.1G_2) + \log_2(n_3 + (1 - a_4)G_3) \\
&- \log_2(n_3 + 0.3G_3) + \log_2(n_4 + G_4) - \log_2(n_4 + (1 - a_4)G_4)
\end{aligned}
\qquad (15)
$$

The first and second derivatives of the objective function are calculated to judge the convexity of the function:

$$\frac{\partial R}{\partial a_4} = \left[\frac{G_4 n_3 - G_3 n_4}{(G_3 + n_3 - a_4 G_3)(n_4 + G_4 - a_4 G_4)} \right] \times \frac{1}{\ln 2} \qquad (16\text{-}a)$$

$$\frac{\partial^2 R}{\partial a_4^2} = \left[\frac{(-2A_3 A_4 - A_4 n_3 - A_3 n_4 + 2A_3 A_4 a_4)(A_4 n_3 - A_3 n_4)}{\left(A_3(n_4 + A_4 - 2A_4 a_4 - n_4 a_4 + A_4 a_4^2) + n_3(n_4 + A_4 - A_4 a_4)\right)^2} \right] \times \frac{1}{\ln 2}$$

$$(16\text{-}b)$$

In summary, it is not difficult to conclude that R is a concave function.

3.2 Maximum Throughput Optimization Based on QoS and Interference Temperature Constraints

As can be seen from the above equation, the objective function to be optimized is a concave function, which can be solved by convex optimization method. The following is the transformation of constraint conditions:

$$SINR_1 \geq SINR_1^{th} \Rightarrow n_1 SINR_1^{th} - a_1 G_1 \leq 0 \qquad (17\text{-}a)$$

$$SINR_2 \geq SINR_2^{th} \Rightarrow (n_2 + a_1 G_2)SINR_2^{th} - a_2 G_2 \leq 0 \qquad (17\text{-}b)$$

$$SINR_3 \geq SINR_3^{th} \Rightarrow (n_3 + a_1 G_3 + a_2 G_3)SINR_3^{th} - a_3 G_3 \leq 0 \qquad (17\text{-c})$$

$$SINR_4 \geq SINR_4^{th} \Rightarrow (n_4 + G_4(a_1 + a_2 + a_3))SINR_4^{th} - a_4 G_4 \leq 0 \qquad (17\text{-d})$$

$$a_1 p_s \leq p_1^{th} \Rightarrow a_1 p_s - p_1^{th} \leq 0 \qquad (17\text{-e})$$

$$a_2 p_s \leq p_2^{th} \Rightarrow a_2 p_s - p_2^{th} \leq 0 \qquad (17\text{-f})$$

$$\Gamma \leq \Gamma^{th} \Rightarrow \Gamma - \Gamma^{th} = \frac{\sum_3^{i=1} a_i p_s |h_i|^2}{k} - \Gamma^{th} \leq 0 \qquad (17\text{-g})$$

In general, Lagrange multiplier method is generally used when solving convex optimization problems, and Lagrange multiplier (λ, β, η) is required to be non-negative. In addition, a_1, a_2 has been assumed for the optimization problems in this paper, so the Lagrange function is as follows:

$$
\begin{aligned}
L(a_4, \lambda, \beta, \eta) &= R + \lambda_1 \Big[(n_3 + 0.3G_3)SINR_3^{th} - (0.7 - a_4)G_3\Big] \\
&+ \lambda_2 \Big[(n_4 + (1 - a_4)G_4)SINR_4^{th} - a_4 G_4\Big] \\
&+ \beta_1 \Big[(0.7 - a_4)P_s - P_s^{th}\Big] + \beta_2 \Big[a_4 P_s - P_4^{th}\Big] \\
&+ \eta \left[\frac{0.1G_1 + 0.2G_2 + (0.7 - a_4)G_3 + a_4 G_4}{k} - \Gamma^{th}\right]
\end{aligned}
\qquad (18)
$$

To facilitate the calculation, the above equation is converted to a dual function, and x is minimized to obtain the lower bound of $L(a_4, \lambda, \beta, \eta)$, thus obtaining the dual function $g(\lambda, \beta, \eta)$:

$$g(\lambda, \beta, \eta) = \min_{a_4} L(a_4, \lambda, \beta, \eta) \qquad (19)$$

Then maximize $g(\lambda, \beta, \eta)$ to approximate the minimum of the original function.

$$\max_{(\lambda \geq 0, \beta \geq 0, \eta \geq 0)} g(\lambda, \beta, \eta) \qquad (20)$$

After the above transformation, the maximum value obtained by the dual function is less than or equal to the minimum value of the original function. In order to make these two values equal, the following *KKT* conditions should be met:

$$\frac{\partial L}{\partial a_4} = \frac{\partial R}{\partial a_4} + \lambda_1 G_3 - 2\lambda_2 G_4 - \beta_1 P_s + \beta_2 P_s + \eta \left(\frac{G_4 - G_3}{k}\right) = 0 \qquad (21\text{-a})$$

$$\frac{\partial L}{\partial \lambda_1} = (n_3 + 0.3G_3)SINR_3^{th} - (0.7 - a_4)G_3 = 0 \qquad (21\text{-b})$$

$$\frac{\partial L}{\partial \lambda_2} = (n_4 + (1 - a_4)G_4)SINR_4^{th} - a_4 G_4 = 0 \qquad (21\text{-c})$$

$$\frac{\partial L}{\partial \beta_1} = (0.7 - a_4)P_s - P_s^{th} = 0 \tag{21-d}$$

$$\frac{\partial L}{\partial \beta_2} = a_4 P_s - P_4^{th} = 0 \tag{21-e}$$

$$\frac{\partial L}{\partial \eta} = \frac{0.1G_1 + 0.2G_2 + (0.7 - a_4)G_3 + a_4 G_4}{k} - \Gamma^{th} = 0 \tag{21-f}$$

The Lagrange dual function must be a concave function, so the sub-gradient descent method is introduced to get the optimal Lagrange multiplier:

$$\lambda_i^{(k+1)} = \lambda_i^{(k)} - \mu^{(k)} \frac{L(\lambda_i)}{L'(\lambda_i)} \tag{22-a}$$

$$\beta_i^{(k+1)} = \beta_i^{(k)} - \nu^{(k)} \frac{L(\beta_i)}{L'(\beta_i)} \tag{22-b}$$

$$\eta_i^{(k+1)} = \eta_i^{(k)} - o^{(k)} \frac{L(\eta_i)}{L'(\eta_i)} \tag{22-c}$$

where μ, ν, o is the iteration step of sub-gradient descent method. According to the KKT conditions above, the expression of optimal power a distribution of SU_3 and SU_4 can be solved:

$$a_4 = \frac{2G_3G_4 + G_4n_3 + G_3n_4 + \sqrt{(2G_3G_4 + G_4n_3 + G_3n_4)^2 - 4G_3G_4 \left[\frac{G_3n_4 + G_3G_4 + n_3n_4}{+ \frac{G_4G_3 - G_3G_4}{\ln 2 \left(\lambda_1 G_3 - 2\lambda_2 G_4 - \beta_1 P_s + \beta_2 P_s + \eta \left(\frac{G_4 - G_3}{k} \right) \right)}} \right]}}{2G_3G_4} \tag{23-a}$$

$$a_3 = 0.7 - \frac{2G_3G_4 + G_4n_3 + G_3n_4 + \sqrt{(2G_3G_4 + G_4n_3 + G_3n_4)^2 - 4G_3G_4 \left[\frac{G_3n_4 + G_3G_4 + n_3n_4}{+ \frac{G_4G_3 - G_3G_4}{\ln 2 \left(\lambda_1 G_3 - 2\lambda_2 G_4 - \beta_1 P_s + \beta_2 P_s + \eta \left(\frac{G_4 - G_3}{k} \right) \right)}} \right]}}{2G_3G_4} \tag{23-b}$$

Algorithm 1 performs $(m + 1)$ iterative solution through constraint conditions (13-a), (13-b), (13-c), (13-d) and (13-e) to generate a feasible solution set. Algorithm 1 uses an approximate nonconvex function that increases with each iteration and returns an increasing sequence of target values. Since the feasible solution set is convex, algorithm 1 converges to a finite value.

Table 1. Algorithm pseudocode.

Algorithm: Solve the maximum communication throughput(R) of multiple users
Require: $n_1, n_2, n_3, n_4, h_1, h_2, h_3, h_4, SINR_1^{th}, SINR_2^{th}, SINR_3^{th}, SINR_4^{th}, P_s, P_1^{th}, P_2^{th}, P_3^{th}, P_4^{th}, \Gamma^{th}$
Initialize: $m=0$
Suppose: $a_1 = 0.1, a_2 = 0.2, a_3 = 0.7 - a_4, a_4 = a_4$
Ensure: a_3, a_4
1. while communication was not interrupted
2. Repeat the following steps
3. Solve (12) subject to (13-a) (13-b) (13-c) (13-d) (13-e) iteratively for a_3 and a_4
4. $m=m+1$
5. until Convergence
6. end while

Table 2. System simulation parameters.

Parameter	Value
CRN-PU	2
CRN-SU	4
Channel model PU	slow Rayleigh fading
Channel model SU	slow Rayleigh fading
Propagation model	Range Propagation Loss
Noise	AWGN
$a1$	0.1
$a2$	0.2
$n_1 = n_2 = n_3 = n_4$	1
$h1$	8
$h2$	7
h_3	6
h_4	5

4 Simulation Result

This paper mainly uses MATLAB to realize the simulation results in CRN-NOMA hybrid network. With the help of the optimization toolbox and Monte Carlo program in MAT-LAB, the theoretical curves of OMA and OFDMA were obtained, and compared with CRN-NOMA to verify the accuracy of the derived expressions. Table 1 above shows the values of common parameters mentioned in this article. The simulation diagram obtained by using MATLAB simulation will be shown below. As expected, the proposed scheme shows improvements in total spectral efficiency and undetected probability compared to other schemes, as shown in Figs. 2, 3 and 4. On the other hand, the worst outcome in terms of the variables analyzed was OMA's policy, which demonstrated the necessity and benefits of using CRN-NOMA (Table 2).

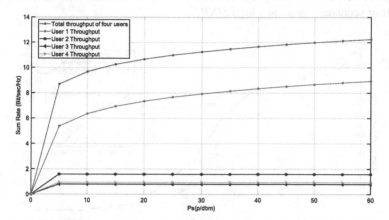

Fig. 2. Data throughput comparison graph for each sub-user.

As shown in Fig. 2, the transmission power of *SBT* fluctuates between 0dbm-60dbm. In order to ensure that edge users get higher power allocation, simulation analysis is carried out under the condition that sub-users meet the minimum threshold of 0.5bit/Hz. As can be seen from Fig. 2, as the transmission power of *SBT* increases, the power distribution method proposed in this paper presents the throughput of each user and the total throughput of all users in the system under the condition of multi-user communication.

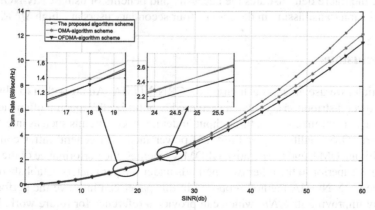

Fig. 3. Comparison of the *SINR* and the total transmission rate of OMA, OFDMA and the algorithm in this paper.

As shown in Fig. 3, when the *SINR* is lower than 18db, the throughput of OMA and OFDMA is better than that of the proposed algorithm. When the *SINR* is between 18db-25db, the total throughput of the proposed algorithm is higher than OMA, but still lower than OFDMA. When the *SINR* is higher than 25db, the total throughput of the proposed algorithm is higher than OMA and OFDMA. In summary, the figure demonstrates the necessity and benefits of using CRN-NOMA for communication transmission in the case of four secondary users at a high *SINR*.

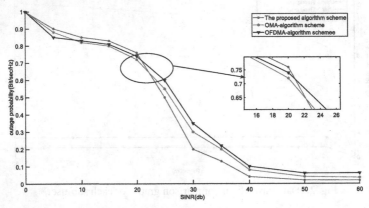

Fig. 4. Comparison of *SINR* and outage probability of OMA, OFDMA and proposed algorithms in this paper.

As shown in Fig. 4, when the *SINR* is lower than 22db, the interrupt probability of OMA and OFDMA algorithm is better than that of the algorithm proposed in this paper. When the SINR is at 21db, the outage probability of the proposed algorithm is better than OMA, but still lower than OFDMA. When the *SINR* is higher than 22db, the outage probability of the proposed algorithm is better than OMA and OFDMA. In summary, the figure demonstrates the necessity and benefits of using CRN-NOMA for communication transmission in the case of four secondary users at a high *SINR*.

5   Conclusions

In this article, we use an approach based on CRN-NOMA. An algorithm to obtain the optimal power distribution coefficient is studied to optimize the spectral efficiency. This algorithm can maximize system throughput under many constraints such as interference temperature, QoS quality, power limit and power factor. In general, after comparing with traditional OMA and cooperative OFDMA schemes, the performance of the system algorithm is superior to the other two methods under the parameters established in this paper. The CRN-NOMA method proposed in this paper can improve the performance of *PBT* by improving its *SINR*, which can provide a reference for future work. Further increases in the number of users can be proposed to determine the robustness of the system as the network expands.

Acknowledgement. The authors would like to thank the anonymous reviewers for their selfless reviews and valuable comments, which have improved the quality of our original manuscript.

Funding Statement. This work was partially supported by the National Natural Science Foundation of China (No.61876089, No. 61771410), by the Talent Introduction Project of Sichuan University of Science & Engineering (No. 2020RC22), by the Zigong City Key Science and Technology Program (No. 2019YYJC16), by the Teaching Reform Research Project of Sichuan University of Science & Engineering (JG-2121), by the Enterprise Informatization and Internet of Things Measurement and Control Technology Sichuan Provincial Key Laboratory of universities (No.2020WZY01).

Conflicts of Interest. The authors declare that they have no conflicts of interest to report regarding the present study.

References

1. Khan, I., Al-Wesabi, F.N., Obayya, M.: An optimized algorithm for cr-mimo wireless networks. Computers, Materials & Continua **71**(1), 697–715 (2022)
2. Sun, Y.: Deep learning-based long-term power allocation scheme for NOMA downlink system in S-IoT. IEEE Access **7**, 86288–86296 (2019)
3. Seyman, M.N.: Symbol detection based on back tracking search algorithm in mimo-noma systems. Comput. Syst. Sci. Eng. **40**(2), 795–804 (2022)
4. Almohamad, A.: A novel downlink im-noma scheme. IEEE Open J. Commun. Soc. **2**, 235–244 (2021)
5. He, X., Song, Y., Xue, Y., Owais, M., Yang, W.: Resource allocation for throughput maximization in cognitive radio network with noma. Comput., Mater. Continua **70**(1), 195–212 (2022)
6. Agarwal, A.: Outage probability analysis for NOMA downlink and uplink communication systems with generalized fading channels. IEEE Access **8**, 220461–220481 (2020)
7. Abd-Elnaby, M.: Capacity and fairness maximization-based resource allocation for downlink noma networks. Comput., Mater. Continua **69**(1), 521–537 (2021)
8. Han, T.: On downlink NOMA in heterogeneous networks with non-uniform small cell deployment. IEEE Access **6**, 31099–31109 (2018)
9. Abd-Elnaby, M., Alsharif, S., Alhumyani, H., Alraddady, F.: Lowest-opportunities user first-based subcarrier allocation algorithm for downlink noma systems. Intell. Autom. Soft Comput. **30**(3), 1033–1048 (2021)
10. Liu, X., Wang, Y., Liu, S., Meng, J.: Spectrum resource optimization for NOMA-based cognitive radio in 5G communications. IEEE Access **6**, 24904–24911 (2018)
11. Nandan, N., Majhi, S., Wu, H.: Secure beamforming for MIMO-NOMA-based cognitive radio network. IEEE Commun. Lett. **22**(8), 1708–1711 (2018)
12. Chen, X., Jia, R.: Ng: On the design of massive non-orthogonal multiple access with imperfect successive interference cancellation. IEEE Commun. **67**(3), 2539–2551 (2019)
13. Zhou, F., Wu, Y., Liang, Y.: State of the art, taxonomy, and open issues on cognitive radio networks with NOMA. IEEE Wirel. Commun. **25**(2), 100–108 (2018)
14. Dong, Y.F.: Research on non-orthogonal multiple access technology based on relay selection in cognitive radio networks. M.S. dissertation, Yantai University, China (2019)

Resource Allocation for D2D Communication Underlaying Cellular Network

Zhen Zeng[1], Xiaoli He[1(✉)], Lun Li[3], Yu Song[2], Hongwei Li[1], HaiMin Yi[1], and XiaoDong Yin[1]

[1] School of Computer Science, Sichuan University of Science and Engineering, Zigong 643000, China
392275464@qq.com

[2] Department of Network Information Management Center, Sichuan University of Science and Engineering, Zigong 643000, China

[3] China Mobile Group Sichuan Company Limited Zigong Branch, Zigong 643000, China

Abstract. At present, resource allocation schemes based on cellular users and D2D users have been widely concerned by the society. With the development of society, the number of cellular users and D2D users has been increasing, but the frequency spectrum resources of users have not been reasonably allocated. Therefore, we propose a spatial matching algorithm (SMA) based on spatial region division, which divides cellular regions and realizes the reuse of user spectrum resources within the region to obtain the optimal solution of resource allocation. Finally, numerical simulation results show that the SMA resource allocation strategy is more efficient than Distance Constrained Resource Allocation (DCRA) algorithm.

Keywords: D2D communication · Resource allocation · Cellular network

1 Introduction

With the explosion of smart devices and communication users, the current transmission rate and traffic of cellular systems are increasing rapidly, which will make the shortage of spectrum resources more serious. In order to solve this problem, it is urgent to improve the transmission rate of cellular users and D2D users. It is reported that mobile traffic will exceed monthly 120 exabytes in 2018, an increase of about 12 times over 2012 [1]. However, with the continuous research of researchers, a new technology, D2D communication technology emerged. D2D communication in cellular network is mainly used for local business processing, realizing direct communication between two mobile users without going through the base station or core network. It can improve the spectrum efficiency of the whole system through the flexible reuse of radio resources [2]. Therefore, it can also improve the spectrum utilization and the overall performance and capacity of the system, consume low power, and provide guaranteed quality of service. It is expected to be adopted by the next generation of cellular networks.

© The Author(s), under exclusive license to Springer Nature Switzerland AG 2022
X. Sun et al. (Eds.): ICAIS 2022, LNCS 13338, pp. 94–106, 2022.
https://doi.org/10.1007/978-3-031-06794-5_8

In many scenarios, we observed that a lot of D2D users were not occupying the spectrum all the time, they were mostly in a standby state. Therefore, we consider using these standby users to assist active users in data transmission. However, we also need to consider two issues. The first is whether the standby user is willing to help the active user with the data transfer. The second problem is that in complex scenarios, the distance between users usually limits the communication quality of the channel, and the interference from cellular users to D2D users and from D2D users to other D2D users.

1.1 Related Works

Based on the cellular network, many scholars have carried out a detailed study on the interference generated by D2D communication, and most of them believe that the interference is caused by D2D users using spectrum resources for channel transmission. D2D communication in a cellular network can occur on the cellular spectrum or unlicensed spectrum. Most of the current literature suggests using the cellular spectrum for D2D and cellular communications. Co-channel interference between cellular users and D2D users is a major problem. Some resource allocation methods can alleviate interference and improve spectrum efficiency and energy efficiency, but their implementation principles are basically complicated [3–5]. Orthogonal D2D and cellular communication on the specified cellular spectrum can completely avoid such interference [6], but compared with other schemes, the disadvantages are also obvious: the spectral efficiency is lower. In order to solve the problem of co-channel interference, some researchers propose an algorithm based on graph coloring to make use of the weighted priority of spectrum resources so that a single cellular user resource can be reused by multiple D2D users [7].

In recent years, a lot of research has been done on collaborative D2D communication. Previous research on cooperative D2D communication focuses on spectrum and power allocation when instantaneous channel state information (CSI) is available. In practice, however, only statistical CSI is available. In order to allocate spectrum and power with statistical CSI, system performance (such as outage probability, average reachable rate) of cellular and D2D users need to be analyzed [8]. Most of these papers have not mentioned the region division scheme of cellular users, so we propose a channel aware space matching algorithm. By this algorithm, the previously unordered cellular users are confined to a circular area and divided into several equally large fan areas. In addition, efficient power control minimizes the negative effects of interference and achieves the promised benefits of D2D communication. Two power control schemes, namely power control Scheme 1 (PCS 1) and Power control Scheme 2 (PCS 2), were proposed in [9] to reduce interference and provide performance analysis.

In order to expand the system throughput and ensure the fairness of resource allocation for D2D users, [10] We formulate an optimization problem and find the optimal cache probability and beginning-segment size that maxi mise the cache-throughput probability of beginning-segments. [11] proposes a joint algorithm time scheduling and power control. The main idea is to effectively maximize the number of allocated resources in each scheduling period with satisfied quality of service requirements. The constraint problem is decomposed into time scheduling and power control subproblems. An interference minimization algorithm based on odd-even number of antennas is proposed [12]. The cellular connection precoding matrix is generated by minimizing the interference power of the base station to the non-target receiver. Then, the interference suppression matrix of cellular connection is obtained by maximum SNR criterion. Finally, the internal interference is eliminated by linear interference alignment and the maximum degree of freedom is obtained.

Classical communication theory has revealed the great benefits of equipping users with multiple antennas in wireless channels. In particular, multiple antennas can enhance the ability to interfere between cells, which is the main cause of rate decline in dense cellular networks. However, in current cellular microwave systems, comparative studies of the benefits of user-side MIMO are limited because it is difficult for end users to equip many antennas due to the size limitations of user equipment [13–15]. Therefore, we consider whether cooperative communication can improve the communication capability of cellular users in devices with few antennas. How much performance will be improved through this collaborative approach? These problems require us to reach a conclusion through algorithm calculation and data simulation.

1.2 Contributions

In this study, different from previous studies, we propose a channel-aware space matching algorithm, which divides users in a certain area and then transmits data with the assistance of standby users. Therefore, spectrum resource allocation is carried out under multiple constraints such as minimum transmission threshold, multiplexing parameters, channel state and maximum transmission power. More specifically, our main contributions to this work are summarized as follows:

First, we divide cellular users using channel-aware space matching algorithm to reduce the number of cellular users in each region.

Then, the convex optimization algorithm is used to determine the nature of the problem, and standby users are deployed to assist active users in communication, so as to improve the communication performance of cellular users and reduce interference.

Finally, the effectiveness of the algorithm is verified by numerical simulation. Numerical simulation results show that the channel awareness matching algorithm can achieve better communication performance when there are many antenna lines and the multiplexing parameter is 1.

1.3 Organization of the Paper

The rest of this article is organized as follows. The second part establishes system and network model, including system model and mathematical model. The third part proposes the solution to this problem. Numerical results are given. In Sect. 4. Finally, the fifth section summarizes this paper.

2 System Model

This paper mainly uses the uplink of cellular users and D2D users, because compared with the downlink, the reuse of the spectrum resources of the uplink makes the disturbance between users less. The model is shown below.

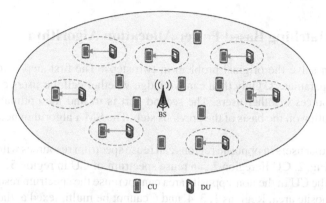

Fig. 1. System model of D2D communication underlaying cellular network.

We consider the following scenario: a base station with L antennas, k active users in a circular area of diameter R. In order to simplify the scenario, each user is equipped with only one antenna, because the presence of multiple antenna colleagues will also affect the communication channel. In this paper, we propose a distributed MIMO scheme based on channel-aware spatial matching algorithm to improve the communication performance of cellular users.

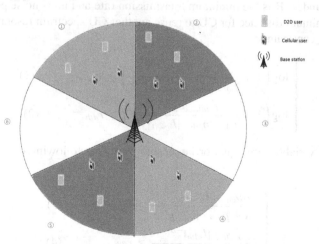

Fig. 2. System model of energy-aware space matching algorithm.

As shown in Fig. 1, the system activity is divided into two phases. In the first phase, the base station sends target data to the active user, and the standby user listens to the data sent by the base station to the active user. In the second phase: The standby user sends the monitored data to the active user to facilitate data processing and improve efficiency. MIMO technology improves the data transmission rate and energy efficiency of the entire system.

3   Space Matching Based Power Allocation Algorithm

The SMA can solve the original problem in two steps. The first step is to obtain the multiplexing parameters. Only then can we judge whether cellular users can reuse the spectrum resources of other users. The second part is to find the optimal solution of power distribution on the basis of the previous step. The SMA algorithm needs to follow two rules:

First, Cellular users in opposite regions can reuse spectrum resources with each other. As shown in Fig. 2, CU in region 2 can reuse spectrum of CU in region 5.

Second, The CU in the non-opposite area cannot reuse the spectrum resources of the CU in the opposite area. Regions 1, 3, 4, and 6 cannot be multiplexed at the same time.

The SMA should determine the spectrum reuse parameter X. As we all know, due to the fading characteristics of wireless communication, the distance between users is the main factor restricting the channel quality. Therefore, how to ensure good channel quality and less interference in the state of communication, is particularly important. If cellular users can reuse spectrum resources. According to SMA multiplexing rules, the opposite region of CU multiplexing is sufficiently distant from the same CU spectrum. Therefore, the interference between CU can be approximately ignored. cth represents CU in one region and dth represents CU in the opposite region. Lc-B represents the distance from cth CU to base station B, Pcth represents the transmission power of cth CU. α represents the path loss index. R is the minimum transmission rate and n0 is noise power. On this basis, the minimum distance for CU to reuse another CU spectrum resource must meet the following constraints:

$$
\begin{cases}
\log\left(1 + \dfrac{p_{cth} \cdot |L_{c-B}|^{-\alpha}}{n_0 + p_{dth} \cdot |L_{d-B}|^{-\alpha}}\right) \geq r_{cth}, & (1) \\[4mm]
\log\left(1 + \dfrac{p_{dth} \cdot |L_d|^{-\alpha}}{n_0 + p_{cth} \cdot |L_{c-d}|^{-\alpha}}\right) \geq r_{dth}. & (2)
\end{cases}
$$

When all variables are equal or larger than zero, the following conversion can be performed.

$$
\begin{cases}
\dfrac{p_{cth} \cdot |L_{c-B}|^{-\alpha}}{n_0 + p_{dth} \cdot |L_{d-B}|^{-\alpha}} \geq \tilde{r}_{dth}, & (3) \\[4mm]
\dfrac{p_{dth} \cdot |L_{dth}|^{-\alpha}}{n_0 + p_{cth} \cdot |L_{c-d}|^{-\alpha}} \geq \tilde{r}_{dth}. & (4)
\end{cases}
$$

where $\tilde{r}_{cth} = \exp(\tilde{r}_{cth}) - 1$, $\tilde{r}_{dth} = \exp(\tilde{r}_{dth}) - 1$, We obtain the following formula:

$$\begin{cases} p_{cth} \geq \tilde{r}_{cth}(p_{dth} \cdot |L_{dth}|^{-\alpha} + n_0) \cdot |L_{c-B}|^{\alpha}, & (5) \\ |L_{c-d}| \geq \left(\dfrac{p_{dth} \cdot |L_{dth}|^{-\alpha} - n_0\tilde{r}_{dth}}{\tilde{r}_{dth} \cdot p_{cth}} \right). & (6) \end{cases}$$

Take Pcth into Lc-d

$$\begin{aligned} |L_{c-d}| &\geq \left(\frac{p_{dth} \cdot |L_{dth}|^{-\alpha} - n_0\tilde{r}_{dth}}{\tilde{r}_{dth} \cdot \tilde{r}_{cth}(p_{dth} \cdot |L_{d-B}|^{-\alpha} + n_0) \cdot |L_{c-B}|^{\alpha}} \right)^{-1/\alpha} \\ &\geq \left[\left(\frac{|L_{dth}|^{-\alpha}}{\psi} \right) \left(1 - \frac{\phi \cdot |L_{dth}|^{-\alpha} + n_0 \cdot \psi \cdot \tilde{r}_{dth}}{\psi \cdot |L_{dth}|^{-\alpha} \cdot p_{dth} + \phi \cdot |L_{dth}|^{-\alpha}} \right) \right]^{-1/\alpha} \end{aligned} \quad (7)$$

where ψ represents $\tilde{r}_{dth} \cdot \tilde{r}_{cth} \cdot |L_{d-B}|^{-\alpha} \cdot |L_{c-B}|^{\alpha}$, φ represent $\tilde{r}_{dth} \cdot \tilde{r}_{cth} \cdot |L_{c-B}|^{\alpha} \cdot n_0$. Then we consider the worst case, that is, the transmission power between CU is the least and the channel quality is the worst. The following conclusions are obtained:

$$d_{cd} = |L_{\tilde{c}\tilde{d}}| \geq \left(\frac{p_{\tilde{d}} \cdot |L_{\tilde{d}}|^{-\alpha} - n_0\tilde{r}_{dth}}{\tilde{r}_{dth} \cdot \tilde{r}_{cth}\left(p_{\tilde{d}} \cdot |L_{\tilde{d}-B}|^{-\alpha} + n_0 \right) \cdot |L_{\tilde{c}-B}|^{\alpha}} \right)^{-1/\alpha} \quad (8)$$

3.1 Problem Analysis

Based on the above research, this paper proposes a channel capacity maximization solution in the scenario of CU reusable DU spectrum resources. Where, the reuse parameter $X = \{xcth, dth\}$ (xcth, dth $= 0,1$) is defined. If $X = 1$, it means that the dj-th CU has multiplexed the spectrum resources of the cth CU in the opposite region. If $X = 0$, it means that the spectrum resources of the cth CU in the oppo-site region are not multiplexed by dth CU. The mathematical model is established as follows:

$$P1 : \max_{X, P_C, P_D} R_{sum}(X, P_C, P_D), \quad (9)$$

$$s.t. \log(1 + R_{cth}) \geq r_{cth}, (\forall cth \in \Phi C), \quad (9a)$$

$$\log(1 + R_{dth}) \geq r_{dth}, (\forall dth \in \Phi D), \quad (9b)$$

$$0 \leq p_{cth} \leq P_{cth}^{\max}, \quad (9c)$$

$$0 \leq p_{dth} \leq \min\{P_{dth}^{\max}\}, \quad (9d)$$

$$\sum_{cth} x_{cth,dth} \leq 1, (\forall dth \in \Phi D), \quad (9e)$$

$$\sum_{dth} x_{cth,dth} \leq m, (\forall cth \in \Phi C), \quad (9f)$$

$$x_{cth,dth} \in \{0, 1\}, \quad (9g)$$

Rsum is the sum of the channel capacity of all users in the region, Rci is the SNR of the cth CU, and rdth is the SNR of the dth CU. Eqs. 2–3 represent the minimum power threshold of the transmission rate that cth and dth should achieve respectively. Formula 4 represents whether dth CU multiplexes the spectrum resources of cth CU, and Formula 5 represents that a CU cannot be multiplexed by more than m opposite regions of CU.

3.2 Resource Allocation

In the second step, after obtaining the integer value of multiple index X, appropriate power is allocated among the matched CU to maximize the transmission rate of the entire network. Therefore, due to the spectrum orthogonality of different CUs, the system transmission rate maximization problem can be divided into N sub-problems.

$$\max_{\{p_{cth}, P_{dth}\}} \log(1 + R_{cth}) + \sum_{dth=1}^{N_D} \tilde{x}_{cth,dth} \log(1 + R_{dth}), \tag{10}$$

$$s.t. \ \log(1 + R_{cth}) \geq \tilde{r}_{cth}, \tag{10a}$$

$$\log(1 + R_{dth}) \geq \tilde{r}_{dth}, \tag{10b}$$

$$0 \leq p_{cth} \leq P_{cth}^{\max}, \tag{10c}$$

$$0 \leq p_{dth} \leq \min\{P_{dth}^{\max}\}, \tag{10d}$$

By substituting variables, $p_{cth} = e^{\tilde{pc}}, p_{dj} = e^{\tilde{pd}}$:

$$\max_{\{\tilde{P}_{cth}, \tilde{P}_{dth}\}} \hat{f}_{cth}\left(\hat{X}, \widetilde{p_C}, \widetilde{P_D}\right) + \sum_{dj=1}^{N_D} \hat{x}_{cth,dth} \widetilde{f_{dth}}\left(\hat{X}, \widetilde{P_C}, \widetilde{P_D}\right), \tag{11}$$

$$s.t. \ \tilde{f}_{cth}\left(\hat{X}, \tilde{P}_{cth}, \tilde{P}_D\right) \geq r_{cth}, \tag{11a}$$

$$\tilde{f}_{dth}\left(\hat{X}, \tilde{P}_C, \tilde{P}_D\right) \geq r_{dth}, \tag{11b}$$

Algorithm: SMA
(1) for cth = 1 to C do
(2)   for dth = 1 to D do
(3)   if cth and dth satisfy the matching rules and smaller than d_{cd}
(4)   delete cth from C;
(5)   Update: $\{r_{cth}, r_{dth}\}$;
(6)   else
(7)   dth = dth + 1;
(8)   end
(9)   end
(10) end

4 Simulation Result

Considering the large number of CU in real world scenarios, this will undoubtedly increase the difficulty of simulation. So, we set up a small-scale scenario where there are only 5 active users in a sector with multiple DU (from 2 to 10). In order to verify the effectiveness of the algorithm, DCRA algorithm proposed by Gong Wenrong [16] is introduced for comparison. The matching probability and average transmission rate obtained by the SMA algorithm adopted in this paper are shown in Fig. 2 and Fig. 3 (Table 1).

In the course of the simulation experiment, it can be clearly seen from Fig. 3 that SMA-RANDOM is usually able to obtain matching performance second only to SMA-BEST. Considering the minimum safe multiplexing distance, matching parameters, and channel status parameters between CU and DU, different performance curves in the three states occur.

At the same time, we observed that SMA still achieved better performance when compared to the other two algorithms. SMA can obtain good matching performance for the following reasons: First, the CU of SMA can only be multiplexed by one DU, so there is less noise interference after multiple DU multiplexed CU affects the matching parameters and channel status parameters. Second, DCRA-AR and DCRA-PSA do not involve the division of time-frequency resources, which is easy to cause DU multiplexing to be reused to CUs under the same time-frequency resources, resulting in reduced spectrum resources and increased interference between DU.

Table 1. Simulation scenario parameters.

Description	Value
Cellular radius	500 m
Noise power	116 dBm
Numbers of cellular user	30
Numbers of D2D user	15
Path loss model	$32.4 + 20*\log(L/1000)$
Cellular bandwidth	18 MHz
Distance of D2D pair	50 m
User noise figure	9 db
BS noise figure	5 db

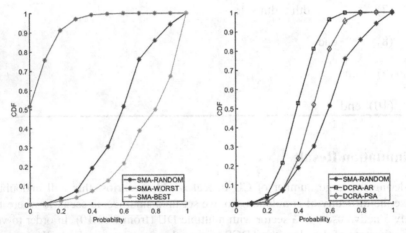

Fig. 3. The matching probability.

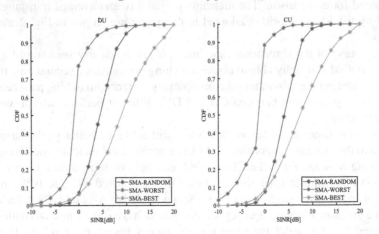

Fig. 4. The sinr figure of SMA.

As shown in Fig. 4, the matching probability affects the sinr, and the higher the matching probability, the higher the sinr obtained under the algorithmic condition. From the sinr images of DU and CU, we can see that the derivatives and performance of the two images are roughly similar. Overall, SMA-WORST's worst performance was expected, as its reuse conditions were also more stringent. At the same time, SMA-BEST achieved optimal sinr performance, while SMA-RANDOM achieved suboptimal sinr performance. As we all know, the larger the sinr, the more obvious the improvement in the communication quality of the DU or CU. For the SMA-RANDOM and SMA-BEST curves, the main difference between the two is that the latter has a 66.7% chance of a sinr of 0-10 dB, while the odds of reaching greater than 10 dB are 24.2%. This is because SMA-BEST select cues with the smallest Euclidean distances, which have a smaller path fading, so higher sinr values can be achieved.

As can be seen from Fig. 5, the SMA algorithm obtains optimal sinr performance, DCRA-PSA obtains suboptimal sinr performance, and DCA-AR has the worst performance among the three algorithms. Similar to the image of Fig. 4, the curves of DU and CU are roughly the same, because CU and DU are paired, and When the DU is present, CU is present. Therefore, we take THE sinr image analysis of DU. As far as the sinr images of DCRA-AR and DCRA-PSA are concerned, the performance of the two is relatively close, because although DCRA-PSA and DCRA-AR divide the dedicated spectrum for some CUs, there are also cases where CUs are not reused, so the performance improvement is not obvious. When we compare the two algorithms of DCRA with SMA, we can see that the performance of SMA is optimal. Taking the 0-10dB range as an example, the probability of SMA is 89.9%, while the probability of DCRA-AR is 62.3%, and the probability of DCRA-PSA is 70.2%. This is because the SMA adopts a strategy of separate multiplexing, and there will be no case where one CUs in DCRA is reused by multiple DU. This also leads to the use of SMA algorithm for communication, the noise interference generated by multiple DU under the same CU is also minimal, so that the noise interference in the whole scene is also minimal.

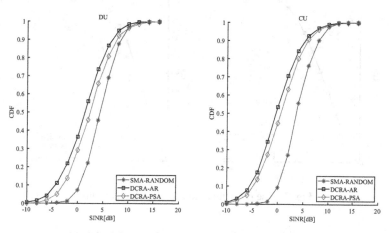

Fig. 5. The sinr figure of each algorithm.

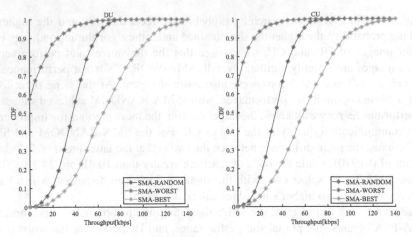

Fig. 6. The throughput figure of SMA.

As can be seen from Fig. 4, SMA-BEST's sinr performance is the best, and Fig. 6 reflects a corresponding throughput relationship. In terms of the throughput image of the DU, in the tested scene, after using the SMA-WORST algorithm, 70% of the DU has a throughput of 0 and cannot complete normal communication. SMA-RANDOM and SMA-BEST have a throughput of 0 without DU, and both can com-plete normal communication. However, the latter obviously has a larger throughput range, reaching a maximum of 140 kbps, which is 75% higher than the former's 80 kbps. SMA-RANDOM, on the other hand, is 100% larger than SMA-WORST's 40 kbps, suggesting that the former can generally provide more stable and faster communication conditions.

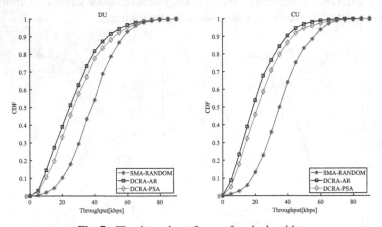

Fig. 7. The throughput figure of each algorithm

As can be seen from Fig. 7, the throughput performance of SMA is generally better than that of the DCRA two algorithms. In the image of the throughput of DU, we can see that in the 60-80 kbps range, the curves of DCRA-PSA and SMA roughly coincide, indicating that the limit performance of the two algo-rithms is relatively close. However, when we look at the 20-50 kbps range, 56.2% of the former's DU can fall in this range, while the latter has 69% of the DU in this range, indicating that the SMA in this range has a 12.8% increase in throughput performance compared to DCRA-PSA. Compared to DCRA-AR's 53.5%, the performance is improved by 15.5%. The DCRA-PSA performance improvement compared to DCRA-AR is not significant because PSA only allocates dedicated spectrum resources for some cellular users, but it is not necessarily used for communication in the scene, and there is also interference caused by multi-DU multiplexing.

5 Conclusion

In this paper, we study the scheme of using SMA resource allocation in the scenario of single DU multiplexing a single CU. In order to meet the resource allocation in this scenario, we propose a corresponding resource allocation algorithm that is called SMA. By setting a minimum safe multiplexing distance, the noise interference generated during multiplexing is reduced, and different time-frequency resources are divided into different areas, so as to improve the spectrum utilization of equipment in the same area. Finally, in a series of simulations, we add two algorithms of DCRA to compare, which confirms that the proposed algorithm can effectively improve the communication performance of the partitioned scenario, and points out the advantages of the proposed algorithm.

Acknowledgment. The authors would like to thank the anonymous reviewers for their selfless reviews and valuable comments, which have improved the quality of our original manuscript.

Funding Statement. This work was partially supported by the National Natural Science Foundation of China (No.61876089, No. 61771410), by the Talent Introduction Project of Sichuan University of Science & Engineering (No. 2020RC22), by the Zigong City Key Science and Technology Program (No. 2019YYJC16), by the Teaching Reform Research Project of Sichuan University of Science & Engineering (JG-2121), by the Enterprise Informatization and Internet of Things Measurement and Control Technology Sichuan Provincial Key Laboratory of universities (No.2020WZY01).

Conflicts of Interest. The authors declare that they have no conflicts of interest to report regarding the present study.

References

1. Wang, F., Li, Y., Wang, Z., Yang, Z.: Social-community-aware resource allocation for D2D communications underlaying cellular networks. IEEE Trans. Veh. Technol. **65**(5), 3628–3640 (2016)
2. Doppler, K., Rinne, M., Wijting, C., Ribeiro, C.B., Hugl, K.: Device-to-device communication as an underlay to LTE-advanced networks. IEEE Commun. Mag. **47**(12), 42–49 (2009)
3. Feng, D., Lu, L., Yuan-Wu, Y., Li, G.Y., Feng, G., Li, S.: Device-to-device communications underlaying cellular networks. IEEE Trans. Commun. **61**(8), 3541–3551 (2013)

4. Xu, C.: Efficiency resource allocation for device-to-device underlay communication systems: a reverse iterative combinatorial auction based approach. IEEE J. Sel. Areas Commun. **31**(9), 348–358 (2013)
5. Lin, X., Andrews, J.G., Ghosh, A.: Spectrum sharing for device-to-device communication in cellular networks. IEEE Trans. Wireless Commun. **13**(12), 6727–6740 (2014)
6. Pei, Y., Liang, Y.C.: Resource allocation for device-to-device communications overlaying two-way cellular networks. IEEE Trans. Wireless Commun. **12**(7), 3611–3621 (2013)
7. Hamid, A.K., Al-Wesabi, F.N., Nemri, N., Zahary, A., Khan, I.: An optimized algorithm for resource allocation for d2d in heterogeneous networks. Comput., Mater. Continua **70**(2), 2923–2936 (2022)
8. Ahamad, R.Z., Javed, A.R., Mehmood, S., Khan, M.Z., Noorwali, A.: Interference mitigation in d2d communication underlying cellular networks: towards green energy. Comput., Mater. Continua **68**(1), 45–58 (2021)
9. Anjum, N., Yang, Z., Khan, I., Kiran, M., Wu, F.: Efficient algorithms for cache-throughput analysis in cellular-d2d 5g networks. Comput., Mater. Continua **67**(2), 1759–1780 (2021)
10. Al-Wesabi, F.N., Khan, I., Alamgeer, M., Al-Sharafi, A.M., Choi, B.J.: A joint algorithm for resource allocation in d2d 5g wireless networks. Comput., Mater. Continua **69**(1), 301–317 (2021)
11. Bashir, S., Khan, I., Al-Wesabi, F.N., Nemri, N., Zahary, A.: An optimized algorithm for d2dmimo 5g wireless networks. Comput., Mater. Continua **68**(3), 3029–3044 (2021)
12. Cao, Y., Jiang, T., Wang, C.: Cooperative device-to-device communications in cellular networks. IEEE Wireless Commun. **22**(3), 124–129 (2015)
13. Spencer, Q.H., Swindlehurst, A.L., Haardt, M.: Zero-forcing methods for downlink spatial multiplexing in multiuser MIMO channels. IEEE Trans. Signal Process. **52**(2), 461–471 (2004)
14. Li, Y., Kan, H.: Complex Orthogonal Designs with Forbidden 2×2 Submatrices. IEEE Trans. Inf. Theory **58**(7), 4825–4836 (2012)
15. Liu, X., Li, Y., Kan, H.: On the minimum decoding delay of balanced complex orthogonal designs. IEEE Trans. Inf. Theory **61**(1), 696–699 (2015)
16. Gong, W., Pang, L., Wang, J.: Distance constrained resource allocation algorithm of D2D communication under-laying cellular networks. J. Xi'an Univ. Sci. Technol. **40**(3), 492–497 (2020)

Application Research of Safety Helmet Detection Based on Low Computing Power Platform Using YOLO v5

Mengxi Chen[1], Rong Kong[2], Jianming Zhu[1], Lei Wang[3], and Jin Qi[1(✉)]

[1] School of Internet of Things, Nanjing University of Posts and Telecommunications, Nanjing 210003, China
qijin@njupt.edu.cn

[2] College of Automation and College of Artificial Intelligence, Nanjing University of Posts and Telecommunications, Nanjing 210003, China

[3] RWTH Aachen University, Aachen 52056, Germany

Abstract. Nowadays, long-distance and small target detection has become a research hotspot in computer vision. There are various potential dangers in the construction site with complex environment, and safety accidents often occur because of not wearing safety helmet. Due to the large number of personnel and the changeable environment, the traditional manual inspection and video surveillance have some problems, such as poor detection efficiency and lack of timeliness. In this paper, we propose an improved YOLO v5 method and deployed on Raspberry Pi. Firstly, an attention mechanism is introduced to solve the problem that the backbone network is not sensitive to feature differences; Secondly, the loss function is improved and GFocal Loss is used to train the model. In this paper, the helmet is carried out on the Raspberry Pi, and the experimental results show that the improved YOLO v5 algorithm is better than the original algorithm to detect the target, which is helpful to the practical deployment of intelligent transportation, traffic flow and other application scenarios.

Keywords: Target detection · Raspberry Pi · YOLO v5 · Helmet detection

1   Introduction

With the continuous development of cities and the emergence of large-scale high-rise buildings, casualties caused by non-compliance with construction rules and regulations occur frequently, resulting in a large number of casualties and property losses. Construction safety has gradually become a problem that cannot be ignored. Among them, the wearing of safety helmet is the basic protection and guarantee measure in construction. Wearing safety helmet correctly can protect the safety of construction workers to a certain extent, and even avoid some accidents. Therefore, it is necessary to check whether the safety helmet is

© The Author(s), under exclusive license to Springer Nature Switzerland AG 2022
X. Sun et al. (Eds.): ICAIS 2022, LNCS 13338, pp. 107–117, 2022.
https://doi.org/10.1007/978-3-031-06794-5_9

worn during the engineering operation [1,2]. At present, the construction site mainly relies on manual inspection by management personnel and surveillance video for detection [3]. This method may cause missed detection and error detection due to camera location, construction operation type, personnel location and other factors. The real-time monitoring of whether the construction workers wear safety helmets through the target detection method can not only achieve safety supervision, but also reduce the labor cost of traditional methods.

Because of its low resolution and less information, long-distance target detection is difficult to extract effective features [4], so it has gradually become a hot and difficult point in the field of target detection. At the same time, with the rapid development of deep learning theory and technology [5], many deep learning networks and various mechanisms have been applied to target detection, which makes a great breakthrough in the performance of target detection algorithms [6]. SSD (Single Shot Multibox Detector) proposed by Liu et al. uses large-scale feature maps to detect small objects and uses small-scale feature maps to detect larger objects [7]; Kong et al. proposed Hyper multi-scale feature fusion network, which clips interesting features in different scale feature maps and detects targets through these multi-scale features [8]; Xu et al. proposed Reasoning-RCNN on the basis of Fast R-CNN network, which constructs a knowledge graph to encode the context relationship and uses a priori context relationship to improve the performance of target detection [9]. Yan et al. proposed a feature pyramid network based on special attention mechanism, which improves the performance of small target detection by generating target features of different sizes into a feature pyramid [10].

In order to facilitate the deployment of remote detection, we choose the Raspberry Pi as the carrier and applies the detection algorithm to the Raspberry Pi for the identification and detection of the safety cap. We used the YOLO v5 algorithm and improves it. In this paper, we use the attention mechanism to improve the insensitivity of backbone network to feature differences and use GFocal Loss instead of Focal Loss to train and experiment on raspberry pie. The experimental results show that the improved algorithm has a better recognition rate in safety helmet detection.

2   Algorithm Analysis

2.1   YOLO

Due to the inefficiency of the two-stage target detection algorithm, Redmon et al. proposed YOLO v1 in 2015 [11]. The algorithm removes the candidate box to extract branches and realizes feature extraction, candidate box classification and regression through the same non-branching deep convolution network, which makes the network structure simpler, but sacrifices the accuracy of the algorithm to a certain extent. Then, in view of the shortcomings of YOLO v1, Redmon and Farhadi proposed an improved model YOLO v2 [12]. The core idea is to improve the detection accuracy through batch normalization, high-resolution classifier, direct target frame position detection, multi-scale training and other operations, and train the Darknet-19 network composed of 19 convolution and 5 pooling layers to extract features to reduce the amount of computation. The subsequently published YOLO v3 [13–15] is improved on the basis of YOLO v2, using a new Darknet-53 residual network and FPN(Feature Pyramid network) [16] for multi-scale fusion prediction, which reduces the computational complexity of the model and increases the network depth to 53 layers to improve the detection accuracy. YOLO v4 [17] is an improved version of YOLO v3, which adopts SPP(Spatial Pyramid Pooling) and PANet(Path Aggregation Network) structure in the feature pyramid structure. YOLO v5 was also proposed a few months later. Although the official paper has not been published and the test comparison with YOLO v4 has not been given, the test effect of YOLO v5 on the COCO data set is more reliable, so it is also favored by many researchers.

YOLO series is a regression method based on deep learning, which solves object detection as a regression problem rather than a classification problem. From the point of view of its characteristics, it has the characteristics of high speed, small model, strong generalization ability and so on.

2.2   YOLO v5

YOLO v5 is divided into four versions according to the depth and width of the network: YOLO v5s [21], YOLO v5m, YOLO v5l and YOLO v5x. The structure of YOLO v5 is similar to that of YOLO v4, as shown in Fig. 1:

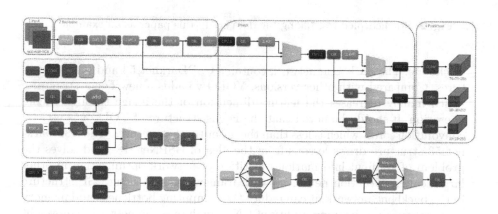

Fig. 1. YOLO v5 network structure.

The YOLOv5 network structure is mainly divided into four parts:

– Input: The input end uses the data enhancement method Mosaic to input the training set. After the images of the data set are randomly scaled, distributed and cut, any four pictures are selected for stitching, as shown in Fig. 2. This method can improve the detection effect of long-distance small targets to a certain extent. The detection dataset is enriched by using Mosaic, which improves the robustness of the detection network and can reduce the training cost. In addition, YOLO v5 adds an Auto Learning Bounding Box Anchors. In the training, the prediction box is output on the basis of the initial anchor frame and compared with the ground truch to calculate the gap between the two and update them in reverse to achieve the iteration of network parameters. In addition, most target detection algorithms scale the original image to a unified ruler for detection, while YOLO v5 reduces information redundancy by adding the least black edges through adaptive image scaling.

Fig. 2. Stitched pictures, taking the data set in this paper as an example.

- Backbone: The backbone network contains CSPDarknet_53 and Focus structures. Compared with other versions, YOLO v5 adds a new Focus structure, which mainly increases the feature dimension of the image through slicing operation. It should be noted that the Focus structure of YOLO v5s uses 32 convolution cores, which is less than the other three structures. The CSPDarknet_53 structure draws lessons from the idea of CSPNet [18], and solves the problem of gradient information repetition of network optimization in other large-scale convolution neural network frameworks. By using CSP structure in the backbone network, it can reduce the computing bottleneck and memory cost, enhance the learning ability of CNN, maintain the network lightweight while maintaining accuracy. Among them, YOLO v5s network designs two kinds of CSP structures, CSP1_X structure is applied to backbone network, and CSP2_X structure is applied to Neck.
- Neck: The Neck part not only contains CSP2_X structure, but also adopts SPP module and FPN+PAN (Pyramid Attention Network) structure. The maximum pool method is used in the SPP module, and finally the feature images of different scales are operated by concat. FPN fuses the top feature information with the backbone network feature information through downward sampling, and then PAN samples upward to achieve further strong

positioning feature transmission, the two are combined to obtain information about the characteristics of the network.

– Prediction: Including loss function calculation and NMS(Non-maximum suppression). The loss function consists of three parts: GIoU(Generalized Intersection over Union) Loss function, Confidence Loss Function $Loss_{Obj}$ and Localization Loss function. By using NMS to eliminate the redundant prediction box and retain the prediction box with the highest confidence as the detection result, the target detection process is completed.

3 Algorithm Improvement

3.1 SENet

SENet(Squeeze-and-Excitation Networks) [19] is a module that regulates the channel attention mechanism, which was proposed by Hu et al. and won the championship of the ImageNet classification competition in 2017. Its function is to improve the attention level of useful features by learning the correlation between various feature channels and according to the different weights of channels. By reducing the attention of the unimportant information in the current detection task, the network can pay more attention to the useful information in the global information, so as to improve the accuracy of the target detection algorithm. In this paper, the SENet module is introduced into the CSPDark-net_53 of the backbone network to solve the problem that the network model is not sensitive to feature differences caused by the original algorithm scanning all areas of the image with the same attention.

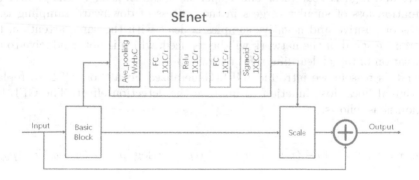

Fig. 3. SENet module structure.

The structure of the SENet module is shown in Fig. 3, and the operation is mainly divided into two phases: Squeeze and Excitation. The Squeeze operation is to perform global pooling on the input feature map (H,W,C) through global average pooling, the pooling size is (H,W), and output $(1 \times 1 \times C)$ size feature map. The Excitation operation is to get the weight coefficient of each channel through the learning of the full connection layer on the basis of the feature graph obtained by the compression operation, and then use the sigmoid function to normalize the weights of each channel to (0,1). Finally, the output result of SENet and the result of Basic block are scaled to realize the weighting of each channel characteristic. Where H,W,C are the length, width and number of channels of the global feature graph, r is the reduction coefficient, and when r is 8 or 16, the network calculation and performance are relatively optimal [20].

3.2 Generalized Focal Loss

In the part of confidence loss function, YOLO v5 network uses Focal loss function [22] to solve the problem of serious imbalance between positive and negative samples. The definition of Focal Loss is as follows:

$$FL(p,y) = \{-\alpha(1-p)^{\gamma}\log(p), \gamma = 1 - (1-\alpha)p^{\gamma}\log(1-p), \gamma = 0 \quad (1)$$

where γ is an adjustable focusing parameter, and $\gamma \in \{0,1\}$, p represents the probability that the category label is 1, and $p \in [0,1]$.

The original Focal loss function focuses on the learning of low-quality samples, which leads to the update efficiency of the parameters of the target detection model and affects the subsequent detection results. In the long-distance small target detection, there is often the problem of imbalance between the foreground class and the background class, because of the long distance of the builders in the construction environment, as a result, the target to be detected is very small, the resolution of collected pixels is low, and the representation ability of local details and information is poor, resulting in a great imbalance in the number of positive and negative samples. The deeper the network layer is, the greater the information loss of smaller targets in the process of downward sampling is. If the loss of positive and negative samples is dealt with the same attention, the convergence speed of the network will be reduced, which is not conducive to the preservation of target learning information [23].

For this reason, we introduce GFL(Generalized Focal Loss) [24] to replace the original Focal loss function to improve the detection effect. The GFL loss function is as follows:

$$GFL(p_{yl}, p_{yr}) = -|y - (y_l p_{yl} + y_r p_{yr})|^{\beta} ((y_r - y)\log(p_{yl}) + (y - y_l)\log(p_{yr}))$$
$$(2)$$

where $y \in [0,1]$ is continuous and represents the IoU score of the positive sample, when $y = 0$, it represents the negative sample, when $0 < y \leq 1$, it represents the positive sample, and $y_l \leq y \leq y_r$; where β is a super parameter of scaling factor, which is used to control the weight reduction rate. By extending the FL, when the predicted value deviates from the label y, the scaling factor will become larger and the resulting weight will become larger, the network will spend more time to learn the sample, and the scaling factor tends to 0; the probability sum of p_{y_l} and p_{y_r} is 1, and the final prediction is the linear combination of the two, as shown in the formula 3:

$$y = y_l p_{y_l} + y_r p_{y_r} \ (y_l \leq y \leq y_r) \tag{3}$$

The global minimum is achieved by GFL, and the joint representation of classification score and quality estimation is directly input as the NMS score in the reasoning process. Finally, the network will focus on high-quality samples to improve the update efficiency of model parameters, and then improve the convergence speed of the network.

4 Result

4.1 Experimental Environment

This experiment based on the embedded low computing power platform Raspberry Pi 4B. With Broadcom 64-bit high-performance processor, the main frequency is up to 1.8Ghz, include 4G RAM, 64G ROM, essentially an embedded minicomputer, It's a size of Credit Card, the Peak power consumption is 10w, and can powered by power bank or lithium battery. Its complete hardware architecture allows the Raspberry Pi to run a full Linux version system. With a full-featured python environment on it. The python files trained on the server can be directly transferred to the Raspberry Pi to run, so there is no difficulty in transplantation, and it is convenient and fast to deploy.

The hardware environment based on Raspberry Pi 4B as the core computing node, OV7255 camera for Image capture, and power supply by the power bank. The software environment based on the official Raspbian system, which is the compiled version of Debian on ARM Platform, and optimizes the kernel for Raspberry Pi, include python IDE. The training of Yolo V5 is completed on the server side. The completed training file is directly copied to the Raspberry Pi to run.

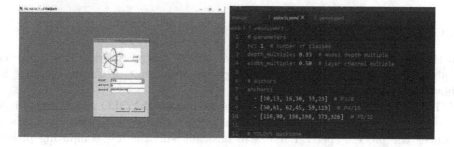

Fig. 4. Schematic environment of Raspberry Pi.

Since the Raspberry Pi is not configured with a display screen, we connected to the Raspberry Pi with RDP protocol to configuration the experimental environment. After the setup is completed, place the equipment to the construction site and find a suitable location for Image capture.

4.2   Model Training

Using the Safety Helmet Wearing-Dataset database, the images cover various scenes, including 9044 human wearing safety helmet and 111514 normal head (non-wearing or negative), and all images are labeled with labelimg to indicate the target area and category. Figure 5 shows some images in the database, with a total of 7581 images. According to the ratio of 8:2, images divided into 5957 in the training set and 1624 in the verification set.

Fig. 5. Images in the database.

The training hardware environment including Intel(R) Xeon(R) CPU E5-2680 v3 @2.50GHz. NVIDIA Tesla K80 graphics card. Software environments including the server with Ubuntu 14.04.6 operating system, CUDA10.1 and cuDNN7.6.5 to accelerate the training. We use the Python 3.6 as the coding language and the PyCharm as IDE environment, based on the Pytorch 1.8.0. network framework. Before training, configured the relevant parameters of the model and set the training times epoch to 100. Then the trained model file is copied to the Raspberry Pi 4B and run the results to verified.

4.3   Result Analysis

In this paper, we use Precision, Recall and mAP (mean Average Precision) as evaluation indexes. Comparison the experimental result of the two models is shown in Table 1.

It can be observe from the table data the improved YOLO v5 algorithm has a certain improvement in mAP. Although the increased attention mechanism reduces the process speed, but it still basically suit the low computing power platform.

The experimental results of the improved YOLO v5 algorithm are shown in Fig. 6(b), and the experimental results of the traditional YOLO v5 algorithm are shown in Fig. 6(a). By comparing the detection results of the experiment, it can be found that the original algorithm only detects a few targets which are close to each other, and misses three small targets which are farther away, while the improved algorithm in this paper detects all 11 targets, which effectively reduces the missing rate and enhance the construction safety.

Table 1. Experimental results.

Models	Precision/%	Recall/%	mAP-0.5/%
YOLO v4	91.65	85.21	89.81
YOLO v5	91.91	85.5	90.77
Improved-YOLO v5	**92.24**	**87.32**	**91.11**

(a) Detection results of traditional YOLO v5s (b) Detection results of improved YOLO v5s algorithm   gorithm

Fig. 6. Applied on Raspberry Pi.

The Focal loss function in the original algorithm has some problems. For instance, the imbalance numbers of positive and negative samples made the long-distance detection with low Precision, other is the original algorithm has only three detection layers, which leads to the low confidence of the output prediction frame and the problem of missing detection and failing to detect long-distance targets. We improved the Focal loss function; the detection effect is significantly improved. Based on the analysis, this article shows that the effect of long-distance helmet detection is better than the traditional YOLO v5. Considering the low Computing-Rate of Raspberry Pi, YOLO v5s can be selected as the backbone network. It can not only reduce network complexity and uplift the detection speed, but also identify the relevant objects with a more accurate detection rate. Through experimental verification, it is feasible to deploy YOLO v5 in Raspberry Pi and carry out helmet detection application during construction.

5 Conclusion

An improved YOLO v5 target detection network model for helmet detection in construction scenarios is proposed in this paper. The model is fully trained on the server by using the training dataset, and then the trained model file deployed on the Raspberry Pi for detection experiments. By import the SENet module in the backbone network, enhance the attention degree of useful information in global information. The Precision rate of the long-distance safety helmet is improved. To train the module with Generalized Focal Loss to replace the

Focal Loss confidence function, the Raspberry Pi long-distance target detection mAP are improved. In future research, author will focus on how to improve the detection speed under low Computing-Rate of Raspberry Pi with an acceptable Precision rate. At the same time, study the detection performance under different illumination conditions and how to improve it. To facilitate application in some actual scenarios.

Acknowledgements. Thanks for the support and help of the team when writing the paper. Thanks to the reviewers and experts of your magazine for their valuable opinions on the article revision. This author has provided great inspiration when writing.

Conflicts of Interest. The authors declare that they have no conflicts of interest to report regarding the present study.

References

1. Hu, J., Gao, X.W., Wu, H.F., et al.: Detection of workers without the helments in videos based on YOLO V3. In: 2019 12th International Congress on Image and Signal Processing, BioMedical Engineering and Informatics (CISP-BMEI), pp. 1–4 (2019)
2. Zhou, Q., Qin, J., Xiang, X., Tan, Y., Xiong, N.N.: Algorithm of helmet wearing detection based on at-YOLO deep mode. Comput. Mater. Continua **69**(1), 159–174 (2021)
3. Deng, B.Y. Lei, X.C., Ye, M.: Safety helmet detection method based on YOLO v4. In: 2020 16th International Conference on Computational Intelligence and Security (CIS), pp. 155–158 (2020)
4. Alghassab, M.A.: Defect detection in printed circuit boards with pre-trained feature extraction methodology with convolution neural networks. Comput. Mater. Continua **70**(1), 637–652 (2022)
5. Yuan, J.J., Hu, Y.L., Sun, Y.F., et al.: Summary of small target detection methods based on deep learning. J. Beijing Univ. Technol. **47**(3), 293–302 (2021)
6. Li, Y.N.: A review of deep learning target detection methods. China New Commun. **23**(9), 159–160 (2021)
7. Redmon, J., Divvala, S., Girshick, R., et al.: You only look once: unified, real-time object detection. In: 2016 IEEE Conference on Computer Vision and Pattern Recognition (CVPR), Las Vegas, NV, USA, pp. 779–788 (2016)
8. Liu, W., et al.: SSD: single shot multibox detector. In: Leibe, B., Matas, J., Sebe, N., Welling, M. (eds.) ECCV 2016. LNCS, vol. 9905, pp. 21–37. Springer, Cham (2016). https://doi.org/10.1007/978-3-319-46448-0_2
9. Kong, T., Yao, A., Chen, Y., Sun, F.: HyperNet: towards accurate region proposal generation and joint object detection. In: Proceedings of the IEEE Conference on Computer Vision and Pattern Recognition, pp. 845–853 (2016)
10. Xu, H., Jiang, C., Liang, X., Lin, L., Li, Z.: Reasoning-RCNN: unifying adaptive global reasoning into large-scale object detection. In: Proceedings of the IEEE/CVF Conference on Computer Vision and Pattern Recognition, pp. 6419–6428 (2019)

11. JYan, J., Zhao, L., Diao, W., Wang, H., Sun, X.: AF-EMS detector: improve the multi-scale detection performance of the anchor-free detector. Remote Sensing **13**(2), 160 (2021)

12. Redmon, J., Farhadi, A.: YOLO9000: better, faster, stronger. In: Proceedings of the IEEE Conference on Computer Vision and Pattern Recognition, pp. 7263–7271 (2017)

13. Redmon, J., Farhadi, A.: Yolov3: an incremental improvement. arXiv:1804.02767 (2018)

14. Wang, Y., Jia, K., Liu, P.: Impolite pedestrian detection by using enhanced YOLOV3-tiny. J. Artif. Intel. **2**(3), 113 (2020)

15. Liu, Q., Lu, S., Lan, L.: Yolov3 attention face detector with high accuracy and efficiency. Comput. Syst. Sci. Eng. **37**(2), 283–295 (2021)

16. Seferbekov, S., Iglovikov, V., Buslaev, A., Shvets, A.: Feature pyramid network for multi-class land segmentation. In: Proceedings of the IEEE Conference on Computer Vision and Pattern Recognition Workshops, pp. 272–275 (2018)

17. Bochkovskiy, A., Wang, C.Y., Liao, H.Y.M.: YOLOV4: optimal speed and accuracy of object detection. arXiv:2004.10934 (2020)

18. Wang, C.Y., Liao, H.Y.M., Wu, Y.H., Chen, P.Y., Hsieh, J.W., Yeh, I.H.: CSPNet: a new backbone that can enhance learning capability of CNN. In: Proceedings of the IEEE/CVF Conference on Computer Vision and Pattern Recognition Workshops, pp. 390–391 (2020)

19. Hu, J., Shen, L. and Sun, G.: Squeeze-and-excitation networks. In: Proceedings of the IEEE Conference on Computer Vision and Pattern Recognition, pp. 7132–7141 (2018)

20. Mao, Y.H., He, Z.Z., Liu, L.L.: Pruning based on separable convolutions for object tracking. J. Xi'an Jiaotong Univ. 1–8 (2020)

21. Ashraf, A.H., et al.: Weapons detection for security and video surveillance using CNN and YOLO-v5s. Comput. Mater. Continua **70**(2), 2761–2775 (2022)

22. Lin, T.Y., Goyal, P., Girshick, R., He, K., Dollár, P.: Focal loss for dense object detection. In Proceedings of the IEEE International Conference on Computer Vision, pp. 2980–2988 (2017)

23. Tan, S., Lu, G., Jiang, Z., Huang, L.: Improved YOLOv5 network model and application in safety helmet detection. In 2021 IEEE International Conference on Intelligence and Safety for Robotics (ISR), pp. 330–333 (2021)

24. Li, X., et al.: Generalized focal loss: learning qualified and distributed bounding boxes for dense object detection. In: Advances in Neural Information Processing Systems, pp. 21002–21012 (2020)

Application Research of MES in Intelligent Manufacturing Training Factory

Zhou Li[1] , Guwei Li[1(✉)] , and Zhengyuan Li[2]

[1] Zhejiang Dongfang Polytechnic, WenZhou 325000, China
3168897@qq.com
[2] Nagoya City University, Nagoya 23100-2, Japan

Abstract. With the continuous impact of the epidemic, the decline of the demographic dividend and the intensification of market competition, the traditional manufacturing industry urgently needs to transform and upgrade to intelligent manufacturing, the demand for high-skilled talents in intelligent manufacturing is growing, and the talent training tasks undertaken by high-skilled talent training bases all over the country are increasing day by day. Taking a training factory of intelligent manufacturing high-skilled talents in Wenzhou as a sample, this paper studies the application of MES in the training base, discusses the information construction ideas of talent training base, and promotes the high-quality development of high-skilled talent training in the base.

Keywords: Intelligent manufacturing · Training base · MES

1 Introduction

In the 1990s, the American management community put forward the concept of MES (Manufacturing Execution System) to establish a "real-time information channel" between planning and production to be responsible for production management and scheduling performance [1]. MES improves the competitiveness of manufacturing industry by controlling all factory resources (including materials, equipment, personnel, process instructions and facilities), and provides a method to systematically integrate functions such as quality control, document management and production scheduling on a unified platform. MES connects the preceding with the following, and eliminates the fault between the planning layer and the field control layer.

In order to change the situation of manufacturing industry being "a large-scale industry but a technologically weak one in the world", China proposes 'Made in China 2025' strategy [2]. Through 10 years of efforts, China will step into the ranks of manufacturing power. One of the main strategic lines is the integration of informatization and industrialization, Internet + and intelligent manufacturing. The foundation is that enterprises must first realize the digital chemical factories. As an automatic control execution system, MES is one of the indispensable technologies in the construction of intelligent factory, the core of digital chemical factory and the booster of Made in China 2025. Revitalizing the manufacturing industry is the key to the sound development of the economy,

© The Author(s), under exclusive license to Springer Nature Switzerland AG 2022
X. Sun et al. (Eds.): ICAIS 2022, LNCS 13338, pp. 118–127, 2022.
https://doi.org/10.1007/978-3-031-06794-5_10

which requires a large number of multi-level and high-quality skilled workers. The public training base needs to coordinate the cultivation of skilled talents training and provide basic talents and human resources support for industrial transformation and upgrading and the realization of the strategic goal of "Made in China 2025". This paper studies the application of MES of Public Training Center for High-skilled Talents of Zhejiang Provincial Industry Education Integration Demonstration Base in talent training in intelligent manufacturing training factory, discusses the information construction ideas of talent training base, and promotes the high-quality development of high-skilled talents training in the base.

2 Requirement Analysis

2.1 Various Types of Equipment and Data from Complex Sources

At present, there are 13 training areas in the training factory, including traditional bench work area, lathe work area, milling work area, grinding work area, mold precision processing area and other mechanical training areas. There are also CNC precision machining area, industrial design training center, electrical control comprehensive training area, advanced control technology comprehensive training area, industrial drive control technology training area, electromechanical integration system comprehensive training area, robot application technology training area, intelligent manufacturing production training center and other electrical training areas. The factory has dozens of different types of equipment, such as drilling machine, vice bench, general lathe, milling machine, grinder, EDM machine tool, CNC feeding wire-cut machine, CNC high-speed small hole EDM machine, industrial engraving machine, drilling machine, CNC centerless grinder, precision inner hole grinder, fluid polishing machine, press, inclined CNC lathe, 4-axis vertical machining center and 3-axis vertical machining center. In this case, it is difficult for the traditional manual scheduling mode give full play to the effective utilization rate of equipment.

2.2 Complex Structure and Different Foundations of Training Objects

Based on higher vocational colleges, the training factory provides vocational skill training services [3] for college students and social personnel. According to the preliminary planning of the training factory and the needs of social development for skilled talents, there are mainly the following three kinds of training objects. The first is students in higher vocational colleges. Focusing on the skill requirements of talent training plans, consolidate theoretical knowledge, strengthen skills and improve skills, comprehensive quality and professional quality in practical trainings of real operating environment. The second is enterprises employees. Employees in original posts urgently need to update knowledge and improve skills while the enterprise is reforming and innovating the production chain. The training factory formulates and implements corresponding training plans and returns eligible trainees to the enterprise, thus realizing the orientation training and output. The third is the laid-off and unemployed personnel in cities and towns and surplus rural labors. The big data shows that the number of the registered unemployed personnel is 40,000 and the registered unemployment rate is 1.79% in cities and towns of Wenzhou in 2020. And also there are previously unemployed social personnel and surplus rural labors. Because such personnel generally have low cultural levels and technical levels, the base can make full use of their advantages of openness and public welfare to improve their knowledge and skills, help the job transfer and post taking and maintain the stable and harmonious development of the local society. The foundations of above kinds of training objects are different, and it is hard to achieve the best training effects by relying on the mode of manual scheduling.

2.3 Different Training Contents and Durations and Large Temporary Changes

As for students in higher vocational colleges, the training period is long, the main training contents are skill operation and post training, especially the new knowledge, process and method closely related to their majors, and it is to train the practical and thought abilities of students and their abilities to analyze and solve problems and train the high-quality skilled talents [4] facing the forefront of production. As for on-the-job employees of enterprises, the training is mainly in the slack season of production and spare time on the premise of minimum impact on the normal production of enterprises, including: enterprise development strategies, rules and regulations, enterprise culture, post responsibilities, basic working knowledge and post skills, working attitude and outlook on life and values. As for trainings carried out for laid-off and unemployed personnel, the training factory shall take the skill operation, market adaptability and innovation and entrepreneurship ability as the core in combination with the actual conditions of laid-off and unemployed personnel according to the social needs for types of talents, and focus on the short-term centralized training to mainly train their abilities of survival and development. The training contents are mainly the basic post knowledge and post skills. The training factory has multiple short-term training projects, which are characterized by large temporary changes and strong randomness, and it cannot make the fast response in the targeted, practical and operational manner by relying on the mode of manual scheduling.

3 MES Construction Goals

3.1 Efficient and Automatic Scheduling, and Automatic Matching with Long-Term and Short-Term Training Projects

The training factory is characterized by multiple varieties of equipment, small batches and different schedules, and managers shall spend a lot of energy in mastering the on-site production information and various conditions occurred, but the effects are still limited [5]. Through the advanced planning and scheduling and capability assessment, the MES can accurately calculate the production and processing capacity of each station, continuously optimize and improve the business process and reasonably arrange the executable and optimal production execution plan, which provides the real, reliable data basis for the fine management of on-site practical training and the practical and effective data foundation and measuring tools for the analysis on the improvement of equipment utilization rate.

3.2 Automatic Supervision of Site Production Information, Automatic Warning of Delayed Orders and Active Declaration Acceptance of Exception

Through automatic site data collection, the MES timely and accurately collects the production progress, quality information, equipment operation status, personnel working hours and other information of the workshop production site, thus realizing information transparency and maintaining the coordinated and smooth operation of all stations in the training factory. By strictly controlling the development and retention time of the training items at each station, an automatic warning is given in case of abnormal detention. The training instructors shall deal with it in time, notify the supervisor if necessary, and quickly dredge and solve it [6]. Trainees can also actively declare exceptions to trigger warning and get the help of training instructors and supervisors.

3.3 Elimination of Information Islands to Reach System Integration

The construction of MES system in the training factory will connect the equipment, resources, information, etc. [7]. of the training factory in series to establish a unified digital production and scheduling integration platform, integrate with PLM system, MDC system and CMM of the whole training base, share the system information resources, and completely solve the problem of "information island" formed by the complex system of the factory.

4 Detailed Design of Production Management Information System Based on MES

4.1 Application of Artificial Fish Swarm Algorithm

Introduction to artificial fish swarm algorithm. The artificial fish swarm algorithm is a new Fangsheng optimization algorithm proposed by Li Xiaolei and others based on the research on the intelligent behavior of animal groups in 2002. The algorithm simulates the foraging behavior of fish swarms according to the characteristic that the place with the largest number of fish in the water area is the place with the most nutrients in the water area to realize the optimization [8]. The algorithm mainly uses the three basic behaviors of fish: foraging, clustering and tail-tracking. The top-down optimization mode is used, starting from the construction of individual bottom behavior, to reach the highlighting global optimal value in the group through the local optimization of each individual in the fish swarms. The top-down optimization idea is used for this method [9]; firstly, the perception and behavior mechanism of a single individual is designed, and then one or a group of entities are placed in the environment to solve problems in the interaction of the environment [10]. The artificial fish is an abstract and virtualized entity of real fish, encapsulating its own data and a series of behaviors, which can accept the stimulation information of the environment and make corresponding activities. Its environment depends on solution space of the problem and the state of other artificial fish [11]. Its behavior at the next moment depends on its own state and environment state, and it also affects the environment by its own activities, and then affects the activities of other artificial fish (See Fig. 1).

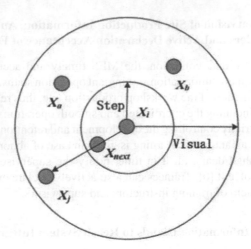

Fig. 1. Visual Field.

The external perception of artificial fish is realized by vision. In the model of artificial fish, the following methods are used to realize the virtual vision of artificial fish:

$$X_v = X + \text{Visuan1} * \text{Rand}() \tag{1}$$

$$X_{\text{next}} = X + \frac{X_v - X}{||X_v - X||} * \text{Step} * \text{Rand}() \tag{2}$$

where, Rand () represents a random function, generating random numbers between 0 and 1, and Step represents the step length.

The billboard is a place to record the individual state of the best artificial fish. After each iteration, each artificial fish compares its current state with the state recorded in the billboard [12]. If it is better than the state in the billboard, it updates the state in the billboard with its own state; otherwise, the state of the billboard remains unchanged. When the iteration of the whole algorithm ends, the value of the billboard is the optimal solution [13]. The behavior evaluation is a way to reflect the autonomous behavior of fish. There are two methods for evaluation when solving optimization problems: One is to select the optimal behavior execution; the other is to select the better optimization direction. For solving the maximum value, the back tracking method is used, that is, the clustering, tail-tracking and other behaviors are simulated. The best optimization is selected for the value after the action. The default behavior is foraging. Iteration termination condition: The usual method is to judge that the mean variance of the value obtained for consecutive times is less than the allowable error; or judge that the number of artificial fish gathered in a certain area reaches a certain proportion [14]; or the mean value obtained for several consecutive times does not exceed the extreme value found; or the maximum iteration time is limited. If the termination conditions are met, output the optimal record of the billboard; otherwise, continuously perform the iteration (See Fig. 2).

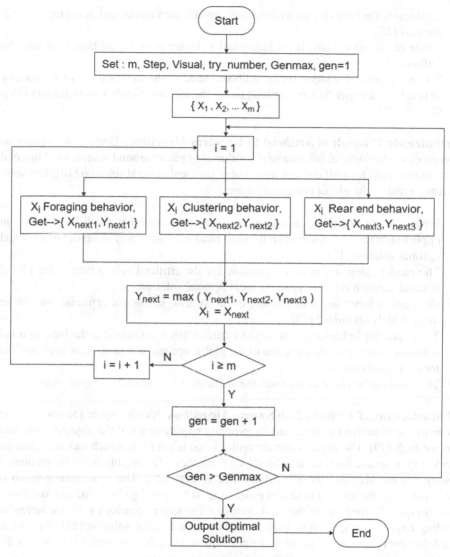

Fig. 2. Algorithm Flow Chart.

Steps of artificial fish swarm algorithm:

① Initialization settings, including population size NN, initial position of each artificial fish, visual field of artificial fish VisualVisual, step length step step, crowding factor δδ, number of repetitions try – numberTry – number.

② Calculate the fitness value of each individual in the initial fish swarm, and give the optimal artificial fish state and its value to the billboard.

③ Evaluate each individual and select the behavior to be performed, including foraging, clustering, tail-tracking and random behavior.

④ Implement the behavior of artificial fish, update themselves and generate new fish swarms [15].
⑤ Evaluate all individuals. If an individual is better than the billboard, update the billboard to that individual.
⑥ When the optimal solution on the billboard reaches the satisfactory error boundary or reaches the upper limit of iteration times, the algorithm ends, otherwise go to step ③.

Optimization Principle of Artificial Fish Swarm Algorithm. During the optimization process, the artificial fish swarm algorithm may gather around several local optimal solutions to make the artificial fish jump out of the local optimal solution [16]. The main factors to realize the global optimization are:

① When the number of repetitions in the foraging behavior is small, it provides an opportunity for the artificial fish to move randomly, so it may jump out of the local optimal solution [17].
② The random step size makes it possible for the artificial fish to turn to the global optimal solution on the way to the local optimal solution.
③ Congestion factor $\delta\delta$ limits the size of the swarm, so that the artificial fish can be more widely optimized [18].
④ The clustering behavior can make the artificial fish less trapped in the local optimal solution converge in the direction of the global optimal solution, so as to escape the local optimal solution.
⑤ Tail-tracking behavior accelerates the artificial fish to swim to a better state.

Characteristics of Artificial Fish Swarm Algorithm. It only requires to compare the value of the objective function, and the property requirements of the objective function are not high [19]. The requirement for initial value is not high, which can be generated randomly or set as a fixed value, with strong robustness. The requirements for parameter setting are not high and the allowable range is large [20]. The convergence speed is slow, but it has the ability of parallel processing. It has good global optimization ability and can quickly jump out of the local optimum. For some occasions with low intensive reading requirements, it can be used to quickly get a feasible solution [21]. It does not need the strict mechanism model of the problem, or even the accurate description of the problem, which extends its application scope.

The system applies artificial fish swarm algorithm to discrete production scheduling problem, finally optimizing the quality of dynamic scheduling results of the workshop [22].

4.2 MES Functional Architecture Design

Considering unfixed training project cycle, diversified training projects and other characteristics, the precision and timeliness in the order execution process are strictly controlled so as to further improve the utilization rate of training equipment [23]. Through the digital, information-based and intelligent transformation of the production workshop, the resource consumption will be reduced, the product quality will be improved, the process control will be strengthened, the execution efficiency will be improved, and a new intelligent manufacturing mode of transparent management of the whole production process will be created. The server side is planned to be subject to three-tier architecture development. The first layer is the presentation layer. The Js front-end framework of Google is used to complete the construction of various functional module frameworks, which are used to manage the production plan of the system. Instructors in each training room can carry out relevant detailed operations according to their respective training project requirements and course arrangements. The second layer is the business logic layer, which is based on Java Web framework to analyze the internal business logic relationship between various production and management tasks such as production process and quality management mode. It includes plan exclusion, plan assessment, warning management, logistics management, completeness registration, exception registration, etc. The third layer is the data management layer, that is, various data structures, data collection methods, etc. of the workshop production management system [24]. The data management layer is constructed by hibernate framework. The client refers to various management modules directly operated by various production personnel and management personnel in different stations, equipment and control consoles of the workshop. The client is based on the front-end framework AngularJs and developed based on the browser. On the web side of the control console, MVC design pattern is adopted based on AngularJs framework. The basic process is that the browser requests all kinds of data of REST specifications from the server through HTTP request. These data are temporarily stored in the browser by internal cache, and then interacted with the model layer. The controller layer connects the view layer and the model layer, so that users carry out interactive operation through the view layer.

4.3   MES Functional Module Design

MES consists of seven functional modules and several sub-functional modules. The data management module is an important index to measure the application effect of the system, reflecting the level of automation management [25]; the plan management module includes several sub-modules such as plan information management, project warning management, training project material calculation, etc.; the training factory process management module includes sub-modules such as production process management, requisition and return of products, production manpower information[26]; the procurement business management module mainly includes the entry and inquiry of material purchase orders, raw material information and raw material price. The operation of product quality management is mainly to meet the requirements of training projects for product quality; the sub-module of inventory business management mainly includes inventory information inquiry, inventory alarm setting and other operations [27]; the sales business management module includes sub-modules such as sales order, return information and inquiry of sales information. System management mainly includes the operation of user and database backup [28]. For aided teaching, this system strengthens the data transmission of the production equipment controller PLC, collects and analyzes the basic information of the equipment and the production status information in real time, matches the production progress indicators after sorting, pushes the knowledge points of the current progress to the station receiving end, and pushes warning icons to students and practical training instructors when deviation or serious deviation from the indicators is detected, so as to be of great help to practical training teaching guidance [29].

5   Conclusion

Combine with the current practice of training factory management, to further strengthen the analysis and research of MES and the construction of training factory information management platform, so that the cost control is more accurate and reasonable [30]. At the same time, through the collection and analysis of relevant cost data, the level of cost management and performance appraisal in the base can be continuously improved. It has played a very important role in reducing training cost, improving training efficiency, etc. It is of important reference value for the construction of other similar public training bases.

References

1. Erdemir, E., Altun, A.A.: A new metaheuristic approach to solving benchmark problems: hybrid salp swarm jaya algorithm. Comput., Mater. Continua **71**(2), 2923–2941 (2022)
2. Mahmoud, S., Salman, A.: Cost estimate and input energy of floor systems in low seismic regions. Comput., Mater. Continua **71**(2), 2159–2173 (2022)
3. Almazroi, A.A., Sher, R.: Covid-19 cases prediction in Saudi Arabia using tree-based ensemble models. Intell. Autom. Soft Comput. **32**(1), 389–400 (2022)
4. Fang, W., Pang, L., Yi, W., Sheng, V.S.: Attef: convolutional lstm encoder-forecaster with attention module for precipitation nowcasting. Intell. Autom. Soft Comput. **30**(2), 453–466 (2021)
5. Huang, C., Huang, C.: Cvae-gan emotional ai music system for car driving safety. Intell. Autom. Soft Comput. **32**(3), 1939–1953 (2022)
6. Rudniy, A.: Data warehouse design for big data in academia. Comput., Mater. Continua **71**(1), 979–992 (2022)
7. Wang, Y.: Hybrid efficient convolution operators for visual tracking. J. Artificial Intell. **3**(2), 63–72 (2021)
8. Wang, Q.Y., Dong, H.B.: Book retrieval method based on QR code and CBIR technology. J. Artificial Intell. **1**(2), 101–110 (2019)
9. Ju, X.: An Overview of Face Manipulation Detection. J. Cyber Secur. **2**(4), 197–207 (2020)
10. Jiang, L., Fu, Z.: Privacy-preserving genetic algorithm outsourcing in cloud computing. J. Cyber Secur. **2**(1), 49–61 (2020)
11. Xia, S.: Application of Maya in film 3D animation design. In: 2011 3rd International Conference on Computer Research and Development, pp. 357–360 (2011)
12. Can, G., Odobez, J., Gatica-Perez, D.: Maya codical glyph segmentation: a crowdsourcing approach. IEEE Trans. Multimedia **20**(3), 711–725 (2018)
13. Kinsman, J., Asher, D.: Orbital dynamics of highly probable but rare Orionid outbursts possibly observed by the ancient Maya. Mon. Not. R. Astron. Soc. **493**(1), 551–558 (2020)
14. Pei, S., Chang, K.: Odd ramanujan sums of complex roots of unity. IEEE Signal Process. Lett. **14**(1), 20–23 (2007)

15. Jakelic´, D., Moura, A.A.D.: Tensor products, characters, and blocks of finite-dimensional representations of quantum affine algebras at roots of unity. Int. Math. Res. Notices **2011**(18), 4147–4199 (2011)
16. Zhu, M.: Regular representations of quantum groups at roots of unity. Int. Math. Res. Not. **2010**(15), 3039–3065 (2010)
17. Alshambri, H.A., Alassery, F.: Securing fog computing for e-learning system using integration of two encryption algorithms. J. Cyber Secur. **3**(3), 149–166 (2021)
18. Xu, H., Du, C., Guo, Y., Cui, Z., Bai, H.: A generation method of letter-level adversarial samples. J. Artificial Intell. **3**(2), 45–53 (2021)
19. Jin, K., Wang, S.: Image denoising based on the asymmetric Gaussian mixture model. J. Internet Things **2**(1), 1–11 (2020)
20. Zhou, Y., He, J., Yang, H.: Bfs parallel algorithm based on sunway taihulight. J. New Media **3**(2), 63–72 (2021)
21. He, J., Wang, C., Wu, H., Yan, L., Lu, C.: Multi-label Chinese comments categorization: comparison of multi-label learning algorithms. J. New Media **1**(2), 51–61 (2019)
22. Albahli, S., Nabi, G.: Defect prediction using akaike and bayesian information criterion. Comput. Syst. Sci. Eng. **41**(3), 1117–1127 (2022)
23. Wang, X., Wang, Q.: Design and research of intelligent alcohol detector based on single chip microcomputer. J. Internet Things **2**(3), 121–127 (2020)
24. Palpandi, S., Meeradevi, T.: Development of efficient classification systems for the diagnosis of melanoma. Comput. Syst. Sci. Eng. **42**(1), 361–371 (2022)
25. Fang, W., Zhang, W., Shan, L., Assefa, B., Chen, W.: Ldpc code's decoding algorithms for wireless sensor network: a brief review. J. New Media **1**(1), 45–50 (2019)
26. Zhou, Y., Luo, W.W.: A QR data hiding method based on redundant region and BCH. J. Big Data **3**(3), 127–133 (2021)
27. Sheng, Y.F., Chen, W.D., Wen, H., Lin, H.J., Zhang, J.J.: Visualization research and application of water quality monitoring data based on ECharts. J. Big Data **2**(1), 1–8 (2020)
28. Yang, H.L., Hu, C.Q., Li, G.W., Fan, J.C.: A fire escape simulation system based on the dijkstra algorithm. Comput. Syst. Sci. Eng. **39**(3), 365–372 (2021)
29. Chen, Y., Lan, W.H., Wang, C.: Application of MES system in offshore oil and gas field production management. J. Big Data **1**(2), 47–54 (2019)
30. Jiang, Y., et al.: A new method based on evolutionary algorithm for symbolic network weak unbalance. J. Internet Things **1**(2), 41–53 (2019)

Design of Temperature Monitoring System Using Distributed Intelligent CAN Bus Networks

Yu Su[1,2,3], Lingjuan Hou[2,3(✉)], Sinan Li[1], and Zhaochang Jiang[1]

[1] The 54th Research Institute, China Electronics Technology Group Corporation, Shijiazhuang 050081, China
su_yu01@163.com

[2] School of Management, Tianjin Normal University, Tianjin 300387, China
lingjuan258@163.com

[3] Graduate School, Sehan University, Mokpo 58613, South Korea

Abstract. Temperature sensing and control remain challenges since temperature is a critical index of the increasingly growing in agriculture and smart planting. CAN (Controller Area Network) bus, due to its high stability, anti-interference ability, timeliness, adaptability to complex industrial environment, good performance, it has been widely used industrial communication among networked instrument. In this project a STC89C52 microcontroller is selected as the master chip, using as an independent CAN controller SJA1000, PCA82C250 as the CAN bus driver to achieve CAN bus communication, designed and implemented based on CAN bus network multi-node temperature monitoring system, including the master node controller, from the node controller and PC server-side procedures. The system in real time from a node can collect temperature sensor DS18B20 temperature signal transmitted via the CAN controller SJA1000 CAN controller to the receiver, and then before sending the master node, the master node receives the signal can be displayed on the LCD screen, you can also via RS-232 bus serial transmission to the host computer program computer display, the other computer can also send commands through the host computer to control the master/slave node, enabling on-line monitoring distributed CAN bus network in site-specific farming.

Keywords: Controller Area Network bus (CAN-bus) · Temperature sensor · Temperature measurement and conditioning · Fieldbus · Embedded systems (ES)

1 Introduction

Over the past few years, the rapid development of 5G communication, Internet of things (IoT), artificial intelligence (AI), big data, and mobile Internet technologies have revolutionized the agricultural cultivation in many ways, and speeded up the successful applications of smart farming and precision agriculture, in which many controlling, monitoring, and tracking systems based on IoTs have been developed to explicate the network of physical objects integrated in various sensors to measure different quantities of the temperature, soil, and air conditions to control a suitable environment for enhancing the efficiency and quality of agricultural products, industrial farming and small-scale

© The Author(s), under exclusive license to Springer Nature Switzerland AG 2022
X. Sun et al. (Eds.): ICAIS 2022, LNCS 13338, pp. 128–141, 2022.
https://doi.org/10.1007/978-3-031-06794-5_11

home agriculture [1, 2]. So, Temperature sensing and control remain a challenge because temperature is also a critical index of the increasingly growing in agriculture and smart farming [3, 4]. Recently, plenty of new industrial temperature sensors are designed around SoCs inside Zynq, including ring-oscillator and the flip-flop element, to undergo hard environmental conditions [5–7], so arms at detecting temperature changes in less than 1 ms as fast as possible to achieve the thermal protection of a logic area of the chip in an absolute way.

Various digital temperature sensors were developed for precision agriculture, e.g., a smart sensor with temperature compensation capacity was employed to monitor the impact of industrial, agricultural, or urban activities on water quality in real time [8–10]. To measure and distribute the amount of required water in farm fields, Vunnava et al. proposed an IoT-based hydration system which consists of MCU microcontrollers to know temperature and other parameters, and manage automatically the water usage which ensures the reducing of human labor and the saving of water resources [11–13]. A temperature control system was implemented by using aeroponics that consists of several chambers where the temperature variation was 29–32.9 °C for the cultivated plant growth in urban farming [14]. Through the estimation of the root-zone soil moisture with remote sensing data, including soil-air temperature difference, canopy-air temperature difference, land surface temperature, etc., in order to manage the phenological behavior and energy balance of the plants [15, 16].

Many devices with multiple sensors that are embedded in the machine's Controller area network bus (CAN-bus) that is one of the fieldbuses. Fieldbus is a kind of data bus of serial digital multipoint communication between automatic control systems installed in the production field. It is a kind of bus topology network applied in the lowest level of production which is realized the information communication by connecting single distributed network node of measurement or monitoring device with bus [17–19]. Fieldbus has the characteristics of openness, interoperability and interoperability, intelligent and functional autonomy of field devices, highly decentralized system structure and adaptability to field environment. In fact, CAN-bus is a kind of serial communication network that supports distributed control or real-time control effectively [20]. CAN bus has the advantages of simple structure, high stability, strong anti-interference ability, expansibility, good openness, real-time and adaptability to complex industrial environment, so it is widely used in industrial networked instrument communication where a mixed H∞/LQR robust controller based on CAN model is established for the marine electric propulsion system [21].

The efficiency metrics is introduced for the quantifying flexibilities in terms of energy consumptions and silicon areas in the architectural applications. However, there exist several problems in security and privacy, Bauer et al. [22] proposed a modular, CAN't, for collaborative tasks in site-specific farming. In order to reducing energy consumption, a new edge-fog-cloud architecture that process the plant data including temperature, moisture, irrigation, etc., from smart sensors real-time operation [23]. Because of its low energy and cheaper, people can employ the sensing devices over smart Bluetooth connections to operate the respective UAVs enabled smart farming-related sensors in the future applications. Lau et al. [24] studied the temperature distribution of the common bulbs available in farming by mimicking the experimental model of broilers. In Ref. [25], the wireless transponder based on EM4325 chip was designed to analyze the leaf-to-air temperature difference, so as to monitor the water stress status of crops. In this paper, STC89C52 chip is selected as the main control MCU, SJA1000 as the independent CAN controller, PCA82C250 as the CAN bus driver, temperature sensor DS18B20 and so on. A multi node real-time temperature monitoring system based on CAN bus network is designed and implemented for site-specific applications in smart farming.

2 Hierarchical Structure and Representation of CAN Bus

2.1 Hierarchical Structure of CAN Bus

The data transmission rate of CAN bus can reach 1 Mbps, and the signal transmission distance can reach 40 m. When the signal transmission distance reaches 10 km, CAN can still provide the data transmission rate as high as 5 Kbps. In order to establish compatibility between two CAN devices, achieve design transparency and implementation flexibility, CAN is divided into different levels [3]: physical layer and data link layer. The hierarchical structure and ISO/OSI reference model have different significances. Logic link control sublayer (LLC) media access control sublayer (MAC) acceptance filtering, overload notification, recovery management data packaging/decoding, frame coding (fill/unfill), media access management error detection error calibration response parallel conversion to serial/serial conversion to parallel.

2.2 Bit Value Representation of CAN Bus

CAN values are two complementary logical numbers: "dominant" (represented by 0) and "recessive" (represented by 1). CAN bus bit numerical expression, CAN_H and CAN_L When the "dominant" and "recessive" bits on the bus are sent at the same time, the final bus value is "dominant". When in "recessive" position, Vcan_H and Vcan_L is fixed to the average voltage and the differential voltage vdiff is approximately 0. The "recessive" bit is sent during the "recessive" bit or bus idle period. The "dominant" state is represented by VDIFF greater than the minimum threshold.

3 Hardware Design of Temperature Monitoring System

3.1 Working Principle of CAN Controller SJA1000

SJA1000 is an independent CAN controller of NXP semiconductor company. It can work in basican and Pelican modes. The working mode can be selected by the CAN mode bit in the clock frequency division register. The default working mode of power on reset is basican mode.

SJA1000 controls the sending and receiving of CAN frame, and its internal structure [5] interface management logic (IML) interprets the commands from CPU, controls the addressing of CAN register, and provides interrupt information and status information to main controller; transmit buffer (TXB) is an interface between CPU and bit stream processor (BSP), which can store a complete message sent to CAN network; receive buffer (rxb, Rxfifo stores the message received from CAN bus. ACF compares the received identifier with the preset value in ACF and decides whether the message should be accepted. The bit stream processor (BSP) controls the data stream sequence generator between TXB, rxfifo and CAN. The bit timing logic (BTL) monitors the serial CAN bus and handles the bit timing related to the bus. The error management logic (EML) is responsible for the error definition on the media access control sublayer. It receives error reports from BSP and then notifies BSP and IML of the error statistics. The CAN bus filter is set to the nodes on the bus. Only when the CAN information frame meets the requirements CAN it pass through, and the rest can be filtered out. Based on the setting of SJA1000 filter in basic CAN mode, with the help of acceptance filter, the CAN controller only allows the received information to be stored in rxfifo when the identification code bit in the received information is equal to the predefined value of acceptance filter.

3.2 Calculation of Baud Rate of CAN Bus Communication

By setting bus timing register 0 (btr0) and bus timing register 1 (btr1), the communication baud rate of CAN bus can be set.

(1) Bus timing register 0 (btr0): bus timing register 0 defines the values of baud rate preset (BRP) and synchronous jump width (SJW). In reset mode, this register is accessible (read/write). In Pelican operation mode, this register is read-only; in Basican operation mode, the value read from this register is always "FFH".

Baud rate preseter (BRP) and bit field BRP make the cycle of CAN system clock programmable and determine their bit timing. The CAN system clock is calculated by the following formula:

$$t_{SCL} = 2 \times t_{SCL} \times (32 \times BRP.5 + 16 \times BRP.4 \\ + 8 \times BRP.3 + 4 \times BRP.2 + 2 \times BRP.1 + BRP.0 + 1) \tag{1}$$

where t_{SCL} is the frequency period of SJA1000 crystal oscillator:

$$t_{SCL} = 1/f_{XTAL} \tag{2}$$

The purpose of setting SJW is to compensate the phase offset during the clock oscillation cycle of different controllers. Any bus controller must resynchronize at the edge of the currently transmitted signal. SJW defines the maximum number of clock cycles that each bit cycle can be shortened or extended by resynchronization

$$t_{SJW} = t_{SCL} \times (2 \times SJW.1 + SJW.0 + 1) \tag{3}$$

(2) Bus timing register 1 (btr1) defines the length of a bit period, the location of sampling points and the number of samples at each sampling point. In reset mode, this register is accessible (read/write). In Pelican operation mode, this register is read-only. When reading this register in basic can operation mode, the value read is always 'FFH'.

Time period 1 (tseg1) and time period 2 (tseg2). Tseg1 and tseg2 determine the number of clocks and the position of sampling points for each bit. The calculation is as follows:

$$t_{TSEG2} = t_{SCL} \times (4 \times TSEG2.2 + 2 \times TSEG2.1 + TSEG2.0 + 1) \tag{4}$$

$$t_{TSEG1} = t_{SCL} \times (8 \times TSEG1.3 + 4 \times TSEG1.2 + 2 \times TSEG1.1 + TSEG1.0 + 1) \tag{5}$$

$$t_{TSEG2} = t_{SCL} \times (4 \times TSEG2.2 + 2 \times TSEG2.1 + TSEG2.0 + 1) \tag{6}$$

Baud rate of SJA1000 [4]

$$\text{Baud rate} = 1/t_{bit}, \ t_{bit} = (t_{SYNCSEG} + t_{TSEG1} + t_{TSEG2}) \tag{7}$$

The Overall structure of 1 bit cycle CAN communication baud rate range:

$$1/(t_{bit} + t_{SJW}) \leq \text{Baud} \leq 1/(t_{bit} - t_{SJW}) \tag{8}$$

3.3 CAN Bus Driver

The mainstream drivers of CAN bus include PCA82C250, TJA1040, tja1050, tja1041, tja1054, etc. among them, tja1041 and tja1054 also have fault tolerance function, which can carry out simple bus fault diagnosis, such as bus line short circuit, etc. [3]. Taking PCA82C250 as an example, this design drives part of limited current circuit, which can prevent TXD from short circuit to power, ground or load. The 82C250 adopts two-wire differential drive, which helps to suppress the transient interference in the harsh electrical environment.

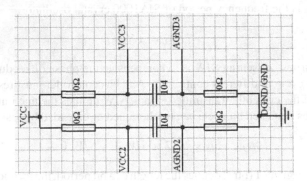

Fig. 1. Power supply circuit to SJA1000

3.4 Modu Hardware Design

1) *Design of system power supply module.* Analog circuit involves weak and small signal, but the threshold level of digital circuit is higher, so the requirement of power supply is lower than that of analog circuit. In the system with both digital circuit and analog circuit, the noise produced by digital circuit will affect the analog circuit and make the small signal index of analog circuit worse. The way to overcome this problem is to separate analog ground and digital ground. The system uses USB power supply, and its output is +5 V, as shown in Fig. 1. The LED in the figure is used to show whether it is powered on (the light is on when it is powered on), and the two capacitors in the figure are used for filtering. The output +5 V power supply can output 3.3 V DC through an ams1117/3.3 voltage regulator, as shown in Fig. 2, which is used to isolate the power supply between digital ground and analog ground.

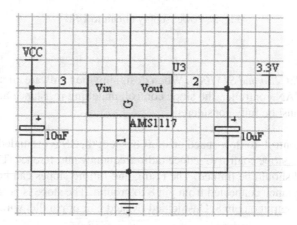

Fig. 2. Regulated output (3.3 V)

2) *CAN controller SJA1000 and MCU connection circuit.* The connection circuit between CAN controller SJA1000 and MCU is shown in Fig. 2. If rx1 level is higher than rx0, read dominant level, otherwise read recessive level. Through the con6 port, you can choose whether rx1 is connected to VREF or DGND, as shown in Fig. 3. SJA1000 crystal circuit, address/data multiplexing bus, etc. The address/data multiplexing bus of SJA1000 is led out through CON1, which can be connected to port P0 of 8051. The address/data multiplexing function of port P0 is used.

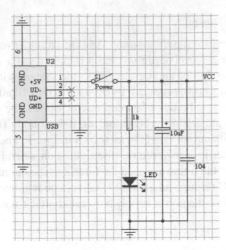

Fig. 3. Power supply circuit to USB

3) *Circuits of 82C250 and SJA1000.* When designing the hardware circuit of CAN bus driver and CAN controller, the slope control, matching resistance and electrostatic protection must be fully considered.

(1) Slope control: for low speed or short bus length, RS is grounded through resistance → slope control to reduce radio frequency interference. The slope of rise and fall should be limited. The rising and falling slopes can be controlled by the resistance connected from pin 8 to ground. The slope is proportional to the current output on pin 8. Unshielded twisted pair or parallel wire can be used as the bus.

(2) There can only be one pair of matching resistors at both ends of CAN bus. If there are only two nodes on the bus, both nodes should be connected with matching resistors. When there are multiple nodes, only two of them can use matching resistor.

(3) Electrostatic protection (ESD) "electrostatic discharge". All CE devices are required: IEC 61000–4-2 level 4, 8 kV (contact discharge) and 15 kV (non-contact discharge), so as to avoid the CAN bus being damaged by ESD and other transient changes.

4) *Design of minimum system board for single chip microcomputer.* Any circuit needs power and ground. First, connect the 40th pin of 8051 MCU to 5V power VCC and the 20th pin to GND [6].

(1) Clock oscillation circuit: 8051 already has an oscillation circuit, as long as a crystal is connected to xtal1 and xtal2 pins, as shown in Fig. 4. 8051 hardware reset circuit, 1602 LCD is omitted. If the internal oscillation circuit of 8051

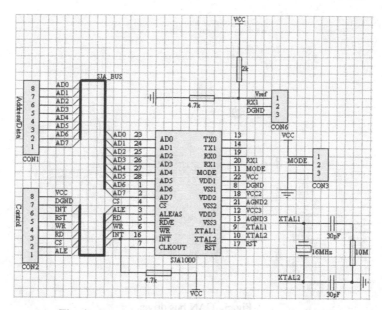

Fig. 4. Connection circuit between SJA1000 and MCU

is not used, the external clock pulse generation circuit can also be used, as shown in Fig. 5. The 7-pin clkout of SJA1000 can generate clock pulse signal, which comes from the internal oscillator of SJA1000 and can be divided by programming. Therefore, for this system, the external clock pulse can be provided through the 7th pin clkout of SJA1000 (Fig. 6).

5) RS232 Serial communication. The hardware circuit of RS232 uses Maxim's MAX232 chip [11] to realize RS232 communication. The connection circuit of other single-chip microcomputers is shown in Fig. 7.

6) *DS18B20 Temperature sensor.* DS18B20 digital thermometer [12] provides 9-bit temperature reading. Its shape is similar to triode. It has three main data components: 1) 64 bit laser ROM; 2) temperature sensitive device; 3) non volatile temperature alarm trigger th and TL. DS18B20 adopts single bus interface, and can't use memory and control operation before ROM operation is established. After preliminary trial of sequence diagram, write sequence diagram, read sequence diagram, Rom operation, etc.: read ROM, match ROM, search ROM, skip ROM, alarm search, the following formula can be used to calculate actual temperature:

$$Temprature(T) = Temp\_Read - 0.25 + \frac{Count\_Per\_C - Count\_Remain}{Count\_Per\_C} \tag{9}$$

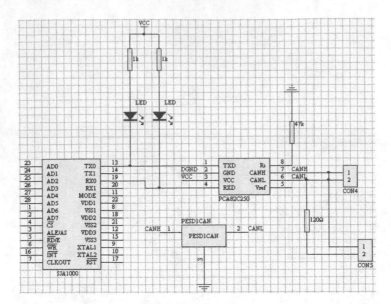

Fig. 5. CAN bus driver

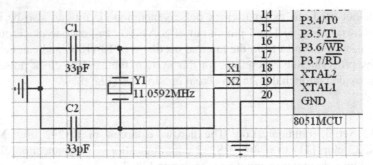

Fig. 6. Internal oscillation circuit

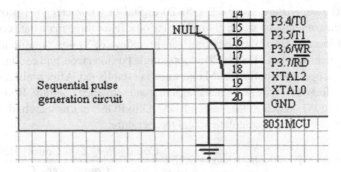

Fig. 7. External oscillation circuit

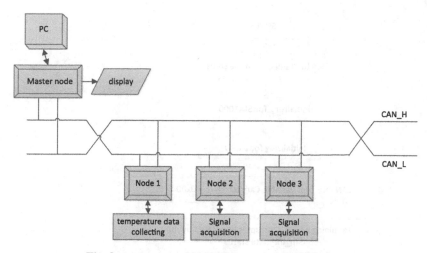

Fig. 8. Multi-nodes CAN communication acquisition

3.5 Multiple Nodes Communication with CAN Bus

The schematic diagram of CAN communication between nodes is shown in Fig. 8. The temperature acquisition module transmits the collected temperature signal to node 1 through DS18B20 temperature sensor. When node 1 judges that the bus is idle, it sends the CAN data frame to the master node. The master node sends the transmitted signal to the LCD module for display, and also sends the signal to the upper computer interface on the PC through RS-232 serial Display. The PC CAN also send instructions to each node. After receiving the data frame sent by the host, each node judges whether the received information is to be sent to itself through the acceptance filter. If it is received, it will be received. If not, it will be filtered. When each node receives the instruction sent by the master node, it will perform the corresponding operation according to the instruction.

4 Software Design of Temperature Monitoring System

The software design includes CPU initialization, SJA1000 initialization, CAN bus receiving/sending, temperature acquisition module DS18B20 initialization, instruction writing to DS18B20, data reading from DS18B20, LCD display module, host computer display and other parts of the program design. In the initialization process, each processing function first obtains the address of the corresponding register, and then assigns the command value to the address Detailed design flow chart is omitted. Figure 9 and Fig. 10 CPU initialization flow chart and processing function flow chart in initialization.

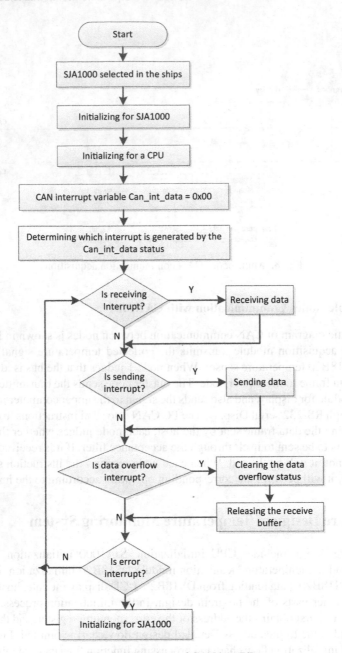

Fig. 9. Flowchart of CAN bus T/R

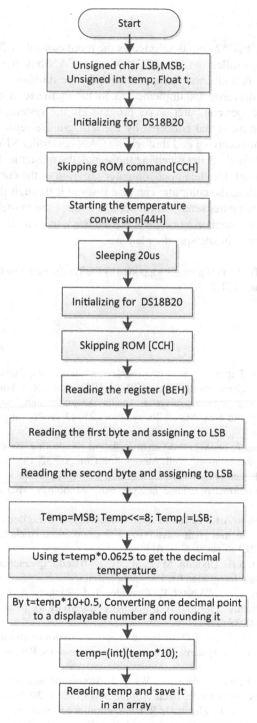

Fig. 10. Flowchart of temperature collection

5   Conclusion

In this work, the STC89C52 chip is selected as the main control MCU, SJA1000 as the independent CAN controller and PCA82C250 as the CAN bus driver to realize CAN bus communication. A multi node temperature real-time monitoring system based on CAN bus network is designed and implemented, including master node controller, slave node controller and upper computer server program. In the system, the slave node can transmit the temperature signal collected by the temperature sensor DS18B20 to the CAN controller of the receiving end through the CAN controller SJA1000 in real time, and then to the master node. After receiving the signal, the master node can display it on the LCD screen, or send it to the upper computer program of the computer through the RS-232 bus. In addition, the computer can also display it through the CAN controller SJA1000. The host computer sends instructions to control the master/slave node, so as to realize the real-time monitoring of CAN bus network that can be applied to control the temperature changes in site-specific planting.

Acknowledgments. The work is partially supported by the Tianjin Planning Project of Philosophy and Social Science (No. TJGL20–018).

References

1. Kassim, M.R.M.: IoT applications in smart agriculture: issues and challenges. In: 2020 IEEE Conference on Open Systems (ICOS), pp. 19–24. IEEE Press, New York (2020)
2. Monica, K.M.: Design and study of system on chip design for signal processing applications in terms of energy and area. Mater. Today: Proc. 31–42 (2021). https://doi.org/10.1016/j.matpr.2021.07.221
3. Khan, A.A., Khan, F.A.: A cost-efficient radiation monitoring system for nuclear sites: designing and implementation. Intell. Autom. Soft Comput. **32**, 1357–1367 (2022)
4. Lefebvre, C.A., Montero, J.L., Rubio, L.: Implementation of a fast relative digital temperature sensor to achieve thermal protection in Zynq SoC technology. Microelectron. Reliab. **79**, 433–439 (2017)
5. Ompal, V.M., Mishra, A.K.: FPGA integrated IEEE 802.15.4 ZigBee wireless sensor nodes performance for industrial plant monitoring and automation. Nucl. Eng. Technol. (2022). https://doi.org/10.1016/j.net.2022.01.011
6. Saidi, A., Othman, S.B., Dhouibi, M., et al.: FPGA-based implementation of classification techniques: a survey. Integration **81**, 280–299 (2021)
7. McDowell, K., Zhong, Y., Webster, K., Gonzalez, H.J., Zachary, A., CamiloMora, T.: Comprehensive temperature controller with internet connectivity for plant growth experiments. HardwareX **10**, e00238 (2021)
8. Halder, S., Conti, M., Sajal, K.D.: A holistic approach to power efficiency in a clock offset based intrusion detection systems for controller area networks. Pervasive Mob. Comput. **73**, 101385 (2021)
9. Liang, S., Wang, D., Wu, J., Wang, R., Wang, J.: Method of bidirectional LSTM modelling for the atmospheric temperature. Intell. Autom. Soft Comput. **30**, 701–714 (2021)
10. Peng, H., Zhu, X., Yang, L., Zhang, G.: Robust controller design for marine electric propulsion system over controller area network. Control. Eng. Pract. **101**, 104512 (2020)

11. Bauer, J., Helmke, R., Bothe, A., Aschenbruck, N.: CAN't track us: adaptable privacy for ISOBUS controller area networks. Comput. Stan. Interfaces **66**, 103344 (2019)
12. Maddikunta, P.K.R., et al.: Unmanned aerial vehicles in smart agriculture: applications, requirements, and challenges. IEEE Sens. J. **21**, 17608–17619 (2021)
13. Akram, V.K., Challenger, M.: A smart home agriculture system based on Internet of Things. In: 10th Mediterranean Conference on Embedded Computing (MECO), pp. 1–4. Budva, Montenegro (2021)
14. Thakare B.D., Rojatkar, D.V.: A review on smart agriculture using IoT. In: 6th International Conference on Communication and Electronics Systems (ICCES), pp. 500–502. Coimbatre, India (2021)
15. Gong, H., et al.: The data acquisition and control system based on IoT-CAN bus. Intell. Autom. Soft Comput. **30**, 1049–1062 (2021)
16. Vunnava, S.L., Yendluri, S.C., Dhuli, S.: IoT based novel hydration system for smart agriculture applications. In: 10th IEEE International Conference on Communication Systems and Network Technologies (CSNT), pp. 505–509. IEEE Press (2021)
17. Lau K.X., et al.: Temperature distribution study for Malaysia broiler house. In: 2nd International Conference on Smart Sensors and Application (ICSSA), pp. 69–73. Kuching, Malaysia (2018)
18. Palazzi, V., Gelati, F., Vaglioni, U., Alimenti, F., Mezzanotte, P., Roselli, L.: Leaf-compatible autonomous RFID-based wireless temperature sensors for precision agriculture. IEEE Topical Conf. Wireless Sensors and Sensor Networks (WiSNet), pp. 1–4. IEEE Press (2019)
19. Alahi, M.E.E., Xie, L., Mukhopadhyay, S., Burkitt, L.: A Temperature compensated smart nitrate-sensor for agricultural industry. IEEE Trans. Indu. Electron. **64**, 7333–7341 (2017)
20. Islam, S.U., Jan, S., Waheed, A., Mehmood, G., Zareei, M., Alanazi, F.: Land-cover classification and its impact on Peshawar's land surface temperature using remote sensing. Comput. Mater. Continua **70**, 4123–4145 (2022)
21. Alharbi, H.A., Aldossary, M.: Energy-efficient edge-fog-cloud architecture for IoT-based smart agriculture environment. IEEE Access **9**, 110480–110492 (2021)
22. Jamhari, C.A., Wibowo, W.K., Annisa, A.R., Roffi, T.M.: Design and Implementation of IoT system for aeroponic chamber temperature monitoring. In: Third International Conference on Vocational Education and Electrical Engineering (ICVEE), pp. 1–4. Surabaya, Indonesia (2020)
23. Fitrianto Rahmad, I., Tanti, L., Puspasari, R., Ekadiansyah, E., Fragastia, V.A.: Automatic monitoring and control system in Aeroponic plant agriculture. In: 8th International Conference on Cyber and IT Service Management (CITSM), pp. 1–5. Pangkal, Indonesia (2020)
24. Aktas, A., Üstündağ, B.B.: Soil moisture monitoring of the plant root zone by using phenology as context in remote sensing. IEEE J. Sel. Top. Appl. Earth Obs. Remote Sens. **13**, 6051–6063 (2020)
25. Udutalapally, V., Mohanty, S.P., Pallagani, V., Khandelwal, V.: sCrop: a novel device for sustainable automatic disease prediction, crop selection, and irrigation in internet-of-agro-things for smart agriculture. IEEE Sens. J. **21**(16), 17525–17538 (2021). https://doi.org/10.1109/JSEN.2020.3032438

Distant Supervised Relation Extraction Based on Sentence-Level Attention with Relation Alignment

Jing Li[1], Xingjie Huang[1], Yating Gao[1], Jianyi Liu[2(✉)], Ru Zhang[2], and Jinmeng Zhao[1]

[1] State Grid Information and Telecommunication Branch, Beijing, China
[2] School of Cyberspace Security, Beijing University of Posts and Telecommunications, Beijing 100876, China
liujy@bupt.edu.cn

Abstract. Current distant supervised relation extraction algorithms based on neural network deep learning always label a large number of irrelevant sentences as valid data or sentences as wrong relation because of their overly broad assumptions. Although many scholars have proposed some methods to reduce the influence of distant supervision noise and their optimization methods, such as organizing sentences into bag of sentences and introducing attention mechanism, they still cannot obtain a good feature vector of a bag of sentences. In this paper, we propose an attention-weight allocation algorithm for sentences inside a bag of sentences based on relative alignment. Compared with previous methods, it can better capture the similarity of sentences to relative vectors, and better extract relationships in sentences under distant supervision. On the standard dataset, the proposed model has improved by 2.5%, 2.4%, 2.8% and 2% compared with the PCNN_ATT model, P@100, P@200, P@300 and AUC indexes, respectively.

Keywords: Distant supervision · Attention mechanism · Relation alignment

1 Introduction

Relation Extraction (RE) is the core task of text mining and information extraction. It mainly uses text data modeling to automatically extract semantic relation triples $< e_1, r, e_2 >$ from natural language text. Among them, e_1 and e_2 are entities, and r is the target relation category to obtain effective semantic knowledge. It is widely used in information retrieval, automatic question and answer, knowledge base construction, semantic network, knowledge graph, visual question answering and other fields.

At present, the main methods of relationship extraction include deep learning relationship extraction model based on supervised and distant supervised. The supervised relational extraction algorithm is limited by the amount of training data and the difficulty of labeling. The relationship extraction method based on remote supervision can make full use of unlabeled unstructured data, and has more application prospects and practical significance. However, the remote supervision method always labels a large

© The Author(s), under exclusive license to Springer Nature Switzerland AG 2022
X. Sun et al. (Eds.): ICAIS 2022, LNCS 13338, pp. 142–152, 2022.
https://doi.org/10.1007/978-3-031-06794-5_12

number of irrelevant sentences as valid data or sentences as false relationships due to its overly broad assumptions. The commonly used methods to reduce the influence of noise from remote supervision include multi-instance learning: organize sentences into bag of sentences and propose the hypothesis of "at least one" [1], which holds that at least one sentence in a bag of sentences is correctly marked. During training, only learn the most likely labeled sentences in a bag of sentences. Based on the probability distribution of this sentence, perform objective function calculation and back propagation to optimize the network. The problem with the "at least one" hypothesis is that most of the training data in the bag of sentences is ignored through the overly strong hypothesis.

In this paper, a sentence-level attentional mechanism for relation alignment is proposed. Considering the noise problem of remote supervision, all sentences in a bag of sentences are aligned with all relations, and a more accurate feature representation vector of bag of sentences is obtained.

2 Related Work

The main difficulty of supervised relation extraction is the extraction of sentence features. With the support of a data set with better annotation quality, it can now achieve a more ideal effect. However, the manually labeled data is always limited and requires a lot of manpower from relevant practitioners. In order to solve the problem of insufficient labeled data, Mintz et al. [2] proposed a labeling method called Distant Supervision. This method uses the existing knowledge base to heuristically align the existing triples in the knowledge base with the corpus, thereby automatically obtaining a large amount of annotation data. However, the distant supervision hypothesis is too absolute. According to this hypothesis, as long as there are two entities in the knowledge base in a sentence and there is a relation R between the two entities in the knowledge base, it is considered that the sentence expresses the relation R between the two entities and marks it as R. This absolute assumption also brings a large amount of noise to the remotely supervised labeled data set.

In order to solve the problem of noise caused by distant supervision, the current main method is to organize all sentences marked with the same triplet and the sentence feature vector after sentence feature extraction into a bag of sentences, and further learn the difference between real mark and noise from the bag of sentences containing several positive samples and noise. On how to use the other bag to deal with noise, different researchers have put forward various algorithms, multi-instance learning was first proposed by Ridel et al. in literature [3], the method employs a looser assumption, the assumption that contain the same of entity for the relationship between R and the labeling of all the sentences, there are at least a couple of really expressing the relationship between R. The above learning methods mostly rely on manual features or features annotated by external annotation tools as sentence features, which seriously depend on the accuracy of annotation, which will also lead to error propagation problems.

The problem with "at least one" hypothesis is that the strong hypothesis ignores most of the training data in the bag of sentences. The attentional mechanism was introduced into natural language processing by Bahdanau et al. in reference [4]. The mechanism of soft attention between bag of sentences was proposed by Lin [5] et al. in 2016. The similarity score of each sentence relative to the relation feature vector was obtained by alighting the sentences in the bag of sentences respectively with the feature vector of the relation represented by the bag of sentences. Finally, the similarity score of all sentences is normalized to the corresponding weight of each sentence by softmax function, and the feature representation of bag of sentences can be obtained by the weighted sum of all sentences. Experimental results show that this kind of soft attention mechanism makes better use of the information of all sentences in the whole bag of sentences and achieves better relationship extraction effect.

Subsequent researchers have also improved this attention mechanism, Lin's selective attention mechanism was improved by Ji et al. [6] in 2017. Unlike Lin, which uses a trainable relational feature vector to express it, Ji uses the feature of word2vec word vector [7], similar to "France" - "Paris" = "China" - "Beijing", to use the difference between the head and tail solid word vectors as the feature vector of the relation between them, and uses a better relational feature vector to calculate the similarity. More accurate similarity weight of each sentence and relation is obtained, and more accurate feature representation vector of each bag of sentences is also obtained. However, considering that distant supervision uses a very broad assumption, through the study of distant supervision data set, this paper finds that the "at least one" assumption is still too broad. In many bags of sentences, none of the instances is correctly labeled. At this time, the alignment with the marked relation vector does not guarantee to obtain a true and reliable weight distribution among bag of sentences, which also results in a failure to obtain a good bag of sentence feature vector. Based on the above analysis, this paper proposes a new sentence-level attention mechanism for relation alignment. Considering the noise problem of distant supervision, all sentences in a bag of sentences are aligned with all relations, and a more accurate feature representation vector of bag of sentence is obtained.

Vaswani et al. proposed the self-attention mechanism in literature [8], which can better capture the dependencies between words in long-distance sequences and greatly reduce the computing time and improve the computing efficiency through parallelization. Transformer networks and BERT language models with self-attention mechanisms at their core also achieve the best results for machine translation, conversation and various downstream tasks. Du et al. proposed a two-dimensional soft attention mechanism in literature [9], which comprehensively considered the different distributions of sentences in multiple feature spaces in the calculation of attention weight, and achieved good results. Q. Yue [10] et al. proposed The FastText-BiGRU-Dual Attention model. The FastText-BiGRU-Dual Attention model is composed of BiGRU and Dual Attention. The model focuses on words that have a decisive effect on sentence relation extraction. And captures relational semantic words and direction words.

Although pre-trained language models like BERT have achieved relatively good results in NLP tasks, when extracting relationships in specific fields, K. Ding [11] et al. found the performances of these BERT-based models on Chinese specific-domain corpora are not as effective as on English datasets. For the extraction of entities and relations in specific domains, K. Ding et al. proposed a hybrid framework based on a knowledge-enriched and span-based network. This model combines the dependency structure and can effectively use external vocabulary and syntactic knowledge for joint extraction of specific Chinese fields.

In order to capture the long-distance dependence of semantics and the semantic interaction between two entities, J. Sun [12] et al. proposed joint self-attention bi-LSTM (SA-Bi-LSTM) to model the internal structure of sentences. The model can obtain the importance of each word in the sentence without relying on additional information. S. Zhao [13] et al. proposed a dynamic cross-modal attention network (CMAN) for uniting entities and REs. In the application of extracting semantic relations between entities, it overcomes the problem of insufficient cross-modal interaction.

3 Method

Aiming at the shortcomings of predecessors that only consider each similarity with the current relationship in the distantly supervised bag of sentence coding, this paper proposes a bag of sentences internal sentence attention weight distribution algorithm based on relation alignment. Align each sentence with all relations to be classified, and then calculate the similarity of sentence vector and relation vector, and then get the distribution of each sentence on all relations, and also get the bag of sentence vector of each bag of sentence on all relations. Thus, the information of each sentence in the bag of sentence can be better integrated, and the noise information of remote supervision can be better used.

3.1 Method Description

The traditional inter-bag of sentences selective attention mechanism is based on the premise that the labeling of the bag of sentences is correct: that is, at least one sentence in the bag of sentences correctly expresses the relationship that the remote supervision labels the bag of sentences. However, in practice, this premise is not necessarily correct. Then, the weights are assigned according to the similarity between each sentence in the bag of sentences and the annotation relation vector. Finally, the weighted sum of each sentence is taken as the feature vector of the bag of sentences, and then the distribution probability of the feature of a bag of sentences on 53 relations is mapped through the full connection layer. This way of learning only considers the influence of a relationship on the bag of sentences, which is far from enough.

The feature extraction algorithm of bag of sentences proposed in this paper considers the similarity between any sentence in bag of sentences and all relations, so there are 53 feature vectors in a bag of sentences, which are the weighted sum of sentences in bag of sentences aligned with different relations. In this way, the feature distribution of each bag of sentences considers all relationship vectors, rather than only aligning the annotation relationship vectors. Compared with the traditional method, it makes more full use of the noise information. In this paper, PCNNs model is used as the sentence feature extractor, combined with the sentence level attention mechanism of relationship alignment, which can extract the short-term features of sentences by combining CNN and the long-term dependence of sentences by self-attention mechanism, and a new relationship extraction model is constructed (Fig. 1).

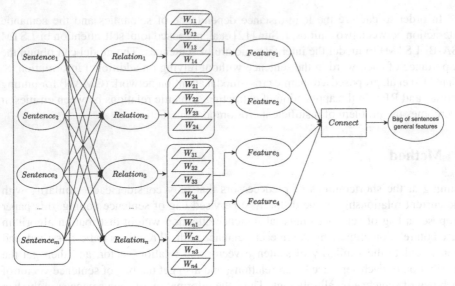

Fig. 1. Structure diagram of relational extraction model based on attention mechanism of relational aligned sentences.

3.2 Word Embedding Layer

For the relational extraction task, the input is a sentence, which can also be called word sequence. The word embedding layer converts every word in the sentence from one-hot encoding to low-dimensional dense word vector. For an input sentence (word sequence) $S = [c_1, c_2, \ldots, c_l]$, where c_i represents the one-hot vector of the i-th word and l represents the length of the sentence.

For the input data, this paper uses the word vector pretrained by Word2Vec as the low dimensional vector to be converted for each word. Think of each one-hot vector as a search index, and find the corresponding Word2Vec vector from the pretrained word vector matrix. Then, each word c_i is mapped to the corresponding word vector wv_i. Finally, a sentence in the form of word vectors is represented by $S = [wv_1, wv_2, \ldots, wv_l]$.

3.3 Position Embedding Layer

In the context of relational extraction, the most important information in a sentence is two entities, so this paper also adds each word into the word vector to the relative position information of the two entities in the sentence, which also provides the sentence structure information. In the data preprocessing, entities in the data in this paper have been marked. After word segmentation, this paper traverses each sentence and enforces each word with a three-dimensional vector $[d_1, d_2]$, where d_1 and d_2 represent the relative distance of the head entity and the tail entity of the word respectively.

In the network, this paper dynamically maintains two relative distance embedding matrices. Just like word embedding, this paper uses the position embedding matrix to map the two relative position information corresponding to each word to two low-dimensional dense vectors. This step is called position embedding (Position Embedding, PE), two phases and one position the information obtained three or two position embedding vectors PE_1 and PE_2 respectively. s is the same as loading the pretrained word vector matrix. In this paper, the relative position embedding matrix is randomly initialized, and these two positions embedding matrices are dynamically updated during training. A word c_i undergoes word embedding and position embedding, and finally the final representation of the word $w_i = [wv_i; PE_{i1}; PE_{i2}; PE_{i3}]$ is obtained, and its dimension is d_w.

3.4 Sentence Coding Layer

In this paper, the classical PCNNs neural network is used to encode sentence features. For an input sentence (word vector sequence) $S = \{w_1, w_2, \ldots, w_l\}$, a set of convolution kernels $\{f_1, f_2, \ldots, f_k\}$ with the same width of $width_f$ are used to conduct one-dimensional convolution operations on the sentence matrix respectively. The size of each convolution kernel f_i is $d_{f_i} \in R^{width_f * d_w}$. Through padding, the feature map $F = \{q_1, q_2, \ldots, q_k\}$ with the same length of sentence is obtained. Each q_i is a one-dimensional vector of length l, which is obtained by convolution of the sentence by the convolution kernel f_i. The size of F is $k \times l$. For each convolution result q_i, the feature vector of sentence structure information is obtained by maximizing the pool before, between and after entity pairs. After segmented maximum pooling, each q_i becomes a three-dimensional vector sentence feature. Finally, the feature vector of the sentence $sen(d_{sen} \in R^{3*k})$ can be obtained by connecting each q_i.

3.5 Bag of Sentences Coding

The traditional selective attention mechanism aligns the sentences with the marking relation vector, and obtains the similarity score of each sentence relative to the marking relation vector r_i. After softmax normalization, the weight of each sentence in the bag of sentences is obtained. Then all sentences in each bag of sentences are weighted and summed to get the final bag of sentences representation vector. Such a selective attention mechanism believes too much that the mark of a bag of sentences must be aligned with at least one sentence, and directly considers the probability distribution of all sentences in the case of marking, and does not consider that each sentence should be marked as other relations. Observation of the distant supervised dataset shows that there are many bags of sentences in which no sentence is labeled correctly, so it makes no sense for all sentences to be similarly aligned with the bag of sentences marker vector. In this paper, all sentences in each bag of sentence are aligned with all relational vectors, and then the weight distribution of sentences in the bag of sentence under all marked conditions is obtained. Finally, the weighted summation is performed to obtain the bag of sentences vector representation of all relations aligned. In this case, according to the different vector representations of the bag of sentences, through the full connection layer mapping to the probability distribution of bag of sentences on all relations. The specific calculation details are as follows:

A bag of sentences contains j sentence feature vector sen. For a sentence sen_m, align it with all relation vectors r_n, $n = 1 \sim n_{relation}$ and calculate the alignment score:

$$bag = \{sen_1, sen_2, \ldots, sen_j\} \tag{1}$$

$$\text{Score}_{mn} = \text{align}(\text{sen}_m, r_n) \tag{2}$$

$$\text{align}(a, b) = a^T b \tag{3}$$

Get the score of a sentence sen_m for all relations and the alignment score of all sentences and all relations in a bag of sentences

$$\text{score}_m = \{\text{score}_{m1}, \text{score}_{m2}, \ldots \text{score}_{mn_{\text{relation}}}\} \tag{4}$$

$$\text{score} = [\text{score}_1, \text{score}_2, \ldots, \text{score}_j]^T \tag{5}$$

For each column of score, use softmax for normalization to obtain the weight distribution D_p in the bag of sentences aligned with relation n.

$$D_p = \text{softmax}([\text{score}_{1p}, \text{score}_{2p}, \ldots, \text{score}_{jp}]) \tag{6}$$

Using this weight distribution, the feature representation of the bag of sentences aligned with relation n in the bag of sentences is obtained, and finally the feature representation of the bag of sentences corresponding to all relations of the bag of sentences is obtained.

$$\text{bag}_n = D_p^T \text{bag} \tag{7}$$

$$\text{bag} = \{\text{bag}_1, \text{bag}_1, \ldots, \text{bag}_{\text{relation}}\} \tag{8}$$

For the bag of sentences representation corresponding to each relationship in the bag of sentences, this paper calculates the similarity score o corresponding to each bag of sentences representation:

$$o_t = r_t^T \text{bag}_t + b_t \tag{9}$$

After the softmax layer, this paper obtains a probability distribution representation of a bag of sentences:

$$P(t|\text{bag}) = \frac{\exp(o_t)}{\sum_{t'=1}^{n_{\text{relation}}} \exp(o_{t'})} \tag{10}$$

It should be noted that this paper uses the same relationship vector to calculate the similarity between sentences and bag of sentences. The similarity is calculated in the way of dot product. The larger the dot product of bag of sentences feature vector and relation vector, it shows that after aligning each sentence in the bag of sentences with all relations, not only the error of false marking is considered at the bag of sentences level, but also the possible relations of more sentences are considered. In terms of network structure, all relations are introduced into forward propagation and back propagation of a bag of sentences in forward propagation. The soft attention mechanism of single relation alignment of Lin and Ji only considers the alignment of one relation vector in each bag of sentences vector, so only one relation vector is introduced into forward propagation. Therefore, when learning through back propagation, only the parameters of this corresponding relation vector will be updated. However, the introduction of all relationship vectors for alignment will make the network update not only the real relationship vector but also the wrong relationship vector during the back propagation. Therefore, the attention mechanism of multi-relation alignment will be more efficient in model training. Updating all relation vectors each time will also enable this paper to get a more accurate representation of relation vectors. For other NLP tasks, it also has a certain enlightening effect.

3.6 Objective Function and Optimization

The relationship extraction model of the multi-relational alignment attention mechanism in this paper still uses the cross-entropy function as the loss function of the network to measure the difference between the network output and the actual situation:

$$J(\theta) = - \sum_{(g,k)\in T} \log P(k|g; \theta) \tag{11}$$

T represents all training data, and θ represents all parameters of the neural network model: word vector, position vector, weight and bias of all convolution kernels in piece-wise maximum pooling convolutional neural network, and relational vector matrix. This paper uses the SGD method to update the network parameters.

4 Experiments

This paper will compare the proposed PCNN_RA_ATT model with the baseline model PCNN_ATT, PCNN_MLSSA model on the standard data set, and verify the effectiveness of the innovation points through a series of commonly used indicators. A comparative experiment was conducted on the NYT-10 remote supervision data set to verify the effectiveness of the improvement in sentence selection at the bag-level sentence.

4.1 Datasets

The experiment uses the distant supervision standard data set NYT-10 published by Del et al. [3]. This data set aligns the triples in the Freebase knowledge base with the corpus of the New York Times through a remote monitoring strategy. Using web crawler technology, crawled all the articles on the New York Times website from November 2009 to January 2010, extracted all sentences from them, and marked them with the Stanford NER (Named Entity Recognition) tool All entities that exist in freebase. There are a total of 52 relationships in NYT-10 data set plus one NA relationship. The training set contains 522,611 sentences, 281,270 pairs of entities, and 18252 triples. The testing set, consisting of 172,448 sentences, 96,678 entity pairs, and 1950 triples, has now become the standard evaluation data set for a large number of distant supervised relationship extraction methods.

4.2 Hyperparameter Settings

This paper uses CBOW to train a 50-dimensional word2vec word vector on NYT-10 corpus. In addition, the dimension of the position embedding is set to 20, and the dimension of the hidden state vector is set to 230. In this paper, SGD learner is used to update network parameters, the learning rate is 0.1, and the batch size is 60.

4.3 Experimental Results

The RA_ATT algorithm proposed in this paper is compared with the sentence-bag-based attention mechanism proposed by Lin and multidimensional sentence-bag-based attention mechanism proposed by Du on nyT-10, a distant supervised standard dataset. In order to be fair, this paper uses PCNNs as the sentence feature extractor, and compares the MLSSA2 model combining the bag-level attention mechanism, PCNN_ATT, and the multi-PCNN and multidimensional bag-level attention mechanism. The P-R curves of the three models are shown in Fig. 2. The P@N and AUC indicators of each model are listed in Table 1.

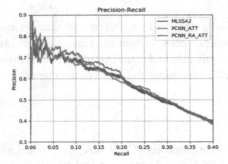

Fig. 2. Effect of relational extraction model based on relational alignment attention mechanism

As can be seen from Fig. 2 and Table 2, the accuracy of relation extraction model PCNN + RA_ATT based on relation alignment attention mechanism is significantly higher than that of PCNN_ATT and MLSSA2 when Recall is less than 0.2. Since then, the accuracy is similar, but always higher than the other two models. In addition, the overall AUC index is also better, indicating that the capture of features in bag of sentences is more accurate after the introduction of multi-relation alignment mechanism. However, due to the problem of remote supervision of mislabeling, the attentional mechanism at the level of multi-relation alignment is still limited when Recall is large.

Table 1. Comparison of the accuracy rate of P@N and the area under the P-R curve AUC at different.

Method	P@100	P@200	P@300
PCNN + RA_ATT	0.7510	0.7343	0.7070
PCNN + ATT	0.7326	0.7164	0.6877
MLSSA2	0.7033	0.6808	0.6602

Table 2. Extraction accuracy rate on each relationship.

Algorithm	Relationship	Accuracy
PCNN + RA_ATT	/location/location/contains	0.5278
	/people/person/nationality	0.4986
	/people/person/place_lived	0.2116
	/business/person/company	0.3991
	/location/administrative_division/country	0.3317
PCNN + ATT	/location/location/contains	0.4669
	/people/person/nationality	0.4604
	/people/person/place_lived	0.1734
	/business/person/company	0.3611
	/location/administrative_division/country	0.3089
MLSSA2	/location/location/contains	0.4699
	/people/person/nationality	0.4514
	/people/person/place_lived	0.1684
	/business/person/company	0.3517
	/location/administrative_division/country	0.3005

5   Conclusion

In order to solve the problems of noise data generated by mislabeling due to the over-broad assumption of noise labeling in remote supervision strategy, and the effect of single relation alignment on training efficiency, this paper designs an attentional mechanism for sentence and relation alignment in bag of sentences. Compared with the traditional method, this method can upgrade the optimization learning of a single relation vector in back propagation to the optimization learning of all relation vectors, which improves the learning efficiency of the network and is intuitively more consistent with cognition. A sentence feature that aligns with one relation should not refer to the expression of other relations. Compared with the baseline algorithm PCNN ATT and MLSSA on the standard data set, it can be seen that the proposed method better deals with and utilizes the distant supervised noise information to some extent and can achieve better relationship extraction effect.

Acknowledgement. The authors would like to thank the anonymous referees for their valuable comments and helpful suggestions. The work is supported by Science and Technology Project of the State Grid Information & Telecommunication Branch, "The research and technology for multi-Scenario Oriented security protection framework" (52993920002J).

References

1. Zeng, D., Liu, K., Chen, Y., Zhao, J.: Distant supervision for relation extraction via piecewise convolutional neural networks. In: Proceedings of the 2015 Conference on Empirical Methods in Natural Language Processing, pp. 1753–1762 (2015)
2. Mintz, M., Bills, S., Snow, R., Jurafsky, D.: Distant supervision for relation extraction without labeled data. In: Proceedings of the Joint Conference of the 47th Annual Meeting of the ACL and the 4th International Joint Conference on Natural Language Processing of the AFNLP, pp. 1003–1011 (2009)
3. Riedel, S., Yao, L., McCallum, A.: Modeling relations and their mentions without labeled text. In: Balcázar, J.L., Bonchi, F., Gionis, A., Sebag, M. (eds.) ECML PKDD 2010. LNCS (LNAI), vol. 6323, pp. 148–163. Springer, Heidelberg (2010). https://doi.org/10.1007/978-3-642-15939-8_10
4. Bahdanau, D., Cho, K., Bengio, Y.: Neural machine translation by jointly learning to align and translate. arXiv preprint arXiv:1409.0473 (2014)
5. Lin, Y., Shen, S., Liu, Z.: Neural relation extraction with selective attention over instances. In: Proceedings of the 54th Annual Meeting of the Association for Computational Linguistics, vol. 1, pp. 2124–2133 (2016)
6. Ji, G., Liu, K., He, S., Zhao, J.: Distant supervision for relation extraction with sentence-level attention and entity descriptions. In: Proceedings of the AAAI Conference on Artificial Intelligence, vol. 31, no. 1, pp. 3060–3066 (2017)
7. Mikolov, T., Sutskever, I., Chen, K., Corrado, G.S., Dean, J.: Distributed representations of words and phrases and their compositionality. In: Advances in neural information processing systems, pp. 3111–3119 (2013)
8. Vaswani, A., Shazeer, N., Parmar, N.: Attention is all you. In: Advances in neural information processing systems, pp. 5998–6008 (2017)
9. Du, J., Han, J., Way, A., Wan, D.: Multi-level structured self-attentions for distantly supervised relation extraction. arXiv preprint arXiv:1809.00699 (2018)
10. Yue, Q., Li, X., Li, D.: Chinese relation extraction on forestry knowledge graph construction. Compu. Syst. Sci. Eng. **37**(3), 423–442 (2021)
11. Ding, K., Liu, S., Zhang, Y., Zhang, H., Zhang, X.: A knowledge-enriched and span-based network for joint entity and relation extraction. Comput. Mater. Continu. **68**(1), 377–389 (2021)
12. Sun, J., Li, Y., Shen, Y., Ding, W., Shi, X.: Joint self-attention based neural networks for semantic relation extraction. J. Inform. Hiding Privacy Protect. **1**(2), 69–75 (2019)
13. Zhao, S., Hu, M., Cai, Z., Z, Liu, F.: Dynamic modeling cross-modal interactions in two-phaseprediction for entity-relation extraction. IEEE Trans. Neural Netw. Learn. Syst. (2021) https://doi.org/10.1109/TNNLS.2021.3104971

Dual Attention Mechanisms Based Auto-Encoder for Video Anomaly Detection

Jiatao Gu, Jing Zeng, and Genlin Ji[✉]

School of Computer and Electronic Information, Nanjing Normal University, Nanjing, China
glji@njnu.edu.cn

Abstract. Video anomaly detection refers to the identification of abnormal behaviors that do not conform to normal patterns. Reconstruction of video frames based on auto-encoder is the current mainstream video anomaly detection method. If frames have higher reconstruction error than the threshold, these frames will be treated as the anomalous frames. However, auto-encoders lack attention to global information and channel dependence. The attention mechanism enables the neural network to accurately focus on input-related elements and becomes an important part of the neural network. In order to focus the feature of both channel and spatial dimensions, we propose dual attention mechanisms based auto-encoder (DAMAE) for video anomaly detection. After each down-sampling, the feature map is operated by two kinds of attention processing. The feature map is divided into specific groups. Every individual group can autonomously enhance its learnt expression and suppress possible noise. By fusing channel attention and spatial attention, DAMAE is able to capture the pixel-level pairwise relationship and channel dependence. Compared with traditional auto-encoder in the process of each up-sampling, the feature with channel attention and spatial attention can reconstruct the normal pattern of the video better. Experimental results show that our method is superior to other advanced methods, which proves the effectiveness of our method.

Keywords: Video anomaly detection · Auto-encoder · Attention mechanisms

1 Introduction

Video anomaly detection refers to the identification of abnormal events in a video that do not conform to the expected appearance or behavior. Anomaly detection of video data has become a hot topic of computer vision and has been widely concerned by scholars. However, the definition of "anomaly" in video anomaly detection is vague, there is no obvious boundary between normal events and abnormal events, and the same event will have different anomaly attributes in different environmental scenarios. This is not feasible to collect all the anomaly data and video anomaly detection becomes a very challenging task. A typical method to solve the problem of video anomaly detection is to build a model using normal data. Test data is considered abnormal when it deviates significantly from the model.

© The Author(s), under exclusive license to Springer Nature Switzerland AG 2022
X. Sun et al. (Eds.): ICAIS 2022, LNCS 13338, pp. 153–165, 2022.
https://doi.org/10.1007/978-3-031-06794-5_13

Methods of video anomaly detection can be roughly divided into two categories: methods of learning spatiotemporal activity patterns based on hand-craft features and methods [1, 2] based on deep learning. Early researchers learned patterns of spatiotemporal activity based on hand-craft features, such as color, texture, and light flow [3]. Refactoring events by learning dictionaries, normal events have a small refactoring error and exception events have the opposite. However, the internal changes of most hand-craft features are subject to certain external influences, such as lighting and deformation. These hand-craft features cannot be well summarized in complex surveillance video scenes. In addition, some researchers use trajectory features to represent normal patterns [4, 5]. Tacks with similar spatial and velocity patterns are grouped to create semantic scene patterns to detect abnormal events [6] because it can describe the dynamic information of foreground objects. Moreover, a variable-sized cell structure is constructed by researchers [7]. However, these methods are not reliable in complex and crowded scenarios. In recent years, deep learning has been widely used in image classification [8, 9], object detection [10, 11] and anomaly detection [12]. Video anomaly detection based on deep learning can be divided into reconstruction and prediction. Reconstruction is to reconstruct the current frame by modeling the normal mode using encoder-decoder structure and large reconstruction errors are regarded as abnormal frames. For example, Hasan et al. [12] proposed a two-dimensional convolution auto-encoder to build normal frames by superposing frames in the channel. Prediction is to predict the next frame of the input video, and predict the future frame by using the historical frame to model the normal mode. Liu et al. [13] used a generation model to predict future frames and used reconstruction errors as an indicator of anomalies. However, the convolution operation of traditional auto-encoder tends to miss the global information and channel information in the frame through the convolution kernel. It is difficult for traditional auto-encoders to extract channel dependence features and spatial relational features. The performance of auto-encoder decreases in the testing phase because the normal video frame cannot be reconstructed well in the training phase.

We proposed dual attention mechanisms based auto-encoder for video anomaly detection. In the process of sampling under each layer, the sub-feature is conducted with dual attention mechanisms. In the process of reconstructing video frames, we fuse sub-features with channel dependency and spatial relations. Thus, the auto-encoder is able to accurately capture relevant elements of the sub-feature and reconstructs normal frames of video better. The main contributions of this paper can be summarized as follows:

(1) We proposed dual attention mechanisms based auto-encoder for video anomaly detection. Through fusing channel attention and spatial attention, the model is able to capture the pixel-level pairwise relationship and channel dependency.
(2) The feature maps are divided into specific groups. Every individual group can autonomously enhance its learnt expression and suppress possible noise. Robust features can be extracted from feature maps.
(3) Compared with traditional auto-encoder, the AUC has been improved in benchmark datasets. The experimental results demonstrate the effectiveness and efficiency of our method.

2 Related Work

In this section, we review the current video anomaly detection methods in deep learning and the mechanism of attention in computer vision.

2.1 Deep Learning Based Anomaly Detection

Video anomaly detection based on deep learning is the most common method in recent years. Hasan et al. [12] proposed two-dimensional convolution auto-encoder to learn the rule of time information, but two-dimensional convolution lacks motion information and cannot reflect motion characteristics. Luo et al. [14] proposed to combine convolutional neural network with LSTM to learn the appearance and motion information of normal frames. Subsequently, Liu et al. [13] proposed a video prediction framework, using the past frame to predict the future frame. Because neural network has strong generalization ability, abnormal frame can be predicted as normal frame. Sultani et al. [15] proposed to take video clips as examples of multi-example learning (MIL) for video anomaly detection. The training set requires equal normal data and abnormal data, and the method is not feasible because the abnormal data is very sparse.

2.2 Attention Mechanisms

The attention mechanism aims to ignoring irrelevant information and focus on important information. Attention mechanisms are widely used in computer vision, such as target tracking [16], classification [17], segmentation [18], identification [19] and recognition [20]. More and more attention has been paid to the introduction of attention mechanism in video anomaly detection. Fan et al. [21] proposed a saliency shift perceptual convolution LSTM, which can effectively capture video saliency dynamics by learning human attention-shifting behaviors. Nasaruddin et al. [22] used three-dimensional convolutional neural networks to find attention regions from spatiotemporal information to learn abnormal behaviors. Wang et al. [23] proposed a GAN recognition model with attention mechanism to improve the generation quality of future frames. Zhang et al. [24] designed generative adversarial networks by combining super-resolution and self-attention mechanisms. Self-attention is introduced on the basis of discriminator to enhance the difference between normal events and abnormal events. However, self-attention only focuses on the relevance in the spatial dimension of image and ignores the relevance in the channel dimension of image.

There are mainly two types of attention mechanisms most commonly used in computer vision [25]: channel attention [26] and spatial attention both of which strengthen the original features by aggregating the same feature from all the positions with different aggregation strategies. Based on these observations, some studies, including GCNet [27] and CBAM [28] integrated both spatial attention and channel attention into one module and achieving significant improvement. ECA-Net [29] simplifies the process of computing channel weights in SE block by using a 1-D convolution. SA-Net [30] fuses different attention modules in a lighter and more efficient way.

3 Method

The process of video anomaly detection can be divided into two steps: training phase and testing phase. The main idea of our proposed method is that: in the training phase, the model is only trained with normal video frames. We use DAMAE model to learn normal pattern of these video frames. In the testing phase, when abnormal frames are inputted, DAMAE is expected to put low regular scores on them. If a score is lower than the threshold, we judge the video frame is abnormal.

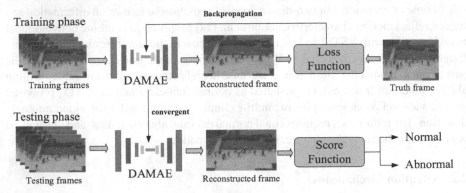

Fig. 1. The process of method.

Algorithm 1 DAMAE-VAD

Input: Training video frames FS, testing video frames TS, the number of training epoches N

Output: the trained model's parameters set θ

1 **If** frame in FS do:

2   frame = Transform(frame)   // normalized RGB values from [0, 255] to [-1, 1]

3 **For** i = 0 to N do: // train the model N epochs

4   Take five successive frames from $I_t, I_{t+1}, I_{t+2}, I_{t+3}, I_{t+4}$ in F

5     $\hat{I}_{t+4}$ = $DAMAE_i(I_t, I_{t+1}, I_{t+2}, I_{t+3})$ // generate $\hat{I}_{t+4}$

6   reconstruct_loss = $F_{loss}(I_{t+4}, \hat{I}_{t+4})$ // calculated reconstruction loss

7     $DAMAE_{i+1}$= BP($DAMAE_i$, reconstruct_loss) //update model

8   **if** $DAMAE_{i+1}$ is convergent: // end the training if the model converges

9         $DAMAE_{trained}$ = $DAMAE_{i+1}$

10   θ = parameter($DAMAE_{trained}$)   // obtain model parameters set

11   **else** i=i+1

12 **For** each frame I_{test} in TS do:

13   Score = S($I_{test}, DAMAE_{trained}(I_{test})$)   // calculate the normal score

14   **if** Score < threshold:

15   the frame I_{test} is abnormal

16   **else** the frame I_{test} is normal

17 **return** θ

DAMAE-VAD based on dual attention mechanisms auto-encoder is proposed. An overview of our method is illustrated in Fig. 1.

For the purpose of enhancing learnt expression and suppressing possible noise, channels are divided into specific groups to realize channel attention and spatial attention mechanisms, respectively. After that, we aggregate all sub-futures. A channel shuffle operation is used to enable information communication between different sub-futures during aggregating. In this way, we can capture the pixel-level pairwise relationship and channel dependency. We propose a video anomaly detection algorithm DAMAE-VAD based on dual attention mechanism auto-encoder, as shown in Algorithm 1.

3.1 Dual Attention Mechanisms Based Auto-Encoder

DAMAE contains three main parts, encoder, decoder and dual attention mechanisms unit. The functions of these three components are as follows: 1) The encoder extracts features by gradually reducing the spatial resolution. 2) The decoder is used to reconstructs the frame by increasing the spatial resolution. 3) Attention mechanisms unit is employed to strengthen the capture of spatial relationship and channel dependency.

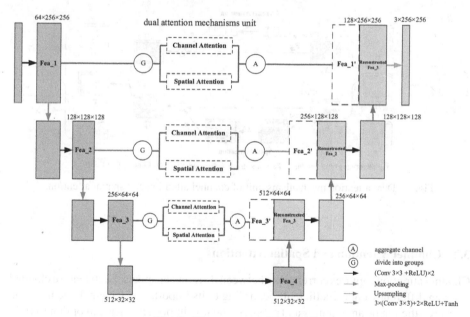

Fig. 2. The structure of DAMAE

Traditional auto-encoder confronts with the gradient vanishing problem and information imbalance in each layer. To avoid this issue, U-Net is proposed by adding a shortcut between a high level layer and a low level layer with the same resolution. Different from U-Net, each layer of the encoder and decoder in DAMAE is added a skip connection which is conducted with spatial and channel attention. Thus, DAMAE can extract channel correlation and spatial correlation from sub-features. We divide the channel into specific groups. Within each group the channels are divided into two sections. Channel attention operation is conducted in one section and spatial attention operation is conducted in the other. In the end, all the channels are aggregated with shuffle operation to fuse cross-group information along channel dimensions. The structure of DAMAE is shown in Fig. 2.

A layer of encoder extracts a feature map $X \in \mathbb{R}^{C \times H \times W}$, where C, H, W represents the channel number, spatial height and width. In our dual attention mechanisms unit, we split X into G groups following channel dimension, $X = [X_1, \ldots X_G], X_k \in \mathbb{R}^{C/G \times H \times W}$. The group feature captures a specific semantic response in the training process. The group feature is split into two branches along the channels dimension, i.e. $X_{k_1}, X_{k_2} \in \mathbb{R}^{C/2G \times H \times W}$.

We generate the corresponding importance coefficient for each sub-feature through an attention unit. Then one branch X_{k_1} is used to perform channel attention operation in order to exploiting the inter-relationship of channels. The other branch X_{k_2} is used to perform spatial attention in order to exploiting the inter-relationship of features. The dual attention mechanisms unit is showed in Fig. 3.

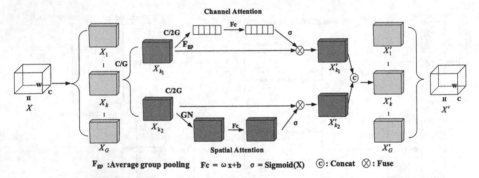

Fig. 3. Dual attention mechanisms unit of channel attention and spatial attention.

3.2 Channel Attention and Spatial Attention

Channel attention captures correlations between different channels. Each feature channel is given different weight coefficients according to its importance. Channel attention can reinforce the important features and suppress the less important ones. An option to fully capture channel-wise dependencies is utilizing the SE block proposed in [31]. However, to get a lightweight and suppress possible noise, we firstly embed the global information by simply using global averaging pooling (GAP) to generate channel-wise statistics as $s \in \mathbb{R}^{C/2G \times 1 \times 1}$.

$$S = \mathcal{F}_{gp}(X_{k_1}) = \frac{1}{H \times W} \sum_{i=1}^{H} \sum_{j=1}^{W} X_{k_1}(i,j) \tag{1}$$

Then, corresponding importance coefficient is created to be learnable. We employ a simple gating mechanism with sigmoid activation to obtain the output of channel attention.

$$X'_{k_1} = \sigma(\mathcal{F}_c(s)) \cdot X_{k_1} = \sigma(W_1 s + b_1) \cdot X_{k_1} \tag{2}$$

The shape of W_1, W_2, b_1, b_2 are $\mathbb{R}^{C/2G \times 1 \times 1}$. Spatial attention captures spatial dependencies between any two positions in a feature map. The spatial information in the original picture is transformed into another space through the spatial conversion module. Weights are generated for each position to enhance specific target areas of interest while weakening irrelevant background areas. We use Group Norm (GN) over X_{k_2} to obtain spatial-wise statistics. The final output of spatial attention is obtained by

$$X'_{k_2} = \sigma(W_2 \cdot GN(X_{k_2}) + b_2) \cdot X_{k_2} \tag{3}$$

After that, all the sub-features are aggregated. Finally, similar to ShuffleNetv2 [31], we adopt a "channel shuffle" operator to enable cross-group information flow along the channel dimension. The final output of our model is the same size of X, making model easy to be integrated with modern architectures.

3.3 Anomaly Detection

Let I denotes the actual frame, $\hat{I}$ denotes the reconstructed frame. To train our model, we use intensity loss $\mathcal{L}_{int}$ and structural similarity loss $\mathcal{L}_{ssim}$ balanced by λ_t and λ_s as follows:

$$\mathcal{L} = \lambda_t \mathcal{L}_{int} + \lambda_s \mathcal{L}_{ssim} \tag{4}$$

Given the loss function, our model can be able to reconstruct the frame $\hat{I}$ as similar as the actual frame I. We use smooth l_1 loss which is shown in Eq. (5) to compare pixel-wise intensity loss $\mathcal{L}_{int}$.

$$\mathcal{L}_{int} = f_{L_1}(\hat{I} - I) \tag{5}$$

$$f_{L_1}(x) = \begin{cases} \frac{1}{2}x^2, & |x| < 1 \\ |x| - \frac{1}{2}, & otherwise \end{cases} \tag{6}$$

The value of x is the difference between predicted and ground truth values.

SSIM is structural similarity between the two frames. $\mathcal{L}_{ssim}$ is calculated by the brightness, contrast and structure of the reconstructed frame as follows:

$$\mathcal{L}_{ssim}(I, \hat{I}) = \frac{(2\mu_I \mu_{\hat{I}} + C_1)(\sigma_{I,\hat{I}} + C_2)}{(\mu_I^2 + \mu_{\hat{I}}^2 + C_1)(\sigma_I^2 + \sigma_{\hat{I}}^2 + C_2)} \tag{7}$$

Among SSIM function, μ_I is the mean value of the actual frame I, $\mu_{\hat{I}}$ is the mean value of the reconstructed frame $\hat{I}$, $\sigma_{I,\hat{I}}$ is the covariance between the actual frame I and the reconstructed frame $\hat{I}$, σ_I^2 is the variance of the actual frame I, $\sigma_{\hat{I}}^2$ is the variance of the reconstructed frame $\hat{I}$, C_1, C_2 are two constants which are used to avoid the occurrence of zero denominator.

The regular score of reconstruction is used to determine the anomaly, as shown in Eq. (8)

$$Score(t) = \frac{S(t) - S_{min}(t)}{S_{max}(t)} \tag{8}$$

A lot of related works have shown that PSNR can increase the gap between normal and abnormal events compared with MSE under the same circumstances. We use PSNR to evaluate the quality of reconstructed frames and PSNR score is defined as:

$$S(t) = PSNR = 10log_{10}\frac{I_{max}^2}{MSE} \tag{9}$$

Obviously, the higher value of the regularity score signifies the lower level of the anomaly. If the regular score of the reconstructed frame at time t is lower than the threshold, the abnormal event is believed to occur at that time.

4 Experiment

4.1 Experiment Settings

Datasets. Our proposed method is evaluated on two main benchmark datasets, including UCSD Ped2, CUHK Avenue. 1) The UCSD Pedestrian 2 (Ped2) dataset contains 16 training videos and 12 testing videos with 12 abnormal events. The event is normal in training frames. All of abnormal cases are in testing frames about vehicles such as bicycles and cars. The frame resolution is 360×640 pixels. 2) CUHK Avenue dataset contains 16 training videos and 21 testing ones with a total of 47 abnormal events, including throwing objects, loitering and running.

Evaluation Metrics. We evaluate our methods using the area under the ROC curve (AUC). The ROC curve is obtained by varying the threshold for the anomaly score. A higher AUC value represents better anomaly detection performance.

Implementation Details. In our experiments, all video frames are resized to 256×256 and pixel values are normalized to $[-1,1]$. In the training phase, the Adam is adopted as optimizer and learning rate is set as 0.0002. The λ_t and λ_s are set as 0.84 and 0.16. The number of batch size is 4. Training epochs are set as 400 on Ped2 and avenue by default. We implemented DAMAE in pytorch and experiments are conducted with four Nvidia 3080 GPUs.

4.2 Experimental Results

We compare our model with other models for anomaly detection on UCSD Ped2 and CUHK Avenue in Table 1.

Table 1. Comparison of AUC and EER performance with other models.

Method	UCSD Ped2		CUHK Avenue	
	AUC(%)	EER(%)	AUC(%)	EER(%)
MPPCA29 [32]	69.3	30.0	–	–
SF30 [33]	55.6	42.0	–	–
SF + MPPCA [34]	61.3	36.0	–	–
ConvAE [12]	90.0	21.7	70.2	25.1
STAE32 [35]	91.2	16.7	80.9	24.4
GMMAE [36]	92.2	12.6	83.4	22.7
MemAE [37]	94.1	–	83.3	–
TSC [38]	92.2	–	83	–
Ours	94.9	12.6	84.9	21.7

Four consecutive video frames are inputted in our model. The model outputs fifth reconstructed frame. As shown in Fig. 4, we calculate the loss between the reconstructed frame and the real frame to draw the normal score graph of UCSD ped2 datasets. The position of normal and abnormal frames can be seen directly. In Fig. 4, the number of video frame is represented by the abscissa and the corresponding law score of each frame represented by the ordinate.

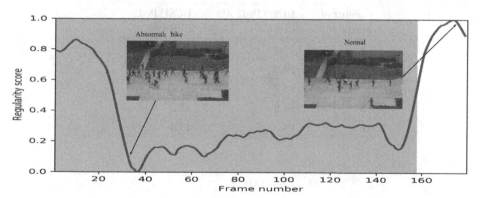

Fig. 4. Regularity score of each frame in one video sequence.

The graph illustrates that the smaller the score, the higher the probability of abnormal frame. Also, the red area in that graph represents the real label (Ground-truth) when the exception occurs in the dataset.

4.3 Ablation Experiment

In order to analyze the performance of the anomaly detection after channels were divided into groups, we compare DAMAE with the model which is without channel groups. For purpose of analyzing the performance of channel attention, we compare the DAMAE with the model which is without channel attention. Through comparing the area under the ROC curve of three (see Fig. 5), it can be seen that DAMAE has a better performance.

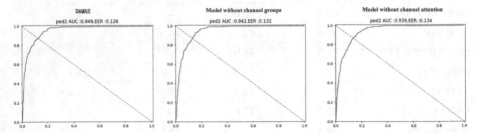

Fig. 5. DAMAE compares with two models without channel groups and channel attention.

We evaluate the effect of the number of groups on the model. The Table 2 shows that the number of groups has different effects on the performance of the model. When the number of groups equals two, the model has the best performance on UCSD Ped2. Meanwhile, the number of groups can't be set too large. When the number of groups equals sixteen, the performance of the model deteriorates dramatically.

Table 2. AUC and EER performance with different number of groups.

Number of groups	UCSD Ped2 AUC(%)	UCSD Ped2 EER (%)
1	94.4	13.2
2	**94.9**	**12.6**
4	94.7	13.1
8	94.8	12.2
16	94.3	13.4

5   Conclusion

In this paper, we propose dual attention mechanisms based auto-encoder to detect the anomaly events in videos. Channel is divided into specific groups. For the purpose of capturing the pixel-level pairwise relationship and channel dependency, channel attention and spatial attention are performed respectively in each group. In this way, our model enhances its learnt expression and suppresses possible noise. Intensity loss and structural similarity loss are employed to enable the model to reconstruct high-quality normal frames. If frames get a lower regularity score than threshold, these frames are treated as the anomalous frames. Extensive experimental on two benchmark datasets demonstrate our proposed method performs well. However, the fusion of channel attention and spatial attention is naive and needs to be improved in DAMAE. It is still a challenge to train a scene-adaptive attention model to resolve video anomaly detection.

Funding Statement. This work was supported by the National Science Foundation of China under Grant No. 41971343.

References

1. Cong, Y., Yuan, J., Liu, J.: Sparse reconstruction cost for abnormal event detection. In: The 24th IEEE Conference on Computer Vision and Pattern Recognition, CVPR 2011, Colordo Springs, CO, USA, 20–25 June 2011, pp. 3449–3456. IEEE Computer Society (2011)
2. Lu, C., Shi, J., Jia, J.: Abnormal event detection at 150 FPS in MATLAB. In: ICCV, pp. 2720–2727. IEEE Computer Society (2013)
3. Zhao, B., Fei-Fei, L., Xing, E.P.: Online detection of unusual events in videos via dynamic sparse coding. In: CVPR, pp. 3313–3320. IEEE Computer Society (2011)
4. Tung, F., Zelek, J.S., Clausi, D.A.: Goal-based trajectory analysis for unusual behaviour detection in intelligent surveillance. Image Vis. Comput. **29**(4), 230–240 (2011)
5. Shi, Y., Tian, Y., Wang, Y., Huang, T.: Sequential deep trajectory descriptor for action recognition with three-stream CNN. IEEE Trans. Multim. **19**(7), 1510–1520 (2017)
6. Wang, X., Tieu, K., Grimson, E.: Learning semantic scene models by trajectory analysis. In: Leonardis, A., Bischof, H., Pinz, A. (eds.) ECCV 2006. LNCS, vol. 3953, pp. 110–123. Springer, Heidelberg (2006). https://doi.org/10.1007/11744078_9
7. Xu, Z., Zeng, X., Ji, G., Sheng, B.: Improved anomaly detection in surveillance videos with multiple probabilistic models inference. Intell. Autom. Soft Comput. **31**(3), 1703–1717 (2022)
8. Chen, W., Xie, D., Zhang, Y., Pu, S.: All you need is a few shifts: Designing efficient convolutional neural networks for image classification. In: CVPR, pp. 7241–7250. Computer Vision Foundation/IEEE (2019)
9. Xue, Z.: Semi-supervised convolutional generative adversarial network for hyperspectral image classification. IET Image Process. **14**(4), 709–719 (2020)
10. Crawford, E., Pineau, J.: Spatially invariant unsupervised object detection with convolutional neural networks. In: AAAI, pp. 3412–3420. AAAI Press (2019)
11. Liu, Z., Shi, S., Duan, Q., Zhang, W., Zhao, P.: Salient object detection for RGB-D image by single stream recurrent convolution neural network. Neurocomputing **363**, 46–57 (2019)
12. Hasan, M., Choi, J., Neumann, J., Roy-Chowdhury, A.K., Davis, L.S.: Learning temporal regularity in video sequences. In: CVPR, pp. 733–742. IEEE Computer Society (2016)
13. Liu, W., Luo, W., Lian, D., Gao, S.: Future frame prediction for anomaly detection - A new baseline. In: CVPR, pp. 6536–6545. Computer Vision Foundation/IEEE Computer Society (2018)
14. Luo, W., Liu, W., Gao, S.: Remembering history with convolutional LSTM for anomaly detection. In: ICME, pp. 439–444. IEEE Computer Society (2017)
15. Sultani, W., Chen, C., Shah, M.: Real-world anomaly detection in surveillance videos. In: CVPR, pp. 6479–6488. Computer Vision Foundation /IEEE Computer Society (2018)
16. Xiang, X., Ren, W., Qiu, Y., Zhang, K., Lv, N.: Multi-object tracking method based on eficient channel attention and switchable atrous convolution. Neural Process. Lett. **53**(4), 2747–2763 (2021)
17. Li, P., Chen, P., Xie, Y., Zhang, D.: Bi modal learning with channel-wise attention for multi-label image classification. IEEE Access **8**, 9965–9977 (2020)

18. Hou, G., Qin, J., Xiang, X., Tan, Y., Xiong, N.N.: Af-net: A medical image segmentation network based on attention mechanism and feature fusion. Comput. Mater. Continua **69**(2), 1877–1891 (2021)
19. Li, Y., Wang, X.: Person re-identification based on joint loss and multiple attention. Intell. Autom. Soft Comput. **30**(2), 563–573 (2021)
20. Prabhu, K., SathishKumar, S., Sivachitra, M., Dineshkumar, S., Sathiyabama, P.: Facial expression recognition using enhanced convolution neural network with attention mechanism. Comput. Syst. Sci. Eng. **41**(1), 415–426 (2022)
21. Fan, D., Wang, W., Cheng, M., Shen, J.: Shifting more attention to video salient object detection. In: CVPR, pp. 8554–8564. Computer Vision Foundation/IEEE (2019)
22. Nasaruddin, N., Muchtar, K., Afdhal, A., Dwiyantoro, A.P.J.: Deep anomaly detection through visual attention in surveillance videos. J. Big Data **7**(1), 87 (2020)
23. Wang, C., Yao, Y., Yao, H.: Video anomaly detection method based on future frame prediction and attention mechanism. In: CCWC, pp. 405–407. IEEE (2021)
24. Zhang, W., Wang, G., Huang, M., Wang, H., Wen, S.: Generative adversarial networks for abnormal event detection in videos based on self-attention mechanism. IEEE Access **9**, 124847–124860 (2021)
25. Fu, J., Liu, J., Tian, H., Li, Y., Bao, Y., Fang, Z., Lu, H.: Dual attention network for scene segmentation. In: CVPR, pp. 3146–3154. Computer Vision Foundation/IEEE (2019)
26. Deng, L., Wang, X., Jiang, F., Doss, R.: Eeg-based emotion recognition via capsule nework with channel-wise attention and lstm models. CCF Trans. Pervasive Comput. Interact. **3**(4), 425–435 (2021)
27. Cao, Y., Xu, J., Lin, S., Wei, F., Hu, H.: Gcnet: Non-local networks meet squeeze-excitation networks and beyond. In: ICCV Workshops, pp. 1971–1980. IEEE (2019)
28. Ma, B., Wang, X., Zhang, H., Li, F., Dan, J.: CBAM-GAN: generative adversarial networks based on convolutional block attention module. In: Sun, X., Pan, Z., Bertino, E. (eds.) ICAIS 2019. LNCS, vol. 11632, pp. 227–236. Springer, Cham (2019). https://doi.org/10.1007/978-3-030-24274-9_20
29. Wang, Q., Wu, B., Zhu, P., Li, P., Zuo, W., Hu, Q.: Eca-net: Efficient channel attention for deep convolutional neural networks. In: CVPR, pp. 11531–11539. Computer Vision Foundation/IEEE (2020)
30. Zhang, Q., Yang, Y.: Sa-net: Shuffle attention for deep convolutional neural networks. In: ICASSP, pp. 2235–2239. IEEE (2021)
31. Ma, N., Zhang, X., Zheng, H.-T., Sun, J.: ShuffleNet V2: practical guidelines for efficient CNN architecture design. In: Ferrari, V., Hebert, M., Sminchisescu, C., Weiss, Y. (eds.) Computer Vision – ECCV 2018. LNCS, vol. 11218, pp. 122–138. Springer, Cham (2018). https://doi.org/10.1007/978-3-030-01264-9_8
32. Mahadevan, V., Li, W., Bhalodia, V., Vasconcelos, N.: Anomaly detection in crowded scenes. In: CVPR, pp. 1975–1981. IEEE Computer Society (2010)
33. Mehran, R., Oyama, A., Shah, M.: Abnormal crowd behavior detection using social force model. In: CVPR, pp. 935–942. IEEE Computer Society (2009)
34. Kim, J., Grauman, K.: Observe locally, infer globally: A space-time MRF for detecting abnormal activities with incremental updates. In: CVPR, pp. 2921–2928. IEEE Computer Society (2009)
35. Chong, Y.S., Tay, Y.H.: Abnormal event detection in videos using spatiotemporal autoencoder. In: Cong, F., Leung, A., Wei, Q. (eds.) ISNN 2017. LNCS, vol. 10262, pp. 189–196. Springer, Cham (2017). https://doi.org/10.1007/978-3-319-59081-3_23
36. Fan, Y., Wen, G., Li, D., Qiu, S., Levine, M.D., Xiao, F.: Video anomaly detection and localization via gaussian mixture fully convolutional variational autoencoder. Comput. Vis. Image Underst. **195**, 102920 (2020)

37. Gong, D., Liu, L., Le, V., Saha, B., Mansour, M.R., Venkatesh, S., van den Hengel, A.: Memorizing normality to detect anomaly: Memory-augmented deep autoencoder for unsupervised anomaly detection. In: ICCV, pp. 1705–1714. IEEE (2019)
38. Luo, W., et al.: Video anomaly detection with sparse coding inspired deep neural networks. IEEE Trans. Pattern Anal. Mach. Intell. **43**(3), 1070–1084 (2021)

Radar Fusion Monocular Depth Estimation Based on Dual Attention

JianYu Long, JinGui Huang[✉], and ShengChun Wang

Hunan Normal University, Changsha 410006, China
hjg@hunnu.edu.cn

Abstract. In this article, we explore the integration of multimodal data into monocular depth estimation. Monocular depth estimation is performed by fusing RGB data with sparse radar data. Since the existing fusion method does not take into account the correlation between the two types of data in the channel and in space, it lacks the representation of the global information relationship on the channel and in space. Therefore, we propose a feature fusion module (DAF) based on the dual attention mechanism. The dual attention fusion module improves the global information representation capability of the model by modeling the dynamic and non-linear relationship of the two kinds of data in the channel and space, adaptively recalibrates the response to each feature, and maximizes the use of radar data. At the same time, DAF can reduce noise interference in radar data by weighting features, avoiding the loss of secondary details caused by filtering operations, and alleviating the problem of excessive noise in radar data. Finally, due to the influence of the complex weather environment and the model itself, it is difficult for the model to obtain an effective feature representation in the complex weather environment. Therefore, we introduced a batch loss function to enable the model to focus on feature extraction in a complex environment, so as to obtain a more accurate representation of feature information. It reduces model errors and speeds up the convergence of the model. The experiment was conducted on the recently released nuScenes dataset, which provides data records of the entire sensor suite of autonomous vehicles. Experiments prove that our method is superior to other fusion methods.

Keywords: Monocular depth estimation · Radar · Attention · nuScenes

1 Introduction

Depth estimation is a fundamental problem in the field of computer vision, and it has a wide range of applications in the fields of robotics, augmented reality, three-dimensional reconstruction, real-time positioning and map construction, and autonomous driving. Before the advent of deep learning, traditional depth sensors were usually used to obtain depth, including physical equipment such as lidar, structured light-based sensors, and stereo cameras. However, changes in the environment will cause great errors in the depth results of the above-mentioned similar depth sensors. At the same time, due to the high

© The Author(s), under exclusive license to Springer Nature Switzerland AG 2022
X. Sun et al. (Eds.): ICAIS 2022, LNCS 13338, pp. 166–179, 2022.
https://doi.org/10.1007/978-3-031-06794-5_14

cost of the depth sensor, it cannot be applied to various fields on a large scale, which makes the development and research of this field very difficult.

In recent years, with the continuous development of deep learning, convolutional neural networks have been proven effective in image feature extraction. Therefore, convolutional neural networks have been widely used in various fields of computer vision. Researchers have begun a large number of attempts to use convolutional networks to deal with the problem of depth prediction, mainly in the field of monocular depth estimation, and have made more prominent progress. Monocular depth estimation predicts the depth by using an RGB picture or a picture from only one viewing angle, and estimates the distance of each pixel relative to the shooting source. It has lower cost, more flexible applications, and most of the image data in real life is single-view data. However, compared with binocular and multi-eye depth estimation, it lacks the limitation of depth information, so that the prediction results cannot meet the requirements of accuracy and reliability in real applications. Therefore, how to constrain the output of monocular depth in deep learning becomes a challenge.

To solve this problem, researchers first use task transformation to estimate depth, and predict depth by converting monocular depth estimation tasks into other visual tasks. For example, through view synthesis to predict a picture of another viewing angle, the monocular depth estimate is converted into a binocular depth, and the depth is obtained by calculating the disparity of the two views. Secondly, depth prediction is carried out through multi-task combination, and the depth prediction task is combined with other tasks. It uses the results of other tasks or its intermediate features to constrain the output of depth prediction and improve accuracy. For example, depth prediction and semantic segmentation are performed on an RGB picture at the same time. The result of depth prediction improves the accuracy of semantic segmentation, and the result of semantic segmentation supplements the edge information missing in depth prediction. The two cooperate and promote each other. In addition to task transformation and multi-task combination, researchers also use multi-modal data to limit the depth output. Some methods use sensors to obtain information about the current environment and use it as input information to predict depth. The most commonly used is lidar, which can provide more 3D information about the current environment, but it is very sensitive to weather conditions. And the cost is very expensive. In contrast, radars that have the advantages of low cost and better adaptability are more suitable for popularization in the real world. In fact, radar has already been widely used on various mechanical equipment, which provides a prerequisite for our work of fusing radar data for depth prediction.

This article aims to study how to fuse radar data in the task of depth estimation. We propose a dual attention fusion module to improve the model's global information representation ability, recalibrate the response to each feature, and fully extract the channel correlation and spatial correlation of the two types of data. The batch loss function is introduced to improve the feature extraction ability of the model in a complex weather environment, and obtain more accurate feature information representation, thereby improving the accuracy of the model and speeding up the convergence of the model. It further proves the effectiveness of integrating radar data into monocular depth estimation to ensure the accuracy and reliability of monocular depth estimation.

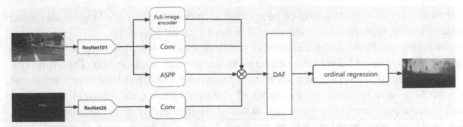

Fig. 1. Overall structure. The dual attention fusion module proposed by DAF for us will be introduced in detail in Sect. 3.

2   Related Work

In recent years, with the rapid development of neural networks, convolutional neural networks have been proven to have strong image comprehension capabilities and have been widely used in subsequent work. Eigen et al. [1] designed a multi-stage multi-scale prediction network based on CNN. The network is divided into two stages. The first stage uses a global view of the scene to predict the overall depth map structure, and the second stage, it edits the rough predictions produced in the first stage to align with local details. On the basis of this work, they expanded the network into a three-scale network to improve the resolution of the output, and it can be applied to three different computer vision problems: depth estimation, surface normal vector estimation, and semantic segmentation [2]. Laina et al. [3] proposed a fully connected residual network that uses small convolutions instead of large convolutions to achieve upsampling, solves the checkerboard effect, and uses reverse Huber as the loss function to achieve better results. Fu et al. [4] transformed the depth prediction into an ordinal regression problem by discretizing the depth, which accelerated the network convergence speed.

Considering the high cost of acquiring tags required for training, Zheng et al. [5] proposed T2Net, which includes an image translation network that can synthesize pictures for prediction, reducing the data requirements. Ji et al. [6] designed a depth estimation network based on a generative adversarial network, and generated more annotated images through a small number of annotated depth images. Godard et al. [7] pioneered the use of disparity to predict depth, predicting another view through one view, and finally converting the disparity between the two into a depth map. In the video depth estimation, Zhou et al. [8] predict the camera pose based on the changes in the front and back frames of the video, so as to obtain views from multiple perspectives, and obtain the parallax by stereo matching. Jiao et al. [9] combined attention-driven loss, focused the network's attention, and proposed a semantic segmentation and depth estimation collaborative unit to improve prediction accuracy. On this basis, in order to avoid bleeding artifacts, Zhu et al. [10] designed a three-dimensional mask. Srinivasan et al. [11] pioneered the use of the camera's aperture as supervision information, introduced two microaperture rendering functions, and used the input image and predicted depth to simulate the depth of field effect caused by the real camera aperture to train the depth estimation network.

In terms of multi-modal data, Mal et al. [12] first used Lidar data fusion, fusing the two along the channel. Ma et al. [13] proposed an early fusion method in shallow

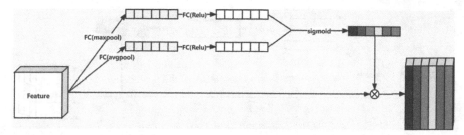

Fig. 2. Channel attention calculation module (CAM).

convolutional blocks. Jaritz et al. [14] adopted a late fusion method and combined the features of different modes to perform multi-task learning to improve overall performance. Lin et al. [15] first introduced radar data to dense depth prediction, which proved the effectiveness of radar data in depth prediction. On this basis, Lo et al. [16] took the radar data as input to improve the accuracy of the model, and used the ordinal regression network as the model to turn the depth prediction into an ordinal regression problem.

Attention mechanism is an important concept in deep learning. It was first applied to the field of machine translation by Bahdanau [17] and achieved good results. Since then, the attention mechanism has been widely used in fields such as natural language processing and computer vision. Xu et al. [18] proposed a structured attention model, which combined it with a conditional random field, weighted fusion of the multi-scale information of the convolutional network, and fully extracted the scale information that contributed more to the result. Li et al. [19] proposed a classification network based on deep attention, which uses channel attention and adds higher weights to more important channels. Since then, the self-attention mechanism [20–23] has become more popular in the fields of natural language processing and computer vision.

3 Method

This part will introduce in detail the method of monocular depth estimation based on the attention radar fusion. The overall network structure is shown in Fig. 1. In our method, ResNet26 and ResNet101 [31] perform feature extraction on radar data and RGB images, respectively. The dual attention fusion module is used for feature fusion. The deep ordinal regression network is used as the skeleton of deep prediction, and the fused feature map is used as the prediction input. The loss function is composed of ordinal regression loss and batch loss.

3.1 Radar Data

Compared with lidar, radar relies on transmitting and receiving radio waves to obtain data, the transmitted signal is more susceptible to interference, the transmission range is short and the resolution is low. Therefore, if you want to apply radar data to dense depth estimation, there are the following limitations:

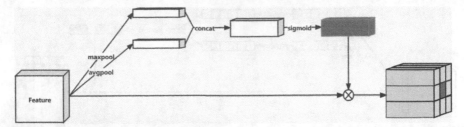

Fig. 3. Spatial attention calculation module (SAM).

1. Sparseness: On the projected image plane, the radar data points are extremely rare, much lower than the lidar data, and it is difficult to provide help for dense estimation.
2. Limited vertical field of view: Due to the limitation of the sensor, the vertical range of the radar measurement is only between a certain height range, which will lead to the lack of guidance from the radar data in the data blank area, and the wrong estimation of the depth.
3. Noise: Because the radar's radio wave signal is easily interfered by external signals, there will be a lot of noise in the radar data.

In order to solve these problems, we introduced a radar data preprocessing strategy [16]. It merges multiple frames of radar into the same image plane, alleviating the sparseness of radar data, and improving the range of the vertical field of view by fusing radar data of different heights. However, due to the fusion of multiple radar data into a single radar data, this also causes a single radar data to have more noise. When solving the problem of noise, if it is simply filtered, it will cause some minor details to be mistakenly regarded as noise and be filtered out. Therefore, we propose a dual attention fusion module, which reduces the model's response to noise, increases the weight of important features, and ensures that secondary details are not lost.

3.2 Deep Ordinal Regression Network

Deep Ordinal Regression Network for Monocular Depth Estimation [4], DORN for short, is a monocular depth estimation model based on encoder-decoder, using ResNet101 as the feature extractor of the network. It proposes a prediction method of ordinal regression, using spacing-increasing discretization (SID) to discretize the depth, transform the original depth prediction problem into an ordered regression problem, and train it through ordinal regression loss. In order to obtain more scale feature information, DORN uses Atrous Spatial Pyramid Pooling (ASPP) to extract multi-scale information of different receptive fields, removes down-sampling, and expands convolution to improve resolution and obtain more detailed information.

3.3 Attention Mechanism

The attention mechanism is a deep learning method that has been widely used in recent years. It can make the model have the ability to focus on its input or a subset of features,

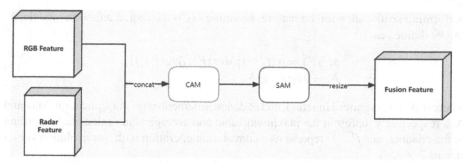

Fig. 4. Dual attention fusion module (DAF), CAM and SAM respectively indicate that the features are calculated for channel attention and spatial attention.

and quickly focus on the input subset that has a greater impact on the result. It can reduce the influence of other interference points on the results, speed up the convergence of the model, and improve the accuracy of the model. The attention mechanism is mainly divided into channel attention and spatial attention. First, given input feature map is $F \in R^{C*H*W}$ and output feature map is $F' \in R^{C*H*W}$. Next, we introduce channel attention and spatial attention respectively.

Channel Attention

Channel attention was first proposed in SENet [29], which extracted a weight map by analyzing the different importance of each channel. Different weights determine the degree of attention the model pays to each channel. It considers each channel of the feature as a feature detector [30], and we need to pay attention to which feature detector is meaningful for our task through channel attention. As shown in Fig. 2, When channel attention is performed on feature, we first compress the input feature into a one-dimensional vector with the number of channels, then calculate the channel attention through nonlinear transformation, and finally multiply it with the input feature to get the final feature. Assume that M_C is the channel attention module, F' can be defined as:

$$M_C(F) = \sigma(MLP(MaxPool(F)) + MLP(AvgPool(F)))$$
$$F' = M_C(F) \otimes F$$

(1)

where σ denotes sigmoid function, MLP is a multi-layer perceptron with a hidden layer, and $\otimes$ denotes element-wise multiplication.

Spatial Attention. When a person looks at a picture, the first thing people see is not the whole picture, but a part of the picture, and this part is the key part or focus part of the image. Because the importance of each spatial location information in the image is different. Based on this principle, spatial attention is proposed, which can help the model focus on more important spatial regions and capture features that are more critical to the task. Different from channel attention, spatial attention generates a spatial attention map by using the spatial internal relationship of features, which determines that the model should focus on the important features of the feature map. As shown in Fig. 3, when performing spatial attention on feature, assuming M_S is the spatial attention module, F' can be defined as:

$$M_S(F) = \sigma\left(f^{7\times7}\left(\left[Max(F); Avg(F)\right]\right)\right)$$
$$F' = M_S(F) \otimes F \tag{2}$$

where σ denotes sigmoid function, and $\otimes$ denotes element-wise multiplication. Max and Avg respectively represent the maximum value and average value calculated according to the channel, and $f^{(7\times7)}$ represents a convolution operation with a convolution kernel size of 7×7.

It is worth mentioning that due to the loss of location information and detailed information due to downsampling, when we compress the model, we use average pooling and maximum pooling to obtain the final attention matrix, which is used to capture different features to compensate for the loss of location information and detailed information [28].

3.4 Dual Attention Fusion Module

When realizing the fusion of radar and RGB feature maps, because there are many noise points in the radar map itself, although some noise points can be removed by filtering operations, there are still residues and some secondary details may be filtered out. When performing feature fusion, if all points are not filtered and all points maintain the same weight, the presence of noise will seriously affect the accuracy of prediction. At the same time, without considering the influence of noise, after assigning different weights to each spatial region and each channel of the two feature maps, the results of depth prediction are different. Because the two kinds of data have a certain correlation in channel and space, the fusion of space and channel with different response degrees will produce different fusion characteristics and produce different depth prediction results. To improve the accuracy of prediction, it is necessary to fully consider the relevance of the two types of data in the channel dimension and the spatial dimension to generate a high-quality fusion feature map. Therefore, we propose a dual attention fusion module (DAF), which suppresses the influence of noise, finds the best combination of channel and space fusion between the two, and maximizes the promotion of fusion of radar data.

The dual attention fusion module mainly includes spatial attention fusion and channel attention fusion. As shown in Fig. 4, it connects the channel attention and spatial attention sequence together, and encodes the correlation between the two data in the channel and space to the output feature. Adaptively adjust the response to each feature to avoid the loss of detailed information and the error of noise. The module first connects the radar feature map and the RGB feature map in the channel dimension, and then uses the channel attention and spatial attention to adjust the feature weights to obtain the final fusion feature map. given RGB feature map is $F_{rgb} \in R^{c_1 * H * W}$ and Radar feature map is $F_{radar} \in R^{c_2 * H * W}$, We can formulate DAF as follows:

$$F_{fusion} = Concat\left(F_{rgb}, F_{radar}\right)$$
$$Y' = M_C\left(F_{fusion}\right) \otimes F_{fusion}$$
$$Y'' = M_S\left(Y'\right) \otimes Y' \tag{3}$$

where M_C and M_S represent channel attention and spatial attention respectively, Concat operation represents channel merging, and $\otimes$ denotes element-wise multiplication. Y'' is the final output fusion feature map.

3.5 Loss Function

The overall loss function consists of two parts:

$$L_{all} = L_{ord} + L_{batch} \tag{4}$$

where L_{ord} is ordinal regression loss [4]. and L_{batch} is defined as:

$$L_{batch} = \frac{1}{n}\sum_{i=1}^{n} w_i * \left(|y_i - \hat{y}_i|\right) + \frac{1}{n}\sum_{i=1}^{n} |y_i - \hat{y}_i|$$

$$w_i = \frac{e^{|y_i - \hat{y}_i|}}{\sum_{i=1}^{n} e^{|y_i - \hat{y}_i|}} \tag{5}$$

where n is the number of all pixels with the depth value of depth image and w_i is the modulating factor obtained by the result of each sample's the deviation in a batch. This loss is called Batch Loss [24], and it is mainly to make the model quickly focus on complex samples, improve the feature extraction ability of the model under complex weather conditions, and obtain more accurate feature information representation, thereby improving the accuracy of the model and speeding up the convergence of the model.

3.6 Implementation Details

This article uses the deep learning framework PyTorch [25] to implement the algorithm, using 4 Nvidia GTX1080Ti training. The epoch and batch sizes are 40 and 3, respectively, the initial learning rate is 0.0001, and a polynomial decay strategy with a power of 0.8 is adopted, and the minimum is 0.00001. With the SGD optimizer, the momentum and weight decay are 0.85 and 0.0005, respectively. The depth of ordered regression is set between 1 m-80 m. For other settings such as RGB image enhancement and image trimming, please refer to [16].

4 Experiment

In this section, we will evaluate the method we proposed, explore the structure and using time of the method, and compare the final model with the baseline to prove the effectiveness of our method. [16] as the baseline for experimental comparison.

4.1 Dataset

We use the recently released nuScenes [27] dataset as the model dataset. nuScenes is a large public data set for autonomous driving developed by the Motional team. It contains data records of the entire sensor suite of autonomous vehicles, including RGB maps and lidar data. As well as radar data, the shooting scenes are Boston and Singapore. The

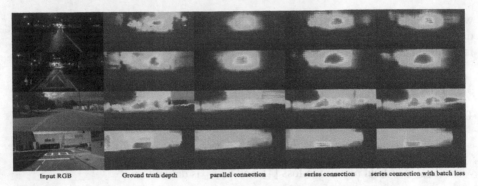

Input RGB   Ground truth depth   parallel connection   series connection   series connection with batch loss

Fig. 5. Comparison result graph of different dual attention model.

data set collects 1000 driving scenes, each scene is 20 s, each scene has 40 key frames, and they are all manually annotated. Among them, 850 scenes are officially divided into training sets, and the remaining 150 scenes are test sets. We divided 850 scenes into 765 training scenes and 85 verification scenes according to the [16] segmentation method, and got 30731 training and 3418 verification pairs, and divide the verification scene into three categories: day, night, and rain.

4.2 Evaluation Metrics

In our experiments, we use the most commonly used metrics in depth estimation [15, 16, 26] to measure the effect of the model.

1. Root Mean Square Error (RMSE):

$$\sqrt{\frac{1}{|N|} \sum_{p_i \in N} |y_{gt}(p_i) - y(p_i)|^2}$$

2. Mean Absolute Relative Error (AbsRel):

$$\frac{1}{|N|} \sum_{p_i \in N} |y_{gt}(p_i) - y(p_i)| / y_{gt}(p_i)$$

3. δ_1 threshold:

$$\delta_1 = |\{y_{gt}(p_i) : \max\left(\frac{y_{gt}(p_i)}{y(p_i)}, \frac{y(p_i)}{y_{gt}(p_i)}\right) < 1.25\}| / |N|$$

where y and y_{gt} represent the prediction result and ground truth, N represents the collection of pixels on the ground truth, p_i represents the pixel, $p_i \in N$, and $y(p_i)$ represents the depth value corresponding to the pixel p_i.

4.3 Comparison of Different Dual Attention Model

In order to find the best dual attention fusion model to achieve high-quality fusion of radar data and RGB data, we explored the connection structure of channel attention and spatial attention. The first is to use the two in parallel, perform channel attention and spatial attention on the input features, and then add the output of the two as the final feature map. The second is to use in series, first use the input feature map for channel attention, and then use the result of the channel attention as the input of spatial attention, and then get the final feature map. In Table 1, the use of dual attention in series is significantly better than parallel, which can more fully extract important features, make the fusion of features more refined, and improve the expressiveness of the model.

At the same time, in order to prove the effectiveness of batch loss, we conducted comparative experiments on a more effective series connection model. As can be seen in Fig. 5, the use of batch loss series connection model can achieve better results. It can improve the expression ability of the model in complex scenes, obtain finer feature details, and have high performance benefits.

Table 1. Comparison of different dual attention model.

Connection method	$\delta_1\uparrow$	RMSE↓	AbsRel↓
Parallel connection	0.877	5.525	0.110
Series connection	0.882	5.293	0.110
Series connection with batch loss	**0.891**	**5.083**	**0.104**

4.4 Comparison of Different Attention Timing

In order to find a better time to use the dual attention fusion module, we did a comparative experiment on the use time of DAF. First, after using DAF on the radar feature map and the RGB feature map, the output results of the two are connected as fusion features. This method is called early attention. Secondly, after connecting the radar feature map and the RGB feature map, and then use DAF to output the fusion feature, it is called late attention. As shown in Fig. 6, compared with late attention, early attention has larger errors at different depths. Although early attention can fully extract the features in the radar feature map and the RGB feature map, it ignores the correlation between the two types of data, resulting in the extracted radar feature cannot be used as a supplement to the RGB feature. Instead, the radar data became noise, which seriously interfered with the prediction results. From the data given in Table 2, we can also see that late attention is far better than early attention. Late attention can fully consider the correlation between the two types of data, positively encode fusion features, generate high-quality fusion features, and improve the utilization of radar data.

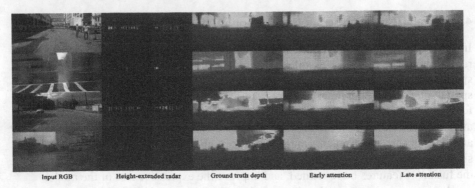

Fig. 6. Comparison result graph of different attention timing.

Table 2. Comparison of different attention timing.

Timing	$\delta_1\uparrow$	RMSE$\downarrow$	AbsRel$\downarrow$
Early attention	0.865	5.569	0.122
Late attention	**0.889**	**5.150**	**0.106**

4.5 Comparison of Different Weather Condition

In contrast to the baseline, we conducted experiments in three different scenes: day, night, and rain. From Table 3, we can see that our method is better than the baseline. Due to the influence of lighting conditions on the RGB map, the RGB map cannot provide more useful depth information, and the radar data can well compensate for the loss caused by the RGB map, so the improvement effect is more prominent in the dark night environment. The DAF module we proposed can better fuse radar data, fully correlate the two types of data, and maximize the utilization of radar data. At the same time, batch loss can also make the network better focus on the complex weather phenomenon of dark night, promote the fusion of radar data, quickly capture some details that are easy to be overlooked, and improve the accuracy of prediction (Fig. 7).

Table 3. Comparison between different weather conditions.

Method	$\delta_1\uparrow$			RMSE$\downarrow$			AbsRel$\downarrow$		
	Day	Night	Rain	Day	Night	Rain	Day	Night	Rain
DORN	0.887	0.764	0.865	5.150	7.122	5.637	0.110	0.169	0.118
Baseline	**0.906**	0.784	0.891	4.845	6.856	5.268	0.100	0.164	0.106
Ours	0.905	**0.794**	**0.894**	**4.756**	**6.614**	**5.096**	**0.100**	**0.157**	**0.103**

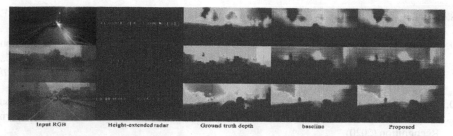

Input RGB   Height-extended radar   Ground truth depth   baseline   Proposed

Fig. 7. Comparison results of different weather conditions, Height-extended radar represents the radar data of extended 5 frames.

5 Conclusion

We propose a dual-attention-based fusion module of radar data and RGB data, which is applied to monocular depth estimation, and batch loss is introduced. By encoding the correlation between the two kinds of data, the quality of feature fusion is improved, and the adaptive response of DAF to the feature is used to suppress the interference of noise. Through experiments, the optimal combination of dual attention models was selected, and the influence of different attention timings on the fusion effect was compared, which proved that late attention is better than early attention. And through experiments under different weather conditions, it is proved that our fusion method can obtain more performance gains and produce better results under complex weather conditions.

Funding Statement This work is supported by the Key Research and Development Program of Hunan Province (No.2019SK2161) and the Key Research and Development Program of Hunan Province (No.2016SK2017).

References

1. Eigen, D., Puhrsch, C., Fergus, R.: Depth Map Prediction from a Single Image using a Multi-Scale Deep Network. MIT Press (2014)
2. Eigen, D., David, Fergus, R.: Predicting depth, surface normals and semantic labels with a common multi-scale convolutional architecture. In: Proceedings of the IEEE international conference on computer vision, pp. 2650–2658 (2015)
3. Laina, I., et al.: Deeper depth prediction with fully convolutional residual networks. In: Fourth International Conference on 3d Vision. IEEE (2016)
4. Fu, H., et al.: Deep Ordinal Regression Network for Monocular Depth Estimation. In: 2018 IEEE/CVF Conference on Computer Vision and Pattern Recognition. IEEE (2018)
5. Zheng, C., Cham, T.J., Cai, J.: T2Net: synthetic-to-realistic translation for solving single-image depth estimation tasks. In: Proceedings of the European Conference on Computer Vision (ECCV) (2018)
6. Ji, R., et al.: Semi-supervised adversarial monocular depth estimation. IEEE Trans. Pattern Anal. Mach. Intell. 1–1 (2019)
7. Godard, C., Aodha, O.M., Brostow, G.J.: Unsupervised monocular depth estimation with left-right consistency. Compu. Vis. Pattern Recognit. (2017)

8. Zhou, T., et al.": Unsupervised learning of depth and ego-motion from video. In: 2017 IEEE Conference on Computer Vision and Pattern Recognition (CVPR). IEEE (2017)

9. Jiao, J., Cao, Y., Song, Y., Lau, R.: Look deeper into depth: monocular depth estimation with semantic booster and attention-driven loss. In: Ferrari, V., Hebert, M., Sminchisescu, C., Weiss, Y. (eds.) ECCV 2018. LNCS, vol. 11219, pp. 55–71. Springer, Cham (2018). https://doi.org/10.1007/978-3-030-01267-0_4

10. Zhu, S., Brazil, G., Liu, X.: The edge of depth: explicit constraints between segmentation and depth. In: Proceedings of the IEEE/CVF Conference on Computer Vision and Pattern Recognition (2020)

11. Srinivasan, P.P., et al.: Aperture supervision for monocular depth estimation. In: Proceedings of the IEEE Conference on Computer Vision and Pattern Recognition (2018)

12. Mal, F., Karaman, S.: Sparse-to-dense: depth prediction from sparse depth samples and a single image. In: IEEE International Conference on Robotics and Automation (ICRA) (2018)

13. Ma, F., Cavalheiro, G.V., Karaman, S.: Self-supervised sparse-to-dense: self-supervised depth completion from lidar and monocular camera. In: 2019 International Conference on Robotics and Automation (ICRA). IEEE (2019)

14. Jaritz, M., De Charette, R., Wirbel, E., Perrotton, X., Nashashibi, F.: Sparse and dense data with CNNs: depth completion and semantic segmentation. In: 2018 International Conference on 3D Vision (3DV). IEEE (2018)

15. Lin, J.-T., Dai, D., Gool, L.V.: Depth estimation from monocular images and sparse radar data. In: IEEE International Conference on Intelligent Robots and Systems (IROS) (2020)

16. Lo, C.-C., Vandewalle, P.: Depth estimation from monocular images and sparse radar using deep ordinal regression network. In: International Conference on Image Processing (ICIP) (2021)

17. Bahdanau, D., Cho, K., Bengio, Y.: Neural machine translation by jointly learning to align and translate. arXiv preprint arXiv:1409.0473 (2014)

18. Dan, X., et al.: Structured attention guided convolutional neural fields for monocular depth estimation. In: IEEE Conference on Computer Vision and Pattern Recognition (CVPR). IEEE (2018)

19. Li, R., et al.: Deep attention-based classification network for robust depth prediction. In: Asian Conference on Computer Vision. Springer, Cham (2018)

20. Vaswani, A., et al.: Attention is all you need. Adv. Neural Inf. Process. Syst. 2017

21. Dosovitskiy, A., et al.: An image is worth 16×16 words: transformers for image recognition at scale. arXiv preprint arXiv:2010.11929 (2020)

22. Liu, Z, et al.: Swin transformer: hierarchical vision transformer using shifted windows. arXiv preprint arXiv:2103.14030 (2021)

23. Ranftl, R, Bochkovskiy, A., Koltun, V.: Vision transformers for dense prediction. In: Proceedings of the IEEE/CVF International Conference on Computer Vision (2021)

24. Pei, M.: MSFNet:Multi-scale features network for monocular depth estimation. arXiv preprint arXiv:2107.06445 (2021)

25. Paszke, A., et al.: PyTorch: an imperative style, high-performance deep learning library. Adv. Neural. Inf. Process. Syst. 32, 8026–8037 (2019)

26. Siddiqui, S.A., Vierling, A, Berns K.: Multi-modal depth estimation using convolutional neural networks. In: 2020 IEEE International Symposium on Safety, Security, and Rescue Robotics (SSRR), pp. 354–359 (2020)

27. Caesar, H., et al.: nuScenes: a multimodal dataset for autonomous driving. In: IEEE Conference on Computer Vision and Pattern Recognition (CVPR) (2020)

28. Woo, S., et al.: CBAM: convolutional block attention module. Eur. Conf. Comput. Vis. (2018)

29. Jie, H., et al.: Squeeze-and-excitation networks. IEEE Trans. Pattern Anal. Mach. Intell. 99 (2017)

30. Zeiler, M.D., Fergus, R.: Visualizing and understanding convolutional neural networks. In: European Conference on Computer Vision (2013)
31. He, K., Zhang, X., Ren, S., Sun J.: Deep residual learning for image recognition. In: 2016 IEEE Conference on Computer Vision and Pattern Recognition (CVPR). IEEE (2016)

Application of Artificial Intelligence in Financial Risk Management

Wanting Hu[1] and Yixian Chen[2(✉)]

[1] Canvard College, Beijing Technology and Business University, Beijing 100000, China
[2] China Electronic Product Reliability and Environmental Testing Research Institute,
Guangzhou 511370, China
chenyixian@ceprei.com

Abstract. With the progress of the times, artificial intelligence (AI) technology is becoming more and more mature. Being widely used in China, AI plays an indispensable role in various fields. However, to further intelligent financial risk management, consistent innovation needs to be made in financial risk management system. A fire-new intelligent financial prevention and control system cannot be built without making the best of AI to strengthen the control and management of financial risk, which is not only a major topic but an inevitable trend of innovation in financial risk management. From the perspective of financial risk management, combined with relevant data research, this paper discusses the application status and potential risks of AI in financial risk management, puts forward corresponding countermeasures and suggestions, and finally analyzes the application requirements of AI in financial risk in the future, striving to improve China's financial risk management system by offering some meaningful reference.

Keywords: Artificial intelligence · Financial risk management · Application analysis

1 Introduction

In 2017, the State Council issued the "Development Planning for a New Generation of Artificial Intelligence", proposing that by 2025, the core industrial scale of AI will exceed 400 billion yuan, which will drive the related industrial scale to exceed five trillion yuan and further expand the scope of AI application nationwide to promote leapfrog innovation and development of various industries [1]. As financial risk management features data intensive analyses and model prediction analyses, it exists a natural adhesion with AI. Domestic and foreign technology giants have invested considerable resources in financial sector and delivered a series of results. But these technological achievements, essentially, have two sides, that is, they have both advantages and disadvantages. The same is true of AI technology. When applied to financial risk management, it can give play to its advantages while facing many difficulties. Though current research has presented analyses on the application status and difficulties of AI in financial sector mainly in terms of technical risks and privacy protection, there is a lack of research findings on the

© The Author(s), under exclusive license to Springer Nature Switzerland AG 2022
X. Sun et al. (Eds.): ICAIS 2022, LNCS 13338, pp. 180–188, 2022.
https://doi.org/10.1007/978-3-031-06794-5_15

potential risks, difficulties, and solutions for AI application in financial risk management. Hence, it is better to see essence through phenomena. It is of great significance to explore AI application in financial risk management against the development background of it in China.

2 Application Status of AI in Financial Risk Management

2.1 Inevitable Trend of AI Intervention in Financial Risk Prevention and Control System

In recent years, with the rapid development of storage technology and communication technology, some data that could have been cleared regularly can be stored permanently. The information gap caused by information asymmetry proves to be an essential factor in determining the total amount of information. The application of big data technology in information gap has become a crucial direction of current research. Complex financial information integration aiming to manage and control financial risks can be realized by analyzing massive data with the help of AI deep learning system. The application of AI will dramatically reduce labor costs and improve the business processing ability of financial risk management. With the promulgation of a series of policy documents such as the "Provisions of the Supreme People's Court on Several Issues Concerning the Application of Law in the Trial of Private Lending Cases", small and micro enterprises in financial sector have been vigorously restricted [2]. Nowadays, AI-aided finance has become a major trend in the development of the financial risk management.

2.2 Based on Data-Driven Mode

In the early days, under the background of backward scientific research level, scientists believed that the only way to intelligentize machine was to make them think like humans. Numerous experiments all ended in failure. By then, they had realized that machines can never think like human brains, and what they really need to do is to solve the problems that human brains can solve. Thus, scientists explored a new scheme, that is, using data to drive AI. Under the traditional financial model, the earnings of commercial banks are mainly from the balance of the interest rate between loan and deposit from individuals or enterprises. This financial model bears many risks. For example, a lender may fail to repay the loan on time, which will exert a significant influence on the bank; and some banks may even go bankrupt directly in serious cases. Since ancient times, banks have basically carried out risk control and management through risk avoidance. The so-called risk avoidance is to avoid the risk of overdue repayment as much as possible by restricting the loans to individuals or some small enterprises lacking adequate repayment capacity. Successful risk avoidance is naturally down to the analyses of user data through AI. In other words, risk control and management can be further improved in a data-driven mode. Overall, the main form of financial risk management in the future should be: "Internet + Big data + AI + Risk management".

2.3   Successful Application Cases of AI in Financial Risk Management

The innovative applications of AI in financial risk management system are emerging one after another. "Sesame Credit" and "Ant Micro Loan" are successful cases at the individual and enterprise level respectively. Alibaba Group applied AI technology to an array of services including AntSure, Huabei, Jiebei, Zhima Credit, cutting down the fictitious trading rate to one tenth and the document review time from one day to one second. Moreover, 100% of the user service consists of intelligent customer service and human assisted consultation, and the accuracy of response by robots has been improved from 67% to over 80%. Additionally, Jingdong Group has developed Shakespeare's artificial intelligence system, which can generate thousands of recommended copywriting for numerous commodities in one second. Besides, its intelligent evaluation system can automatically recommend dozens of projects to JD Crowdfunding platform on a daily basis. Furthermore, JD AI NeuHub has been built to share the AI capabilities extracted from JD's massive scenes and data with the pubic in an all-round way. Here is another example. Abe Al financial assistant, developed by Amazon, can supply functions like conversational banking business, financial management, financial business support by integrating into multiple communication programs [3].

3   Potential Risks of AI Application in Financial Risk Management

3.1   Technical Risks

First, the current AI technology is still in the exploration stage, and it is inevitable to encounter many potential risks resulted from technical problems. For instance, with the widespread use of AI in banking industry, a number of banks have adopted face swiping technology to withdraw money from ATM. But the accuracy and security of face recognition still need to be further tested. Second, AI technology has not yet been mature enough. In recent years, black swan phenomena have occurred in financial markets from time to time. The speed of machine in-depth learning is not fast enough to catch up with the rhythm of financial markets, especially the occurrence of financial risks. In the meantime, some defects and loopholes in algorithms also lead to a huge gap between schemes, investment suggestions and actual situations of markets. The two factors above contribute to investors' losses. Third, due to the influence of technical reserves, capital scale, talents and other factors, many small and medium-sized financial enterprises or organizations in China have neither the will nor the ability to apply AI technology. Thus, AI application is proceeding very slowly without remarkable results. For example, instead of positively incorporating financial technology into strategic planning, many urban commercial banks subjectively have been forced to push forward AI application and lacked supporting hardware equipment or software architecture. Beyond that, if a large number of investors employ the same algorithm and calculation model, financial stability faces challenges in view of the pre-input algorithm program of AI in financial markets. Additionally, if AI transactions meet algorithm transaction failure or error, they will not only result in wrong data analyses and decision failures, but also affect relevant business activities, which impede the smooth completion of financial transactions, bring huge losses to financial consumers, and seriously affect the stability of the whole financial market in severe cases.

3.2 Information Security Risks

The increasingly fierce market competition forces many consumers financial institutions to explore and deepen AI application. They have raced to transform from traditional financial institutions to the direction of digitalization and intelligence. They "deeply excavate" personal information of financial consumers through technology to up the marketing success rate and anti-fraud rate. At the same time, they also steal and abuse consumers' private information by means of "big data", "AI", etc. What's more, many even illegally trade and disclose financial consumer's information, which have seriously damaged consumers' legitimate rights and interests. First of all, the disclosure of personal private information may get financial consuming subjects into trouble and sometimes even lose their jobs. For consumer finance application of AI, effective policies and procedures must be worked out to ensure consumers' information safe, otherwise, leakage of personal privacy is likely to cause social equity problems. For example, the abuse of big data and AI analysis can easily bring about information leakage when data masking is used improperly, giving rise to a variety of derivative problems. Therefore, fintech companies and other types of consumer financial institutions should make every effort to avoid any private information disclosure. Secondly, illegal trading and abuses of personal information turn out to be a "trample" on the rights of financial consumers and a "destruction" of social relations. The reason why a human can be regarded as an independent individual is that he/she has perfect independent legal personality and enjoys independent rights to personal relationships and property relationships protected by law. As an independent right object, personal information is sure to play an important part in personal rights and should be protected by legal norms. However, in the era of AI, with the assistance of "Big data" and "AI", illegal trading and abuses of personal information conducted by many consumers financial institutions keep bothering customers on cellphones or in test messages normally using "malicious collection" and "violent collection" as excuses. Such never-ending conduct without the consent of the person concerned has not only brought great damage to the social life of financial consumers, but also resulted in ruthless damage to their rights [4].

3.3 Risks at the Regulatory Level

As a "double-edged sword", AI can provide great development opportunities for financial industry, but also bring about a significant threat to legal and regulatory work of this field. With the continuous progress of the industry, some traditional financial institutions (such as commercial banks) should strictly abide by various regulations and set necessary management indicators, such as capital adequacy ratio and deposit reserve ratio, etc. Sometimes these targets may get off track, but financial innovation should never go over the provisions of the existing laws and regulations and financial institutions should never carry out "regulatory arbitrage" under"regulatory vacuum" [5]. Firstly, the increasingly complicated financial supervision objects make it difficult to define responsible subjects. The subjects of financial supervision generally consisting of natural person, legal person or other organizations constitute the basis of the current financial legal supervision system. However, as AI technology develops rapidly, for accounts regarding ownership as collective subject, it is often found that the subject of crime may be an "intelligent agent" rather than a specific legal subject in most cases when tracing criminals according to the current "see-through" regulatory principle. Under the existing legal supervision system, China's legal norms have not directly and clearly stipulated the nature of AI legal subject, the responsibility identification in financial risk events caused by AI failures, or the ruling of causal relationship between illegal acts and the harm results relating to AI application in financial scenarios. All in all, China is facing a legislation shortage in AI application in financial sector. Secondly, the costs and difficulties of financial supervision are becoming greater. Both AI and finance features professionalism and complexity. Thus, the comprehensive application of AI in financial sector will double the complexity of finance and make it more difficult to implement financial supervision.

3.4 Legal and Regulatory Risks and Institutional Risks

First of all, the in-depth application of AI in financial sector requires legal basis. However, whether in the standardization of regulatory laws or in the relevant detailed regulatory policies and rules, China still stays at the level of Internet finance and has not issued systematic and standardized laws and regulations. The lack of laws and regulations in AI application makes the regulatory boundary relatively blurred. Many business models related to AI can only be formulated by referring to the laws and regulations in traditional finance and Internet finance. It is hard to identify responsibility for a lack of legal ground once disputes occur. Secondly, the innovative application and development of AI has posed new challenges to the financial supervision system. Although China has issued an array of relevant guidance, it is still necessary to further refine the relevant support policies among different sectors and improve the "legal gap" and "supervision vacuum" of finance industry related to AI application. Thirdly, the deepening application of AI in financial markets has brought about changes in financial operation mode and supervision mode. How to keep pace with the times and constantly perfect the legal system are also crucial topics that relevant authorities need to place emphasis on.

4   Countermeasures and Suggestions on the Rational Use of AI in Financial Risk Management

4.1 Train High-Tech Talents and Improve the Level of Information Technology

As the competition in financial industry in AI era is heating up day by day, the first problem to be solved in financial risk management is the fierce competition for talented people. All kinds of financial institutions are competing for composite talents that are well versed in AI and financial risk management with all their strength. Under the background of serious imbalance between supply and demand in the talent market, there is a need to strengthen the comprehensive education of liberal arts and science as well as the integration of theory and practice. Besides, we should focus on the comprehensive development of "government, customer, university, and research institution", and promote the proliferation of compound talents excelling in both financial risk management and AI. Since the present AI technology is machine intelligence based on data and algorithm, it is featured by complexity and uncertainty. At present, AI technology is not yet mature, and its technical level is still limited. Instead of becoming the advantages of AI, machine learning and deep learning have become "program bugs" amplified by technology which cannot be thoroughly understood with the current technical level and cognitive ability, let alone fully predict its risks. Therefore, it is necessary to strengthen the research level of basic disciplines in AI and conduct scientific research from the basic technical levels of machine learning, deep learning and artificial neural network. First, enterprises, universities and scientific research institutes should be guided to strengthen the research on basic topics in AI from the viewpoint of policy. For instance, some AI innovation demonstration areas planned to be built are eligible to get support like tax breaks, etc. China should encourage the practical application of AI from practical use to basic research. Second, based on the demands of AI industry, China should keep perfecting the basic industry standards related to AI, participate in the compilation of AI training materials, set up qualification examination for AI industry, and encourage employees to make breakthroughs and innovations in basic disciplines. Finally, as the "bridgehead" of basic research on AI, colleges and universities need to play an exemplary role in enhancing basic discipline research on AI. They should not only stay in the "face-saving project" of setting up AI institutes or laboratories in colleges and universities countrywide but build a multi-level talent system and deepen the research on basic disciplines of AI, preventing various financial risks from the source by strengthening the integration of theory and financial practice [6].

4.2 Consolidate Information Data Security of AI

Big data is the technical basis for the deepening of artificial intelligence, while social credit investigation is the data cornerstone for the development of financial risk management. Only the data obtained by financial institutions are really big data, because these data proves to be large in amount, broad in range and muti-dimensional. The application of AI technology in consumer financial risk management can improve efficiency. First of all, the financial industry lacks a unified social credit investigation system. Financial information sharing has not been available in China. "Muti-platform Loan" is nothing new and "joint debt risk" has increasingly become a common development pain point of the industry. Therefore, it is necessary to actively build a unified social credit investigation system nationwide. All kinds of market subjects engaged in financial business should be incorporated in the credit investigation system with the help of AI technology, so as to fully realize data sharing of all financial institutions and further consolidate the data foundation of AI. Secondly, the "homogenization" of big data, especially the "homogenization" of data base and data model, is rooted in the limited data sources of financial sector. It is necessary to further open big data. On the one hand, it requires all kinds of financial institutions in China to effectively integrate with the credit investigation system of the people's Bank of China. On the other hand, to effectively get big data out of homogenization, there is need to break market data monopoly by liberalizing the application for social credit investigation license. In addition, a national unified social credit investigation system should be built through AI technology, and a proactive, operational and post-operational oversight system based on credit should also be set up. Legislatures should make basic preparations for the promulgation of personal bankruptcy law and personal bankruptcy system. Financial institutions should guard against risks like moral hazard and adverse selection from "vicious debtors".

4.3 Build a New "See-Through" Intelligent Regulatory System

To strengthen AI financial supervision, instead of following the traditional unilateral legal governance, China should promote the two-wheel drive of "AI governance + legal governance". Due to the lag, rigidity and blankness of traditional legal governance, it is necessary to establish and improve the legal norms of AI finance at legislative level, strengthen the risk prediction and evaluation of AI, and formulate industry standards and ethical norms, so as to realize the legal governance of AI finance at legal and industry norm level. Secondly, the self-discipline role of industry associations should be brought into play in the development of new business forms of scientific and technological finance. Authorities related should guide influential financial industry associations to establish and improve a self-discipline mechanism clarifying the rights and obligations of financial enterprises for AI application in financial risk management. At the same time, a management system combining government regulation, industry self-discipline and market constraints, should be built to promptly figure out and make up loopholes, ensuring the sound and orderly development of financial markets, controllable risks and full implementation of supervision. Finally, regulatory authorities should increase the research on AI and other financial technologies, unify the relevant standards for AI application in the banking industry as early as possible, establish a special regulatory response group, and enhance network security.

4.4 Build a Relatively Perfect System of Laws and Regulations to Standardize AI Development

Legislatures should establish and perfect laws and regulations related to AI, refine specific policies, identify the scope and direction of application of policies and regulations, and standardize the specific application of AI, so as to provide support for a wide and rapid promotion of AI in financial markets. Meanwhile, related authorities should keep pace with the times and constantly improve the legal system of new technology and business according to the actual development of financial risk management business to avoid disconnection between technology and law.

5 Application Requirements of AI in Future Financial Risks

5.1 Optimize Intelligent Model Algorithm and Improve the Supervision Ability of Financial Institutions

For financial institutions, although AI technology has optimized financial supervision model and risk management, there is still great potential to tap. AI algorithms and technologies are just what need to be continuously optimized in the future. Only by establishing a better model closing to the actual market and simulating real transactions can the risk management ability of financial institutions be further improved. Moreover, the "interpretability" of AI technology in financial risk management should be paid more attention to. That is, we should not only apply AI technology to financial risk management, but also let users better understand the technical principle and the operation principle of the model in AI application.

5.2 Strengthen Intelligent Data Analyses and Maintain the Fairness and Order of Financial Markets

Fairness, efficiency and order are undoubtedly the most important for financial markets. The powerful data processing, data analysis and data mining functions of AI have significantly improved the efficiency of financial markets, weakened the information asymmetry in the market as well as consolidated the fairness of financial markets. Besides, the introduction of "intelligent supervision" has improved the security of transactions in financial markets, cracked down on financial frauds and crimes, and maintained the stable order of financial markets. To ensure the fairness, efficiency and order of financial markets, the strengths of AI technology in data analysis in the future should be given full play, and great data resource asymmetry among different individuals and institutions and regulatory loopholes caused by unsound intelligent supervision technology and modes should be avoided.

5.3 Develop Intelligent Forecasting Models to Monitor Systemic Risks in Financial System

The rapid development and comprehensive application of AI technology will exert an influence on the structure of the whole financial risk management system, changing the importance of various institutions in the original system, developing new forms of financial institutions, and even increasing the unknown systemic risks of the whole system. Widespread use of AI technology, increasing reliance on AI technology and convergence trend appears in AI technology, will greatly endanger the whole financial system once decision failure and technical error happen. Relying solely on the reliability of AI technology and strengthening analysis ability is not enough to cope with systematic risks. An intelligent prediction model should be developed to per-judge the possible systematic risks brought by AI technology by using AI to predict AI.

6 Conclusion

Being in the initial stage of development, AI has enormous development potential and application prospect in financial risk management. At this stage, AI application in financial risk management is just partially replacing the relatively simple labor in financial management system for it is only a kind of relatively primary "intelligence". As for the grasp, prediction and supervision of financial markets, accurate and reliable results have not yet been achieved through AI technology. The paper preliminarily summarizes the application status of AI in financial risk management, analyzes the potential risks of AI application, puts forward corresponding countermeasures and suggestions and explores its future application requirements and prospect. In a word, in order to truly embrace the arrival of "intelligent finance", great efforts should be made in tapping the potentials of AI application in financial risk management. Only technological progress can promote the qualitative leap of application products and really stimulate the vitality of "intelligent finance".

References

1. Yu, X., Peng, Y.: Application and Challenges of Artificial Intelligence in the Field of Financial Risk Management. South China Finance (2017)
2. Zhao, Y.: Reasonable application of artificial intelligence in the field of financial risk management. Enterp. Reform Manage. **000**(011), 8–9 (2018)
3. Zhang, B.: Application and challenges of artificial intelligence in the field of financial risk management. Mark. Obs. **790**(02), 33 (2020)
4. Li, S.: Discussion on innovative application and challenges of artificial intelligence in the field of financial risk management. Invest. Guidance Public **322**(02), 77–78 (2019)
5. Liu, T.: Artificial intelligence and financial risk prevention-based on the research on prevention of bank card crimes. Qinghai Finance **10**, 39–43 (2018)
6. Rao, D.: Research on financial risk avoidance based on artificial intelligence. CPCFan **000**(002), 154 (2018)

Research on Commercial Sector Electricity Load Model Based on Exponential Smoothing Method

Huifeng Yan[1], Xuyang Yu[1](✉), Dawei Li[2], Ying Xiang[1], Jian Chen[2], Zhiyong Lin[2], and Jingwen Shen[3]

[1] State Grid Hunan Electric Power Company, Changsha 410006, China
yuxuyang@126.com

[2] State Grid Hunan Electric Power Company Economic and Technical Research Institute, Changsha 410006, China

[3] State Grid Information and Communication Company of Hunan Changsha, Changsha 410006, China

Abstract. This article mainly proposes a forecasting model based on time series. Exponential smoothing is a kind of time series analysis method. Exponential smoothing is a model that combines old and new information. Different ratios of old and new information are given to predict future phenomena. Appropriate weight parameters will more accurately predict the electricity consumption of China's residents, which provides an important basis and reference for promoting China's power resource conservation and promoting the development of national energy. This article briefly describes the basic theoretical knowledge about exponential smoothing method, using exponential smoothing method, select typical park user electricity consumption data for training and forecasting, to verify the superiority of exponential smoothing method for forecasting data. Finally, according to the research results of this article, it can be used as a reference for future decision-making.

Keywords: Electricity consumption · Exponential smoothing method · Predictive analysis · Weight parameter

1 Introduction

1.1 Research Background

Electricity occupies a vital position in the entire economic and ecological fields of China People's lives are closely related. In order to study the different regions, different time domain residents of electricity, we can select different features of the park as a research object, wherein the total amount of electricity load user parks the top 4 of company A, company B, company C, company D as a typical representative, carried out the research on the forecasting method of the park user's power load.

At present, electricity is still an important energy source in our country. A reasonable forecast of user power consumption can not only reduce energy waste but also adjust the power generation load of the power supply plant [1]. Time series analysis can be used

© The Author(s), under exclusive license to Springer Nature Switzerland AG 2022
X. Sun et al. (Eds.): ICAIS 2022, LNCS 13338, pp. 189–205, 2022.
https://doi.org/10.1007/978-3-031-06794-5_16

to make reasonable forecasts of user power consumption. Time series is based on time, arranging events at each point in time into a set of sequences, and using this sequence to study and predict future phenomena. Exponential smoothing ES (Exponential Smoothing) is the most commonly used forecasting method. Compared with single exponential smoothing SES (Single Exponential Smoothing) and double exponential smoothing DES (Double Exponential Smoothing), triple exponential smoothing TES (Triple Exponential Smoothing) adapted to analyze the time series of the general problem [2, 3]. At the same time, TES can be used for sequences that have trends and seasons. Therefore, this article chooses ES based on the time series method to construct a forecasting model to more accurately predict the electricity consumption of each park user, which will provide a more reliable basis for power development.

1.2 Current Status of Time Series Research

Time series TS (Time Series) is a method for predicting the statistical law, law mining data may be analyzed. Robert G. Brown proposed the exponential smoothing method in the early 1870s [4]. He found that the time series has certain laws, and the latest information reflects the future trend to a certain extent. Winter was founded in the 1960s and has the ability to predict trend patterns and seasonal patterns. Current, ES is a commonly used method in our life and production used to predict, which is closely related to the accuracy of forecasting and smoothing coefficient, the order to determine the appropriate coefficient by experience and experiments are crucial. In 2013, Siddharth Arora proposed the important influence of seasonal load on short-term load forecasting [14], which can more accurately calculate forecast data.

Forecasting methods are mainly divided into qualitative methods and quantitative methods. Qualitative methods include expert meeting, analogy forecasting and Delphi method. They are suitable for long-term forecasting. Generally, when there is less historical data, they rely on the judgment of experts to make forecasts. They are highly subjective, so they are effective. Mainly limited by the technical level of some experts, the practicability and reliability will be relatively low. Quantitative methods mainly include linear regression forecasting method, nonlinear regression forecasting method, trend external estimation method, moving average method, exponential smoothing method, adaptive filtering method, stationary time series forecasting method, etc. They are generally suitable for medium and short-term forecasting.

1.3 Research Exponential Smoothing

ES has many advantages: First, ES only based on historical data can predict future data [5]. ES is a time series analysis method based on the moving average method [6], without discarding the past data, but slowly reducing the weight of the data [7].

ES is commonly used in the short-term prediction, all forecasting techniques, ES is the use of a more extensive. Compared with the traditional full-period average method and moving average method, ES is compatible with long-term data and recent data [8], and allocates a larger proportion to recent data.

ES is a smooth forecasting model. According to the characteristics of the data, the exponential smoothing method is divided into SES, DES and TES. SES can be used for relatively stable data. DES can also be applied to time series with a linear trend. Compared with the above two exponential smoothing methods, TES increases the seasonal effect factor.

2 Exponential Smoothing Algorithm

2.1 Exponential Smoothing

The most basic smooth forecast of time series forecasting is a simple time series. Smoothing prediction is to use average behavior to remove some random effects in the time series, so that TS becomes smooth and smooth.

The calculation formula of simple TS is:

$$S(T + 1) = (1/N) * \sum X(I) \tag{1}$$

wherein, X(I) are the I actual data value of a, S(T + 1) is the predicted value of the next period, N is the number, T is the predicted time.

Simple smoothing is a forecasting method that uses averages to predict future data. According to different needs, different types of averages are used.

ES is developed on the basis of the moving average method. First, the smooth value can be calculated, and then the time series model is used to predict the future development trend. This method is more in line with the actual situation, and the calculation method and logic of the model They are easier to understand, and the prediction results are more stable. By selecting training data for different times of exponential smoothing, choosing the trend of forecasting data and the effect of fitting, choosing a better exponential smoothing method. The basic formula of ES is:

$$\widehat{x_t} = \alpha(0)_t^{(0)} + (1 - \alpha)\widehat{x_{t-1}}, t = 1, 2 \cdots, n \tag{2}$$

where x_t is the predicted value of exponential smoothing at time t, x_t0 is the actual value at time t, $x\_(t - 1)$ is the predicted value of exponential smoothing at time t–1, a is the smoothing coefficient, and its value range is [0,1], it is very important to determine an appropriate smoothing coefficient. For data with relatively large fluctuations, the smoothing coefficient is generally larger, giving the latest information more weight. In the actual prediction, we select the appropriate smoothing coefficient through the accuracy of the prediction. Since SES cannot adapt to all situations, DES and TES are improved and developed on this basis.

2.2 Exponential Smoothing Model

The exponential smoothing model ESM (Exponential Smoothing Model) is one of the most commonly used time series forecasting methods in our production and economy. EMS is commonly used for short- and medium-term forecasting. EMS can reduce the influence of abnormal data on the prediction results, and is simple, stable and easy to operate [11].

When ES forecasts the data of the next period, it must consider the data indicators of the previous period and the current period at the same time. Higher allocation of scale factor to recent data, it will be more realistic, more accurate forecasting phenomenon, fitting better. There are three commonly used classifications of exponential smoothing: single exponential model, double exponential model and triple exponential model.

Single exponential model. The single exponential has only one parameter, which is suitable for the prediction of relatively stable time series, and is also called the stationarity prediction method. The principle is to give a larger weight ratio to the most recent data, give a smaller weight ratio to the early historical data, and get the predicted value based on the historical data.

Smoothing formula: with y_t to represent the actual data values, using S_t is represented predictable events specific value of the current time, which is t smoothed value at the point S_t is calculated as follows:

$$S\_t = ay\_(t-1) + (1-a)S\_(t-1)(0 < a \leq 1, t \geq 3) \tag{3}$$

Initialization: exponential smoothing is an initial prediction value S_2, two methods may S_2 is initialized, one is $S_2 = y_1$, there is a previous select the actual average value. Forecast formula: the exponential smoothing formula at time $T+1$ is:

$$S_t = ay_{t-1} + (1-a)S_{t-1}(0 < a \leq 1, t \geq 3) \tag{4}$$

The exponential smoothing formula at time $T+i$ is:

$$S_{t+i} = ay_{t+i-1} + (1-a)S_{t+i-1}(0 < a \leq 1, t \geq 3) \tag{5}$$

where i represents the point in time.

Exponential smoothing equation can be expanded, the smoothing formula to replace S_{t-1}, as follows:

$$S_t = ay_{t-1} + (1-a)[ay_{t-2} + (1-a)S_{t-2}] = ay_{t-1} + a(1-a)y_{t-2} + (1-a)^2 S_{t-2} \tag{6}$$

Substituting the values in S in turn, until S_2, the following formula can be obtained:

$$S_t = a\sum_{i=1}^{t-2}(1-a)^{i-1}y_{t-i} + (1-a)^{t-2}S_2(t \geq 2) \tag{7}$$

$a(1-a)^i$ has been decreasing, and the proportion of early historical data is getting smaller and smaller.

Quadratic exponential smoothing model. The one-time exponential model is suitable for a stable time series without a trend, but a smoothing model is not suitable when the demand sequence has an upward or downward trend.

Quadratic exponential smoothing is a method designed for a trending demand sequence to calculate the parameters of an equation with a linear trend. The second smoothing is to perform another smoothing on the basis of the first smoothing. The formula is as follows:

$$\begin{cases} S_t^2 = \alpha S_t^1 + (1 - \alpha) S_{t-1}^2 \\ S_t^2 = \alpha X_{t-1} + (1 - \alpha) \widehat{x_{t-1}} = \widehat{x_t} \end{cases} \tag{8}$$

S_t^2 is the average of the quadratic exponent and α is the smoothing coefficient. The prediction equation is as follows:

$$\widehat{x_{i+\tau}} = a_i + b_i \tau \tag{9}$$

where τ is the prediction timeout, the theorem of exponential smoothing is:

$$\alpha_t = 2S_t^1 - S_t^2, b_t = \frac{\alpha}{1 - \alpha}(S_t^1 - S_t^2) \tag{10}$$

Forecasting formula:

$$\widehat{x_{t+\tau}} = a_t + b_t \tau = \left(2 + \frac{\alpha \tau}{1 - \alpha}\right) S_t^1 - \left(1 + \frac{\alpha}{1 - \alpha}\right) S_t^2 \tag{11}$$

Quadratic predictions are clearly more accurate for trending data than for first smoothing cubic exponential model. When the time series value is nonlinear, neither the first exponential smoothing model nor the second exponential smoothing model is applicable, then the cubic exponential model is developed, and the third exponential model is smoothed again on the basis of the second smoothing. Its formula is shown as follows:

$$S_t^3 = \alpha S_t^2 + (1 - \alpha) S_{t-1}^3 \tag{12}$$

The prediction formula of cubic smoothing model is shown below:

$$\widehat{x_{t+\tau}} = a_t + b_t \tau + c_t \tau^2 \tag{13}$$

When the time series is not linear, using cubic smoothing model will get more accurate prediction data.

2.3 Evaluation Criteria for Model Accuracy

The accuracy of model prediction represents whether the selection of this model is suitable for our data scenario. The methods of prediction accuracy include prediction error, average error, percentage error, average absolute error, average percentage error, error standard deviation and mean square error. Choosing a suitable exponential smoothing model can reduce errors and improve the accuracy of prediction.

The accuracy of the prediction result is closely related to the selected smoothing coefficient and fitting effect. The more accurate prediction results, the predicted and the predicted image data and the fit of the actual data and the image on the high. In this article, the Mean Absolute Error (MAE) is used to evaluate the quality of the prediction model. MAE is the average of the absolute value of the error between each observation and the arithmetic mean:

$$\Delta = (|\Delta 1| + |\Delta 2| + \cdots + |\Delta n|)/n \tag{14}$$

The above is a set of observation data, Δ is MAE, $\Delta 1, \Delta 2 \cdots \Delta n$ is the absolute error of each measurement. A better smoothing coefficient will reduce M AE, and the actual value will be closer to the predicted value.

3   Establish an Exponential Smoothing Model

3.1   Three Times Exponential Smoothing Method

TES is smoothed again on the basis of the second exponential smoothing. According to the cyclical and seasonal characteristics of the data, a corresponding model is constructed. The mathematical model of TES is:

$$Y_{t+T} = a_t + b_t T + a_t T^2 \tag{15}$$

$$a_t = 3S_t^{(1)} - 3S_t^{(2)} + S_t^{(3)} \tag{16}$$

$$b_t = \frac{\alpha}{2(1-\alpha)^2}[(6-5\alpha)S_t^{(1)} - 2(5-4\alpha)S_t^{(2)} + (4-3\alpha)S_t^{(3)}] \tag{17}$$

$$b_t = \frac{\alpha}{2(1-\alpha)^2}\left[S_t^{(1)} - 2S_t^{(2)} + S_t^{(3)}\right] \tag{18}$$

$$S_t^{(1)} = \alpha y_t + (1-\alpha)S_{t-1}^{(1)} \tag{19}$$

$$S_t^{(2)} = \alpha S_t^{(1)} + (1-\alpha)S_{t-1}^{(2)} \tag{20}$$

$$S_t^{(2)} = \alpha S_t^{(1)} + (1-\alpha)S_{t-1}^{(3)} \tag{21}$$

In the above formula, Y_{t+T} represents the predicted value of the user's power consumption at t + T, and T represents the predicted number of periods in the future, a_t, b_t, b_t represents a smoothing factor, $S_t^{(1)}$, $S_t^{(2)}$, $S_t^{(2)}$ indicates the SES, the DES and TES smoothed values of, α represents a smoothing factor [11–13].

3.2 Construction of Model

Import data first. This paper studies user power consumption data from January 2019 to August 2020, and selects user power consumption data from four campuses: Deloitte, company D, company B, and company C Data processing. The data is divided into a training set (2019 years) and test set (2020 years), by 2019 trained in good smoothing coefficient data. The smoothing coefficient can be calculated from 0.01 to 0.99 through an experimental algorithm to get a better smoothing coefficient. Determination of the initial value. The initial data is the average of the actual data in the last four periods. Calculate the smoothing value. Calculate the smooth value according to the above formula.

3.3 Forecast Electricity Consumption

According to the forecast model, forecast the electricity consumption of users in the four parks of company A, company D, company B and company C in 2020, and calculate the forecasted value and actual value of MAE, and summarize the forecasting effect of the data and the degree of curve fitting, And make an error comparison between the pre-epidemic period, the peak period of the epidemic and the recovery period of the epidemic.

4 Exponential Smoothing Method Applied to Electricity Consumption Forecasting

The exponential smoothing method is applied in many fields because of its easy operation and good stability. Through the experiments in this chapter, the exponential smoothing method is applied to the prediction of user power consumption. The average error of the predicted data and the actual data to verify the accuracy and the feasibility model [9, 10].

4.1 Implementation of the Method and Data Selection

The experimental data are selected from the national grid provided by Hunan Electric Power Company 2019 January to 2020 August Red Star district electricity user data. Among the top 4 in the total power load of park users, company A, company B, company C, and company D are the typical representatives to conduct research on the prediction method of park user power load.

The four campus users of electricity divided into a training set and test set to 2019 in 1 January to 2019 in 12 months for the training set, in order to get the basis to predict the 2020 user data for electricity. With 20 is. 19 minimum error between the actual value of the data and the predicted value of the optimal smoothing coefficient, the 2020 annual epidemic preliminary data into data (. 1 dated), the peak of the outbreak of the data (2 dated, 3 month) and a data recovery epidemic (4 months 5 months 6 months 7 months, eight months, nine months), the error is calculated, the error comparison of three different periods of error and four different zone, and determining the epidemic The impact of different types of parks on forecast data. This paper implements two exponential smoothing experiments to predict the electricity consumption of users in the four parks in 2020. In this paper, the parameter comparison method is used to determine the optimal smoothing coefficient, the optimal parameters are tested to predict the data, the predicted value is calculated, and the actual data and the predicted data error result are calculated at the same time.

Judging from the current data on commercial districts, some of the established commercial districts have undergone major changes in their operating methods, and the data quality is uneven, which is not conducive to verification as a typical representative. The Red Star commercial district is a large emerging commercial district with good data quality. It is helpful to establish a stable analysis model and to verify the correctness of the experiment. Through the analysis of the electricity consumption data of all users in the Red Star business district, four parks were finally selected as typical parks. Among them, Deloitte mainly manages large-scale commercial complexes, company D mainly manages large- scale residential communities, company B belongs to a large state-owned property group, and company C is a large telecom operator company. This experiment is mainly to predict and verify the short-term (1 day, 96 time points, one point every 15 min).

4.2 Data Preprocessing

The initial data is that the four campuses are mixed together, and they are out of order, and some data are missing. Therefore, certain data needs to be processed to prepare for the subsequent prediction of residential electricity load.

The initial data has a certain lack and confusion, which will affect the accuracy of the data to a certain extent. The initial data cannot be directly manipulated with time series, so certain preprocessing must be performed on the initial data.

The initial data includes user code, user name, date, time and power load. Because each park selects a fixed user for experimentation, the user code data item is removed. The date and time of the merger, representing a special fixed point in time. Remove items irrelevant to the data to improve efficiency and effectiveness.

Data segmentation: The data of different parks will be segmented. The 2019 data will be used as the training set, and the 2020 data will be used as the test set. The test set is divided into the pre-epidemic period, the peak period of the epidemic, and the period of recovery from the epidemic. Missing data: The missing data has a greater impact on the prediction results, so it must be filled in. The data at the same time point in the previous day is filled in the missing data. Time format: combine the date and time into a certain point in time. Each point in time corresponds to an electricity load, and the electricity load keeps three decimal places.

4.3   Experimental Design

Experimental Module. The experiment in this paper is to predict the residential electricity load of four different parks, which is divided into three modules, data input, data analysis and data output. As shown below (Fig. 1):

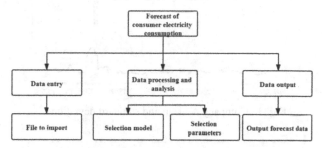

Fig. 1. Experiment module diagram.

To save the data form is stored in excel table, file import mode used to read the data. It was chosen for ESM model, the parameter error comparison method, to choose the best parameters. Finally, enter the forecast data for the three periods of the pre-epidemic period, the peak period of the epidemic and the recovery period of the epidemic respectively, and calculate the MAE of the predicted value and the actual value. The following figure shows the flow chart (Figs. 2, 3, 4, 5 and 6):

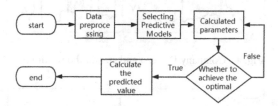

Fig. 2. Flow chart of experiment.

Experimental Function Diagram. The following are four parks on time line graph to display the electricity load and data entry, 2019 years. 1 dated. 1 Day to 2020 years. 9 dated. 9 days, every 15 min a measurement large amount of data. The overall actual power consumption of the four parks can be seen from the figure below, as shown in the figure:

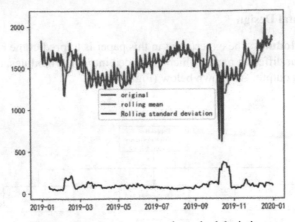

Fig. 3. Company A mean and standard deviation.

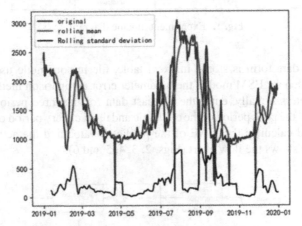

Fig. 4. Company D mean and standard deviation.

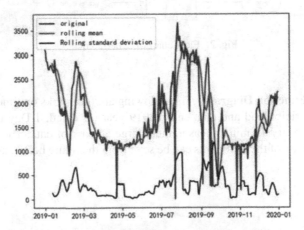

Fig. 5. Company B mean and standard deviation.

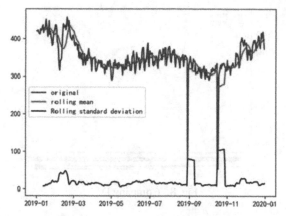

Fig. 6. Company C mean and standard deviation.

The above figure shows the rolling average and standard deviation of the actual electricity load of 4 business district users in 2019. The rolling window is set to 12 days. It is obvious from the figure that the time series data is not stable and fluctuates greatly.

The following figure shows 2020 years. 1 dated. 1 comparative one day predicted and actual values of the power consumptions, as follows (Figs. 7, 8 and 9):

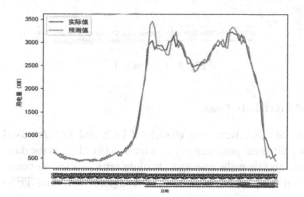

Fig. 7. Company A.

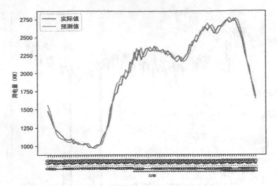

Fig. 8. Company D.

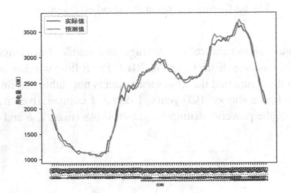

Fig. 9. Company B.

4.4 Forecast of Electricity Load

In the experiment of this article, two models of DES and TES are used to predict the user's power load, different parameters are selected according to the data characteristics of different parks, and then the average absolute error is used to compare the impact of the epidemic on the prediction results and compare DES And TES two prediction models.

Experimental Data for Quadratic Exponential Smoothing. Four Star Circle Park 2019 on. 1 January to 2020 in 8 electricity load months as the data of this experiment, the use of DES on 2020 electricity load in prediction. The following is a table for the integration of the forecast results. The data is measured every 15 min, and a short-term forecast of one day is made. The data of 2019 is used to predict the data of the next day in 2020, and the forecast result is obtained. And show its prediction error. As follows (Table 1):

Table 1. Data error table DES of company A.

Company A		
Period	Mean absolute error	Label
Pre epidemic period	65.31	High
Epidemic recovery period	254.86	Low
Epidemic peak	185.41	Low

The above table shows the error between the forecasted data and actual data of company A 2020 in different periods. It can be seen that the error between the predicted data and actual data in the early stage of the epidemic is relatively small. At the peak of the epidemic, due to the national government restricting people's going out, this has led to a certain amount of electricity consumption in a series of large shopping malls such as company A. The degree of reduction, during the recovery period of the epidemic, its electricity consumption slowly returned to normal. The smoothing parameter in the experiment is obtained by the parameter comparison method to obtain a more reasonable value. For the data characteristics of Deloitte, 0.66 is selected as the smoothing coefficient of the second exponential smoothing (Tables 2 and 3).

Table 2. Data error table DES of company D.

Company D		
Period	Mean absolute error	Label
Pre epidemic period	110.2	High
Epidemic recovery period	253.9	Low
Epidemic peak	148.56	Low

Table 3. Data error table DES of company B.

Company B		
Period	Mean absolute error	Label
Pre epidemic period	200.53	High
Epidemic recovery period	381.92	Low
Epidemic peak	271.12	Low

The above table is the forecasted and actual electricity consumption data of D Company Limited Property Company in 2020. In the early stage of the epidemic, the forecasting effect was better and the error was low. During the peak of the epidemic, the electricity consumption of residents decreased to a small extent. Overall, During the epidemic, company D did not show any significant changes in its electricity consumption.

For the characteristics of company D Property Data, the smoothing coefficient of the second exponential smoothing is 0.51.

The above is the error data between the predicted electricity consumption and actual electricity consumption of Company B, a state-owned enterprise in 2020. The epidemic has a small impact on Company B, with a small reduction in electricity consumption. According to the 2019 data set training, 0.57 is obtained as the smoothing coefficient of the second exponential smoothing (Table 4).

Table 4. Data error table DES of company C.

Company C		
Period	Mean absolute error	Label
Pre epidemic period	218.5	High
Epidemic recovery period	632.91	Low
Epidemic peak	529.16	Low

During the epidemic, company C's electricity consumption showed a substantial increase, and the error was also large. During the epidemic, online class and online office became our main way of life, which greatly promoted the development of the Internet. With the general development of 5G, the power consumption of mobile companies has reached a peak again. For the data training of company C in 2019, 0.34 was obtained as the smoothing coefficient of the second exponential smoothing.

From the results of the above table, it is found that in the early stage of the epidemic, the accuracy of the prediction results is relatively high; during the peak of the epidemic, due to the impact of the epidemic, many factories, shopping malls and other places closed their business, and at the same time promoted the wide application of the network, making the prediction results more accurate. The accuracy rate has decreased to a certain extent; during the recovery period of the epidemic, the accuracy rate of its electricity load forecasting slowly returned to normal.

Experimental Data of Three Exponential Smoothing. Use TES to for 2020 predict electricity consumption in different regions at different times, and also of short-term forecast, based on 2019 data to predict the next day's data and forecast data continuously generated by iteration to get 2020 years 1 month to 8 forecast data of the month, The error analysis between forecast data and actual data is summarized in the following tables (Tables 5, 6, 7 and 8).

Table 5. Data error table TES of company A.

Company A		
Period	Mean absolute error	Label
Pre epidemic period	48.28	High
Epidemic recovery period	246.36	Low
Epidemic peak	156.32	Low

Table 6. Data error table TES of company D.

Company D		
Period	Mean absolute error	Label
Pre epidemic period	89.52	High
Epidemic recovery period	219.35	Low
Epidemic peak	165.52	Low

Table 7. Data error table TES of company B.

Company B		
Period	Mean absolute error	Label
Pre epidemic period	139.27	High
Epidemic recovery period	217.39	Low
Epidemic peak	156.32	Low

Table 8. Data error table TES of company C.

Company C		
Period	Mean absolute error	Label
Pre epidemic period	139.27	High
Epidemic recovery period	472.41	Low
Epidemic peak	409.38	Low

The above is the error table summarized by the four parks using TES. Through calculation, 0.46, 0.35, 0.39, and 0.2 are obtained as the smoothing coefficients for the secondary exponential smoothing of Deloitte, company D and company A There is a certain degree of difference in errors between epidemic and non-epidemic periods.

4.5 Algorithm Analysis

The experiment in this paper uses the MAE between the predicted data and the actual data and the fitting curve of the predicted value and the actual value to measure the quality of the ES two methods in predicting the user's power load. Through the above two comparative experiments and the data characteristics of the four parks, it is found that TES is more suitable for predicting the electricity consumption of residents. During the non-epidemic period, the MAE between the predicted data and the actual data is small, and the comparison curve between the two is also similar. ES itself is a prediction method used to study TS, and different models are selected according to the different characteristics of its data. When using the ES method, the most important point is to select the appropriate parameters to get a higher prediction accuracy. This experiment is a short-term forecast, with a 15- minute interval as a one-day forecast. According to the trend sequence, seasonal sequence, and residual sequence, it is found that the data has the characteristics of periodicity and seasonality, which is in line with the scope of application of the algorithm in this paper.

However, this experiment has certain limitations. The data fitting effect during the epidemic is not good, and the impact of sudden factors on the power consumption of users is not taken into account, which makes the accuracy of the prediction results low and there is room for improvement.

5 Summary and Outlook

This experiment uses ES to predict the electricity load of users in the business circle. The predicted results can provide a certain reference for power grid companies and power plants, improve economic efficiency, maintain reliable power supply, and promote the development of new energy sources.

This article builds a forecasting model around the power load of the four parks in the Red Star business district, mines effective data and obtains useful information. In the experiment, the python language was used to establish a prediction model. According to the output data table and data picture, the data characteristics and the comparison curve between the prediction and the actual were displayed, and the superiority of the model was verified according to the experimental results.

This paper applies the time series to predict the user's power load, and the use of appropriate weights can more accurately predict the power consumption, but there are still some shortcomings in the experiment, and further research is needed. In the next step, we will explore the improvement of data mining under the influence of the long-term epidemic. The direction of exploration will shift from the commercial economic circle to the economic relevance of the urban economic circle and the industrial economy.

References

1. Huang, W., Zhang, Y., Huang, Y.: Research on power generation forecast of thermal power plant based on dynamic cubic exponential smoothing method. Mod. Electron. Technol. **43**(17), 147–154 (2020)

2. Fang, Y., Yu, F., Xiang, G., Wang, X.: The cubic exponential smoothing model based on grey theory predicts the f-CaO content of hot steel slag during natural aging. Bull. Chin. Ceram. Soc. **38**(03), 634–648 (2019)
3. Tang, G., Zhang, F., Lu, W., Peng, J., He, L., Li, Y.: Application of exponential smoothing method in the prediction of measles incidence. Pract. Prev. Med. **25**(06), 757–759 (2018)
4. Li, D.: Establishment and Realization of the Prediction Model for the Development Level of Modern Agricultural Equipment in Xinjiang Production and Construction Corps. Shihezi University, Xinjiang Uygur Autonomous Region (2016)
5. Xie, X., Zheng, Z., Wang, J., Chun, C.: Cloud forecast model based on exponential smoothing and cubic convolution time network. On Commun. **40**(08), 143–150 (2019)
6. Jia, M.: Research and Application of Time Series Analysis Method Based on Machine Learning. Xi'an University of Science and Technology, Shaanxi Province (2020)
7. Wei, S.: Forecast of air quality in Taiyuan city based on the triple exponential smoothing method. Sci. Educ. J. **27**, 167–169 (2019)
8. Cao, J.: Research on the Prediction Model of Expressway Traffic Flow. Zhejiang University of Science and Technology, Zhejiang Province (2020)
9. Tian, Y., Zhang, X., Cheng, G., Wang, N., Li, F.: Improved clustering and LSTM predicted long-term residential load. Henan Power **S2**, 58–63 (2020)
10. Wei, L., Zhang, J.: Study analysis electricity load based on the depth of belief networks. Electron. Des. Eng. **29**(04), 43–47 (2021)
11. Liu, W., Qin, Y., Dong, H., Yang, Y., Tian, Z.: Highway passenger traffic volume prediction of cubic exponential smoothing model based on grey system theory. In: 2nd International Conference on Soft Computing in Information Communication Technology. Atlantis Press (2014)
12. Gao, H., Zhang, D.: Fractal and three exponential smoothing traffic flow forecasting model. Nanjing Univ. Posts Telecommun. (Natural Science) **38**(06), 63–67 (2018)
13. Gong, X., Guo, J.: Based on cubic exponential smoothing shanghai brand auction monthly average price forecast. Univ. Shanghai Sci. Technol. **40**(01), 27–32 (2018)
14. Scotch, C.G., Murgulet, D., Constantz, J.: Time-series temperature analyses indicate conduction and diffusion are dominant heat-transfer processes in fine sediment, low-flow streams. Sci. Total Environ. **768** (2021)
15. Chen, A., Tong, L., Zheng, C., Xu, Z., Liu, Y., Xie, C.: Research on the economic development of business districts based on power data. Power Supply **38**(04), 6–10 (2021)

Research on Dynamic Monitoring of Train Running Part Using Integrated Detection System

Sha Wen[1]($\boxtimes$) (iD), Qingmao Ren[2], Yunzhi Shao[2], and Binhui Tang[1]

[1] Chengdu Jincheng University, Chengdu 610097, China
1677095905@qq.com
[2] Chengdu Senchuan Technology Co., Ltd., Chengdu 610041, China

Abstract. With the rapid development of the rail transit industry, the safety and reliability of train is a prerequisite to ensure the development of rail transit technology. In train maintenance work, the running part has many components and various reasons of failure, so how to detect breakdown for running part is always a prominent challenge in train maintenance work. Through the ground based integrated detection system for running train, data digging and analysis, machine learning algorithm, this paper researches the breakdown detection of two key transmission components: traction motor, gearbox. According to the root causes and characteristics of breakdown in above components, we design a breakdown detection system with an evaluation criteria to ensure that the system can detect the breakdown in train running part accurately in the early stage.

Keywords: Train running part · Dynamic monitoring · Thermal diagnosis · Noise monitoring · Infrared thermal imaging

1 Introduction

Along with the operation and large-scale construction of railway industry in China, the railway industry has entered a new era, it develops very fast with the direction of more automotive, more intelligence. At the same time, it is also facing a big challenge: how to ensure safety. According to the analysis of the causes of train accidents, most of them are caused by the breakdown of train parts, especially the transmission system and the running part of train [1], which is very critical to the lives of thousands of passengers. Because there is no skirt at the bottom of the train, all important equipment and parts at the bottom of the train are exposed, so the maintenance worker has to check all of those components. The current way of check is that maintenance workers check the status of those components by visual inspection in daily base only. In this way, only some visible serious faults can be found, and the initial faults of components cannot be investigated and found. In addition, due to the large number of parts in the whole train and the hidden location of some parts at the bottom of the train, it is very difficult to inspect all parts at the bottom of the train in daily maintenance, which may cause missed inspection and repair of those critical parts. Therefore, some faults can be found by the specific checking device in the periodic maintenance phase or overhaul stage [2] only. In recent years,

© The Author(s), under exclusive license to Springer Nature Switzerland AG 2022
X. Sun et al. (Eds.): ICAIS 2022, LNCS 13338, pp. 206–216, 2022.
https://doi.org/10.1007/978-3-031-06794-5_17

China has invested a lot of monitoring and detecting equipment and facilities in train stations, detection stations and line boundaries to ensure the safety of train operation, and these investment has played an important role in safety insurance. However, we need pay more attention on safety insurance work, such as, monitoring the working status of key components of train, timely troubleshooting hidden dangers, fault discovery at early stage and timely early warning danger, [3] remedying the disadvantages of conventional train maintenance approach, applying more and more complete, safe and reliable fault detection methods to the daily maintenance of train, then we can improve the operational efficiency and safety insurance capability of rail transit in China.

2 System Overview

According to the fault characteristics of key components of the train, the ground based integrated detection system for running train collects the information of temperature, image and noise for key components of train through different sensors, and analyzes the collected data with technologies such as optical thermal fusion and acoustic wave spectrum analysis, Through the big data analysis, we get one optimized fault detecting model for key components of train, finally realize the "ground" to "train" monitoring [4].

The ground based integrated detection system adopts modular design (as shown in Fig. 1), and the whole system is divided into four layers: perception layer, network layer, processing layer and application layer. Each layer uses the adjacent lower layer services, and the path of data flow is from bottom to top.

The perception layer of the system is composed of various intelligent sensors. Its main task is to collect the basic data of running train (including train number, ambient temperature and passing time), optical/thermal image data, vibration data and sound data, so that to generate effective original data for analysis. In order to monitor the breakdown of key components at the bottom of train when train is running, this system installs infrared thermal imaging sensors, optical imaging sensors and sound sensors beside the rail [5]. When train passes through the equipment on the rail, two optical and thermal combined cameras (as shown in Fig. 2) located between the rails collect the entire optical image data and thermal image data of the bottom parts of the train from the front and back angles. The sound sensors located between the rails (as shown in Fig. 3) collect the sound signals of the components at the left and right bottom of the train.

The network layer of this system uses the data communication network to provide multiple types and highly reliable data transmission channels for data. The processing layer mainly provides the storage and intelligent analysis of original data, analyzes and understands the original data through data interaction, distribution and mining technology, and generates advanced abstract data which is convenient for further analysis in the application layer. The application layer mainly provides two types of services: one is real-time monitoring for running train, which draws the temperature diagram of the bearings on both sides of the whole train according to the maximum temperature of each bearing on both sides of train, which intuitively reflects whether there is abnormal bearing in this train; The second is to provide the service of data analysis center, through in depth analysis of the data transmitted from the processing layer, diagnose the health

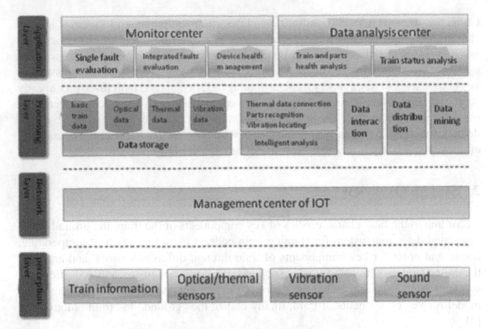

Fig. 1. Modules of system.

Fig. 2. Optical and thermal combined cameras.

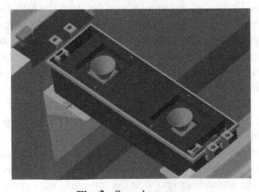

Fig. 3. Sound sensors.

status of train components according to different fault evaluation criteria, and find the hidden dangers of train components in advance.

3   Detection and Analysis of Breakdown on Running Parts of Train

During the running of train, the power and transmission parts provide power for the train. Its transmission principle is: the rotation of the traction motor drives the coupling to rotate, the coupling drives the gear in gearbox to rotate, and the gear drives the wheel set to rotate, then transmit the power for train. During the process of power transmission, the structure and performance of traction motor, coupling and gearbox at the bottom of train will directly affect the reliability, power and safety of train's operation. The failure causes and characteristics of two key components: traction motor and gearbox at the bottom of train, will be discussed in detail below. According to the different failure characteristics of different components, we will provide different failure detection approach and evaluation criteria.

3.1   Fault Detection of Traction Motor

Traction motor is the critical device of train operation. Its working principle is to convert electric energy into mechanical energy to provide power for train operation. Figure 4 is the picture of traction motor of train. Due to different structure and working environment of traction motor, the actual breakdowns caused by various failure are also different. At the early stage of traction motor breakdown, the traction motor will have different fault symptoms compared with normal status, such as abnormal noise and temperature [6]. Therefore, in order to find the failure of traction motor timely at early stage, we can monitor some specific indicators of traction motor, once we find out the different status, we can detect the fault of traction motor.

Fig. 4. Traction motor of train.

Since rolling bearings are usually used for traction motors of train, bearing is one of the parts where traction motor will breakdown [7]. When the bearing breakdowns, the bearing structure of the traction motor will be damaged, so the motor shaft will have abnormal sound and temperature. This system monitors the surface temperature and operation noise of running traction motor, consider these two indicators to judge if this traction motor has fault or not. [8] In order to collect the optical, thermal and acoustic data of traction motor, the system installs different sensors besides the rail [9]. When the train pass the device, the monitor range for traction motor is shown in Fig. 5.

Fig. 5. Monitor range for traction motor.

The system collects the surface temperature and generate thermal picture of traction motor through the integrated optical and thermal camera besides the rail. The thermal picture is shown in Fig. 6.

Fig. 6. Thermal picture of traction motor.

At the same time, the system has two sound sensors installed on the rail. System device collects the acoustic data generated by the running traction motor in real time by these two sound sensors under the motor and gear. We proceed huge amount of acoustic data: pre-processing, noise reduction and neural network model training, then establish an optimized fault evaluation model to realize the intelligent fault identification of motor.

The system gives different weight to thermal analysis result (temperature index TL) and acoustic analysis (sound index CL) result, then calculate the fault index (FL) using TL and CL. If the following fault evaluation criteria are met, the system will report the traction motor as a fault.

(1) breakdown alert: FL $\geq$ FLset; or the number of Continuous early warning is greater than or equal to Nset. Where FLset1 = 2.0, Nset = 3.
(2) early warning: FL $\geq$ FLset2. Where FLset2 = 1.0.

3.2 Fault Detection of Gearbox

As the power transmission device between traction motor and wheel set, gearbox is a key check point in maintenance work. The gearbox contains complex and wearing parts such as gears and rolling bearings. Since the gearbox transmits power and drives train, at same time supports the rotating parts of the gearbox [10], so normally it will have several faults, like: working flank peeling, scratching, corrosion, cracking and collision [11]. According to statistics, the parts failure ratio in the gearbox is shown in Table 1:

Table 1. Failure ratio of each part in gearbox.

Failure parts	Gear	Bearing	Rotation axis	Box	Fastening parts	Oil seal
Proportion	60%	19%	10%	7%	3%	1%

We can see from Table 1 that the failure of gear parts accounts for 60% of the total failure of gearbox, which is the major failure of gearbox [12]. There are several major faults will cause the gear breakdown, such as: broken teeth, pitting corrosion and abrasion. When the above faults occur, abnormal gear meshing noise will occur during train running, and bring in abnormal higher temperature at the gearbox [13]. Therefore, the fault detection principle of gearbox is the same as that of traction motor. Thermal data analysis and acoustic data analysis are used to evaluate and analyze the gearbox parts of running train. The monitor range of gearbox is shown in Fig. 7:

Fig. 7. Monitor range of gearbox.

The thermal and optical images of the gearbox can be generated through the integrated optical and thermal device besides the rail. The captured infrared thermal image of the gearbox is shown in Fig. 8:

Fig. 8. Infrared thermal image of gearbox.

At the same time, the system installs two sound sensors besides the rail. System device collects the acoustic data generated by the operation of the gearbox in real time [14]. We proceed huge amount of acoustic data: pre-processing, noise reduction and neural network model training, then establish an optimized fault evaluation model to realize the intelligent fault identification of gearbox, and give the sound index (CL).

The system gives different weight to thermal analysis result (temperature index TL) and acoustic analysis (sound index CL) result, then calculate the fault index (FL) using TL and CL. If the fault index of one gearbox ≥ FLset (FLset = 3.0), the system will report this gearbox as a breakdown gearbox.

4   Research on Key Technologies

4.1   Optical-Thermal Fusion Technology

The fusion of optical-gram and thermal-gram is to use machine vision technology to map the key parts in an optical diagram to the corresponding area in a thermal diagram.

We assume that a position matrix for each pixel in an optical diagram of the surface of key parts is expressed as below:

$$
\begin{bmatrix}
w_{11} & w_{12} & \cdots & w_{1n} \\
w_{21} & w_{22} & \cdots & w_{2n} \\
\cdots & \cdots & \cdots & \cdots \\
w_{m1} & w_{m2} & \cdots & w_{mn}
\end{bmatrix}
$$

where, Wmn represents the position coordinates of the pixel in row m and column n in the optical diagram of the key parts.

Furthermore, the position matrix of each pixel in the thermal diagram of same parts is expressed as below:

$$
\begin{bmatrix}
I_{11} & I_{12} & \cdots & I_{1n} \\
I_{21} & I_{22} & \cdots & I_{2n} \\
\cdots & \cdots & \cdots & \cdots \\
I_{m1} & I_{m2} & \cdots & I_{mn}
\end{bmatrix}
$$

where, Imn represents the position coordinates of the pixel in row m and column n in the thermal diagram of same parts.

Furthermore, we install the optical sensor and thermal sensor in a constant distance, when train passes them in a certain speed, the position gap of same pixel in optical diagram and thermal diagram is a constant:

$$I_{ij} = W_{ij} + I$$

where, Iij represents the coordinate of pixel (i, j) in the thermal diagram of key parts, Wij represents the coordinate of pixel (i, j) in the optical diagram of same parts, I represents the position gap of same pixel in both diagrams, it's a constant too.

In this way, the optical-thermal data can be displayed visually, as shown in below Fig. 9:

Fig. 9. Optical-thermal fusion image.

4.2 Optical Fiber Vibration Detection Technology

In order to collect noise data of key parts in train, we use optical fiber vibration sensor, it is a vibration sensing demodulation scheme based on 3 × 3 couplers. We can realize the passive homodyne phase demodulation of interferometric optical fiber sensor with phase demodulation method of 3 × 3 couplers. Compared with other phase demodulation technologies, the advantage is this approach does not need any modulation component; has larger dynamic range of demodulated signal; can realize all optical fiber sensing.

The structure of this module is shown in Fig. 10. The light injected from the laser reaches 3 × 3 coupler after passing through the circulator C1, divided into two beams of light into Faraday rotating mirror and vibrating film respectively. The unused branch of the 3 × 3 coupler is used to eliminate reflection. One beam of light is reflected back after entering the Faraday rotating mirror by the coupler, and the other beam of light is transmitted to the mass block through the optical fiber. Under the external vibration, the reflective film will undergo elastic deformation. The reflected light carries the external information back to the coupler from the optical fiber and interferes with the light reflected from the Faraday rotating mirror in the coupler. The interference

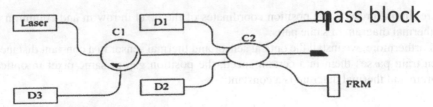

Fig. 10. Fiber vibration sensor based on 3 × 3 coupler.

light is divided into three beams, two of them are received by detector 1 and detector 2 respectively, and the third beam reaches detector 3 through circulator.

3 channels of signals to be demodulated can be expressed as:

$$I_n = A + B \cdot cos\left[\varphi(t) - \frac{2\pi}{3}(n-1)\right]$$

(1) Where, I is the intensity of three output signals, A and B are the light intensity coefficients, where n = 1,2,3, $\varphi(t) = \Phi(t) - \psi(t)$, $\varphi(t)$ is the vibration signal, $\psi(t)$ is the phase error caused by environmental changes. Multiply the sum of the three signals by – 1/3, and add it to each I respectively to remove the DC component of the signal, then we can get:

$$\begin{cases} a = Bcos\varphi(t) \\ b = Bcos\left[\varphi(t) - \frac{2\pi}{3}\right] \\ b = Bcos\left[\varphi(t) - \frac{4\pi}{3}\right] \end{cases}$$

(2) Multiply each one of three channels of signal removed DC component by the differential difference of the other two channels, we can get:

$$\begin{cases} d = \sqrt{3}B^2\dot{\varphi}(t)cos^2\varphi(t) \\ e = \sqrt{3}B^2\dot{\varphi}(t)cos^2\left[\varphi(t) - \frac{2\pi}{3}\right] \\ f = \sqrt{3}B^2\dot{\varphi}(t)cos^2\left[\varphi(t) - \frac{4\pi}{3}\right] \end{cases}$$

(3) Add the d,e,f three signals together, we can get:

$$Q = d + e + f = \frac{3\sqrt{3}B^2}{2}\dot{\varphi}(t)$$

(4) In formula 4, there is an uncertainty factor B. we can construct a sum of squares of three signals removed DC component as below:

$$\begin{cases} M = a^2 + b^2 + c^2 = \frac{3B^2}{2} \\ P = \frac{Q}{M} = \sqrt{3}\dot{\varphi}(t) \end{cases}$$

(5) In this way can remove the influence of uncertain factor B, finally we can demodulate and get the vibration signal by integrating P. As shown in the Fig. 11:

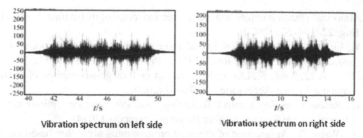

Vibration spectrum on left side   Vibration spectrum on right side

Fig. 11. Vibration spectrum.

When the useful vibration signal is obtained, we can use the pattern recognition method of machine learning to find the suspicious fault signal spectrum. This is different from the traditional practice. The working principle of traditional TP mostly starts with modulation, filtering, separation of frequency domain and amplitude direction; Pattern recognition will start from the whole, use the original data and confirmed fault data collected by the TP system of the Railway Bureau, and find out the fault mode through the machine recognition SVN classification algorithm.

5 Summary

Currently, the rail transit industry is still in the stage of rapid development. Ensuring the operation safety of train and timely discovering train's faults at early stage are the key challenges that the industry needs to break through. Based on the ground based integrated detection system, this paper makes an in-depth research on the dynamic monitoring of train running parts. By installing the various sensors between rails, the system can completely monitor the acoustic, optical, thermal and other data of the key parts at the bottom of the running train. The original data is transmitted to the remote data analysis center for analysis and processing through the data communication network to obtain the fault information of parts. The paper also analyzes the fault root causes and characteristics of the traction motor, gearbox at the bottom of train, and gives different faultw detection schemes and fault evaluation criteria for above key parts, so as to ensure that the system can accurately identify and analyze the breakdown parts at the bottom of train and find the hidden dangers of train faults in time, It provides a big technical help for the maintenance and repair of train.

References

1. Liu, Z., Tang, N., Lv, M.: Breakthrough and innovation of key parts of rail transit equipment. China Ind. Inf. **10**, 42–47 (2020)
2. Hua, L., Xie, Q., Liu, C., Liu, C., Liu, F.: Research on real-time monitoring and analysis system of urban rail transit vehicles. Urban Fast Rail Transit **33**(01), 134–138 (2020)
3. Song, J.: Condition monitoring system of urban rail transit vehicles and equipment. Railway Comput. Appl. **30**(02), 68–73 (2021)
4. Zhou, Q.: Research on Reliability Analysis and Maintenance Mode Decision of Metro Bogie system. Beijing Jiaotong University (2019)

5. Li, Y.: Abnormal vibration in maintenance of traction motor of metro train. Electron. Technol. Softw. Eng. **22**, 199–200 (2020)
6. Ding, Y., Liao, A.: Study on reliability of rolling bearing of traction motor of rail transit vehicle bogie. Urban Rail Transit Res. **22**(06), 115–119 (2019)
7. Cheng, H., Wu, L., Song, S., Liu, J.: Research on fault diagnosis method of traction motor. Intern. Combust. Engine Accessories **14**, 76–77 (2020)
8. Zhao, L.: Research on Key Control Technology and Performance Optimization of Metro Traction Electric Drive System. Beijing Jiaotong University (2014)
9. Wang, X., Wang, Q.: Application of dynamic programming algorithm based on model predictive control in hybrid electric vehicle control strategy. J. Internet Things **2**(2), 81–87 (2020)
10. Yang, G.P., Joshi, C.: Seo: Improving the detection rate of rarely appearing intrusions in network-based intrusion detection systems. Comput. Mater. Continua **66**(2), 1647–1663 (2021)
11. Haider, A., Khan, M.A., Rehman, A., Rahman, M.U., Kim, H.S.: A real-time sequential deep extreme learning machine cybersecurity intrusion detection system. Comput. Mater. Continua **66**(2), 1785–1798 (2021)
12. Jin, L., Meng, Q., Liang, S.: Operation optimal control of urban rail train based on multi-objective particle swarm optimization. Comput. Syst. Sci. Eng. **42**(1), 387–395 (2022)
13. Jin, L., Meng, Q., Liang, S.: Model of a composite energy storage system for urban rail trains. Comput. Syst. Sci. Eng. **40**(3), 1145–1152 (2022)

Identification of Terrace Boundaries from DEMs Using Multidirectional Hill-Shading

Peng Liu[1], Kai Zeng[2], Ji Dai[2], and Wen Dai[3,4(✉)]

[1] School of Marine Technology and Surveying and Mapping, Jiangsu Ocean University, Lianyungang 222000, China
[2] Department of Industrial and Mining Architecture, Bijie Vocational and Technical College, Bijie 551700, China
[3] School of Geographical Sciences, Nanjing University of Information Science and Technology, Nanjing 210044, China
dwdaerte@163.com
[4] Institute of Earth Surface Dynamics (IDYST), University of Lausanne, 1015 Lausanne, Switzerland

Abstract. Mapping and monitoring terraces are important for maintaining agricultural production and evaluating soil-and-water conservation. However, mapping all boundaries of individual terraces is still a challenge. In this study, a multidirectional hill-shading method based on digital elevation models (DEMs) is proposed for terrace boundary mapping. First, hill-shading in four directions was simulated using 1-m DEM. Second, the mean brightness image of four hill-shading maps was calculated. Meanwhile, according to the brightness difference between terrace boundaries and terrace areas, a threshold was used to identify terrace boundaries from the mean brightness image. Third, loess shoulder lines extracted by the positive-negative terrain method were used to remove non-terraced areas (noise area). Finally, terrace boundaries were obtained by vectorization and compared with reference data. Results from two study areas in the Loess Plateau of China show that the producer's accuracy (PA) and user's accuracy (UA) ranged from 80.07% to 83.08% and 75.42% to 78.17%, respectively. The proposed method is practicable and applicable for terrace boundary mapping. This work is beneficial to terraced land maintenance, agricultural production management, and monitoring soil erosion.

Keywords: Terrace boundaries · Shade relief · Digital elevation model (DEM) · Multidirectional hill-shading · Linear feature detection · Terrain analysis

1 Introduction

Agricultural terraces are beneficial to agricultural production as well as soil-and-water conservation [1, 2]. Compared with slope land, terraces enhance water infiltration, reduce soil erosion risks, and improve biodiversity by increasing landscape diversity [3, 4]. Due to these advantages, terraces are widely distributed around the world.

© The Author(s), under exclusive license to Springer Nature Switzerland AG 2022
X. Sun et al. (Eds.): ICAIS 2022, LNCS 13338, pp. 217–226, 2022.
https://doi.org/10.1007/978-3-031-06794-5_18

Detecting and mapping terrace is important for maintaining agricultural production and evaluating soil-and-water conservation. Field investigation and visual interpretation [5, 6] are the most classical methods since they are simple, direct, and highly accurate. However, it's time-consuming, costly and unsuitable for long-term monitoring in large areas.

Recently, with the advances in remote sensing technology [7–11], some image-based methods were proposed for automatic detection of terraces. These methods can be summarized into two categories: 1) pixel-based method [12–15]. This method is achieved by using spectral, shape, and textural features from imagery. The performance of pixel-based method is easily affected by land covers; 2) Object-based image analysis (OBIA) [16–18]. The OBIA method is superior to pixel-based method because the analysis unit transfers from pixels to objects [19, 20]. OBIA improved the classification accuracy by combining spectral information with spatial information of target features [21].

While the classification accuracy of image-based methods has been greatly improved, the three-dimensional features of terraces cannot be measured from images. However, most of image-based methods only focused on terrace area mapping and failed to outline all boundaries for individual pieces. Terraces are always at risk from gully or gravity erosion [22, 23]. Changes in each individual terrace boundary are a significant sign of erosion occurs. Hence, detecting all boundaries of terraces is crucial for terrace mapping.

With the continuous improvement and development of the technology and method of digital elevation model (DEM), digital terrain analysis methods have been widely used in various industries. Early DEMs have low resolution (e.g., 30 m SRTM DEM) that cannot capture the terrace boundaries. The development of unmanned Aerial Vehicle (UAV) has made it possible to quickly obtain high-resolution DEMs, which records the information of the terrace pieces.

Hill-shading, also known as shade relief, is a mature technique for terrain expression enhancement based on digital elevation models (DEMs) [24]. It has been successfully applied to topographic feature extraction in recent years [25, 26], which shows the potential for terrace boundaries mapping. Accordingly, this paper aimed to develop a terrace boundaries mapping method based on hill-shading.

2   Areas and Data

Two study areas located in the Loess Plateau of China were employed to develop the method (Fig. 1). The Wucheng area (39°16′28.15″N, 111°34′26.06″E) located in Pianguan County, Shanxi Province, with elevations ranging from 1238 to 1450 m, covering 0.32 km^2. The other site, the Zhifang area (36°43′46.59″N, 109°14′49.01″E), located in southern Ansai County, Shaanxi Province, with elevations ranging from 1129 to 1415 m, covering 3.42 km^2.

The 1-m DEMs and 0.3-m digital orthophoto maps (DOMs) for the two areas were obtained by unmanned aerial vehicle (UAV) photogrammetry. The DEM of the Zhifang area was generated on 15 March 2016 and the UAV used in this area was a quadcopter platform with vertical take-off and landing (VTOL), model md4–1000 (microdrones GmbH, Siegen, Germany). The DEM of the Wucheng area was generated on 27 April 2018. The UAV used in this area was a quadcopter platform with VTOL, model inspire-1pro (SZ DJI Technology Co., Ltd., Shenzhen, China).

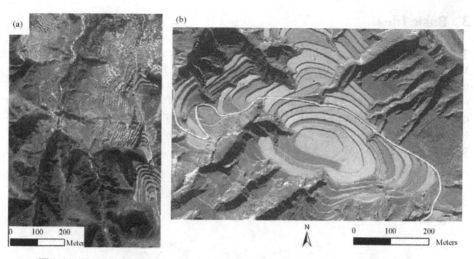

Fig. 1. Study area: (a – b) are image of Zhifang and Wucheng areas, respectively.

The terraces are mostly distributed around the top of the mountain or on the slopes, the original terrain usually has a certain slope, and the modified terraces are usually flat and straight, which can usually be divided into horizontal terraces, slope terraces, and reverse slope terraces, but either one has the following characteristics: 1) General characteristics of terraces The terraced terrain has three characteristics: "inheritance, regularity, and variability". The terraced terrain is gradually formed by artificially modifying various natural slope terrains. Although the slope and slope length of the original slope have been changed to a large extent, in the overall morphology of the slope, the macroscopic topographic characteristics of the original natural slope are still maintained, and the general pattern of terrain undulating has not changed, and all the transformations are only changes to the microscopic morphology of the ground. Therefore, the terraced terrain has the inheritance of natural terrain. The artificially modified terraced terrain is characterized by flat extension and arrangement rules in the horizontal direction, and step-like undulation in the vertical direction, and the height of the terraced fields of each class is basically the same, with obvious regularity. Terraces are often located on hillside slopes, which are strongly affected by the erosion of gully traceability, and once a terraced field collapses, it will often produce a domino effect, resulting in the destruction of the entire slope terraces. Changes in land use types will also change the terraces. Therefore, its morphology and distribution have certain instabilities over time, that is, the terraced terrain is volatile. 2) Measurable features: The terraced surface is flat and straight, and there are often relatively clear boundary lines; the terraced surface has no slope (horizontal terraces) or a small slope (slope terraces, reverse slope terraces); the terraced field slope surface is non-flat; the terraced field ridge often has a large slope.

3   Basic Idea

The brightness degree of a hill-shading map is influenced by surface slope and aspect. When the simulated light shines on the terrace area, the brightness difference between terrace boundary and area is obvious, as the slope is generally very high in the boundary (Fig. 2). The brightness difference can be used for identifying terrace boundaries. However, terraces are generally distributed on different sides of hillslope (Fig. 2). in order to detect terrace boundaries as complete as possible, the multidirectional hill-shading method was proposed.

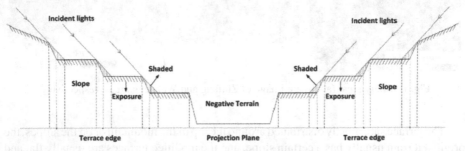

Fig. 2. Diagram of hill-shading.

The DEM hill-shading method is usually to calculate the relative radiation value of each grid cell which can represent by illumination or greyscale [25]. The commonly used formula is as follow [27]:

$$E = 255 \times (\cos \theta_z \times \cos \emptyset_s + \sin \theta_z \times \sin \emptyset_s \times \cos(\theta_A - \emptyset_A)) \tag{1}$$

where E is the brightness degree; θ_z and θ_A is the simulated zenith and aspect angle, respectively; $\emptyset_s$ and $\emptyset_A$ is slope and aspect degree of local terrain, respectively.

The illumination shading simulation results in a light-exposed, backlit surface darkening, and the degree of brightness and darkness is affected by the slope and aspect of the surface.

According to the morphological characteristics of the terraced terrain, the surface of the terraces is usually flat and straight, while the ridges are steeper and non-straight, so when simulating the dim sum of the DEM, the simulation results usually show a clear contrast between light and dark. By means of a series of operations such as threshold segmentation and length filtering of the halo difference between the terraced surface and the terraced field, the terraced field can be automatically identified and extracted, as shown in Fig. 1. At the same time, when the azimuth of the light source simulated by the illumination halo is changed to the opposite direction, the slopes on both sides of the valley can be automatically extracted, as shown in Fig. 2. In order to ensure that the fields of different aspects can be well extracted, two pairs of orthogonal directions of the light source, that is, four directions of the light source simulation.

4   Workflow

The workflow of the multidirectional hill-shading method is shown in Fig. 3 as follows:

(I)   Hill-shading in four directions was simulated using DEM. In order to identify terrace boundaries as much as possible, the four aspect angles used in the simulation should be perpendicular to each other, such as 45°, 135°, 225°, 315°.

(II)   The mean brightness image of four hill-shading maps was calculated. Then, terrace boundaries can be clearly observed in the image due to its low brightness. According to the brightness difference between the terrace boundary and terrace area, a threshold was used to identify terrace boundary form the mean image. The threshold formula is as follow:

$$t = 180 - d \tag{2}$$

where t is the threshold; d is the standard deviation of the mean image

(III)   After threshold segmentation, the result was a binary image, where value 1 means terrace boundaries, and value 0 means background. However, some noise remained in the image. Hence, loess shoulder lines extracted by the positive-negative terrain method [28] were used to remove non-terraced areas (noise area). The final results were obtained by vectorization of the segmented binary image.

(IV)   The DOMs were used to generated reference data by visual interpretation. The performance of the proposed method was validated by comparing its results with the reference data. Producer's accuracy (PA) and User's accuracy (UA) [29, 30], which have been widely used in assessing the accuracy of feature identification, were employed in this study. In order to calculate the indices, the detection results (raster) are converted to vector by ArcGIS 10.5. Then, a buffer is constructed around each reference boundary. Given the DEM resolution was 1 m, the extracted boundaries that fall within the 1 m buffer zone are regarded as "correct detection"; otherwise, called "incorrect detection". Finally, we can calculate these indices. The formulas are as follows:

$$PA = \frac{L_m}{L_e} \tag{3}$$

$$UA = \frac{L_m}{L_r} \tag{4}$$

where L_m indicates correct detection and is the total length of the extracted risers that match the reference risers; L_r is the total length of the reference boundaries; L_e is the total length of the extracted boundaries.

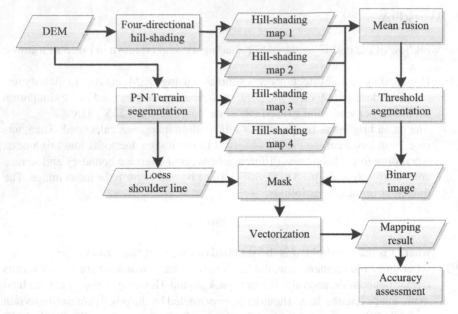

Fig. 3. Workflow.

5 Results and Discussion

In this study, the zenith angle of illumination source was 45°, and the aspect angles were 45°, 135°, 225°, and 315°, respectively (Fig. 4a-d). The brightness of hill-shading maps varied with the aspect angle changing. However, the brightness difference between the terrace boundary and area always existed. After mean fusion (Fig. 4e) and threshold segmentation, terrace boundaries can be clearly observable in the binary image (Fig. 4f).

The final mapping results were obtained by vectorization of the binary image. Most of terrace boundaries were correctly detected (Fig. 5). In order to validate the performance of the multidirectional hill-shading method, 1-m buffer zone of reference data was generated because the DEM resolution was 1 m. When extracted terrace boundaries fell within the 1-m buffer zone of reference data, it was regarded as 'correct detection'; otherwise, they were termed as an 'incorrect detection'. Then, two indices i.e. producer's accuracy (PA) and user's accuracy (UA) were employed for quantitative accuracy assessment. As Table 1 shows, The PA and UA ranged from 80.07% to 83.08% and 75.42% to 78.17%, respectively. The acceptable results validated the applicability of the multidirectional hill-shading method.

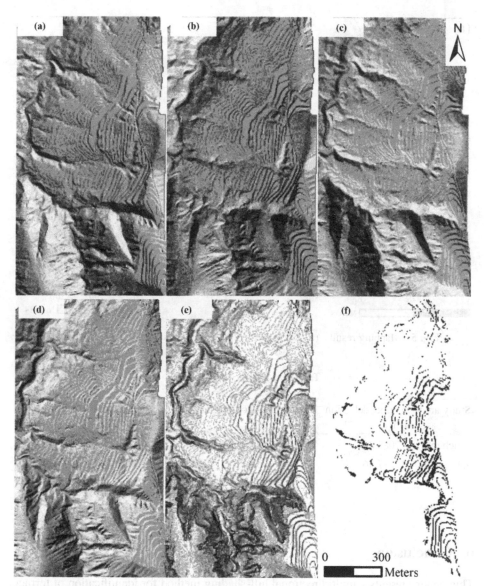

Fig. 4. Hill-shading results in Zhifang area: (a - d) hill-shading map with aspect of 45°, 135°, 225° and 315°, respectively; (e) mean image; (f) segmented binary image.

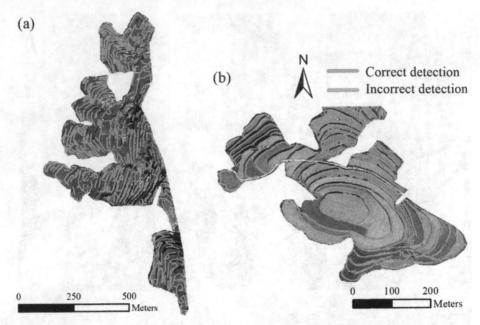

Fig. 5. Mapping results: (a - b) result of Zhifang and Wucheng area, respectively.

Table 1. Accuracy assessment.

Study area	Correct detection (m)	Incorrect detection (m)	Reference data (m)	PA (%)	UA (%)
Wucheng	7088.83	8532.72	9068.60	83.08	78.17
Zhifang	20217.46	25249.20	26806.36	80.07	75.42

6 Conclusion

This paper presents a multidirectional hill-shading method for identification of terrace boundaries from DEMs. Results from two study areas in the Loess Plateau of China show that the PA and UA ranged from 80.07% to 83.08% and 75.42% to 78.17%, respectively. The proposed method is practicable and applicable for terrace boundary mapping.

In the process of implementing the proposed method, parameters, such as the height angle, azimuth angle and threshold segmentation, are involved. to improve the applicability of the method, this paper analyzes the parameters and gives the method of parameter determination, which provides an operable basis for the application of the method in other regions.

This work is beneficial to terraced land maintenance, agricultural production management, and monitoring soil erosion.

Conflicts of Interest. The authors declare that they have no conflicts of interest to report regarding the present study.

Funding Statement. We are grateful for the financial support provided by the National Natural Science Foundation of China [grant numbers 41771415 and 41871313].

References

1. Gao, H., Li, Z., Li, P., Jia, L., Zhang, X.: Quantitative study on influences of terraced field construction and check-dam siltation on soil erosion. J. Geog. Sci. **22**, 946–960 (2012)
2. European-Commission: The Common Agricultural Policy: A Partnership Between Europe and Farmers, p. 16. Publications Office of the European Union Luxembourg (2012)
3. Fu, B.: Soil erosion and its control in the Loess Plateau of China. Soil Use Manag. **5**, 76–82 (1989)
4. Van Wesemael, B., Poesen, J., Benet, A.S., Barrionuevo, L.C., Puigdefabregas, J.: Collection and storage of runoff from hillslopes in a semi-arid environment: geomorphic and hydrologic aspects of the aljibe system in Almeria Province. Spain. Journal of Arid Environments **40**, 1–14 (1998)
5. Liu, X.Y., Yang, S.T., Wang, F.G., Xing-Zhao, H.E., Hong-Bin, M.A., Luo, Y.: Analysis on sediment yield reduced by current terrace and shrubs-herbs-arbor vegetation in the Loess Plateau. J. Hydraul. Eng. **45**, 1293–1300 (2014)
6. Agnoletti, M., et al.: Traditional landscape and rural development: comparative study in three terraced areas in northern, central and southern Italy to evaluate the efficacy of GAEC standard 4.4 of cross compliance. Italian J. Agrono. **6**, 16 (2011)
7. Mao, Y., Li, K., Mao, D.: Application of wireless network positioning technology based on gps in geographic information measurement. Journal of New Media **2**, 131–135 (2020)
8. Lotfy, K., El-Bary, A.A., Tayel, I., Alebraheem, J., Asad, S.: The hyperbolic two temperature semiconducting thermoelastic waves by laser pulses. Computers, Materials and Continua **67**, 3601–3618 (2021)
9. Brezulianu, A., Geman, O., Arif, M., Chiuchisan, I., Wang, G.: Epidemiologic evolution platform using integrated modeling and geographic information system. Computers, Materials and Continua **67**, 1645–1663 (2021)
10. Arputham, C., Nagappan, K., Russeliah, L.B., Russeliah, A.S.: Mammographic image classification using deep neural network for computer-aided diagnosis. Intel. Automa. Soft Compu. **27**, 747–759 (2021)
11. Renukadevi, T., Saraswathi, K., Prabu, P., Venkatachalam, K.: Brain image classification using time frequency extraction with histogram intensity similarity. Comp. Sys. Sci. Eng. **41**, 645–660 (2022)
12. Li, Y., Gong, J., Wang, D., An, L., Li, R.: Sloping farmland identification using hierarchical classification in the Xi-He region of China. Int. J. Remote Sens. **34**, 545–562 (2013)
13. Martínez-Casasnovas, J.A., Ramos, M.C., Cots-Folch, R.: Influence of the EU CAP on terrain morphology and vineyard cultivation in the Priorat region of NE Spain. Land Use Policy **27**, 11–21 (2010)
14. Dai, W., Hu, G., Huang, N., Zhang, P., Yang, X., Tang, G.: A contour-directional detection for deriving terrace ridge from open source images and digital elevation models. IEEE Access **7**, 129215–129224 (2019)
15. Pal, N.R., Pal, S.K.: A review on image segmentation techniques. Pattern Recogn. **26**, 1277–1294 (1993)

16. Zhao, H., et al.: Extraction of terraces on the Loess Plateau from high-resolution DEMs and imagery utilizing object-based image analysis. ISPRS Int. J. Geo Inf. **6**, 157 (2017)
17. Diaz-Varela, R., Zarco-Tejada, P.J., Angileri, V., Loudjani, P.: Automatic identification of agricultural terraces through object-oriented analysis of very high resolution DSMs and multi-spectral imagery obtained from an unmanned aerial vehicle. J. Environ. Manage. **134**, 117–126 (2014)
18. Li, M., Stein, A., Bijker, W., Zhan, Q.: Region-based urban road extraction from VHR satellite images using binary partition tree. Int. J. Appl. Earth Obs. Geoinf. **44**, 217–225 (2016)
19. Duro, D.C., Franklin, S.E., Dubé, M.G.: A comparison of pixel-based and object-based image analysis with selected machine learning algorithms for the classification of agricultural landscapes using SPOT-5 HRG imagery. Remote Sens. Environ. **118**, 259–272 (2012)
20. Blaschke, T.: Object based image analysis for remote sensing. ISPRS J. Photogramm. Remote. Sens. **65**, 2–16 (2010)
21. Drăguţ, L., Tiede, D., Levick, S.R.: ESP: a tool to estimate scale parameter for multiresolution image segmentation of remotely sensed data. Int. J. Geogr. Inf. Sci. **24**, 859–871 (2010)
22. Wen, Y., Gao, P., Xingmin, M.U., Zhao, G., Sun, W.: Effect of rainfall intensity on rill erosion on terrace wall. Research of Soil & Water Conservation **25**, 6–10 (2018)
23. Dai, W., et al.: Integrated edge detection and terrain analysis for agricultural terrace delineation from remote sensing images. Int. J. Geogr. Inf. Sci. **34**, 484–503 (2020)
24. Horn, B.K., Schunck, B.G.: Determining optical flow. In: 1981 Technical symposium east, pp. 319–331. International Society for Optics and Photonics (1981)
25. Na, J., et al.: Bidirectional DEM relief shading method for extraction of gully shoulder line in loess tableland area. Phys. Geogr. **39**, 368–386 (2018)
26. Yang, X., Li, M., Na, J., Liu, K.: Gully boundary extraction based on multidirectional hill-shading from high-resolution DEMs. Trans. GIS **21**, 1204–1216 (2017)
27. Yoëli, P.: The mechanisation of analytical hill shading. Cartogr. J. **4**, 82–88 (1967)
28. Zhou, Y., Tang, G., Yang, X., Xiao, C., Zhang, Y., Luo, M.: Positive and negative terrains on northern Shaanxi Loess Plateau. J. Geog. Sci. **20**, 64–76 (2010)
29. Mäkinen, V., Oksanen, J., Sarjakoski, T.J.I.J.o.G.I.S.: Automatic determination of stream networks from DEMs by using road network data to locate culverts. **33**, 291–313 (2019)
30. Schütze, H., Manning, C.D., Raghavan, P.: Introduction to information retrieval. Cambridge University Press (2008)

Graph Regularization Based Multi-view Dictionary Learning for Person Re-Identification

Yang Dai[✉] and Zhiyuan Luo

Nanjing University of Information Science and Technology, Nanjing 210044, China
zgjsycfndy2015@163.com

Abstract. Person re-identification (re-ID) is an attractive task, while it has not yet reached the realistic applications. Most existing re-ID methods based on supervised scenario achieve satisfactory performance, which is mainly due to the requirement for a large number of paired-annotated training images with cross cameras. Nonetheless, this limits their generalization ability in real-world scene because of the huge annotation cost. We propose a graph regularization based dictionary learning for unsupervised re-ID. Specifically, in order to alleviate the difference between different cameras, we first project the samples under different cameras into a common space through asymmetric projections, i.e., specific projection for each camera. Then we construct a constraint item which is called Laplacian regularization via the visual similarity matrix to exploit the cross-view identity-discriminative information. In addition, we also extend our model to multi-view scene which aims at learning different dictionary for various visual features due to the confidence of the similarity matrix constructed from a single view is limited. In our experiments, the effectiveness of the proposed method has been manifested on several re-ID datasets.

Keywords: Unsupervised person re-identification · Laplacian graph regularization

1 Introduction

Person re-identification (re-ID) [10,14] is a task that attempts to retrieve a person of interest across multiple non-overlapping cameras, which is playing a major role in smart city and security monitoring system. Today it is still considered being an open problem, the matching accuracy of re-ID mainly influenced by several factors, such as lighting, posture, viewing angle and occlusion variation. Previous researches focus on supervised learning, a common solution is to learn a discriminative metric [2,22,38,47,56] by minimizing the within-class distances and simultaneously maximizing the between-class distances, or develop a non-linear version by kernel trick [7,27,51] for further enhancements. However, numerous labelled training images need to be taken in this situation which

© The Author(s), under exclusive license to Springer Nature Switzerland AG 2022
X. Sun et al. (Eds.): ICAIS 2022, LNCS 13338, pp. 227–239, 2022.
https://doi.org/10.1007/978-3-031-06794-5_19

depends on manual labeling, accordingly these supervised methods cannot be applied straight in the real-world scenario.

To directly make use of the cheap unlabeled pedestrian images taken by the surveillance camera network, some unsupervised methods [17,53,59] have been proposed, but the recognition effect is obviously lower than the supervised one. In the absence of the supervision of paired pedestrian images, it is tough for the model to effectively model the huge discrepancy between cameras. Regrettably, all manual-/deep-descriptors cannot extract the "essential characteristics" of pedestrian image, i.e., features that are truly unrelated to the variations of lighting, posture, viewing angle or occlusion which are mostly caused by cross-camera setting.

In our paper, we introduce asymmetric projection transformation to explicitly project pedestrian images captured by different cameras into a common subspace to alleviate the distribution divergence, and then use dictionary learning to achieve high-quality discriminative semantic features of pedestrian images. Due to the lack of identity labels, we can only use visual similarity to mine the potential category discrimination information of pedestrian images across different cameras by injecting a Laplacian regularization into the dictionary learning objective function. Considering that the discrimination learned from a single-view is limited, we learn multiple dictionary models guided by several visual features, thus a higher accuracy can be attained. This is because different visual features concern about particular characteristics of pedestrian images, e.g., some pay attention to the colour level information, the matching results given by the corresponding model are more similar in colour, and some pay attention to the texture level information, thus the results given by the corresponding model are more similar in texture. In this way, the matching result voted jointly by all models may be more precise. The contributions we make can be summarized in two aspects:

(1) We propose a graph regularization based dictionary learning model for unsupervised person re-ID. Our model learns cross-view asymmetric projections for each camera and maps original samples into a common space such that the identity-discriminative information can be preserved.

(2) We extend our model to learn several dictionaries from multiple feature views to give voting jointly. Because multi-view features of an image can be transformed into several codings with inhomogeneity discriminability, their combination can help provide a better matching result (Fig. 1).

2   Related Work

2.1   Supervised Person Re-ID

Researchers mainly concern about the performance improvement of supervised person re-identification in which a host of labeled cross-camera pedestrian image pairs are needed. Traditional methods mainly focus on two research directions, including feature extraction [5,34,35] and metric learning [22,47]. The former attempts to extract or learn invariant and discriminative person features, the latter aims to learn a metric matrix that can effectively reflect the relation

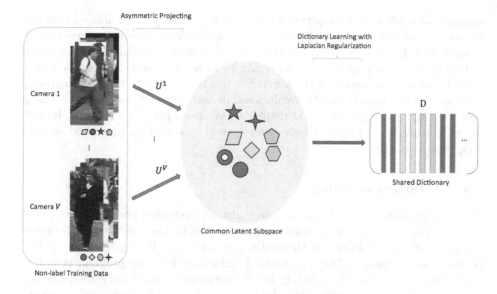

Fig. 1. Single-view learning process.

(distance or similarity) between data samples, consequently the distribution of the same class samples can be more compact, and the distribution of the different class samples can be further far away in the new feature space based on the learned metric matrix. Since deep learning shined in the ImageNet Challenge, it has been utilized widely in person re-identification. A series of re-ID models [3,55] based on CNN networks have been subsequently proposed, from representation learning [25,54] to local feature learning [31,42], and then attention mechanism [20,21,46] has also been assembled, the deep learning method has refreshed the matching accuracy over and over again, but deep learning models need to be fully trained on a large-scale dataset, and a small training set may cause the model to collapse.

2.2   Unsupervised Person Re-ID

The earliest traditional unsupervised methods try to design descriptors manually [4,8,22] that have invariant properties to environment variations, e.g., paper [22] proposes a local maximum occurrence descriptor, which maximizes the occurrence of local features in horizontal stripes to make a stable representation against illumination and viewpoint changes. After obtaining the features, we can do matching instantly but with extremely poor performance. Hence, some researches [58,59] try to do significance analysis to find more accurate matching images that belong to the same pedestrian, e.g., paper [59] intensively divides the image into blocks by slide window and extracts 32-dimensional LAB color histogram and 128-dimensional SIFT [30] descriptor from each block, then uses adjacency constrained patch matching to build salience map for each image to support accurate matching between image pairs. Different from above handcraft features, some researches [16,17] try to learn advanced semantic features by dictionary learning, e.g., paper [17] introduces a Laplacian regularization term into the dictionary learning framework, trying to mine the potential positive image pairs by iteratively updating the similarity matrix. Owing to the deep learning, especially the development of convolutional neural networks, some deep learning based unsupervised person re-ID methods have been proposed recently, including clustering-based pseudo labels generation [11,24] and unsupervised domain adaptation [12,36].

2.3   Dictionary Learning

Dictionary learning algorithm aims to learn an over-complete dictionary, that each original training signal can be approximated by the linear combination of a few atoms, i.e., columns in the dictionary. Let $X = [x_1, x_2, ..., x_m] \in R^{n \times m}$ be the training images, the conventional dictionary learning problem is to find a dictionary $D = [d_1, d_2, ..., d_k] \in R^{n \times k}$ containing k dictionary atoms and a sparsity representation matrix $Y = [y_1, y_2, ..., y_m] \in R^{k \times m}$ which subjects to the constraint $X \approx DY$ by solving $\min\limits_{D, \{y_i\}} \sum\limits_{i=1}^{m} \|x_i - Dy_i\|_2^2 + \lambda \sum\limits_{i=1}^{m} \|y_i\|_1$ in an unsupervised form, where the first accumulation item is to minimize the reconstruction error and the second is to constrain the sparsity of reconstruction coefficients. To introduce supervision signals in person re-ID, paper [19] proposes a general framework for cross-camera projective dictionary learning which assumes that a pair of images and patches from the same pedestrian but two cameras should have similar dictionary codings. To learn the intrinsic relationship of different cameras and different features, paper [34] proposes a multi-view based coupled dictionary pair learning strategy which learns person coding from color and texture level. To apply into unsupervised scenes, Laplacian regularization is suggested in paper [17] to pull up the distances of images with similar appearances.

3   Ours

3.1   Problem Definition

Suppose we collect m images in total from V cameras as training data and the p-th $(p = 1, ..., V)$ camera provides m_p images, thus we have $m = m_1 + ... + m_V$. The whole training set is denoted as $X = [x_1^1, ..., x_{m_1}^1, ..., x_1^V, ..., x_{m_V}^V] \in R^{d \times m}$, where each column $x_i^p \in R^d$ $(i = 1, ..., m_p; p = 1, ..., V)$ represents the feature of the i-th image from the p-th camera, and denote by $\mathbf{x}^p = [x_1^p, ..., x_{m_p}^p] \in R^{d \times m_p}$ all images from the p-th camera, accordingly we also have $X = [\mathbf{x}^1, ..., \mathbf{x}^V]$. Our destination is to learn V transformations and one dictionary, i.e., $U^1, ..., U^V$ and D, where $U^p \in R^{d \times r}$ $(p = 1, ..., V)$ projects the original representation x_i^p into a common space R^r to alleviate the deviation of distribution between different cameras and then we learn the optimal dictionary $D \in R^{r \times k}$, in which k represents the number of dictionary atoms from R^r. Let $\mathbf{y}^p = [y_1^p, ..., y_{m_p}^p] \in R^{k \times m_p}$ denote the sparse coding of $\mathbf{x}^p$, such that the sparse coding of X can be denoted as $Y = [\mathbf{y}^1, ..., \mathbf{y}^V]$. Note, given any matrix M, we use $M_{:,i}/M_{i,:}$ to denote the i-th column/row of M and $M_{i,j}$ to represent the element which is located in the i-th row and j-th column of M.

3.2   Modelling

Using conventional dictionary learning formulation, $U^1, ..., U^V$ and D can be estimated as:

$$\min_{U^1,...,U^V,D} F_{reconstruct} = \sum_{p=1}^{V} \|(U^p)^T \mathbf{x}^p - D\mathbf{y}^p\|_F^2 + \lambda_1 \|Y\|_2^2 \tag{1}$$

$$s.t. \|D_{:,i}\|_2^2 \leq 1, \ (U^p)^T \Sigma^p U^p = I,$$

in which the constraint $\|D_{:,i}\|_2^2 \leq 1$ enforces the learned dictionary atoms to be compact, and the quasi-orthogonal constraint $(U^p)^T \Sigma^p U^p = I$ ensures that the mapping $U^p \ (p = 1, ..., V)$ will not simply be zero, note that $\Sigma^p = \mathbf{x}^p (\mathbf{x}^p)^T / m_p + \alpha I$ and I represents the identity matrix which is added to avoid the singularity problem of the covariance matrix encountered in optimization. The quasi-orthogonal constraint can be further relaxed to $\sum_{p=1}^{V} (U^p)^T \Sigma^p U^p = VI$. Denote $\widetilde{U} = [(U^1)^T, ..., (U^V)^T]^T$ and $\widetilde{\Sigma} = diag\{\Sigma^1, ..., \Sigma^V\}$, we can rewrite the relaxed quasi-orthogonal constraint by $\sum_{p=1}^{V} (U^p)^T \Sigma^p U^p = \widetilde{U}^T \widetilde{\Sigma} \widetilde{U} = VI$, and denote $\widetilde{X} = diag\{\mathbf{x}^1, ..., \mathbf{x}^V\}$, then the first item in Eq. (1) becomes $\sum_{p=1}^{V} \|(U^p)^T \mathbf{x}^p - D\mathbf{y}^p\|_F^2 = \|\widetilde{U}^T \widetilde{X} - DY\|_F^2$. Considering that the learned asymmetric projections can be arbitrarily diverse and inconsistent, which are not what we exactly expect, in fact transformations from different cameras should be inherently correlated and homogeneous. Hence, we add a consistency constraint $F_{consistency} = \sum_{p \neq q} \|U^p - U^q\|_F^2$ to strike a balance, it can be rewritten as

$$tr(\widetilde{U}^T S \widetilde{U}), \text{ where } S = \begin{bmatrix} (V-1)I & \cdots & -I \\ \vdots & \ddots & \vdots \\ -I & \cdots & (V-1)I \end{bmatrix}.$$

It is clear from Eq. (1) that the conventional dictionary learning model only cares about how to reconstruct samples by dictionary and sparse coding in an unsupervised form, the model can not learn discriminative dictionary atoms with no supervision signal, consequently the learned sparse coding is meaningless for matching people across different cameras. To overcome this problem, we introduce graph Laplacian regularization $F_{graph} = \sum_{i,j}^{m} W_{i,j} \|Y_{:,i} - Y_{:,j}\|_2^2$ to exploit cross-camera identity discriminative information, where $W_{i,j} = \frac{(X_{:,i})^T X_{:,j}}{\|X_{:,i}\|\|X_{:,j}\|}$ if $X_{:,i}, X_{:,j}$ come from different cameras and $X_{:,i}$ is among the κ-nearest neighbours of $X_{:,j}$ or vice versa, otherwise $W_{i,j} = 0$, note that W is a symmetric matrix. We use adjacent matrix W to represent a soft cross-camera correspondence relationship which is determined by weak visual similarity between training samples. F_{graph} can be rewritten as $tr(YLY^T)$ where $L = Q - W$ is the Laplacian matrix and Q is a degree matrix, w.r.t. $Q_{i,i} = \sum_j W_{i,j}$. Finally, we get our model below:

$$\min_{\widetilde{U},D} F = F_{reconstruct} + \lambda_2 F_{consistency} + \lambda_3 F_{graph}$$

$$= \|\widetilde{U}^T \widetilde{X} - DY\|_F^2 + \lambda_1 \|Y\|_2^2 + \lambda_2 tr(\widetilde{U}^T S \widetilde{U}) \tag{2}$$

$$+ \lambda_3 tr(YLY^T) \quad s.t. \|D_{:,i}\|_2^2 \leq 1, \ \widetilde{U}^T \widetilde{\Sigma} \widetilde{U} = VI.$$

After solving the optimization of Eq. (2), we can learn the optimal $U^1, ..., U^V$ and D. Given a test sample x_i^p which comes from the p-th camera, its coding can be calculated by optimizing the following LASSO problem [45]:

$$(y_i^p)^* = \arg\min_{y_i^p} \|(U^p)^T x_i^p - Dy_i^p\|_2^2 + \lambda \|y_i^p\|_2^2, \tag{3}$$

it is easy to know that $(y_i^p)^* = (D^T D + \lambda I)^{-1} D^T (U^p)^T x_i^p$.

3.3   Optimization

Although the optimization problem in Eq. (2) is non-convex for $\widetilde{U}$, D and Y simultaneously, we develop an alternative minimization strategy to solve it by executing the following three steps repeatedly until convergence:

1) Update Y: For fixed $\widetilde{U}, D$, the objective function becomes

$$\min_Y \|\widetilde{U}^T \widetilde{X} - DY\|_F^2 + \lambda_1 \|Y\|_F^2 + \lambda_3 tr(YLY^T). \tag{4}$$

First, we calculate its partial derivative which gives $\frac{\partial(\cdot)}{\partial Y} = -2D^T \widetilde{U}^T \widetilde{X} + 2D^T DY + 2\lambda_1 Y + 2\lambda_3 YL$, and then set it to zero to obtain the optimal solution of Y, thus we got a standard Sylvester equation $(D^T D + \lambda_1 I)Y + Y\lambda_3 L = D^T \widetilde{U}^T \widetilde{X}$ which can be solved by Bartels-Stewart algorithm [6].

2) Update $\widetilde{U}$: For fixed D, Y, the objective function becomes

$$\min_{\widetilde{U}} \|\widetilde{U}^T \widetilde{X} - DY\|_F^2 + \lambda_2 tr(\widetilde{U}^T S \widetilde{U}) \quad s.t. \widetilde{U}^T \widetilde{\Sigma} \widetilde{U} = VI. \tag{5}$$

The orthonormality constraint on $\widetilde{U}$ leads to the convex problem which can be solved by Stiefel manifold [49] optimization technique. Denote $D = \widetilde{U}^T \widetilde{X} A$ for some $A \in R^{m \times k}$, then transform the objective function which subject to an equality constraint into a Lagrange function $\mathcal{L} = \|\widetilde{U}^T \widetilde{X} - \widetilde{U}^T \widetilde{X} AY\|_F^2 + \lambda_2 tr(\widetilde{U}^T S \widetilde{U}) + tr(\Lambda^T(VI - \widetilde{U}^T \widetilde{\Sigma} \widetilde{U}))$ by introducing a Lagrange multiplier matrix Λ (a diagonal matrix). Same as step 1), we take derivative of $\mathcal{L}$ and set it to zero which gives $\frac{\partial \mathcal{L}}{\partial \tilde{U}} = (2\tilde{X}\tilde{X}^T - 2\tilde{X}Y^T A^T \tilde{X}^T - 2\tilde{X}AY\tilde{X}^T + 2\tilde{X}AYY^T A^T \tilde{X}^T)\tilde{U} + 2\lambda_2 S\tilde{U} - 2\tilde{\Sigma}\tilde{U}\Lambda = 0$, thus we get $\tilde{\Sigma}^{-1}(\tilde{X}\tilde{X}^T - \tilde{X}Y^T A^T \tilde{X}^T - \tilde{X}AY\tilde{X}^T + \tilde{X}AYY^T A^T \tilde{X}^T + \lambda_2 S)\tilde{U} = \tilde{U}\Lambda$, then we can solve this eigen decomposition problem to obtain the optimal solution of $\tilde{U}$.

3) Update D: For fixed $\tilde{U}, Y$, the objective function becomes

$$\min_D ||\tilde{U}^T \tilde{X} - DY||_F^2 \quad s.t. ||D_{:,i}||_2^2 \leq 1. \tag{6}$$

We can learn basis of dictionary by using Lagrange dual method [18], consequently the analytical solution of D can be computed as $D^* = \tilde{U}^T \tilde{X}Y^T(YY^T + \Lambda^*)^{-1}$, in which $\Lambda^* = diag\{\lambda_1^*, ..., \lambda_k^*\}$ is a diagonal matrix constructed of all the optimal dual variables $\lambda_1, ..., \lambda_k$, also we denote these dual variables as a column vector $\overrightarrow{\lambda} = [\lambda_1, ..., \lambda_k]^T$, it can be updated by $\overrightarrow{\lambda} := \overrightarrow{\lambda} - H^{-1}g$ iteratively until convergence, where $H = -2(\tilde{U}^T \tilde{X}Y^T(YY^T + \Lambda)^{-1})^T(\tilde{U}^T \tilde{X}Y^T(YY^T + \Lambda) \odot (YY^T + \Lambda)^{-1}$ and $g = ((\tilde{U}^T \tilde{X}Y^T(YY^T + \Lambda)^{-1}) \odot (\tilde{U}^T \tilde{X}Y^T(YY^T + \Lambda)^{-1}))^T \overrightarrow{1} - 1$, notice that $\odot$ represents element-wise dot of two matrices and $\overrightarrow{1} = [1, ..., 1]^T$.

Algorithm 1: A complete person re-ID process based on our method

---

Input: Train set, query set, gallery set, λ, λ_1, λ_2, λ_3, max iteration number T, threshold *eps*

Output: The multi-view jointly matching results

1 Initialisation: objective function value $O_0 = 0$, iteration index $t = 1$, fusion score matrix $S = 0$;

2 **foreach** v_i **do**

3   Extract visual feature X_{v_i} of train set;

4   Construct Laplacian matrix L_{v_i} according to X_{v_i};

5   **while** $O_t - O_{t-1} > eps$ *and* $t < T$ **do**

6   Update Y_{v_i} according to Eq. (4);

7   Update $\tilde{U}_{v_i}$ by Eq. (5);

8   Update D_{v_i} using Eq. (6);

9   **end**

10   Evaluate $Y_{v_i}^q$ and $Y_{v_i}^g$ of query set and gallery set according to Eq. (3);

11   Calculate $S_{v_i} = (Y_{v_i}^q)^T Y_{v_i}^g$;

12   Accumulate $S = S + w_{v_i} \cdot S_{v_i}$;

13   Reset $O_0 = 0$ and $t = 1$;

14 **end**

15 **return** the rank-1 accuracy of CMC calculated with S

3.4 Multi-view Jointly Matching

Now we can learn several dictionary models according to Eq. (2) for multiple visual features (multi-view) and combine their effects in person re-ID at the step of computing similarity scores. In details, we first calculate the L2-normalized coding of query set and gallery set, denoted as $Y_{v_i}^q$ and $Y_{v_i}^g$ respectively for a specific model under view v_i $(i = 1, ..., n)$ according to Eq. (3), then we can calculate the similarity score matrix $S_{v_i} = (Y_{v_i}^q)^T Y_{v_i}^g$ between them by matrix multiplication, thus we can obtain the final score matrix $S = \sum_i^n w_{v_i} \cdot S_{v_i}$ by score-level fusion where w_{v_i} $(i = 1, ..., n)$ is the fusion coefficient (we summarise all steps of our method in Algorithm 1). Finally, we can obtain the multi-view jointly matching results based on their ranking and promising results can be achieved. In experiments, we also try to cascade a variety of visual features together to form one fusion feature, but the result was lower than the fusion at the score level.

4 Experiments

4.1 Experiments Settings

In our experiments, we use four visual features $(n = 4)$, i.e., WHOS [26], LOMO [22], GOG [35] and JSTL [53]. Because of the great long dimension of these features which will bring huge computation cost, especially for LOMO and GOG, we need to do PCA (Principal Component Analysis) before feeding the data into our model, specifically, 90% of the energy is preserved. The parameters of our model are set as follows: in Eq. (2), $\lambda_1 = 0.0001$, $\lambda_2 = 0.1$, $\lambda_3 = 0.2$, in Eq. (3), $\lambda = 0.1$. In addition, parameter α in the quasi-orthogonal constraint of Eq. (1) is set as $\dfrac{\sum\limits_{p}^{V} tr(\mathbf{x}^p (\mathbf{x}^p)^T / m_p)}{d \times V}$, the projection space dimension r is set as the length of feature after PCA, the number of dictionary atoms k is approximately set as $1.35 * r$, the max iteration number $T = 20$, threshold $eps = 0.001$, the fusion coefficients of the score matrices for different view are all set equal to 1 and κ (nearest neighbours) is set as 3. The Cumculative Matching Characteristic (CMC) is used for evaluating our model.

4.2 Comparative Results

Three benchmarks are listed to verify the validity of our approach, including Dic [17], ISR [26] and CAMEL [53]. Experiments are conducted on four widely used datasets, i.e., VIPeR, PRID, CUHK01 and Market1501. From Table 1 we can observe that our method outperforms these benchmarks.

VIPeR is a single-shot dataset, which contains 632 image pairs of people captured by two cameras. Although it has been tested by many researchers, it is still one of the most challenging datasets. In our setting, VIPeR is randomly splitted into two sets of 316 image pairs separately for training and testing and the matching result is obtained by averaging over 10 splits.

PRID has two version, we use the version in which each person only has one image in our experiments. There are 749 labelled people but only 200 of them appear in both two cameras, we randomly choose 100 people out of the 200 to construct the training set, and the remaining people in each camera are used for testing, specifically, the remaining 100 people in one camera with total 100 images are used as probe set, and the remaining 649 people in another camera with total 649 images are used as gallery set. The matching result is also obtained by averaging over 10 splits.

CUHK01 consists of 971 people, every person has two images in each camera i.e., multi shot. In each data split, we follow the standard setting: 486 persons are selected randomly for training, while other 485 persons for test. The matching result is also obtained by averaging over 10 splits.

Market1501 contains 32668 images of 1501 labeled persons from six cameras. We comply with the setting in [60], specifically, 12936 person images of 751 identities are used for training, 3,368 person images of 750 identities are used as query set and 19,732 person images of 750 identities are used as gallery set.

Table 1. Rank-1 matching accuracy of our unsupervised approach.

Datasets	VIPeR	PRID2011	CUHK01	Market1501
Dic [17]	29.6	21.1	52.9	50.2
ISR [26]	27.0	17.0	–	40.3
$CAMEL$ [53]	30.9	–	61.9	54.5
$Ours$	37.1	35.8	65.5	54.8

To further show the superiority of our method compared to others, we extend it to the supervised scenario and denote as $Ours_s$, which also represents the ceiling of our unsupervised model. Giving labels of the training data, we can construct a precised Laplacian regularization F_{graph} to guide the model to learn the correspondence across cameras, in which $W_{i,j} = 1$ if $X_{:,i}$ and $X_{:,j}$ have the same identity label, otherwise $W_{i,j} = 0$. We compare our supervised version with three other methods, i.e., the supervised version of Dic (denote as Dic_s), CVDCA [9] and the supervised version of CAMEL (denote as $CAMEL_s$). From Table 2, we notice that it is comparable to others.

Table 2. Rank-1 matching accuracy of our model under supervised setting.

Datasets	VIPeR	PRID2011	CUHK01	Market1501
Dic_s [17]	38.9	25.2	–	–
$CVDCA$ [9]	37.6	–	60.9	52.6
$CAMEL_s$ [53]	33.7	–	62.7	55.0
$Ours_s$	58.9	42.6	74.8	56.3

5 Conclusion

In this work, we proposed a graph regularization based dictionary learning framework for unsupervised person re-ID. For each single view, our method will learn transformations for all cameras respectively which can alleviate discrepancy of data to pull up the distance of the same pedestrian under different cameras. A common dictionary which can be used to represent samples with advanced semantic properties that shared by all cameras. Furthermore, we and extend our method to multi-view scene, where the Discriminating ability learned from multiple visual features can be accumulated. Experiments on four benchmark datasets show that the proposed model truly improves the performance of unsupervised person re-ID.

References

1. Aharon, M., Elad, M., Bruckstein, A.: K-SVD: an algorithm for designing overcomplete dictionaries for sparse representation. IEEE Trans. Signal Process. **54**(11), 4311–4322 (2006)
2. Ali, T.M.F., Chaudhuri, S.: Maximum margin metric learning over discriminative nullspace for person re-identification. In: Ferrari, V., Hebert, M., Sminchisescu, C., Weiss, Y. (eds.) ECCV 2018. LNCS, vol. 11217, pp. 123–141. Springer, Cham (2018). https://doi.org/10.1007/978-3-030-01261-8_8
3. Alsaedi, N.H., Jaha, E.S.: Dynamic audio-visual biometric fusion for person recognition. Comput. Mater. Continua **71**(1), 1283–1311 (2022)
4. Baabou, S., Bremond, F., Fradj, A., Farah, M.A., Kachouri, A.: Hand-crafted system for person re-identification: a comprehensive review. In: SM2C' (2017)
5. Bak, S., Charpiat, G., Corvée, E., Brémond, F., Thonnat, M.: Learning to match appearances by correlations in a covariance metric space. In: Fitzgibbon, A., Lazebnik, S., Perona, P., Sato, Y., Schmid, C. (eds.) ECCV 2012. LNCS, vol. 7574, pp. 806–820. Springer, Heidelberg (2012). https://doi.org/10.1007/978-3-642-33712-3_58
6. Bartels, R.H., Stewart, G.W.: Solution of the matrix equation ax+ xb= c [f4]. Commun. ACM **15**(9), 820–826 (1972)
7. Cao, M., Chen, C., Hu, X., Peng, S.: Towards fast and kernelized orthogonal discriminant analysis on person re-identification. Pattern Recognit. **94**, 218–229 (2019)
8. Chahla, C., Snoussi, H., Abdallah, F., Dornaika, F.: Learned versus handcrafted features for person re-identification. Int. J. Pattern Recognit Artif Intell. **34**(04), 2055009 (2020)
9. Chen, Y.C., Zheng, W.S., Lai, J.H., Yuen, P.C.: An asymmetric distance model for cross-view feature mapping in person reidentification. IEEE Trans. Circuits Syst. Video Technol. **27**(8), 1661–1675 (2016)
10. Dai, Y., Luo, Z.: Review of unsupervised person re-identification. J. New Media **3**(4), 129 (2021)
11. Fan, H., Zheng, L., Yan, C., Yang, Y.: Unsupervised person re-identification: clustering and fine-tuning. ACM Trans. Multimedia Comput. Commun. Appl. (TOMM) **14**(4), 1–18 (2018)

12. Ge, Y., Zhu, F., Zhao, R., Li, H.: Structured domain adaptation for unsupervised person re-identification. arXiv preprint arXiv:2003.06650 (2020)
13. Gu, S., Zhang, L., Zuo, W., Feng, X.: Projective dictionary pair learning for pattern classification. In: Advances in Neural Information Processing Systems, pp. 793–801 (2014)
14. Jiang, T.: A review of person re-identification. J. New Media **2**(2) (2020)
15. Jin, X., Lan, C., Zeng, W., Chen, Z.: Global distance-distributions separation for unsupervised person re-identification. In: Vedaldi, A., Bischof, H., Brox, T., Frahm, J.-M. (eds.) ECCV 2020. LNCS, vol. 12352, pp. 735–751. Springer, Cham (2020). https://doi.org/10.1007/978-3-030-58571-6_43
16. Kodirov, E., Xiang, T., Fu, Z., Gong, S.: Person re-identification by unsupervised ℓ_1 graph learning. In: Leibe, B., Matas, J., Sebe, N., Welling, M. (eds.) ECCV 2016. LNCS, vol. 9905, pp. 178–195. Springer, Cham (2016). https://doi.org/10.1007/978-3-319-46448-0_11
17. Kodirov, E., Xiang, T., Gong, S.: Dictionary learning with iterative laplacian regularisation for unsupervised person re-identification. In: BMVC, vol. 3, p. 8 (2015)
18. Lee, H., Battle, A., Raina, R., Ng, A.Y.: Efficient sparse coding algorithms. In: Advances in Neural Information Processing Systems, pp. 801–808. Citeseer (2007)
19. Li, S., Shao, M., Fu, Y.: Cross-view projective dictionary learning for person re-identification. In: Twenty-Fourth International Joint Conference on Artificial Intelligence (2015)
20. Li, W., Zhu, X., Gong, S.: Harmonious attention network for person re-identification. In: Proceedings of the IEEE Conference on Computer Vision and Pattern Recognition, pp. 2285–2294 (2018)
21. Li, Y., Wang, X.: Person re-identification based on joint loss and multiple attention mechanism. Intel. Autom. Soft Comput. **30**(2), 563–573 (2021)
22. Liao, S., Hu, Y., Zhu, X., Li, S.Z.: Person re-identification by local maximal occurrence representation and metric learning. In: Proceedings of the IEEE Conference on Computer Vision and Pattern Recognition, pp. 2197–2206 (2015)
23. Liao, S., Li, S.Z.: Efficient PSD constrained asymmetric metric learning for person re-identification. In: Proceedings of the IEEE International Conference on Computer Vision, pp. 3685–3693 (2015)
24. Lin, Y., Dong, X., Zheng, L., Yan, Y., Yang, Y.: A bottom-up clustering approach to unsupervised person re-identification. In: Proceedings of the AAAI Conference on Artificial Intelligence, vol. 33, pp. 8738–8745 (2019)
25. Lin, Y., et al.: Improving person re-identification by attribute and identity learning. Pattern Recogn. **95**, 151–161 (2019)
26. Lisanti, G., Masi, I., Bagdanov, A.D., Del Bimbo, A.: Person re-identification by iterative re-weighted sparse ranking. IEEE Trans. Pattern Anal. Mach. Intell. **37**(8), 1629–1642 (2014)
27. Lisanti, G., Masi, I., Del Bimbo, A.: Matching people across camera views using kernel canonical correlation analysis. In: Proceedings of the International Conference on Distributed Smart Cameras, pp. 1–6 (2014)
28. Liu, C., Gong, S., Loy, C.C., Lin, X.: Person re-identification: what features are important? In: Fusiello, A., Murino, V., Cucchiara, R. (eds.) ECCV 2012. LNCS, vol. 7583, pp. 391–401. Springer, Heidelberg (2012). https://doi.org/10.1007/978-3-642-33863-2_39
29. Liu, J., Zha, Z.J., Chen, D., Hong, R., Wang, M.: Adaptive transfer network for cross-domain person re-identification. In: Proceedings of the IEEE/CVF Conference on Computer Vision and Pattern Recognition, pp. 7202–7211 (2019)

30. Lowe, D.G.: Distinctive image features from scale-invariant keypoints. Int. J. Comput. Vis. **60**(2), 91–110 (2004)
31. Luo, H., Jiang, W., Zhang, X., Fan, X., Qian, J., Zhang, C.: AlignedReID++: dynamically matching local information for person re-identification. Pattern Recogn. **94**, 53–61 (2019)
32. Ma, B., Su, Yu., Jurie, F.: Local descriptors encoded by fisher vectors for person re-identification. In: Fusiello, A., Murino, V., Cucchiara, R. (eds.) ECCV 2012. LNCS, vol. 7583, pp. 413–422. Springer, Heidelberg (2012). https://doi.org/10.1007/978-3-642-33863-2_41
33. Ma, B., Su, Y., Jurie, F.: Covariance descriptor based on bio-inspired features for person re-identification and face verification. Image Vis. Comput. **32**(6–7), 379–390 (2014)
34. Ma, F., Zhu, X., Liu, Q., Song, C., Jing, X.Y., Ye, D.: Multi-view coupled dictionary learning for person re-identification. Neurocomputing **348**, 16–26 (2019)
35. Matsukawa, T., Okabe, T., Suzuki, E., Sato, Y.: Hierarchical gaussian descriptor for person re-identification. In: Proceedings of the IEEE Conference on Computer Vision and Pattern Recognition, pp. 1363–1372 (2016)
36. Mekhazni, D., Bhuiyan, A., Ekladious, G., Granger, E.: Unsupervised domain adaptation in the dissimilarity space for person re-identification. In: Vedaldi, A., Bischof, H., Brox, T., Frahm, J.-M. (eds.) ECCV 2020. LNCS, vol. 12372, pp. 159–174. Springer, Cham (2020). https://doi.org/10.1007/978-3-030-58583-9_10
37. Patel, V.M., Qiu, Q., Chellappa, R.: Dictionaries for image-based recognition. In: 2013 Information Theory and Applications Workshop (ITA), pp. 1–8. IEEE (2013)
38. Pedagadi, S., Orwell, J., Velastin, S., Boghossian, B.: Local fisher discriminant analysis for pedestrian re-identification. In: Proceedings of the IEEE Conference on Computer Vision and Pattern Recognition, pp. 3318–3325 (2013)
39. Prates, R., Schwartz, W.R.: Kernel cross-view collaborative representation based classification for person re-identification. J. Vis. Commun. Image Represent. **58**, 304–315 (2019)
40. Shen, Y., Lin, W., Yan, J., Xu, M., Wu, J., Wang, J.: Person re-identification with correspondence structure learning. In: Proceedings of the IEEE International Conference on Computer Vision, pp. 3200–3208 (2015)
41. Suh, Y., Wang, J., Tang, S., Mei, T., Lee, K.M.: Part-aligned bilinear representations for person re-identification. In: Ferrari, V., Hebert, M., Sminchisescu, C., Weiss, Y. (eds.) Computer Vision – ECCV 2018. LNCS, vol. 11218, pp. 418–437. Springer, Cham (2018). https://doi.org/10.1007/978-3-030-01264-9_25
42. Sun, Y., Zheng, L., Yang, Y., Tian, Q., Wang, S.: Beyond part models: person retrieval with refined part pooling (and a strong convolutional baseline). In: Ferrari, V., Hebert, M., Sminchisescu, C., Weiss, Y. (eds.) ECCV 2018. LNCS, vol. 11208, pp. 501–518. Springer, Cham (2018). https://doi.org/10.1007/978-3-030-01225-0_30
43. Syed, M.A., Jiao, J.: Multi-kernel metric learning for person re-identification. In: 2016 IEEE International Conference on Image Processing (ICIP), pp. 784–788. IEEE (2016)
44. Tay, C.P., Roy, S., Yap, K.H.: AaNet: attribute attention network for person re-identifications. In: Proceedings of the IEEE/CVF Conference on Computer Vision and Pattern Recognition, pp. 7134–7143 (2019)
45. Tibshirani, R.: Regression shrinkage and selection via the lasso. J. Royal Stat. Soc. Ser. B (Methodological) **58**(1), 267–288 (1996)

46. Wang, C., Zhang, Q., Huang, C., Liu, W., Wang, X.: Mancs: a multi-task attentional network with curriculum sampling for person re-identification. In: Ferrari, V., Hebert, M., Sminchisescu, C., Weiss, Y. (eds.) ECCV 2018. LNCS, vol. 11208, pp. 384–400. Springer, Cham (2018). https://doi.org/10.1007/978-3-030-01225-0_23

47. Wang, H., Zhu, X., Gong, S., Xiang, T.: Person re-identification in identity regression space. Int. J. Comput. Vis. **126**(12), 1288–1310 (2018)

48. Wei, L., Zhang, S., Gao, W., Tian, Q.: Person transfer GAN to bridge domain gap for person re-identification. In: Proceedings of the IEEE Conference on Computer Vision and Pattern Recognition, pp. 79–88 (2018)

49. Wen, Z., Yin, W.: A feasible method for optimization with orthogonality constraints. Math. Program. **142**(1), 397–434 (2013)

50. Wu, A., Zheng, W.S., Lai, J.H.: Unsupervised person re-identification by camera-aware similarity consistency learning. In: Proceedings of the IEEE/CVF International Conference on Computer Vision, pp. 6922–6931 (2019)

51. Xiong, F., Gou, M., Camps, O., Sznaier, M.: Person re-identification using kernel-based metric learning methods. In: Fleet, D., Pajdla, T., Schiele, B., Tuytelaars, T. (eds.) ECCV 2014. LNCS, vol. 8695, pp. 1–16. Springer, Cham (2014). https://doi.org/10.1007/978-3-319-10584-0_1

52. Yang, X., Wang, M., Tao, D.: Person re-identification with metric learning using privileged information. IEEE Trans. Image Process. **27**(2), 791–805 (2017)

53. Yu, H.X., Wu, A., Zheng, W.S.: Cross-view asymmetric metric learning for unsupervised person re-identification. In: Proceedings of the IEEE International Conference on Computer Vision, pp. 994–1002 (2017)

54. Zhai, Y., Guo, X., Lu, Y., Li, H.: In defense of the classification loss for person re-identification. In: Proceedings of the IEEE/CVF Conference on Computer Vision and Pattern Recognition Workshops (2019)

55. Zhang, G., Ge, Y., Dong, Z., Wang, H., Zheng, Y., Chen, S.: Deep high-resolution representation learning for cross-resolution person re-identification. IEEE Trans. Image Process. **30**, 8913–8925 (2021)

56. Zhang, L., Xiang, T., Gong, S.: Learning a discriminative null space for person re-identification. In: Proceedings of the IEEE Conference on Computer Vision and Pattern Recognition, pp. 1239–1248 (2016)

57. Zhao, H., et al.: Spindle Net: person re-identification with human body region guided feature decomposition and fusion. In: Proceedings of the IEEE Conference on Computer Vision and Pattern Recognition, pp. 1077–1085 (2017)

58. Zhao, R., Ouyang, W., Wang, X.: Person re-identification by salience matching. In: Proceedings of the IEEE International Conference on Computer Vision, pp. 2528–2535 (2013)

59. Zhao, R., Ouyang, W., Wang, X.: Unsupervised salience learning for person re-identification. In: Proceedings of the IEEE Conference on Computer Vision and Pattern Recognition, pp. 3586–3593 (2013)

60. Zheng, L., Shen, L., Tian, L., Wang, S., Wang, J., Tian, Q.: Scalable person re-identification: a benchmark. In: Proceedings of the IEEE International Conference on Computer Vision, pp. 1116–1124 (2015)

LTDTS: A Lightweight Trash Detecting and Tracking System

Zijun Yu, Jin Liu[✉], and Xingye Li

College of Information Engineering, Shanghai Maritime University, Shanghai, China
jinliu@shmtu.edu.cn

Abstract. Community environment is one of the focuses of urban governance. And the phenomenon of residents littering in violation of community regulations is one of the most prominent problems in the management of the community environment. However, the existing methods, whether it is time-consuming and labor-intensive human management or action detection-based system that still cannot achieve a good balance between accuracy and real-time performance, cannot solve this outstanding problem well. At the same time, the more commonly used object detection-based systems also have poor performance due to the complexity of the model and system architecture. To address these issues, we propose a novel lightweight trash detection system. The system uses an improved yolov5 algorithm, which is more suitable for the detection of small targets like litter. In addition, we novelly proposed two methods called tracking object transmission and video backtracking, combined with the tracking algorithm based on kernelized correlation filter, we successfully achieved accurate localization of littering pedestrians. So far, our model has been experimented on several small public datasets and our self-designed community littering dataset. What's more, our system has also been put into use in some communities, with initial results that are acceptable, which successfully verified the feasibility of our method.

Keywords: Object detection · Pedestrian tracking · Trash detection system

1 Introduction

Community environmental governance is a critical component of the urban governance system. The most prominent problem in community environmental management is the phenomenon of littering by residents. There are three types of management systems now in use: manual-based, action recognition model-based, and object detection model-based.

Manual-based Method. Manual management monitoring is the traditional as well as the most common means currently used, mainly through manual inspection of the scene to find, or through the surveillance cameras to capture the record of littering behavior. However, this manual means of management requires a lot of human and material resources, detection efficiency is not high, and by the weather, personnel leave and working hours, and other external factors.

© The Author(s), under exclusive license to Springer Nature Switzerland AG 2022
X. Sun et al. (Eds.): ICAIS 2022, LNCS 13338, pp. 240–250, 2022.
https://doi.org/10.1007/978-3-031-06794-5_20

Action Recognition Model-based Method. The approach attempts to use deep learning models to capture certain human behaviors. [1] loads a violence detection system on a drone that captures and identifies violent actions such as kicking, stabbing, or choking in a crowd. In a recent study, [2] explores deep learning architecture of CNNs and inception V4 to detect and recognize violence, improved by the keyframe extraction.

Object Detection Model-based Method. The method mainly uses deep learning models to detect and identify pedestrian and garbage targets and then combines other functional modules depending on the system task requirements. In order to identify construction waste generated during urban construction, [3] uses an improved YOLOV2 model to do waste detection and identification, and transplants it to a front-end embedded module to manage thousands of monitoring front-ends with IoT and back-end servers. [4] presents a low-cost scheme capable of locating litter targets in low-altitude images from cell phones during autonomous patrol missions by UAVs. [5] proposes a new real-time small object detection algorithm based on YOLOV3, which improves the small object detection accuracy by FPNs. [6] conducted garbage detection experiments and analysis on MASK-RCNN, YOLOV4, and YOLOV4-tiny, and determined to embed YOLOV4-tiny into the garbage collection robot.

Overall, with the development of AI technology, the management model of manual detection is gradually being replaced by the management model based on deep learning models. Among the deep learning models, the technology of action recognition models is not mature enough and has only achieved good results in academic research. This method's detection accuracy and hardware consumption make it unsuitable for usage in specific projects, instead increasing workload due to mistaken or missing recognition. Object detection is commonly used at this stage, and in the studies of [3, 4, 6], the models performed well in terms of detection effectiveness and migration into the system.

In this paper, we proposed a lightweight litter detection and tracking system (LTDTS). The system is divided into two main modules, which are target detection module and target tracking module. The location of the garbage is first detected by the target detection module and the location information is passed to the tracking module. Based on the location information of the garbage, the tracking module tracks backward to the moment when the resident throws the garbage. The detection module in this paper uses the modified yolov5 model, and the tracking module uses the KCF tracking algorithm. Extensive experiments show that the proposed method achieves good results in the dataset presented in this paper. LTDTS is also in use in several communities and has been well received. The major contributions of our research can be summarized as follows:

(1) We propose a lightweight deep learning-based trash detection and tracking system (LTDTS).
(2) We introduce a new dataset of the community refuse collection scenarios RCP-2021.
(3) For the dataset presented in this paper, we propose an improved yolov5 model with good results.

2 Related Work

This section discusses the existing work in the field of object detection and object tracking. Comparing the previous work, we choose the most suitable module for our system.

Object Detecting Methods. There exist two mainstream types of detection models: anchor-based and anchor-free detectors. Anchor-based detectors can be further classified into two-stage and single-stage based on their structure. Two-stage anchor detectors (e.g., R-CNN series [7–10], TSD [21]) consisting of region proposal networks (RPNs) and classifiers are firstly proposed for the object detection task. A large number of foreground and background region proposals are first generated by RPNs, and then the objects in the proposals are classified by the classifier. For real-time object detection, one-stage anchor-based detectors (e.g., YOLO series [12–14]) are proposed to predict both bboxes categories at the same time, thus eliminating the need for RPNs. Recently, anchor-free detectors such as CornerNet [18] have also been proposed to remove anchored priors. These models predict the locations of key points (corner, center of mass, or extreme points) and then group them into the same bbox if they are geometrically aligned. In addition, transformers (e.g., DETR series [16, 17]) have also been developed for object detection without anchor generation or non-maximum suppression (NMS), achieving the performance on par with the above CNN-based detectors. Similar to the transformers, [15] uses a new multi-scale convolution model based on multiple attention to achieve significant results on classification. [23] proposed a multi-lane capsule network with strict-squash (MLSCN) for classifying images with complex background. With the gradual increase of multimodal training tasks in recent years, an increasing number of research have incorporated natural language processing (e.g., knowledge graph applications [20], relationship extraction [11], question classification [28]) to improve performance in visual tasks. [19] proposed a novel Reasoning-RCNN, which takes into account semantic links and infers between observed items.

Object Tracking Methods. The methods are generally divided into two categories: correlation filter-based methods and deep learning-based methods. Correlation filters were early applied to signal to process. The main principle is to calculate the correlation between two signals. The earliest tracking algorithm using correlation filters is MOSSE [24], after which KCF [25], DSST [26], ECO [27], etc. received widespread attention. The DNNs currently used for object tracking are Autoencoders (AE), Convolutional Neural Networks (CNN), and Recurrent Neural Networks (RNN). DLT [22] is an early well-known object tracking algorithm based on deep learning, and other representative algorithms include MDNet [29], SiamFC [30], SiamRPN [31].

In the system designed in this paper, the object detection module uses the yolov5 model improved for the new dataset, and the tracking module uses the traditional KCF algorithm. In the next section, we will start to describe the methodology of this paper specifically.

3   Method

In this section, we first introduce RCP-2021, a small objective-based dataset proposed in the paper, and the corresponding modifications to the anchor. After that, the loss function and KCF algorithm will be presented. Finally, we will give a detailed description of LTDTS.

3.1   RCP-2021 Dataset

Traditional datasets are dominated by large objects with few or unevenly distributed small objects, and a large number of small objects are concentrated in a small part of the image. This unbalanced sample distribution structure causes the trained model to be more inclined to large objects. To solve this problem, we produced RCP-2021, which is dominated by small objects, from community surveillance camera videos as experimental data. In previous work, some approaches (e.g., MSMC-CGAN [33], CMTGAN [34]) have used generative adversarial network to generate new pictures. However, compared to the collected images, the images generated by GANs is not good enough.

The RCP-2021 dataset has a total of 8000 images, including 6400 images and 25,500 annotations in the training set; 800 images and 3,500 annotations in the validation set; and 800 images in the test set. The image samples in the RCP-2021 dataset are shown in Fig. 1 Altogether, there are 6 classes in labeling objects: 0: people, 1: bicycle, 2: car, 3: bags, 4: boxes, 5: bottle. The image samples in the RCP-2021 dataset are shown in Fig. 1.

Fig. 1. Randomly selected images from the RCP-2021 dataset.

3.2   Anchor Redesign

The initial anchor size used by yolov5 is clustered from the object box size in the COCO dataset. The disparities in object size between the RCP-2021 dataset and the COCO dataset are shown in Table 1, with little items making up the majority of the RCP-2021 dataset. As a result, the original anchor size does not work with the RCP-2021 dataset.

The anchor size is redesigned using the KMeans++clustering algorithm [35] to increase the object box and anchor matching probability. The KMeans++algorithm is divided into two steps.

Table 1. Quantitative comparison of object sizes between RCP-2021 and COCO.

Size	COCO (%)	RCP-2021 (%)
Small	41.43	78.67
Medium	34.32	17.42
Large	24.24	3.91

The first step is to determine the initial values of K cluster centers:
The distance s is defined as (1):

$$s(box, centroid) = 1 - IoU(box, centroid) \tag{1}$$

where 'box' is the target box and 'centroid' is the cluster center. The distance from all points to the nearest cluster center is S(x), and P(x) represents the probability of each point to becomes the next cluster center (2):

$$P(x) = \frac{S(x)^2}{\sum_{i=1}^{N} S(x_i)^2} \tag{2}$$

According to the probability, the roulette wheel selection (the greater the distance, the greater the probability of being selected as cluster center) is repeated until K cluster centers $C = \{C_1, C_2,..., C_K\}$ are selected.

The second step is to cluster the initial cluster centers selected in the first step:

Each sample is separated into the set to which the nearest cluster center belongs, with K cluster centers divided into K sets. The new cluster center is determined using the average value of all samples in each set, and each sample is partitioned into the set with the shortest distance from the new cluster center; the average value of the samples in each set is then recalculated. Repeat the preceding process until the average value change is less than a given threshold, and the new anchor size is K cluster centers.

3.3 Loss Function

In a recent study, [32] proposed a new power IoU loss function, called α-IoU, which can consistently outperform existing IoU-based losses and provide more robustness for small datasets. Therefore, we decide use the α-IoU to replace GIoU in yolov5.

The more general form of α-IoU is defined as formula:

$$L_{\alpha-IoU} = 1 - IoU^{\alpha} + P^{\alpha}(B, B^{gt}) \tag{3}$$

where $\alpha > 0$ and $P^{\alpha}(B, B^{gt})$ denotes any penalty term computed based on B and B^{gt}.

3.4 KCF Tracking

Because of its excellent efficiency and competitive performance, we utilize the Kernelized Correlation Filter (KCF) as our baseline method. KCF is used for single-object tracking in [25]. Training samples $x_i(w, h) \in \{0, \ldots, W - 1\} \times \{0, \ldots, H - 1\}$, are recorded by cyclic shifts of picture patches x with size $W \times H$ pixels, and the classifier is learned in the Fourier domain. x is clipped around the middle of the target. For each sample x_i, the predicted label $y_i(w, h)$ follows a Gaussian function with values ranging from 0 to 1. For a centered target, y_i will be 1, while for other regions that shift away from the target center, it will be 0. The goal for KCF training is to find a function $f(z) = w^T z$ that minimizes the squared error between samples x_i and their regression target y_i as follows:

$$\min_{\omega} \sum_i (f(x_i) - y_i)^2 + \lambda ||\omega||^2 \tag{4}$$

where the regularization parameter λ is used to prevent overfitting. ω is the optimal value to minimize Eq. (4). Then Eq. (4) is rewritten as Eq. (5) by kernel function mapping x_i to the Hilbert space.

$$\min_{\omega} \sum_i | < \varphi(x_i, \omega) > -y_i|^2 + \lambda ||\omega||^2 \tag{5}$$

where λ is the mapping function with kernel $\mathcal{K}$, $\mathcal{K}(x, x') = \langle \varphi(x), \varphi(x') \rangle$. After mapping, the solution ω for Eq. (4) can be expressed as:

$$\min_{\omega} \sum a_i \phi(x_i) \tag{6}$$

Then the problem is turned to solve the classifier coefficients α. Following the circulate matrix structure and convolution theorem in [36], coefficient α is solved as:

$$F(\alpha) = \left(\frac{F(y)}{F(k^x) + \lambda} \right) \tag{7}$$

where F is the Fourier transform, $y = \{y_i(w, h) | (w, h) \in \{0, \ldots, W - 1\} \times \{0, \ldots, H - 1\}\}$. $k^x = \mathcal{K}(x, x')$ is computed by Gaussian kernel in the Fourier domain.

For an image patch z with size $W \times H$ in a new frame $t + 1$, where z is cropped in the search window around object location, the confidence response is computed as:

$$\hat{y}(z) = F^{-1}(F(k^Z) \odot F(\alpha)) \tag{8}$$

where $\odot$ is the element-wise product, $k^z = \mathcal{K}(z, \hat{x}_i)$ is the kernel distance between regression sample z, and the learned object appearance $\hat{x}_i$. The place where the maximum response R occurs determines the final target location, and the response R is formulated as $R = max\hat{y}(z)$.

3.5 LTDTS

In the LTDTS designed in this paper, the function of the system is to determine whether a video sequence contains a resident's littering behavior, and to obtain the time frame when the resident threw down the litter. In order to achieve this function, we divide the system into two parts: first, the trash target detection module, which is mainly responsible for confirming the location information of the trash thrown down by the residents; and the trash target tracking module, which is responsible for tracking the trash target and locating it to a certain moment when the trash was thrown down. The purpose of our trash tracking is also to capture the positive face of people. Here we adopt the ideas of tracking target shifting and video back tracking, i.e., the original tracking of residents is shifted to trash target tracking, and video back tracking is to rewind the frames of the current video.

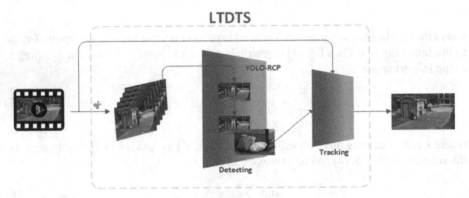

Fig. 2. Framework diagram of the LTDTS.

The framework flow chart of the system is shown in Fig. 2. A video is chopped into numerous video frames after it is entered into the system. The YOLO-RCP model is then used to detect trash from these video frames. If there is garbage in the scene and it is identified, the tracking module uses the location information of the trash as input, together with the original input video, to create a picture of the moment the resident throws the trash down. The resident's front face, if present, is also caught during this process.

4 Experiment

We carried out our experiments on the RCP-2021 dataset to test our method. The testing environment was conducted on one single Nvidia GTX 3090Ti graphic card with 16GB memory, and an Intel(R) Core (TM) i7-7700 3.60 GHz.

As shown in Table 2, to verify the effectiveness of the two improved methods, ablation experiments are used for testing. The experiment retains the improved methods that need to be tested and shields other methods that may affect the test module. The first is to reset the anchor size. By comparing the data of yolov5s and M1 in Table 2, we find that the new anchor size increases the mAP of the model from 53.05 to 54.76%, which shows that setting a reasonable anchor size according to the characteristics of the dataset can effectively increase the detection precision of the model. The second is to use α-IoU to replace the GIoU bounding box loss function. By comparing M1 and M2, it was found that the improvement of the α-IoU loss function increases the mAP of the model from 53.05 to 56.24%. Finally, the model M3, which is called YOLO-RCP, trained by integrating all methods in the same network achieved the best test results. Compared with yolov5s, the mAP of M3 increased from 53.05 to 58.11%.

Table 2. Ablation study of two improvements on RCP-2021 dataset.

method	New anchor	α-IoU	Precision	Recall	mAP50
Yolov5s	✘	✘	79.19	81.62	53.05
M1	✓	✘	80.51	83.27	54.76
M2	✘	✓	81.06	84.23	56.24
M3	✓	✓	82.35	85.91	58.11

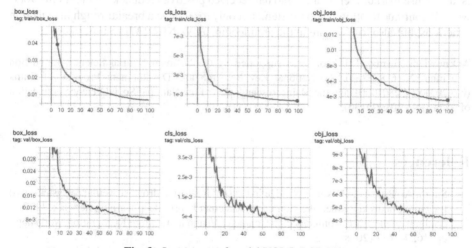

Fig. 3. Loss curve of model YOLO-RCP(M3).

Figure 3 shows the loss curves of the model training, with the top half being the train loss and the bottom half being the validation loss. Figure 4 shows the results of the trash detection module and tracking module.

The left depicts the moment when the trash detection module recognizes rubbish in video frames. The identification result is presented in the middle figure, where the waste is clearly framed out, indicating that the garbage's position information is obtained. The trash is tracked to the person who is placing the trash down in the rightmost figure, and it is evident that the resident in the figure is dropping the rubbish on the ground.

Fig. 4. The results of two module, the left is original picture, the middle is detection result, the right is tracking result.

5　Conclusion

We presented a lightweight litter detection and tracking system (LTDTS) in this research. The target detection module and the target tracking module are the two major modules of the system. The target detection module detects the location of the garbage first, and the location information is transmitted to the tracking module. The tracking module works backwards from the moment the resident throws the rubbish based on the garbage's location information. The modified yolov5 model is used in the detection module, while the KCF tracking technique is used in the tracking module. Extensive testing demonstrates that the proposed strategy performs well on the dataset described in this paper. LTDTS is also in use in a number of areas and has received positive feedback. In the future work, we will continue to optimize the system, not only to achieve a breakthrough in detection functions, but also to innovate in the architecture as VANET [37] in ITS.

Acknowledgements. This work was supported by the National Natural Science Foundation of China (No.61872231), the National Key Research and Development Program of China (No.2021YFC2801000), and the Major Research plan of the National Social Science Foundation of China (No.20&ZD130).

References

1. Singh, A., Patil, D., Omkar, S.N.: Eye in the sky: Real-time drone surveillance system (dss) for violent individual identification using scatternet hybrid deep learning network. In: Proceedings of the IEEE Conference on Computer Vision and Pattern Recognition Workshops, pp. 1629–1637 (2018)
2. Ahmed, M., Ramzan, M., Khan, H.U., Iqbal, S., Khan, M.A.: Real-time violent action recognition using key frames extraction and deep learning. Computers, Materials & Continua **69**(2), 2217–2230 (2021)
3. Liu, Y., Ge, Z., Lv, G., Wang, S.: Research on automatic garbage detection system based on deep learning and narrowband internet of things. J. Phys: Conf. Ser. **1069**, 12032 (2018)
4. Kraft, M., Piechocki, M., Ptak, B., Walas, K.: Autonomous, onboard vision-based trash and litter detection in low altitude aerial images collected by an unmanned aerial vehicle. Remote Sensing **13**(5), 965 (2021)
5. Sun, W., Dai, L., Zhang, X., Chang, P., He, X.: RSOD: Real-time small object detection algorithm in UAV-based traffic monitoring. Appl. Intell. (2021). https://doi.org/10.1007/s10 489-021-02893-3

6. Kulshreshtha, M., et al.: OATCR: outdoor autonomous trash-collecting robot design using yolov4-tiny. Electronics **10**(18), 2292 (2021)
7. Cai, Z., Vasconcelos, N.: Cascade r-cnn: delving into high quality object detection. In: Proceedings of the IEEE Conference on Computer Vision and Pattern Recognition, pp. 6154–6162 (2018)
8. Girshick, R.: Fast r-cnn. In: Proceedings of the IEEE International Conference on Computer Vision, pp. 1440–1448 (2015)
9. He, K., Gkioxari, G., Dollár, P., Girshick, R.: Mask r-cnn. In: Proceedings of the IEEE International Conference on Computer Vision, pp. 2961–2969 (2017)
10. Ren, S., He, K., Girshick, R., Sun, J.: Faster r-cnn: towards real-time object detection with region proposal networks. Adv. Neural. Inf. Process. Syst. **28**, 91–99 (2015)
11. Liu, J., Yang, Y., He, H.: Multi-level semantic representation enhancement network for relationship extraction. Neurocomputing **403**, 282–293 (2020)
12. Redmon, J., Divvala, S., Girshick, R., Farhadi, A.: You only look once: unified, real-time object detection. In: Proceedings of the IEEE Conference on Computer Vision and Pattern Recognition, pp. 779–788 (2016)
13. Redmon, J., Farhadi, A.: YOLO9000: better, faster, stronger. In: Proceedings of the IEEE Conference on Computer Vision and Pattern Recognition, pp. 7263–7271 (2017)
14. Bochkovskiy, A., Wang, C.Y., Liao, H.Y.M.: Yolov4: optimal speed and accuracy of object detection. arXiv:2004.10934 (2020)
15. Yang, Y., Xu, C., Dong, F., Wang, X.: A new multi-scale convolutional model based on multiple attention for image classification. Appl. Sci. **10**(1), 101 (2020)
16. Carion, N., Massa, F., Synnaeve, G., Usunier, N., Kirillov, A., Zagoruyko, S.: End-to-end object detection with transformers. In: European Conference on Computer Vision, pp. 213–229. Springer, Cham (2020)
17. Zhu, X., Su, W., Lu, L., Li, B., Wang, X., Dai, J.: Deformable detr: deformable transformers for end-to-end object detection. arXiv:2010.04159 (2020)
18. Law, H., Deng, J. Cornernet: Detecting objects as paired keypoints. In: Proceedings of the European Conference on Computer Vision (ECCV), pp. 734–750 (2018)
19. Xu, H., Jiang, C., Liang, X., Lin, L., Li, Z.: Reasoning-rcnn: unifying adaptive global reasoning into large-scale object detection. In: Proceedings of the IEEE/CVF Conference on Computer Vision and Pattern Recognition, pp. 6419–6428 (2019)
20. Gong, P., Liu, J., Yang, Y., He, H.: Towards knowledge enhanced language model for machine reading comprehension. IEEE Access **8**, 224837–224851 (2020)
21. Song, G., Liu, Y., Wang, X.: Revisiting the sibling head in object detector. In: Proceedings of the IEEE/CVF Conference on Computer Vision and Pattern Recognition, pp. 11563–11572 (2020)
22. Wang, N., Yeung, D.Y.: Learning a deep compact image representation for visual tracking. Advances in Neural Information Processing Systems (2013)
23. Chang, S., Liu, J.: Multi-lane capsule network for classifying images with complex background. IEEE Access **8**, 79876–79886 (2020)
24. Bolme, D.S., Beveridge, J.R., Draper, B.A., Lui, Y.M.: Visual object tracking using adaptive correlation filters. In: 2010 IEEE Computer Society Conference on Computer Vision and Pattern Recognition, pp. 2544–2550. IEEE (2010)
25. Henriques, J.F., Caseiro, R., Martins, P., Batista, J.: High-speed tracking with kernelized correlation filters. IEEE Trans. Pattern Anal. Mach. Intell. **37**(3), 583–596 (2014)
26. Danelljan, M., Häger, G., Khan, F., Felsberg, M.: Accurate scale estimation for robust visual tracking. In: British Machine Vision Conference. Nottingham (2014)
27. Danelljan, M., Bhat, G., Shahbaz Khan, F., Felsberg, M.: Eco: efficient convolution operators for tracking. In: Proceedings of the IEEE Conference on Computer Vision and Pattern Recognition, pp. 6638–6646 (2017)

28. Liu, J., Yang, Y., Lv, S., Wang, J., Chen, H.: Attention-based BiGRU-CNN for Chinese question classification. J. Ambient. Intell. Humaniz. Comput. **13**, 1–12 (2019). https://doi.org/10.1007/s12652-019-01344-9

29. Nam, H., Han, B.: Learning multi-domain convolutional neural networks for visual tracking. In: Proceedings of the IEEE Conference on Computer Vision and Pattern Recognition, pp. 4293–4302 (2016)

30. Bertinetto, L., Valmadre, J., Henriques, J.F.: Fully-convolutional siamese networks for object tracking. In: European Conference on Computer Vision, pp. 850–865. Springer (2016)

31. Li, B., Yan, J., Wu, W., Zhu, Z., Hu, X.: High performance visual tracking with Siamese region proposal network. In: Proceedings of the IEEE Conference on Computer Vision and Pattern Recognition, pp. 8971–8980 (2018)

32. He, J., Erfani, S., Ma, X., Bailey, J., Chi, Y., Hua, X.S.: A family of power intersection over union losses for bounding box regression. Advances in Neural Information Processing Systems, p. 34 (2021)

33. Liu, J., Gu, C., Wang, J., Youn, G., Kim, J.-U.: Multi-scale multi-class conditional generative adversarial network for handwritten character generation. J. Supercomput. **75**(4), 1922–1940 (2017). https://doi.org/10.1007/s11227-017-2218-0

34. Wang, H., Wang, J., Bai, K., Sun, Y.: Centered multi-task generative adversarial network for small object detection. Sensors **21**(15), 5194 (2021)

35. Arthur, D., Vassilvitskii, S.: k-means++: the advantages of careful seeding. Stanford (2006)

36. Chu, Q., Ouyang, W., Li, H., Wang, X., Liu, B., Yu, N.: Online multi-object tracking using CNN-based single object tracker with spatial-temporal attention mechanism. In: Proceedings of the IEEE International Conference on Computer Vision, pp. 4836–4845 (2017)

37. Jiang, X., Yu, F.R., Song, T., Leung, V.C.: Resource allocation of video streaming over vehicular networks: a survey, some research issues and challenges. IEEE Trans. Intell. Transp. Syst. (2021). https://doi.org/10.1109/TITS.2021.3065209

Deep Learning Feature-Based Method for FY3 Image Inpainting

Li Feng[1], Feihu Huang[1], Yan Zhang[2], and Jinrong Hu[1]([✉])

[1] Department of Computer Science, Chengdu University of Information Technology,
Chengdu 610225, China
hjr@cuit.edu.cn

[2] Satellite Meteorological Center (NSMC), China Meteorological Administration (CMA),
Beijing 100086, China

Abstract. The atmospheric ozone layer plays an important role in the interaction of extraterrestrial environmental systems. Obtaining complete ozone data can help relevant scientific researchers better analyze the state of the ozone layer and predict its impact on global or local climate. Due to the operating orbit and other factors, the polar weather satellite may lose some data when collecting data. We use an encoder-decoder convolutional neural network to repair missing data, and use a discriminant network to judge the quality of the data. The model showed amazing performance on a test set that was not related to the training set.

Keywords: Data quality control · Ozone · Deep learning · Generative adversarial network

1 Introduction

Ozone is a trace gas [1] in the earth's atmosphere, mainly distributed in the upper atmosphere or stratosphere, 10 ~ 50 km from the ground. When ultraviolet light passes through the stratosphere, most of it is absorbed by the ozone layer. Therefore, ozone is the earth's umbrella, protecting life on Earth from the destruction of ultraviolet rays. However, for more than a decade, the earth's ozone layer is being destroyed. Therefore, it is necessary to monitor stratospheric ozone [2]. Satellite ozone detector [3] has the obvious advantages of covering a large space and being less affected by weather changes in terms of time and space, making satellite ozone detection become an important means to monitor global ozone changes. FY3A satellite [4] launched in 2008 and FY3B satellite launched in 2010 are equipped with Total Ozone Unit (TOU) [5] developed by China for Ozone detection. TOU is a digital camera that uses ultraviolet rays from sunlight to create images. Ultraviolet light from the sun hits the atmosphere at the earth's surface. Some of the ultraviolet light is absorbed by ozone in the atmosphere, which protects life on Earth from the destruction of ultraviolet rays. However, the TOU instrument was affected by some abnormalities, resulting in missing ozone product data, as shown in Fig. 1. This brings great inconvenience to scientific research based on ozone layer data.

© The Author(s), under exclusive license to Springer Nature Switzerland AG 2022
X. Sun et al. (Eds.): ICAIS 2022, LNCS 13338, pp. 251–263, 2022.
https://doi.org/10.1007/978-3-031-06794-5_21

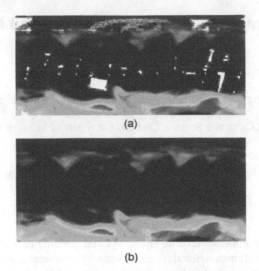

(a)

(b)

Fig. 1. Comparison before and after repairing the data. (a) is a TOU product that contains missing data. (b) is TOU products that have been repaired.

In this paper, a quality control algorithm for ozone missing data based on deep learning is proposed to repair the missing data. This method is based on generative adversarial network to repair the missing images. The network is composed of generator and discriminator. Generator is composed of Encoder, Residual Block and Decoder. Discriminator uses PatchGAN [6] structure. In the supervised method, this experiment made some improvements.

First, the MSR dataset was destroyed using a manufactured mask, and then the destroyed MSR images were put into the RN model for training (Fig. 2). The model is used to repair TOU images of FY3.

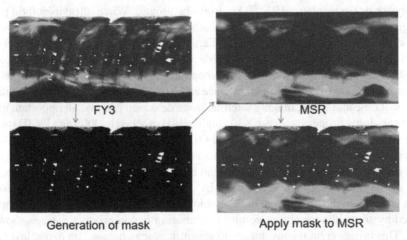

FY3   MSR

Generation of mask   Apply mask to MSR

Fig. 2. The production process of the data set

2 Related Work

Image repair refers to the process of reconstructing missing or damaged parts of an image. It is widely used in life. For example, when there are cracks in photos or scratches and dust spots in films, image repair can be used to prevent further deterioration of image quality. On the other hand, image repair can also be used for image editing. For example, when adding or deleting elements, we remove unnecessary image content and fill the gap after removal with reasonable image content. The existing image repair methods are mainly based on sequence and deep learning.

2.1 Image Inpainting Based on Sequence

Sequence - based image repair mainly includes sample - based and diffusion - based methods [7]. The basic idea of sample-based restoration is to find similar image blocks on the original image and fill them in the positions to be repaired. This method can not only fill the missing area of any size, but also repair the texture details of the damaged part. A number of sample-based fixes have been proposed. For example, Criminisi et al. [8]. proposed a texture-based algorithm for removing occlusion in pictures. It is mainly realized by repeating the following three steps: calculating the priority of edge pixels, finding the best matching block, and copying. The basic idea of diffusion based restoration is to use the edge information of the region to be repaired to determine the direction of diffusion, and then use the diffusion mechanism to diffuse the known information to the region with repair [9]. This method is mainly used for repairing small scale image damage, such as small scratches in photos. Typical methods include [10] 's BSCB(Bertalmio Sapipez Caselles Ballester) model, which uses third-order partial differential equations to simulate smooth transmission process. And The CDD(Curvature diffusion-Diffusion) model proposed by Chan et al. [11].

2.2 Image Repair Based on Deep Learning

In recent years, with the development of deep learning technology and hardware devices, researchers have proposed many image restoration methods based on deep learning, and achieved success in some aspects. Deep convolutional Neural network (CNN) shows great potential in image restoration [12]. CNN consists of one or more convolution layers, pooling layers and full connection layers. The purpose of convolution is to extract different features of the input. The pooling layer mainly carries out subsampling on the feature maps learned by the convolutional layer. There are two types of pooling, namely maximum pooling and average pooling. The full connection layer is used for final model tasks such as classification, regression, and so on. LeNet [13], as the first successful convolutional neural network, was implemented by Yann LeCun et al. in the 1990s, mainly applied in the field of identifying numbers and postal codes. The Alex [14] convolutional neural network proposed by Alex et al. is popular in the field of computer vision. Its structure is very similar to LeNet, but it has more network layers and uses layered convolutional layers to acquire features. In 2014, GoogLeNet [15], proposed by Szeged et al., significantly reduced the number of parameters in the network. The main contribution of VGGNet proposed by Karen et al. is to show that the depth of the network is a key part of the excellent performance of the algorithm. The Residual Network was realized by He Kaiming et al. It uses special jump links and makes heavy use of Batch normalization. Generative Adversarial Networks (GANs) [16], proposed by Goodfellow et al. in 2014, are widely used in computer fields as a Generative model, such as image repair, image denoising and image generation. Generative adversarial network consists of two important parts: generator and discriminator. During training, the generator is used to generate data in order to "fool" the discriminator. The discriminator determines whether the image is real or machine-generated, in order to find "fake data" made by the generator. As the Convolutional network has stronger fitting and expression capabilities, Alec et al. introduce generators and discriminators into CNN and propose Deep Convolutional GAN [17], which improves the quality of samples and the speed of convergence and has achieved great results.

2.3 Supervision Methods

The training methods of deep learning algorithms can be divided into three categories: supervised learning, semi-supervised learning and unsupervised learning. In supervised learning, the value of the target variable, that is, the label data, must be given so that the learning algorithm can discover the relationship between the input features and the target variable. So supervised learning has clear goals and knows what results you want [18]. Unsupervised learning does not require a given value of the target variable. The algorithm learns from the unlabeled data, trying to find hidden structures to build a model describing certain relationships between samples of the data set. In semi-supervised learning, the algorithm combines labeled data and unlabeled data to train and generate an appropriate output model.

3 Method

3.1 Method of Supervision in this Paper

In this experiment, the missing data to be repaired were used as feature data and the complete data as label data. The data to be repaired is called P_mask and the complete data is called P_original, then

$$P\_mask = P\_original \odot (1 - mask) \tag{1}$$

$\odot$ is the dot product. When P_mask data passes through the network to generate a new image, the generated image is called Pred. P_original$\odot$ Mask is used to supervise Pred$\odot$mask to control network training (Fig. 3).

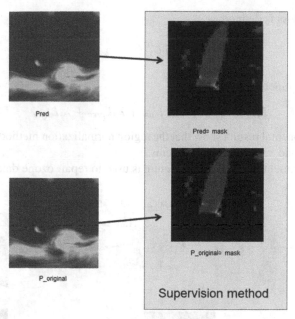

Fig. 3. Supervision method

3.2 Network Model

Most image restoration methods based on deep learning are trained by Feature Normalization, but Normalization in spatial dimension ignores the impact of damaged areas on Normalization, such as mean and variance drift. As a result of this defect, [19] puts forward a new method of regional Normalization. According to the input mask, the spatial pixels are divided into damaged regions and undamaged regions, and the mean and variance of the two regions are calculated to normalize, so as to solve the problem of mean and variance drift.

The image generator of EdgeConnect network [20] was used as the backbone generator in the literature, and the whole generating network was composed of encoder, Residual block and decoder. This structure can effectively reduce the complexity of feedback neural network. The main purpose of the generator is to generate an image similar to the original image according to the image to be completed and then patch the corresponding position image block to the image to be completed.There has been Basic Region Normalization (RN-B) module in the encoder and Learnable Region Normalization (RN-L) module in the residual and decoder. The discriminant was PatchGAN. Meanwhile, its loss function is used, including four parts: adversarial loss, perceptual loss, style loss and l1 loss. The adversarial loss is defined as

$$L_{adv} = E_{(I_{gt}, C_{comp})} \log[D(I_{gt}, C_{comp})] + E_{C_{comp}} \log[1 - D(I_{pred}, C_{comp})] \quad (2)$$

The style loss is defined as

$$L_{style} = E_j[||G_j^{\varphi}(I_{pred}) - G_j^{\varphi}(I_{gt})||_1] \quad (3)$$

The perceptual loss is defined as

$$L_{prec} = E[\sum_i \frac{1}{N_i} ||\varphi_1^{(i)}(I_{gt}) - \varphi_1^{(i)}(I_{pred})||_1] \tag{4}$$

Our overall loss function is

$$L_G = \lambda_{l_1} L_{l_1} + \lambda_{adv} L_{adv} + \lambda_p L_{prec} + \lambda_s L_{style} \tag{5}$$

The final experimental results show that the region normalization method can effectively solve the mean and variance drift problems.

In this experiment, the network structure is used to repair ozone data (Fig. 4).

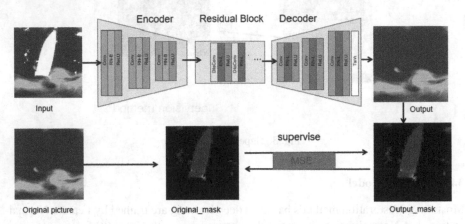

Fig. 4. Illustration of our inpainting model and supervision method

4 Experiment

The implementation of the experiment will be explained from three aspects: data set, experimental details and evaluation methods. There are three data sets used, namely TOU data set, MSR data set and MSR_fy_mask data set. The last data set is the training data of the experiment, and the production process will be described in detail below.

4.1 Dataset

FY3 dataset. The ozone data observed by TOU on FY3A and FY3B satellites are called TOU total ozone product. The main data contents include observation time, geographical location, solar direction, satellite observation direction, total ozone, total ozone inversion quality control code, etc. TOU provides a daily map of total global ozone. However, due to some unavoidable reasons of the instrument, there are some gaps in the total ozone map, as shown in Fig. 5, and our work is to recover these missing ozone data. The Tou products of Fy3A in this experiment are from 2008 to 2014, and the Tou products of Fy3B are from 2010 to 2017, with a total of 4917 cases. The image size is 360 by 720 pixels.

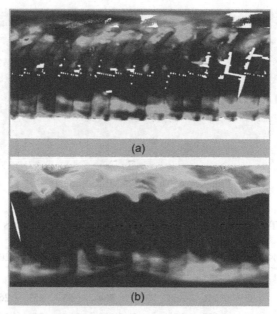

Fig. 5. TOU products with the missing data. (a) is the total TOU ozone product of FY3A on August 9, 2008. (b) is the total TOU ozone product of FY3B on March 5, 2013. Missing data is shown in white.

MSR dataset. In order to restore the image of Tou product, a very important data set is used in this experiment., It is called multi sensor reanalysis (MSR) [21]. It contains almost three decades of corrected satellite ozone data. It uses satellite instruments such as TOMS, SBUV, GOME, SCIAMACHY, OMI and GOME-2, and has identified and collected 14 total ozone satellite data sets. The study also used two other sets of data sets, ground total ozone dataset named WOUDC and effective ozone temperature dataset named ECMWF. The generation of the data set is divided into two steps: firstly, the small system deviation in the satellite data is corrected by taking the ground observation average as the true value. Then, all satellite data are assimilated by Kalman filter technology, and finally an ozone data set with a complete 30-year cycle is obtained.

We used the data from 2008 to 2018 (see Table 1). The image size was 360 * 720 pixels, a total of 4016 cases (Fig. 6).

MSR_fy_mask dataset. The mask used in this experiment was generated by TOU products. The mask of TOU products is extracted to form a FY_mask dataset (Fig. 7). The making method of mask is as follows:

$$m = \begin{cases} 0, 1 > fy > 0 \\ 1, fy = 1 \end{cases} \qquad (6)$$

where, fy represents TOU pixel value, 0 represents black and 1 represents white, that is, empty.

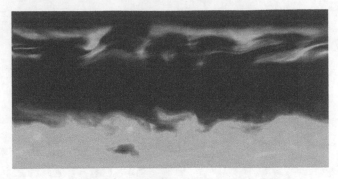

Fig. 6. An example of MSR products

Table 1. Number of fy3 and MSR data in different years

	2008	2009	2010	2011	2012	2013	2014	2015	2016	2017	2018	Total
FY3A	181	364	365	365	363	362	133					2133
FY3B			359	361	360	358	364	356	357	269		2784
MSR	366	365	365	365	366	365	365	365	366	365	363	4016

The mask is then applied randomly to the MSR data, making it a missing picture. Specific methods are as follows:

$$MSR' = MSR \odot (1 - mask) \tag{7}$$

This ensures the accuracy of the model for FY3 data repair.

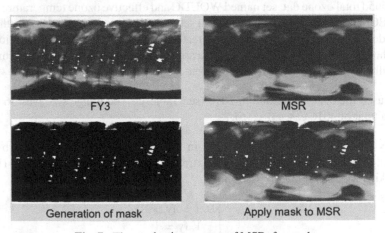

Fig. 7. The production process of MSR_fy_mask

During the generation of mask dataset, we have done some data preprocessing. First of all, we found that there were some completely missing data in the TOU product of FY3, and the FY_mask obtained was an all-white image. We made statistics on the data in this situation, and there were 801 images in total, which would certainly cause some errors in the experiment. To avoid this error, we filtered the images. In addition, we also found that TOU the north and south poles of products, namely the both ends up and down on the image there are different levels of large area is missing, hope our present work will only missing a small area of the image in the middle of the area, if the blank of the north and south poles are directly related to the data model to join in training, will have a larger effect on the recovery of the experimental effect. Therefore, we removed the north and south polar regions of all TOU product images according to different missing conditions, and cut out 60 pixels at the top, 60 pixels at the bottom and 30 pixels at the upper and lower ends of the image. Thus, the mask image from X is 300*720 pixels (Fig. 8).

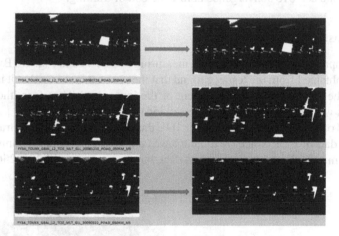

Fig. 8. Preprocess of Fy_mask

In order to make the experiment robust, we do data enhancement work as shown in Fig. 9. The ROC of the region of interest was obtained randomly from MSR images and

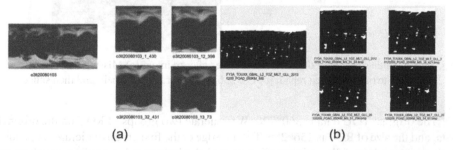

(a)   (b)

Fig. 9. Expansion of data volume. (a) is the clipping of MSR data. (b) is the clipping of mask data

FY_mask images. The region size was 256*256, and 10 ROC were randomly obtained from each image. This increases the amount of data involved in training tenfold.

4.2 Experimental Details

Although the amount of data is expanded through data enhancement, we use transfer learning for better results. A 300,000 Places dataset was used as the pretrained model for this experiment. The model was iterated on the Places dataset for 43 times.

This experiment was carried out on the Linux server of Win10 Professional edition. The hardware configuration of the server was CPU(Intel I7-7700K), four GPUs (Nvidia RTX2080Ti), and software configuration was CUDA, Anaconda3, Pytorch, Python3.7, etc. The MSR_fy_mask dataset was trained, the image size was 256*256, and the batch-size of the training was 10. Adam optimizer [22] was used for optimization. Exponential decay rate $\beta 1 = 0$, $\beta 2 = 0.9$ and learning rate 10–4 were set. We train RN network with 500 epochs and achieve convergence before the end of training.

4.3 Contrast

We first compared our method with data measuring 360 by 720 in Fig. 10. By observing the images obtained from the test, we found that the use of this shows that it is necessary to modify the size and data enhancement of the input data. Therefore, the following experiments will uniformly input the size of 256*256.

The goal of this experiment is to repair TOU data. Therefore, we use the trained model to test TOU data of FY3. Since we did not have complete TOU data for comparison, we made some minor adjustments to the test data, but the size was still 256*256.

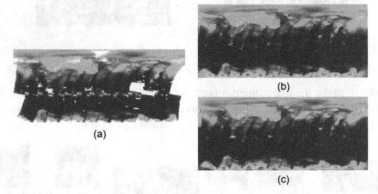

Fig. 10. Inpainting results of data of different sizes after training. (a) Missing data. (b) Use 360 * 720 pictures to train and then repair. (c) Use 256 * 256 to train and repair, and then splice.

The original TOU data is 360*720. We generate two groups of ROC on the original data, and the size of ROC is 256*256. The top edge of the first group of pictures coincides with the top edge of the original picture, and the bottom edge of the second group coincides with the bottom edge of the original picture, as shown in Fig. 11. This value is bound to form an overlap area between the two groups of images. We just need to calculate the coincidence of the overlapping areas to know how well the repair is. In this experiment, peak Signal to Noise Ratio (PSNR), structural similarity index measure (SSIM) [23] and L1 loss were used to calculate the degree of coincidence.

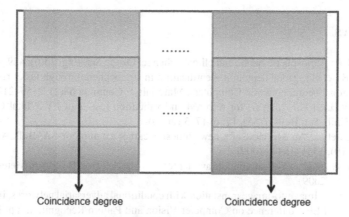

Coincidence degree   Coincidence degree

Fig. 11. Evaluation method

To prove the feasibility and superiority of this experimental method, our method was compared and analyzed with existing restoration networks like EdgeConnect(EC) [19], Contextual Attention(CA) [24] and Partial Convolution(PC) [25] (see Table 2).

Table 2. Comparison results of the different methods

	PSNR	SSIM	L1 loss
EC	30.0235	0.9438	0.0047
CA	27.0855	0.9622	0.00612
PC	46.4722	0.9398	0.0049
Ours	57.4349	0.9984	0.0005

5   Conclusion

In this experiment, a model trained by MSR data was proposed to repair the missing ozone data of TOU. The model used is a generative adversarial network, the generator is the encoding and decoding structure, and the discriminator is the PatchGan structure. Before the training, a series of pre-processing for the input data, including data enhancement, data cleaning, data cutting, etc. By comparing the visual effect, peak signal-to-noise ratio (PSNR), structural similarity and L1 loss of the restored images on MSR data set with other algorithms, the results show that the proposed method has a better effect on the restoration of FY3 missing ozone data.

Funding Statement. This study is supported by the National Key R&D Program of China (Grant No. 2020YFA0608004).

References

1. Shine, K.P.: Atmospheric ozone and climate change. Ozone Sci. Eng. **23**(6), 429–435 (2001)
2. Aslam, B., et al.: Ozone depletion identification in stratosphere through faster region-based convolutional neural network. Computers, Materials & Continua **68**(2), 2159–2178 (2021)
3. Wang, W.H., et al.: Analysis for retrieval and validation results of FY-3 Tatal Ozone Unit (TOU). Chin. Sci. Bull **17**(55), 1726–1733 (2010)
4. Dong, C., et al.: An overview of a new chinese weather satellite FY-3A. Bull. Am. Meteor. Soc. **90**(10), 1531–1544 (2009)
5. Wang, Y.M., et al.: FY-3 satellite ultraviolet total ozone detector. Bull. Am. Meteor. Soc. **23**, 3778–3783 (2009)
6. Isola, P., et al.: Image-to-image translation with conditional adversarial networks, In: Proceedings of the IEEE Conference on Computer Vision and Pattern Recognition, pp. 1125–1134 (2017)
7. Liu, Q., Xiang, X., Qin, J., Tan, Y., Tan, J., Luo, Y.: Coverless steganography based on image retrieval of DenseNet features and DWT sequence mapping. Knowl.-Based Syst. **192**, 105375–105389 (2020)
8. Criminisi, A., Pérez, P., Toyama, K.: Region filling and object removal by exemplar-based image inpainting. IEEE Trans. Image Process. **13**(9), 1200–1212 (2004)
9. Zhang, J., Qi, X., Myint, S.H., Wen, Z.: Deep-learning-empowered 3d reconstruction for dehazed images in iotenhanced smart cities. Computers, Materials & Continua **69**(2), 2809 (2021)
10. Bertalmio, M., et al.: Image inpainting. In: Proceedings of the 27th Annual Conference on Computer Graphics and Interactive Techniques, pp. 417–424 (2000)
11. Chan, T.F., Shen, J.: Nontexture inpainting by curvature-driven diffusions. J. Vis. Commun. Image Represent. **12**(4), 436–449 (2001)
12. Chen, J., Zhou, Z., Pan, Z., Yang, C.: Instance retrieval using region of interest based cnn features. Journal of New Media **1**(2), 87–99 (2019)
13. LeCun, Y., et al.: Gradient-based learning applied to document recognition. Proc. IEEE **86**(11), 2278–2324 (1998)
14. Krizhevsky, A., Sutskever, L., Geoffrey, E.H.: Imagenet classification with deep convolutional neural networks. Adv. neural Info. Process. Sys. **25**, 1097–1105 (2012)
15. Szegedy, C., et al.: Going deeper with convolutions. In: Proceedings of the IEEE Conference on Computer Vision and Pattern Recognition, pp. 1–9 (2015)
16. Goodfellow, I., et al.: Generative adversarial nets. Adv. Neural. Inf. Process. Syst. **27**, 2672–2680 (2014)
17. Radford, A., Luke, M., Soumith, C.: Unsupervised representation learning with deep convolutional generative adversarial networks. arXiv preprint arXiv **1511**(06434) (2015)
18. Hu, X., et al.: A semantic supervision method for abstractive summarization. Computers, Materials & Continua **69**(1), 145–158 (2021)
19. Yu, T., et al.: Region normalization for image inpainting. Proc. AAAI Conf. Artif. Intell. **34**(07), 12733–12740 (2020)

20. Nazeri, K., et al.: Edgeconnect: generative image inpainting with adversarial edge learning. arXiv preprint arXiv **1901**(00212) (2019)
21. Van Der, A.R.J., Allaart, M.A.F., Eskes, H.J.: Multi sensor reanalysis of total ozone. Atmos. Chem. Phys. **10**(22), 11277–11294 (2010)
22. Kingma, D.P., Ba, J.: Adam: a method for stochastic optimization. arXiv preprint arXiv **1412**(6980) (2014)
23. Wang, Z., et al.: Image quality assessment: from error visibility to structural similarity. IEEE Trans. Image Process. **13**(4), 600–612 (2004)
24. Yu, I., et al.: Generative image inpainting with contextual attention. In: Proceedings of the IEEE Conference on Computer Vision and Pattern Recognition, pp. 5505–5514 (2018)
25. Liu, G., et al.: Image inpainting for irregular holes using partial convolutions. In: Proceedings of the European Conference on Computer Vision (ECCV), pp. 85–100 (2018)

Let the Big Data Speak: Collaborative Model of Topic Extract and Sentiment Analysis COVID-19 Based on Weibo Data

Tianjie Luo[1], Ran Li[1(✉)] ⓘ, Zhe Sun[1], Fuqiang Tao[1], Manoj Kumar[2], and Chao Li[1]

[1] Cyberspace Institute of Advanced Technology, Guangzhou University, Guangzhou 510006, China
liran@gzhu.edu.cn
[2] University of Petroleum and Energy Studies, Dehradun 248007, India

Abstract. Micro-blog is an important medium of emergency communication. The topic and emotion analysis of micro-blog is of great significance in identifying and predicting potential problems and risks. In this paper, a collaborative analysis model of emotion and topic mining is constructed to analyze the users' sentiment and the topics they care about, Firstly, we use SO-PMI to construct domain sentiment lexicon and extract topics with LDA. Then we use the collaborative model to analyze sentiment and topic. The results showed that the model we proposed can present the features of sentiment and topic of user concerns. And through text clustering and sentiment analysis, it is found that the attitude of users towards the COVID-19 has gone through three stages, namely, a period of fluctuating tension and anxiety, a period of slowly rising solidarity and a period of stable self-confidence with little fluctuation, on the whole, positive is greater than negative, positive than negative state.

Keywords: Emergency · COVID-19 · Sentiment classification · Topic mining · Collaborative model

1 Introduction

1.1 A Subsection Sample

Nowadays, the Internet has changed the way in which emergencies are transmitted. Everyone can share their own views and become the producers of Internet information without the restrictions of time and space. Internet social platform plays an important role in the information exchange port in the major events in the economic, social and cultural fields. It is of great significance to analyze the hot spots and sentimental evolution characteristics of public health emergencies, such as the COVID-19 epidemic sweeping the world in 2020.

At present, researches on sentiment analysis of emergencies mainly focus on the classification of user sentiment by using different sentiment analysis methods [1–3], and the analysis of sentimental communication mechanism and communication network in

© The Author(s), under exclusive license to Springer Nature Switzerland AG 2022
X. Sun et al. (Eds.): ICAIS 2022, LNCS 13338, pp. 264–275, 2022.
https://doi.org/10.1007/978-3-031-06794-5_22

public opinion of emergencies [4–6]. These researches mainly focus on the evolution of sentimental situation by dividing stages and subjects, visually displaying sentimental evolution by constructing sentimental maps in different periods of public opinion development [7], analyzing the mechanism and differences of sentimental communication of different subjects [8], constructing various models such as sentimental evolution to analyze the evolution of public opinion [9], etc. However, in the face of serious emergency, single topic mining or sentiment analysis cannot meet the actual needs. The research results on how to conduct thematic sentiment and topic content mining are relatively few.

In order to solve the problem that the topic and sentiment of COVID-19 hot news and emergent events are difficult to distinguish, we propose a sentiment analysis method based on domain lexicon, which uses SO-PMI algorithm to expand the sentiment words, enhancing the domain applicability of lexicon. The complex context of Chinese text and the phenomenon of polysemy often lead to some errors in the sentiment analysis method based on the sentiment dictionary, therefore, this paper also proposes a topic mining and sentimental analysis of the emergency analysis method. Using the techniques of Data pre-processing, feature extraction and Word Cloud visualization to mine the hot topics of the target data, then using co word analysis, LDA topic model, PaddlePaddle based sentiment analysis algorithm to analyze the target data, mining the trend of topic evolution of unexpected events. Finally, we get the general sentimental trend of the data, the core theme of each period, and the sentimental evolution process with time. The main contributions of this paper are as follows:

- A domain sentiment lexicon was constructed to enhance the domain applicability of the Chinese micro blog about the COVID-19.
- Construct a collaborative analysis model of sentiment and topic mining to analyze the sentiment and topic characteristics of typical emergencies during the epidemic period of COVID-19.
- Combined with the sentiment distribution characteristics in the event cycle of COVID-19, the sentiment development trend of emergent events was analyzed.

2 Related Works

Current research on emergency sentiment analysis mainly focuses on the unsupervised method based on sentiment lexicon and the supervised method based on machine learning.

Many scholars and institutions have compiled some comprehensive Chinese and English sentiment lexica, including: SentiWordNet, LIWC, NTUSD, Hownet, and DLUT-Sentiment ontology [10]. SentiWordNet is the most famous sentiment lexicon in English by classifying the entries in WordNet and labelling the sentiment weight of positive and negative words. The LIWC English sentiment lexicon uses a large number of regular expressions to describe sentimental words and gives comprehensive information on the part of speech, antonyms, commendations, positive and negative of each entry. The HowNet sentiment lexicon published by HowNet contains Chinese and English sentiment lexica. NTUSD lexicon includes 2,810 positive words and 8,276 negative words with high accuracy. DLUT-Sentiment ontology is a Chinese sentiment lexicon which is manually sorted and annotated. The lexicon describes a Chinese word or phase from different perspectives, including information on part of speech type, sentiment category, sentimental intensity and polarity. However, the generally constructed sentiment lexicon is not rich in the domain field, and the emergency words are changeable, so its effect is not satisfactory.

In the face of complex major events, a single topic mining or emotion analysis cannot meet the actual needs. Some scholars combine topic extraction with emotion analysis to comprehensively analyze the hot spots and the evolution of public opinion [11].

Due to the complex in serious emergencies, there are some errors to the results of sentiment analysis based on sentiment lexicon, thus the accuracy is not ideal. As another popular method of sentiment analysis, machine learning-based sentiment analysis can be more effective in emergency texts with complex contexts. Roy et al. [12] used PLSA model to extract sub topics in different time periods, obtain the emotional tendency value of each sub topic in a time series, and finally draw the emotional change trend of the whole topic. An Sreenivasulu et al. [13] divided the stages according to the evolution cycle of public opinion, combined word2vec with K-means clustering to extract the subject feature words of each stage, and carried out fine-grained emotion analysis for each stage. Wang et al. [14] proposed a fast-clustering method of microblog topics, and studied the extraction of hot topics and emotional trend analysis over a period of time. Zhao et al. [15] extracted sub topics using LDA and analyzed the emotional trend of each sub topic with the help of emotional dictionary. From the above research results, the existing research mainly determines the theme content of the text through emergencies, and then classifies the theme sentimentally. There are relatively few researches on the correlation analysis of topic sentiment and topic content for the COVID-19.

3 Model

In this paper, we analyze the microblog data around the topic of "COVID-19", and constructs the collaborative model of sentiment and topic mining, as shown in Fig. 1 below. Firstly, preprocess the text data, expand the exclusive domain of the existing basic sentiment lexicon by using SO-PMI algorithm, and construct the domain sentiment lexicon. Then the text clustering algorithm is used to classify the topic, and then PaddlePaddle is used to analyze the sentiment and trend of the extracted topic.

3.1 Domain Sentiment Lexicon Construction

Most of the previous researches of microblog sentiment analysis used the extended general lexica, while the texts studied in this paper have strong pertinence and applicability in the field of emergencies, and the contents of sentiment analysis are network comment texts. There are unique sentimental words in different fields. The sentiments expressed by these words cannot be ignored, and they are not included in the basic lexicon. Therefore, it is necessary to expand the exclusive domain of the basic lexicon. We use sentiment orientation point mutual information algorithm (SO-PMI) [16] to select the extended sentiment words from the actual COVID-19 related micro-blog, then we get the sentiment words in the COVID-19 field, some of them are depicted in Table 1 below.

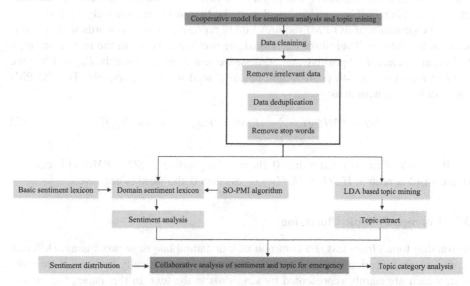

Fig. 1. Cooperative model of sentiment analysis and topic mining.

Table 1. COVID-19 sentiment word table.

No.	Sentiment word	Sentiment polarity	Part of speech
1	疫情(epidemic)	-1	n
2	新型冠状病毒(COVID-19)	-1	n
3	确诊(confirmed)	-1	v
4	隔离(isolated)	-1	v
5	口罩(mask)	-1	n
6	超级传播者(super spreader)	-1	n
7	医护人员(paramedics)	1	n
8	抗击(fight)	1	v
...	...	...	...

SO-PMI is a further application of pointwise mutual information (PMI) in sentiment analysis, which uses PMI to evaluate the semantic orientation (SO) of the words to be classified. PMI is used to measure the interdependence between the words w_1 and w_2. The PMI formula is as follows:

$$PMI(w_1, w_2) = \log \frac{P(w_1 w_2)}{P(w_1) \cdot P(w_2)} \tag{1}$$

where $P(w_1 w_2)$ represents the co-occurrence probability of w_1 and w_2. $P(w_1)$ and $P(w_2)$ represent the probability that appear alone. The larger the $PMI(w_1, w_2)$, the greater the correlation between w_1 and w_2. And the sentiment polarity of them are more consistent. When $PMI(w_1, w_2)$ is greater than 0, the two words are related. When $PMI(w_1, w_2)$ is equal to 0. The two words are independent of each other, neither related nor mutually exclusive. When $PMI(w_1, w_2)$ is less than 0, the two words are mutually exclusive.

The calculation of SO-PMI requires highly representative seed words with obvious sentiment tendency. Therefore, we ranked the sentiment words in the texts from high to low, and selected 50 positive and 50 negative sentiment seed words. P_{w_i} and N_{w_i} are used to represent the i-th positive and negative seed word, respectively. The SO-PMI formula for w is written as:

$$SO - PMI(w) = \sum_{i=1} [PMI(w, P_{w_i}) - PMI(w, N_{w_i})]$$ (2)

If $SO - PMI(w)$ is greater than 0, the word is positive. If $SO - PMI(w)$ is equal to 0, the word is neutral. If $SO - PMI(w)$ is less than 0, the word is negative.

3.2 Emergency Topic Clustering

Extracting topics from text is a common task in natural language processing. Different from text classification, topic extraction requires to automatically find topics from the text, which are mainly represented by keywords in the text. In this paper, the images in microblog are ignored in the topic extracting, only the discussion topic and texts are used. We use the LDA [17] topic model to mine the topic of the texts.

The LDA probability topic model proposed by Beli et al. is usually used to model large-scale document data. The LDA model is a three-layer structure of word-topic-document. The idea comes from the basic assumption that documents are made up of multiple implicit topics, which are made up of several specific feature words. The advantage of LDA model is that it has a clear internal structure and is trained by unsupervised method. It is suitable for classifying a large amount of data. The generation of the LDA model is shown in Fig. 2 below:

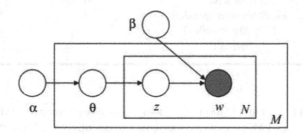

Fig. 2. LDA graph model.

In a document set, the parameters α reflect the relative intensity between potential topics. The larger the document, the more topics it contains, and vice versa. β is the probability distribution for all potential topics, and the bigger β is, the more words the topic contains, and vice versa. θ represents the weight of the potential topic in the target document, W is the word vector representation of the target document, and Z is the number of potential topics assigned to each term in the document. Suppose m is a potential topic, w_i is the i-th word in the document, then the probability that w_i belongs to m is:

$$P(w_i) = \sum_{m=1}^{k} P(w_i|z_i = m)P(z_i = m) \tag{3}$$

where $P(w_i|z_i = m)$ is the probability that the word w_i belongs to the potential topic m, $P(z_i = m)$ is the topic probability of the document.

In practice, the accurate calculation of the LDA model is more complex. Hence, we use the most common Gibbs sampling method to estimate the parameters, and the parameters are set as $\alpha = 0.5$, $\beta = 0.1$. The number of iterations is 300, and the number of clusters is $K = 10$. The selection of the optimal number of clusters can be calculated by the probability of word selection or the degree of perplexity [18]. We use the word cloud map to verify the topic clustering effect, at the same time, we can also visually display the hot words in the microblog. In a word cloud, the size of a word is determined by its frequency of occurrence, so the word cloud can be highlighted for high-frequency words. The key words in COVID-19 micro-blog are shown in Fig. 3 below. In our dataset, the word "COVID-19"is the most frequently mentioned term in microblog. And words such as "prevention and control", "Wuhan", "new cases", and "confirmed cases" also frequently appear on popular microblogs.

Fig. 3. Topic cloud chart of Covid-19.

3.3 Topic-Sentiment Fusion Analysis

Public sentiment analysis, which is related to the attitude of users on the Internet, plays a vital role in the development of events. While in the face of complex major events, single topic mining or sentiment analysis cannot meet the actual needs. Hence, in this paper, we use the ERINE pre-training model embedded in PaddlePaddle to process the sentiment of text data and excavate the multi-meaning sentiment of emergency. First of all, the text arranged by time is processed by word segmentation, and the domain sentiment lexicon above is used for word segmentation, entity extraction, and sentiment analysis. Then, according to the comparison results of positive and negative sentiment values in a single text, the se tendency of all texts was divided into three categories: positive, negative and neutral. Firstly, the collected micro-blog data were classified by sentiment, and the different sentiment distribution of the micro-blog data was obtained. The different sentiment text samples were sorted out, to achieve the collaborative analysis of emotion and theme.

4 Experiments

In this section, we will first introduce the datasets and evaluation indexes. Then, the proposed model is verified in the COVID-19 epidemic emergency data set, and compared with the baseline model, the reported results are the optimal results.

4.1 Dataset and Evaluation Index

In this paper, we use the dataset of "Sentiment recognition of Internet users during the COVID-19". The dataset collects data according to 230 subject keywords related to "COVID-19", captures a total of 1 million microblog data from January 1, 2020 to February 20, 2020, and manually labels 100,000 of them.

In order to eliminate the influence of other unnecessary factors, the training set used in each model is consistent with the test set. Among them, 80% of the data set is used as the training set, and the remaining 20% is used as the testing set. Precision, recall and Macro-F1 are used as the evaluation indexes, which are referred to as P, R and F1 values respectively.

$$P = \frac{TP}{TP + FP} \tag{4}$$

$$R = \frac{TP}{TP + FN} \tag{5}$$

$$F1 = \frac{2 \times P \times R}{P + R} \tag{6}$$

where TP represents the amount of data when both the actual value and the predicted value are positive. FP represents the amount of data when the actual value is negative and the predicted value is positive. FN represents the amount of data when the actual value is positive and the predicted value is negative. Calculate the $F1$ value for each category and average it to get macro-$F1$. The larger the value of $F1$, the better the classifying effect of the model is.

4.2 Experiment Results and Analysis

Effect Analysis of Domain Sentiment Lexicon. After pre-processing, 1,000 microblogs were randomly selected as the test set. Three people annotate the sentiment of these texts, and the results with the largest number of labels are counted as the final sentiment polarity of the microblog. For comparison, we choose the DLUT-Sentiment ontology which is recognized to be the state-of-art as the baseline. The results are shown in Figs. 4 and 5 below.

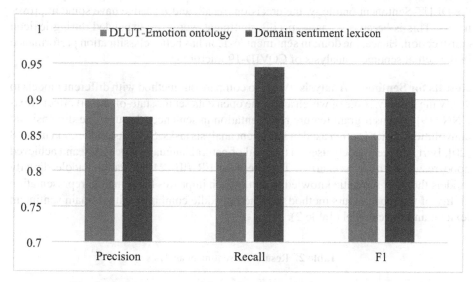

Fig. 4. Performance comparison of sentiment lexicon (positive texts).

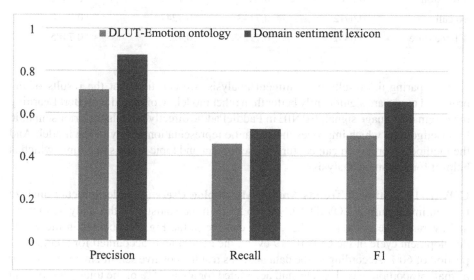

Fig. 5. Performance comparison of sentiment lexicon (negative texts).

As can be seen from Figs. 4 and 5, the domain sentiment lexicon has greatly improved the sentiment analysis performance of positive texts Fig. 4 and negative texts Fig. 5. In terms of positive sentiment, the precision of our domain sentiment lexicon is nearly the same to the baseline lexicon, while the recall and $F1$ value have grown significantly. For the negative texts, our domain sentiment lexicon is better in classifying. Compared with the DLUT-Sentiment ontology, the precision, recall, and $F1$ value have some improvements. This is because domain-specific sentiment words are expanded during lexicon construction. Hence, the domain sentiment lexicon has better classification performance in the actual sentiment analysis of COVID-19 microblog.

Results for Sentiment Analysis. We also compare our method with different models to verify the validity, some of which are in the open data set for state-of-the-art effect. Text-CNN [19] obtains n-gram feature representation in sentences through one-dimensional convolution, which is often used in sentiment analysis tasks. Since its publication in 2018 [20], Bert has been widely used in the field of natural language processing and achieved good results in many scenarios. The pre-train ERNIE [21] in PaddlePaddle directly models the prior semantic knowledge unit, which improves the semantic representation ability of the model. Ours method use PaddlePaddle combined with domain sentiment lexicon and topic model (Table 2).

Table 2. Results for sentiment analysis.

	Text-CNN	BERT	PaddlePaddle	Ours
Precision	0.6703	0.7009	0.7301	0.7452
Recall	0.6912	0.7143	0.7241	0.7518
F1-measure	0.6852	0.7128	0.7257	0.7485

Comparing the results of sentiment analysis, we can find that the results of the proposed model are significantly better than other models. Compared with Bert Learning the original language signal, ERNIE in PaddlePaddle directly models the prior semantic knowledge unit, which improves the semantic representation ability of the model. And the method we proposed can capture the sentiment and topic at the same time, which is helpful for sentiment analysis.

COVID-19 Sentiment Trends Among Micro-blog Users. In order to better analyze the sentiment during COVID-19, we made a simple statistic in the daily sentiment, and averaged the analysis results. As we can see in the Fig. 5(a) below, in the whole development cycle of the COVID-19 event, the neutral texts accounted for a large proportion of 60%. According to the data analysis results, positive sentiment accounted for a small proportion in each cycle, and accounted for about 15% of the total microblog in each cycle. The proportion of negative sentiment tendency gradually decreased with the development of the event. As can be seen from this sudden topic event, the overall trend of this event is positive. In addition, we also calculated the average daily sentiment value as shown in Fig. 5(b), we can find that from Jan. 1 to Feb. 20, the attitude of netizens toward the "COVID-19" was generally positive. During these 50 days, there are 46 days when the sentiment analysis is positive, which is greater than 0. And only 4 days when the sentiment analysis value is less than 0, which tends to be negative. The attitude of the netizens towards the "COVID-19" can be divided into three stages during this period. The first stage is from Jan. 1 to Jan. 20, the netizens' mood fluctuated greatly and became more unstable, with positive and negative sentiments alternating. The second stage is from Jan. 20 to Feb. 3, during which the netizens' mood has gradually increased from negative to positive. The third stage is from Feb. 3 to Feb. 20, during which the netizens' mood is stable in a positive and positive state with little fluctuation. Therefore, the overall attitude of netizens towards COVID-19 is positive. Although there was a big fluctuation in the previous stage, netizens' attitude gradually improved and stabilized in a positive mood (Fig. 6).

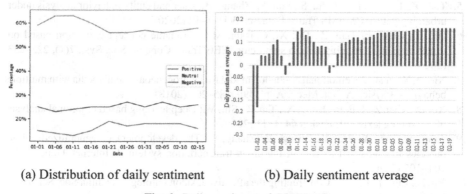

(a) Distribution of daily sentiment   (b) Daily sentiment average

Fig. 6. Daily sentiment of COVID-19

5 Conclusion

In this paper, we present a method combining sentiment and topic mining to analyze the sentiment of COVID-19. We use the SO-PMI Algorithm is used to extend the basic lexicon and construct a domain sentiment lexicon suitable for COVID-19. Then we extract the topics with LDA, which enriches the research method of collaborative analysis of sentiment and topic mining. According to the topic of COVID-19 emergency, this paper classifies the users' sentiment, and gets the trend of the users' sentimental change. The results show that using the collaborative analysis model of sentiment and topic mining to label the training data is helpful to build consistent labeling principles and enhance the precision of sentiment classifier. The method of this paper can effectively excavate the sentiment and theme of the emergency, summarize the development of the hot news, and provide ideas for the future disaster response, emergency and so on.

Acknowledgement. This work was supported in part by the National Natural Science Foundation of China (No. 62002077), in part by Guangdong Basic and Applied Basic Research Foundation (No. 2020A1515110385) and Guangzhou Science and Technology Plan Project (202102010440).

Conflicts of Interest. The authors declare that they have no conflicts of interest to report regarding the present study.

References

1. Van, L.T., Nguyen, Q.H., Dao, T.: Emotion recognition with capsule neural network. Comput. Syst. Sci. Eng. **41**(3), 1083–1098 (2021)
2. Oglah, M., Asghar, S.: Sentiment analytics: extraction of challenging influencing factors from covid-19 pandemics. Intell. Autom. Soft Comput. **30**(3), 821–836 (2021)
3. Albahli, A.S., et al.: COVID-19 public sentiment insights: a text mining approach to the Gulf countries. Comput. Mater. Continua **67**(2), 1613–1627 (2021)
4. Gu, Z., et al.: Epidemic risk assessment by a novel communication station based method. IEEE Trans. Netw. Sci. Eng. **9**(1), 332–344 (2021)
5. Tian, Z., Luo, C., Lu, H., Su, S., Sun, Y., Zhang, M.: User and entity behavior analysis under urban big data. ACM/IMS Trans. Data Sci. **3**(1), 1–19 (2020)
6. Qiu, J., Chai, Y., Tian, Z., Du, X., Guizani, M.: Automatic concept extraction based on semantic graphs from big data in smart city. IEEE Trans. Comput. Soc. Syst. **7**(1), 225–233 (2020)
7. Xiong, X., et al.: An emotional contagion model for heterogeneous social media with multiple behaviors. Physica A Stat. Mech. Appl. **490**, 185–202 (2018)
8. Xu, D., Tian, Z., Lai, R., Kong, X., Tan, Z., Shi, W.: Deep learning based emotional analysis of microblog texts. Inf. Fusion **64**, 1–11 (2020)
9. Tang, Y., Liu, W., He, Y., Zhang, Y., Zhang, F.: The development of generalized public bicycles in China and its role in the urban transportation system. J. Internet Things **2**(3), 101–107 (2020)
10. Xu, L., Lin, H., Pan, Y.: Constructing the affective lexicon ontology. J. China Soc. Sci. Tech. Inf. **27**(2), 180–185 (2008)
11. Luo, C., Tan, Z., Min, G., Gan, J., Shi, W., Tian, Z.: A novel web attack detection system for internet of things via ensemble classification. IEEE Trans. Ind. Inform. **17**(8), 5810–5818 (2021)
12. Roy, K.C., Ahmed, M.A., Hasan, S., Sadri, A.M.: Dynamics of crisis communications in social media: spatio-temporal and text-based comparative analyses of twitter data from hurricanes Irma and Michael. In: 17th International Conference on Information Systems for Crisis Response and Management, pp. 812–824. IEEE, Virginia, USA (2020)
13. Sreenivasulu, M., Sridevi, M.: Comparative study of statistical features to detect the target event during disaster. Big Data Mining Anal. **3**(2), 121–130 (2020)
14. Wang, X.F., Sheng, S., Lu, Y.: Analyzing public opinion from microblog with topic clustering and sentiment intensity. Data Anal. Knowl. Discov. **2**(6), 37–47 (2018)
15. Zhao, C.Y., Wu, Y.P., Wang, J.M.: Twitter text topic mining and sentiment analysis under the belt and road initiative. Libr. Inf. Serv. **19**, 119–127 (2019)
16. Turney, P.D., Littman, M.L.: Measuring praise and criticism: inference of sematic orientation from association. ACM Trans. Inf. Syst. **21**(4), 315–346 (2003)
17. Blei, D.M., Andrew, A.Y., Jordan, M.I.: Latent Dirichlet allocation. J. Mach. Learn. Res. **3**(1), 993–1022 (2003)
18. Zareie, A., Sheikhahmadi, A., Jalili, M.: Identification of influential users in social networks based on users' interest. Inf. Sci. **493**, 217–231 (2019)
19. Kim, Y.: Convolutional neural networks for sentence classification. In: 2014 Conference on Empirical Methods in Natural Language Processing, pp. 1746–1751. ACL, Doha, Qatar (2014)

20. Devlin, J., Chang, W.W., Lee, K., Toutanova, K.: BERT: pre-training of deep bidirectional transformers for language understanding. In: 2019 Conference of the North American Chapter of the Association for Computational Linguistics, pp. 4171–4186. ACL, Minneapolis, Minnesota (2019)
21. Zhang, Z.Y., Han, H., Liu, Z.Y., Jiang, X., Sun, M.S., Liu, Q.: ERNIE: enhanced language representation with informative entities. In: 57th Annual Meeting of the Association for Computational Linguistics, pp. 1441–1451. ACL, Florence, Italy (2019)

An Improved Cuckoo Search Algorithm Using Elite Opposition-Based Learning and Golden Sine Operator

Peng-Cheng Li[1], Xuan-Yu Zhang[1], Azlan Mohd Zain[2], and Kai-Qing Zhou[1(✉)]

[1] College of Information Science and Engineering, Jishou University, Jishou 416000, China
kqzhou@jsu.edu.cn
[2] UTM Big Data Centre, Universiti Teknologi Malaysia, 801310 Skudai, Malaysia

Abstract. The existing cuckoo search (CS) algorithm has the drawbacks of slow convergence speed, low convergence accuracy, and easy to fall into local optimum. An improved cuckoo search algorithm is proposed in this manuscript to overcome the mentioned shortages using elite opposition-based learning and golden sine operator (EOBL-GS-CS). The modifications could be summarized from two aspects. On the one hand, the elite opposition-based learning (EOBL) mechanism is employed to improve the diversity and quality of the population, preventing the algorithm from falling into the local optimum. On the other hand, the golden sine operator accelerates the algorithm's convergence speed and improves the algorithm's optimization ability. In the verification part, 14 unimodal and multimodal benchmark functions are used to highlight the characteristics of the proposed algorithm. The experimental results show that, compared with the standard CS and other variants, the EOBL-GS-CS has a faster convergence speed, higher solution accuracy, and significantly improved optimization performance.

Keywords: Cuckoo search · Elite opposition-based learning · Golden sine operator · Function optimization · Modification

1 Introduction

The Cuckoo Search algorithm, proposed by Yang and Deb in 2009, is a new swarm intelligence optimization algorithm for the obligate brood parasitic behavior of some cuckoo species [1]. Due to the characteristics of strong versatility, few parameters, simple implementation, the CS has been gained fruitful applications in industrial domains, such as photovoltaic system optimization [2], image processing [3–5], engineering optimization [6–8], signal processing [9], cloud computing [10].

However, the CS algorithm has some problems: slow convergence speed, poor population diversity, and low global search efficiency. In past years, various CS variants have been discussed to improve CS performances. Wang et al. [11] proposed a hybrid particle swarm optimization and cuckoo search (PSO-CS) algorithm. In each iteration of the algorithm, the PSO is first used to update individual velocity and position. Then the CS algorithm is used to the individual position update again. The experiment shows

© The Author(s), under exclusive license to Springer Nature Switzerland AG 2022
X. Sun et al. (Eds.): ICAIS 2022, LNCS 13338, pp. 276–288, 2022.
https://doi.org/10.1007/978-3-031-06794-5_23

that the PSO-CS algorithm has better optimization ability than the CS algorithm. Lim et al. [12] proposed a hybrid cuckoo search-genetic algorithm (CSGA) to optimize the hole-making operations. Naik et al. [13] proposed an adaptive Cuckoo Search (ACS) algorithm to implement face recognition through selecting step size based on iteration number and fitness value without Levy distribution. Sheikholeslami et al. [14] proposed a hybrid algorithm combining harmony search algorithm (HS) and CS algorithm to optimize the design of water distribution system for improving the global optimization ability of CS algorithm. Mlakar et al. [15] proposed a novel hybrid self-adaptive CS algorithm, which extended the original CS by adding three features, i.e., a balancing of the exploration search strategies, a self-adaptation of cuckoo search control parameters, and a linear population reduction. The experimental results reveal the algorithm's effectiveness, but the optimal parameters are still needed to obtain by many experiments. At present, the improvement of CS has achieved good results, but the existing algorithm still has some problems, such as slow convergence speed and low global search efficiency. Inspired by the above literature, this paper proposes an improved CS algorithm using elite opposition-based learning and golden sine operator (EOBL-GS-CS) to improve the convergence speed and optimization ability of the CS algorithm. The primary thinking of this paper is listed below.

1. The elite opposition-based learning mechanism to increase population diversity and avoid falling into the local optimum;
2. The golden sine operator is used to accelerate the algorithm's convergence speed and global searchability.

In addition, 14 typical benchmark functions are selected to verify the feasibility of the EOBL-GS-CS algorithm. The experimental results show that the performance of the EOBL-GS-CS algorithm is significantly better than that of the CS algorithm and its variants.

This paper is arranged as follows: The Sect. 2 mainly introduces the standard CS algorithm. Section 3 presents details of the improved cuckoo algorithm using elite opposition-based learning and golden sine operator. Section 4 tests the EOBL-GS-CS algorithm and verifies the algorithm's performance using 14 benchmark functions. The Sect. 5 summarizes the entire paper.

2   The Standard CS Algorithm

In the CS algorithm, Yang et al. [1] assumes cuckoo's spawning behavior as the following three ideal states to facilitate the simulation of cuckoo's breeding habit.

1. Each cuckoo lays one egg at a time and randomly places it into a host's nest;
2. In a group of nests, the best nests with high-quality eggs will carry over to the next generation;
3. The number of nests available is constant, and the probability that the host bird will find parasitic cuckoo egg is p_a.

Based on the above three ideal states, the updating formula of position and path of cuckoo exploring host nest is given as follows:

$$X_i^{t+1} = X_i^t + \alpha \oplus Levy(\lambda), i \in [1, N] \tag{1}$$

where X_i^{t+1} and X_i^t represent the position of the i_{th} nest in iteration t and iteration $t + 1$; $\alpha > 0$ is used to control step size; $\oplus$ refers to entry-wise multiplications; $Levy(\lambda)$ is the random walk through a $Levy$ flight [16], and the formula of $Levy(\lambda)$ is illustrated shown as Eq. (2), and N is the number of nests.

$$Levy(\lambda) \sim \frac{u}{|v|^{1/\beta}} \times \left\{ \frac{\Gamma(1 + \beta) \sin(\pi\beta/2)}{\Gamma[(1 + \beta)/2]2^{(\beta-1)/2}\beta} \right\}^{1/\beta} \tag{2}$$

where u and v follow the standard normal distribution; β is a constant, and it's generally 1.5; $\Gamma(\cdot)$ refers to gamma function; To facilitate calculation, the calculation formula of α is described as follows:

$$\alpha = \alpha_0 \times (X_i^t - X_{best}^t) \tag{3}$$

where α_0 is a constant, and it's generally 0.01; X_{best}^t is the best solution among all X_i at iteration t.

p_a is the probability that the host bird finds alien eggs. If alien eggs are found, the host bird will abandon these eggs or build a new nest. In other words, the CS algorithm generates a random number r after position updating through Eq. (1). If $r > p_a$, the selective random walk is adopted to update the nest position. Otherwise, the nest position remains unchanged.

Based on the above operations, the entire implementations of a standard CS algorithm could be divided into following steps as follows:

Step 1: Set the population size N, search space dimension D, the maximum number of iterations, and other parameters. Randomly initialize the nest position $X_i = (x_{i,1}, x_{i,2}, \cdots, x_{i,D}), i \in [1, N]$. Defining the objective function $f(X)$.

Step 2: Calculate the fitness function value of each nest and find the nest with the best fitness function value among all the current nests.

Step 3: Random walk based on $Levy$ distribution. Keep the current best nest. For each remaining nest, the Eq. (1) is used to update the position and get the new nest. Retain the nest with the best fitness function value by comparing the fitness function value of the new nest with that of the original one.

Step 4: Selective random walk. After updating the position, If $r > p_a$, the nest position will be updated randomly. Otherwise, the nest position will remain unchanged.

Step 5: If the maximum number of iterations or search accuracy is met, move to 6. Otherwise, move to step 3.

Step 6: Output the position of the global optimal bird's nest.

3 The EOBL-GS-CS Algorithm

3.1 Elite Opposition-Based Learning Mechanism

Opposition-Based Learning (OBL) [17] is proposed by Tizhoosh in 2005. Tizhoosh's research shows that the probability of the opposition solution being closer to the global optimum is 50% higher than the current solution. This mechanism can effectively increase the diversity and quality of the population and avoid the algorithm falling into the local optimum. At present, this mechanism has been applied to improve a variety of algorithms and has achieved good results. Zhou et al. [18] proposed an improved flower pollination algorithm using OBL, which improves the ability of the algorithm to jump out of the local optimum. Tubishat et al. [19] proposed an improved salp swarm algorithm based on OBL, which effectively improved the diversity and global convergence of the algorithm. The main idea of the OBL can be summarized as generating the opposition solution of the current solution, and selecting the optimal group of individuals from the population composed of the current solution and its opposition solution to enter the next iteration.

Suppose $X_i = (x_{i,1}, x_{i,2}, \cdots, x_{i,D})$ is a solution in the current population, D is the dimension of search space, $x_{i,j} \in [a_j, b_j], j \in [1, D]$, and its opposition solution $\overline{X}_i = (\overline{x}_{i,1}, \overline{x}_{i,2}, \cdots \overline{x}_{i,D})$ is defined as follows:

$$\overline{x}_{i,j} = a_j + b_j - x_{i,j} \tag{4}$$

Because the opposition solution generated by OBL is not necessarily easier to search for the globally optimal solution than the current solution. In response to this problem, elite OBL (EOBL) was proposed. Compared with the OBL mechanism, the EOBL uses the characteristics of the elite individual (optimal individual in the population) that contain more practical information than ordinary individuals and uses the elite individual in the current population to construct opposition population to increase the diversity of the population. And select the optimal group of individuals from the new population composed of the current population and the opposition population to enter the next iteration. The elite opposition-based learning mechanism can be described as follows: Suppose the elite individual in the current population is $X_i^e = (x_{i,1}^e, x_{i,2}^e, \cdots, x_{i,D}^e)$, for each individual $X_i = (x_{i,1}, x_{i,2}, \cdots, x_{i,D})$, the elite opposition solution $\overline{X}_i^e = (\overline{x}_{i,1}^e, \overline{x}_{i,2}^e, \cdots \overline{x}_{i,D}^e)$ of X_i is defined as follows:

$$\overline{x}_{i,j}^e = k \times \left(da_j + db_j\right) - x_{i,j}^e \tag{5}$$

where $i \in [1, N]$, N is the population size, $j \in [1, D]$, D is the dimension of search space, $k \in (0, 1)$ and k is a generalized coefficient, $da_j = \min(x_{i,j})$, $db_j = \max(x_{i,j})$, and $[da_j, db_j]$ is the dynamic boundary of the j_{th} dimensional search space. If $\overline{x}_{i,j}^e$ is outside the range of the dynamic boundary, it is reset using the method of random generation as follows:

$$\overline{x}_{i,j}^e = rand\left(da_j, db_j\right) \tag{6}$$

3.2 Golden Sine Operator

Golden Sine Algorithm [20] (Gold-SA) is a mathematical heuristic algorithm, which is inspired by the sine function in trigonometric functions. The Gold-SA algorithm combines the sine function and golden section coefficient to perform an iterative search. The algorithm has good robustness and convergence speed. Using the special relationship between the sine function and the unit circle, there is an equivalent relationship between scanning all points on the sine function and scanning all points on the unit circle. Scanning the unit circle through the sine function is similar to exploring the search space, thus making the optimization area of the algorithm more comprehensive. In addition, the Gold-SA algorithm introduces the golden section coefficient in position update and comprehensively searches for regions that can produce high-quality solutions during each iteration, which speeds up the algorithm's convergence speed and enhances the algorithm's local development capabilities.

The core process of the Gold-SA algorithm is the update process of the solution. First, the positions of N individuals are randomly generated. It is assumed that each solution of the optimization problem corresponds to the individual position in the search space as $X_i^t = (x_{i,1}, x_{i,2}, \cdots, x_{i,D})$, $i \in [1, N]$, where X_i^t represents the i_{th} position in the D-dimensional space at iteration t. $G_{best} = (g_1, g_2, \cdots, g_D)$ represents the globally optimal solution. At the t_{th} iteration, the position update formula of the i_{th} individual could be calculated as follows:

$$X_i^{t+1} = X_i^t \times |\sin(R_1)| + R_2 \times \sin(R_1) \times |x_1 \times G_{best} - x_2 \times X_i^t| \qquad (7)$$

where R_1 is a random number between 0 and 2π to determine the moving distance of the individual in the next iteration. R_2 is a random number between 0 and π to determine the position update direction of the i_{th} individual in the next iteration; x_1 and x_2 are utilized into the coefficients which are obtained by the golden section number, these coefficients narrow the search space and lead the individual to approach the optimal value gradually, and ensure the convergence of the algorithm. A golden section number is an irrational number defined as τ. x_1 and x_2 are defined as follows:

$$x_1 = b + (a - b) \times \tau \qquad (8)$$

$$x_2 = a - (a - b) \times \tau \qquad (9)$$

In this paper, the values of x_1 and x_2 are $-\pi$ and π, respectively.

3.3 Improvement of CS

In our EOBL-GS-CS, the EOBL mechanism is use to increase the diversity of the population, and the group selection mechanism is used to sort the current solution and the elite opposition solution according to fitness values and select the best N individuals to form the next generation population for improving the quality of the population. First, for the initial population, the EOBL can increase the diversity of the initial population and lay the foundation for a better global search. Secondly, for each generation of the population, the EOBL can be generated far away from the local minimum value. The opposition solution of the value point guides the algorithm to jump out of the local optimum and enhances the algorithm's global search capability; Finally, the EOBL adopts dynamic boundary tracking search mode to obtain a gradually reduced search space, which is beneficial to improve the convergence progress of the CS algorithm and speed.

In addition, based on retaining the *Levy* flight and selective random walk of the basic cuckoo algorithm, the Gold-SA is used to update the position of the bird's nest again. The golden sine operation is performed on the position of the entire bird's nest at the later stage of each iteration of the algorithm to promote the rapid spread of information in the population, enable the general individual and the optimal individual to exchange information, fully absorb the position difference information with the optimal individual, optimize the optimization method of the algorithm, and accelerate the convergence speed of the algorithm. Performing golden sine operations on individuals can increase the diversity of the population, ensure individuals jump out of the local optimum, and reduce the possibility of the algorithm falling into the local optimum.

The entire EOBL-GS-CS algorithm includes following steps.

Step 1: Define an objective function $f(X)$, initialize the population size N, the search space dimension D, the maximum number of iterations T, the discovery probability p_a, and the upper and lower bounds of the search space.

Step 2: Generate the initial population of N host nests $X_i = (x_{i,1}, x_{i,2}, \cdots, x_{i,D})$, $i \in [1, N]$. Calculate the fitness value $f_i = f(X_i)$ of each host nest, select the best nest position X_{best} and the best fitness value f_{min}.

Step 3: Use Eq. (5) to calculate the opposition solution of the elite individual to form an elite opposition population and select the first N individuals from the current population and the elite opposition population to construct a new population according to the fitness value sorting.

Step 4: Random walk based on *Levy* distribution. Keep the current best nest. For each remaining nest, the Eq. (1) is used to update the position and get the new nest for each remaining nest. Compare the fitness function value of the new nest with that of the original nest and retain the nest with the best fitness function value.

Step 5: Selective random walk. After updating the positions, if $r > p_a$, the nest position is updated randomly. Otherwise, the nest position will remain unchanged.

Step 6: For each nest, Eq. (7) is used to update the position to obtain a new nest. Then, retaining the nest with the best fitness value by comparing the fitness value of the new nest and the original nest.

Step 7: Calculate the fitness value of all nests according to the objective function, and record the best nest position X_{best} and the best fitness value f_{min}.

Step 8: If the maximum number of iterations or search accuracy is met, move to step 9. Otherwise, move to step 3.

Step 9: Output the position of the global optimal bird's nest.

The operation flowchart of the EOBL-GS-CS algorithm is illustrated as shown in Fig. 1.

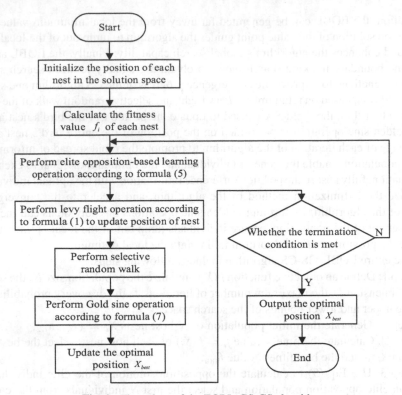

Fig. 1. Flow chart of the EOBL-GS-CS algorithm.

4   Simulation Experiments and Result Analysis

4.1   Benchmark Functions

Fourteen benchmark functions are selected in this manuscript to test the optimization performance of the proposed algorithm by comparing the optimization results among the basic CS algorithm, ACS algorithm [13], MCS algorithm [21], and the EOBL-GS-CS. The benchmark functions are divided into two parts: unimodal function and multimodal function. Among them, F1–F6 are unimodal functions, F7–F14 are multimodal functions. The dimensions of the test functions are all 30. It runs 30 times independently for different algorithms, and the experimental results are calculated from three aspects, which are the average, the best value, and standard deviation (Table 1).

4.2   Experimental Environment and Parameter Settings

These experiments are executed by following environment: the operating system is Winodws10, the CPU is Intel(R) Core(TM) i7-4710HQ CPU @ 2.50 GHz, the memory is 16 GB, and the simulation software is MATLAB R2020b. The population size of these four CS and CS variants is 15, the maximum number of iterations is 500, and other parameters settings of each algorithm are shown in Table 2.

Table 1. Benchmark functions.

No	Mathematical representation	Dim	Range of search	Theoretical optima
F1	$f(x) = \sum_{i=1}^{D} x_i^2$	30	$[-100,100]$	0
F2	$f(x) = \sum_{i=1}^{D} |x_i| + \prod_{i=1}^{D} |x_i|$	30	$[-10,10]$	0
F3	$f(x) = \sum_{i=1}^{D-1} \left[100\left(x_{i+1} - x_i^2\right)^2 + (x_i - 1)^2 \right]$	30	$[-5,10]$	0
F4	$f(x) = \sum_{i=1}^{D} (|x_i + 0.5|)^2$	30	$[-100,100]$	0
F5	$f(x) = \sum_{i=1}^{D} i x_i^4 + random[0, 1)$	30	$[-1.28,1.28]$	0
F6	$f(x) = \sum_{i=1}^{D} i x_i^2$	30	$[-10,10]$	0
F7	$f(x) = \sum_{i=1}^{D} -x_i \sin\left(\sqrt{|x_i|}\right)$	30	$[-500,500]$	$-$ 12569.487
F8	$f(x) = \sum_{i=1}^{D} \left[x_i^2 - 10\cos(2\pi x_i) + 10 \right]$	30	$[-5.12,5.12]$	0
F9	$f(x) = -20\exp\left(-0.2\sqrt{\frac{1}{D}\sum_{i=1}^{D} x_i^2}\right)$ $- \exp\left(\frac{1}{D}\sum_{i=1}^{D}\cos(2\pi x_i)\right) + 20 + e$	30	$[-32,32]$	0
F10	$f(x) = \frac{1}{4000}\sum_{i=1}^{D} x_i^2 - \prod_{i=1}^{D}\cos\left(\frac{x_i}{\sqrt{i}}\right) + 1$	30	$[-600,600]$	0
F11	$f(x) = \frac{\pi}{D}\left\{ 10\sin(\pi y_1) + \sum_{i=1}^{D-1}(y_i - 1)^2\left[1 + 10\sin^2(\pi y_{i+1})\right] + (y_D - 1)^2 \right\}$ $y_i = 1 + \frac{x_i + 1}{4}$ $u(x_i, a, k, m) = \begin{cases} k(x_i - a)^m, x_i > a \\ 0, -a < x_i < a \\ k(-x_i - a)^m, x_i < a \end{cases}$	30	$[-50,50]$	0
F12	$f(x) = 0.1\left\{ \sin^2(3\pi x_i) + \sum_{i=1}^{D}(x_i - 1)^2\left[1 + \sin^2(3\pi x_i + 1)\right] \right.$ $\left. + (x_i - 1)^2\left[1 + \sin^2(2\pi x_i)\right] \right\} + \sum_{i=1}^{D} u(x_i, 5, 100, 4)$	30	$[-50,50]$	0
F13	$f(x) = \sum_{i=1}^{D} |x_i \sin x_i + 0.1 x_i|$	30	$[-10,10]$	0
F14	$f(x) = \frac{\sin^2\sqrt{\sum_{i=1}^{D} x_i^2} - 0.5}{1 + 0.001 \times \sum_{i=1}^{D} x_i^2} + 0.5$	30	$[-10,10]$	0

Table 2. Parameters setting of four algorithms.

Algorithm	Parameters
CS	$N = 15, \beta = 1.5, \alpha_0 = 0.01, p_a = 0.25$
ACS	$N = 15, \beta = 1.5, p_a = 0.25$
MCS	$N = 15, \beta = 1.5, \alpha_{min} = 0.1, \alpha_{max} = 1.5, p_a = 0.25$
EOBL-GS-CS	$N = 15, \beta = 1.5, \alpha_0 = 0.01, p_a = 0.25$

4.3 Experimental Results and Analysis

In the selected functions, the F1–F6 are generally used to test the local development capabilities of the algorithm. According to the experimental results, for F1–F2, the optimization performance of EOBL-GS-CS is significantly better than the other three algorithms, all indicators are ahead of the other three algorithms, the optimization capabilities of ACS and MCS are ranked as the second position, and the optimization of CS The effect is the worse. For F3, the optimization results of the four algorithms are not ideal. The optimal value of ACS is better than EOBL-GS-CS, but the robustness of the ACS algorithm is poor, and the stability of EOBL-GS-CS is the best. For F4, these algorithms can all converge to the theoretical optimal value, but the EOBL-GS-CS is better than MCS and ACS from the mean and standard deviation. For F5–F6, the optimization performance of EOBL-GS-CS is significantly better than the other three algorithms, and all can converge to the theoretical optimal value. The accuracy of MCS and ACS is the second, and that of the CS is the worst. Overall, for the unimodal function, the optimal value and average value of EOBL-GS-CS are the best compared to the other three algorithms, and from the standard deviation, the stability of EOBL-GS-CS is better.

On the other hand, the F7–F14 are generally used to evaluate the global optimization capability of the algorithm. For F7, the four algorithms are not ideal. The optimal and average values of EOBL-GS-CS are better than the other three algorithms, but the stability is poor; For F8–F14, the EOBL-GS-CS shows the best global optimization ability their average and stability are better than the other three algorithms. For the three test functions of F8, F10, and F14, the EOBL-GS-CS can converge to the theoretical optimal value. In addition, the standard deviation of EOBL-GS-CS is better than the other three algorithms, and it further indicates that the EOBL-GS-CS has more feasibility ability. The above analysis shows that the global optimization ability of EOSL-GS-CS is better than that of other three algorithms (Table 3).

The experiment selected the iterative convergence curve of the test function to verify the convergence of the EOBL-GS-CS. This article only lists the iterative convergence curves of eight test functions, F1, F3, F6, F7, F9, F11, F12, and F13, depicted in Figs. 2, 3, 4, 5, 6, 7 and 8.

Figures 2, 3 and 4 reveal the iterative convergence curve obtained by testing the four algorithms on the single-mode functions F1, F3, and F6. It can be seen that for F1 and F6, the convergence speed and convergence accuracy of the EOBL-GS-CS are significantly better than the other three algorithms. For F3, the convergence accuracy of the four algorithms is not much different, and none of them converges to the globally optimal value. However, the convergence speed of EOBL-GS-CS is significantly better than the other three functions. Figures 5, 6, 7, 8 and 9 record the iterative convergence curves obtained by the four algorithms while optimizing the functions F7, F9, F11, F12, and F13. From these four figures, it can be seen that the EOBL-GS-CS algorithm is compared with the other three, and the algorithm has better convergence speed and convergence accuracy.

Table 3. Simulation results of benchmark functions.

Statistic	Algorithm	F1	F2	F3	F4	F5	F6	F7
Best	EOBL-GS-CS	0	**4.4338E−233**	26.4372	0	0	0	**204.1851**
	MCS	0.0894	0.9448	34.3848	0	1.5340E−04	0.0889	4.2330E+03
	ACS	0.0019	0.0208	9.6592	0	2.6152E−08	2.8792E−04	3.3555E+03
	CS	2.4726	1.4218	135.4930	13	1.0303E−04	0.5787	3.6803E+03
Mean	EOBL-GS-CS	0	**2.5285E−210**	**27.0454**	0	0	0	**1800.9959**
	MCS	0.2112	1.9854	88.4638	1.4333	6.8629E−04	0.2880	5.2402E+03
	ACS	0.0131	0.1465	89.1805	0.5333	3.5074E−06	0.0016	5.7959E+03
	CS	25.8713	4.7578	505.7363	55.6333	0.0028	2.9487	4.5887E+03
Std	EOBL-GS-CS	0	0	**0.4068**	0	0	0	1185.8414
	MCS	0.0867	0.9216	39.2559	1.4065	4.9217E−04	0.1003	413.4571
	ACS	0.0180	0.1646	49.8331	1.0743	8.2833E−06	0.0014	729.5543
	CS	22.6073	3.7861	392.4850	38.5473	0.0037	2.5749	**361.2226**

Statistic	Algorithm	F8	F9	F10	F11	F12	F13	F14
Best	EOBL-GS-CS	0	**8.8818E−16**	0	**3.8241E−06**	**6097E−05**	**8.0649E−226**	0
	MCS	91.6958	0.6573	0.3775	1.0703	0.2250	4.3357	0.0444
	ACS	103.7813	0.0658	0.0089	1.6859	0.0415	0.7954	0.0253
	CS	65.9922	3.7173	0.9911	5.0170	12.4816	5.8374	0.0468
Mean	EOBL-GS-CS	0	**8.8818E−16**	0	**0.0012**	**0.0224**	**3.9914E−209**	0
	MCS	131.1557	2.1480	0.7223	4.5804	0.5274	8.8115	0.0598
	ACS	138.6677	1.0979	0.1568	179.3263	744.4827	8.5119	0.0566
	CS	97.8951	6.9597	1.1691	12.2808	3.3359E+03	9.2290	0.0742
Std	EOBL-GS-CS	0	0	0	**0.0020**	**0.0389**	0	0
	MCS	17.3641	0.7193	0.1824	2.2483	0.2703	2.2897	0.0096
	ACS	21.1330	1.4543	0.1386	933.7348	4.0223E+03	3.9338	0.0136
	CS	17.7408	2.2255	0.1407	6.0021	8.2705E+03	1.5682	0.0144

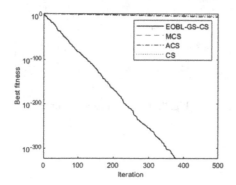

Fig. 2. F1 optimization curve.

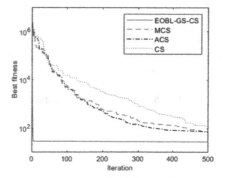

Fig. 3. F3 optimization curve.

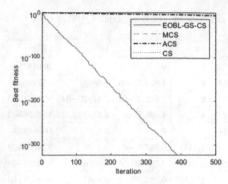

Fig. 4. F6 optimization curve.

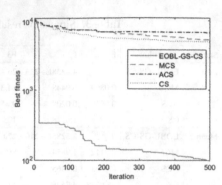

Fig. 5. F7 optimization curve.

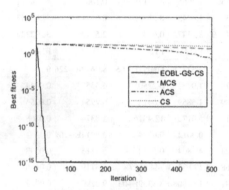

Fig. 6. F9 optimization curve.

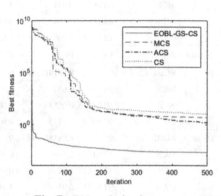

Fig. 7. F11 optimization curve.

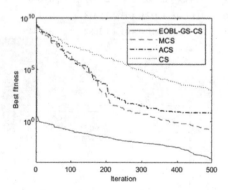

Fig. 8. F12 optimization curve.

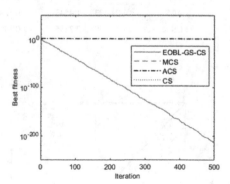

Fig. 9. F13 optimization curve.

5 Conclusion

This paper proposes an EOBL-GS-CS algorithm using elite opposition-based learning and a golden sine operator to solve the drawbacks of the standard CS algorithm. The elite opposition-based learning mechanism is introduced to enhance the population diversity and prevent falling into the local optimum. At the same time, the golden sine operator is used to improve the convergence speed and global search efficiency. In order to verify the effectiveness of the algorithm, comparative experiments are carried out among the EOBL-GS-CS, MCS, ACS, and CS algorithms, and the 14 benchmark functions are utilized to test the performance of these algorithms. The experimental results show that the algorithm has a faster convergence speed and convergence accuracy.

Funding Statement. This work was supported by the National Natural Science Foundation of China (No. 62066016), the Research Foundation of Education Bureau of Hunan Province, China (No. 21C0383), the Natural Science Foundation of Hunan Province, China (No. 2020JJ5458).

References

1. Yang, X.S., Deb, S.: Cuckoo search via Lévy flights. In: 2009 World Congress on Nature & Biologically Inspired Computing (NaBIC), pp. 210–214. IEEE, Coimbatore (2009)
2. Mosaad, M.I., Abed El-Raouf, M.O., Al-Ahmar, M.A., Banakher, F.A.: Maximum power point tracking of PV system based cuckoo search algorithm; review and comparison. Energy Procedia **162**, 117–126 (2019)
3. Malik, M., Azim, I., Dar, A.H., Asghar, S.: An adaptive SAR despeckling method using cuckoo search algorithm. Intell. Autom. Soft Comput. **29**(1), 165–182 (2021)
4. Zhang, X.R., Zhang, W.F., Sun, W., Sun, X.M., Jha, S.K.: A robust 3-d medical watermarking based on wavelet transform for data protection. Comput. Syst. Sci. Eng. **41**(3), 1043–1056 (2022)
5. Vasudevan, N., Nagarajan, V.: Efficient image de-noising technique based on modified cuckoo search algorithm. J. Med. Syst. **43**(10), 1–20 (2019)
6. Yang, X.S., Deb, S.: Engineering optimisation by cuckoo search. Int. J. Math. Model. Numer. Optim. **1**(4), 330–343 (2010)
7. Durbhaka, G.K., Selvaraj, B., Mittal, M., Saba, T., Rehman, A., Goyal, L.M.: Swarm-lstm: condition monitoring of gearbox fault diagnosis based on hybrid lstm deep neural network optimized by swarm intelligence algorithms. Comput. Mater. Continua **66**(2), 2041–2059 (2021)
8. Nageswari, D., Kalaiarasi, N., Geethamahalakshmi, G.: Optimal placement and sizing of distributed generation using metaheuristic algorithm. Comput. Syst. Sci. Eng. **41**(2), 493–509 (2022)
9. Patwardhan, A.P., Patidar, R., George, N.V.: On a cuckoo search optimization approach towards feedback system identification. Digital Signal Process. **32**, 156–163 (2014)
10. Kumar, M.S.: Hybrid cuckoo search algorithm for scheduling in cloud computing. Comput. Mater. Continua **71**(1), 1641–1660 (2022)
11. Wang, F., Luo, L., He, X.S., Wang, Y.: Hybrid optimization algorithm of PSO and Cuckoo Search. In: 2011 2nd International Conference on Artificial Intelligence, Management Science and Electronic Commerce (AIMSEC), pp. 1172–1175. IEEE, Zhengzhou (2011)
12. Lim, W.C.E., Kanagaraj, G., Ponnambalam, S.G.: A hybrid cuckoo search-genetic algorithm for hole-making sequence optimization. J. Intell. Manuf. **27**(2), 417–429 (2014). https://doi.org/10.1007/s10845-014-0873-z

13. Naik, M.K., Panda, R.: A novel adaptive cuckoo search algorithm for intrinsic discriminant analysis based face recognition. Appl. Soft Comput. **38**, 661–675 (2016)
14. Sheikholeslami, R., Zecchin, A.C., Zheng, F., Talatahari, S.: A hybrid cuckoo–harmony search algorithm for optimal design of water distribution systems. J. Hydroinf. **18**(3), 544–563 (2016)
15. Mlakar, U., Fister Jr., I., Fister, I.: Hybrid self-adaptive cuckoo search for global optimization. Swarm Evol. Comput. **29**, 47–72 (2016)
16. Barthelemy, P., Bertolotti, J., Wiersma, D.S.: A Lévy flight for light. Nature **453**(7194), 495–498 (2008)
17. Tizhoosh, H.R.: Opposition-based learning: a new scheme for machine intelligence. In: International Conference on Computational Intelligence for Modelling, Control and Automation and International Conference on Intelligent Agents, Web Technologies and Internet Commerce (CIMCA-IAWTIC 2006), vol. 1, pp. 695–701. IEEE, Vienna, Austria (2005)
18. Zhou, Y., Wang, R., Luo, Q.: Elite opposition-based flower pollination algorithm. Neurocomputing **188**, 294–310 (2016)
19. Tubishat, M., Idris, N., Shuib, L., Abushariah, M.A., Mirjalili, S.: Improved Salp Swarm Algorithm based on opposition based learning and novel local search algorithm for feature selection. Expert Syst. Appl. **145**, 113122 (2020)
20. Tanyildizi, E., Demir, G.: Golden sine algorithm: a novel math-inspired algorithm. Adv. Electr. Comput. Eng. **17**(2), 71–78 (2017)
21. Ong, P., Zainuddin, Z.: Optimizing wavelet neural networks using modified cuckoo search for multi-step ahead chaotic time series prediction. Appl. Soft Comput. **80**, 374–386 (2019)

Model Study on Integrated Thermal Management System of New Energy Bus

Zhiguo Li, Bojing Cheng(✉), and Ying Wang

Hunan Automotive Engineering Vocational College, Zhuzhou 412000, China
20430690@qq.com

Abstract. As new energy vehicles are gradually popularized, the safety of new energy vehicles is also getting more and more attention, and the thermal management system, as the key to ensure the normal operation of new energy key assemblies, is also getting more and more attention in its related research. This thesis takes the plug-in new energy bus powertrain integrated thermal management system development project as the research object, starts from the powertrain thermal modeling analysis, studies the integrated thermal management system model design and intelligent control strategy, explores the method of considering practical factors used to establish the integrated thermal management system control model, takes the thermal management system's lowest energy consumption as the main purpose, to determine the relevant parameters, and is used to optimize the system control strategy. The simulation and test platform is constructed to simulate and analyze the solved parameters, to guide the actual design for the selection and matching of system components and the verification of the real vehicle, to verify the feasibility of the intelligent control strategy, to optimize the system integration, and to provide reference for the development of new models or new systems.

Keywords: New energy vehicles · Thermal management system · Integration · Simulation analysis

1 Introduction

With the gradual promotion of new energy vehicles, especially in the field of public transportation, the proportion of new energy vehicles is increasing, coupled with the new trend of state-run bus transportation in rural areas, the promotion of new energy buses for rural passenger transportation is also imperative [1]. But at present, there are few researches on the design of new energy buses that pay attention to rural road conditions, and rural road conditions have higher requirements for the "three electric" systems of new energy vehicles, and the corresponding thermal management system requirements are also higher. This paper focuses on the design of new energy bus powertrain thermal management system applicable to rural road conditions [2].

In recent years, there have been a number of new energy vehicle fires and spontaneous combustion incidents. The Tsinghua University team found that the large reduction in the critical point of thermal runaway caused by high-power fast charging is the main

© The Author(s), under exclusive license to Springer Nature Switzerland AG 2022
X. Sun et al. (Eds.): ICAIS 2022, LNCS 13338, pp. 289–300, 2022.
https://doi.org/10.1007/978-3-031-06794-5_24

cause of current electric vehicle fires. While seeking breakthroughs in battery materials and charging technology, an efficient, energy-saving and reliable thermal management system for the whole vehicle has gradually become a hot spot [1]. If the key electrical equipment such as electric drive system, power battery system and related controller of new energy vehicles work in unsuitable temperature environment for a long time, it will lead to the decrease of its working efficiency, performance and cycle life, which will affect the performance of the whole vehicle and lead to the decrease of driving range and even cause safety accidents [3]. The introduction of a suitable thermal management system can improve such problems, such as thermal management of the electric drive system and thermal management of the battery system. The electric air-conditioning system for new energy vehicles is a thermal management system based on the design of traditional automobile air-conditioning, plus key components such as batteries, motors, and electric controls. They are powered by the limited capacity of the vehicle power battery, so its design principle is to ensure that each managed component can work within the normal temperature range, while reducing the overall energy consumption as much as possible [4].

2 Integrated Thermal Management System Structure

The key to the matching design of the thermal management system lies in the accurate acquisition of parameters, and the key point of accurate acquisition of parameters lies in the establishment and analysis of thermal management models. With the emergence of CAD/CAE-type software, simulation modeling has gradually been recognized by the industry, coupled with the relevant experience and empirical parameters accumulated in the physical design, it can effectively improve design efficiency and design costs [5].

This paper focuses on the analysis of the new energy vehicle motor drive thermal management system, engine thermal management system and other thermal management system accessories; and introduces the establishment of the thermal management model of the power drive system and the calculation of related parameters. The integrated thermal management system of the plug-in new energy bus powertrain in rural road conditions is studied by the actual project to explain the architecture and working logic of the powertrain integrated thermal management system [6]. After that, the simulation model is established and explained based on AME sim, and the control method is designed for the next chapter and lays the foundation for optimization work. The related parameters of the established thermal system model can provide a reference for the subsequent design and matching of the heat dissipation system (heat exchange system). Because the power battery of the plug-in model studied in this thesis is a stand-alone water-cooled system, this paper does not do the relevant research, but focuses on the plug-in hybrid power assembly to do the relevant analysis. As shown in Fig. 1, it is the three-dimensional model diagram of the thermal management system of the hybrid powertrain studied in this paper. It is used in the plug-in new energy bus suitable for rural road conditions studied in this article, specifically the motor (drive motor and generator), the engine, the integrated controller and other assemblies, as well as the related heat dissipation system [7].

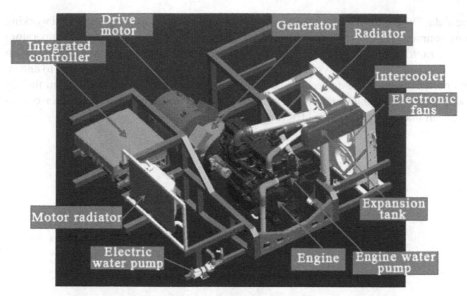

Fig. 1. Powertrain and thermal management system structure diagram.

3 Motor System Thermal Management Model Analysis

The power of the new energy vehicle is provided by the electric drive system, the performance of the system to meet certain conditions: high power, output range of voltage, strong overload capacity, high efficiency and good cooling performance and other conditions. The electric motor, motor controller and power converter constitute the electric drive system. The drive system generates a large amount of heat in the process of power operation. If the heat cannot be dissipated efficiently in real time, the temperature of the drive system will continue to rise, and the continuous high temperature condition will seriously affect the efficiency and service life of the whole system [8]. The specific performance of the motor running heat makes the temperature rise, resulting in uneven heating of various parts of the motor. When the ambient temperature reaches a certain condition, the physical characteristics of the metal materials in the motor system will produce changes, such as the mechanical strength of the material deterioration, insulation material insulation capacity failure. The motor controller includes many electronic devices, especially concentrated in the power drive module. The heat loss during work will continue to dissipate heat and increase the ambient temperature. High temperature will affect the work efficiency of the parts, shorten the life of their electronic components, and even cause them to burn out, thus causing the motor drive system to fail to operate normally. Therefore, the study of the thermal management system of the drive motor of new energy vehicles has its own research necessity [9].

3.1 Motor Thermal Model Analysis

When a new energy vehicle is working, the drive motor uses the motor controller and transmission system to convert electrical energy into mechanical energy to drive the vehicle. During the working process, due to the change in its working mode and working environment, the motor will produce a lot of energy loss, which will cause the temperature of the motor to continue to rise. A reasonable and effective thermal management system can keep the drive motor system in the appropriate working temperature range to ensure its normal operation. At present, the drive motor thermal management system mainly adopts air-cooled and water-cooled methods, and this paper focuses on the water-cooled thermal management system [10] (Fig. 2).

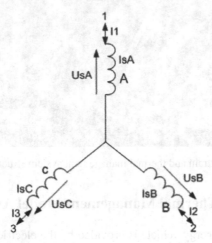

Fig. 2. Drive motor star connection.

The heat loss of the motor is determined by the Joule loss as:

$$D_h = R_s \times I_{sd}^2 + R_s \times I_{sq}^2 \tag{1}$$

where, I_{sd}, I_{sq} can be calculated by the relevant equations.

The test of permanent magnet synchronous motor resistance can be tested by the method of bridge as follows, which can be obtained:

$$R_1 = R_A + R_B, \quad R_2 = R_C + R_B, \quad R_3 = R_A + R_C \tag{2}$$

In general, $R_A = R_B = R_C$, so the phase resistance is:

$$R_S = \left[(R_1 + R_2 + R_3 \div 3] \div 2 \tag{3}$$

After specifying the drive motor thermal model, further analysis of the heat transfer model is required. Based on practical engineering applications, the drive motor thermal model is simplified. In this step, the temperature of the components in the system is regarded as uniform, the state of the object is assumed to be unchanged during the heat transfer process, and the heat transfer process is assumed to be linear.

$$C(T(\varphi) - T(\varphi_0)) = \int_{t0}^{\varphi} q_1 |(\tau) - q_2(\tau) d\tau| \tag{4}$$

The formula for an object with a mass M and a specific heat capacity Cp is $C = M \times Cp$, C is the heat capacity constant, and the unit is J/K. A derivation of the above formula can be obtained (Table 1):

$$C\frac{dT}{dt} = (q_1(\varphi) - q_2(\varphi)) \qquad (5)$$

Combined with Eq. 1, the temperature variation equation of the PM synchronous motor can be transformed into:

$$M_m Q_{in}\frac{dT_e}{dt} = -\rho_w C_w q_{vw} T_e - T_\gamma \qquad (6)$$

where, M_m indicates the mass of the motor; C_m indicates the specific heat capacity of the motor; $q_{v,w}$ indicates the volume flow rate of the thermal management fluid; C_w indicates the specific heat capacity of the thermal management fluid; Q_{in} indicates the heat of the motor; T_e indicates the inlet temperature of the heat sink; T_r indicates the outlet temperature of the heat sink; ρ_w indicates the density of the thermal management fluid.

Table 1. Thermal management system parameters table.

Thermal model parameters	Value
Thermal management system thermal management fluid volume V	20 L
Heat management fluid density w	1.071 kg/m^3
Thermal management fluid specific heat capacity C_W	4.18 kJ/(kg °C)
Flow rate of thermal management fluid $q_{v,w}$	$1.0 * 10^4 \text{ m}^3/\text{s}$
The quality of the radiator	32 kg
Specific heat capacity of radiator	0.88 kJ/(kg °C)
Radiator equivalent resistance R	0.25 K/W
Motor quality m	250 kg
Motor specific heat capacity C_m	0.48 kJ/(kg °C)
Ambient temperature T_e	20 °C
Specific heat capacity of air Cp, a	1.005 kJ/(kg °C)
Air density (under 20 degrees)	1.205 kg/m^3

The research object described in this article includes motor heating, which mainly includes two parts, namely, the generator and the motor of the hybrid powertrain. Combined with the specific content studied in this paper, the relevant parameters were determined as follows. Combined with the motor heat loss model, it lays the foundation for the subsequent thermal management system modeling simulation and the whole vehicle powertrain thermal management system test [11].

3.2   Controller Thermal Management Model Analysis

The plug-in new energy bus described in this paper adopts the integrated controller TP5 as the high-voltage drive control system. As shown in Fig. 3. The integrated controller contains the motor drive control system, the insulation monitor, DC/AC, the whole vehicle controller, and other components (Table 2).

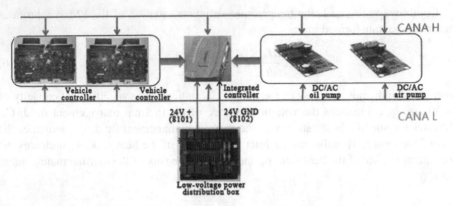

Fig. 3. All-in-one controller composition schematic.

Table 2. All-in-one controller parameters.

Point binomial	Parameters
Bus voltage	200 V–720 V
Rated capacity	120 kVA × 2 + 5 kVA × 2 + 3 kVA
Peak capacity	200 kVA × 2 + 7.5 kVA × 2 + 3 kVA
Protection level	IP67
Weight	35 kg
Volume	50 L
Dimensions	565 × 515 × 205
Scope of application	8 m–12 m Bus, Highway bus, Scenic spot bus; 8 t–12 t Logistics vehicle

Considered the actual heat generation ratio, the heat generation loss of other components in the integrated controller was ignored in the controller thermal management modeling analysis, and the model processing was simplified only for the motor controller module. According to the actual situation of the object under study, the following formula was chosen to calculate the heat production of the motor controller [12]:

$$P_{MCU} = \frac{P_{out}}{\eta_{MCU}}(1 - \eta_{MCU}) \qquad (7)$$

where, P_{MCU} indicates the motor controller heat production power, P_{out} indicates the motor controller output power, and η_{MCU} indicates the motor controller efficiency.

The heat dissipation $Q_{m驱}$ of the drive motor is 4 KW, the heat dissipation $Qm发$ of the generator is 32 KW, and the heat dissipation $Q_{m控}$ of the controller is 3 KW. Motor/controller cooling system heat dissipation:

$$P_{MCU} = \frac{P_{out}}{\eta_{MCU}} (1 - \eta_{MCU}) \qquad (8)$$

3.3 Engine Heat Balance Model Analysis

In this thesis, the engine is a supercharged diesel engine with a rated power of 125 kW, a rated speed of 2600 r/min, a maximum torque of 600 N-m at 1300–1700 r/min, a displacement of 3.8 L and a compression ratio of 17.2:1.

The following empirical formula is used to calculate the engine water jacket heat dissipation Q_w:

$$Q_w = \left(A \cdot g_e \cdot \frac{N_e h_n}{3600} \right) \qquad (9)$$

where: A indicates the percentage of actual heat transferred from the engine to the cooling system versus the heat energy of the fuel, the range of values for diesel engines is 0.18–0.25, and the current value is 0.24; g_e is the engine fuel consumption rate, the data provided by the engine manufacturer. g_e takes the value of 0.195 kg/KW-h, Ne indicates the rated power of engine, 125 kW, and h_n is the low calorific value of fuel, the value of diesel is taken as 41870 kJ/kg.

Combining the above, we can calculate $Q_W = (0.24 \times 0.195 \times 125 \times 41870)/3600 = 68$ KW.

4 Integrated Thermal Management Simulation Modeling Based on AME Sim

Lab AME Sim (Advanced Modeling Environment for Simulation of Engineering Systems) is a platform for system modeling and simulation in interdisciplinary fields. Users can build complex system models on the platform, and then perform in-depth analysis and simulation operations, and can also test the static and dynamic performance of the research system, or a single component on the platform by adjusting parameters. As shown in Fig. 4, the AME sim interface diagram.

4.1 Motor Thermal Management System Modeling

The motor thermal management model mainly consists of two models: the motor and the inverter model. The motor model is shown in Fig. 5, where interfaces 1–4 are electrical data interface, speed-torque interface, copper loss and iron loss interface, respectively, which are indicated as the main heat sources of permanent magnet synchronous motors.

The inverter module is shown in Fig. 6 diagram. Here the main parameters are the voltage drop of the transistor, the diode voltage and the resistance value.

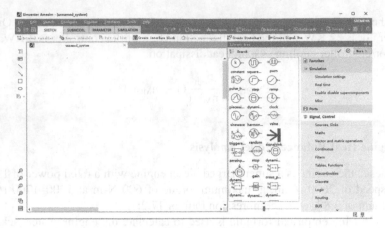

Fig. 4. AME sim interface diagram.

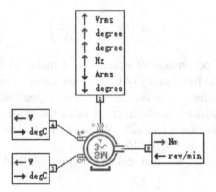

Fig. 5. Motor model.

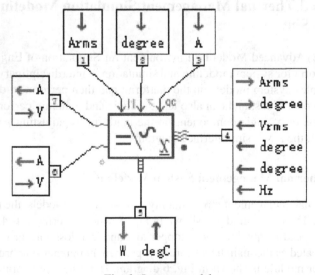

Fig. 6. Inverter model.

4.2 Engine Thermal Management System Modeling

The engine thermal management system model is selected from the AME sim component library, as shown in Fig. 7. Combined with the previous model analysis content and related parameters to complete the model parameter settings, the engine, radiator and water pump models make up the engine thermal management system model. According to the relevant manuals and references, No. 1 represents the speed input interface and torque output interface, No. 2 represents the emission data output interface, No. 3 represents the average effective pressure BMEP, maximum and minimum torque data output interface, No. 4 represents the interface to receive the control signal from the controller, No. 5 represents the environmental parameters input interface, No. 6 represents the combustion heat loss and engine wall temperature data interface, No. 7 represents the engine coolant temperature input interface, and No. 8 represents the interface of friction loss and oil temperature data.

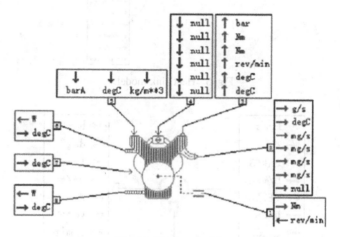

Fig. 7. Engine model.

In the AME sim library, the radiator and fan are integrated to facilitate user-friendly use. In this paper, the radiator model diagram is shown in 3–5, with interfaces 1–5 representing the natural air temperature and flow rate interface, tank connection interface, coolant inlet, fan speed signal interface, and coolant outlet, respectively (Fig. 8).

The water pump model diagram is shown in Fig. 9. Interface 3 is the speed and torque data interface, Flow rate, pressure loss parameters and efficiency curves under different working conditions are important parameters of the pump.

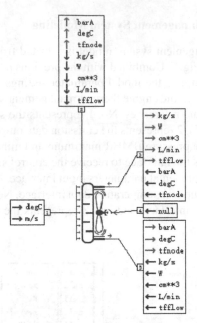

Fig. 8. Heat sink model.

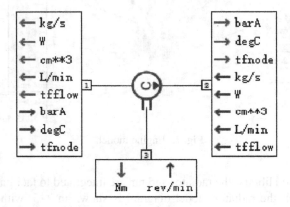

Fig. 9. Water pump model.

4.3   Integrated Thermal Management System Simulation Model

The integrated thermal management system studied in this paper is logically analyzed to show that the heat dissipation of the engine, motor and inverter is handled by temperature conduction devices that transfer the heat to the thermal management system for cooling. The temperature information is collected through sensors and processed and analyzed by the whole vehicle controller to control whether the cooling fan is turned on or not. A water pump in the system also accelerates the circulation of coolant to assist in heat dissipation. The working principle is shown in Fig. 10.

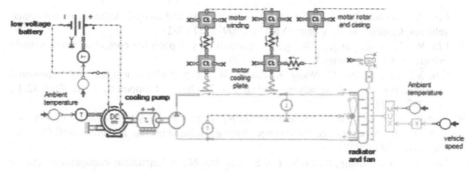

Fig. 10. Working principle diagram of integrated thermal management system.

5 Summary and Shortcomings

In this paper, we focused on the thermal model analysis of the powertrain integrated thermal management system and performed simulation modeling illustration. In the process of thermal model analysis, we focused on analyzing the heat generation mechanism of the main heat sources of the system, i.e., electric motor (drive motor and generator) and engine, and calculated the corresponding parameters for the subsequent modeling and control system design with the actual situation. In the thermal model simulation modeling, the key system thermal model was analyzed and the overall simulation model was established, which was used for the subsequent control system design and simulation, and laid the foundation for the real vehicle verification. In addition, there are some shortcomings in this paper. Some of the research methods in this paper were simplified in modeling and analysis, and only a small number of models were analyzed in the control method design, and more models need to be added for subsequent processing and analysis.

Funding Statement. This research is supported by Natural Science Foundation of Hunan Province (2020JJ6093).

References

1. Gong, H., Li, J., Ni, R., Xiao, P., Ouyang, H., et al.: The data acquisition and control system based on IoT-can bus. Intell. Autom. Soft Comput. **30**(3), 1049–1062 (2021)
2. Thamizhazhagan, P., Sujatha, M., Umadevi, S., Priyadarshini, K., Parvathy, V.S.: Ai based traffic flow prediction model for connected and autonomous electric vehicles. Comput. Mater. Continua **70**(2), 3333–3347 (2022)
3. Khan, N.A., Jhanjhi, N.Z., Brohi, S.N., Almazroi, A.A., Almazroi, A.A.: A secure communication protocol for unmanned aerial vehicles. Comput. Mater. Continua **70**(1), 601–618 (2022)
4. Uthathip, N., Bhasaputra, P., Pattaraprakorn, W.: Application of anfis model for Thailand's electric vehicle consumption. Comput. Syst. Sci. Eng. **42**(1), 69–86 (2022)
5. Fu, Z., Hu, P., Li, W., Pan, J., Chu, S.: Parallel equilibrium optimizer algorithm and its application in capacitated vehicle routing problem. Intell. Autom. Soft Comput. **27**(1), 233–247 (2021)

6. Lee, J., Lee, S., Choi, H., Cho, H.: Time-series data and analysis software of connected vehicles. Comput. Mater. Continua **67**(3), 2709–2727 (2021)
7. Liu, W., Tang, Y., Yang, F., Wang, J.: Research on CO pollution control of motor vehicle exhaust. J. Internet Things **1**(2), 71–76 (2019)
8. Liu, X., Xu, S., Yang, C., Wang, Z., Zhang, H.: Deep reinforcement learning empowered edge collaborative caching scheme for internet of vehicles. Comput. Syst. Sci. Eng. **42**(1), 271–287 (2022)
9. Manjusha, M., Sivarani, T.S., Jerusalin, C.J.: Application of fuzzy fopid controller for energy reshaping in grid connected PV inverters for electric vehicles. Intell. Autom. Soft Comput. **32**(1), 621–641 (2022)
10. Su, S., Tian, Z., Liang, S., Li, S., Du, S., Guizani, N.: A Reputation management scheme for efficient malicious vehicle identification over 5G networks. IEEE Wirel. Commun. **27**(3), 46–52 (2020)
11. Cao, Y.Q., Tan, C., Ji, G.L.: A multi-label classification method for vehicle video. J. Big Data **2**(1), 19–31 (2020)
12. Osibo, B., Zhang, C., Xia, C., Zhao, G., Jin, Z.: Security and privacy in 5G internet of vehicles (IoV) environment. J. Internet Things **3**(2), 77–86 (2021)

Chinese Sentence Similarity Calculation Based on Modifiers

Fangling Wang[1], Shaoqiang Ye[1], Diwen Kang[1], Azlan Mohd Zain[2],
and Kaiqing Zhou[1]([✉])

[1] College of Information Science and Engineering, Jishou University, Jishou 416000, China
kqzhou@jsu.edu.cn
[2] UTM Big Data Centre, Universiti Teknologi Malaysia, 801310 Skudai, Malaysia

Abstract. To compute the similarity of Chinese sentences accurately, a revised Chinese sentence similarity approach is proposed though enhancing the importance of the modifiers of stem of sentence. After extracting the modified part of the sentence by Language Technology Platform (LTP), this part of each structure could be removed the longest common substring, to better capture the similarities of modified parts. The entire method includes three phases, which are to split the sentences into principal and predicate object structures using the syntactic analysis tool, to generate modifiers and sentence stem vectors and calculate the similarity between the vectors using the Word2Vec, and to obtain the similarity between two sentences by weighting each part. Experimental results on 200 sentences of the LCQMC dataset and corresponding analysis reveal that the proposed method can obtain more accurate similarity calculation results by effectively gaining the modified part - which affects the whole sentence meaning effectively-of the sentence structure.

Keywords: Chinese sentence similarity · Word2Vec · Syntactic structure · Word vector · Natural language processing

1 Introduction

Text similarity is the degree of similarity between the given two texts [1]. The similarity between texts can be considered as a weighted calculation of the similarity between each sentence. Because of the complexity of human language, calculating the similarity of natural language needs to account for the difference between words and the relevance between semantics. There are many approaches to calculate the similarity of words and semantics, and the application achieves fruitful results. Recently, text similarity calculation has been mainly applied to information retrieval [2, 3], text categorization [4], Spam blocking [5], document clustering [6], answering question system [7, 8], plagiarism detection [9], machine translation [10], recommendation system [11, 12], answers evaluation [13], detection of malicious urls [14] Sentiment analysis [15] and so on.

© The Author(s), under exclusive license to Springer Nature Switzerland AG 2022
X. Sun et al. (Eds.): ICAIS 2022, LNCS 13338, pp. 301–310, 2022.
https://doi.org/10.1007/978-3-031-06794-5_25

As a traditional method, the similarity calculation method utilizing the lexical is implemented by computing the similarity between texts based on matching the words or strings of the text. Generally, there are three similarity calculation approaches based on the lexical, which are the Longest Common Sequence (LCS) [16], edit distance [17], and Jaccard distance [18]. Calculating the common subsequence of two sentences is the most original text similarity calculation, which is to compare the proportion of the largest substrings included in two sentences. The edit distance measures text similarity by counting how many additions, deletions, or changes could be converted into the same sentence. Furthermore, the Jaccard distance transforms two texts into the corresponding set of words and measures the similarity between texts by calculating the similarity between the sets.

Although the lexical-based text similarity calculation is easy to implement, it could exist misjudgment in the process of similarity calculation because it is insufficient and difficult to obtain the relationship between words and measure the similarity between sentences according to the semantic of sentences accurately. Therefore, accurately obtaining the relationship between words in sentences when using the lexical-based method to calculate the sentences' similarity is still a research hotspot. The currently mainstream method of obtaining the relationship between words includes two steps: splitting the sentences into a subject, predicate, and object structure and weighting the similarity of the whole sentence by calculating the lexical similarity of the same structure. Vector Space Models (VSM) is widely used to express a text completely to represent the text as a vector for obtaining the text-similarity between texts [19]. Moreover, it is found that the meaning of the primary sentence modifiers could be wholly changed sometimes, especially to settle the complement of the object in calculating the similarity calculation [20]. Inspired by this idea, this paper proposes an improved similarity calculation method through calculating the differences between sentences by the modification parts of stem structure in a sentence using the Language Technology Platform (LTP) and Word2Vec. A case study using the LCQMC dataset is carried out to illustrate the feasibility and correctness of the proposed method. The experiment results demonstrate that the proposed method can effectively improve the accuracy of sentences similarity calculation by self-comparison and comparison experiments with existing methods.

The rest parts of this manuscript are organized as follows. Section 2 introduces the VSM briefly. Section 3 describes the proposed method. Section 4 shows the proposed approach's performance by a case study. Section 5 concludes the whole paper.

2   Related Concepts

Vector Space Models (VSM), presented by Salton et al., is used to represent the text content as vectors in space and to express the semantic similarity between texts utilizing spatial vectors. Computing text similarity using the VSM could be roughly divided into three steps: featuring item extraction, calculating the similarity between the feature terms, and weighting the similarity obtained by the feature terms.

2.1 Feature Term Extraction

The stem of the whole sentence is usually used to depict the structure of the subject-predicate-object. The existing text similarity calculation methods based on the sentence structure are widely discussed because the method considers the similarity between words and easy to understand the meaning of the text in expression.

Syntactic analysis is the process of annotating a complete sentence using a syntactic analyzer. There are two standard Chinese syntax analyzers, which are Stanford Parser [21] and the LTP [22].

By analyzing the dependence relationship between the various components in the sentence, the stem of the whole sentence could be accurately extracted to make the similarity more accurate. This paper adopts the LTP to analyze the Chinese sentence. And Table 1 lists the relationships between the parts of the Chinese sentence using the LTP and the corresponding abbreviations.

Table 1. Abbreviations and the corresponding meanings

Abbreviation	Meaning
HED	The core of the sentence
SBV	Subject-verb
VOB	Verb-object
ATT	Attribute
IOB	Indirect-object
RAD	Right adjunct
LAD	Left adjunct
CMP	Complement
DBL	Double

A simple case of analyzing the stem of a Chinese sentence using LTP' is shown in Fig. 1:

Example sentence 1: 请大家检查一下自己的学号。

Fig. 1. Dependency tree of sentence

As shown in Fig. 1, the stem of the sentence is "请确认学号", and the remain parts "大家" and "自己" are marked as the modifiers for "确认" and "学号". These two modifiers are also considered in the process of similarity calculation.

2.2 Calculate the Similarity Between the Features

Before calculating the similarity, it needs to generate a vector representation for each part first. Word2Vec is employed in this paper to calculate the vectors for each part. Word2Vec is proposed by Mikolov et al. [23] to represent the words as vectors. The sense of two words trained based on the characteristics is more relevant whiling the distance between the vectors is closer.

Two weighting methods are used to calculate the similarity of a sentence while obtaining the vector representation of the words using VSM. One is to sum or average each word vector directly, and the other is to weight the word Term Frequency-Inverse Document Frequency (TF-IDF) according to the proportion of words in the text [24].

After obtaining a VSM representation of the sentences, the similarity could be computed by the cosine similarity. The formula of the cosine similarity is illustrated by Eq. 1

$$similarity(x, y) = \cos(\overline{x} \cdot \overline{y}) = \frac{\overline{x} \cdot \overline{y}}{\|\overline{x}\| \|\overline{y}\|} \tag{1}$$

2.3 Feature Item Weighting

Calculating the similarity of the entire sentence from the similarity of the feature vector is the process of weighting feature items. The existing weighting methods are mainly TF-IDF and its improved algorithms. The TF-IDF algorithm is a statistical method to judge the importance of words according to the frequency of words in the corpus. TF-IDF is divided into two aspects, TF is the word frequency is the number of words, and IDF is the reverse text frequency, the higher the frequency of words appearing in the text, the smaller their weight. The TF-IDF is calculated as Eq. 2.

$$TFIDF = TF \times IDF \tag{2}$$

After obtaining the weight values corresponding to the word vector, the similarity between the whole sentences could be gained by computing the weighted averaging.

3 The Proposed Method

The proposed modified Chinese sentence similarity calculation approach could be divided into three main phases, which are preprocessing, calculate vector similarity, and feature item weighting.

3.1 Pro-processing

After obtaining sentence pairs from the dataset, this approach uses LTP to analyze the dependencies of each sentence separately, and the content of each part is stored separately for getting the stem part of each sentence. In the sentence stem, it takes the predicate verb of the sentence as the root node of the whole sentence and the remaining subject and object as the leaf nodes, respectively. Furthermore, the subject-predicate-object of a sentence is considered as the featured item of a sentence.

3.2 Calculate Vector Similarity

Compared with the existing similarity methods using the sentence stem, the primary modification of the proposed algorithm is to consider the difference between the modified parts. Therefore, two strategies are used to solve mentioned problems and improve the accuracy of similarity. On the one hand, the determination will be executed to judge whether the leaf node exists. If there are leaf nodes, the similarity of the root node and the leaf node are saved separately due to the different influences and weights on the sentence similarity calculation. On the other hand, a hybrid method combines the feature items and the modified parts of the feature items to remove the two modified parts through the string matching rules and to calculate the remaining parts of the vectors.

3.3 Feature Item Weighting

Due to the modification proposed in Sect. 3.2, The root of a sentence clearly expresses the content of a sentence, so the root node of the sentence is assigned a relatively heavily weighted. In this case, there is no leaf we are considering, so the similarity calculation of the two sentences can be expressed in Eq. 3.

$$Sim_{s1,s2} = 0.7 * Sim_{root} + 0.3 * Sim_{others} \tag{3}$$

When leaf nodes exist, the method in this paper considers the same weight of the leaf node and the root node of the sentence, so the similarity calculation of the two sentences can be expressed by Eq. 4.

$$Sim_{s1,s2} = 0.4 * Sim_{root} + 0.4 * Sim_{leaves} + 0.2 * Sim_{others} \tag{4}$$

According to the Eqs. 3 and 4, the Sim_{root}, Sim_{leaves}, and Sim_{others} represent the similarity of the root node, the similarity of the leaf node, and the similarity of other components of the sentence, respectively.

The flowchart of the entire algorithm is demonstrated as shown in Fig. 2.

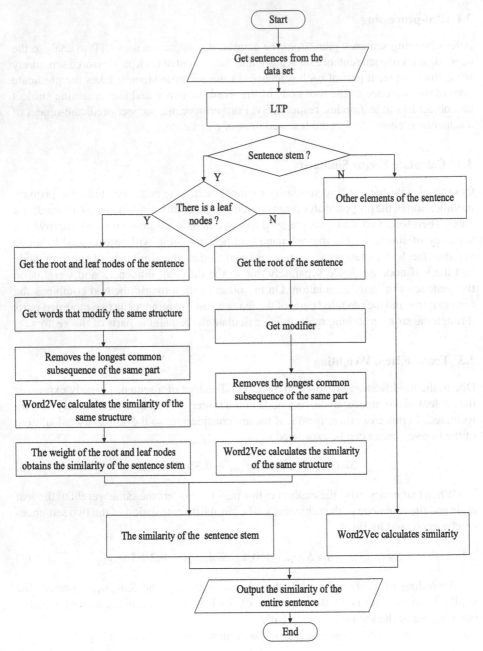

Fig. 2. The algorithm flow chart

4   Case Study

This paper proposes a method based on syntactic structure and Word2Vec to remove the longest common substring of sentence components. The test set used in the paper contains a total of 12,500 pairs of sentences which from the Chinese Q&A matching data set of Harbin Institute of Technology [25]. The first 200 pairs of successfully segmented sentences in the test set are intercepted to calculate the similarity. Then the F-Measure is used to judge the pros and cons of the proposed method.

The precision rate is calculated to reflect how many samples whose predictions are positive are correct. The calculation could be obtained from the Eq. 5.

$$P = \frac{TP}{TP + FP} \times 100\% \tag{5}$$

Recall is used to calculate for reflecting how many positive samples are predicted correct. The recall could be calculated by the Eq. 6.

$$R = \frac{TP}{TP + FN} \times 100\% \tag{6}$$

The contradiction between the precision rate and the recall rate is also needed to be consider comprehensively. F-Measure is one of the most common methods, which is computed by formula 7.

$$F = \frac{2PR}{P + R} \times 100\% \tag{7}$$

The similarity calculation method based on sentence structure and modifiers proposed in this paper has an accuracy of 87.5% when the similarity threshold is 0.6. At the same time, the values of precision and recall are 0.9277 and 0.8021, respectively. After obtaining the values of precision and recall, the F-measure is 0.8603. Furthermore, a comparative test is developed to verify the ability to remove the same part of the modifier. The first step of this experiment is to tag each part. Table 1 records the tags of the parts of the sentence.

In Table 1, besides sentences HED, SBV, and ATT, the remaining relationships are marked as OTHERS. After splitting the sentence, the modification part of the host and predicate is not a simple word sometimes. The original calculation of multiple modifiers does not make an exact discovery of the similarities and similarities of the modification part, so after computing the HED and SBV, the experiment results reveal whether ATT and OTHERS remove the same part of the similarity. The experimental results are listed in Table 2.

Table 2 shows that the proposed algorithm can improve the accuracy of the similarity calculation and remove the same part of the modifier effectively, especially for the parts describing each structure. Hence, the proposed algorithm can accurately capture the impact of the modified part on the whole sentence during the sentence similarity calculation while indicating that the modified part of the sentence structure can significantly affect the meaning to be expressed in the sentence.

Table 2. Experimental data comparison.

	Accuracy	F-measure
The same part is not removed entirely	73.5%	0.6827
Only the same part of the OTHERS was removed	80.5%	0.7958
Only the same part of the ATT was removed	84.0%	0.8222
Remove the same part of the ATT, OTHERS	87.5%	0.8603

A comparison among the proposed method with the correctness rate and F values of similar methods is given, as shown in Table 3.

Table 3. Performance comparison of sentence similarity calculation methods

Algorithm	Accuracy	F-measure
Wang [26]	47.5%	0.6237
Li [27]	82.0%	0.8043
Ours	87.5%	0.8603

The results indicate that our method can also effectively improve the accuracy of similarity calculation, indicating that modifiers will significantly affect the similarity between sentences in the similarity calculation process. And the value of F of our method is much higher than that of the other two methods, indicating that the similarity calculation method proposed in this paper is more effective. It further verifies the necessity of considering modifiers when calculating similarity and brings a theoretical basis for calculating the similarity of subsequent sentences.

5 Conclusion

The semantic similarity calculation algorithm based on the syntactic structure and the modification words fully considers the different effects of the modifiers on the meaning of the sentence, instead of just performing the similarity calculation of the words in the same structure and calculating the similarity between words using Word2Vec, which can better distinguish the differences and similarities of word meanings and achieve good experimental results. In addition, this method is also applicable when the number of Chinese sentences is not large. It is a further exploration of traditional Chinese sentence similarity calculation methods. However, the semantic similarity calculation algorithm also has some disadvantages, for sentences that fail to segment successfully, this method still has some shortcomings. It cannot accurately obtain the similarity between sentences, and some sentence components cannot be considered in the similarity calculation. Therefore, how to use LTP for more accurate word segmentation and find a more accurate tool to segment Chinese sentences are the focus of our follow-up research, because it is related to our subsequent sentence similarity calculation.

Acknowledgements. This work was supported by the National Natural Science Foundation of China (No. 62066016), the Research Foundation of Education Bureau of Hunan Province, China (Nos. 21C0363 and 21C0383), the Natural Science Foundation of Hunan Province, China (No. 2020JJ5458), and the Jishou University Graduate Research and Innovation Project (No. JDY20021).

References

1. Gomaa, W.H., Fahmy, A.A.: A survey of text similarity approaches. Int. J. Comput. Appl. **68**(13), 13–18 (2013)
2. Alonso, I., Contreras, D.: Evaluation of semantic similarity metrics applied to the automatic retrieval of medical documents: an UMLS approach. Expert Syst. Appl. **44**, 386–399 (2016)
3. Asiri, Y.: Short text mining for classifying educational objectives and outcomes. Comput. Syst. Sci. Eng. **41**(1), 35–50 (2022)
4. Madani, Y., Erritali, M., Bengourram, J., Sailhan, F.: A multilingual fuzzy approach for classifying Twitter data using fuzzy logic and semantic similarity. Neural Comput. Appl. **32**(12), 8655–8673 (2020)
5. Venkatraman, S., Surendiran, B., Kumar, P.A.R.: Spam e-mail classification for the internet of things environment using semantic similarity approach. J. Supercomputing **76**(2), 756–776 (2020)
6. Meymandpour, R., Davis, J.G.: A semantic similarity measure for linked data: an information content-based approach. Knowl. Based Syst. **109**, 276–293 (2016)
7. Chergui, O., Begdouri, A., Groux-Leclet, D.: Integrating a Bayesian semantic similarity approach into CBR for knowledge reuse in community question answering. Knowl. Based Syst. **185**, 104919 (2019)
8. Al-Besher, A., Kumar, K., Sangeetha, M., Butsa, T.: Bert for conversational question answering systems using semantic similarity estimation. Comput. Mater. Continua **70**(3), 4763–4780 (2022)
9. Luo, L., Ming, J., Wu, D., Liu, P., Zhu, S.: Semantics-based obfuscation-resilient binary code similarity comparison with applications to software plagiarism detection. In: Proceedings of the 22nd ACM SIGSOFT International Symposium on Foundations of Software Engineering, pp. 389–400. Association for Computing Machinery, Hong Kong, China (2014)
10. Seki, K.: Cross-lingual text similarity exploiting neural machine translation models. J. Inf. Sci. **47**(3), 404–418 (2021)
11. Wang, R., Cheng, H.K., Jiang, Y., Lou, J.: A novel matrix factorization model for recommendation with LOD-based semantic similarity measure. Expert Syst. Appl. **123**, 70–81 (2019)
12. Palaniappan, L., Selvaraj, K.: Profile and rating similarity analysis for recommendation systems using deep learning. Comput. Syst. Sci. Eng. **41**(3), 903–917 (2022)
13. Vij, S., Tayal, D., Jain, A.: A machine learning approach for automated evaluation of short answers using text similarity based on WordNet graphs. Wirel. Pers. Commun. **111**(2), 1271–1282 (2020)
14. Atrees, M., Ahmad, A., Alghanim, F.: Enhancing detection of malicious URLs using boosting and lexical features. Intell. Autom. Soft Comput. **31**(3), 1405–1422 (2022)

15. Abas, A.R., Elhenawy, I., Zidan, M., Othman, M.: Bert-CNN: a deep learning model for detecting emotions from text. Comput. Mater. Continua **71**(2), 2943–2961 (2022)
16. Chen, Y., Lu, H., Li, L.: Automatic ICD-10 coding algorithm using an improved longest common subsequence based on semantic similarity. PLoS ONE **12**(3), e0173410 (2017)
17. Mohammad, A.S., Jaradat, Z., Mahmoud, A.A., Jararweh, Y.: Paraphrase identification and semantic text similarity analysis in Arabic news tweets using lexical, syntactic, and semantic features. Inf. Process. Manage. **53**(3), 640–652 (2017)
18. Ru, C., Tang, J., Li, S., Xie, S., Wang, T.: Using semantic similarity to reduce wrong labels in distant supervision for relation extraction. Inf. Process. Manage. **54**(4), 593–608 (2018)
19. Salton, G., Wong, A., Yang, C.S.: A vector space model for automatic indexing. Commun. ACM **18**(11), 613–620 (1975)
20. Gu, Q.: A study on modifiers in the English language. J. Lang. Teach. Res. **10**(6), 1312–1317 (2019)
21. Klein, D., Manning, C.D.: Accurate unlexicalized parsing. In: Proceedings of the 41st Annual Meeting of the Association for Computational Linguistics, pp. 423–430. Association for Computational Linguistics, Sapporo, Japan (2003)
22. Che, W., Li, Z., Liu, T.: LTP: a Chinese language technology platform. In: Coling 2010: Demonstrations, pp. 13–16. Coling 2010 Organizing Committee Beijing, China (2010)
23. Mikolov, T., Chen, K., Corrado, G., Dean, J.: Efficient estimation of word representations in vector space. arXiv preprint arXiv:1301.3781 (2013)
24. Joachims, T.: A probabilistic analysis of the Rocchio algorithm with TFIDF for text categorization. Carnegie-Mellon University of Pittsburgh, PA Department of Computer Science (1996)
25. Liu, X., et al.: LCQMC: a large-scale Chinese question matching corpus. In: Proceedings of the 27th International Conference on Computational Linguistics, pp. 1952–1962. Association for Computational Linguistics, Santa Fe, New Mexico, USA (2018)
26. Wang, W., Liang, D., Office, T.S.: Chinese sentence similarity computing based on semantic dependency matching. J. Shenzhen Inst. Inf. Technol. **12**(01), 56–61 (2014)
27. Li, B., Liu, T., Qin, B., Li, S.: Chinese sentence similarity computing based on semantic dependency relationship analysis. Appl. Res. Comput. **12**(12), 15–17 (2003)

Animation Generation Technology Based on Deep Learning: Opportunities and Challenges

Zunfu Wang[1], Fang Liu[1(✉)], and Xue Zhang[2]

[1] School of Design, Hunan University, Changsha, China
fangl@hnu.edu.cn
[2] Nissan Technology Center, Canton, USA

Abstract. More and more information relies on animation videos for dissemination nowadays, but the traditional animation or video production process requires a lot of manpower and time to draw and set the actions of characters. The continuous progress of deep learning technology, especially the continuous development of the Generative Adversarial Networks, has made semi-automated or automated animation production possible. In this paper, we investigated the animation generation technology based on artificial intelligence technology, analyzed the existing technical means and solutions, pointed out the problems and challenges in the current research field, and looked forward to future technological development.

Keywords: Animation generation · Deep learning · Animation effect

1 Introduction

Animation works can convey a large amount of information to the audience in a short period of time, which is unmatched by static images. According to relevant statistics, more than 50% of the information currently mainly relies on video information for dissemination [1]. The short, flat, and fast characteristics of video works make it the best information dissemination carrier in the streaming media era. The production of animation or video is time and resource-intensive, and the production cost is prohibitive. The development of artificial intelligence technology is constantly changing this status. Through automated generation methods, monotonous and tedious repetitive tasks can be replaced, and creative animators can focus more on creative creation.

The production of the animation started from the continuous movement born from the flipbook, and in the 19th century, Edward Muybridge used multiple cameras to photograph the world's first set of continuous movements for a running horse. Then, at the end of the 19th century and the beginning of the 20th century, real modern animation appeared, and it has matured to nowadays [2]. Animations need animators to manually decompose and draw the motion for a series of frames. This requires an animator to have superb drawing skills, and enough kinematics knowledge, only in this way can animation be produced with realistic movements and reasonable behavior.

© The Author(s), under exclusive license to Springer Nature Switzerland AG 2022
X. Sun et al. (Eds.): ICAIS 2022, LNCS 13338, pp. 311–325, 2022.
https://doi.org/10.1007/978-3-031-06794-5_26

Artificial intelligence technology represented by deep learning has brought more efficient and scientific possibilities for animation production. The developer of Pixar Animation set out to build a tool called Midas Creature that can automatically perform animation tasks such as walking motion generation [1]. Adobe is also working on issues related to the automatic synchronization of lip movements and speech in animated characters [1]. Intelligent technologies, on the one hand, can help reduce the burden of animators, and make them focus on more core creative work; on the other hand, they can also break through the boundaries of traditional creativity and bring unpredictable inspiration to creative work.

In this paper, we pay more attention to the overall motion animation generation technology of characters or objects, because this is the basis for pushing intelligent automation technology to higher-level applications. We reviewed the animation automatic generation technologies, investigated the technical methods used, and the related tools and data sets that are publicly available; after that, we discussed the problems and challenges faced by the animation generation technology based on artificial intelligence technology in different dimensions. Then, we discussed the future direction of technology development and proposed the works that can be improved in the future.

2   Approaches in Animation Generation

In the real world, motion is widespread and common. The same is true in the field of animation, animations include not only the physical movement of the object itself but also the appearance and color changes (for example, the sky has different colors at different times of the day). Therefore, different strategies need to be adopted to generate realistic animation effects for different objects. At present, in the fields of computer vision and

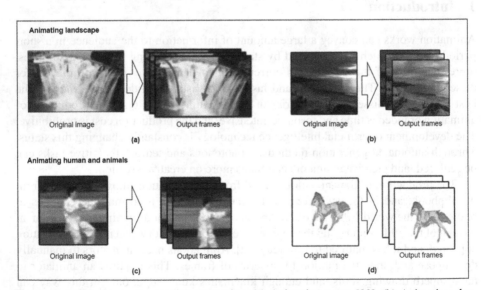

Fig. 1. Research cases of animation generation. (a) Animating water [20]. (b) Animating sky, clouds, water [15]. (c) animating a person [48]. (d) Animating a horse [53].

computer graphics, human motion and natural landscape are the most popular research objects. There are few researches on other objects. Therefore, this paper will mainly analyze the related research on the generation of natural scenery animation and the generation of characters and animals. Figure 1 shows some study cases in this field.

2.1 Animating Landscape

When observing static natural images, humans can distinguish the objects in the picture and can imagine their moving scenes in the brain, such as the flowing of water, the floating of clouds, the color change of the sky, etc. This kind of imagination based on human prior knowledge helps people understand and perceive contents beyond static images. In the field of computer graphics and machine vision, the generation of static images to dynamic videos is a research hotspot and difficulty at this stage. Relevant research has made great progress but still faces many challenges.

Early attempts to animate natural scenes in a single image were a procedural method called random motion texture [3]. This method generates simple quasi-periodic motions of individual components, such as swaying trees, rippling water, and swaying boats. Human users need to manually adjust the parameters of each component to generate motion animations. With the advancement of algorithms and computing power, related studies based on technologies such as databases, rule bases, and deep learning algorithms have gradually been applied to this field. According to the different research methods adopted, we divide related research into two categories: rules and data-based generation methods, deep learning-based methods, and we will present the description of them respectively.

Rules and Data-Based Generation Methods. The landscape image animation generation technology based on rules and data usually needs a rule library and a template library based on datasets, and generates motion animations for specific objects through the user's input and designation. This method relies heavily on large-scale datasets and huge computing resources, and usually requires users to use heavy manual processes to specify, for example, alpha masks, flow fields, and fluid regions.

Makoto et al. [4] proposed a system that allows users to design continuous flow animations from still fluid images. The basic idea is to apply the fluid motion extracted from the video example to the target image. This system first decomposes the video example into three components: average image, flow field and residual. Then, the user specifies the equivalent letter on the target image, manually draws the rough flow field, and the system uses the estimated gradient of the target image to automatically refine it. The user semi-automatically transfers the residual to the target image. Then, the system approximates the average image and synthesizes the animation on the target image by adding the transmitted residuals and distorting them according to the user-specified flow field. Finally, the system adjusts the appearance of the generated animation by applying histogram matching. The system is mainly aimed at the animation generation of rivers, waterfalls, fires, and smoke.

Makoto and Anjyo et al. [5] proposed a method of synthesizing fluid animation from a single image using a fluid video database. The user inputs the target painting or photo of the fluid scene, and extracts the alpha mask of the fluid area of interest in the scene.

This method allows the user to generate fluid animation from the input image and input some additional commands regarding the direction or velocity of the fluid. Using the fluid instance database, the core algorithm automatically assigns fluid videos to each part of the target image. This method can process various paintings and photos of rivers, waterfalls, fires, and smoke.

Makoto and Dobashi et al. [6] provide a system for quickly creating water scene animation in a single image. This method needs to rely on water scene video database and video retrieval technology. Based on a given input image, the user is required to specify the alpha mask and the direction of movement of the region of interest. After that, the system retrieves suitable candidate videos from the database and creates candidate animations for each region of interest as input images and retrieved. At the same time, the system allows the user to interactively control the speed of the desired animation and select the appropriate animation. After selecting the animation for all areas, the generated animation is completed. Finally, the user can optionally apply a texture synthesis algorithm to restore the appearance of the input image.

Prashnani et al. [7] provide a static image animation generation method based on sample videos, which can generate animation effects for static images, including trees, water, smoke, grass, and candle fire. This method requires the user to provide a motion video with similar objects, and set the outline of the animated region of interest (ROI) in the input image and the corresponding outline around the similar appearance area in the example video. Afterwards, by adopting the method based on Euler phase, the phase information in the sample video is collected and the motion in it is transferred to the input image.

This kind of rules and data-based static image animation generation method usually requires the construction of a certain scale database, and the motion effects that can be generated are also relatively limited, and it is not easy to transfer to other object animation generation applications. At the same time, the user is usually required to manually specify the sports field, whether it is through the alpha mask, the flow field, or the fluid area. Although this method requires user interactive input, and usually the amount of calculation is relatively large, an interactive-based generation method can make users have certain expectations of the output results, especially in [5], the user can input control the direction and speed of fluid movement, which is very necessary in the traditional animation production process.

Deep Learning-Based Methods. The landscape image animation generation technology based on rules and data usually needs a rule library and a template library based on datasets, and generates motion animations for specific objects through user's input and designation. This method relies heavily on large-scale datasets and huge computing resources, and usually requires users to use heavy manual processes to specify, for example, alpha masks, flow fields, and fluid regions.

In the past few years, great progress has been made in learning-based methods [8]. Some models based on Generative Adversarial Networks (GAN) [9–12] and models based on Conditional Change Auto-Encoder (CVAE) [13, 14] can automatically generate videos based on the input image content. The use of deep neural networks to learn video representation and prediction of future frames has become a very active research area [15–19]. Most of the early work focused on using a deep neural network (DNN) with recursive units (GRU or LSTM) and training it in an unsupervised way to use pixel-level prediction to obtain the next frame of image [16, 19]. Natural scenery image animation usually includes changes in color and light and shadow in addition to the physical movement of the object itself over a long period of time. In some studies, only short-term movement changes are concerned. Such studies cannot generate long-term time-lapse animation; while other studies are aimed at generating more realistic time-lapse animation videos, which needs to pay attention to the changes in movement and external relations over a long period of time.

A fully automatic method for converting still natural images into real animation loop videos is proposed [20]. This method targets scenes of continuous fluid movement, such as flowing water and billowing smoke. This method uses a priori neural network to extract the motion field from the image, calculates the motion of the particles in the motion field through Euler motion description, and finally decodes the picture of the continuous motion frame. This method can achieve very realistic fluid motion effects and can generate high-resolution motion videos. But the research only focused on the movement itself, and could not form the effect of cloud or sky color change.

A method of generating motion video for the sky and water in natural images is proposed in [21]. This method uses convolutional neural networks to learn motion and appearance in automatic time-lapse videos, and uses decoupling control to predict them. The future uncertainties in the two predictions are dealt with by introducing latent codes. This method can only achieve better results when the sky and water surface in the image are large and the boundary is relatively obvious, otherwise, it will also distort other objects.

By extending the StyleGAN model, the time-lapse scenery video generation for static scenery images is realized in [15]. This method can be trained on a mixed data set of static scenery images and scenery animations, and can effectively solve the problem of insufficient training data. This method can generate more realistic scenery animation effects, but when the color of the object in the picture is close to the sky or water surface, there may be errors in the judgment of the movement field.

An end-to-end outdoor image time-lapse video generation method is proposed in [8]. This method is based on a conditionally generated confrontation network to learn the correlation between the lighting changes of outdoor scenes and the time of day. This method also has the problems of inaccurate judgment of the boundary of the sports field and color distortion.

The FGLA model is proposed to generate high-quality and realistic natural image time-lapse video by learning fine-grained motion embedding for landscape animation in [22]. The model consists of two parts: (1) Motion encoder, which embeds time-delay motion in a fine-grained manner. (2) A motion generator used to generate real motion to set the animation of the input image.

A self-supervised end-to-end model is proposed to generate time-lapse video from a single image and reference video in [23]. The key idea is to extract time-varying styles and features from the reference video and transfer them to the input image, And through the use of noise-like damping, flow loss, and video discriminator to ensure the time consistency and authenticity of the synthesized video.

A two-stage method based on Generative Adversarial Networks (GAN) is proposed to generate high-resolution real time-lapse videos for outdoor still images in [24]. In the first stage, a video with realistic content is generated for each frame, and in the second stage Enhance the video generated in the first stage to make it closer to the real video in terms of motion dynamics. And, in order to further increase the vivid motion in the final generated video, the Gram matrix is used to model the motion more accurately.

Relevant methods based on deep learning have made great progress, and can generate more realistic motion animations for part of the content in natural scenery pictures. However, the current related research mainly focuses on the movement of fluids such as smoke, water, clouds, fog, etc., while there are relatively few studies on the movement of flowers, plants, and trees, which is mainly due to the relatively large differences between these categories of objects, The form of motion in the real world is more complex and changeable. In addition, the existing related methods based on deep learning still have room for improvement in the generation effect. For example, in the division of sports fields, some methods will also distort other objects in the picture, resulting in unrealistic results. This may be due to the limited size of the training data set. Secondly, the results of some methods will have problems such as blur, unrealistic distortion, and color distortion. Finally, the resolution of the video generated by the learning-based method is often relatively low and cannot reach the application level, which is also limited by the current computing power.

Landscape Image Dataset. In the research on the generation of landscape image animation based on learning, the dataset plays a key role. It not only serves as a common basis for measuring and comparing the performance of competing algorithms, but also pushes the field to solve increasingly complex and challenging problems. At present, the datasets collected in related research are mainly as Table 1.

Table 1. Basic information of landscape datasets.

Name	Counts	Description	Image size
Sky Time-lapse dataset [24–28]	35000	Videos of dynamic sky scenes	128 × 128
DTLVDB dataset [29]	450	Landscapes time-lapse videos	/
AMOS dataset [13]	17million	Images taken from outdoor webcams	Most are 320 × 240
Time-Release-D dataset [22]	16874	Video clips with different scene categories	40% 1280 × 720, 30% 1920 × 1080
Webcam Clip Art Dataset [30]	580000	Images taken from 54 outdoor webcam sequences	At least 640 × 480

Animation Effect Evaluation. The evaluation methods of the animation effect of natural scenery image generation mainly include qualitative evaluation and quantitative evaluation. The qualitative evaluation mainly includes the following methods: 1. Comparison of image effects through manual review and baseline; 2. Investigation of the authenticity and naturalness of the generated video effects by the participants through questionnaires and other methods [14, 29]. Quantitative evaluation methods use different strategies according to different research objects and scopes. The commonly used evaluation indicators are mainly: FID [31], PSNR, SSIM [32], LPIPS [33].

2.2 Animating Human and Animals

Characters and animals are usually the protagonists in animation, and their motion animation generation is quite different from the animation generation of natural scenery. The main points are: 1. Characters and animals have their own laws of motion characteristics, such as running, walking, jumping, etc., this has a lot to do with its own bone structure. Therefore, the representation of skeletal animation is usually used as a representation of the movement mode. 2. The appearance of characters or animal characters basically does not change much, unlike clouds in natural scenery, but it is difficult to infer multi-angle images of characters or animal characters, and usually requires images from multiple angles as input, which is a possible way to generate more accurate images in different angles.

Similar to the dynamic effect generation of landscape images, the generation of character animation mainly involves two dimensions: movement and appearance. At present, the movement of character animation mainly includes feature extraction and learning based on motion capture data and motion video data. The appearance of character animation usually requires a given input, or predicted based on images. Next, we will analyze based on the two dimensions mentioned above: motion capture data-based methods and motion video data-based methods.

Motion Capture Data-Based Methods. The method based on motion data capture is the data-driven character animation technology, which uses motion capture data for interactive character control and generates motion animation effects for the character [34]. Traditional data-based methods include methods based on the motion graph structure, finite state machines, and so on. Various techniques based on classic machine learning, such as K-nearest neighbor (KNN), principal component analysis [35–38], radial basis function (RBF) [39, 40], Reinforcement Learning [41], and Gaussian Process (GP) [42–44]. Most of them are based on classic machine learning methods. The methods of learning technology all have scalability issues: they first require a lot of data preprocessing, including motion classification and alignment. The deep learning technology based on neural network has attracted the attention of related researchers due to its scalability and high runtime performance. Related research mainly includes:

A real-time character control mechanism based on phase function neural network is proposed in [45]. The system takes the previous state of the character and the geometry of the scene as input user controls, and automatically generates high-quality motions to achieve the required user controls. The entire network is trained on a large data set in an end-to-end manner, which consists of walking, running, jumping, and climbing suitable for virtual environments. It allows characters to adapt to different geometric environments, such as walking and running on rugged terrain, climbing large rocks, jumping over obstacles, and squatting under low ceilings.

Zhang et al. [34] proposed a pattern-adaptive neural network architecture to control the movement of quadrupeds. The system consists of a motion prediction network and a gated network. In each frame, the motion prediction network calculates the state of the character in the current frame based on the state of the previous frame and the control signal provided by the user. The system can learn consistent expert weights across various aperiodic/periodic actions from unstructured motion capture data in an end-to-end manner.

In addition to being used in the field of character animation generation, motion generation through motion data is often used as a motion control strategy for biomimetic robots. Luo et al. [46] proposed a CARL quadruped robot control system, which uses a generative confrontation neural network to extract motion data from motion data to learn control strategies. By using a model-based controller to simulate different animal gaits, without any real-world fine-tuning, four different animal gaits can be generated on the A1 robot [47].

To generate character animation through motion data, an object model with control bones is required, and the data is aligned with the character. At the same time, in the data collection stage, complicated marking point positioning and data processing are required. Image-based deep learning character animation generation technology can avoid these shortcomings.

Motion Video Data-Based Methods. Generating high-quality video from static images is challenging because it requires learning an appropriate representation of the object, such as a 3D model of the face or human body. This task also needs to accurately extract the motion pattern from the driving video and map it to the object. Therefore, most objects are specific. The depth model can effectively transfer the motion patterns between human subjects in the video [48, 49], or transfer facial expressions from one person to another [50]. However, these methods have limitations: for example, they rely on pre-trained models to extract object representations that require expensive ground truth data annotations [11, 51, 52].

Siarohin et al. [53] proposed a model framework that can generate animation from objects in static images (faces, humans). It uses a self-supervised learning strategy, so it does not use any annotations or a priori about the specific object to be animated information. In order to support complex movements, a representation consisting of a set of learned key points and their local affine transformations is used. The generator network models the occlusion generated during the target motion and combines the appearance extracted from the source image with the motion derived from the driving video.

Chan et al. [51] proposed a method of transferring the appearance image of a character to a video to synthesize a character video of a specific action, such as dancing. In order to transfer motion, the method extracts pose from the source object and apply the learned pose to appearance mapping to generate the target object.

A deep neural network for predicting future frames in natural video sequences is proposed in [54]. It can predict the facial expression movement and body movement of the person in the image. The model is based on the encoder-decoder convolutional neural network and convolutional LSTM for pixel-level prediction, which independently captures the spatial layout of the image and the corresponding temporal dynamics. By independently modeling motion and content, predicting the next frame is simplified to convert the extracted content features into the next frame content through the identified motion features, thereby simplifying the prediction task.

A novel image animation deep learning framework is proposed in [48], which can generate animation videos that are consistent with the reference video actions based on the input images and reference videos. The method is implemented by a deep architecture that separates appearance and motion information. The framework consists of three main modules: 1. unsupervised training of keypoint detectors to extract object keypoints, 2. for sparse keypoints, a dense motion prediction network that generates a dense heat map to better encode motion information, 3. a motion transmission network, which uses the motion heat map and appearance information extracted from the input image to synthesize the output frame. This method can generate good motion animation for facial expression movement, character movement, animal movement, etc. However, there is still a problem of inaccurate appearance migration.

The learning method based on image vision can realize the generation of character animation in an end-to-end manner, but the technology based on video prediction cannot generate long-term video sequences, and the method based on reference video has the problem of partial distortion of appearance and motion. Which still needs further research and exploration.

Motion Dataset. The dataset of character animation includes two types: motion capture dataset and video dataset. The motion datasets disclosed in related research are as shown in Table 2.

Table 2. Basic information of motion datasets.

Name	Counts	Description	Image size
Dog motion dataset [34]	/	30 min of unstructured dog motion capture data	/
Bair dataset [55]	41226	Videos of Sawyer's robotic arm pushing various objects onto the table	64 × 64
Tai-Chi dataset [56]	4500	Tai Chi video clips downloaded from Youtube	64 × 64
UCF101 dataset [57]	13200	Videos in 101 different action categories	320 × 240
MGif dataset [48]	1269	Gifs of animals from Google	256 × 256

Animation Effect Evaluation. The evaluation method of the character movement animation effect is similar to the evaluation method in Sect. 2.1, which also includes the same qualitative evaluation and quantitative evaluation. LPIPS and SSIM are also used in the quantitative evaluation. In addition, for human posture evaluation, many studies [48, 49] use the human posture estimator in [58].

3   Problems and Challenges in Animation Generation

Although some progress has been made in deep generative models in recent years, automatically generating high-quality videos from a single landscape image is still a challenging task. This mainly lies in: 1. The movement (for example, moving clouds) and appearance (for example, the color of the sky changing over time) in the natural scene have different time scales. 2. Movement in natural scenery has greater uncertainty. For example, the color and shape of clouds are varied, and the direction of movement can also be diverse. 3. Objects in natural scenery images or video content are difficult to label, therefore, the training of the model can only be carried out through self-supervised or unsupervised learning methods at present. 4. Motion in general natural landscape scenes is highly complex, involving perspective effects, occlusion, and transients.

The generation of character animations such as characters and animals is more complicated than the animation generation of natural scenery images. This is mainly due to: 1. there are many types of characters and animals, and each animal has its own unique characteristics and patterns of movement behavior. It is difficult to make a dataset for each animal; 2. For image-based methods, when characters and animals are in motion, there are occlusion problems (occlusion of their own body parts, front and back occlusion in multi-role, etc.). It is difficult to infer images from multiple angles from angled images, and there is often a problem of distortion; 3. For character animation generation, the clothes of the characters are changeable, and the wrinkles on the clothes will also follow the state of motion. The different effects have different effects, which also brings difficulties to deep learning; 4. For the method based on the motion data set, the movement marker data of the character can still be collected, but for a variety of animals, the marker point tracking is unrealistic; 5. For insects and other animals, because it is not easy to capture the motion of the motion markers, only the image-based method can be used to learn the motion mode, but the insect posture recognition is difficult and difficult to achieve a better tracking effect.

4   Research Opportunities

The animation effect generation technology of natural scenery can be applied to many fields, such as the production of dynamic photos, animation production, and multimedia content production. However, the results achieved at present are still relatively limited, and learning-based methods have greater uncertainty. We summarize the research opportunities as follow:

1) *Editable and Predictable Generation Results.* For example, users cannot judge the direction and form of movement of clouds in the generated video. In the future, interactive technology may enable users to the output results are controlled to achieve better expectations. In addition, due to the limitation of the data set and data scale, the existing related scale basically can achieve relatively few animation effects, such as only the movement of water and clouds. In the future, it may be possible to achieve a variety of sports effects through transfer learning. Finally, the current related research mainly focuses on real natural images. In the future, it may be possible to realize the generation of animation effects in artwork images through style transfer and so on.

2) *Realistic 3D Reconstruction.* Through the generation of character animation driven by motion data, more realistic and natural virtual character motion effects can be generated. But this usually requires a prototype of a virtual character in advance, and usually a 3D character. In the future, it may be possible to use 3D motion capture technology to generate realistic motion animations for two-dimensional characters through dimensionality reduction processing of data. The current image-based character animation generation technology cannot recommend multi-angle images of characters well. Perhaps it is possible to generate multi-angle image inferences for virtual characters by adding relevant modules. For example, [59] DECA reconstructs a 3D head model with detailed facial geometry from an input image, and the resulting 3D head model can be easily animated. Huang et al. [60] use several images from different angles as the rabbit to generate various target poses. Image-based character animation has the problem of background distortion, which may be avoided by mating technology [61].

3) *New Objects and Actions.* The current related research is mostly focused on human actions. There is little research on the animation generation of insects and birds. As far as we know, certain progress has been made in insect pose tracking and recognition [62–64, 66, 67]. In the future, it will be able to automatically generate motion animations for these objects through related motion feature learning methods.

4) *New Animation Types.* The current research mainly focuses on the movement of the object, while there are relatively few studies on the process and physical changes. For example, [65] learns the process of specific types of physical changes from time-lapse videos, such as melting, flowering, baking, and decay. This specific type of physical change video can be automatically generated for the input image. The animation generation of physical processes in the future may also be an important research direction.

5 Conclusions

The animation generation technology has broad application prospects. With the continuous improvement of the quality of the generated results, we believe that this will greatly change the traditional animation production method. We introduce the animation generation technology for natural landscape images, human images, and animal images respectively, analyze the existing technical methods, and enumerate the commonly used datasets in related research fields. At present, the animation generation technology based on artificial intelligence still has problems such as difficulty in dataset production and poor animation generation effect. This is due to the complexity of the movement on the one hand, and the insufficient of current technology and computing power on the other hand. We believe that in future, editable and predictable generation methods, realistic 3D reconstruction technology based on 2D images, new moving objects and motion methods, and new animation types, will be the future research opportunities in the future. We will continue to pay attention to the development trends in related fields, and carry out specific technical applications and discussions.

Funding Statement. This work is supported by The National Key Research and Development Program of China (2019YFB1405702).

References

1. State of AI in Animation (2020). https://blog.adobe.com/en/publish/2019/06/11/state-of-ai-in-animation.html#gs.fftul3
2. He, S.Q., He, Y.Y.: Analysis of the development of Chinese animation and American animation. Times Rep. **07**(1), 48–49 (2021)
3. Chuang, Y.Y., Goldman, D.B., Zheng, K.C., Curless, B., Salesin, D.H., Szeliski, R.: Animating pictures with stochastic motion textures. In: SIGGRAPH 2005: ACM SIGGRAPH 2005, NY, USA, pp. 853–860 (2005)
4. Okabe, M., Anjyo, K., Igarashi, T., Seidel, H.P.: Animating pictures of fluid using video examples. Comput. Graph. Forum **28**(2), 667–686 (2009)
5. Okabe, M., Anjyo, K., Onai, R.: Creating fluid animation from a single image using video database. Comput. Graph. Forum **30**(7), 1973–1982 (2011)
6. Okabe, M., Dobashi, Y., Anjyo, K.: Animating pictures of water scenes using video retrieval. Vis. Comput. **34**(3), 347–358 (2016). https://doi.org/10.1007/s00371-016-1337-6
7. Prashnani, E., Noorkami, M., Vaqueri, D., Sen, P.: A phase-based approach for animating images using video examples. Comput. Graph. Forum **36**(6), 303–311 (2017)
8. Nam, S., Ma, C., Chai, M., Brendel, W., Xu, N., Kim, S.J.: End-to-end time-lapse video synthesis from a single outdoor image. In: Proceedings of the IEEE/CVF Conference on Computer Vision and Pattern Recognition (CVPR), Long Beach, CA, pp.1409–1418 (2019)
9. Bychkovsky, L., Paris, S., Chan, E., Durand, F.: Learning photographic global tonal adjustment with a database of input/output image pairs. In: IEEE Conference on Computer Vision and Pattern Recognition (CVPR), Colorado Springs, USA, pp. 97–104 (2011)
10. Matusik, W., Loper, M., Pfister, H.: Progressively-refined reflectance functions from natural illumination. Render. Tech. **1**(2), 1 (2004)
11. Wang, T., et al.: Video-to-video synthesis. In: Advances in Neural Information Processing Systems, vol. 1, no. 1, pp. 1152–1164 (2018)
12. Xu, X., Wan, L., Liu, X., Wong, T.T., Wang, L., Leung, C.S.: Animating animal motion from still: In: ACM SIGGRAPH Asia 2008, Suntec, Singapore, pp. 1–8 (2008)
13. Jacobs, N., Roman, N., Pless, R.: Consistent temporal variations in many outdoor scenes. In: IEEE Conference on Computer Vision and Pattern Recognition (CVPR), Minneapolis, Minnesota, USA, pp. 1–6 (2007)
14. Li, Y., Liu, M.-Y., Li, X., Yang, M.-H., Kautz, J.: A closed-form solution to photorealistic image stylization. In: Ferrari, V., Hebert, M., Sminchisescu, C., Weiss, Y. (eds.) ECCV 2018. LNCS, vol. 11207, pp. 468–483. Springer, Cham (2018). https://doi.org/10.1007/978-3-030-01219-9_28

15. Logacheva, E., Suvorov, R., Khomenko, O., Mashikhin, A., Lempitsky, V.: DeepLandscape: adversarial modeling of landscape videos. In: Vedaldi, A., Bischof, H., Brox, T., Frahm, J.-M. (eds.) ECCV 2020. LNCS, vol. 12368, pp. 256–272. Springer, Cham (2020). https://doi.org/10.1007/978-3-030-58592-1_16

16. Srivastava, N., Mansimov, E., Salakhudinov, R.: Unsupervised learning of video representations using LSTMs. In: International Conference on Machine Learning, Lile, France, pp. 843–852 (2015)

17. Villegas, R., Yang, R., Hong, J., Lin, S., Lee, X.: Decomposing motion and content for natural video sequence prediction. arXiv:1706.08033 (2017)

18. Mathieu, M., Couprie, C., LeCun, Y.: Deep multi-scale video prediction beyond mean square error. arXiv:1511.05440 (2015)

19. Finn, C., Goodfellow, I., Levine, S.: Unsupervised learning for physical interaction through video prediction. In: Advances in Neural Information Processing Systems, vol. 29, no. 1, pp. 64–72 (2016)

20. Holynski, A., Curless, B., Seitz, S., Szeliski, R.: Animating pictures with Eulerian motion fields. In: Proceedings of the IEEE/CVF Conference on Computer Vision and Pattern Recognition (CVPR), Virtual, USA, pp. 5810–5819 (2021)

21. Endo, Y., Kanamori, K., Kuriyama, S.: Animating landscape: self-supervised learning of decoupled motion and appearance for single-image video synthesis. arXiv:1910.07192 (2019)

22. Xue, H., Liu, B., Yang, H., Li, J., Luo, J.: Learning fine-grained motion embedding for landscape animation. In: Proceedings of the 29th ACM International Conference on Multimedia, NY, USA, pp. 291–299 (2021)

23. Cheng, C., Chen, H., Chiu, W.: Time flies: animating a still image with time-lapse video as reference. In: Proceedings of the IEEE/CVF Conference on Computer Vision and Pattern Recognition (CVPR), Seattle, WA, USA, pp. 5641–5650 (2020)

24. Xiong, W., Luo, W., Ma, L., Liu, W., Luo, J.: Learning to generate time-lapse videos using multi-stage dynamic generative adversarial networks. In: Proceedings of the IEEE Conference on Computer Vision and Pattern Recognition (CVPR), Salt Lake City, UT, USA, pp. 2364–2373 (2018)

25. Vondrick, C., Pirsiavash, H., Torralba, A.: Generating videos with scene dynamics. In: Advances Neural Information Processing Systems (NIPS), Barcelona, Spain, pp. 613–621 (2016)

26. Villegas, R., Yang, Y., Zou, Y., Sohn, S., Lin, X., Lee, H.: Learning to generate long-term future via hierarchical prediction. In: International Conference on Machine Learning (ICML), Sydney, Australia, pp. 3560–3569 (2017)

27. Karpathy, A., Toderici, G., Shetty, S., Leung, T., Sukthankar, R., Li, F.: Large-scale video classification with convolutional neural networks. In: IEEE Conference on Computer Vision and Pattern Recognition (CVPR), Columbus, OH, USA, pp. 1725–1732 (2014)

28. Funke, C., Gatys, L., Ecker, A., Bethge, M.: Synthesising dynamic textures using convolutional neural networks. arXiv:1702.07006 (2017)

29. Shih, Y., Paris, S., Durand, F., Freeman, W.: Data-driven hallucination of different times of day from a single outdoor photo. ACM Trans. Graph. (TOG) 32(6), 1–11 (2013)

30. Lalonde, J., Efros, A., Narasimhan, S.: Webcam clip art: appearance and illuminant transfer from time-lapse sequences. ACM Trans. Graph. (TOG) 28(5), 1–10 (2009)

31. Heusel, M., Ramsauer, H., Unterthiner, T., Nessler, B., Hochreiter, S.: GANs trained by a two time-scale update rule converge to a local Nash equilibrium. In: NeurIPS, Long Beach, CA, pp. 6626–6637 (2017)

32. Unterthiner, T., Steenkiste, S., Kurach, S., Marinier, R., Michalski, S., Gelly, S.: Towards accurate generative models of video: a new metric & challenges. arXiv:1812.01717 (2018)

33. Zhang, R., Isola, P., Efros, A., Shechtman, E., Wang, O.: The unreasonable effectiveness of deep features as a perceptual metric. In: IEEE Conference on Computer Vision and Pattern Recognition (CVPR), Salt Lake City, UT, USA, pp. 586–595 (2018)

34. Zhang, H., Starke, S., Komura, T., Saito, J.: Mode-adaptive neural networks for quadruped motion control. ACM Trans. Graph. (TOG) 37(1), 1–11 (2018)

35. Chai, J., Hodgins, J.: Performance animation from low-dimensional control signals. ACM Trans. Graph. 24(3), 686–696 (2005)

36. Min, J., Chai, J.: Motion graphs++: a compact generative model for semantic motion analysis and synthesis. ACM Trans. Graph. 31(6), 153–166 (2012)

37. Safonova, A., Hodgins, J., Pollard, N.: Synthesizing physically realistic human motion in low-dimensional, behavior-specific spaces. ACM Trans. Graph. 23(3), 514–521 (2004)

38. Tautges, J., et al.: Motion reconstruction using sparse accelerometer data. ACM Trans. Graph. 30(3), 1–18 (2011)

39. Kovar, L., Gleiche, M.: Automated extraction and parameterization of motions in large data sets. ACM Trans. Graph. 23(3), 559–568 (2004)

40. Rose, C., Cohen, M., Bodenheimer, B.: Verbs and adverbs: multidimensional motion interpolation. IEEE Comput. Graph. Appl. 18(5), 32–40 (1998)

41. Safonova, A., Hodgins, J.: Construction and optimal search of interpolated motion graphs. ACM Trans. Graph. 26(3), 106–120 (2007)

42. Grochow, K., Martin, S., Hertzmann, A., Popović, Z.: Style-based inverse kinematics. ACM Trans. Graph. 23(3), 522–531 (2004)

43. Ikemoto, L., Arikan, O., Forsyth, D.: Generalizing motion edits with Gaussian processes. ACM Trans. Graph. 28(1), 1–1 (2009)

44. Mukai, T., Kuriyama, S.: Geostatistical motion interpolation. ACM Trans. Graph. 24(3), 1062–1070 (2005)

45. Holden, D., Komura, T., Saito, J.: Phase-functioned neural networks for character control. ACM Trans. Graph. (TOG) 36(4), 1–13 (2017)

46. Luo, Y., Soeseno, J., Chen, T., Chen, W.: CARL: controllable agent with reinforcement learning for quadruped locomotion. ACM Trans. Graph. (TOG) 39(4), 1–38 (2020)

47. Li, T., Won, J., Ha, S., Rai, A.: Model-based motion imitation for agile, diverse and generalizable quadupedal locomotion. arXiv:2109.13362 (2021)

48. Siarohin, A., Lathuilière, S., Tulyakov, S., Ricci, E., Sebe, N.: Animating arbitrary objects via deep motion transfer. In: Proceedings of the IEEE/CVF Conference on Computer Vision and Pattern Recognition (CVPR), Long Beach, CA, USA, pp. 2377–2386 (2019)

49. Bansal, A., Ma, S., Ramanan, D., Sheikh, Y.: Recycle-GAN: unsupervised video retargeting. In: Ferrari, V., Hebert, M., Sminchisescu, C., Weiss, Y. (eds.) ECCV 2018. LNCS, vol. 11209, pp. 122–138. Springer, Cham (2018). https://doi.org/10.1007/978-3-030-01228-1_8

50. Wiles, O., Koepke, A.S., Zisserman, A.: X2Face: a network for controlling face generation using images, audio, and pose codes. In: Ferrari, V., Hebert, M., Sminchisescu, C., Weiss, Y. (eds.) ECCV 2018. LNCS, vol. 11217, pp. 690–706. Springer, Cham (2018). https://doi.org/10.1007/978-3-030-01261-8_41

51. Chan, C., Ginosar, S., Zhou, T., Efros, A.: Everybody dance now. In: The European Conference on Computer Vision (ECCV), Munich, Germany, pp. 5933–5942 (2018)

52. Balakrishnan, G., Zhao, A., Dalca, A., Durand, F., Guttag, J.: Synthesizing images of humans in unseen poses. In: IEEE Conference on Computer Vision and Pattern Recognition (CVPR), Salt Lake City, UT, USA, pp. 8340–8348 (2018)

53. Siarohin, A., Lathuilière, S., Tulyakov, S., Ricci, E., Sebe, N.: First order motion model for image animation. In: Advances Neural Information Processing Systems (NIPS), Vancouver, Canada, pp. 7137–7147 (2019)

54. Villegas, R., Yang, J., Hong, S., Lin, X., Lee, X.: Decomposing motion and content for natural video sequence prediction. arXiv:1706.08033 (2017)

55. Ebert, F., Finn, C., Lee, A., Levine, S.: Self-supervised visual planning with temporal skip connections. In: CoRL, California, USA, pp. 344–356 (2017)
56. Tulyakov, S., Liu, M., Yang, X., Kautz, J.: MoCoGAN: decomposing motion and content for video generation. In: IEEE Conference on Computer Vision and Pattern Recognition (CVPR), Salt Lake City, UT, USA, pp. 1526–1535 (2018)
57. Soomro, K., Zamir, A., Shah, M.: UCF101: a dataset of 101 human actions classes from videos in the wild, vol. 2, no. 11. Center for Research in Computer Vision (2012)
58. Cao, Z., Simon, T., Wei, S., Sheikh, Y.: Realtime multi-person 2D pose estimation using part affinity fields. In: IEEE Conference on Computer Vision and Pattern Recognition (CVPR), Honolulu, HI, USA, pp. 7291–7299 (2017)
59. Feng, Y., Feng, H., Black, M., Bolkart, T.: Learning an animatable detailed 3D face model from in-the-wild images. ACM Trans. Graph. (TOG) **40**(3), 1–13 (2021)
60. Huang, Z., Han, X., Xu, J., Zhang, T.: Few-shot human motion transfer by personalized geometry and texture modeling. In: Proceedings of the IEEE/CVF Conference on Computer Vision and Pattern Recognition (CVPR), Virtual, USA, pp. 2297–2306 (2021)
61. Sengupta, S., Jayaram, V., Curless, B.: Background matting: the world is your green screen. In: Proceedings of the IEEE/CVF Conference on Computer Vision and Pattern Recognition (CVPR), Seattle, WA, USA, pp. 2291–2300 (2020)
62. Mathis, M., Mathis, A.: Deep learning tools for the measurement of animal behavior in neuroscience. Curr. Opin. Neurobiol. **60**(1), 1–11 (2020)
63. Pereira, T., et al.: Fast animal pose estimation using deep neural networks. Nat. Methods **16**(1), 117–125 (2019)
64. Lauer, J., Zhou, M., Ye, S.: Multi-animal pose estimation and tracking with DeepLabCut. bioRxiv (2021)
65. Zhou, Y., Berg, T.L.: Learning temporal transformations from time-lapse videos. In: Leibe, B., Matas, J., Sebe, N., Welling, M. (eds.) ECCV 2016. LNCS, vol. 9912, pp. 262–277. Springer, Cham (2016). https://doi.org/10.1007/978-3-319-46484-8_16
66. Lee, S.: A study on classification and detection of small moths using CNN model. Comput. Mater. Contin. **71**(1), 1987–1998 (2022)
67. Alsaedi, N., Jaha, E.: Dynamic audio-visual biometric fusion for person recognition. Comput. Mater. Contin. **71**(1), 1283–1311 (2022)

Variations of Solar Radiation in Typical Resource Regions of China During 1961–2016

Wenzheng Yu[1](✉), Mingxuan Zhu[1,2], Aodi Fu[1], Li Shao[2], Haitao Liu[2], Tianliang Chen[2], and Hanxiaoya Zhang[3]

[1] School of Geographical Sciences, Nanjing University of Information Science and Technology, Nanjing 210044, China
ywzheng519@126.com

[2] School of Environmental Science and Engineering, Nanjing University of Information Science and Technology, Nanjing 210044, China

[3] Faculty of Science, The University of Auckland, Auckland 1010, New Zealand

Abstract. Based on the total solar radiation, horizontal direct radiation and scattered radiation data of six typical resource regions in China from 1961 to 2016, this paper focuses on analyzing the variation trend of solar radiation by using climate tendency estimation method, cumulative anomaly method, Morlet wavelet analysis method and Mann-Kendall mutation analysis method. The results are as follows: in addition to the Zhengzhou six typical resources scattered radiation in a downward trend, basic and change rule and the plane direct radiation and total radiation change law basic similar, Kashgar, the level of the direct radiation decreases in Lhasa, Golmud trends, by contrast, the level of the direct radiation level direct radiation biggest drop in Zhengzhou. The mutation years were mainly concentrated in the 1980s and 1990s.

Keywords: Horizontal direct radiation · Scattered radiation · Mutation analysis

1 Introduction

Over the past 100 years since the Industrial Revolution, carbon emission activities such as fossil energy burning, cement production and deforestation have resulted in the continuous increase of atmospheric carbon-containing greenhouse gas concentration, which may lead to global warming [1]. The dependence of human beings on fossil energy has seriously threatened the existence of human beings. At the same time, the increase of energy gap has forced the increase of international disputes and the increase of economic instability. Under the background of environment and current human existence, countries all over the world have taken the development of low-carbon economy as their best development mode. It has become a new trend of global economic and social development to reduce the use of non-renewable energy and vigorously develop sustainable energy [2]. And plentiful renewable energy as an inexhaustible energy, human can free use, won the eyes of the world, it is hoped that through the development of renewable energy to maintain long-term sustainable development, and the solar energy with its

© The Author(s), under exclusive license to Springer Nature Switzerland AG 2022
X. Sun et al. (Eds.): ICAIS 2022, LNCS 13338, pp. 326–347, 2022.
https://doi.org/10.1007/978-3-031-06794-5_27

unique advantage and become the focus of attention, solar energy is the fastest growing in recent years, the most dynamic of renewable energy. In the future, renewable energy mainly based on solar energy will occupy a dominant position in the world energy consumption [3–5]. During the long-term evolution of the Earth's climate system, solar radiation is closely related to the earth's climate system [6, 7]. Solar radiation plays an important role in coping with climate change, economic and social development and energy structure adjustment [8].

International extensive ground observation of solar radiation reaching the ground began in the late 1950s (after the International Geophysical Year of 1957–1958) [9]. At the same time, top-down satellite remote sensing observation of the earth's radiation balance was gradually carried out [10]. Many researchers have analyzed and discussed the changes of surface radiation in their own country, region and even the world. Analysis of root-distance ground radiation observations by Wild [11] et al. found that during 1950–1990, ground solar radiation in most parts of the world showed a decreasing trend, which is the so-called global "dimming". Other previous studies also found this phenomenon, but the decreasing amplitude was different. Gilgen et al. [12] and Liepert [13] suggested an average reduction of 1.3% or 7 W/m^2 per decade, while Stanhill et al. [14] suggested a reduction of 2.7% or 5/m^2 per decade. In particular, Wild [15] pointed out that from the mid to late 1980s until 2000, this "dimming" phenomenon was no longer sustained in the Northern and southern hemisphere, such as Australia and Antarctica. Instead, there was a gradual increase in the amount of solar radiation reaching the ground, which is called global "brightening". China's meteorological departments began to observe the solar radiation on the ground in the 1950s, and researchers analyzed the basic characteristics of long-term changes of the solar radiation on the ground in China from the observation data of more than 50 years [16]. It is found that the overall variation of surface solar radiation in most regions of China in the past 50 years showed a decreasing trend from 1960 to 1990, and then gradually increased from 1990. Xu Qun [17] studied the variation of solar radiation in winter from 1959 to 1987 in China and found that solar radiation decreased by 3.9% every 10 years during the period. Zha Liangsong [18] studied the spatio-temporal variation of surface solar radiation in China during 1971–1990, and concluded that the surface solar radiation in China decreased by 5.3 W/m^2 per decade on average during 1971–1990. Che et al. [19] studied the changes of solar radiation on the ground in China during the 40 years from 1961 to 2000, and found that solar radiation began to increase in the late 1980s, but the increase range was not given.

The above researchers provide theoretical and methodological support for the study of solar radiation, but there are few studies on the variation degree of solar radiation in China's typical resource areas. Therefore, this paper selected the data of total solar radiation, horizontal direct radiation and scattered radiation from 1961 to 2016 from the first level radiation stations in six regions (Beijing, Mesozoic-cenozoic, Golmud, Lhasa, Kashgar and Zhengzhou). The climate trend estimation method, cumulative anomaly method, Morlet wavelet analysis method and Mann-Kendall mutation analysis method were used to analyze the variation degree of solar radiation in typical resource areas of China.

2 Research Methods

2.1 Climate Tendency Estimation Method

In this paper, climate tendency rate and relative variability of climate tendency are adopted to express the change trend of radiation [19]. The climate tendency rate is calculated as follows:

$$x_i = a + b_t \quad (i = 1, 2, \cdots, n) \tag{1}$$

where, x_i represents a climate variable with a sample size of n, and t_i represents the corresponding time of x_i. The unitary linear regression between x_i and t_i is established [20]. A is the regression constant, b is the regression coefficient, and the significance is judged by whether the t test of α is 0.05. The formula for calculating the relative variability of climate tendency is [21]:

$$k = [(b/a) \times 50] \times 100\% \tag{2}$$

where, k is the relative variability of climate tendency as a unit of 50 years, a is the regression constant, and b is the regression coefficient [22].

2.2 Cumulative Anomaly Analysis

The cumulative anomaly is used to represent the linear fluctuation of trend change. For sequence X, the cumulative anomaly of t at a certain time is expressed as [20]:

$$x_t = \sum_{i=1}^{n} (x_i - \bar{x})(t = 1, 2, \cdots, n) \tag{3}$$

where

$$\bar{x} = \frac{1}{n} \sum_{i=1}^{n} x_i \tag{4}$$

2.3 Morlet Wavelet Analysis

Periodic analysis of solar radiation is carried out by Morlet wavelet. Given Morlet wavelet function $\varphi(t)$, continuous Morlet wavelet transform of time series $f(t) \in L^2(R)$ is defined as [23, 24]:

$$W_f(a, b) = \int_{-\infty}^{+\infty} f(t)\varphi(\frac{t - b}{a})dt \tag{5}$$

In the formula, $W_f(a, b)$ is the Morlet wavelet transform coefficient. Two-dimensional contour map of $W_f(a, b)$ can be drawn by b as abscissa and a as ordinate to analyze the multi-time scale variation characteristics of time series. $\varphi(t)$ is the complex conjugate function of $\varphi(t)$; a is the scale factor (frequency domain), reflecting the period length of Morlet wavelet; b is the time factor, reflecting the shift.

Integrate the square of all Morlet wavelet transform coefficients $W_f(a, b)$ of A in the time domain, namely, the square difference of Morlet wavelet Var(a):

$$\text{Var(a)} = \int_{-\infty}^{+\infty} |W_f(a, b)|^2 db \tag{6}$$

The change process of Morlet wavelet square difference scale a is called Morlet wavelet square difference diagram, which reflects the distribution of wave energy with scale. The scale corresponding to energy significantly is the main periodic component existing in a given time series.

2.4 Mann-Kendall Mutation Analysis

For time series x with n sample sizes, construct an order column:

$$S_k = \sum_{i=1}^{k} r; \ (k = 2, 3, \cdots, n) \tag{7}$$

S_k is the cumulative number whose value at time i is greater than that at time j, where

$$r_i = \begin{cases} +1 & x_i > x_j \\ 0 & Otherwise \end{cases} \ (j = 1, 2, \cdots, n) \tag{8}$$

Under the assumption of random independence of time series, define statistics:

$$UF_k = \frac{[s_k - E(s_k)]}{\sqrt{Var(s_k)}} \quad (k = 1, 2, \cdots, n) \tag{9}$$

where $UF_k = 0$, $E(s_k)$, $Var(s_k)$ are the mean and variance of cumulative s_k. When x1, x2, xn are independent of each other and have continuous distribution, they can be calculated by the following formula:

$$E(s_k) = \frac{n(n+1)}{4} \tag{10}$$

$$Var(s_k) = \frac{n(n-1)(2n+5)}{72} \tag{11}$$

UF_i is the standard normal distribution. It is the statistical sequence calculated according to time series x order $x_1, x_2, \cdots, x_n$. Given significance level α, if $UF_i = -UF_k$, k = n, n−1... 1, $UB = 0$ [25, 26].

3 Site Solar Radiation Analysis

3.1 Analysis of Climate Tendency Rate and Relative Variability of Climate Tendency

Direct Radiation from the Sun's Horizontal Plane. Table 1 for Beijing, Zhengzhou, Golmud, Kashgar, Lhasa, Mesozoic-cenozoic six typical resources area site of radiation in the sun direct radiation plane of climate tendency rate and climate tend to be relatively change rate, can be seen from the table, there are only three cities of Beijing, Lhasa, Zhengzhou in the sun direct radiation through the plane of the α = 0.05 significance test, It can be seen from the relative trend variability that the annual solar horizontal direct radiation pair variability of Beijing, Lhasa and Zhengzhou are all negative values, indicating that the annual solar horizontal direct radiation of the three cities gradually decreases with time. Among them, the annual solar horizontal direct radiation decreases the most in Zhengzhou, with the relative climate trend variability of −35.7%/50a. It can be seen from the trend rates that the climate trend rates of Beijing, Lhasa and Zhengzhou are all negative, and the climate trend rate of Zhengzhou is the lowest. The average annual solar horizontal direct radiation decreases by 198.1 MJ every 10 years. It can be seen from the analysis that the annual solar horizontal direct radiation of typical radiation stations in resource areas shows a downward trend.

Table 1. Climate tendency rate and relative variability of annual solar horizontal radiation.

Site	Relative variability of climatic trends per 50 years/(%)	Propensity rates per 10 years /(MJ)	Trend rate linear regression curve	Significance tests on time scales
Beijing	−25.2	−164.7	$y = -16.468x + 3266.9$	-0.731^{**}
Lhasa	−9.9	−107.6	$y = -10.762x + 5422.3$	-0.293^{*}
Zhengzhou	−35.7	−198.1	$y = -19.806x + 2777.7$	-0.819^{**}
Mesozoic-cenozoic	−3.4	−30.6	$y = -3.0641x + 4451.1$	-0.075
Golmud	2.3	19.6	$y = 1.9629x + 4316.8$	0.129
Kashgar	−3.1	−19.0	$y = -1.9031x + 3104.6$	-0.090

Note: ** indicated a significant correlation at 0.01 level (bilateral); * represents a significant correlation at the level of 0.05 (bilateral)

Radiation Scattered by the Sun. Table 2 for Beijing, Golmud, kashi, Lhasa, Zhengzhou, Mesozoic-cenozoic sites in six typical resources area radiation scattering solar radiation climate tendency rate and relative rate of change climate, from the table we can see, only Beijing, Zhengzhou, Golmud, Kashgar, Lhasa in five cities scattering solar radiation through the α = 0.05 significance test. The relative trend variability of the annual solar scattered radiation of the other four cities except Zhengzhou is negative, indicating that the annual solar scattered radiation of the four cities except Zhengzhou gradually decreases with time. Kashgar has the largest decline in annual solar scattered radiation, and its climate relative variability is −16.3%/50a. The relative trend variation of annual solar scattered radiation in Zhengzhou is 31.3%/50a, indicating that the annual solar scattered radiation in Zhengzhou is gradually increasing. From the trend rate, we can see that the climate trend rate of Beijing, Golmud, Kashgar and Lhasa are all negative, Golmud has the lowest climate trend rate, and the annual solar scattered radiation decreases by 93.4 MJ on average every 10 years, while Zhengzhou has a positive climate trend rate. The analysis shows that the annual solar scattered radiation of Beijing, Golmud, Kashgar and Lhasa shows a decreasing trend, while that of Zhengzhou shows a rising trend, which may be related to the aggravation of environmental pollution in Zhengzhou.

Table 2. Climate tendency rate and relative variability of annual solar scattered radiation over the surface.

Site	Relative variability of climatic trends per 50 years /(%)	Propensity rates per 10 years /(MJ)	Trend rate linear regression curve	Significance tests on time scales
Beijing	−5.2	−25.9	$y = -2.5886x + 2504.7$	−0.324*
Golmud	−16.3	−93.4	$y = -9.3432x + 2873$	−0.423**
Kashgar	−12.8	−73.5	$y = -7.3466x + 2873$	0.748**
Lhasa	−12.4	−62.7	$y = -6.2675x + 2532.4$	−0.052
Zhengzhou	31.3	140.0	$y = 14.004x + 2236.9$	−0.681**
Mesozoic-cenozoic	−4.8	−20.3	$y = -2.0288x + 2126.1$	−0.564**

Note: ** indicated a significant correlation at 0.01 level (bilateral); * represents a significant correlation at the level of 0.05 (bilateral)

3.2 Analysis of Decadal Anomalies

Direct Radiation from the Sun's Horizontal Plane. According to the classification criteria for the decadal anomaly of surface solar horizontal direct radiation in Table 3, the decadal anomaly of annual solar horizontal direct radiation passing $\alpha = 0.05$ significance test site was classified, and the classification results were shown in Table 4. It can be seen from the table that the horizontal direct radiation of Beijing, Lhasa and Zhengzhou showed an obvious upward trend from 1961 to 1970. From 1971 to 1980, the horizontal direct radiation of Beijing, Zhengzhou and Lhasa showed an upward trend, among which Beijing and Zhengzhou showed an obvious upward trend. From 1981 to 1990, the horizontal direct radiation of Beijing showed a decreasing trend, Lhasa showed an obvious decreasing trend, and Zhengzhou showed an increasing trend. From 1991 to 2000, the horizontal direct radiation of Beijing, Lhasa and Zhengzhou showed a downward trend. From 2001 to 2010, the horizontal direct radiation of Beijing and Zhengzhou showed a strong trend, while the horizontal direct radiation of Lhasa showed a rising trend. From 2011 to 2016, Beijing, Lhasa and Zhengzhou all showed a downward trend. In conclusion, from the 1960s to the 1980s, the horizontal direct radiation of typical resource areas showed an upward trend. However, after the 1980s, the annual direct radiation of the solar horizontal plane basically showed a downward trend, indicating that there are some other factors affecting the annual direct radiation of the solar horizontal plane in these cities in recent years, which may be the air pollution or haze weather caused by urbanization.

Table 3. Standard for classification of decadal anomalies of surface solar horizontal direct radiation.

Trend type	Percentage of anomaly (%)
Dropped significantly	−20 ~ −10
Significantly lower	10 ~ −1
No significant change	−1 ~ 1
Rise significantly	1 ~ 10
Increased significantly	10 ~ 20

Radiation Scattered by the Sun. According to the classification criteria in Table 5, the interdecadal anomalies of annual solar scattered radiation passing $\alpha = 0.05$ significance test sites were classified. It can be seen from the table that the solar scattered radiation showed a significant downward trend during 1961–1970 except for Zhengzhou, while Beijing, Golmu, Kashgar and Lhasa all showed an upward trend. Lhasa has a significant upward trend. From 1971 to 1980, the annual solar scattered radiation of Lhasa and Zhengzhou showed an increasing trend, while that of the other three cities showed a decreasing trend. From 1981 to 1990, the annual solar scattered radiation of Beijing and Kashgar showed a decreasing trend, and that of Lhasa. The variation of annual solar scattered radiation in Zhengzhou is not obvious, but the annual solar scattered radiation in Golmud is on the rise. From 1991 to 2000, the annual solar scattered radiation of Beijing, Golmud, Kashgar and Lhasa showed a decreasing trend, while that of Zhengzhou was not obvious. From 2001 to 2010, the annual solar scattered radiation of Golmud, Kashgar and Lhasa showed a decreasing trend, while that of Beijing showed no obvious change trend, but that of Zhengzhou showed an increasing trend. From 2011 to 2016, the annual solar scattered radiation in Golmud and Kashgar showed a downward trend, while the annual solar scattered radiation in Beijing and Lhasa showed an obvious upward trend, while the annual solar scattered radiation in Zhengzhou showed an obvious upward trend. In conclusion, since the 1960s, the annual solar scattered radiation in Zhengzhou has decreased significantly to increase significantly, indicating that the environmental changes in Zhengzhou are great. Before the 1980s, the annual solar scattered radiation of the five typical resource areas showed an upward trend, but after the 1990s, it showed a downward trend (Table 6).

Table 4. Classification of interdecadal anomalies at sites where annual solar horizontal direct radiation passed the α = 0.05 significance test.

Trend type	Percentage of anomaly (%)	1961–1970	1971–1980	1981–1990	1991–2000	2001–2010	2011–2016
Dropped significantly	−20 ~ −10			Lhasa			
Significantly lower	−10 ~ −1			Beijing	Beijing, Lhasa, Zhengzhou	Beijing, Zhengzhou	Beijing, Lhasa, Zhengzhou
No significant change	−1 ~ 1						
Rise significantly	1 ~ 10		Lhasa	Zhengzhou		Lhasa	
Increased significantly	10 ~ 20	Beijing, Lhasa, Zhengzhou	Beijing, Zhengzhou				

Table 5. Standard for classification of decadal anomalies of surface solar scattered radiation

Trend type	Percentage of anomaly (%)
Dropped significantly	−20 ~ −10
Significantly lower	10 ~ −1
No significant change	−1 ~ 1
Rise significantly	1 ~ 10
Increased significantly	10 ~ 20

Table 6. Classification of decadal anomalies at sites where annual surface solar scattered radiation passes the α = 0.05 significance test

Trend type	Percentage of anomaly(%)	1961–1970	1971–1980	1981–1990	1991–2000	2001–2010	2011–2016
Dropped significantly	−20 ~ −10	Zhengzhou					
Significantly lower	−10 ~ −1		Lhasa, Zhengzhou	Beijing, Kashgar	Beijing, Golmud, Kashgar, Lhasa	Golmud, Kashgar, Lhasa	Golmud, Kashgar
No significant change	−1 ~ 1			Lhasa, Zhengzhou	Zhengzhou	Beijing	Beijing, Lhasa
Rise significantly	1 ~ 10	Beijing, Golmud, Kashgar	Beijing, Golmud, Kashgar	Golmud		Zhengzhou	
Increased significantly	10 ~ 20	Lhasa					Zhengzhou

3.3 Cumulative Anomaly Analysis

Direct Radiation from the Sun's Horizontal Plane. It can be seen from Fig. 1 that the variation trend of annual solar horizontal direct radiation in Beijing and Zhengzhou is basically similar, showing a significant upward trend from the 1960s to the 1980s and a significant downward trend after the 1990s. Golmud and Kashgar have similar trends in the variation of direct solar radiation in the horizontal plane, both of which showed a slow decreasing trend before 1990's and a slow increasing trend after 1990's. The general trend of annual direct solar radiation in the horizontal plane is not obvious. The trend of direct solar horizontal radiation in Mesozoic-cenozoic is not obvious. The annual solar horizontal direct radiation of Lhasa showed a significant upward trend before the 1970s, a significant downward trend from the 1980s to the 1990s, and no significant change trend after the 1990s. Based on the analysis of the cumulative anomaly of the annual solar horizontal direct radiation in typical resource areas, it can be seen that the annual solar horizontal direct radiation of most of the stations in typical resource areas basically shows a trend of increasing first and then decreasing, and the changes are concentrated in the 1980s and 1990s.

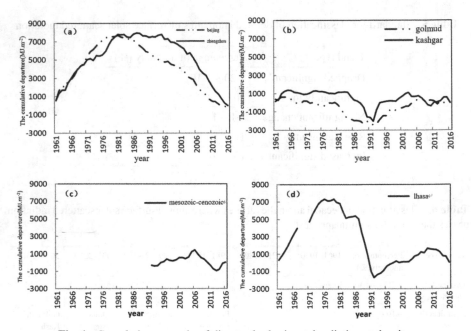

Fig. 1. Cumulative anomaly of direct solar horizontal radiation at the site.

Radiation Scattered by the Sun. It can be seen from the cumulative anomaly chart of annual solar scattered radiation in Fig. 2 that the variation trend of annual solar scattered radiation in Beijing and Lhasa is basically similar, with an upward trend before 1980s and a downward trend after 1990s, but the overall variation trend is not obvious. The trend of solar scattered radiation in Mesozoic-cenozoic is not obvious. The variation trend of annual solar scattered radiation in Golmud and Kashgar is similar, which shows an upward trend before 1990's and a downward trend after 1990's. Zhengzhou had a downward trend before the 1970s, rose slowly from the 1970s to the 21st century, and then rose rapidly. Area of typical resource years accumulated scattering solar radiation anomaly map analysis, we can see the four typical resources except Zhengzhou and Mesozoic-cenozoic zone site in solar diffuse radiation basic present the change trend of decline after rising first, and the concentration changes in the 20th century 80s and 90s. Zhengzhou scattered radiation is on the rise in recent years. It may be due to environmental pollution caused by industrial development.

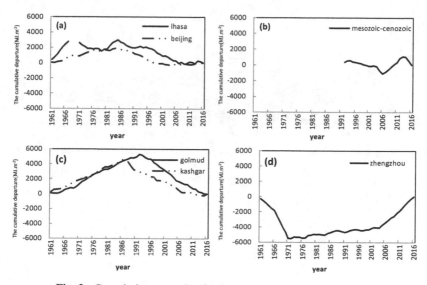

Fig. 2. Cumulative anomaly of solar scattered radiation at the site.

3.4 Morlet Wavelet Analysis

Annual Variation of Total Solar Radiation. Matlab was used to draw the Morlet wavelet periodic variation diagram and Morlet wavelet square difference diagram of the total radiation amount in Beijing, Golmu, Kashgar, Lhasa and Zhengzhou during 1961–2016, as shown in Fig. 3. Figure 3 (1) shows that the annual variation of total solar radiation in Beijing mainly exists in 2a and 12a main cycles. It can be seen from Fig. 3 (2) that the interannual variation of Golmud's total solar radiation mainly has three main cycles: 8a, 16a and 26a. It can be seen from Fig. 3 (3) that the annual variation of total solar radiation in Kashgar mainly has two main cycles of 8a and 18a, and the variation trend of solar radiation is similar to Golmud, and the variation time is basically similar. It can be seen from Fig. 3 (4) that the interannual variation of solar radiation in Lhasa

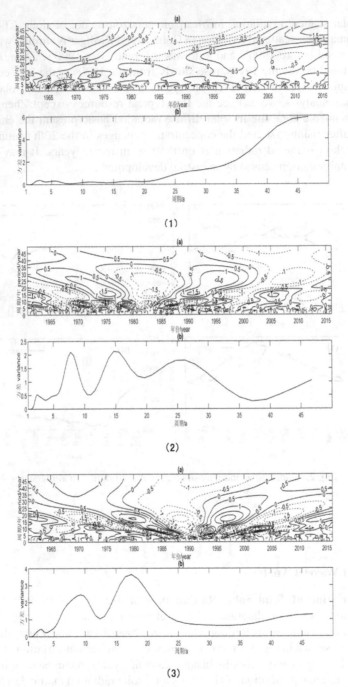

Fig. 3. The Morlet wavelet transform and Morlet wavelet square difference of the annual total solar radiation at ground level passing the significance test α = 0.05 (1), (2), (3), (4) and (5) are the Morlet wavelet transform and Morlet wavelet square difference of Beijing, Golmud, Kashgar, Lhasa and Zhengzhou respectively.

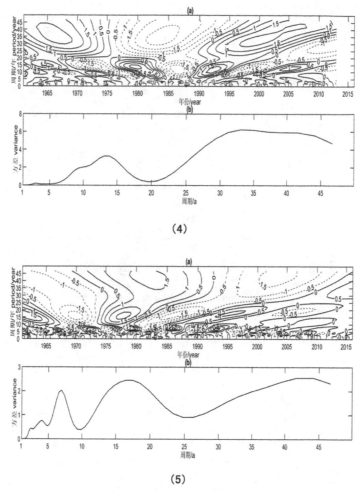

Fig. 3. continued

mainly has two main cycles of 14a and 35a. It can be seen from Fig. 3 (5) that the annual variation of total solar radiation in Zhengzhou mainly has two main cycles of 7a and 17a.

Direct Radiation from the Sun's Horizontal Plane. Matlab was used to draw the Morlet wavelet periodic variation diagram and Morlet wavelet square difference diagram of horizontal direct radiation amount in Beijing, Golmu, Kashgar, Lhasa and Zhengzhou during 1961–2016, as shown in Fig. 4. From Fig. 4 (1), we can see that the annual variation of direct solar horizontal radiation in Beijing mainly exists in the main cycle of 2a and 27a. It can be seen from Fig. 4 (2) that the annual variation of direct solar horizontal radiation in Lhasa mainly has a main period of 12a and 32a. It can be seen from Fig. 4 (3) that the annual variation of direct solar horizontal radiation in Zhengzhou mainly has two main cycles of 14a and 28a.

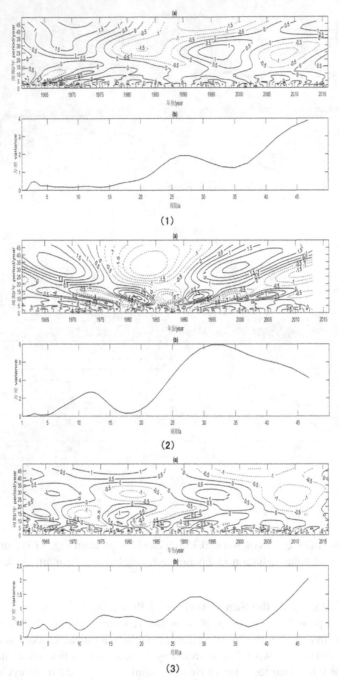

Fig. 4. The Morlet wavelet transform and Morlet wavelet square difference of direct solar horizontal radiation in the year of surface passing the significance test α = 0.05 (1), (2), (3), (4) and (5) are the Morlet wavelet transform and Morlet wavelet square difference of Beijing, Lhasa and Zhengzhou respectively.

Radiation Scattered by the Sun. Matlab was used to draw the Morlet wavelet periodic variation diagram and Morlet wavelet square difference diagram of the total radiation amount in Beijing, Golmu, Kashgar, Lhasa and Zhengzhou during 1961–2016, as shown in Fig. 5. From Fig. 5 (1), we can see that the annual variation of total solar radiation in Beijing mainly has a main cycle of 8a and 43a. It can be seen from Fig. 5 (2) that the interannual variation of Golmud's total solar radiation mainly exists in 18a and 44a main cycles, among which, at the scale of 44a. In Fig. 5 (3), the interannual variation of total solar radiation in Kashgar mainly exists in the main periods of 7a, 17a and 44a, and the variation trend of solar radiation is similar to Golmud and the variation time is basically similar. Figure 5 (4) The interannual variation of solar radiation in Lhasa mainly has two main cycles of 2a and 14a, among which, at 14a scale. In Fig. 5 (5), the interannual variation of total solar radiation in Zhengzhou mainly has two main cycles of 7a and 29a, among which periodic oscillation occurs at 29a scale.

3.5 Mutation Analysis

Annual Variation of Total Solar Radiation. Mann-Kendall mutation test was conducted for the annual total solar radiation of the five cities that passed the $\alpha = 0.05$ significance test, and the test results are shown in Fig. 6. The UF curve showed that the total solar radiation in Beijing was lower than the critical line of -0.05 after 1980s, and the total solar radiation in Beijing had a significant downward trend. The intersection of UF and UB showed that the mutation year was 1977. Before the 1990s, Golmud oscillated at the critical line of 0.05 with no obvious change trend, and then it was lower than -0.05. Solar radiation showed a significant downward trend, and the mutation year was 1996. In the 1980s, Kashgar oscillated at the critical line of 0.05 with no obvious change trend, and then it was lower than -0.05. Solar radiation showed a significant downward trend, and the mutation year was 1977. Before the 1970s, Lhasa oscillated at the critical line of 0.05 with no obvious change trend, but after the 1970s and 1980s, it was below the critical line of -0.05. The solar radiation showed a significant decreasing trend, and the mutation year was 1972. Since the 1960s, Zhengzhou has been oscillating at the critical line of 0.05, and the variation trend of total solar radiation is not obvious, and the mutation year is 1995. The mutation years were mainly concentrated in the 1980s and 1990s.

Direct Radiation from the Sun's Horizontal Plane. Figure 7 shows the Mann-Kendall mutation test results of the annual solar horizontal direct radiation of the ground passing the significance test $\alpha = 0.05$. The UF curve shows that the annual solar horizontal direct radiation of Beijing is lower than the critical line of -0.05 after 1980s, and the annual solar horizontal direct radiation of Beijing has a significant downward trend after 1980s. According to the intersection of UF and UB, the mutation year was 1978. From the 1950s to the 1970s, Lhasa was above the critical line of 0.05, showing an upward trend, but it was below -0.05 after the 1970s and 1980s. The annual direct solar horizontal radiation showed a significant downward trend, and the mutation year was 1976. Before the 1980s, Zhengzhou oscillated at the critical line of 0.05, and the variation trend of annual solar horizontal direct radiation was not obvious. After that, it was always below the critical

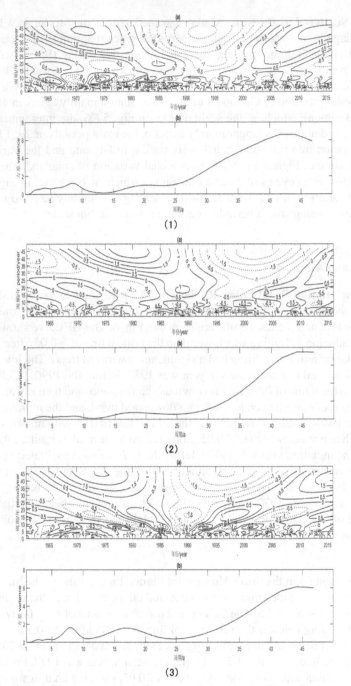

Fig. 5. The Morlet wavelet transform and Morlet wavelet square difference of annual solar scattered radiation from the surface with $\alpha = 0.05$ significance test (1), (2), (3), (4) and (5) are the Morlet wavelet transform and Morlet wavelet square difference of Beijing, Golmud, Kashgar, Lhasa and Zhengzhou respectively.

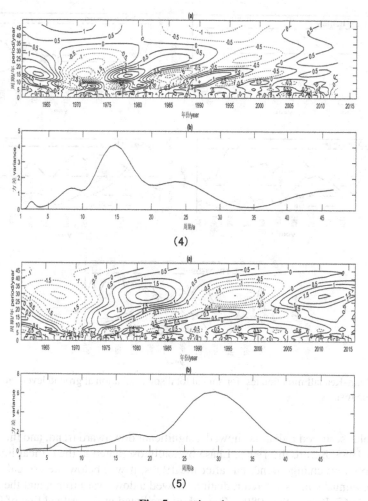

Fig. 5. continued

line of −0.05, and the annual solar horizontal direct radiation decreased significantly, and the mutation year was 1988. The mutation years were mainly concentrated in the 1980s and 1990s.

Radiation Scattered by the Sun. The UF curve in Fig. 8 (a) shows that the annual solar scattered radiation in Beijing fluctuated at the critical boundary of 0.05 before 1990s, with no obvious change trend. After 1990s, it was lower than the critical boundary of −0.05, with a significant decreasing trend. Before the 21st century, Golmud oscillated at the 0.05 critical line with no obvious change trend, and then it was lower than − 0.05. The annual solar scattered radiation showed a significant downward trend, and the mutation year was 1992. Before the 1990s, Kashgar oscillated at the critical line of 0.05 with no obvious change trend, and then it was below the critical line of −0.05. The

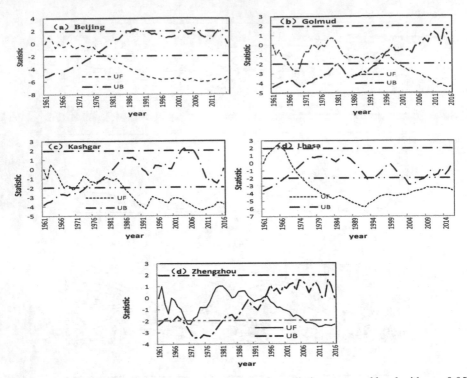

Fig. 6. Mann-Kendall mutation test for annual total solar radiation at ground level with α = 0.05 significance test.

annual solar scattered radiation showed a significant downward trend, and the mutation year was 1983. Before the 1990s, Lhasa basically oscillated at the critical line of 0.05 with no obvious change trend, but after the 1990s, it was below the critical line of − 0.05. The annual solar scattered radiation showed a downward trend, and the mutation year was 1967. Before the 1980s, Zhengzhou oscillated at the critical line of 0.05 with no obvious change trend, but after the 1980s, it was higher than the critical line of 0.05, and the annual solar scattered radiation showed a significant upward trend, which may be related to environmental changes in Zhengzhou. The mutation year was 1998. The mutation years were mainly concentrated in the 1980s and 1990s.

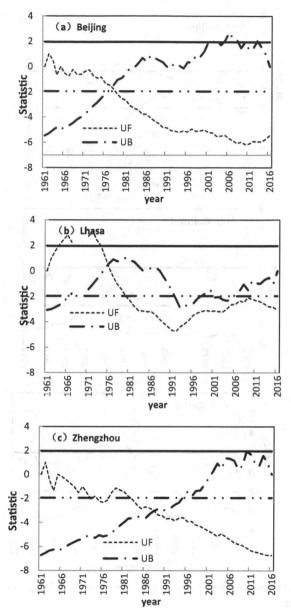

Fig. 7. Results of Mann-Kendall mutation test for annual direct solar horizontal radiation at ground level with $\alpha = 0.05$ significance test

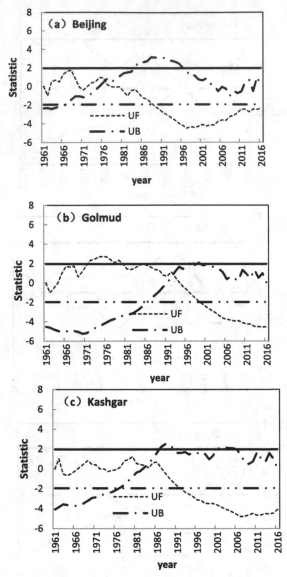

Fig. 8. Results of Mann-Kendall mutation test for surface annual solar scattered radiation with α = 0.05 significance test.

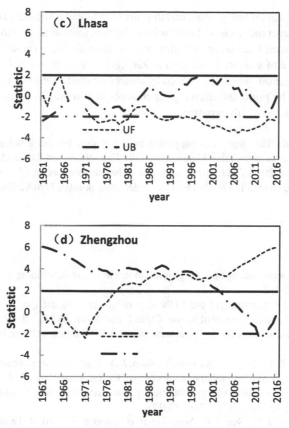

Fig. 8. continued

4 Conclusion

Based on the first-level radiation stations in Beijing, Mesozoic-cenozoic, Golmud, Lhasa, Kashgar and Zhengzhou, this paper studied the variation characteristics of total solar radiation, horizontal direct radiation, scattered radiation and inclination Angle in recent 56 years. Combined with the impact of photovoltaic power generation on the ecological environment, the following conclusions were drawn: Six typical resource area in the overall trend of solar total radiation is declining, most have been lowered after the change trend of solar total radiation began to decline since the 1990s, the biggest drop in Beijing, the other five cities except Mesozoic-cenozoic change year basic concentrated in the 80s–90s of the 20th century, and cumulative anomaly analysis results are basically identical. The period is basically 2-8a, 12-18a. In the six typical resource areas, the annual solar horizontal direct radiation showed a downward trend, with the largest decline in Zhengzhou. It can be seen from the cumulative anomaly and abrupt change years that the solar horizontal direct radiation was mainly concentrated in the 1980s and 1990s, and the variation law of the direct solar radiation was basically similar to that of the total solar radiation. In the six typical resource areas except Zhengzhou, the annual solar scattered radiation showed a decreasing trend, and the variation law was similar to the variation law of annual solar direct radiation and total solar radiation, indicating that there was a certain relationship between total solar radiation and horizontal direct radiation and scattered radiation. The rise of scattered radiation in Zhengzhou may be related to environmental changes in Zhengzhou, which are caused by many circumstances, such as environmental problems caused by pollutant discharge or changes in climate environment. The reasons for these changes are worth exploring.

Acknowledgement. This work was supported by the National Natural Science Foundation of China Study on "the Second Tibet Plateau Scientific Expedition and Research Program (STEP) under grant number 2019QZKK0804", and "the dynamic mechanism of grassland ecosystem response to climate change in Qinghai Plateau under grant number U20A2098."

References

1. Cao, K.: Renewable energy power generation in the UK is developing rapidly. Energy Res. Util. **2**, 18 (2020)
2. Fu, C.: Global governance of the EU's response to climate change: an external decision-making model and the causes of action. Chin. J. Eur. Stud. **30**(01), 65–80 (2012)
3. Fang, H.: Low-carbon economy' overview and its development in China. Econ. Vis. **3**, 45–46 (2009)
4. Lin, Z., Feng, Z.X., Zhang, Z.X., Hao, Y., Shen, X.Y.: Carbon peak and carbon neutralization: China's action to combat global climate change. Explor. Free Views **9**, 4–177 (2021)
5. Shen, Y.B.: Development of the solar energy resource assessment methods in China. Adv. Meteorol. Sci. Technol. **7**(1), 77–84 (2017)
6. Chen, C., Chen, Z.H., Sun, P.J.: Advances in calculation method of the optimal tilted angle for PV array in solar resource assessment. Adv. Meteorol. Sci. Technol. **7**(04), 60–65 (2017)
7. Qi, Y., Fang, S.B., Zhou, W.Z.: Variation and spatial distribution of surface solar radiation in China over recent 50 years. Acta Ecol. Sin. **34**(24), 7444–7453 (2014)
8. Zhang, H.W.L., Zhang, Q., Liu, C.L.: Evaluation and analysis of solar energy resources in Dongying city. J. Zhejiang Agric. Sci. **06**, 1404–1405 (2011)
9. Wild, M., Gilgen, H., Roesch, A.: From dimming to brightening: decadal changes in Solar radiation at Earth's surface. Science **3**(08), 847–850 (2005)
10. Zhong, Q.: Advance on research on surface radiation climatology: some problems of retrieval of surface radiation budget from satellite. Adv. Earth Sci. **11**(3), 238–244 (1966)
11. Gilgen, H., Wild, M., Ohmura, A.: Means and trends of shortwave irradiance at the surface estimated from global energy balance archive data. J. Clim. **11**(02), 61 (1998)
12. Liepert, B.G.: Observed reductions of surface solar radiation at sites in the United States and worldwide from 1961 to 1990. Geophys. Res. Lett. **29**, 1421 (2002)
13. Ulgen, K.: Optimum tilt angle for solar collectors. Energy Sour. **28**(13), 1171–1180 (2007)
14. Stanhill, G., Cohen, S.: Global dimming: a review of the evidence for a widespread and significant reduction in global radiation with discussion of its probable causes and possible agricultural consequences. Agric. For. Meteorol. **1**(07), 2552–3278 (2001)
15. Shen, Y.B., Zha, Z.C., Shi, G.Y.: The progress in variation of surface solar radiation, factors and probable climatic effects. Adv. Earth Sci. **23**(9), 915–923 (2008)
16. Xun, Q.: The remarkable change of winter solar radiation in China during recent 29 years. Sci. China **10**(1), 112–120 (1990)

17. Zha, L.S.: A study on spatial and temporal variation of solar radiation in China. Scientia Geographica Sinica **03**, 41–46 (1996)
18. Che, H.Z., Shi, G.Y., Zhang, X.Y.: Analysis of 40 years of solar radiation data from China. Geophys. Res. Lett. **16**(03), 232–237 (1961)
19. Ma, J.Y., Luo, Y., Shen, Y.B.: Regional long-term trend of ground solar radiation in China over the past 50 years. Scientia Sinica (Terrae) **42**(10), 1597–1608 (2012)
20. Wei, F.Y.: Modern Climate Statistics Diagnosis and Prediction Technology. China Meteorological Press, Beijing (2007)
21. Wang, M.Q., Zou, Q.M., Huang, W.Q.: Study on intermittent optimal regulation of solar panel installation. Acta Energiae Solaris Sinica **36**(01), 113–119 (2015)
22. Gao, J., Lin, X.: Mathematical interpolation and correction of three-dimensional modelling of high-speed railway. Intell. Autom. Soft Comput. **26**(05), 1023–1034 (2020)
23. Zou, M.L., Liu, Z.X., Chen, X.Y.: A meaningful image encryption algorithm based on prediction error and wavelet transform. J. Big Data **1**(03), 151–158 (2019)
24. Jayashree, N., Bhuvaneswaran, R.S.: A robust image watermarking scheme using z-transform, discrete wavelet transform and bidiagonal singular value decomposition. Comput. Mater. Contin. **58**(01), 263–285 (2019)
25. Liu, Y., Liu, L., Yan, Y., Feng, H., Ding, S.: Analyzing dynamic change in social network based on distribution-free multivariate process control method. Comput. Mater. Contin. **60**(03), 1123–1139 (2019)
26. Ping, H.: Study of assessment method based on coupling factor of casualty in earthquake disasters in Guangdong area. Comput. Syst. Sci. Eng. **35**(03), 191–199 (2020)

Quantum Fuzzy K-Means Algorithm Based on Fuzzy Theory

Min Hou[1], Shibin Zhang[1,2(✉)], and Jinyue Xia[3]

[1] School of Cybersecurity, Chengdu University of Information Technology, Chengdu 610225, China
cuitzsb@cuit.edu.cn
[2] Advanced Cryptography and System Security Key Laboratory of Sichuan Province, Chengdu 610255, China
[3] International Business Machines Corporation (IBM), New York 14201, USA

Abstract. Cluster analysis is used to classification according to their different charac-teristics, affinity, and similarity. Because the boundary of the relationship between things is often unclear, it is inevitable to use the fuzzy method to perform cluster analysis. In this paper, according to the cross fusion of "fuzzy theory + K-means algorithm + quantum computing", a quantum fuzzy k-means algorithm based on fuzzy theory is proposed for the first time, which can classify samples with lower time complexity and higher ac-curacy. Firstly, the training data sets and the classified sample points can be encoded into quantum states, and swap test is used to calculate the similarity between the classified sample points and k cluster centers with high parallel computing abilities. Secondly, the similarity is stored with the form of quan-tum bits by using the phase estimation algorithm. The Grover algorithm is used to search the cluster points with the highest membership degree and de-termine the category of the test samples. Finally, by introducing quantum computing theory, the computation complexity of the proposed algorithm is improved, and the space complexity of the proposed algorithm is reduced. By introducing fuzzy theory, the proposed algorithm can deal with uncertain problems efficiently, the scope of application of the algorithm is expanded, and the accuracy is improved.

Keywords: Quantum k-means · Quantum computing · Fuzzy theory

1 Introduction

With the rapid development of big data, all walks of life are generating a large amount of data every day. The forms of data include numbers, images, sounds, etc., and the organization methods are also different. In 1989, Fayyad proposed database knowledge discovery, which defines the process of identifying and proposing knowledge from the data set [1]. Cluster analysis, regression analysis and discriminant analysis are the three major methods of multivariate data analysis. As an unsupervised machine learning tech-nology, clustering divides the data into several classes according to the given similarity

© The Author(s), under exclusive license to Springer Nature Switzerland AG 2022
X. Sun et al. (Eds.): ICAIS 2022, LNCS 13338, pp. 348–356, 2022.
https://doi.org/10.1007/978-3-031-06794-5_28

measure, so that the data similarity in the same class is high, while the data similarity between different classes is low [2]. K-means is a classical clustering algorithm, which has been widely used since it was proposed. S. Park et al. Proposed an enhanced koced routing protocol with k-means algorithm [3]. Puthige et al. Detected the safest route through hazard index calculation and K-means clustering [4]. H. He et al. Proposed a detection method based on K-means and complex network [5]. T. M. ghazal et al. Compared the performance of K-means clustering algorithms with different distance metrics [6]. However, in the era of big data, the huge amount of data has brought great challenges to the speed of K-means clustering [7]. M. Zidan et al. Proposed a quantum algorithm based on Hamming distance [8].

Since quantum computing was proposed, it has attracted the attention of many researchers because of its powerful parallel computing ability. Grover proposed a search algorithm for the disordered databases (Grover algorithm), which fully shows the advantages of quantum computing [9]. In 1983, Gamache and Davies proposed quantum Fourier transform. Compared with classical Fourier transform, its computational complexity is exponentially reduced [10]. Lloyd et al. Proposed the quantum k-means algorithm, which can achieve efficient data clustering [11]. Pan Jian Wei's team implemented and verified the quantum k-means algorithm on a small light quantum computer for the first time [12]. Buhrman et al. Combined quantum computing with machine learning and proposed a new method to calculate similarity [13]. However, with the improvement of the efficiency of machine learning algorithms, its shortcomings are becoming more and more obvious. Although the computer has a very fast computing speed, it is helpless when facing the fuzzy state with unclear extension. Facing the problems of uncertainty, imprecision, and incomplete information, how should the computer do it? Researchers propose to use membership degree, non-membership degree, hesitation degree, and other indicators to describe uncertainty problems. In 1983, Atanassov put forward the intuitionistic fuzzy set theory [14]. In 2002, Li et al. Studied the properties, operations, correlations, correlation functions, and clustering methods of direct fuzzy sets [15]. In 2011, Beliakov et al. Proposed a new construction method based on Lukasiewicz triangular norm, simplifying and expanding the existing structure [16]. Aiming at the problems of uncertainty, imprecision, and incomplete information, this paper combines quantum computing theory with fuzzy theory proposes a quantum fuzzy k-means algorithm combined with quantum computing theory.

This part introduces the introduction and related work; The second part introduces the related theories, including classical k-means algorithm, fuzzy theory, and quantum computing theory; In the third part, the quantum fuzzy k-means algorithm is described in detail; Finally, the efficiency and accuracy of the proposed algorithm are analyzed.

2 Basic Knowledge

In this section, we briefly introduce the Classical k-means algorithm, fuzzy classification, and quantum computing-related knowledge.

2.1   Classical K-Means Algorithm

Given a data set $X = \{x_1, x_2, \ldots, x_n\}$, n is the number of samples in the data set. The data set is divided into k categories, and the cluster center is $c = \{c_1, c_2, \ldots, c_k\}$, c_i is the i-th cluster center, x_j is the j-th sample, and the characteristic dimension of each sample is d, x_{jr} representing the r-th eigenvalue of the j-th data. The clustering process of the K-means algorithm is as follows:

(1)   K samples are randomly selected from data set X as the initial clustering center c.
(2)   For each data point x_j, calculate the similarity to k clustering centers.
(3)   The sample x_j is classified into the greatest similarity cluster centers.
(4)   Recalculate the new cluster center after (2) (3) steps for all the samples in the data set X.
(5)   Determine whether the condition for the end of clustering is reached, and if so, the clustering ends, otherwise, go back to step (2).

2.2   Fuzzy Classification

If the data set X is divided into k classes, the classification result corresponds to a matrix $U = (u_{ij})_{k \times n}$, x_j belongs to a certain class with a certain degree of membership, a single sample belongs to a certain class with different membership degrees.

$$U = \begin{bmatrix} u_{11} & \cdots & u_{1n} \\ \vdots & \ddots & \vdots \\ u_{k1} & \cdots & u_{kn} \end{bmatrix} \tag{1}$$

Matrix $U = (u_{ij})_{k \times n}$ meets three conditions:

(1) $u_{ij} \in [0, 1]$, Matrix elements take values between 0 and 1.
(2) $\sum_{i=1}^{k} u_{ij} = 1$, The sum of membership degrees belonging to each category in each column is 1.
(3) $\sum_{j}^{n} u_{ij} > 0$, The samples belong to various types in varying degrees.

2.3   Quantum Computing

Phase Estimation.   Quantum phase estimation uses two registers. The first register contains t qubits with an initial state of $|0\rangle$. The t is related to the number of digits of $|\varphi\rangle$. The initial state of the second register is of $|u\rangle$, and contains the number of qubits required to store. Phase estimation is divided into four stages:

(1)   First, apply the H gate to the first register.
(2)   Then apply the controlled u gate to the second register.
(3)   Apply inverse Fourier transform to the first register.
(4)   Measure the state of the first register.

The circuit diagram is as follows (see Fig. 1).

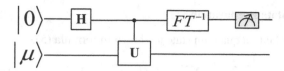

Fig. 1. Circuit of the phase estimation.

Quantum Search Algorithm. Grover algorithm, sometimes called quantum search algorithm, refers to an unstructured search algorithm running on a quantum computer. It is one of the typical algorithms of quantum computing. It has polynomial acceleration. Grover search algorithm is divided into two steps:

(1) Phase Inversion. This step is mainly to flip the probability amplitude x^* into a negative number, while others remain unchanged. The x^* is the target we are looking for.
(2) Inversion about the Mean. Handle αx becomes $2\mu - \alpha x$. This is asking me to turn my present state to the future μ Flip.

Then we can get the result by iterating these two steps.

Projection Measurement. The projection measurement is described by a Hermite operator M representing the observability in the system, and has spectral decomposition.

$$M = \sum_{m} mP_m \tag{2}$$

where P_m is the projection operator on the Eigenspace M of the eigenvalue m, and the measurement result corresponds to the eigenvalue m. For status $|\psi\rangle$, the probability of measuring the result m is

$$p(m) = \langle\psi|p_m|\psi\rangle \tag{3}$$

After measurement, the status changes to

$$\frac{p_m|\psi\rangle}{\sqrt{p(m)}} \tag{4}$$

Projection measurement is a special case of general measurement. Restrictions are added to the general measurement: 1) M_m is the Hermite operator; 2) When $M_m M_{m'} = M_m \partial_{mm'}$ then gets the projection measurement (at this time, M_m is equivalent to p_m, pay attention to the idempotency of the projection operator).

3   Quantum Fuzzy K-Means Algorithm

The matrix composed of k cluster centers is $c = \{c_1, c_2, \ldots, c_k\}$, $c_i = \{c_{i1}, c_{i2}, \ldots, c_{id}\}$, $i = 1, 2, \ldots, k$. Set the dataset as $X = \{x_1, x_2, \ldots, x_n\}$, n is the number of samples in the data set, $x_j = \{x_{j1}, x_{j2}, \ldots, x_{jd}\}, j = 1, 2, \ldots, n$. The characteristic dimension of each sample is d.

3.1 Quantum State Preparation

x_0 can be prepared into a quantum state as shown in formula (5).

$$|x_0\rangle = \frac{1}{\sqrt{d}}\sum_{r=1}^{d}\sum_{j}^{k}\mu_{0j}|r\rangle\left(\sqrt{1-x_{0r}^2}|0\rangle + x_{0r}|1\rangle\right)|1\rangle \qquad (5)$$

The k cluster centers are prepared into the quantum state shown in formula (6).

$$|c\rangle = \sum_{i=1}^{k}\frac{1}{\sqrt{k}}\sum_{j=1}^{k}|i\rangle\mu_{ij}|k\rangle\frac{1}{\sqrt{d}}\sum_{r=1}^{d}|r\rangle\times\left(\sqrt{1-c_{ir}^2}|0\rangle + c_{ir}|1\rangle\right)|1\rangle \qquad (6)$$

3.2 Similarity Calculation

To calculate the similarity between x_i and c_i, we can use the controlled switching gate to calculate the fidelity between quantum states to estimate the similarity. The control switching gate is used to calculate the similarity of quantum states $|x_0\rangle$ and $|c\rangle$ is shown in Fig. 2.

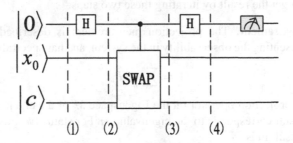

Fig. 2. Circuit of the Control-SWAP test.

The calculation process is as follows:

(1) Initial state: $|0\rangle|x_0\rangle|c\rangle$;
(2) Application H gate: $\frac{1}{\sqrt{2}}(|0\rangle + |1\rangle)|x_0\rangle|c\rangle$;
(3) Perform Swap operation: $\frac{1}{\sqrt{2}}(|0\rangle|x_0\rangle|c\rangle + |1\rangle|c\rangle|x_0\rangle)$;
(4) Application H gate again: $\frac{1}{2}|0\rangle(|x_0\rangle|c\rangle + |c\rangle|x_0\rangle) + \frac{1}{2}|1\rangle(|x_0\rangle|c\rangle - |c\rangle|x_0\rangle)$;

3.3 Projection Measurement

Use a measurement operator $M_1 = |1\rangle\langle1|$ to observe the quantum state $|\phi\rangle$.

$$P(M_1) = \langle\phi|M_1|\phi\rangle$$
$$= \frac{1}{4}(((\langle0, x_0, c| + |0, c, x_0\rangle) + (|1, x_0, c\rangle - |1, c, x_0\rangle))$$
$$\times |1\,1|((|0, x_0, c\rangle + |0, c, x_0\rangle) + (|1, x_0, c\rangle - |1, c, x_0\rangle))$$

$$= \frac{1}{4}((\langle x_0, c| - \langle c, x_0|)(|x_0, c\rangle - |c, x_0\rangle))$$

$$= \frac{1}{4}\left(2 - 2(\langle x_0|c\rangle)^2\right)$$

$$= \frac{1}{2}\left(1 - \langle x_0|c\rangle^2\right) \tag{7}$$

The probability that the first quantum state is 1 is $\frac{1}{2}\left(1 - \langle x_0|c\rangle^2\right)$. The quantum state $|c\rangle$ is the superposition of the quantum states $|c_i\rangle$ of k clustering center points. Therefore $\langle x_0|c\rangle$ is the cosine value of x_0 and c_i. Define $s(x_0, c_i) = \frac{1}{2}(1 - \langle x_0|c\rangle)^2$ to describe the similarity of x_0 and c_i.

The output of the control switch gate can be expressed as:

$$|\varphi\rangle = \frac{1}{\sqrt{k}}\sum_{i=1}^{k}|i\rangle\sum_{j=1}^{n}(\mu_{ij})^2\left(\sqrt{1 - s(x_0, c_i)}|0\rangle + \sqrt{s(x_0, c_i)}|1\rangle\right) \tag{8}$$

3.4 Phase Estimation

Next, the phase estimation algorithm is applied $|\phi\rangle$. Taking the quantum state $|\phi\rangle$ as the input of phase estimation. The steps of the quantum Phase estimation algorithm are as follows:

(1) Prepare initial quantum state, including $|0\rangle^{\otimes k}$ and $|\phi\rangle$. Using H gate in initial state.

$$|\phi_1\rangle = \left(H^{\otimes k} \otimes I\right)|0\rangle^{\otimes k}|\phi\rangle = \frac{1}{\sqrt{2^k}}\sum|x_0 x_1 ... x_{k-1}\rangle|\phi\rangle \tag{9}$$

(2) Use controlled U, $e^{2\pi i\theta}$ is added to the probability range when each qubit is 1.

$$U|\phi\rangle = e^{2\pi i\theta}|\phi\rangle$$

$$|\phi_2\rangle = \frac{1}{\sqrt{2^k}}\sum e^{2\pi i\theta}|x_1 x_2 ... x_{k-1}\rangle|\phi \tag{10}$$

(3) Use QFT^{-1}:$QFT^{-1}|\phi_2\rangle = |\theta\rangle$, θ is the $(\mu_{ij})^2\|x_0 - c_i\|$.
    we can get:

$$|\alpha\rangle = \frac{1}{\sqrt{k}}\sum_{i=1}^{k}|i\rangle\sum_{j=1}^{n}\left|(\mu_{ij})^2\|x_0 - c_i\|\right\rangle \tag{11}$$

We can store the degree of membership and similarity of x_0 and c in the qubit $|\alpha\rangle$.

3.5 Quantum Search Algorithm

Use the Grover algorithm to find the qubits with the greatest similarity and the degree of membership. The steps of the quantum search algorithm are as follows:

(1) In the initial state $|0\rangle^{\otimes k}$ use $H^{\otimes k}$ obtain $|s\rangle = |+\rangle^{\otimes k}$, k is the number of cluster categories.

(2) Repetitive action Grover iteration $G = (2|s\rangle\langle s| - 1)O$, and repeat times are R $\approx \sqrt{k}$.

(3) Measured obtain c_i. It is the final selected classification result.

4 Algorithm Complexity Analysis

Comparison of time complexity and space complexity between the proposed algorithm and the classical algorithm, as shown in Table 1.

Table 1. Comparison of the complexity of two algorithms.

Complexity	Classical	Quantum
Time	$O(nkd)$	$O(n\sqrt{k})$
Space	$n(d + kd + k)$	$(4 + 2log_2d + log_2k)$

4.1 Time Complexity

The main calculation step of the classical k-means algorithm is to calculate the similarity between n sample points and k cluster centers, so the time complexity is $O(nkd)$.

The quantum fuzzy clustering algorithm proposed in this paper uses the control switching gate to calculate the similarity between the sample to be tested and the k clustering centers. The phase estimation algorithm is used to store the similarity and membership into qubits, and the quantum search algorithm is used to find the cluster center with the largest similarity and membership. The time complexity required to find the target cluster center is $\sqrt{k}$, so the time complexity is $O(n\sqrt{k})$. When the number of samples n and eigenvalue k become larger, the more advantages of the quantum algorithm can be reflected.

4.2 Space Complexity

Compared with the basic unit bits of classical information, the basic storage unit of quantum information is called a qubit. In the process of classical information processing, one bit can only store one of the classical states 0 or 1; For quantum information, a qubit state is a vector in a two-dimensional complex space, which can exist continuously and randomly in any superposition state of $|0\rangle$ and $|1\rangle$. Therefore, m qubits can store 2^m information at the same time, under the same bit number.

In a classical algorithm, if a characteristic dimension occupies 1-bit space, n variables have d attributes, nd bit space is required, and occupied nk bit storage membership. In the calculation process of the algorithm, the similarity between n samples and k clusters needs to be calculated, so nkd bit storage space is needed to store the variables in the execution process of the algorithm. So the total storage space $M = nd + nkd + nk = n(d + kd + k)$.

In a quantum algorithm, the memory required for the quantum state of any data point $|x_j\rangle$ is $2 + \log_2 d$ bits (membership is encoded in quantum amplitude), and the memory required for the quantum state of k cluster centers is $2 + \log_2 d + \log_2 k$ bits. Then the maximum memory required in the first step is $4 + \log_2 d + \log_2 k$ bits.

Compared $n(d + kd + k)$ with $4 + \log_2 d + \log_2 k$, we can see that the spatial complexity of the quantum algorithm is reduced exponentially.

5 Conclusion

Quantum fuzzy k-means algorithm introduces quantum computing and fuzzy theory into clustering tasks. The algorithm proposed in this paper mainly goes through four steps: first, prepare the data points to be clustered (including membership) and K clustering center points into quantum states; Secondly, the controlled switching gate is used to calculate the similarity between any data point and K clustering centers; Thirdly, the similarity is stored in qubits by phase estimation; Finally, the quantum search algorithm is used to find the smallest of the K similarity, that is, to find the most similar cluster center.

After analyzing the classic algorithm and the algorithm proposed in this article. we can see that the spatial complexity of the quantum algorithm is reduced exponentially and the time complexity is also reduced.

Acknowledgement. This work is supported by the National Natural Science Foundation of China (No. 62076042), the Key Research and Development Project of Sichuan Province (No. 2021YFSY0012, No. 2020YFG0307, No. 2021YFG0332), the Science and Technology Innovation Project of Sichuan (No. 2020017), the Key Research and Development Project of Chengdu (No. 2019-YF05-02028-GX), the Innovation Team of Quantum Security Communication of Sichuan Province (No. 17TD0009), the Academic and Technical Leaders Training Funding Support Projects of Sichuan Province (No. 2016120080102643).

References

1. Fayyad, U.M., Piatetsky-Shapiro, G., Smyth, P., et al.: Advances in knowledge discovery & data mining. Technometrics **40**(1), 1271414 (1996)
2. Jain, A.K., Murty, M.N., Flynn, P.J.: Data clustering. ACM Comput. Surv. **31**(3), 264–323 (1999)
3. Park, S., Lee, J.Y., Lee, D.: Enhanced KOCED routing protocol with K-means algorithm. Comput. Mater. Contin. **67**(3), 4019–4037 (2021)
4. Puthige, I., Bansal, K., Bindra, C., Kapur, M., Singh, D., et al.: Safest route detection via danger index calculation and k-means clustering. Comput. Mater. Contin. **69**(2), 2761–2777 (2021)
5. He, H., Zhao, Z., Luo, W., Zhang, J.: Community detection in aviation network based on k-means and complex network. Comput. Syst. Sci. Eng. **39**(2), 251–264 (2021)
6. Ghazal, T.M., et al.: Performances of k-means clustering algorithm with different distance metrics. Intell. Autom. Soft Comput. **30**(2), 735–742 (2021)

7. Ding, Y., Qin, X., Liu, L., et al.: An energy-efficient algorithm for big data processing in heterogeneous cluster. J. Comput. Res. Dev. **52**(2), 377–390 (2015)
8. Zidan, M., Eldin, M.G., Shams, M.Y., Tolan, M., Abd-Elhamed, A., Abdel-Aty, M.: A quantum algorithm for evaluating the hamming distance. Comput. Mater. Contin. **71**(1), 1065–1078 (2022)
9. Grover, L.K.: A fast quantum mechanical algorithm for database search. In: 28th Annual ACM Symposium on the Theory of Computing, pp. 212–219 (1996)
10. Gamache, R.R., Davies, R.W.: Theoretical calculations of n2-broadened half-widths using quantum fourier transform theory. Appl. Opt. **22**(24), 4013 (1983)
11. Lloyd, S., Mohseni, M., Rebentrost, P.: Quantum algorithms for supervised and unsupervised machine learning. arXiv:1307.0411 (2013)
12. Cai, X.D., Wu, D., Su, Z.E., et al.: Entanglement-based machine learning on a quantum computer. Phys. Rev. **114**(11), 110504 (2015)
13. Buhrman, H., Cleve, R., Watrous, J., Wolf, R.D.: Quantum fingerprinting. Phys. Rev. Lett. **87**(16), 167902 (2001)
14. Atanassov, K.: Intuitionistic fuzzy sets. Fuzzy Sets Syst. **20**(1), 87–96 (1986)
15. Li, D.F., Chen, C.T.: New similarity measures of intuitionistic fuzzy sets and application to pattern recognition. Pattern Recogn. Lett. **23**(1–3), 219–220 (2002)
16. Beliakov, G., Bustince, H., Goswami, D.P., et al.: On averaging operators for Atanassov's intuitionistic fuzzy sets. Inf. Sci. Int. J. **181**(6), 1116–1124 (2011)

Rolling Bearing Fault Diagnosis Method Based on Multiple Efficient Channel Attention Capsule Network

Kang Wu[1,2] , Jie Tao[1(✉)] , Dalian Yang[3] , Hewen Chen[1,2] , Shilei Yin[1,2] , and Chixin Xiao[4]

[1] School of Computer Science and Engineering, Hunan University of Science and Technology,
Xiangtan 411201, China
caroltaojie@126.com
[2] Hunan Key Laboratory for Service Computing and Novel Software Technology,
Xiangtan 411201, China
[3] Key Laboratory of Mechanical Equipment Health Maintenance, Hunan University of Science
and Technology, Xiangtan 411201, China
[4] University of Wollongong, Wollongong, NSW 2522, Australia

Abstract. In the environment of strong noise, it is very difficult to extract bearing fault characteristics from vibration signals. To solve the problem, this paper proposes a fault diagnosis method based on Multiple Efficient Channel Attention Capsule Network (MECA-CapsNet). Due to diverse scales channel of attention mechanism, MECA-CapsNet can obtain multi-scale channels feature, enhance information interaction between different channels, and fuse key information of diverse scale receptive field. So, our model can effectively abstract the key information of bearing fault characters from noisy vibration signal. To verify the effectiveness of MECA-CapsNet, experiments are carried out on the bearing data set of CWRU. When the signal-to-noise ratio is from 4 dB to −4 dB, the accuracies of MECA-CapsNet are better than typical fault diagnosis methods. Then, T-SNE technology is used to visualize the features extraction process. The visualization result verifies that multiple ECA modules on different scales can effectively reduce noise interference and improve the accuracy of rolling bearing fault diagnosis.

Keywords: Fault diagnosis · Efficient Channel Attention · Capsule network · Information interaction

1 Introduction

In recent years, deep learning algorithms such as deep neural network [1–3], convolutional neural network [4], convolutional auto-encoder network [5], residual network [6], LSTM Network [7] and capsule network [8, 9] have gradually been applied in bearing fault diagnosis and have achieved fruitful results. Compared with traditional methods [10], deep learning methods are more suitable for the requirements of the big data era. Xu et al. [11] proposed a bearing fault diagnosis method combining deep convolutional

© The Author(s), under exclusive license to Springer Nature Switzerland AG 2022
X. Sun et al. (Eds.): ICAIS 2022, LNCS 13338, pp. 357–370, 2022.
https://doi.org/10.1007/978-3-031-06794-5_29

neural network and random forest ensemble learning, which can mine multi-level features of bearing fault and improved fault diagnosis performance of the model. Zhang et al. [12] introduced scaling exponential linear unit and layering into convolutional neural network to construct an enhanced convolutional neural network, which improved feature extraction ability of the model for time-frequency image of bearing vibration signal. Chen et al. [13] used cyclic spectrum to preprocess original vibration signal and obtained more superior features expression combined with CNN. Zhang et al. [14] used wide kernels in first layer of deep convolution neural network which can capture more characteristic information from original vibration signal. Jian et al. [15] constructed a new type of neural network by using wide kernel, CNN and D-S evidence theory, which effectively improve cross-domain adaptability of fault diagnosis. These existing studies mainly use CNN and its improved model to extract fault characteristics from vibration signals and time-frequency distribution graphs. However, these models pay little attention to correlation of different channel features and interaction of cross-channel information. When vibration signal contains strong noise, existing methods will be difficult to extract fault features, and this will affect accuracy and reliability of fault diagnosis.

Attention mechanism comes from human visual research. It selectively focuses on important information and ignores other information in process of cognition. Zhang et al. [16] proposed a channel attention mechanism to find the correlation between feature of various channels and highlight features of important channels. Typical channel attention mechanisms are Squeeze-and-Excitation (SE) module [17] and Efficient Channel Attention (ECA) module [18]. Huan Wang et al. [19] proposed multi attention 1DCNN, which improve the discriminant feature representation by using attention module. Hui Wang et al. [20] combined SE module with CNN to make the model reducing redundant information, and main features can be more prominent. Huang et al. [21] proposed a shallow multi-scale neural network with attention, which used the attention mechanism to select features more effectively for classification. Wang et al. [22] used the SE module to fuse frequency signal features for increasing model's versatility. SE module can learn the correlation of different channel features through two fully connected layers. But the learning process is complex, because SE module adopts feature maps in each channel to interact other channels. ECA module uses one-dimensional convolution operation to optimize fully connected operation in SE module. The feature of current channel only interacts with channel feature of its K domains, which can greatly reduce parameters and decrease model complexity.

Therefore, this paper proposes a bearing fault diagnosis method based on MECA-CapsNet, which applies diverse scales channel attention to extract more comprehensive feature information from noisy vibration signal. Owing to multi-scales convolution, ECA modules can enhance interaction of cross-channel feature information and obtain key channel fusion fault feature information at different scales. In addition, MECA-CapsNet combined with capsule module, vector neurons and dynamic routing algorithm, which can establish correlation between low-level features and high-level features. So MECA-CapsNet could highlight key feature information of bearing faults and improve model's bearing fault diagnosis performance in strong noise environments.

2 Efficient Channel Attention and Capsule Network

2.1 Efficient Channel Attention

In recent years, the channel attention mechanism has been applied to convolutional neural networks, which has great potential in improving network performance. To achieve better performance and reduce model's complexity, the Effective Channel Attention mechanism (ECA module) is proposed. ECA module adopts one-dimensional convolution to effectively realize local cross channel interaction strategy. And the coverage of local cross-channel interaction is decided by adaptive convolution kernel size. The structure of SE module and ECA module is shown as in Fig. 1.

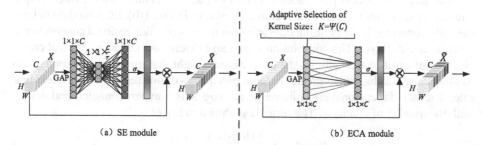

(a) SE module   (b) ECA module

Fig. 1. The structure of SE module and ECA module.

The structure of SE module is shown in Fig. 1(a), which is mainly composed of Global Average Pooling (GAP) layer and a fully connected layer. Among them, C represents channel, W is width, and H express height. The SE module includes two operations, Squeeze and Excitation.

In squeeze operation, gap compresses characteristic information of previous layer into channel descriptor, so that the information from the network global receptive field can be used by its lower layer. That is, the two-dimensional feature maps on each channel become real numbers of global receptive field. The compression operation process is shown in Eq. (1), X are feature maps, and c is channel descriptor.

$$z_c = F_{sq}(X_c) = \frac{1}{W \times H} \sum_{i=1}^{W} \sum_{j=1}^{H} X_c(i, j) \tag{1}$$

After obtaining the global features, an Excitation operation is required to model the importance of different feature channels. The gating mechanism of sigmoid is used here, as shown in Eq. (2).

$$s = F_{ex}(z, W) = \sigma(g(z, W)) = \sigma(W_2 \delta(W_1 z)) \tag{2}$$

In this, $W_1 \in R^{(C/r) * C}$, $W_2 \in R^{C * (C/r)}$. $W_1 \times z$ represents the first fully connected layer operation; the main function control model's complexity by reducing dimensionality. It can be seen from Fig. 1(a) that the dimension has changed from $1 \times 1 \times C$ to 1

$\times$ 1 $\times$ (C/r). r represents the dimensionality reduction coefficient. δ represents ReLU activation function. After the first fully connected layer, the dimension kept unchanged through ReLU layer. The second fully connected layer operation is multiplying with W_2, and the dimension is upgraded to 1 $\times$ 1 $\times$ C. So, the two fully connected layers could reduce parameters and capture more non-linear cross-channel interactive information. s is the weight of C feature maps learned through fully connected layers and nonlinear layers.

Multiplying the learning weight of each channel by the original feature on X, as shown in Eq. (3).

$$\tilde{X}_C = F_{scale}(X_C, S_C) = S_C X_C \tag{3}$$

The learning process pays more attention to channel features with greater weight and suppress unimportant channel features. As shown in Fig. 1(b), ECA module deletes the fully connected layer in SE module and directly uses one-dimensional convolutional layer after GAP layer. The convolution kernel size determines coverage of local cross-channel information interaction. At the same time, weight sharing means that each group has the same weight, which greatly reduces parameters optimizes the network learning rate. The one-dimensional convolution kernel size K is a hyperparameter, and it vary with the number of channels. The formula is shown in Eq. (4).

$$k = \psi(C) = \left| \frac{\log_2(C)}{\gamma} + \frac{b}{\gamma} \right|_{odd} \tag{4}$$

There is a mapping relationship between k and C, that is $C = 2^{\gamma * k - b}$. It is designed to the power of 2 because the number of channels is generally the power of 2. γ and b are designed as 2 and 1 respectively.

2.2 Capsule Network

Network Structure. The Capsule Network transforms traditional scalar neurons into vector neurons and mines the correlation between low-level features and high-level features in a dynamic routing way. The capsule network includes a convolution module and a capsule module. The capsule module consists of PrimaryCaps layer and DigitCaps layer. The structure of Capsule Network is shown in Fig. 2.

The inputs of network are one-dimensional vibration signals. And primitive signal features are extracted by single convolutional layer. Then features are input into capsule module. And vector neurons transform features from scalars into vectors. Between PrimaryCaps layer and DigitCaps capsule layer, a dynamic routing algorithm is used to establish the correlation between low-level capsule and high-level capsule. Finally, the effective classification of rolling bearing fault types is realized. The working principle of capsule is divided into following three steps.

The first step is matrix multiplication of input vector. The neuron u_i and feature matrix W_{ij} are multiplied to obtain prediction vector $U_{j|i}$. u_i contain low-level feature information. W_{ij} contain the space, time and relevance information of low-level and high-level features. As shown in Eq. (5).

$$U_{j|i} = W_{ij} u_i \tag{5}$$

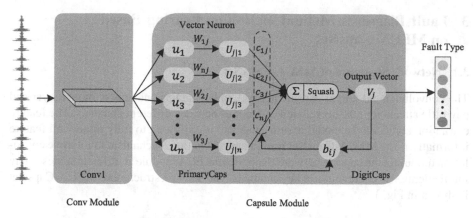

Fig. 2. The structure of capsule network.

The second step is weighted summation of input vectors. The prediction vector $U_{j|i}$ is multiplied by coupling coefficient c_{ij} (weight) and summed to obtain output vector S_j. As shown in Eq. (6).

$$S_j = \sum_i c_{ij} U_{j|i} \tag{6}$$

The third step is nonlinear transformation from vector to vector. The output vector undergoes a non-linear activation function, and squeeze length is less than 1 without changing direction. As shown in Eq. (7).

$$V_j = \frac{\|S_j\|^2}{1 + \|S_j\|^2} \frac{S_j}{\|S_j\|} \tag{7}$$

Dynamic Routing. c_{ij} in Eq. 2 is determined by the dynamic routing algorithm and represents the weight of lower-layer capsules to upper-layer capsules. The purpose is to realize the vector transfer process from lower-layer capsules to upper-layer capsules. As shown in Eq. (8) and Eq. (9).

$$c_{ij} = \text{softmax}(b_{ij}) = \frac{\exp(b_{ij})}{\sum \exp(b_{ij})} \tag{8}$$

$$b_{ij} = b_{ij} + U_{j|i} V_j \tag{9}$$

b_{ij} is initialized to 0. In the process of forward propagation, the correlation between the two is measured according to the dot product of the vector $U_{j|i}$ in the low-level capsule and the vector V_j in the high-level capsule. After the loop iteration of the dynamic routing algorithm, a best set of coupling coefficients is obtained.

3   Fault Diagnosis Method of Rolling Bearing Based on MECA-CapsNet

3.1   Network Structure of MECA-CapsNet

The convolution module of capsule network only contains one convolutional layer and pay little attention to the correlation of features between different channels. The feature extraction ability of the model is restricted, and it is difficult to fully mine fault feature information. The MECA-CapsNet uses channel attention mechanism to improve convolution module of the capsule network. It applies the ECA module at different scales to pay multi attention to the features of key channels. The network structure of MECA-CapsNet is shown in Fig. 3.

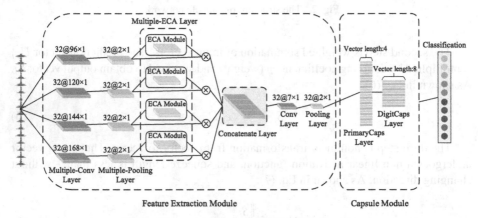

Fig. 3. The network structure of MECA-CapsNet

The feature extraction module of MECA-CapsNet includes Multiple-Conv layer, Conv layer, Multiple-Pooling layer, Pooling layer, Multiple-ECA layer, and concatenate layer. The capsule module includes PrimaryCaps layer and DigitCaps layer. In the feature extraction module, the model directly uses one-dimensional vibration signal as the input of the network. In the Fig. 3, @ is preceded by numbers of channel and followed by kernel size. To obtain the feature information more comprehensively, the Multiple-Conv layer uses four wide kernel convolutions of different sizes. A large convolution kernel corresponds to a large receptive field, which could validly reduce noise interference and improve the anti-noise of the model. So, using large-size convolution kernel can perceive fault feature information. Then, ECA modules with different scales can enhance interaction of cross-channel feature and obtain fault feature from multi-scale key channels. The concatenate layer fuses key channel feature at different scales. In the capsule module, the capsule unit (vector neuron) is constructed by the main capsule layer. Feature scalars are converted into feature vectors and input into DigitCaps layer, and finally 10 vectors with 8 dimensions are output. The 10 vectors correspond to 10 category bearing faults, and the height of vector represent the probability values of 10 types of faults. The loss function uses margin loss.

4 Experimental Verification

4.1 Experimental Data

To verify the effectiveness of MECA-CapsNet in rolling bearing fault diagnosis, this paper uses the public data set of Case Western Reserve University Bearing Data Center to conduct experiments. The experimental bearing is the drive end bearing, and the bearing type is SKF 6205-2RS. Using electric discharge machining technology (EDM) to produce single-point damage on the outer race, inner race, and rolling element of experimental bearing. The diameter of the damage at each location is 0.007 in., 0.014 in., 0.021 in. There are totally 9 category bearing faults. A 16-channel DAT recorder is used to collect the vibration signal with 12 kHz frequency.

There are about 120,000 sample points for each category fault data. And sliding windows are used for continuous overlapping sampling. The size of sliding window is 115. Then every 2048 data points constitute a test sample. The data set expansion method is shown in Fig. 4.

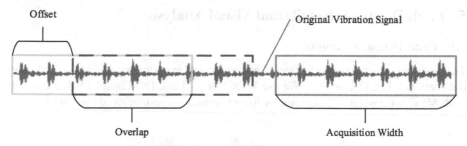

Fig. 4. Data set expansion

Three different loads were included in the experiment such as 1 HP, 2 HP, and 3 HP. There are 9 category bearing states under each load. 1000 samples are collected for each type of fault state. Training set and test set are divided by 7:3. Four data sets are prepared, D1 is samples under load of 1HP, D2 is samples under load of 2HP, D3 is samples under load of 3HP, and D4 mixed the samples of D1, D2, and D3. Ten-dimensional one-hot encoding is used to make samples' labels. The data set information is shown in Table 1. Epoch is set to 150, and batch-size is set to 64. Dropout technology is used in DigitCaps layer to reduce over-fitting.

Table 1. Experimental data set.

Fault labels	Fault classifications	Fault diameter (inch)	Number of samples
0	Normal	0	1000
1	Rolling element fault	0.007	1000
2	Rolling element fault	0.014	1000
3	Rolling element fault	0.021	1000
4	Inner race fault	0.007	1000
5	Inner race fault	0.014	1000
6	Inner race fault	0.021	1000
7	Outer race fault	0.007	1000
8	Outer race fault	0.014	1000
9	Outer race fault	0.021	1000

5   Fault Diagnosis Results and Visual Analysis

5.1   Fault Diagnosis Results

To verify the diagnostic performance of the model, experiments are performed using data sets D1, D2, D3, and D4. We use WDCNN [14] and DC-CapsNet [9] to compare with MECA-CapsNet. The average of five experimental results are shown in Fig. 5.

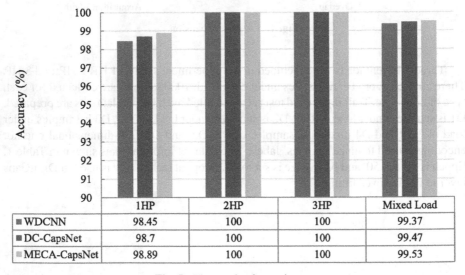

	1HP	2HP	3HP	Mixed Load
■ WDCNN	98.45	100	100	99.37
■ DC-CapsNet	98.7	100	100	99.47
■ MECA-CapsNet	98.89	100	100	99.53

Fig. 5. The result of experiment.

In Fig. 5, the accuracies of MECA-CapsNet bearing fault diagnosis on different data sets have reached 98%. Among them, accuracies on data sets D2 and D3 has reached

100%. The accuracy of MECA-CapsNet reached 99.58% on the mixed data set D4. So MECA-Caps still has good fault recognition accuracy even variable load cases.

5.2 Visual Analysis of Feature Extraction Process

To further verify the effectiveness of MECA-CapsNet and explore its feature extraction process, the t-SNE technology is used to visualize the features of each layer. The experimental data set adopts D4, and result is shown in Fig. 6.

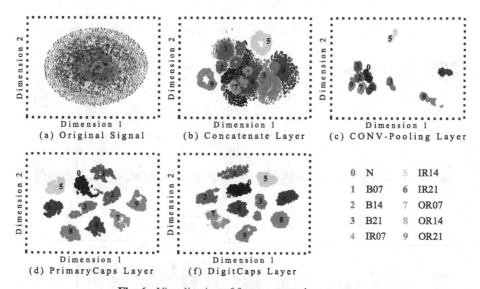

Fig. 6. Visualization of feature extraction process.

Figure 6(a–f) respectively represent the features of original data, connection layer, convolutional layer, PrimaryCaps layer, and DigitCaps layer. Obviously, original data samples emerge chaotic distribution in Fig. 6(a). The ten category samples initially distinguished in concatenate layer as shown in Fig. 6(b). In Fig. 6(c), the samples labeled 5, 3, 8, 6 completely separated from other categories of samples. In PrimaryCaps layer, ten samples are clustered into ten clusters, only samples labeled 0 and 2 have some confused. In Fig. 6(f), DigitCaps layer can distinguish ten samples completely and clearly. So, MECA-CapsNet enhances feature extraction capability through ECA modules.

6 Bearing Fault Diagnosis in Noise Environment

6.1 Fault Diagnosis Results in Noise Environment

To verify fault diagnosis performance of MECA-CapsNet in noise environment, the above two typical deep learning algorithm models are compared with MECA-CapsNet. And a Multi-scale Convolution Capsule network (MC-CapsNet) without ECA modules is constructed to explore the impact of ECA module.

To simulate noise pollution in actual industrial environment, gaussian white noise with different Signal-to-Noise Ratios (SNR) are added to data set. The smaller the value of the signal-to-noise ratio, the higher the noise intensity. Its calculation formula is as shown in Eq. (10). P_{signal} is signal power, P_{noise} is noise power.

$$SNR_{db} = 10 \log_{10} \left(\frac{P_{signal}}{P_{noise}} \right) \qquad (10)$$

The signal waveform with different SNR noises is shown in Fig. 7.

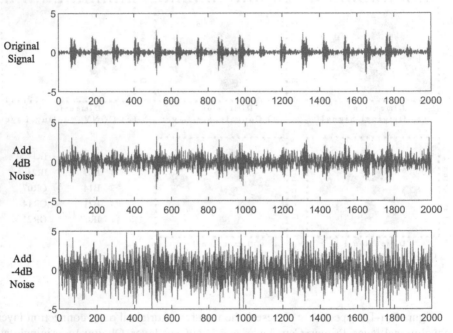

Fig. 7. Original signal, the mixed signal with SNR $= -4$ dB, 4 dB.

The horizontal axis is the number of samples, and the vertical axis is amplitude. It can be seen from the figure that the amplitude of the original signal is more obvious. After adding Gaussian white noise with SNR $= -4$ dB, the vibration features of the original signal are overwhelmed by noise, and it is difficult to determine whether the noise-added signal belongs to the same category as the original signal. Therefore, the difficulty of diagnosing rolling bearing faults in a noise environment with a low SNR will increase significantly.

In this experiment, the mixed load data set D4 is selected. The original signal data is added with Gaussian white noise with SNR $= -4$ dB, -3 dB, -2 dB etc. The experimental results are shown in Fig. 8.

In Fig. 8, MECA-CapsNet achieves 88.56% of bearing fault recognition accuracy in noise with SNR $= -4$ dB, which exceeds WDCNN and DC-CapsNet by 44.33% and 20.81%. Due to advantage of ECA module, accuracy in MECA-CapsNet is 13.33%

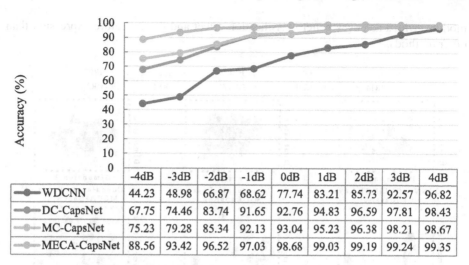

	-4dB	-3dB	-2dB	-1dB	0dB	1dB	2dB	3dB	4dB
WDCNN	44.23	48.98	66.87	68.62	77.74	83.21	85.73	92.57	96.82
DC-CapsNet	67.75	74.46	83.74	91.65	92.76	94.83	96.59	97.81	98.43
MC-CapsNet	75.23	79.28	85.34	92.13	93.04	95.23	96.38	98.21	98.67
MECA-CapsNet	88.56	93.42	96.52	97.03	98.68	99.03	99.19	99.24	99.35

Fig. 8. Fault diagnosis results in noise environment.

higher than MC-CapsNet. Among them, the diagnostic accuracy of DC-CapsNet is better than that of WDCNN, which shows that the capsule network has good resistance. In MECA-CapsNet, bearing fault accuracy reaches 93.42% in noise environment with SNR $= -3$ dB, while WDCNN, DC-CapsNet and MWC-Caps are only 66.87%, 83.74% and 85.34%. When noise intensity drops to 1 dB, MECA-CapsNet's accuracy can reach 99.03%, as other methods only get 83%–95%. When noise intensity drops to 4 dB, WDCNN, DC-CapsNet and MC-CapsNet are lower than 98%, the MECA-CapsNet still keep 99.35%. Therefore, MECA-CapsNet has good anti-noise performance especially in strong noise environments.

6.2 Visual Analysis of Features in Strong Noise Environment

To further verify diagnostic effect of methods, we selected data set C4 with mixed loads, and add gaussian white noise with SNR $= -4$ dB to the data set. Then t-SNE technology is used for feature discrimination visualization in DC-CapsNet, MC-CapsNet and MECA-CapsNet, and the result is shown in Fig. 9.

In Fig. 9, (a) and (d) show feature extraction visualization of DC-CapsNet. (b) and (e) are feature extraction visualization of MC-CapsNet. (c) and (f) present feature extraction visualization MECA-CapsNet. Due to multiscale convolutions, (b) and (c) get better clustering effect than (a). The three models further extract features from ten types of samples. In Fig. 9(d), samples labeled 0, 1, 2, 6 and 8 are still partially confused. In Fig. 9(e), MC-CapsNet is also difficult to completely distinguish samples labeled 0, 2, 6 and 8. In Fig. 9(f), MECA-CapsNet could clearly distinguish ten kinds of data samples. These visualizations show that concatenate layers adopt multi-scale connection layer to extract features, which have more obvious classification trend than single-scale conv-pooling layer. Meanwhile, MECA-CapsNet classification trend is clearer than MC-CapsNet in further information learning. It fully demonstrates the advantages of ECA module, which achieves better classification effect and better feature expression than other methods.

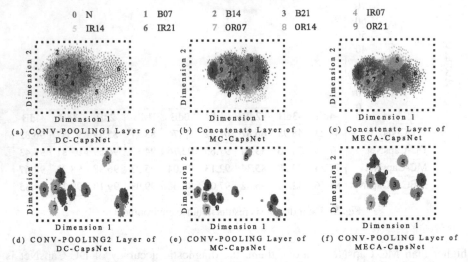

| 0 | N | 1 | B07 | 2 | B14 | 3 | B21 | 4 | IR07 |
| 5 | IR14 | 6 | IR21 | 7 | OR07 | 8 | OR14 | 9 | OR21 |

(a) CONV-POOLING1 Layer of DC-CapsNet

(b) Concatenate Layer of MC-CapsNet

(c) Concatenate Layer of MECA-CapsNet

(d) CONV-POOLING2 Layer of DC-CapsNet

(e) CONV-POOLING Layer of MC-CapsNet

(f) CONV-POOLING Layer of MECA-CapsNet

Fig. 9. Visualize the output features of key layer in feature extraction module.

7 Conclusion

This paper uses Multiple-ECA module to improve capsule network, which applies in bearing fault diagnosis. Multiple-ECA module adopts various scales convolution to abstract features correlation from different channels. So Multiple-ECA can enhance the interaction of cross-channels' information and obtain bearing fault features of multi-scale channels. In capsule module, vector neurons convert feature scalars into a feature vector, and the dynamic routing transmits key feature vectors layer by lay-er. Experimental results show that MECA-CapsNet has stronger anti-noise performance and higher fault diagnosis accuracies than WDCNN, DC-CapsNet and MC-CapsNet. Through visual analysis of features, MECA-CapsNet uses multi-scale convolution combined with ECA module, which can effectively reduce noise interference and improve the accuracy of rolling bearing fault diagnosis in a strong noise environment.

Acknowledgments. The financial support provided from the National Natural Science Foundation of China (11702091), Natural Science Foundation of Hunan Province (2021JJ30267, 2019JJ50156) and Project of Hunan Provincial Department of Education (19B187, HNKCSZ-2020-0316) are greatly appreciated by the authors.

References

1. Gai, J., Shen, J., Hu, Y., Wang, H.: An integrated method based on hybrid grey wolf optimizer improved variational mode decomposition and deep neural network for fault diagnosis of rolling bearing. Measurement **162**, 107901 (2020)

2. Soother, D.K., Kalwar, I.H., Hussain, T., Chowdhry, B.S., Ujjan, S.M., Memon, T.D.: A novel method based on UNET for bearing fault diagnosis. Comput. Mater. Contin. **69**(1), 393–408 (2021)
3. Zhang, K., Lin, B., Chen, J., Wu, X., Lu, C., Tian, L.: Aero-engine surge fault diagnosis using deep neural network. Comput. Syst. Sci. Eng. **42**(1), 351–360 (2022)
4. Zhu, Z., Peng, G., Chen, Y., Gao, H.: A convolutional neural network based on a capsule network with strong generalization for bearing fault diagnosis. Neurocomputing **323**, 62–75 (2019)
5. Chen, S., Yu, J., Wang, S.: One-dimensional convolutional auto-encoder-based feature learning for fault diagnosis of multivariate processes. J. Process Control **87**, 54–67 (2020)
6. Surendran, R., Khalaf, O.I., Romero, C.A.T.: Deep learning based intelligent industrial fault diagnosis model. Comput. Mater. Contin. **70**(3), 6323–6338 (2022)
7. Durbhaka, G.K., Selvaraj, B., Mittal, M., Saba, T., Rehman, A., Goyal, L.M.: Swarm-LSTM: condition monitoring of gearbox fault diagnosis based on hybrid LSTM deep neural network optimized by swarm intelligence algorithms. Comput. Mater. Contin. **66**(2), 2041–2059 (2021)
8. Sabour, S., Frosst, N., Hinton, G.E.: Dynamic routing between capsules. In: Advances in Neural Information Processing Systems, pp. 3859–3869. MIT Press, Long Beach (2017)
9. Yang, P., Su, Y.C., Zhen, Z.: A study on rolling bearing fault diagnosis based on convolution capsule network. J. Vib. Shock **39**(4), 62–68 (2020)
10. Taha, I., Mansour, D.E.A.: Novel power transformer fault diagnosis using optimized machine learning methods. Intell. Autom. Soft Comput. **28**(3), 739–752 (2021)
11. Xu, G., Liu, M., Jiang, Z., Söffker, D., Shen, W.: Bearing fault diagnosis method based on deep convolutional neural network and random forest ensemble learning. Sensors **19**(5), 1088 (2019)
12. Zhang, Y., Xing, K., Bai, R., Sun, D., Meng, Z.: An enhanced convolutional neural network for bearing fault diagnosis based on time–frequency image. Measurement **157**, 107667 (2020)
13. Chen, Z., Mauricio, A., Li, W., Gryllias, K.: A deep learning method for bearing fault diagnosis based on cyclic spectral coherence and convolutional neural networks. Mech. Syst. Signal Process. **140**, 106683 (2020)
14. Zhang, W., Li, C., Peng, G., Chen, Y., Zhang, Z.: A deep convolutional neural network with new training methods for bearing fault diagnosis under noisy environment and different working load. Mech. Syst. Signal Process. **100**, 439–453 (2018)
15. Jian, X., Li, W., Guo, X., Wang, R.: Fault diagnosis of motor bearings based on a one-dimensional fusion neural network. Sensors **19**(1), 122 (2019)
16. Zhang, Y., Li, K., Li, K., Wang, L., Zhong, B., Fu, Y.: Image super-resolution using very deep residual channel attention networks. In: Ferrari, V., Hebert, M., Sminchisescu, C., Weiss, Y. (eds.) ECCV 2018. LNCS, vol. 11211, pp. 294–310. Springer, Cham (2018). https://doi.org/10.1007/978-3-030-01234-2_18
17. Hu, J., Shen, L., Sun, G.: Squeeze-and-excitation networks. In: Proceedings of the IEEE Conference on Computer Vision and Pattern Recognition, Salt Lake City, pp. 7132–7141. IEEE Press (2018)
18. Wang, Q., Wu, B., Zhu, P., Li, P., Zuo, W., Hu, Q.: ECA-Net: efficient channel attention for deep convolutional neural networks. In: IEEE/CVF Conference on Computer Vision and Pattern Recognition, Seattle, pp. 11534–11542. IEEE Press (2020)
19. Wang, H., Liu, Z., Peng, D., Qin, Y.: Understanding and learning discriminant features based on multiattention 1DCNN for wheelset bearing fault diagnosis. IEEE Trans. Industr. Inf. **16**(9), 5735–5745 (2019)
20. Wang, H., Xu, J., Yan, R., Gao, R.X.: A new intelligent bearing fault diagnosis method using SDP representation and SE-CNN. IEEE Trans. Instrum. Meas. **69**(5), 2377–2389 (2019)

21. Huang, T., Fu, S., Feng, H., Kuang, J.: Bearing fault diagnosis based on shallow multi-scale convolutional neural network with attention. Energies **12**(20), 3937 (2019)
22. Wang, Y., Yang, M., Zhang, Y., Xu, Z., Huang, J., Fang, X.: A bearing fault diagnosis model based on deformable atrous convolution and squeeze-and-excitation aggregation. IEEE Trans. Instrum. Meas. **70**, 1–10 (2021)

Research on E-commerce Customer Churn Based on RFM Model and Naive Bayes Algorithm

Yuan Tang, Yupeng Li, and Guang Sun[✉]

Hunan University of Finance and Economics, Changsha 410000, China
sunguang@hufe.edu.cn

Abstract. In recent years, with the rapid development of e-commerce, more and more people are engaged in the e-commerce industry. In order to stand out from numerous e-commerce enterprises and retain customers, it is necessary to achieve accurate marketing, so as to segment the market, locate customer groups, and attract and retain customers through formulating marketing strategies. In this paper, RFM model and Naive Bayes algorithm are used to analyze customer churn. The three indicators of RFM model are relatively independent and have good representativeness for customer classification, and have been widely used in customer classification in various fields. Naive Bayes algorithm can calculate the probability of loss more easily, so the combination of the two can be used to identify which kind of customers are more likely to lose. Thus help enterprises to implement different marketing strategies for different customer groups, in order to save the cost of enterprises, improve the efficiency of enterprises.

Keywords: RFM model · Naive Bayes algorithm · Customer churn forecast

1 Introduction

Precision marketing is a marketing method that enterprises make plans correctly and quickly and constantly change plans to satisfy customers according to their needs. Precision marketing pays the most attention to the word "precision". It delivers accurate products to customers at an accurate time and in an accurate way, so that customers can get satisfactory service, so that suppliers can obtain higher profit margins [1]. The key is to master market segmentation. Only with clear market segmentation [2] can customer groups be accurately positioned and customers can be classified.

There are many publicly published methods of customer classification, and the representative methods include: Carbajal Santiago García et al. classified customers of sporting goods stores through Path Reconstruction [3]. Yadegaridehkordi Elaheh et al. segmented the customers of eco-friendly hotels through multi-criteria and machine learning techniques [4]. Based on the RFM model, Lizheng Jing et al. subdivided e-commerce customers by combining CH clustering to evaluate quality indicators and K-means algorithm [5]. Huilin Yuan et al. RFMPA multi-index customer system and

© The Author(s), under exclusive license to Springer Nature Switzerland AG 2022
X. Sun et al. (Eds.): ICAIS 2022, LNCS 13338, pp. 371–381, 2022.
https://doi.org/10.1007/978-3-031-06794-5_30

improved K-means algorithm to subdivide customers [6]. Haoliang Cui et al. classified social e-commerce customers based on K-means++ algorithm [7]. RFM model is the most popular model used in many customer classification methods. RFM model is a classic model for identifying customer value in the field of marketing. It is used to analyze customer consumption in the observation period (a period before the observation point) at the observation point [8]. It is mainly used in the traditional retail industry and has good characterization in reflecting customer purchase preference [9]. Although RFM model customer consumption behavior analysis results on the frequency of purchase is more accurate and obvious, but for the time consumption frequency is low, purchase frequency is not high amount of regular clients the results of the analysis is relatively fuzzy [10], and in different areas contain indicators are not the same, then you need to improve the RFM model to apply. The scenarios recently used include: Yuqi Chen et al. constructed a popular book evaluation model by combining the improvement of RFM model with book evaluation [11]. Meng Zhao et al. constructed RFMP model based on comment behavior on the basis of traditional RFM model [12]. Weikang Li et al. improved the RFM model and applied the RVMF model to the customer segmentation of online stores [13]. At the same time, RFM model has also been widely used in more subdivided areas. Lingfang Sun et al. established e-commerce recommendation mechanism by combining the RFM model and collaborative filtering [14]. Chengyi Le et al. combined the RFM model with user portraits to conduct research on university library users [15]. Chun Yan et al. improved the SOM neural network model and RFM model to study non-life insurance customers [16]. Zhengang Zhang et al. combined the RFM model with the random actor-oriented model [17]. Ling Wei et al. predicted the loss of MOOC users by improving RFM and GMDH algorithms [18]. Lin Yang et al. combined the RFM model with the random forest algorithm to predict the loss of civil aviation customers more accurately [19].

One of the purposes of customer classification is to identify vulnerable customers. It is known that the cost of developing new customers is 5–6 times that of maintaining existing customers [20]. Therefore, it is of great significance to recover vulnerable users. At present, there are few studies that use RFM model to judge customer churn, and there is no specific study on RFM model to analyze the probability of customer churn. On the basis of studying the RFM model to judge customer churn, this paper combines the RFM model with naive Bayes and focuses on the e-commerce industry with new business models in the 21st century [21] to realize the probability analysis of customer churn, provide reliable basis for retaining customers and facilitate enterprises to take corresponding measures.

2 RFM Model and Naive Bayes Algorithm

2.1 RFM Model

RFM model was proposed by Arthur Hughes of American database research institute in 1994 [22]. It is a customer classification method based on online stores [23]. Currently, the application scenarios mainly include mobile phones, credit cards, securities companies, etc. [24]. Next, we will briefly analyze the RFM model [25].

RFM consists of the following three indicators.

R (Recency) indicates the interval between the last purchase period and the end date of the statistical period.

F (Frequency) indicates the purchase times of a customer during the statistical period. The more times you buy, the more loyal you are and the more likely you are to buy again.

M (Monetary) stands for the total amount of purchases made by customers during the statistical period. In general, the higher the total purchase amount, the more loyal the customer.

The RFM model can divide customer groups into the following eight categories (Figs. 1 and 2).

R	F	M	Customer level
1	1	1	Important value customers
0	1	1	Important to keep customers
1	0	1	Important development customers
0	0	1	Important to retain customers
1	1	0	General value customers
1	0	0	General development customers
0	1	0	General to keep customers
0	0	0	Lost customers

Fig. 1. Customer classification.

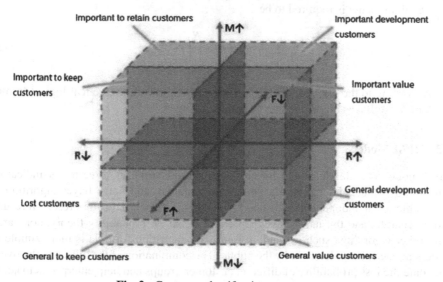

Fig. 2. Customer classification space map.

2.2 Naive Bayes Algorithm

Naive Bayes algorithm is the main algorithm of Bayesianism [26, 27]. It is a classical machine learning algorithm based on the naive assumption [28] that features are independent. It is a direct and powerful probabilistic method [29]. The core idea is to assume that under ideal conditions, all relevant probabilities of classification tasks are known in advance. By comparing the probability of samples in different categories, the optimal category to which the samples belong can be determined [30]. In some areas, its performance is comparable to neural networks and decision tree learning [31].

The following is the naive Bayes algorithm and theorem [32].

Corresponding to the feature vector x_1, x_2, ..., x_m of the given sample X; the probability of the category y of the sample X can be obtained by the Bayesian formula.

$$P(y|x_1, x_2, ..., x_m) = \frac{P(y)P(x_1, x_2, ..., x_m|y)}{P(x_1, x_2, ..., x_m)} \tag{1}$$

Features are independent of each other, and can be obtained as follows.

$$P(y|x_1, x_2, ..., x_m) = \frac{P(y)P(x_1, x_2, ..., x_m|y)}{P(x_1, x_2, ..., x_m)} = \frac{P(y)\prod_{i=1}^{N} P(x_i|y)}{P(x_1, x_2, ..., x_m)} \tag{2}$$

For a given sample, P (x_1, x_2, ..., x_m are constants).

$$P(y|x_1, x_2, ..., x_m) \propto P(y)\prod_{i=1}^{N} P(x_i|y) \tag{3}$$

The final model is required to be.

$$\hat{y} = \arg\max P(y)\prod_{i=1}^{N} P(x_i|y) \tag{4}$$

According to the above modeling process, the following theoretical logical framework of naive Bayes algorithm can be obtained (Fig. 3).

2.3 RFM Model

RFM model as a classic model for customer classification, its three major indicators with relative independence and a good representative, and naive bayes algorithm is applicable to the independence of good indicators, for such indicators research results more accurate, and the naive bayes algorithm based on probability theory, compared with other algorithms such as random forest, Its algorithm formula is more simple to understand, can be understood by the public. The combination of the two can effectively calculate the loss probability of different customer groups and help enterprises to adopt different marketing measures for different customer groups.

Fig. 3. Flow chart of naive Bayes algorithm.

3 Experimental Steps

3.1 Data Preparation

This paper selects the transaction data of Aliyun TIANCHI data website as experimental data. The transaction data of users were imported into Jupyter Notebook for analysis. The total data span is from January 3, 2015 to December 30, 2018, including 9994 data records. The data contains the following fields: commodity ID, payment time, delivery time, buyer ID, buyer nickname, etc. According to the requirements of model construction, three fields of buyer nickname, payment time and actual payment amount were selected to constitute backup data, and a total of 9994 experimental data were obtained (Table 1).

Table 1. Raw data sample.

	Customer name	Order date	Sales
0	Claire Gute	2017-11-08	261.9600
1	Claire Gute	2017-11-08	731.9400
2	Darrin Van Huff	2017-06-12	14.6200
...	...	...	...

3.2 RFM Model Construction

The RFM model was constructed using experimental data. The data collection date was originally set as 13 January 2022 to calculate the index. The calculation results are as follows, where R is the number of days between the latest purchase date and the data collection date. F (Frequency) is the total consumption times of users. (M) Monetary refers to the total amount of money consumed by users (Table 2).

Table 2. Calculation results of index quantity sample.

Customer name	R	F	M
Aaron Bergman	1524	6	886.156
Aaron Hawkins	1121	11	1744.700
Aaron Smayling	1191	10	3050.692
Adam Bellavance	1163	18	7755.620
Adam Hart	1143	20	3250.337

Exploratory analysis is made on the calculated results, and the running results of the program are as follows (Table 3).

Table 3. Exploratory analysis results.

	R	F	M
Count	739.000000	793.000000	793.000000
Mean	1255.773014	12.602774	2896.848500
Std	186.111367	6.242559	2628.670117
Min	1109.000000	1.000000	4.833000
25%	1139.000000	8.000000	1146.050000

(*continued*)

Table 3. (*continued*)

	R	F	M
50%	1184.000000	12.000000	2256.394000
75%	1292.000000	16.000000	3785.276000
Max	2274.000000	37.000000	25043.050000

As can be seen from the figure, there are a total of 793 users after summarizing, with the average of Recency being 1255.77 days, Frequency being 12.60 times and Monetary being 2896.85 yuan. According to the above analysis, the data are divided into regions, and the R, F and M indicators are scored one by one to determine whether the scoring result is greater than the mean value. If it is greater than the mean value, it is 1; if it is less than the mean value, it is 0. Finally, users are classified according to the classical RFM model, and the results are as follows (Table 4).

Table 4. Customer classification results sample.

Customer name	R-score	F-score	M-score	R-score > the men	F-score > the men	M-score > the men	Customer type
Edward Becker	4	3	3	1	1	1	Important value customer
Scot Wooten	3	2	1	1	0	0	General development customer
Guy Phonely	1	1	1	0	0	0	Lost customer

3.3 Combined with Naive Bayes Algorithm

According to the classification of the above customer groups, the lost customer groups are extracted and the mean value and standard deviation of lost customers are calculated (Table 5).

Table 5. Customer churn analysis

	R	F	M
Count	196.00000	196.000000	196.000000
Mean	1427.260204	7.454082	1081.269245
Std	231.883213	3.093904	661.726993
Min	1108.000000	1.000000	4.833000
25%	1233.000000	5.000000	475.839000
50%	1358.000000	7.000000	1039.651000
75%	1540.500000	10.000000	1497.212500
Max	2273.000000	13.000000	2394.025000

Then calculate the mean values of R, F and M of the other seven types of users (Table 6).

Table 6. Other seven types of customer analysis

	R	F	M
Important value customers	1143.929032	19.380645	4920.223203
General value customers	1143.477273	17.295455	1888.671643
Important development customers	1151.151899	10.556962	4362.479223
Important to keep customers	1305.373494	19.469880	5386.354551
General development customers	1146.986755	8.417219	1130.816243
General to keep customers	1328.633333	15.966667	1606.538233
Important to retain customers	1369.618182	10.327273	4161.513700

Combined with Gaussian Naive Bayes algorithm, the churn probability of R, F and M indicators is calculated for the other seven types of users (Table 7).

Finally, the basic formula of naive Bayes algorithm is substituted to get the final conclusion (Table 8).

Table 7. The probability of loss of R, F, M

R	F	M
0.0016734341410082898	0.08387340093102237	$1.1641850028882794e^{-8}$
0.0008240891779219367	0.12302465031031498	0.0006018874986992121
0.0008458775316388757	0.07805425581629265	$2.6951595971178504e^{-9}$
0.0015022047808097782	$6.769826004858919e^{-5}$	$3.7145059389518674e^{-13}$
0.0008111040657287225	$7.48400136213901e^{-5}$	$2.8578936556562513e^{-11}$
0.0015754836437899722	0.002910319523781567	0.000440275537481332
0.0008111040657287225	0.000810773734445775	0.0002864452162800118

Table 8. Churn probability of the other seven categories of users

	The loss probability
Important value customers	$1.1710091090685687e^{-17}$
General value customers	$1.2715153164134549e^{-9}$
Important development customers	$1.201136424389536e^{-12}$
Important to keep customers	$2.5498314676063216e^{-19}$
General development customers	$4.1189398139937196e^{-7}$
General to keep customers	$1.3626455439232312e^{-8}$
Important to retain customers	$1.1029571785724215e^{-11}$

4 Conclusion and Prospect

In the rapidly changing e-commerce industry, enterprise development still follows the 80–20 rule proposed by Italian economist and sociologist Vilfredo Pareto, that is, 20 percent of customers can create 80% of the profits of the enterprise. Given that the cost of acquiring new users is several times higher than the cost of maintaining an old one, retention becomes even more important. The RFM model is commonly used in customer classification, divides customers into eight categories simply and clearly, and then provides different marketing strategies according to different types of users. In the third part of this paper, the prediction of loss probability based on the customer group classified by RFM model combined with naive Bayes algorithm can effectively help enterprises distinguish customers and identify customer value under the circumstance of limited resources, achieve accurate marketing, and efficiently utilize limited resources to maximize the interests of enterprises.

4.1 Conclusion

In the first two parts of this paper, the application of RFM model at home and abroad has done a lot of understanding, and the naive Bayes algorithm has made relevant explanations. In the third part, the naive Bayes algorithm is used to analyze the customer groups classified by RFM model. The results show that compared with the other four categories, the probability of losing general development customers, the probability of losing general to keep customers and the probability of losing general value customers are higher, and the probability of losing general development customers is the highest. Therefore, when making marketing strategies, enterprises should always pay attention to the loyalty of new customers, attract the eyes of new customers, and retain new customers.

4.2 Prospect

RFM model can classify customers with fewer characteristic indexes, which is convenient for enterprises to identify high-value customers quickly. However, it is difficult to determine the weight of the three indicators of THE RFM model. Even though customer groups are divided into eight categories according to the Pareto method, the classification method is still relatively general, and it is still impossible to clearly distinguish the customer groups whose value is in the middle level. Although this paper combined RFM model with naive Bayes algorithm to predict the loss of customer groups, the RFM model itself contained few indicators, so it could not well express the behavior characteristics of customers, and the experimental results obtained still need to be improved. The following experiments can give different weights to the three indicators of the RFM model or increase the consideration indicators of the RFM model to make it more close to the actual results of customer loss, so as to facilitate the adoption of appropriate marketing strategies for the upcoming customer loss, maintain the relationship between customers and enterprises, and achieve accurate marketing.

References

1. Zhu, H.: Analysis of e-commerce precision marketing in the era of big data. Hebei Enterp. **4**, 113–114 (2021)
2. Yang, M.: Analysis of e-commerce precision marketing based on the advantages of big data technology. Chin. Mark. **8**, 189–190 (2021)
3. Customer, S.G.: Customer segmentation through path reconstruction. Sensors **21**(6), 2007 (2021)
4. Yadegaridehkordi, E., Nilashi, M., Bin, M.H.N.: Customers segmentation in eco-friendly hotels using multi-criteria and machine learning techniques. Technol. Soc. **65**, 101528 (2021)
5. Jing, L.Z., Wu, Z.Y.: Research on e-commerce customer segmentation based on improved K-means clustering. J. China Univ. Metrol. **31**(4), 483–489 (2020)
6. Yuan, H.L., Du, J., Li, Y.H.: Research and application of customer segmentation model based on data mining. Comput. Eng. Des. **42**(1), 58–64 (2021)
7. Cui, H., Niu, S., Li, K.: A k-means++ based user classification method for social e-commerce. Intell. Autom. Soft Comput. **28**(1), 277–291 (2021)
8. Moehrle, G.M., Caferoglu, H.: Using semantic patent analysis for the case of camera technology. Technol. Forecast. Soc. Chang. **146**, 776–784 (2019)

9. Xu, X.B., Wang, J.Q., Tu, H.: E-commerce customer segmentation based on improved RFM model. Comput. Appl. **32**(5), 1439–1442 (2012)

10. Ye, B.W., Zhu, Y., Sun, T.Y.: Research on precision marketing of clothing retail based on RFM model. Mod. Mark. **16**, 22–24 (2020)

11. Cheng, Y.Q., Shi, G.L., Zhang, X.X.: Research on evaluation system and influencing factors of popular books in University Library based on modified RFM model. Res. Libr. Sci. **10**, 58–68 (2020)

12. Zhao, M., Qi, J.Y.: Research on customer lifetime value based on purchase behavior RFM and comment behavior RFMP model. Stat. Inf. Forum **29**(9), 91–98 (2014)

13. Li, W.K., Yang, X.B.: Application of an improved RFM model in customer segmentation of online stores. J. China Univ. Metrol. **31**(1), 86–91 (2020)

14. Sun, L.F., Zhang, J.: Electronic recommendation mechanism based on RFM model and collaborative filtering. J. Jiangsu Univ. Sci. Technol. **24**(3), 286–289 (2021)

15. Le, C.Y., Wang, X.: Research on user portrait of University Library based on improved RFM clustering. Libr. Theory Pract. **2**, 75–79 (2020)

16. Yan, C., Liu, L.: Classifying non-life insurance customers based on improved SOM and RFM models. Data Anal. Knowl. Disc. **4**(4), 83–89 (2020)

17. Zhang, Z.G., Luo, T.Y.: Technology opportunity identification based on RFM modeland stochastic actor-oriented model. J. Inf. **40**(1), 54–60 (2021)

18. Wei, L., Guo, X.Y.: Clarifying the connotations of national qualifications framework: a textual analysis of multiple national/regional qualifications frameworks. China **9**, 39–43 (2020)

19. Yang, L., Bai, Z., Kou, Y.G.: Analysis of airline customer churn by random forest algorithm based on rfm model. Comput. Mod. **1**, 100–104 (2021)

20. Hadden, J., Tiwari, A., Roy, R.: Computer assisted customer churn management: state-of-the-art and future trends. Comput. Oper. Res. **34**(10), 2902–2917 (2005)

21. Salamai, A.A., Ageeli, A.A., El-Kenawy, E.M.: Forecasting e-commerce adoption based on bidirectional recurrent neural networks. Comput. Mater. Contin. **70**(3), 5091–5106 (2022)

22. Hughes, A.M.: Strategic Database Marketing. Probus Publishing Company, Röttenbach (1999)

23. Zhao, X., Keikhosrokiani, P.: Sales prediction and product recommendation model through user behavior analytics. Comput. Mater. Contin. **70**(2), 3855–3874 (2022)

24. Xiong, L.: Research on rfm multi-level customer value model based on product classification and its application. M.S. Dissertation (2016)

25. Wu, J., Shi, L., Lin, W.P.: An empirical study on customer segmentation by purchase behaviors using a RFM model and -means algorithm. Math. Probl. Eng. **2020** (2020)

26. Hoff, P.D.: A first course in Bayesian statistical methods. J. Roy. Stat. Soc. **173**(3), 694–695 (2010)

27. Wang, A.P., Zhang, G.Y., Liu, F.: EM algorithm research and application. School Comput. Inf. Technol. **19**(9), 108–110 (2009)

28. Ju, Z.Y., Wang, Z.H.: A Bayesian classification algorithm based on selective patterns. Comput. Inf. Technol.gy **57**(8), 1605–1614 (2020)

29. Subramanian, R.S., Prabha, D.: Ensemble variable selection for Naive Bayes to improve customer behaviour analysis. Comput. Syst. Sci. Eng. **41**(1), 339–355 (2022)

30. Guo, L.: Social network rumor recognition based on enhanced Naive Bayes. J. New Media **3**(3), 99–107 (2021)

31. Butt, A.H., Rovini, E., Dolciotti, C.: Objective and automatic classification of Parkinson disease with Leap Motion controller. BioMed. Eng. OnLine **17**(168), 1–21 (2018)

32. Ma, Y.Z., Zhang, Y., Hou, Y.M.: Study on news classification of COVID-19 based on Naive Bayes. Coll. Inf. Sci. Eng. **17**(14), 120–121 (2020)

A Multi-task Learning Framework for Semantic Segmentation in MLS Point Clouds

Xi Lin[1,2], Huan Luo[1,2(✉)], Wenzhong Guo[1,2], Cheng Wang[3], and Jonathan Li[4]

[1] College of Computer Science and Big Data, Fuzhou University, Fuzhou 350108, Fujian, China
hluo@fzu.edu.cn
[2] Fujian Provincial Key Laboratory of Network Computing and Intelligent Information Processing, Fuzhou University, Fuzhou 350108, Fujian, China
[3] Fujian Key Lab of Sensing and Computing for Smart Cities, School of Informatics, Xiamen University, Xiamen 361005, Fujian, China
[4] Department of Geography and Environmental Management and Department of Systems Design Engineering University of Waterloo, Waterloo, ON N2L 3G1, Canada

Abstract. We study a multi-task learning framework for semantic segmentation in Mobile Laser Scanning (MLS) point clouds. The existing methods on semantic segmentation of point cloud rely on a large number of annotation data. However, manually annotating data is time-consuming and laborious, and the manually annotation efficiency is particularly low. To alleviate those problems, we propose to exploit a multi-task learning framework to reduce the large demand of training samples for implementing semantic labeling of point clouds. Specifically, we design a new neural network containing a backbone network and two branching networks, which accomplish the color prediction and category prediction, respectively. Color prediction, as an auxiliary task, can be easily conducted by exploiting the color information of each 3D point to train the proposed neural network. Here, color information of each point can be easily generated by using the optical images obtained by the cameras equipped in the MLS system. Once the training procedure of color prediction is completed, we only use a small portion of manually-annotated points to fine-tune the branching network of category prediction for each 3D point. To demonstrate the effectiveness and correctness of our proposed framework, we conducted extensive experiments on the colorized point clouds which are collected by a RIEGL VMX450 MLS system. The experimental results show the proposed approach can reach 96.04%. OA and 94.41% mIoU under the supervision of 10% annotation data.

Keywords: Point cloud · Semantic segmentation · Multi-task learning

© The Author(s), under exclusive license to Springer Nature Switzerland AG 2022
X. Sun et al. (Eds.): ICAIS 2022, LNCS 13338, pp. 382–392, 2022.
https://doi.org/10.1007/978-3-031-06794-5_31

1   Introduction

With the rapid development of 3D data acquisition technology, different types of 3D Mobile Laser Scanners (MLS), such as Light Detection and Ranging (LiDAR) scanner [11], are becoming more and more universal. Due to the fact that a LiDAR scanner is an active scanner, the LiDAR scanner is robust in generating high-resolution 3D data regardless of illumination. As a basic data representation, the point cloud can be easily collected by LiDAR scanning devices, and the obtained point cloud has high precision, accurate spatial coordinate information, and rich information is reserved for further investigation. Therefore, point cloud plays an important role in 3D computer vision.

Very recently, deep neural network is introduced to boost the performance of point cloud information extraction. Existing works have proposed a number of frameworks in various fields (e.g. convolutional neural networks [14,21,23], graph neural networks [12,13,24], cyclic neural networks [7,26], etc.) to extract features and accomplish point cloud semantic segmentation. Besides, Gankhuyag et al. [8] proposed to transform the point clouds into 2D depth image through preprocessing to handle the major problem, which is low-quality point clouds that are noisy, cluttered and that contain missing parts in the data. The success of these methods is mainly owing to the deep neural network [19] and a large number of annotated 3D point cloud data [2,15], in which the great number of annotated data is assumed to be usually available. Although many works are still chasing advanced neural network frameworks, we believe that the data annotation problem is a neglected bottleneck. In practice, the labeling of semantic segmentation of point cloud data is time-consuming and laborious and the semantic annotators should be well-trained to build a robust dataset. Moreover, when manually labeling point cloud data, due to the disorder, sparsity and uneven organised of point cloud data, it is inevitable to produce missing labels and wrong labels during manual labeling, which will bring large errors and low accuracy to the learning of neural network.

There are many researches on 2D image semantic segmentation applied to the medical field. Naqvi et al. [17] applied semantic segmentation to biometrics and healthcare. Anand et al. [1] proposed residual u-network for breast tumor segmentation from magnetic resonance images. Af-net [9] utilized attention mechanism and feature fusion to medical image segmentation. What's more, many previous works on semantic segmentation of 2D images used the method of multi-task learning [4]. Bischke et al. [3] used multi-task learning to improve the segmentation predictions of building footprints. Dai et al. [5] proposed Multi-task Network Cascades (MNCs) for accurate and fast instance-aware semantic segmentation. MTI-Net [22] overcome a common obstacle of performance degradation in multi-task networks, and observe that tasks mutually benefit from each other, resulting in significant improvements w.r.t. their single-task counterparts. Peng et al. [18] proposed a multi-task network for cardiac magnetic resonance image segmentation and classification. Compared to networks trained on single task, the performance of these multi-task methods is improved.

In order to reduce the large number of labeled training samples needed by deep learning and boost the performance of semantic labeling, inspired by the multi-task frameworks, we propose a novel multi-task learning method. Specifically, the two tasks are color label prediction and semantic segmentation. Not only the color label prediction task is highly related to semantic segmentation task, but also color labels are easier to obtain compared with semantic labels. Therefore, we use predictive color label as a task with rich training data. Finally, we formulate semantic segmentation tasks as a multi-task learning framework. The multi-task framework contains two outputs where a large number of common model parameters are shared among. We train the model on point cloud data with a fully-supervised color labels and only a small portion of semantic labels. The conducted experiments have supported our views and shown the correctness of the proposed framework. The rest of the paper is outlined as follows. Section 2 contains a discussion about our neural network architectures of multi-task learning. In Sect. 3, Our experiment on VMX450 is introduced. Finally, we give our conclusion in Sect. 4. The main contributions of our proposed multi-task framework is summarized as follows:

- We propose a novel multi-task framework in assisting to boost the performance of semantic segmentation for MLS point cloud. Only a small portion of semantic annotated data is needed to fine-tune neural networks, thus reduce the cost of manually annotating point cloud samples.
- The color label prediction task, as an auxiliary task, is highly related to semantic labeling prediction and can be useful for various applications. Moreover, the color label we use is easy to access from mobile laser scanners.
- We evaluate our network on MLS dataset VMX450, containing real point cloud scenes. The experimental results not only demonstrate that our approach achieves promising performances, but also show as a reference for MLS semantic labeling researchers.

2   Method

Fig. 1. The workflow of the proposed framework.

Given a point cloud scene $s_i = \{p_1, p_2, ..., p_n\}$, each p_i contains three-dimensional coordinate information and color information. The task of semantic segmentation aims at classifying every point in the scene into several regions with specific semantic categories [25].

As shown in Fig. 1, the main stream of our proposed framework can be divided into three components, including color encoding, multi-task training and predicting. Specifically speaking, to obtain a more clean point cloud scene, we first use point cloud filtering to preprocess point clouds. Then we use the color information to encode each input point and assign each point with a color label. After that, the deep learning model is trained under the supervision of generated color labels. And after that we fine-tune the neural network to accomplish semantic labeling only using a small portion of semantic annotations. Finally, We use the trained framework to perform semantic segmentation.

The remainder of the section is organized as follows. In Sect. 2.1, we show how to encode the color label for each point. In Sect. 2.2, the proposed multi-task model is unrolled in detail.

2.1 Color Encoding

Due to the complex measurement environment and the error caused by laser scanners, the acquired original point cloud data may contain a lot of noise. The noise might result in the fact that color and geometry information is not able to be utilized directly. In order to obtain a more accurate color and geometry information, we design a point cloud filtering method on both geometry and color fields. Moreover, to alleviate the huge burden of obtaining semantic labels, we propose a color label generation method. Through the color label generation, each point will obtain a color label. The details will be discussed as follows.

Point Cloud Filtering. The noise comes from two aspects, one is from the geometry aspect, another is from the color aspect. On the one hand, the geometry noise primarily results from complicated background environment. Some objects may be scanned incompletely. Thus the geometry features usually contain redundant information. On the other hand, the color noise results from illumination condition. Thus the color features have more possibility to be extracted incorrectly.

The big challenge of filtering point cloud is to strike a balance between denoising and maintaining the geometry information. To our prior knowledge, the geometry noise is caused by a small part of outliers. Therefore, we remove the geometry outliers directly. However, if we simply remove the color outliers, the geometry information might not be maintained. Therefore, we propose to smooth the color outliers according to their neighbors.

In the beginning, the KDTree [16] is generated according to the point cloud, and the topological relationship of each point is established.

To handle the geometry noise, we use a Radius Outlier Filter to remove the outliers in point cloud scenes. Firstly, we define a radius r. Then for each point p_i, we search the neighbors of p_i in a circle with radius r based on established KDTree. Lastly, as Fig. 2 shows, if the neighbors' number of p_i is less than a threshold d_T, p_i is considered as an outlier and removed from the point cloud scene.

To handle the color noise, we use Neighbor Weighted Filter to smooth the color of outliers. For each point p_i, firstly, we find k neighbors of p_i denoted as

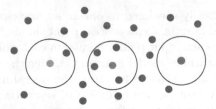

Fig. 2. The example of the Radius Outlier Filter. If the threshold d_T is set to 1, the red point will be regarded as an outlier. If d_T is set to 2, both the red point and orange point will be regarded as outliers. (Color figure online)

$neigh(p_i, k) = \{p_j\}$. Secondly, we use the colors of k neighbors of p_i to decide the new color of p_i based on Eq. (1) and Eq. (2).

$$c_i = \frac{1}{k} \sum_{j=1}^{k} \omega_j c_j \tag{1}$$

$$\omega_j = \frac{e^{-d(p_i, p_j)}}{\sum_{j=1}^{k} e^{-d(p_i, p_j)}} \tag{2}$$

where $d(p_i, p_j)$ represents the distance from neighbor p_j to p_i. ω_j is the weight of p_j to p_i. Equation (2) shows that the more closer the neighbor p_j is, the more influence on p_i the neighbor p_j have.

Color Label Generation. In order to generate color labels for each point, we need to statistically obtain a histogram about the color distribution of point clouds. Firstly We convert RGB channels into a gray channel. The RGB color is formed by proportionally mixing the three primary colors R (red), G (green) and B (blue). Gray value point uses black with different saturation to represent each image point. For example, 8-bit numbers which represent 0–255 are used to represent the "gray" degree. Each point only needs a grayscale value. The conversion of RGB value and gray level is actually the conversion of human eyes' perception of color and brightness. RGB can be converted into gradient according to Eq. (3). Since the distribution of gray value on 0–255 needs to be counted, it needs to be made integer.

$$color = int(\omega_1 R + \omega_2 G + \omega_3 B) \tag{3}$$

where $\omega_1 \sim \omega_3$ are the parameters to mix RGB's value. Note that $\sum_{i=1}^{3} \omega_i = 1$. The color distribution is then obtained according to Algorithm 1. And then the color distribution is divided into K categories. Figure 3 illustrates the division procedure based on salient value ranges. The peaks generally act as the division line. Specifically, if a range contains only a little points, we give them a special color label CL_0 to denote that their categories are uncertain. After that, we traverse each point p_i in the dataset and to see which category range they lay. Finally p_i is given the corresponding color label CL_i.

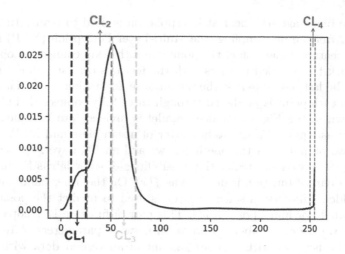

Fig. 3. The example of the color histogram, where there are 4 categories. For those ranges containing less points, we give them a special color label 0 (uncertain label). (Color figure online)

Algorithm 1. Color Histogram Generation

Input:
  the set of point cloud P
Output:
  the color histogram of point cloud H
  initialize H with 256 zcros
  for p in P **do**
    get color code *color* of p using Eq. 3
    $H[color] = H[color] + 1$
  end for
  $H = H/n$
  return H

2.2 Multi-Task Training

The basic framework of our network is shown in Fig. 4. The backbone of our neural network is RandLA-Net [10], since RandLA-Net clearly surpasses state-of-the-art approaches for semantic segmentation.

The native RandLA-Net uses an Encoder-Decoder structure similar to U-net [6], which uses 3D coordinates and attribute features as the input. The corresponding encoder of our network framework contains 5 layers, and the decoder also contains 5 layers. In the encoding stage, each coding layer has an Local Feature Aggregation (LFA) module and random sampling (RS) operation. The LFA module is used to improve the feature dimension of points, and the random sampling is used to reduce the number of points. Only 1/4 points of each coding layer are reserved ($N \rightarrow \frac{N}{4} \rightarrow \frac{N}{16} \rightarrow \frac{N}{64} \rightarrow \frac{N}{256} \rightarrow \frac{N}{512}$), and the feature dimension of each point is increasing ($8 \rightarrow 32 \rightarrow 128 \rightarrow 256 \rightarrow 512 \rightarrow 1024$).

In the decoding stage, the nearest interpolation is used to realize the point up sampling. After the up sampling, the Multi-Layer Perception (MLP) is used to reduce the feature dimension of the points, and the skip connection operation is used to stack the decoded features with the features corresponding to the coding stage, the last native part is the semantic segmentation stage. The semantic category of each point is predicted through three fully-connected (FC) layers.

As shown in the Fig. 4, our deep model is divided into two parts. Taking point cloud as input x, after the last layer of upsampling and MLP, the model contains two outputs. On the one hand, we add an FC Layer. Subsequently, a softmax layer is used to predict the possibilities of color labels for input point cloud. This part of function is denoted as $f(x)$. On the other hand, another FC layer is added. Similarly a softmax layer is used to predict the possibilities of semantic labels for input point cloud. This part of function is denoted as $g(x)$.

Firstly, we use color labels to pre-train network parameters. After that, we fine-tune the network with a small amount of annotated data with semantic labels. Following we will introduce multi-task training in detail.

Train with Color Labels. In order to boost the performance of semantic labeling, we propose to use color labels to pretrain the neural network. According to a related research [20], more similar two tasks are, more beneficial in multi-task learning, and vice versa. Color label prediction is a similar task as semantic label prediction. This is because to some extent, the color distribution can represent the basic feature of categories. For instance, the color of grass is green. In addition, both color and semantic label predictions are the tasks of classification. Therefore, the color label prediction is highly related to semantic label prediction.

In Sect. 2.1, we obtain a large amount of data with color labels. Since every point is assigned a color label, we can firstly train the $f(x)$ part to predict the color labels. In the pretraining stage, the parameters are shared with semantic label prediction task. It is crucial to the work of the training phase. Specifically, the input is the 3D coordinates of the point cloud, and the output is the predicted color label. Through pre-training, the neural network have a better understanding on the common features hidden in data, that is, learn the approximate shapes and colors of each object. We also introduce some penalties to regulate the learning process of predicting color labels. The loss function ℓ_{CE1} is

$$\ell_{CE1} = -\frac{1}{N} \sum_i \sum_{c=1}^{K} CL_i^c \log f(p_i) \tag{4}$$

where K represents the category of color labels. Particularly, for the uncertain color label, loss value is not covered and backpropagated.

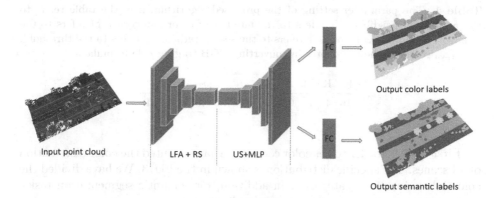

Fig. 4. The proposed framework. FC: Fully Connected layer, LFA: Local Feature Aggregation, RS: Random Sampling, MLP: shared Multi-Layer Perceptron.

Train with Semantic Labels. The pretraining stage not only alleviates our requirements for the number of data with semantic labels to a certain extent, but also makes the model have better generalization ability.

In the formal training stage, we only need to fine-tune, that is, use data with a small amount of semantic labels to adjust the parameters of the pre-trained neural network. The loss function is defined as:

$$\ell_{CE2} = -\frac{1}{N} \sum_i \sum_{c=1}^{M} y_i^c \log g(p_i) \tag{5}$$

where M represents the category of semantic labels. y_{ic} is the true semantic label.

3 Experiment

The dataset used in our experiment was collected by the RIEGL VMX450 mobile LiDAR system on Xiamen Island, China. There are 16 scenes illustrating complex outdoor traffic scenarios in the dataset totally. The number of points in most scene varies from 5 million to 15 million, depending on the traffic scenarios size. All points are provided with both 3D coordinates and color information. We take 8 scenes as the training set. In the remaining 10 scenes, two of them are the validation set and the rest are the test set. In the experiment, we only use 10% of the annotation data.

According to the number of input points in different datasets (about 5 million to 15 million), we train 100 epochs on a single NVIDIA Tesla V100-DGXS GPU with a batch size of 4. The learning rate of pre-training and training start from 0.01 and decays with a rate of 0.05 after every epoch. For the proposed algorithm, the parameter settings are shown in the Table 1. For native RandLA-Net architechture, we set the layer number to be 5, the input points to be 6553, the knn to be 16.

Table 1. The parameter setting of the proposed algorithm. k in the table refers to the number of neighbors. K refers to the number of color categories. M refers to the number of semantic categories. r refers to the search radius. d_T refers to the threshold. $\omega_1, \omega_2, \omega_3$ refers to the parameter in converting RGB to grayscale formula.

k	K	M	r	d_T	ω_1	ω_2	ω_3
16	4	7	0.1	10	0.299	0.587	0.114

First of all, in order to get color coding, we have counted the color distribution of all scenes. The specific distribution is shown in the Fig. 3. We have divided the color labels into four categories. In addition, for semantic segmentation tasks, we train seven categories of segmentation in the scene.

In order to evaluate the performance of our proposed framework in semantic segmentation in 3D point cloud, we conducted three groups of experiments. Specifically, the first group, we use RandLA-Net for training with full supervision. The second group, we use RandLA-Net for training with only 10% annotation data. The last group, we use our multi-task learning network for training with only 10% annotation data. Figure 5 shows the visual results of the experiments we designed.

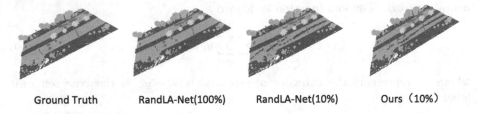

Ground Truth   RandLA-Net(100%)   RandLA-Net(10%)   Ours (10%)

Fig. 5. Example of our semantic segmentation predictions of VMX450.

In addition, we mainly use the mean Intersection-over-Union (mIoU), which is the average IoU of all semantic classes in the entire dataset. Equation (6) is the definition of mIoU. Further, we also provide the overall accuracy (OA) for all points. Equation (7) is the definition of OA. Table 2 quantitatively presents the performance of our network. In general, we performed well regarding to the metrics of average class accuracy (96.04 %) and mIoU (94.41 %). In only 10 % annotation data, it can be seen that our methods are superior to RandLA-Net except grass and road. What's more, IoU of the two categories exceed the fully supervised RandLA-Net, $ie.$, cycas and loght pole.

$$mIoU = \frac{1}{n+1} \sum_{i=0}^{n} \frac{TP}{FN + FP + TP} \tag{6}$$

$$OA = \frac{TP + TN}{TP + FN + FP + TN} \tag{7}$$

Table 2. Semantic segmentation results (%) on VMX450. We compared the IoU of the seven categories in the three experiments.

	OA	mIoU	Road	Grass	Palm tree	Cycas	Brushwood	Loght pole	Vehicle
RandLA-Net	**99.16**	**97.84**	**99.04**	**96.77**	**98.00**	98.04	**96.51**	96.99	**99.55**
RandLA-Net(10%)	96.13	92.25	94.65	85.98	94.45	97.95	89.42	92.61	90.74
Ours(10%)	96.04	94.41	94.23	85.45	96.50	**98.34**	92.50	**97.17**	96.66

4   Conclusion

This paper mainly studies the semantic segmentation of MLS point cloud scene with a small number of annotated data via multi-task learning. Specifically, we have proposed a multi-task learning framework. The two tasks are color label prediction and semantic segmentation. We use point cloud to train the model for color label prediction task, and only a small number of annotated samples are needed for fine-tuning for semantic segmentation task. We verify the significant performance of our network on our VMX450 dataset. To conclude, given a small portion of annotated data, we have provided an effective multi-task learning solution to boost the performance of semantic labeling.

Acknowledgements. This work was supported in part by the National Natural Science Foundation of China under Grant 61801121 and Grant 61972097 and in part by the Natural Science Foundation of Fujian Province, China, under Grant 2019J05034.

References

1. Anand, I., Negi, H., Kumar, D., Mittal, M., Kim, T.h., Roy, S.: Residual u-network for breast tumor segmentation from magnetic resonance images. CMC Comput. Mater. Continua **67**(3), 3107–3127 (2021)
2. Armeni, I., et al.: 3d semantic parsing of large-scale indoor spaces. In: Proceedings of the IEEE Conference on Computer Vision and Pattern Recognition, pp. 1534–1543 (2016)
3. Bischke, B., Helber, P., Folz, J., Borth, D., Dengel, A.: Multi-task learning for segmentation of building footprints with deep neural networks. In: 2019 IEEE International Conference on Image Processing, ICIP, pp. 1480–1484. IEEE (2019)
4. Caruana, R.: Multitask learning. Mach. Learn. **28**(1), 41–75 (1997)
5. Dai, J., He, K., Sun, J.: Instance-aware semantic segmentation via multi-task network cascades. In: Proceedings of the IEEE conference on computer vision and pattern recognition, pp. 3150–3158 (2016)
6. Falk, T., et al.: U-net: deep learning for cell counting, detection, and morphometry. Nat. Methods **16**(1), 67–70 (2019)
7. Fan, H., Yang, Y.: PointRNN: point recurrent neural network for moving point cloud processing (2019). arXiv preprint, arXiv:1910.08287
8. Gankhuyag, U., Han, J.H.: Automatic BIM indoor modelling from unstructured point clouds using a convolutional neural network. Intelli. Autom. Soft Comput. **28**(1), 133–152 (2021)

9. Hou, G., Qin, J., Xiang, X., Tan, Y., Xiong, N.N.: Af-net: a medical image segmentation network based on attention mechanism and feature fusion. CMC-Comput. Mater. Continua **69**(2), 1877–1891 (2021)

10. Hu, Q., et al.: Randla-net: Efficient semantic segmentation of large-scale point clouds. In: Proceedings of the IEEE/CVF Conference on Computer Vision and Pattern Recognition, pp. 11108–11117 (2020)

11. Jaboyedoff, M., et al.: Use of lidar in landslide investigations: a review. Nat. Hazards **61**(1), 5–28 (2012)

12. Lei, H., Akhtar, N., Mian, A.: SegGCN: Efficient 3d point cloud segmentation with fuzzy spherical kernel. In: Proceedings of the IEEE/CVF Conference on Computer Vision and Pattern Recognition, pp. 11611–11620 (2020)

13. Li, G., Muller, M., Thabet, A., Ghanem, B.: DeepGCNS: Can GCNS go as deep as CNNS? In: Proceedings of the IEEE/CVF International Conference on Computer Vision, pp. 9267–9276 (2019)

14. Liu, Y., Fan, B., Xiang, S., Pan, C.: Relation-shape convolutional neural network for point cloud analysis. In: Proceedings of the IEEE/CVF Conference on Computer Vision and Pattern Recognition, pp. 8895–8904 (2019)

15. Mo, K., et al.: Partnet: a large-scale benchmark for fine-grained and hierarchical part-level 3d object understanding. In: Proceedings of the IEEE/CVF Conference on Computer Vision and Pattern Recognition, pp. 909–918 (2019)

16. Moore, A.W.: Effcient memory-based learning for robot control. Technical report, University of Cambridge, Computer Laboratory, New Museums Site, Pembroke Street, Cambridge, CB2 3QG (1990)

17. Naqvi, R.A., Hussain, D., Loh, W.K.: Artificial intelligence-based semantic segmentation of ocular regions for biometrics and healthcare applications (2021)

18. Peng, J., et al.: A multi-task network for cardiac magnetic resonance image segmentation and classification. Intell. Autom. Soft Comput. **30**(1), 259–272 (2021)

19. Qi, C.R., Su, H., Mo, K., Guibas, L.J.: Pointnet: deep learning on point sets for 3d classification and segmentation. In: Proceedings of the IEEE conference on computer vision and pattern recognition, pp. 652–660 (2017)

20. Ruder, S.: An overview of multi-task learning in deep neural networks (2017). arXiv preprint, arXiv:1706.05098

21. Te, G., Hu, W., Zheng, A., Guo, Z.: RGCNN: Regularized graph CNN for point cloud segmentation. In: Proceedings of the 26th ACM international conference on Multimedia, pp. 746–754 (2018)

22. Vandenhende, S., Georgoulis, S., Van Gool, L.: MTI-Net: multi-scale task interaction networks for multi-task learning. In: Vedaldi, A., Bischof, H., Brox, T., Frahm, J.-M. (eds.) ECCV 2020. LNCS, vol. 12349, pp. 527–543. Springer, Cham (2020). https://doi.org/10.1007/978-3-030-58548-8_31

23. Wang, Y., Sun, Y., Liu, Z., Sarma, S.E., Bronstein, M.M., Solomon, J.M.: Dynamic graph CNN for learning on point clouds. ACM Trans. Graphics (tog) **38**(5), 1–12 (2019)

24. Xu, Q., Sun, X., Wu, C.Y., Wang, P., Neumann, U.: Grid-GCN for fast and scalable point cloud learning. In: Proceedings of the IEEE/CVF Conference on Computer Vision and Pattern Recognition, pp. 5661–5670 (2020)

25. Yu, H., et al.: Methods and datasets on semantic segmentation: a review. Neurocomputing **304**, 82–103 (2018)

26. Zhao, J., Liu, C., Zhang, B.: Plstmnet: a new neural network for segmentation of point cloud. In: 2018 11th International Workshop on Human Friendly Robotics, HFR, pp. 42–47. IEEE (2018)

Research on Force Control of Spherical Fruit and Vegetable End-Effector Based on Data-Driven Control Algorithm

Zhenze Liu[1] , Jingquan He[1] , Shoutao Li[1(✉)] , Dikai Dong[1] , Yu Du[2] ,
and Lei Jin[3]

[1] School of Communication Engineering, Jilin University, Changchun 130012, China
list@jlu.edu.cn

[2] Department of Electrical and Computer Engineering, Florida International University,
Miami 33174, USA

[3] Tbea Tianjin Transformers Co., Ltd., Tianjin 300450, China

Abstract. Aiming at the problems of low success rate and large damage in grasping spherical fruits and vegetables, this paper proposed a novel end-effector system based on data-driven control (DDC). According to the actual working conditions, the mechanical structure of the end-effector is designed. The 3D model establishment, kinematics analysis and physical testing of its mechanical structure are completed. Then, using the DDC algorithm, a PID controller and a partial-format dynamic linearization model-free adaptive controller (PFDL-MFAC) are designed to realize the force-tracking control of end-effector system. RecurDyn and Matlab machine-control co-simulation is completed by means of joint modeling and coupling calculation of mechanism and control. It verified the rationality of the mechanical structure and the effectiveness of the control method. The results indicate that the end-effector system designed in this paper can track the desired grasping force well. In terms of end-effector structure and control system design, the problem of non-destructive grasping of spherical fruits and vegetables can be solved.

Keywords: Force control · End-effector · Data-driven

1 Introduction

In the process of robot grasping and handling objects, the end-effector is the part that is in direct contact with the operating object. In order to reduce the damage to the operating object during this process, the design of the end-effector control system has become an important research direction for researchers in this field [1]. In terms of agricultural robots, the complex environment and special circumstances have led to a low success rate of fruit and vegetable grasping and a high damage rate. Non-destructive clamping and grasping have become key technologies in the research of related robots [2–4]. Since the operating object has the characteristics of flexibility, fragility, and fragility, the purpose of force control research on end-effectors is to achieve dexterous and supple

© The Author(s), under exclusive license to Springer Nature Switzerland AG 2022
X. Sun et al. (Eds.): ICAIS 2022, LNCS 13338, pp. 393–404, 2022.
https://doi.org/10.1007/978-3-031-06794-5_32

grasping. This research has significant value not only in agricultural picking, but also in the food processing industry [5]. With robotics, visual recognition algorithms and cutting methods, the end-effector of picking robots has developed rapidly [6–9].

In the field of robotics, force control refers to the control of the output force of the end-effector, or the control of the torque corresponding to the driving joint. In the robot through motion control, the contact force between the end-effector and the operation object is constant or stable within a certain range. Regarding the force control of end-effectors, researchers in this field have carried out a lot of research from mechanical structures and control algorithms [10]. Wang et al. simplified the fruit and vegetable gripping system of the end-effector for fruit and vegetable grasping into an impedance-admittance model, and proposed a grasping force tracking impedance control algorithm for the two-finger end-effector [11]. The designed impedance controller can reduce the damage of fruit and vegetable grasping. Hu et al. found that when the force of the end-effector is loaded, the position control system will affect the force control system, and use the error compensation link to solve the problem of precise control of the grasping force, which has an enlightening effect on the force control of the end-effector [12]. Zuo et al. developed a robot end-effector and proposed an inverse control method based on the Preisach operator, and the active disturbance rejection controller improved the control performance of the rigid end-effector's holding force [13]. The two-fingered flexible manipulator force feedback control system designed by Becedas et al. is applied to the end-effector of a six-degree-of-freedom manipulator to achieve a compliant grasp of fragile objects. The generalized proportional-integral controller improves the force control accuracy of the end-effector [14]. The above researches all need to establish an accurate mathematical model for the end-effector control system. However, the mathematical theoretical analysis and system identification process are complicated and the accuracy of the mathematical model cannot be guaranteed. The traditional force feedback control strategy only pursues the force control accuracy and ignores other dynamic parameters that are not modeled. If the structurally complex end-effector is accurately modeled, the more complex controller designed can affect the stability and robustness of the system.

Model-free adaptive control (MFAC) algorithm is a typical DDC algorithm. Through the design and analysis of the input and output data of the controlled system, the MFAC can realize the parameter self-tuning and structural adaptive control of the unknown nonlinear controlled system [15, 16]. Because this algorithm is robust, does not require any model information, and has a good control effect on nonlinear systems, it is widely used in robots, vehicles and other fields [17, 18].

In this paper, a non-destructive grasping end-effector control system based on DDC is proposed. In terms of the mechanical structure of the end-effector and the design of the control system, the problem of non-destructive grasping of spherical fruits and vegetables is solved. In the first section of this paper, a two-finger arc end-effector with a four-bar linkage mechanism is designed, and a 3D model of the mechanical structure is established. The rationality of the mechanism is verified by kinematic analysis, and the effect of the built end-effector is consistent with the theoretical analysis. In the second section, the algorithm based on DDC is used to realize the force control of the end-effector system, and the typical PID and PFDL-MFAC controllers are designed. The third section mainly uses RecurDyn multi-body system simulation software and Matlab mathematical analysis software to simulate and verify the end-effector system designed in this paper. The results of the joint modeling and coupling calculation of the mechanism and control indicate that the mechanical structure of the end-effector is reasonable and the control algorithm is effective. Finally, the main conclusions of this paper and future research work are given.

2 End-Effector System Design

2.1 Mechanical Design

The robot end-effector is the final actuator of the grasping action. It is connected and fixed by the preset mechanical interface at the end of the manipulator. The rational design of the mechanical structure of the end-effector is very important to achieve the goal of non-destructive grasping.

Considering that the skin of spherical fruits and vegetables is vulnerable, the fingers of the end-effector have a certain enveloping function, which increases the contact area and reduces the contact pressure. Therefore, the curved finger is selected to increase the contact area and reduce grabbing damage [19]. At the same time, a concave-convex texture imitating human fingerprints is designed on the curved surface of the end-effector finger, which can prevent spherical fruits and vegetables from slipping off when they are clamped or transported. The two-knuckle structure is sufficient for grabbing spherical fruits and vegetables, and the control difficulty is small, and the R&D and production costs are low. Therefore, the mechanical structure of the end-effector is shown in Fig. 1, and the mechanical model of the end-effector is established by using the software Solid-Works. The end-effector mechanism includes a transmission mechanism 1, a drive motor 2, a curved surface gripper 3, a parallel four-bar linkage machine 4, a base 5, a connection interface 6 and a force sensor 7.

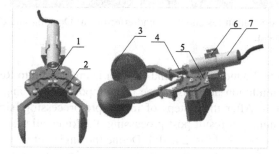

Fig. 1. Structure diagram of the end-effector.

2.2 Kinematics Analysis

The content of the kinematic analysis research of the mechanical structure of the end-effector mainly includes position analysis, velocity analysis and acceleration analysis

[16, 20]. It can determine the motion range and stroke of the two curved fingers of the designed end-effector, and define the motion trajectory of the center of the two curved fingers at key points. From the dynamic analysis point of view, the end-effector system contains a four-bar linkage, which can be simplified as a nonlinear system [21]. In the process of adding end-effector grasping, there are factors such as viscoelasticity of materials, gaps of structures, deformation of rods, etc. These are the complex links that are neglected in mathematical modeling. Therefore, the input and output of the end-effector system designed in this paper have a relatively complex nonlinear relationship.

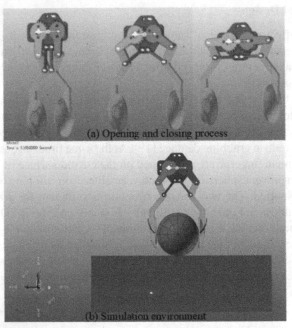

Fig. 2. Kinematics simulation results of the end-effector. (a) Opening and closing process; (b) Simulation environment.

In this paper, the 3D model of the end-effector is imported into RecurDyn software to complete the simulation analysis of the driving point angle, angular velocity and angular acceleration. After three steps of model pre-processing, simulation analysis calculation and simulation result post-processing, the kinematics simulation result of the end-effector is shown in Figs. 2 and 3. Define the angle between the drive rod and the vertical as the end-effector movement angle α, Fig. 2 (a) is the motion state of $\alpha = 0°$, $\alpha = 45°$, $\alpha = 90°$. Figure 2(b) is the simulation environment built by the end-effector. The arc represents the movement trajectory of the two curved finger centers of the key points. The connection point between the steering gear and the actuator in the end-effector system is defined as the driving point, and the angle, angular velocity and angular acceleration of the driving point change with time, as shown in Fig. 3. It can be seen from the kinematics simulation results that the position of the rods of the end-effector mechanism designed in this paper is reasonable, there is no interference between the rods, and the movement trajectory of the key points is consistent with the expectation.

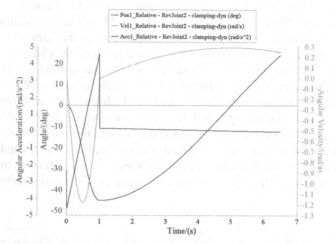

Fig. 3. Driving point angle, angular velocity and angular acceleration.

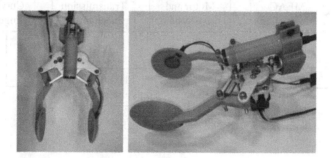

Fig. 4. Physical picture of the end-effector.

2.3 End-Effector

According to the simulated mechanical structure model, a real end-effector with the same scale size was produced. The curved fingers are produced by 3D printing technology, with good results [22]. The size of the arc surface is 47.60 mm in diameter, 2.98 mm in depth, and 2.00 mm in concave-convex texture, as shown in Fig. 4. The hardware test is carried out for the mechanical structure of the end-effector proposed in this paper. The results show that the designed mechanism of the end-effector is compact. It can perform normal opening and closing motions. The end-effector did not appear stuck, which is consistent with the results of kinematics simulation analysis.

3   Based on Data-Driven Control

The adjustment of the grasping force is very important to not damage the spherical fruits and vegetables. After the above analysis, this paper adopts the grasping force control strategy of the end-effector system based on the MFAC control algorithm, as shown in Fig. 5. The end-effector judges the target position through the infrared photoelectric sensor. When the distance is less than the reference position, the end-effector starts to grip spherical fruits and vegetables. The deviation e between the expected force f_d and the actual contact force f is used as the input of the MFAC controller. When the curved surface gripper contacts the spherical fruits and vegetables, the contact force is fed back to the control in real time through the flexible pressure sensor. The control algorithm is embedded in the microcontroller. The output electrical signal controls the motor through the drive system. The motor realizes the actual contact force between the cambered finger and the spherical fruit and vegetable through the transmission mechanism to control the desired tracking force. Thus, the grasping force control of the end-effector system is realized.

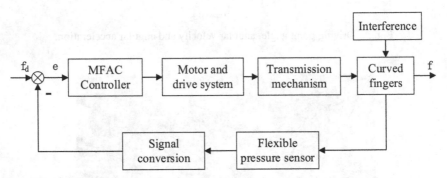

Fig. 5. Force tracking control based on data-driven algorithm.

3.1   Dynamic Linearization

This paper uses MFAC based on the PFDL data model to solve the end-effector system control problem. Since the end-effector system is a SISO nonlinear system, for ease of reading, the general form of single input single output (SISO) nonlinear system PFDL is given below. Consider the following nonlinear system with SISO, as shown in Eq. (1):

$$y(k+1) = f(y(k), ..., y(k - n_y), u(k), ..., u(k - n_u)) \qquad (1)$$

Among them, $u(k) \in R$ and $y(k) \in R$ are the control input contact force and output rotation angle of the system at the time step k respectively. n_y and n_u are both positive integers, and $f(...) : R^{n_u + n_y + 2} \mapsto R$ is a non-linear function.

In the proposed end-effector system, the input of the end-effector system proposed in this paper is the rotation angle of the end-effector drive motor, and the output is the contact force between the grasping object and the end-effector.

Define $U_L(k) \in R^L$ as a vector composed of all control input signals in the sliding time window $[k - L + 1, k]$, as shown in Eq. (2):

$$U_L(k) = [u(k), ..., u(k - L + 1)]^T \tag{2}$$

And when it is $k \geq 0$, there are $U_L(k) = 0^L$, the integer is the control input Linearization length constant; it is a zero vector with a dimension of 0^L.

In order to establish the PFDL data model and use the MFAC strategy, this article puts forward the following assumptions:

Assumption 1: $f(...)$ has continuous partial derivatives with respect to the $(n_y + 2)$ to $(n_y + L + 1)$ variables.

Assumption 2: The system meets the generalized Lipschitz condition, that is, for any $k_1 \neq k_2, k_1, k_2 > 0$ and $U_L(k_1) \neq U_L(k_2)$, there is

$$y(k_i + 1) = f(y(k_i), \ldots, y(k_i - n_y), u(k_i), \ldots, u(k_i - n_u))$$
$$|y(k_1 + 1) - y(k_2 + 1)| \leq b\|U_L(k_1) - U_L(k_2)\| \tag{3}$$

where: $i = 1, 2, b$ is a constant.

Note 1: From a practical point of view, the above assumptions for end-effector systems and other controlled systems are reasonable. This is a typical assumption for nonlinear systems. Assumption 2 is a physical constraint of the end-effector control system. The limited variation of the rotation angle of the end-effector driving motor cannot cause infinite variation of the contact force between the grasped object and the end-effector. From a physical point of view, this is reasonable for real systems.

Theorem 1: Consider a nonlinear system (1) that satisfies Assumptions 1 and 2, given L, when $\|\Delta U_L(k)\| \neq 0$, there must be a time-varying parameter vector $\mathbf{\Phi}_{P,L}(k) \in R^L$, called Pseudo Gradient (PG), in this way, the system (1) can be transformed into a PFDL data model, as shown in Eq. (4):

$$\Delta y(k + 1) = \mathbf{\Phi}_{P,L}^T(k)\Delta U_L(k) \tag{4}$$

Among them $\Delta y(k + 1) = y(k + 1) - y(k)$, $\Delta U_L(k) = U_L(k) - U_L(k - 1)$ and for any time k, $\mathbf{\Phi}_{P,L}(k) = [\mathbf{\Phi}_1(k), ..., \mathbf{\Phi}_1(k)]^T$ is bounded [23].

3.2 PFDL-MFAC Controller

After the end-effector system is dynamically linearized, the PFDL-MFAC control strategy can be designed. Suppose the estimation criterion function of PG is Eq. (5):

$$J(\mathbf{\Phi}_{P,L}(k)) = \left|y(k) - y(k - 1) - \mathbf{\Phi}_{P,L}^T(k)\Delta U_L(k - 1)\right|^2$$
$$+ \mu \left\|\mathbf{\Phi}_{P,L}(k) - \hat{\mathbf{\Phi}}_{P,L}(k - 1)\right\|^2 \tag{5}$$

Among them, is the $\mu > 0$ weight factor, which can punish the excessive change of PG estimation; $\hat{\mathbf{\Phi}}_{P,L}(k)$ is the estimated value of unknown $\mathbf{\Phi}_{P,L}(k)$.

PG uses the matrix inversion theorem to get, as shown in Eq. (6):

$$\hat{\mathbf{\Phi}}_{P,L}(k) = \hat{\mathbf{\Phi}}_{P,L}(k - 1) + \frac{\eta \Delta U_L(k - 1)(y(k) - y(k - 1))}{\mu + \|\Delta U_L(k - 1)\|^2}$$

$$-\frac{\eta \Delta U_L(k-1)(\hat{\boldsymbol{\Phi}}_{P,L}^T(k-1)\Delta U_L(k-1))}{\mu + \|\Delta U_L(k-1)\|^2} \tag{6}$$

$$\hat{\boldsymbol{\Phi}}_{P,L}(k) = \hat{\boldsymbol{\Phi}}_{P,L}(1), \text{ If } \left\|\hat{\boldsymbol{\Phi}}_{P,L}(k)\right\| \leq \varepsilon \text{ or } \|\Delta U_L(K-1)\| \leq \varepsilon \text{ or }$$

$$sign(\Phi_1(k)) \neq sign(\Phi_1(1)) \tag{7}$$

Among them, $\eta \in (0, 2)$; ε is a small positive number; $\hat{\boldsymbol{\Phi}}_{P,L}(1)$ is the initial value of $\hat{\boldsymbol{\Phi}}_{P,L}(k)$. Equation (7) is the added reset algorithm to enhance the ability of the PG estimation algorithm to track time-varying parameters.

In order to estimate the control input of the motor rotation angle, the following criterion function on the control input is listed, as shown in Eq. (8):

$$J(u(k)) = \left|y^*(k+1) - y(k+1)\right|^2 + \lambda|u(k) - u(k-1)|^2 \tag{8}$$

$y^*(k+1) \in R$ outputs the expected value of the contact force between the grasped object and the end-effector, and $\lambda > 0$ is a weighting factor that controls the input change and is a positive coefficient.

Then $u(k)$ can be obtained as shown in Eq. (9):

$$u(k) = u(k-1) + \frac{\rho_1 \hat{\boldsymbol{\Phi}}_1(k)(y^*(k+1) - y(k))}{\lambda + \left|\hat{\boldsymbol{\Phi}}_1(k)\right|^2} - \frac{\hat{\boldsymbol{\Phi}}_1(k)\sum\limits_{i=2}^{L}\rho_i\hat{\boldsymbol{\Phi}}_i(k)\Delta u(k-i+1)}{\lambda + \left|\hat{\boldsymbol{\Phi}}_1(k)\right|^2} \tag{9}$$

Among them $\rho_i \in (0, 1]$, $i = 1, 2, ..., L$.

4   Co-simulation Verification

In this section, the machine-control co-simulation experiment will be carried out by RecurDyn and Matlab software. Through the RecurDyn/Control function interface, it can interact with Simulink data, which realizes the combination of the end-effector mechanical system and the control system [24]. The purpose is to achieve common modeling and coupling calculations to verify the rationality of the mechanical structure of the end-effector system and the effectiveness of the control method. The typical PID control and PFDL-MFAC control are used for the end-effector system respectively, and the co-simulation model is shown in Fig. 6.

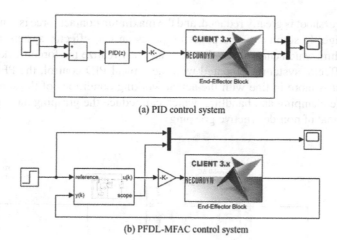

(a) PID control system

(b) PFDL-MFAC control system

Fig. 6. Co-simulation model. (a) PID control system; (b) PFDL-MFAC control system.

Table 1. Controller initial parameters.

Working condition	Controller	Parameter		
7N	PID	$K_p = 0.0002$	$K_i = 0.032$	$K_d = 0$
	PFDL-MFAC	$\hat{\boldsymbol{\Phi}}_{P,L}(0) = [0.1, 0, 0]^T$	$\rho = 0.15$	$\lambda = 40$
		$\eta = 0.5$	$\mu = 1$	$L = 3$
4N	PID	$K_p = 0.00024$	$K_i = 0.042$	$K_d = 0$
	PFDL-MFAC	$\hat{\boldsymbol{\Phi}}_{P,L}(0) = [0.08, 0, 0]^T$	$\rho = 0.1$	$\lambda = 15$
		$\eta = 0.5$	$\mu = 1$	$L = 3$

In co-simulation experiments, for two working conditions with expected pressure values of 7N and 4N, the parameter settings of the typical PID controller and the PFDL-MFAC controller are shown in Table 1. After setting the parameters of the model, the co-simulation is carried out, and the co-simulation results can be obtained as shown in Fig. 7.

The results show that both the typical PID control and the PFDL-MFAC control can realize the force tracking control of the end-effector system, and the steady-state performance of is good. When the expected value is 7N, the adjustment time of the PFDL-MFAC control system is 2.06 s, and the maximum overshoot is 16.4%; the adjustment time of the typical PID control system is 2.37 s, and the maximum overshoot is 30.4%. When the expected value is 4N, the adjustment time of the PFDL-MFAC control system is 2.29 s, and the maximum overshoot is 11.3%; the adjustment time of the typical PID control system is 2.78 s, and the maximum overshoot is 45.8%. Therefore, PFDL-MFAC control system is superior to typical PID control in dynamic response characteristics such as rapidity and overshoot. In addition, after many simulation experiments and analysis, selecting the appropriate value, the PFDL-MFAC control time cost is greater, but the maximum overshoot is greatly reduced, and the maximum contact force is limited within the error range. In summary, this paper proposes an end-effector system based on a DDC algorithm, which can effectively and accurately realize the force-tracking control of the end-effector system. Compared with the typical PID control, the PFDL-MFAC control effect is more in line with the actual working conditions of the spherical fruit and vegetable clamping and handling, which can reduce the grasping damage rate and achieve the goal of non-destructive grasping.

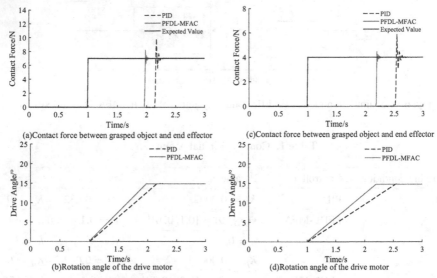

Fig. 7. Simulation results with expected pressure values of 7N and 4N. Expected force 7N: (a) Contact force between grasped object and end effector; (b) Rotation angle of the drive motor;Expected force 4N: (c) Contact force between grasped object and end effector; (d) Rotation angle of the drive motor.

5 Conclusion

In this paper, an end-effector system based on DDC is proposed for the problem of non-destructive grasping of spherical fruits and vegetables. The advantage of this system is that it only needs the input data of the drive motor rotation angle and the output data of the contact force deviation, and does not require any information from the end-effector. The machine-control co-simulation was carried out on RecurDyn and Matlab platforms. The comparative analysis of the simulation results shows that the mechanical structure of the system is reasonable and the control method is effective. When the end-effector system is used to grasp spherical fruits and vegetables, the force tracking control effect of the PFDL-MFAC control algorithm is better than that of the PID control algorithm. In terms of the mechanical structure of the end-effector and the design of the control system, this solution meets the requirements of actual working conditions, and can reduce the damage of the end-effector to fruits and vegetables during the clamping process. In the future, this paper will build an experimental platform for the end-effector system based on the above work. The purpose is to further verify and study the optimization of the proposed data-driven end-effector force control strategy.

References

1. Reinhart, G., Ehinger, C.: Novel robot-based end-effector design for an automated preforming of limb carbon fiber textiles. In: Schuh, G., Neugebauer, R., Uhlmann, E. (eds.) Future Trends in Production Engineering, pp. 131–142. Springer, Heidelberg (2013). https://doi.org/10.1007/978-3-642-24491-9_14
2. Blanes, C., Mellado, M., Ortiz, C., Valera, A.: Technologies for robot grippers in pick and place operations for fresh fruits and vegetables. Span. J. Agric. Res. 9(4), 1130–1141 (2011). https://doi.org/10.5424/sjar/20110904-501-10
3. Li, Q., Hu, T., Wu, C., Hu, X., Ying, Y.: Review of end-effectors in fruit and vegetable harvesting robot. Trans. Chin. Soc. Agric. Mach. 39(3), 175–179 (2008)
4. Wei, J., Dawei, L., Junle, L., Jun, Y., Dean, Z.: Compliance grasp force control for end-effector of fruit-vegetable picking robot. Trans. Chin. Soc. Agric. Eng. 30(9), 19–26 (2014). https://doi.org/10.3969/j.issn.1002-6819.2014.09.003
5. Ilievski, F., Mazzeo, A.D., Shepherd, R.F., Chen, X., Whitesides, G.M.: Soft robotics for chemists. Angew. Chem. 123(8), 1930–1935 (2011). https://doi.org/10.1002/anie.201006464
6. Chien, T.H., Siao, C.Y., Chang, R.G.: A general technique for real-time robotic simulation in manufacturing system. Intell. Autom. Soft Comput. 29(3), 827–838 (2021). https://doi.org/10.32604/iasc.2021.018256
7. El-Shafai, W., Ali, A.M., et al.: Automated Covid-19 detection based on single-image super-resolution and CNN models. Comput. Mater. Contin. 70(1), 1141–1157 (2021). https://doi.org/10.32604/cmc.2022.018547
8. Fang, W., Zhang, F., Sheng, V.S., Ding, Y.: A method for improving CNN-based image recognition using DCGAN. Comput. Mater. Contin. 57(1), 167–178 (2018). https://doi.org/10.32604/cmc.2018.02356
9. Farkh, R., Al Jaloud, K., Alhuwaimel, S., Quasim, M.T., Ksouri, M.A.: Deep learning approach for the mobile-robot motion control system. Intell. Autom. Soft Comput. 29(2), 423–435 (2021). https://doi.org/10.32604/iasc.2021.016219
10. Gijbels, A., Reynaerts, D., Vander Poorten, E.B.: Design of 4-DOF parallelogram-based RCM mechanisms with a translational DOF implemented distal from the end-effector. In: Ceccarelli, M., Glazunov, V.A. (eds.) Advances on Theory and Practice of Robots and Manipulators. MMS, vol. 22, pp. 103–111. Springer, Cham (2014). https://doi.org/10.1007/978-3-319-07058-2_12
11. Wang, X., Xiao, Y., Bi, S., Fan, X., Rao, H.: Design of test platform for robot flexible grasping and grasping force tracking impedance control. Trans. Chin. Soc. Agric. Eng. 31(1), 58–63 (2015). https://doi.org/10.3969/j.issn.1002-6819.2015.01.009
12. Hu, Z., Zhang, X., Zhang, W., Wang, L.: Precise control of clamping force for watermelon picking end-effector. Trans. Chin. Soc. Agric. Eng. 30(17), 43–49 (2014). https://doi.org/10.3969/j.issn.1002-6819.2014.17.006
13. Zuo, W., Song, G., Chen, Z.: Grasping force control of robotic gripper with high stiffness. Trans. Chin. Soc. Agric. Eng. 30(17), 46–49 (2021). https://doi.org/10.1109/TMECH.2021.3081377
14. Becedas, J., Payo, I., Feliu, V.: Two-flexible-fingers gripper force feedback control system for its application as end-effector on a 6-DOF manipulator. IEEE Trans. Rob. 27(3), 599–615 (2011). https://doi.org/10.1109/TRO.2011.2132850

15. Hou, Z., Chi, R., Gao, H.: An overview of dynamic-linearization-based data-driven control and applications. IEEE Trans. Industr. Electron. **64**(5), 4076–4090 (2016). https://doi.org/10.1109/TIE.2016.2636126

16. Hou, Z., Jin, S.: A novel data-driven control approach for a class of discrete-time nonlinear systems. IEEE Trans. Control Syst. Technol. **19**(6), 1549–1558 (2010). https://doi.org/10.1109/TCST.2010.2093136

17. Roman, R.-C., Radac, M.-B., Precup, R.-E., Petriu, E.M.: Virtual reference feedback tuning of MIMO data-driven model-free adaptive control algorithms. In: Camarinha-Matos, L.M., Falcão, A.J., Vafaei, N., Najdi, S. (eds.) DoCEIS 2016. IAICT, vol. 470, pp. 253–260. Springer, Cham (2016). https://doi.org/10.1007/978-3-319-31165-4_25

18. Pezeshki, S., Badamchizadeh, M.A., Ghiasi, A.R., Ghaemi, S.: Control of overhead crane system using adaptive model-free and adaptive fuzzy sliding mode controllers. J. Control Autom. Electr. Syst. **26**(1), 1–15 (2014). https://doi.org/10.1007/s40313-014-0152-4

19. Li, Z., Miao, F., Yang, Z., Chai, P., Yang, S.: Factors affecting human hand grasp type in tomato fruit-picking: a statistical investigation for ergonomic development of harvesting robot. Comput. Electron. Agric. **157**, 90–97 (2019). https://doi.org/10.1016/j.compag.2018.12.047

20. Kim, J.P., Ryu, J.: Inverse kinematic and dynamic analyses of 6-DOF P US type parallel manipulators. KSME Int. J. **16**(1), 13–23 (2002). https://doi.org/10.1007/BF03185151

21. Guo, P.F., Yan, S.Z.: Monte Carlo simulation of motion errors for four-bar linkages with clearances. Tsinghua Univ. Sci. Tech. **47**(11), 1989–1993 (2007)

22. Kang, J., Chen, X., Hu, C., Yang, C.: A small simulated logistics transfer robot car structure design. J. New Media **3**(3), 81 (2021). https://doi.org/10.32604/jnm.2021.017368

23. Cao, R.M., Hou, Z.S.: Simulation study on model-free control method in linear motor control system. J. Syst. Simul. **18**(10), 2874–2878 (2006)

24. Baranov, A.S., Poddubnyi, V.I., Pavlyuk, A.S.: Mechatronic model of tracked vehicle for controlled motion simulation. In: Radionov, A.A., Gasiyarov, V.R. (eds.) RusAutoCon 2020. LNEE, vol. 729, pp. 275–283. Springer, Cham (2021). https://doi.org/10.1007/978-3-030-71119-1_28

Research on ECG Signal Classification Based on Data Enhancement of Generative Adversarial Network

Jian Liu[1(✉)], Xiaodong Xia[1], Xiang Peng[1], Jiao Hui[2], and Chunyang Han[3]

[1] School of Computer and Communication Engineering, University of Science and Technology Beijing, Beijing 100083, China
liujian@ustb.edu.cn

[2] Anti Chemical Command and Engineering Institute of the Chinese People's Liberation Army, Beijing 102205, China

[3] Beijing Satellite Navigation Center, Beijing 100093, China

Abstract. Cardiovascular disease is one of the important diseases endangering human health. Arrhythmia is an important symptom of cardiovascular disease, and ECG is the main diagnostic basis of arrhythmia. At present, in the algorithm research of ECG classification and recognition, due to the small number of samples collected from abnormal signals, the characteristics of abnormal ECG signals can not be well learned, resulting in the low recognition accuracy. This paper proposes an improved Generative Adversarial Network model to enhance the data of a few categories of ECG signals, and then constructs Resnet-seq2seq classification model for classification and recognition. The Generative Adversarial Network uses the game between generator and discriminator to learn the characteristics of a small number of samples. When the Nash equilibrium is reached, the generator automatically generate ECG samples with high similarity to the original data. Resnet network structure learns the features of the ECG signal after data enhancement, and then sends the feature vectors into the seq2seq model for classification and recognition. This paper uses the pattern between patients to divide the data set, and takes the data set after data enhancement as the training set. The results show that the data enhancement based on GAN can effectively improve the classification effect of ECG signals, and the overall classification accuracy is 98.09%, especially in S and F categories.

Keywords: Generative adversarial networks · Convolutional neural network · ECG · Feature learning

1 Introduction

With the development of society and the improvement of people's living standards, cardiovascular disease has become one of the important diseases that endanger people's health. According to the '2021 World Health Statistics Report' released by the World Health Organization [1], cardiovascular disease has become one of the main killers of human beings. Most cardiovascular diseases are often accompanied by arrhythmia,

© The Author(s), under exclusive license to Springer Nature Switzerland AG 2022
X. Sun et al. (Eds.): ICAIS 2022, LNCS 13338, pp. 405–419, 2022.
https://doi.org/10.1007/978-3-031-06794-5_33

including ventricular premature beats, tachycardia, atrial fibrillation, and ECG is one of the main diagnostic methods for detecting arrhythmia [2]. ECG recorded the change of cardiac potential generated by cardiac activity cycle, and had intuitive regularity.

Traditional ECG diagnosis relies mainly on doctors' experience in ECG recognition, which is often time-consuming and laborious. In order to solve this problem, people began to apply machine learning related technologies to the automatic identification and classification of ECG signals. At present, a large number of machine learning algorithms based on Feature Engineering have achieved satisfactory results. Such as Support Vector Machine (SVM), Random Forest (RF), Naive Bayes, Artificial Neural Network and other machine learning classification algorithms [3–6], they classify abnormal ECG signals by extracting the frequency domain features, time domain features, RR interval, wavelet decomposition, high-order statistics (HOS) and other feature information of ECG signals [7]. R. Th et al. [8] used discrete wavelet transform to extract wavelet coefficient features, took the features of each ECG signal as the input of SVM classifier, and achieved 98.67% accuracy in MIT-BIH database test. S. Bhattacharyya et al. [9] used the time series feature extraction library (TSFEL) for feature extraction, the SMOTE method is used for data enhancement, combined RF and SVM, and used weighted majority algorithm (WMA) to classify heartbeat signals to improve the classification effect. F. Bouaziz et al. [10] used the discrete wavelet transform to segment the ECG signal, and realized an automatic ECG classification algorithm based on K-nearest neighbor algorithm (KNN), which achieved 98.71% classification accuracy in the ECG data of MIT-BIH database. Oliveira et al. [11] proposed a method based on Dynamic Bayesian Network (DBN), which can adjust the certainty of beat classification through threshold. On MIT-BIH data set, the Dynamic Bayesian Network with threshold of 0.75 is used to achieve 99% sensitivity and specificity for PVC beat classification. Although ECG signal detection based on machine learning algorithm has achieved very good results, this method requires manual extraction of a large number of feature information, which may lead to information loss. Therefore, these defects limit the overall performance of traditional machine learning algorithms in ECG signals.

With the development of artificial intelligence, deep learning algorithm has made significant breakthroughs, especially convolution neural network has been widely used in medical signal detection. Guo L et al. [12] designed a fusion model architecture of dense connected convolutional neural network (Densenet) and gated recurrent unit (GRU) network to solve the ECG classification between patients. Without complex data preprocessing and feature engineering, the classification performance of supraventricular (SVEB) and ventricular (VEB) abnormal beats is significantly improved. J. Niu et al. [13] used multi-perspective convolutional neural network (MPCNN) to symbolize ECG signals, and realized automatic extraction and classification of ECG signal features, with an overall accuracy of 96.4%. For most of the samples collected from various types of ECG signals, there is a distribution imbalance in the proportion of the number of heart rhythm samples, which makes the detection of abnormal signals often fail to meet the clinical requirements. The imbalance of samples leads to the decrease of the final classification accuracy.

In order to solve the problem of data imbalance, many researchers have proposed different data enhancement methods to overcome this problem. Most of the expansion of

ECG signal data is based on traditional sample sampling techniques, such as: Random over-sampling, Random under-sampling, SMOTE algorithm, etc. [14]. However, these methods have some shortcomings. Under-sampling will lose potentially useful data, and over-sampling may lead to over-fitting. In recent years, Generative adversarial networks have made significant progress in data enhancement, providing new ideas for solving the imbalance problem of arrhythmia data. Since Goodfellow proposed generative adversarial network in 2014, it has been widely used in image data enhancement. Radford A et al. [15] combined convolutional neural network with generative adversarial network to form deep convolutional generative adversarial network (DCGAN). New images were synthesized on different image datasets, and the classification performance was improved by using the generated images. Shota Harada et al. [16] proposed a time series data generation method based on GANs, explored the ability of GANs to generate biological signals with specific categories and characteristics, and introduced canonical correlation analysis (CCA) to analyze potential variables in the method, expressed the relationship between input data and generated data as canonical loads, and used these loads to control the characteristics of the proposed method to generate data. The LSTM neural network model is used to predict the classification accuracy, which proves the effectiveness of this method. In this paper, we propose an improved generative adversarial network DCGAN-BiGRU model for data enhancement. The model learns the characteristics of ECG data after preprocessing, so that it can synthesize a small number of ECG samples to improve the classification accuracy of ECG signals. Then the reliability of the generated data is tested by constructing the classification model of Resnet-seq2seq convolutional neural network.

The rest of this paper is organized as follows: The database, data preprocessing, and related hardware equipment are presented in Sect. 2. The architecture of generating confrontation network model and the Resnet-seq2seq classification model are introduced in Sect. 3. The Sect. 4 gives the experimental results, and finally the Sect. 5 makes a summary of this paper.

2 Prepared

2.1 Datasets

The dataset used in this paper is the Arrhythmia Database (MIT-BIH) data set provided by the Massachusetts Institute of Technology. The MIT-BIH database [17] records 48 ECG data at the frequency of 360 Hz, and each record contains 30 min of ECG information. According to the international standards of the American Association for the Improvement of Medical Devices (AAMI) [18], the 15 types of arrhythmias in the MIT-BIH arrhythmia database can be divided into 5 categories: Normal or bundle branch block (N), Supraventricular ectopic beat (S), Ventricular ectopic beat (V), Fusion beat (F), and Unknown beat (Q). Due to the small number of Unknown beat (Q), this article will not consider this category.

Among the 48 ECG signals, 4 ECG signals (102, 104, 107 and 217) were recorded as rhythmic beat signals, which will not be considered in this modeling. The rest 44 signals were divided into DS1 and DS2 groups according to the classification of inter-patient arrhythmia in this paper [19]. the train set DS1 is: 101, 106, 108, 109, 112, 114, 115,

116, 118, 119, 122, 124, 201, 203, 205, 207, 208, 209, 215, 220, 223, 230; The test set DS2 is 100, 103, 105, 111, 113, 117, 121, 123, 200, 202, 210, 212, 213, 214, 219, 221, 222, 231, 233, 234. Because the individual differences between patients may lead to differences in the same type of arrhythmia signals, the robustness of our model can be better evaluated by using inter-patient classification. Table 1 shows the number of arrhythmia signals for each category after grouping.

Table 1. Number of arrhythmia categories in DS1 and DS2.

Data categories	N	S	V	F	Total
DS1	45770	940	3782	414	50906
DS2	44156	1834	3217	388	49595

2.2 Preprocessing

In general, ecg signal is mainly affected by baseline drift, power frequency interference and electromyographical interference in the acquisition process. These noises will affect the learning of model features and have a negative impact on the recognition of abnormal heart rhythm. In this paper, the wavelet decomposition method [20] is used to denoise the ECG signal, DB5 is selected as the wavelet basis function, 6-scale decomposition is used to remove the first-order, second-order high-frequency noise and sixth-order low-frequency noise, and then the remaining information is reconstructed to obtain the denoised ECG signal.

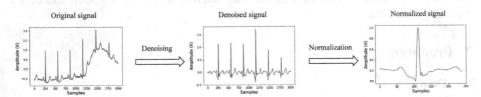

Fig. 1. The preprocessing process of ECG signal.

After the noise was removed from the ECG signal, we divided the long-sequence ECG signal into a single beat. In order to ensure the integrity of the beat, according to the position of the marked R peak in the MIT-BIH database, 120 points were taken forward and 120 points backward, and 240 points were used to characterize a beat. The maximum and minimum normalization is used to normalize the signal. The results are shown in Fig. 1. The single beat data is uniformly converted to the range of [0,1], and the normalization formula is as follows Eq. (1):

$$x = \frac{x - x_{min}}{x_{max} - x_{min}} \tag{1}$$

2.3 Experimental Environment

All the experiments in this paper were carried out based on Intel's I7-2600 processor, and four Titan XP graphics cards were added to accelerate the training. For software, Python3 is used on top of the Ubuntu 16.04 operating system. Scripting language, while introducing TensorFlow1.8 version and keras2.2.4 and other third-party machine learning library under python3.

3 Method

As shown in Fig. 2, shows the flow chart of ecg signal classification in this paper. Firstly, we preprocess the MIT-BIH data set to obtain a single beat signal. Then, a small number of ECG signals are introduced into the generative adversarial network model for training, and a small number of samples are generated for data equalization. Finally, the classification results are input into the classifier.

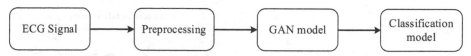

Fig. 2. Frame diagram of ECG signal detection system.

3.1 Data Enhancement Based GAN

Adversarial generative network is a new model of convolutional neural networks, which includes generative model and discriminator model. The generator is responsible for generating the input noise into data similar to the real signal, and Discriminator is responsible for judging the authenticity of the generated data. After several times of training and game between Generator and Discriminator, the data generated by Generator is closer and closer to the real data until the Discriminator cannot distinguish the authenticity of the generated data, and finally reach Nash equilibrium.

In this paper, we propose an improved GAN network structure for data enhancement of ECG signals. According to the DCGAN network structure, we adopt the Wasserstein distance as the loss function and the gradient penalty strategy to improve the stability of the network model. The bidirectional GRU recurrent neural network is introduced into the generator to improve the reliability and similarity of time series generation. Figure 3 depicts the training process of GAN.

In the network model, we use the Wasserstein distance to replace the cross entropy loss function, so that even in the generated data and real data without overlapping, also can better reflect the distance between the two distribution, but at the time of gradient update loss function need to satisfy the continuity conditions, so that greatly reduces the network fitting ability, Therefore, we use the gradient penalty strategy to solve the above problems caused by the continuity constraints. Then our objective function is shown as follows Eqs. (2)–(6):

$$L_{loss} = L_{origin} + L_{gp} \tag{2}$$

$$L_{origin} = \frac{1}{2}\left\{E_{\hat{x} \sim p_g}[D(\hat{x})] - E_{x \sim p_r}[D(x)]\right\} \tag{3}$$

$$L_{gp} = \lambda E_{\overline{x} \sim p_{\overline{x}}}\left[(\|\nabla_{\overline{x}}D(\overline{x})\|_2 - 1)^2\right] \tag{4}$$

where:

$$\hat{x} = G(z) \tag{5}$$

$$\overline{x} = \varepsilon x + (1 - \varepsilon)\hat{x} \tag{6}$$

In the formula, z represents the noise vector, D is the discriminator, G is the generator, and $\overline{x}$ denotes the interpolation sampling between the real data distribution $x \sim p_r$ and the generated data distribution $\hat{x} \sim p_g$. The penalty coefficient $\lambda = 10$, ε is the random number between [0,1].

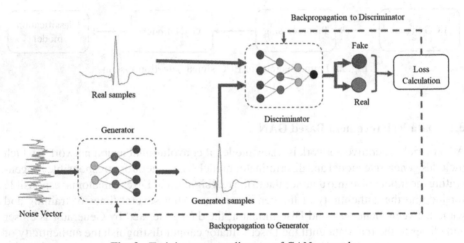

Fig. 3. Training process diagram of GAN network.

In the training process, if all samples are used to train the network, then the categories that generate ECG signals cannot be distinguished. Therefore, we use a separate training network for minority ECG signals to generate minority ECG data to balance the data set. The input of generator G is a random noise of 100×1 dimension obeying Gaussian distribution $Z \sim N(0,1)$. The generator model is mainly composed of four one-dimensional convolution layers, and the number of convolution kernels is divided into 256, 128, 64. The final output convolution kernels are 240, and the size of all convolution kernels is 1 * 6, and the padding is the same. It consists of three up-sampling layers with step size 2 and two bidirectional cyclic neural network GRUs with kernel number 32. Relu and Batch Normalization are used as the activation function of each layer to prevent over-fitting. As a result, Tanh activation function is used to output ECG signals with a length of 240×1 dimension. The input of the discriminator D is a one-dimensional sequence with a length of 240. The model includes three convolution layers, the number of convolution kernels is 32, 64 and 128, respectively. The size of the convolution kernels is 1 * 6, and the step size is 3, and the padding is the same. LeakyRelu is used as the activation function of each layer, the parameter $\lambda = 2$, and Batch Normalization of the leading factor is used as the normalization of the layer. The Dropout process is performed with a Dropout rate of $\alpha = 0.4$ to prevent over-fitting, and the fully connected layer is used as the output. The network architecture of Generator and Discriminator is shown in Table 2.

Table 2. Network structure of generator and discriminator.

Generator				Discriminator			
Layer	Filters	Kernels	Stride	Layer	Filters	Kernels	Stride
Dense	30 * 128	–	1	Conv1D	32	1 * 6	3
Reshape	(30,128)			BN/LeakyReLU	–	–	–
UpSamping	–	–	2	Dropout	–	–	–
Conv1D	256	1 * 6	1	Conv1D	64	1 * 6	3
BN/Relu	–	–	–	BN/LeakyReLU	–	–	–
UpSamping	–	–	2	Dropout	–	–	–
Conv1D	128	1 * 6	1	Conv1D	128	1 * 6	3
BN/Relu	–	–	–	BN/LeakyReLU	–	–	–
UpSamping	–	–	2	Dropout	–	–	–
Conv1D	64	1 * 6	1	Flatten	–	–	–
BN/Relu	–	–	–	Dense	1	–	–
BiGRU	32	–	–				
BiGRU	32	–	–				
Conv1D	240	1 * 6	1				
Tanh	–	–	–				

3.2 Classification Model

In order to verify that the generated data is beneficial to improve our classification accuracy, this paper constructs a hybrid classification model based on Resnet and seq2seq. Resnet module is used to extract the initial features of ECG signals, and then the features are input into the seq2seq classification module. The seq2seq module has two parts: encoder and decoder. The encoder encodes the input features, and the decoder recognizes the input beat information respectively. We introduce the attention mechanism between the encoder and the decoder, which can automatically give each feature to different weight coefficients, so that the model pays more attention to important feature information, so as to improve the accuracy of prediction. The classification model architecture is shown in Fig. 4:

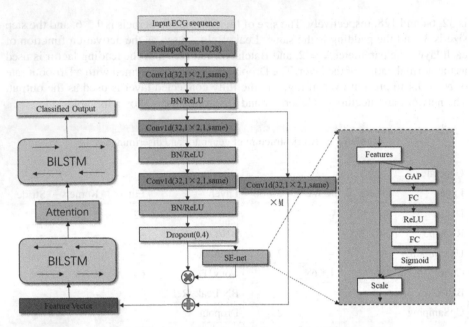

Fig. 4. Resnet-seq2seq classification model architecture.

Resnet Module: In the residual network module, the initial features of ECG signals are extracted from the first layer convolution, and then input into the encoder and decoder modules through M residual modules. In the residual module, the number of M can be adjusted to adjust the function of model performance. If M is too small, the network structure is simple, it can not learn the characteristics of ECG well. If M is too large, the network model is degraded due to the deep number of convolution layers and complex model. Therefore, the parameters of M can be adjusted appropriately to optimize the network.

Encoder and Decoder Module: The module is mainly composed of encoder and decoder. The encoder mainly encodes the signal to form semantic vector. The decoder takes the semantic vector as the initial input, completes semantic conversion through decoding operation, and finally realizes the classification effect. Because the ECG signal has strong timing and is composed according to the sequence of Q wave, R wave and S wave, the encoder and decoder are composed of bidirectional long-term and short-term memory (BiLSTM) network. BiLSTM structure uses the combination of forward propagation and back propagation to capture not only the important characteristics of the previous time period of ECG signal, but also the waveform characteristics of subsequent ECG signal.

Attention Mechanism Module: In this model, there are two parts, local attention mechanism (SE-net) and global attention mechanism. In the residual module, SE-net learns the local morphological features of the ECG signal, focusing on extracting important feature information of single signal. Between the encoder and the decoder, we use

Bahdanau Attention as the global attention mechanism to weight the semantic information extracted by the encoder, so that the decoder does not need to pay attention to all the features of the input signal, and the classification results can be obtained only by calculating the features with higher weights.

Loss function: When constructing the Resnet-seq2seq classification model, the network model parameters increase due to the complexity of the model. In this paper, on the basis of using the cross entropy loss function, the penalty term is introduced to reduce the complexity of the model and prevent over-fitting. The expression of the loss function in this paper is as follows Eq. (7):

$$loss = - \sum_{i=1}^{k} y_i log(p_i) + \beta \sum_{i=1}^{k} w_i^2 \tag{7}$$

where: k is the number of sample types, y_i is the label of sample i, p_i is the probability value predicted as sample i, and w is the model weight, β is the penalty coefficient.

4   The Experimental Results

4.1   Performance Evaluation

In the ECG data generated by GAN network model, we only consider a few samples S, V, F class for data expansion. Three methods for judging the similarity of time series are used to comprehensively evaluate the generated data: (1) Dynamic Time Warping (DTW) [21] (2) Percentage Root mean square Difference (PRD) [22] (3) Root Mean Square Error (RMSE) [23].

In this classification model, accuracy (ACC), accuracy (PPV), sensitivity (SEN) and specificity (SPE) were evaluated. The classification recognition mainly includes true positive (TP), true negative (TN), false positive (FP) and false negative (FN). The calculation method is shown in Eqs. (8)–(11).

$$ACC = \frac{TP + TN}{TP + TN + FP + FN} \tag{8}$$

$$PPV = \frac{TP}{TP + FP} \tag{9}$$

$$SEN = \frac{TP}{TP + FN} \tag{10}$$

$$SPE = \frac{TN}{TN + FP} \tag{11}$$

4.2 Data Enhancement Experimental Analysis

In GAN model training, RMSprop optimizer is used. The learning rate of generator is 0.0006, the learning rate of decider is 0.0002, the smoothing constant is $\alpha = 0.5$, epoch is 200 and batch-size is 64. Three different types of ECG signals were input into the model for training, and the similar data with the original signal was generated by the dynamic game of the generator and the decision maker. In Table 3, the results of the similarity of ECG signals generated by three generation data models are compared. The smaller the value is, the higher the similarity between the generated sequence and the original data is.

As can be seen from Table 3, in DCGAN-BiGRU model, the PRD index of F is larger than that of other models, and the other index values are significantly smaller than those of the other two models. The data indexes of S and V are smaller than those of the other two data generation models. It shows that in the generation of ECG data, the GANs network model using Wasserstein distance as the loss function and gradient punishment is more stable, and the data generated by DCGAN-BiGRU model after introducing bidirectional GRU neural network is more similar to the original ECG signal.

Table 3. Evaluation results of data quality generated by several models.

Model	Category	DTW	PRD	RMSE
DCGAN	S	18.00675	63.4821	0.247752
	V	28.5744	69.77452	0.327756
	F	9.019031	56.53203	0.175713
DCGAN-BiLSTM	S	17.56619	58.04716	0.229904
	V	22.85556	61.24574	0.288245
	F	9.653678	58.24284	0.177979
DCGAN-BiGRU	S	14.00921	50.16172	0.199692
	V	20.75952	58.29548	0.275789
	F	8.286566	57.8493	0.171149

4.3 Data Enhancement Experimental Analysis

In the training process of classification model, Adam optimizer was used, the learning rate was 0.0001, a total of 100 epochs were carried out, and the batch-size was set to 128. We use DS1 as the training set and DS2 as the test set, because the original data set has fewer S, V and F classes, which makes the distribution of types in the training set extremely unbalanced. Therefore, DCGAN-BiGRU network is used for data enhancement to make the number of samples reach 1:1:1:1, and the constructed classification model is used to verify the classification effect. In the classification experiment, we adjust the size of and the evaluation index of classification results to make the classification model achieve the optimal results. Table 4 shows the classification results of the classification model under different M values.

Table 4. Comparison of model classification results under different M.

M	ACC(%)	PPV(%)	SEN(%)	SPE(%)
2	96.02	74.36	75.22	90.97
3	97.75	75.05	**83.99**	94.83
4	**98.09**	**80.63**	83.65	**94.90**
5	98.1	80.49	80.14	93.77
6	97.94	81.05	77.29	93.41
7	97.75	77.32	62.03	90.98
8	97.67	76.75	74.3	91.81

In Table 4, the classification results of M from 2 to 8 are given. With the increasing value of M, the performance of the model continues to improve. It reaches the optimum when M is 4, and then the model performance continues to decline.

In the experiment, the traditional data enhancement method is compared with the DCGAN-BiGRU data enhancement method proposed in this paper, and the classification recognition is carried out under the classification model structure with M = 4. As shown in Table 5, the classification performance of the data enhancement method proposed in this paper is significantly higher than that of the non-data enhancement method and the traditional data enhancement method. Compared with the traditional SMOTE method, the ACC, PPV, SEN and SPE are improved by 1.23%, 22.93%, 6.13% and 2.65% respectively. It can be seen that using DCGAN-BiGRU model to learn the features of the original data and then generate the corresponding category of ECG signals is effective for the classification performance of the model.

Table 5. Category performance comparison in different data balancing modes.

	ACC(%)	PPV(%)	SEN(%)	SEP(%)
Original data	97.76	75.93	56.13	90.18
SMOTE	96.90	65.59	78.79	92.45
DCGAN-BiGRU	98.09	80.63	83.65	94.90

Because the sample size of S, V and F is small, it is not conducive to the learning of classification model features. After using the data enhancement method proposed in this paper, it can be seen from Table 6 that the DCGAN-BiGRU network model constructed in this paper has significantly improved the SEN and PPV of S, V and F, and most classification results reach more than 70%. The SEN of class S is 47.33%, and the PPV of class F is only 29.90%. Due to the small number of classes S and F, in the process of feature learning of generator G, all the features in the test set can not be well learned, and enough feature samples can not be generated, resulting in a slightly low classification accuracy. In future experiments, more samples can be collected to enhance the feature learning of the generator network.

Table 6. Classification effect of each type of beat under DCGAN-BiGRU model.

Class	ACC(%)	PPV(%)	SEN(%)	SPE(%)
N	96.24	97.72	98.07	91.41
S	97.97	95.49	47.33	99.91
V	99.88	99.41	98.73	99.96
F	98.26	29.90	90.46	98.33

In addition, we compare the method proposed in this paper with the method proposed by previous workers. As shown in Table 7. V. Mondjar et al. [24] use multi-feature extraction of ECG signals to construct a multi-support vector machine model to classify ECG signals. The accuracy rate is 94.5%, but the recognition effect of class F is low; Sellami A et al. [25] overcomes the problem of data imbalance by using weighted loss function, and obtains an accuracy of 95.33%, but the accuracy of class S and class F is low; M. Chen et al. [26] used multi-path convolution network and introduced cluster alignment loss and cluster separation loss to increase the discrimination of ECG categories, and obtained an accuracy of 94.35%, but the classification effect of class F was poor; Niu L et al. [27] proposed a new ECG classification method based on adaptive adversarial domain, which solved the problem of insufficient training samples, improved the phenomenon of different data distribution caused by individual differences, and improved the classification accuracy of cross-domain ECG signals with different data distribution, and the classification accura cy reaches 92.3%. By comparing different classification models, this paper adopts the method of data equalization optimization by using GAN network model, which makes the overall classification performance due to other methods. However, the sensitivity of class S is lower than that of other methods, and the accuracy of class F is only 29.90%, which is at a low level and needs to be improved in the follow-up work.

Table 7. The comparison results between this method and other methods.

Class	N		S		V		F	
	PPV	SEN	PPV	SEN	PPV	SEN	PPV	SEN
V. Mondjar [24]	98.20	95.90	49.70	78.10	93.90	94.70	23.60	12.40
A. Sellami [25]	98.80	88.51	30.44	82.04	72.13	92.05	8.60	89.40
M. Chen [26]	98.46	95.34	88.67	78.59	95.00	93.89	8.83	43.81
L. Niu [27]	97.40	93.90	73.20	76.60	57.80	85.10	44.90	38.40
Proposed	97.72	98.07	95.49	47.33	99.41	98.73	29.90	90.46

5 Conclusion

In this paper, a data enhancement method based on generative adversarial network is proposed to solve the problem of unbalanced distribution of ECG signal samples in the classification process. BiGRU neural network model is introduced into the generator to better learn the time series characteristics. The results show that by learning the characteristics of a small number of samples, the Gaussian distribution noise is automatically generated by the generator network, which solves the problem of insufficient number of minority categories in the classification model. Then we construct the Resnet-seq2seq classification model to verify the data enhancement algorithm in this paper. By adjusting the size of M, we select the optimal classification network model. Compared with the traditional data enhancement method and the classification method proposed by other scholars, this paper proves that the data enhancement based on GAN network can effectively improve the classification effect of ECG. However, in the data enhancement method, because the number of minority samples is too small, the generator cannot well learn the feature information about the test set, resulting in low classification accuracy of individual categories. In the future work, we will try to obtain more minority samples for feature learning.

References

1. Sun, L., Wang, Y., Qu, Z., Xiong, N.N.: BeatClass: a sustainable ecg classification system in iot-based ehealth. IEEE Internet Things J. **9**(10), 7178–7195 (2022). https://doi.org/10.1109/JIOT.2021.3108792
2. Alqudah, A.M., Qazan, S., Al-Ebbini, L., Alquran, H., Qasmieh, I.A.: ECG heartbeat arrhythmias classification: a comparison study between different types of spectrum representation and convolutional neural networks architectures. J. Ambient. Intell. Humaniz. Comput. **2021**, 1–31 (2021)
3. Ge, Z., Zhu, Z., Feng, P., Zhang, S., Wang, J., Zhou, B.: ECG-signal classification using svm with multi-feature. In: 2019 8th International Symposium on Next Generation Electronics (ISNE), pp. 1–3 (2019)
4. Aamir, K.M., Ramzan, M., Skinadar, S., Khan, H.U., Tariq, U.: Automatic heart disease detection by classification of ventricular arrhythmias on ecg using machine learning. Comput. Mater. Continua **71**(1), 17–33 (2022)

5. Subashini, A., Sairamesh, L., Raghuraman, G.: Identification and classification of heart beat by analyzing ecg signal using naive bayes. In: 2019 Third International Conference on Inventive Systems and Control (ICISC), pp. 691–694 (2019)
6. Kh-Madhloom, J., Khanapi, M., Baharon, M.R.: Ecg encryption enhancement technique with multiple layers of aes and DNA computing. Intell. Autom. Soft Comput. **28**(2), 493–512 (2021)
7. Dias, F.M., Monteiro, H.L., Cabral, T.W., Naji, R., Kuehni, M., Luz, E.J.D.S.: Arrhythmia classification from single-lead ECG signals using the inter-patient paradigm. Comput. Methods Prog. Biomed. **202**, 105948 (2021)
8. Thilagavathy, R., Srivatsan, R., Sreekarun, S., Sudeshna, D., Priya, P.L., Venkataramani, B.: Real-time ecg signal feature extraction and classification using support vector machine. In: 2020 International Conference on Contemporary Computing and Applications (IC3A), pp. 44–48 (2020)
9. Bhattacharyya, S., Majumder, S., Debnath, P., Chanda, M.: Arrhythmic heartbeat classification using ensemble of random forest and support vector machine algorithm. IEEE Trans. Artif. Intell. **2**(3), 260–268 (2021). https://doi.org/10.1109/TAI.2021.3083689
10. Bouaziz, F., Boutana, D., Oulhadj, H.: Diagnostic of ecg arrhythmia using wavelet analysis and k-nearest neighbor algorithm. In: 2018 International Conference on Applied Smart Systems (ICASS), pp. 1–6 (2018)
11. Oliveira, L.S.C.D., Andreao, R.V., Filho, M.S.: Bayesian network with decision threshold for heart beat classification. IEEE Lat. Am. Trans. **14**(3), 1103–1108 (2016)
12. Guo, L., Sim, G., Matuszewski, B.: Inter-patient ECG classification with convolutional and recurrent neural networks. Biocybern. Biomed. Eng. **39**(3), 868–879 (2019)
13. Niu, J., Tang, Y., Sun, Z., Zhang, W.: Inter-patient ecg classification with symbolic representations and multi-perspective convolutional neural networks. IEEE J. Biomed. Health Inform. **24**(5), 1321–1332 (2020)
14. Karthik, S., Santhosh, M., Kavitha, M.S., Paul, A.C.: Automated deep learning based cardiovascular disease diagnosis using ecg signals. Comput. Syst. Sci. Eng. **42**(1), 183–199 (2022)
15. Radford, A., Metz, L., Chintala, S.: Unsupervised representation learning with deep convolutional generative adversarial networks. arXiv preprint arXiv:1511.06434 (2015)
16. Harada, S., Hayashi, H., Uchida, S.: Biosignal generation and latent variable analysis with recurrent generative adversarial networks. IEEE Access **7**, 144292–144302 (2019)
17. Zheng, Z., Chen, Z., Hu, F.: An automatic diagnosis of arrhythmias using a combination of cnn and LSTM technology. Electronics **9**(1), 121 (2020)
18. Bridgman, E.: Aami: Association for the Advancement of Medical Instrumentation completes recommended practice on decontamination. J. Healthc. Mater. Manage. **9**(1), 78 (1991)
19. Song, X., Yang, G., Wang, K., Huang, Y., Yuan, F., Yin, Y.: Short term ECG classification with residual-concatenate network and metric learning. Multim. Tools Appl. **79**(31), 22325–22336 (2020)
20. Mangathayaru, N., Rani, P., Janaki, V., Srinivas, K., Bai, B.M.: An attention based neural architecture for arrhythmia detection and classification from ecg signals. Comput. Mater. Continua **69**(2), 2425–2443 (2021)
21. Vensko, G., Lieu, K.B., Meloche, S.A., Potter, J.C.: ITT Corp, dynamic time warping (DTW) apparatus for use in speech recognition systems. U.S. Patent 5,073,939 (1991)
22. Ranjeet, K.: Retained signal energy based optimal wavelet selection for denoising of ecg signal using modifide thresholding. In: 2011 International Conference on Multimedia, Signal Processing and Communication Technologies, pp. 196–199. IEEE (2011)
23. Sharma, L.N., Dandapat, S.: Compressed sensing for multi-lead electrocardiogram signals. In: 2012 World Congress on Information and Communication Technologies, pp. 812–816. IEEE (2012)

24. Mondéjar-Guerra, V., Novo, J., Rouco, J., Penedo, M.G., Ortega, M.: Heartbeat classification fusing temporal and morphological information of ECGs via ensemble of classifiers. Biomed. Signal Process. Control **47**, 41–48 (2019)
25. Sellami, A., Hwang, H.: A robust deep convolutional neural network with batch-weighted loss for heartbeat classification. Exp. Syst. Appl. **122**, 75–84 (2019)
26. Chen, M., Wang, G., Ding, Z., Li, J., Yang, H.: Unsupervised domain adaptation for ecg arrhythmia classification. In: 2020 42nd Annual International Conference of the IEEE Engineering in Medicine and Biology Society (EMBC), pp. 304–307 (2020)
27. Niu, L., Chen, C., Liu, H.: A deep-learning approach to ecg classification based on adversarial domain adaptation. Healthcare **8**(4), 437 (2020)

Association Extraction and Recognition of Multiple Emotion Expressed in Social Texts

Jiajun Zou[1], Sixing Wu[2], Zhongliang Yang[3(✉)], Chong Chen[4], Yizhao Sun[5], Minghu Jiang[1], and Yongfeng Huang[3]

[1] School of Humanities, Tsinghua University, Beijing 100084, China
[2] North China Electric Power University, Beijing 100096, China
[3] Beijing National Research Center for Information Science and Technology.
Department of Electronic Engineering, Tsinghua University, Beijing 100084, China
yangzl15@tsinghua.org.cn
[4] North Automatic Control Technology Institute, Taiyuan 030006, China
[5] Multimedia Communications and Signal Processing,
Friedrich-Alexander-Universität Erlangen-Nürnberg, 91058 Erlangen, Germany

Abstract. Detecting the sentiment people present in social media such as tweets is important for politics, commerce, education and so on. The task of multiple emotion recognition in texts is to predict a set of emotion labels that expressed in sentences. There are still some shortcomings in the current works: 1) the dependencies among emotions are not well modeled due to the complex combinatorial features of them, 2) the semantics of emotion labels as well as the semantic correlations between emotion labels and sentences are not fully considered. In this paper, in the purpose of capturing the dependencies between emotions, we propose a new method by using Graph Convolutional Network (GCN) based on a label co-occurrence matrix building from the dataset, and a Convolutional Neural Network (CNN) is used to capture the syntactic and semantic information in the sentences through different convolutional filters, the outputs of GCN and CNN are multiplied together to fuse their features as the last output. Experiments on SemEval2018 Task1: E-c multi-label emotion recognition problem show that metrics have been significantly improved, and our approach obviously obtains the dependencies among emotions described by Pointwise Mutual Information (PMI) which measures the correlations between emotions both in the true test labels and predicted labels.

Keywords: Multi-label emotion recognition · Graph convolutional network · Sentiment analysis · Deep learning

1 Introduction

Nowadays, with the development of Internet, people can express their thoughts, attitudes and emotions through social media such as Twitter, Facebook and

© The Author(s), under exclusive license to Springer Nature Switzerland AG 2022
X. Sun et al. (Eds.): ICAIS 2022, LNCS 13338, pp. 420–430, 2022.
https://doi.org/10.1007/978-3-031-06794-5_34

Weibo. Analyzing these subjective information is an important task in natural language processing (NLP) which has received a lot of attentions from many researchers recently. Sentiment analysis or opinion mining is the computational study of people's opinions, sentiments, emotions, appraisals, and attitudes towards entities such as products, services, organizations, individuals, issues, events, topics, and their attributes [1,5,6,13,17,22], the sentiment can be the polarity or an emotion state such as joy, anger or sadness [9]. The target of sentiment recognition is to recognize the categories of these emotions in sentences.

Judging from the number of emotions in a sentence, we can divide sentiment recognition into single-label recognition and multi-label recognition. Single-label recognition has been extensively studied such as [18,19,23]. However, although the results of single-label sentiment recognition have achieved a superior performance, it ignores the reality that a sentence itself may have multiple emotions at the same time, which result in losing some subjective information during processing these sentences. The task of multiple emotion or multi-label emotion recognition aims to predict a set of emotion labels that expressed in a sentence, which is different from single-label recognition. Due to the combinatorial nature of the emotional output space, that is, the emotions normally cooccur in a sentence with more complex dependencies which is more challenging than single-label task. How to dig out the dependencies between emotions efficiently is a key to solving the problem of multi-label sentiment recognition.

In order to overcome the challenges of multi-label emotion recognition in social texts such as Tweets, there have been several excellent works done by researchers. Most of current methods for this task convert the multi-label recognition problem into a set of binary or multi-class recognition problems, which is called problem transformation, to predict whether each label is or not a true label, and then the predictions are combined into multi-label predictions [9]. A bidirectional Long Short-Term Memory (LSTM) neural network with attention mechanism was used by Baziotis et al. [2] to deal with multi-label emotion recognition task of SemEval-2018 Task1, which won the competition. Their model utilized a set of word2vec word embeddings trained on a large collection of 550 million Twitter messages. Mohammed Jabreel et al. [9] proposed a novel method to transform the problem into a binary recognition problem and exploited a deep learning approach to solve the transformed problem, achieving a new accuracy score on the same dataset. Hardik Meisheri [15] combined three different features generated from deep learning models-a word-level bidirectional LSTM with attention as well as a traditional method in support vector machines. Ji Ho Park et al. [20] transferred the emotional knowledge by exploiting neural network models as feature extractors, they used these representations for traditional machine learning models such as support vector regression and logistic regression to capture the correlations of emotion labels, and it treated the multi-label problem as a sequence of binary recognition problems, thus the current classifier could use previous classifier's output, namely classifier chain [21].

All of the previous works tried to use transformation method to deal with this task and played an important role in multi-label emotion recognition, however, there are still some shortcomings. On the one hand, due to the limitation of predicted emotion label combination, the correlations existing in emotions could not be well modeled or they even lose the dependencies between emotion labels, such as binary relevance [21]. On the other hand, the semantics of emotion labels or even the semantic correlations between the emotion labels and the texts are not considered, and we think it can provide more additional information for multi-label emotion recognition. For example, in sentence "Oh, hidden revenge and anger...I remember the time", the emotion labels for it are "anger" and "disgust", we can obviously find that the labels and the sentence are semantically related, and even label-"anger" appears in it. Therefore, we argue that considering the above two aspects is crucial to achieve the goal of multi-label emotion recognition which motivates us to design a new method to overcome the weakness.

In this paper, we propose a novel Graph Convolutional Network (GCN) [11] based model to capture the label correlations for multi-label emotion recognition with a emotion label co-occurrence matrix. We use a Convolutional Neural Network (CNN) with different convolutional filters to further obtain the syntactic and semantic features in sentences. In order to take advantage of semantic correlations between sentence and labels, we also take the labels' semantics into account which are used as the representations of nodes in the input of GCN. Experiments conducted on SemEval-2018 task 1 dataset show that our approach can improve multi-label emotion recognition metrics, and the dependencies between labels are captured, which are observed through visualization analysis.

This paper is organized as follows: In Sect. 2, we explain the methodology. The experiments and results are reported in Sect. 2. At last, conclusions are presented in Sect. 4.

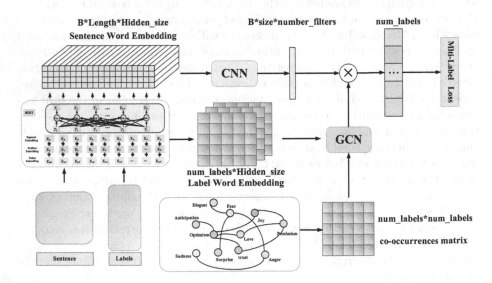

Fig. 1. The proposed multi-label emotion recognition model based on GCN.

2   The Proposed Method

In this Section we will first introduce the overall architecture of the proposed model, then the details of the CNN module and the GCN module which compose the model will be described. At last, we will introduce the output layer.

2.1   Overall Architecture

Assume the input sentence with n words is represented as:

$$S = \{x_1, x_2, ..., x_n\}, \tag{1}$$

x_i is the i-th word in the sentence. The label set is formed as:

$$G = \{g_1, g_2, ..., g_N\}, \tag{2}$$

where N is the number of emotion labels. The goal of this task is to predict a label subset belongs to G according to the input sentence S.

Figure 1 illustrates the overall architecture of the proposed model for the task. In the sake of extracting plentiful features from the input sentence, we adopt Bidirectional Encoder Representation from Transformers (BERT) [4], an excellent pre-trained language model, as the word embedding layer to calculate the embeddings of words in sentences and emotion labels. Then a CNN module is used to capture the local information through several convolutional filters attempting to take full advantage of the syntactic features. According to the dataset, we calculate the co-occurrence matrix of the emotion labels, which is normalized and put into the GCN with emotion label word embeddings, acting as the edge matrix and node matrix, respectively. Then we make the matrices from CNN and GCN multiply each other as the last output, thus fusing the correlations of different emotion labels and the features of sentences.

2.2   CNN Structure

We design a CNN architecture in the model. The input of CNN can be denoted as $H \in \mathbb{R}^{B \times L \times d_B}$, where B is the batch size, L is the max length of sentence we pad, and d_B is the hidden size of BERT.

The convolution operations are applied on these vectors to produce new feature maps. In the proposed model, the convolution operation involves several filters so as to capture different local features, because the emotions are often expressed by a sequence of words in different parts in sentences. We concatenate the results after the convolution. At the first filter, a two-dimensional convolution is used and we employ global max-pooling to obtain the feature r_1:

$$r_1 = \mathbf{F}(H; \theta)) \in \mathbb{R}^{B \times d_m}, \tag{3}$$

where d_m is the number of out channels in CNN, θ indicates model parameters. This operation is the same as the other filters. Thus we can get the last output of the CNN as follows:

$$r = [r_1; r_2; ...; r_n] \in \mathbb{R}^{B \times (d_m \times n)}, \tag{4}$$

where n represents the number of filters.

2.3 GCN Module

GCN [11] is designed to deal with data containing graph structure, which is constructed by nodes and edges. In each GCN layer, a node iteratively aggregates the information from its one-hop neighbors and update its representation [7,12, 25,26].

In this task, we first count all labels in the dataset to construct the label co-occurrence matrix $A \in \mathbb{R}^{k \times k}$ through automatic method. Then we use a GCN to extract the co-occurrence features of emotion labels. For the first layer of GCN, we take the labels' word embeddings $E \in \mathbb{R}^{k \times d_B}$ and normalized label co-occurrence matrix A as the input, which denotes the nodes and edges, respectively, where k is the number of labels. The node features updates as follows:

$$h_i^l = \sigma(\sum_{j=1}^{k} A_{ij} W^l h_j^{l-1} + b^l),$$ (5)

where l is the l-th layer of GCN, h_i and h_j represent the state of node i and j, respectively. W^l is a linear transformation weight, b^l is a bias term, and $\sigma(\cdot)$ is a nonlinear function, such as ReLU. The output of the last layer in GCN is $H \in \mathbb{R}^{k \times (d_m \times n)}$ which represents the aggregated informations among emotion labels.

In this way, the features among emotion nodes can be aggregated through the GCN module.

2.4 The Output of the Whole Model

At last, we make the output of CNN and GCN multiply together as follows:

$$y = rH^T \in \mathbb{R}^k,$$ (6)

where H^T is the transposed matrix of H and y is the last output of the proposed model.

3 Experiments and Results

3.1 Dataset

We evaluated our model on a benchmark dataset: SemEval-2018 Task1 (Affect in Tweets) [16], which contains 10,983 sentences combined with training set (6,838 samples), validation set (886 samples), and testing set (3,259 samples), there are 11 emotion labels in this dataset which are more difficult to conduct recognition task. The statistic of emotion labels in training dataset is shown in Table 1.

We pre-processed each tweet in the dataset like [9], a list of regular expressions was used to recognize the meta information in tweets so as to clean up the unnecessary symbols.

Table 1. The number of labels in training dataset.

Anger	Anticipation	Disgust	Fear	Joy	Love
4282	1916	4563	2124	3876	1401
Optimism	Pessimism	Sadness	Surprise	Trust	Total
3456	1586	3567	760	845	28376

3.2 Compared Models

We compared our model with other five previous related models used to do the this task:

1. **SVM-unigrams** [16]: SVM-unigrams used word unigrams as features and support vector machine to deal with this task.
2. **TCS** [15]: TCS introduced a bidirectional LSTM with attention mechanism in the same task.
3. **PlusEmo2Vec** [20]: PlusEmo2VEc adopted a model with classifier chain and won the third place in SemEval-2018 Task1.
4. **Transformer** [10]: Transformer used a large pre-trained language model to recognize the emotions in sentences.
5. **BNet** [9]: BNet transformed the multi-label task into a binary recognition problem with deep learning, obtaining a better results.

3.3 Evaluation Metrics

In this work, we reported the Jaccard index, Macro-F1 and Micro-F1 for performance evaluation.

When we used the predicted results to calculate the best Macro-F1 and Micro-F1 score, the corresponding thresholds were also selected at the same time, which were represented by *threshold_ma* and *threshold_mi*, respectively, then we took the average of the two thresholds as the last threshold to determine Jaccard index, that was to say, for a sentence, the emotion labels were predicted as positive if the results of them were greater than (*threshold_ma* + *threshold_mi*)/2.

3.4 Training and Parameters Setting

At last, we trained our model by using the multi-label recognition loss as follows:

$$loss = \sum_{j=1}^{k} y_i log(\sigma(\hat{y}_i)) + (1 - y_i)log(1 - \sigma(\hat{y}_i)), \tag{7}$$

where $\sigma(\cdot)$ was the sigmoid function. During training, we used the pre-trained "bert-base-uncased" model, where the number of transformer layers was 12 and hidden size d_B was 768. AdamW [14] was used as the optimizer, the learning rate was set to be 5e-5, and batch size was 4, epoch number was 20. We padded the sentence with the same length of 128. The out channels of CNN was set to be 200, and we adopted 3 convolution filters which size were 2,3 and 4, respectively, the output size of GCN was decided by the number of filters and the out channels of CNN.

3.5 Results

As shown in Table 2, the best results are bolded, we can know obviously that our model performs very well compared to other models on the same dataset especially on Micro-F1 and Macro-F1 indicators which obtain the highest scores, when comes to compare Jaccard index, our model achieves the second place. These results prove our method is effective.

Table 2. Compared results of our model and other models.

Model	Jaccard index	Micro-F1	Macro-F1
SVM-Unigrams [9]	0.442	0.57	0.443
Transfomer [9]	0.577	0.69	0.561
TCS [9]	0.582	0.693	0.53
PlusEmo2Vec [9]	0.576	0.692	0.497
BNet [9]	**0.590**	0.692	0.564
Our model	0.586	**0.701**	**0.587**

We conducted an ablation study to verify the importance of modules in our model. The results are listed in Table 3. When we removed the co-occurrence matrix, the performance of the model was the most worse on Jaccard index. And we replaced GCN with attention mechanism [24], the results were also worse, it was the same as removing CNN. This illustrates the importance of the modules we designed.

Table 3. Ablation study of the proposed model.

	Jaccard index	Micro_F1	Macro_F1
BERT	0.572	0.693	0.573
w/o CNN	0.574	0.694	0.578
w/o Co-oc	0.566	0.686	0.575
Replace GCN with ATT	0.577	0.694	0.565
Whole model	**0.586**	**0.701**	**0.587**

In order to further examine the performance of our model, we calculated the precision score, the recall score and F1 score of every emotion label, which are

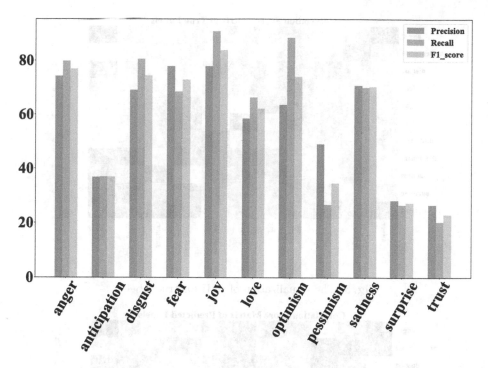

Fig. 2. The performance of our model.

plotted in Fig. 2. As we can see from it, our model clearly recognizes the emotion labels, such as "anger", "disgust", "fear", "joy", "love", "optimism" and "sadness". However, the performances on "anticipation", "pessimism", "surprise" and "trust" are worse. We speculate that the reason for this phenomenon may come from the dataset itself, from Table I, we can see the number of these labels are fewer than others resulting in the model not being able to fully learn the emotional characteristics.

Furthermore, we calculated the Pointwise Mutual Information (PMI) [3] by using the co-occurrence matrix built from the test dataset and predicted emotion labels, the PMI can be written as follows:

$$PMI_{ab} = log\frac{p(a,b)}{p(a)p(b)} = log\frac{p(a|b)}{p(a)}, \tag{8}$$

where positive values indicated that emotion labels occurred together more than would be expected under an independence assumption and negative values indicated that one emotion label tended to appear only when the other did not [8].

The visualization results of PMI for the true emotional labels in test dataset and the predicted results are shown in Fig. 3 and Fig. 4, respectively. Each grid in the pictures represents the correlation of every corresponding pair of labels. The lighter the color, the greater the correlation. From the comparison of the two figures, we can easily find that the image of predicted results is very similar

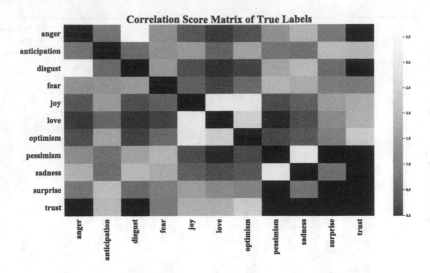

Fig. 3. The visualization of PMI for true labels.

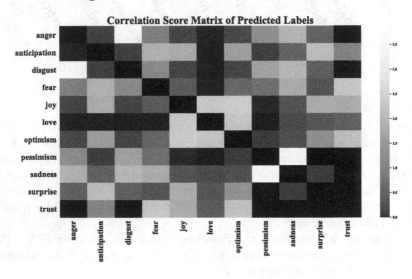

Fig. 4. The visualization of PMI for predicted labels.

to the true labels, meaning our model has captured the dependencies among
the emotion labels. On closer inspection from those figures, we can see that the
relationship between the emotions "anger" and "disgust" and the relationship
between "pessimism" and "sadness" are obvious (the corresponding grid in the
picture is lighter), which can correspond to our real life. Furthermore, the correlations among "joy", "love" and "optimism" are very obvious, which explains

why the samples of "love" is also less but the result is still better than "anticipation", "pessimism", "surprise" and "trust" as shown in Fig. 2, because the model has unearthed the dependences between "love" and "joy" and "optimism".

4 Conclusion

In this paper, we propose a novel method for multi-label emotion recognition based on CNN and GCN. The CNN is used for capturing syntactic and semantic information from sentence word embeddings. In order to effectively mine the correlations characterized by PMI among emotion labels, we build a co-occurrence matrix as well as the labels' word embeddings acting as the inputs of GCN. At last, the product of their results is taken as the final output. Experimental results show that our model outperforms other methods, and the correlations among emotional labels are captured obviously, demonstrating the feasibility and effectiveness of our approach. In the future, it will be expectant to combine other advanced methodologies such as Graph Attention Network to design a better architecture for this task.

Acknowledgements. This work is supported the National Key Research and Development Program of China (No.2018YFC1604000/2018YFC1604002).

References

1. Albahli, A.S., et al.: Covid-19 public sentiment insights: a text mining approach to the gulf countries. Comput. Mater. Continua **67**(2), 913–930 (2021)
2. Baziotis, C., et al.: NTUA-SLP at semeval-2018 task 1: predicting affective content in tweets with deep attentive RNNS and transfer learning (2018). arXiv preprint, arXiv:1804.06658
3. Church, K., Hanks, P.: Word association norms, mutual information, and lexicography. Comput. Linguist. **16**(1), 22–29 (1990)
4. Devlin, J., Chang, M.W., Lee, K., Toutanova, K.: Bert: pre-training of deep bidirectional transformers for language understanding (2018). arXiv preprint, arXiv:1810.04805
5. Hilal, A., Alfurhood, B., Al-Wesabi, F., Hamza, M., Al Duhayyim, M., Iskandar, H.: Artificial intelligence based sentiment analysis for health crisis management in smart cities. Comput. Mater. Continua **71**(1), 143–157 (2022)
6. Hnaif, A.A., Kanan, E., Kanan, T.: Sentiment analysis for Arabic social media news polarity. Intell. Autom. Soft Comput. **28**(1), 107–119 (2021)
7. Hou, X., Huang, J., Wang, G., Huang, K., He, X., Zhou, B.: Selective attention based graph convolutional networks for aspect-level sentiment classification (2019). arXiv preprint, arXiv:1910.10857
8. Islam, A., Inkpen, D.: Second order co-occurrence PMI for determining the semantic similarity of words. In: LREC, pp. 1033–1038 (2006)
9. Jabreel, M., Moreno, A.: A deep learning-based approach for multi-label emotion classification in tweets. Appl. Sci. **9**(6), 1123 (2019)
10. Kant, N., Puri, R., Yakovenko, N., Catanzaro, B.: Practical text classification with large pre-trained language models (2018). arXiv preprint, arXiv:1812.01207

11. Kipf, T.N., Welling, M.: Semi-supervised classification with graph convolutional networks (2016). arXiv preprint, arXiv:1609.02907
12. Lai, Y., Zhang, L., Han, D., Zhou, R., Wang, G.: Fine-grained emotion classification of Chinese microblogs based on graph convolution networks. World Wide Web **23**(5), 2771–2787 (2020)
13. Liu, B.: Sentiment analysis: Mining opinions, sentiments, and emotions. Cambridge University Press (2020)
14. Loshchilov, I., Hutter, F.: Fixing weight decay regularization in Adam (2018)
15. Meisheri, H., Dey, L.: TCS research at semeval-2018 task 1: learning robust representations using multi-attention architecture. In: Proceedings of the 12th International Workshop on Semantic Evaluation, pp. 291–299 (2018)
16. Mohammad, S., Bravo-Marquez, F., Salameh, M., Kiritchenko, S.: Semeval-2018 task 1: affect in tweets. In: Proceedings of the 12th International Workshop On Semantic Evaluation, pp. 1–17 (2018)
17. Twitter Arabic sentiment analysis to detect depression using machine learning. CMC Comput. Mater. Continua **71**(2), 3463–3477 (2022)
18. Mutanov, G., Karyukin, V., Mamykova, Z.: Multi-class sentiment analysis of social media data with machine learning algorithms. Comput. Mater. Continua **69**(1), 913–930 (2021)
19. Pang, B., Lee, L., Vaithyanathan, S.: Thumbs up? sentiment classification using machine learning techniques (2002). arXiv preprint cs/0205070
20. Park, J.H., Xu, P., Fung, P.: Plusemo2vec at semeval-2018 task 1: exploiting emotion knowledge from emoji and# hashtags (2018). arXiv preprint, arXiv:1804.08280
21. Read, J., Pfahringer, B., Holmes, G., Frank, E.: Classifier chains for multi-label classification. Mach. Learn. **85**(3), 333 (2011)
22. Suhail, K., et al.: Stock market trading based on market sentiments and reinforcement learning. CMC-Comput. Mater. Continua **70**(1), 935–950 (2022)
23. Tang, D., Qin, B., Liu, T.: Document modeling with gated recurrent neural network for sentiment classification. In: Proceedings of the 2015 conference on empirical methods in natural language processing, pp. 1422–1432 (2015)
24. Vaswani, A., et al.: Attention is all you need. In: Advances in Neural Information Processing Systems, pp. 5998–6008 (2017)
25. Yao, L., Mao, C., Luo, Y.: Graph convolutional networks for text classification. In: Proceedings of the AAAI Conference on Artificial Intelligence, vol. 33, pp. 7370–7377 (2019)
26. Zhang, C., Li, Q., Song, D.: Aspect-based sentiment classification with aspect-specific graph convolutional networks (2019). arXiv preprint, arXiv:1909.03477

A CNN Based Visual Audio Steganography Model

Ru Zhang, Hao Dong, Zhen Yang[✉], Wenbo Ying, and Jianyi Liu

School of Cyber Space Security, Beijing University of Posts and Telecommunications,
Beijing 100876, China
yangzhenyz@bupt.edu.cn

Abstract. Deep learning based steganography is an important protection for secret message, especially for secret images. For different type of cover and secret message, such as audio cover and secret image, the imperceptibility of steganography can be improved, however, the representation difference between audio cover and secret image becomes a great challenge. In this paper, we propose a visual audio steganography model to based on convolutional neural network (CNN). In our model, we design an audio visualization method with STFT and DWT transformation. Then we exploit ISGAN to build an auto encoder, in order to embed a grayscale image into a segment of audio in the embedding stage. Experimental results show that generated stego audio fidelity is indistinguishable to the listener, and we can extract high-quality grayscale images from stego audio in the extraction stage.

Keywords: Steganography · Audio steganography · Convolutional Neural Network

1 Introduction

The steganography can embed the secret data into the public digital media without changing its perceptual characteristics, and complete the transmission of the secrets through the transmission of the carrier on the open channel. The steganalysis method is to analyze the carrier by fitting statistical characteristics. As time goes by, the development of both domains gradually comes to a bottleneck period. For steganography, it is increasingly difficult to use traditional methods to find a better embedding way to avoid the steganalysis detection.

With the substantial increase in computing power in recent years, deep learning has become popular. Convolutional Neural Networks (CNN) [1], Generative Adversarial Network (GAN) [2], Recurrent Neural Networks (RNN) [3] and other deep learning models have achieved breakthrough results in the fields like image processing, natural language processing, and speech recognition, etc. This has attracted the attention of security researchers, who hope to use deep learning to break through the bottleneck encountered by steganography.

© The Author(s), under exclusive license to Springer Nature Switzerland AG 2022
X. Sun et al. (Eds.): ICAIS 2022, LNCS 13338, pp. 431–442, 2022.
https://doi.org/10.1007/978-3-031-06794-5_35

Through deep learning, the image steganography algorithm can get rid of many expert knowledges of image processing, and achieve higher security using the adversarial training with steganalysis methods. The algorithms that use deep learning to directly generate the stego image can embed the secret image into the cover image and restore the secret image with high quality and good transparency. However, these works raise some new issues. For example, although the generated images have strong anti-analysis capabilities, they are mostly distorted in semantics and are easy to attract human attention. And the restored images might have slight errors, which bring additional noise to the embedded information. Audio, as another widely used digital media, has high redundancy and high data transmission efficiency, and is also suitable for use as a carrier. To embed secret image into cover audio, the representation difference between audio cover and secret image is a main problem to overcome.

To improves some of these problems, we propose a visual audio steganography model based on CNN. Our research is based on ISGAN [4]. And we present a visual audio steganography model based on CNN. The model includes encoder and decoder. The encoder network can embed a gray secret image into a cover audio, and the generated stego audio has good transparency. The decoder can recover the secret image from the stego audio, and the recovered image also has good transparency. In addition, in view of the problem that CNN can only process images, this paper designs audio visualization. Experimental results show that this audio visualization can make CNN process audio objects well.

2 Related Work

2.1 Traditional Steganography Algorithm

There are many types of traditional image steganography algorithms. According to different theories, image steganography can be divided into spatial domain steganography and transform domain steganography.

Least Significant Bits (LSB) is the earliest steganography, which is a kind of airspace steganography. The same type of steganography algorithm includes OPAP (Optimal Pixel Adjustment Process) [5], LSB Matching [6], PPM (Pixel Pair Matching) [7] and so on. The steganography algorithm of image spatial domain has the advantages of large capacity and simple processing. However, due to the disadvantages of spatial steganography, such as poor security and resistance to various processing (such as filtering, compression), researchers have begun to focus on transformation domain.

Another typical image steganography algorithm is based on DCT (Discrete Cosine Tranformation). The steganography in the transform domain has strong security and can resist various compression processing, but the hiding capacity is limited.

With the development of steganalysis technology, the focus of steganography research is not only to reduce the difference in perception of the human visual system, but also to resist the attacks of steganalysis technology. Therefore, the goal of the steganography algorithm is to hide the secret information in areas with complex textures or rich edges according to the properties of the image, i.e., adaptive steganography. Its representative algorithms are HUGO [8], WOW [9], UNIWARD [10], HILL [11], EBS [12], UED [13], etc.

On the other hand, audio steganography provides another choice for information hiding to improve imperceptability. Typical audio steganography also used handmake features to find the best embedding positions and reduce the modification of the audio and reduce the distortion [14].

These steganography algorithms are all based on handmake features and cannot suit for big data environment. Thus, these traditional algorithms cannot achieve better performance in imperceptability in real world, which induce deep learning based algorithms.

2.2 Steganography Algorithm Based on Deep Learning

With deep learning fast develops, researches on steganography algorithms come into the age of deep learning. Volkhonskiy et al. [15] proposed the first image steganography model SGAN (Steganographic GAN) based on deep learning. The generated images have higher security. Yang et al. [16] proposed RNN (Recurrent Neural Network) based linguistic steganography to achieve better imperceptability on natural language steganography. Wang et al. [17] explores autoencoder model based image steganography to achieve higher visual quality. Zhang et al. [18] propose new CNN (Convolutional Nerual Network) structure on image steganalysis to improve the detection ability.

Shi et al. [19] proposed SSGAN (Secure Steganography Based on GAN) on the basis of SGAN. The deep learning model is replaced by DCGAN with WGAN (Wasserstein GAN) [20], which makes the generated images more realistic and their quality higher, and the training speed of the model is further improved. The methods of SGAN and SSGAN do improve the security of the model, but the generated carrier images are mostly distorted in semantics, which attracts channel listeners' attention.

Hayes et al. [21] first proposed a HayesGAN model that directly uses generative adversarial networks to generate secret images. The secret image generated by this model performs well in semantics, but its discriminator D cannot guarantee the correctness of the extracted information, that is, there is a difference between the embedded secret data and the extracted secret data. Based on HayesGAN, Zhu et al. [22] proposed an improved model HiDDeN (Hiding Data With Deep Net-works). This model adds a noise layer. Through adversarial learning, the generated stego images can still extract secret data with high accuracy under attacks such as Gaussian blur, pixel-by-pixel attenuation, cropping, and JPEG compression.

The aforementioned steganography models basically hide secret information in image files. Baluja et al. [23] proposed a steganography model that can hide images in images. The model is based on the autoencoder framework. In the same period, Atique et al. [24] designed a CNN-based model. While this model has a huge payload for complex images, it also guarantees quite high PNSR and SSIM values.

The above two models have large capacity and strong concealment, but the generated dense images have poor security because of color distortion, yellowing and etc. Zhang et al. [4] proposed an ISGAN model that can hide grayscale images in color cover images. The model contains three parts: encoder, decoder and steganalyzer. As shown in Fig. 1, the stego image generated by the ISGAN model is semantically highly consistent with the original cover image, and the problem of color distortion is effectively suppressed.

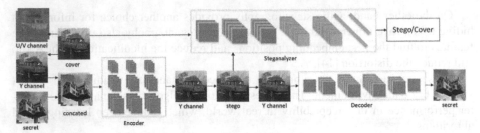

Fig. 1. ISGAN [4] model.

Compared with Atique's work [24], it has stronger transparency and security. But in terms of robustness, it cannot effectively resist scaling attacks.

To embed image secret message into audio cover, we need to analyze the multi-modal steganography to process the audio information and image information in a same information demain. With integrating the data of multiple modalities at different fusion levels, Alsaedi et al. [25] achieves multimodal information fusion. Currently, visual audio steganography still keep an open difficult problem.

3 Method

The research of this paper is carried out on the basis of ISGAN. The ISGAN model based on the encoder-decoder architecture can embed grayscale images on the cover image. The model converts the image from the RGB color space to the YCbCr color space, and then embeds the secret grayscale image of the same size into the Y channel. Although the embedding rate is only one third of that of Baluja et al.'s work [23], it solves the problem of color distortion of the stego image and improves the safety of the model. In view of the excellent performance of this model, we designed a visual audio steganography model based on CNN. The visual processing of the audio carrier facilitates the processing of audio by CNN. The CNN model we proposed can embed a gray-scale secret image into the cover audio, and extract it with high quality.

3.1 Visualization of Audio

CNN performs very well in image recognition tasks. It accepts image pixel matrix as input, reads the matrix in a sliding window mode to learn the features of the image to obtain a feature map, and then inputs it to the next convolutional layer. The digital audio signal is stored in the form of a one-dimensional array, and each semaphore is related before and after, so it is not feasible to directly input the audio signal into the CNN. The data format is inconsistent with the input, and forcibly changing the data format to input the neural network is also inappropriate. Therefore, this paper first considers converting audio signals into frequency domain signals and inputting them into the CNN in the form of a two-dimensional spectrogram. As for the conversion method, we tried windowed short-time Fourier transform (STFT) and discrete wavelet transform (DWT) respectively.

The transformation process of STFT is shown in (1).

$$x_n(k) = \sum_{m=-\infty}^{\infty} x(m)w(n-m)e^{-j\frac{2\pi kn}{N}} \qquad (1)$$

Equation (1) contains a sequence of window functions, that is, w(n-m). The window generally adopts Hann window and slides along with the change of n.

The audio signal is in the form of $a+bi$ complex matrix after STFT, a is a real matrix, and b is an imaginary matrix. In this way, we obtained the two-dimensional features of audio through STFT. In the training process of the model, we can try to embed the secret image into the real matrix.

DWT can divide audio signals into high-frequency signals and low-frequency signals. Low-frequency signals are very important. They often contain signal characteristics, while high-frequency signals give the details or differences of the signal. For a signal containing noise, the energy of the noise component is mainly concentrated in the high-frequency signal. If we remove the high-frequency components of the human voice, it may sound different from the original voice, but we can still know what is said; if we remove enough low-frequency components, we will hear some meaningless sounds. Therefore, in the audio signal, the redundancy of the high-frequency signal component is very high, and the secret image can be embedded in the high-frequency signal component during the training process of the model.

3.2 Autoencoder

The autoencoder is a type of Neural Networks and consists of two parts: an encoder and a decoder. It is traditionally used for high-dimensional feature vector dimensionality reduction or feature learning. The output is infinitely close to the input. As shown in Fig. 2, the compression representation capability of the autoencoder requires that the input data of the network are related to each other. If the input data is completely random, and each input data is completely independent of other input data, then this Compressed representation will be very difficult to learn. During the training process, the autoencoder uses the loss function to measure the original feature representation $(x_1,x_2,x_3,\ldots,x_{100})$ and the reconstructed feature representation $(\hat{x}_1,\hat{x}_2,\hat{x}_3,\ldots,\hat{x}_{100})$, the goal of training is to minimize this loss function.

Our method is to use the convolution neural network (CNN) to build encoder and decoder of our autoencoder. In detail, we use CNN to fuse the secret image into the two-dimensional feature component of the audio signal, and to recover the secret image from the two-dimensional feature component of the stego audio. This process uses the compression learning and representation ability of the autoencoder, and in view of the excellent performance of the ISGAN model in image fusion, we directly uses the autoencoder in the ISGAN network as the basic structure of the model for the next experiment.

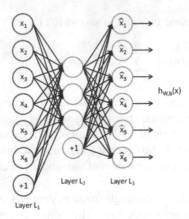

Fig. 2. Autoencoder compression representation example.

The specific structure of the encoder network is shown in Table 1. ConBlock1 represents the 3 × 3 convolutional layer + BN layer + ReLU activation function, and ConBlock2 represents the 1 × 1 convolutional layer + TanH activation function. The input of the encoder is a two-dimensional 128 × 128 matrix. It is composed of a 128 × 128 secret image and a 128 × 128 audio feature. The output is a 128 × 128 stego audio feature map.

Table 1. Architechture of encoder.

Layer	Process	Output size
Input	/	2 × 128 × 128
Layer1	ConBlock1	16 × 128 × 128
Layer2	InceptionBlock	32 × 128 × 128
Layer3	InceptionBlock	64 × 128 × 128
Layer4	InceptionBlock	128 × 128 × 128
Layer5	InceptionBlock	256 × 128 × 128
Layer6	InceptionBlock	128 × 128 × 128
Layer7	InceptionBlock	64 × 128 × 128
Layer8	InceptionBlock	32 × 128 × 128
Layer9	ConBlock1	16 × 128 × 128
Output	ConBlock2	1 × 128 × 128

Compared with the compressed representation function of the encoder network, the decoder network function is relatively simple, and only needs to recover the secret image from the secret audio feature. Its specific structure is shown in Table 2. ConBlock1 represents a 3 × 3 convolutional layer + BN layer, and ConBlock2 represents a 3 × 3 convolutional layer. The input is the stego audio feature of 128×128, and the output is the recovered 128×128 secret image.

Table 2. Architechture of decoder.

Layer	Process	Output size
Input	/	$1 \times 128 \times 128$
Layer1	ConBlock1	$32 \times 128 \times 128$
Layer2	ConBlock1	$64 \times 128 \times 128$
Layer3	ConBlock1	$128 \times 128 \times 128$
Layer4	ConBlock1	$64 \times 128 \times 128$
Layer5	ConBlock1	$32 \times 128 \times 128$
Output	ConvBlock2	$1 \times 128 \times 128$

3.3 Workflow

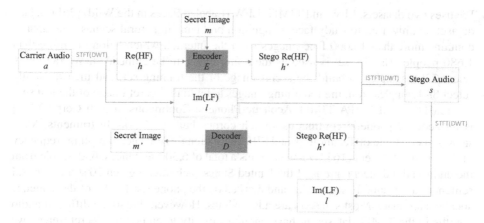

Fig. 3. Algorithm flow.

The entire training process is shown in Fig. 3. First, a batch of cover audios and secret grayscale images are randomly selected from the training set. For each audio and image in batch, perform STFT(DWT) on the cover audio. The real number matrix (high frequency component) h and the secret image are stitched together to form a two-channel image. Then input the two-channel image into the encoder network E to generate the stego real number matrix (the high-frequency component) h'. The stego real number matrix (the high frequency component) h' and the corresponding original imaginary matrix(low frequency component) l form a spectrum graph, and then use the inverse transform to obtain the stego audio s. This is the embedding process. For the extraction process, the stego real number matrix (the high-frequency component) h' obtained after using STFT(DWT) on stego audio is input into the decoder network D to recover the secret image m'. After the embedding and extraction operations are completed, the loss function is used to calculate the error between the stego matrix and the original matrix, and the error between the secret image before embedding and the secret image after extraction. Finally, the parameter gradients of the encoder network and the decoder network are calculated. The optimizer will update the parameters to complete a round of training.

We use h, h' to represent the original feature of 128×128 and the secret feature of 128×128, m, m' to represent the secret image of 128×128 and the recovered secret image of 128×128, respectively, α, β represent hyperparameters, which are used to measure the weight of each loss during training. We take mean square error (MSE) to measure loss. The overall loss function is shown in (2).

$$L\left(h, h^{'}, m, m^{'}\right) = \alpha\left(MSE\|h - h^{'}\|\right) + \beta\left(MSE\|m - m^{'}\|\right) \tag{2}$$

4 Experiments

4.1 Datasets

We uses two datasets, LFW and TIMIT. LFW (Labeled Faces in the Wild) [26] is a face dataset, mainly used to study face recognition problems in natural scenes. The dataset contains more than 13,000 face images from the Internet, which belong to more than 1,680 people. The dataset is used as the secret image to be embedded. We randomly select 2396 samples to build the secret image of the training set, and then randomly select 880 samples from the remaining images to build the secret image of the test set.

TIMIT (The DARPA TIMIT Acoustic-Phonetic Continuous Speech Corpus) [27] is an acoustic-phonetic continuous speech corpus built by Texas Instruments, Massachusetts Institute of Technology and SRI International. The voice sampling frequency of the TIMIT data set is 16 kHz and contains a total of 6,300 sentences. 630 people from the eight major dialect regions of the United States each utter a given 10 sentences. All sentences are manually segmented and marked on the phone level. 70% of the sentence speakers are male. Most speakers are adult whites. However, due to the different audio lengths in the TIMIT dataset, to have enough capacity to embed the secret image, we discarded audios with a length less than 32768. Among the 3276 pieces of audio data remaining after screening, we randomly select 2396 pieces of audio as the carrier data of the training set, and the remaining audio as the test set.

4.2 Results

In our test, each audio is sampled at 16kHz. STFT uses 512 FFT frequency intervals to transform audio with a 10 ms sliding window. The initial learning rate of the model is 1e-4. The batch size is set to 4. The model uses the Adam optimizer [28]. Training is carried out in 100 epochs. After many experimental attempts, the hyperparameters α and β of the model are set to 0.5 and 0.8 respectively.

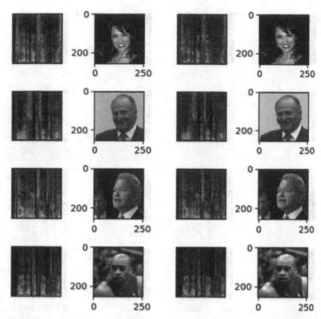

Fig. 4. Experiment performance based on STFT. The first column is the spectrogram of the cover audio, and the second column is the secret image. The third column is the spectrogram of the stego audio, and the fourth column is the recovered secret image.

4.2.1 STFT

After we train the model for 100 epochs, the experimental performance of the STFT-based audio spectrogram is shown in Fig. 4. The first column in the figure is the cover audio spectrogram. The second column is the gray-scale secret image. The third column is the stego audio spectrogram. The fourth column is the recovered secret image. From the experimental results, there is almost no big difference in waveform or color between the secret audio spectrogram and the carrier audio spectrogram. The error between the secret image and the recov-ered secret image is visually invisible. However, the error between the stego audio s and the cover audio a is very different, and the distortion is particularly serious, and the stego audio s is full of noise, and human ears cannot hear any meaningful con-tent. After research, it is found that the problem lies in the STFT process. Although the STFT can reflect the changes of audio signals over time, the redundancy of the trans-formed spectrum is too poor. With any modification, even a very small modification, the spectrum cannot be restored to an audio signal with high quality. Therefore, in the experiment, the secret image is embedded in the audio spectrogram and the result performs well, but the audio signal is seriously distorted when the frequency spectrum is restored to audio by ISTFT.

Fig. 5. Experiment performance based on DWT. The first column is the spectrogram of the cover audio, and the second column is the secret image. The third column is the spectrogram of the stego au-dio, and the fourth column is the recovered secret image.

4.2.2 DWT

However, the performance of the DWT-based audio steganography experiment is excellent, as shown in Fig. 5. From the perspective of the human visual system, there is no significant difference between the secret image and the recovered secret image. There is also no significant difference in the waveform and color between the cover audio spectrogram and the stego audio spectrogram. It is almost indistinguishable for the audience. It can be seen from Table 3 that the PSNR between the secret image and the recovered secret image is slightly inferior to the performance of the ISGAN model, while the PSNR between the cover audio spectrogram and the stego audio spectrogram is very high. But in general, it shouldn't be compared with the ISGAN model, because the carrier object of the ISGAN model is an image, while the carrier object of the model in this paper is audio.

Table 3. PSNR results.

Model	Our	ISGAN
Recovered Image PSNR(db)	51.1717	26.72
Secret Image PSNR(db)	25.6650	25.97

5   Conclusion

In this paper, we propose a visual audio steganography model based on CNNs. The model starts from preprocessing the audio and performs time frequency transformation on the audio. Then the audio two-dimensional frequency domain signal is sent to the autoencoder. In the autoencoder, the encoder network is responsible for embedding the gray secret image into the frequency domain features of the audio to form the stego audio, and the decoder network is responsible for reconstructing the secret image from the features of the stego audio. Our experiments show that the DWT-based method can recover the secret image with high quality. The spectrum of the stego audio and the cover audio are very similar, and the two audios are also indistinguishable aurally, so our algorithm has good transparency.

Acknowledgement. The authors are indebted to anonymous reviewers for their helpful suggestions and valuable comments. The work is supported by the National Key Research and Development Program of China (No. 2019YFB1406504), the National Natural Science Foundation of China (No.U1836108, No.U1936216, No.62002197, No.62001038) and the Fundamental Research Funds for the Central Universities (No.2021RC30).

References

1. Sahiner, B., Chan, H.P., Petrick, N.: Classification of mass and normal breast tissue: a convolution neural network classifier with spatial domain and texture images. IEEE Trans. Med. Imaging **15**(5), 598–610 (2002)
2. Radford, A., Metz, L., Chintala, S.: Unsupervised representation learning with deep convolutional generative adversarial networks. arXiv:1511.06434 (2015)
3. Graves, A., Mohamed, A.R., Hinton, G.: Speech recognition with deep recurrent neural networks. In: 2013 IEEE International Conference on Acoustics, Speech and Signal Processing, pp. 6645–6649. IEEE (2013)
4. Zhang, R., Dong, S., Liu, J.: Invisible steganography via generative adversarial networks. arXiv:1807.0857 (2018)
5. Chan, C.K., Cheng, L.M.: Hiding data in images by simple LSB substitution. Pattern Recogn. **37**, 469–474 (2004)
6. Sharp, T.: An implementation of key-based digital signal steganography. In: International Workshop on Information Hiding, pp. 13–26. Springer, Berlin, Heidelberg (2001)
7. Mielikainen, J.: LSB matching revisited. IEEE Sig. Process. Lett. **13**(5), 285–287 (2006)
8. Pevny, T., Filler, T., Bas, P.: Using high-dimensional image models to perform highly undetectable steganography. In: International Workshop on Information Hiding. Springer, Berlin, Heidelberg, 161–177 (2010)
9. Holub, V., Fridrich, J.: Designing steganographic distortion using directional filters. In: 2012 IEEE International Workshop on Information Forensics and Security (WIFS), pp. 234–239, IEEE (2012)
10. Holub, V., Fridrich, J.: Digital image steganography using universal distortion. In: Proceedings of the first ACM Workshop on Information Hiding and Multimedia Security, pp. 59–68 ACM (2013)
11. Li, B., Tan, S., Wang, M., et al.: Investigation on cost assignment in spatial image steganography. IEEE Trans. Inf. Forensics Secur. **9**(8), 1264–1277 (2014)

12. Wang, C., Ni, J.: An efficient JPEG steganographic scheme based on the block entropy of DCT. In: 2012 IEEE International Conference on Acoustics, Speech and Signal Processing (ICASSP), pp. 1785–1788 (2012)
13. Guo, L., Ni, J., Shi, Y.Q.: Uniform embedding for efficient JPEG steganography. IEEE Trans. Inf. Forensics Secur. **9**, 814–825 (2014)
14. Zhang, X., Sun, X., Sun, X., Sun, W., Jha, S.K.: Robust reversible audio watermarking scheme for telemedicine and privacy protection. Comput. Mater. Cont. **71**(2), 3035–3050 (2022)
15. Volkhonskiy, D., Nazarov, I., Borisenko, B., et al.: Steganographic generative adversarial networks. arXiv:1703.05502 (2017)
16. Yang, Z., Guo, X., Chen, Z., Huang, Y., Zhang, Y.: RNN-Stega: linguistic steganography based on recurrent neural networks. IEEE Trans. Inf. Forensics Secur. **14**(5), 1280–1295 (2018)
17. Wang, Y., Fu, Z., Sun, X.: High visual quality image steganography based on encoder- decoder model. J. Cyber Secur. **2**(3), 115–121 (2020)
18. Zhang, R., Zhu, F., Liu, J., Liu, G.: Depth-wise separable convolutions and multi-level pooling for an efficient spatial CNN-based steganalysis. IEEE Trans. Inf. Forensics Secur. **15**(1), 1138–1150 (2020)
19. Shi, H., Dong, J., Wang, W., et al.: Ssgan: Secure steganography based on generative adversarial networks. In: Pacific Rim Conference on Multimedia, pp. 534–544. Springer, Cham (2017)
20. Arjovsky, M., Chintala, S., Bottou, L.: Wasserstein GAN. In: Proceedings of the 34th International Conference on Machine Learning (ICML), pp. 214–223 (2017)
21. Hayes, J., Danezis, G.: Generating steganographic images via adversarial training. In: Advances in Neural Information Processing Systems, pp. 1954–1963 (2017)
22. Zhu, J., Kaplan, R., Johnson, J., Fei-Fei, L.: HiDDeN: Hiding Data With Deep Networks. In: Ferrari, V., Hebert, M., Sminchisescu, C., Weiss, Y. (eds.) ECCV 2018. LNCS, vol. 11219, pp. 682–697. Springer, Cham (2018). https://doi.org/10.1007/978-3-030-01267-0_40
23. Shumeet, B.: Hiding images in plain sight: deep steganography. In: Proceedings of Advances in Neural Information Processing Systems, vol. 30, pp. 2069–2079 (2017)
24. ur Rehman, A., Rahim, R., Nadeem, S., ul Hussain, S.: End-to-End Trained CNN Encoder-Decoder Networks for Image Steganography. In: Leal-Taixé, L., Roth, S. (eds.) ECCV 2018. LNCS, vol. 11132, pp. 723–729. Springer, Cham (2019). https://doi.org/10.1007/978-3-030-11018-5_64
25. Alsaedi, N.H., Jaha, E.S.: Dynamic audio-visual biometric fusion for person recognition. Computers, Materials & Continua **71**(1), 1283–1311 (2022)
26. Learned-Miller, E., Huang, G.B., Roychowdhury, A., Li, H., Hua, G.: Labeled faces in the wild: a survey. In: Advances in Face Detection and Facial Image Analysis, pp. 189–248, Springer (2016)
27. Garofolo, J.S.: Timit acoustic phonetic continuous speech corpus. Linguistic Data Consortium (1993)
28. Diederik, P. Kingma, Jimmy, Ba. Adam: A Method for Stochastic Optimization. In: The 3rd International Conference for Learning Reoresentations (2015)

A Survey of Multi-label Text Classification Based on Deep Learning

Xiaolong Chen[1], Jieren Cheng[1,2]($\boxtimes$), Jingxin Liu[1], Wenghang Xu[3], Shuai Hua[1], Zhu Tang[1], and Victor S. Sheng[4]

[1] School of Computer Science and Technology, Hainan University, Haikou 570228, China
cjr22@163.com
[2] Hainan Blockchain Technology Engineering Research Center, Hainan University, Haikou 570228, China
[3] School of Cyberspace Security, Hainan University, Haikou 570228, China
[4] Department of Computer Science, Texas Tech University, Lubbock, TX 79409, USA

Abstract. Text classification (TC) is an important basic task in the field of Natural Language Processing (NLP), and multi-label text classification (MLTC) is an important branch of TC. MLTC has undergone a transformation from traditional machine learning to deep learning, and various models with excellent performance have emerged one after another. But at present, the focus of various related researches is also varied, so we combed the excellent research results in the field of MLTC in recent years, and classified them according to the focus of their research. At the same time, we also summarized the relevant data sets and evaluation indicators in the field of multi-label text classification, and made a prospect for the future of the field of MLTC.

Keywords: Natural Language Processing · Text classification · Multi-label · Deep learning

1 Introduction

As one of the important carriers in the information age, text has the characteristics of huge and unstructured. In the mining of text information, named entity recognition [1] and text classification (TC) [2, 3] are all basic tasks. TC refers to categorizing a given text according to preset tags. This text can be a sentence, a paragraph of text, or even a document. TC is also an important link for downstream tasks such as Information Retrieval [4], Emotion Analysis [5], and question answering systems [6–8] in the field of NLP.

According to the number of assignable tags for a single text, it can be divided into single-label text classification and multi-label text classification [9]. Early text classification research is mainly for single-label text, which obviously does not meet most application scenarios. The label of a text has multiple labels with an uncertain number in most problems. Therefore, the focus of text classification research should be on multi-label classification.

© The Author(s), under exclusive license to Springer Nature Switzerland AG 2022
X. Sun et al. (Eds.): ICAIS 2022, LNCS 13338, pp. 443–456, 2022.
https://doi.org/10.1007/978-3-031-06794-5_36

1.1 Contribution

At present, the review papers in the field of multi-label text classification are still in a blank period. We wrote this article in order to fill this gap and made the following contributions:

- We summarized the excellent research results in the field of multi-label text classification in recent years, and classified them according to the different research focuses.
- We summarized the current challenges facing the field of multi-label text classification, and predicted the future development trend for reference.

1.2 Structure

The second section explains the multi-label text classification and briefly describes its development process. In the third section, we summarized the excellent research results in recent years. The fourth section summarizes the data sets that are currently popular in the field of multi-label text classification, and then also introduces the evaluation indicators commonly used in this field. The fifth section summarizes this article and makes an outlook for the future development of the field of multi-label text classification.

2 Background

Multi-label text classification refers to finding a subset that fits the specified text in the label set. The label set $L = \{l_1, l_2, l_3, l_4 \ldots l_n\}$ is set in advance, where l_n represents a label, and n represents the number of labels. Now it is necessary to find an $L_i \in L$ for each t_i in the text set $T = \{t_1, t_2, t_3, t_4 \ldots t_i\}$, and the labels of different texts can be the same. Therefore, multi-label classification can be described as $L = F(T)$, where F is the mapping relationship from text to label, and the mapping relationship is shown in Fig. 1.

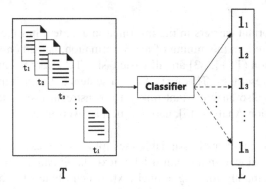

Fig. 1. Text and label mapping.

The processing flow of multi-label text classification tasks can be mainly divided into: text preprocessing, text representation, and multi-label classification. The flowchart is shown in Fig. 2. Text preprocessing refers to a series of operations such as removal of stop words, word segmentation, and part-of-speech restoration on the original data set, but currently there are very mature technologies for the above processing. If you need word segmentation, you can directly use jieba [10], HanLP [11] and other ready-made tools, researchers do not need to spend too much energy on this research. Text representation is the cornerstone of the field of natural language processing. Since machines cannot directly recognize natural language, it is the job of text representation to convert natural text into an expression that can be understood by machines. At present, text representations generally use distributed expression methods. Related research can be traced back to Word2Vec [12] developed by Google, but the feature vector dimension of this model is too high, which will cause excessive calculation. The current mainstream model is BERT [13], and the subdivided areas can be fine-tuned on the basis of BERT.

The research on multi-label text classification can be traced back to Binary [14] proposed by M.R. et al. in 2004. The model adopts the idea of problem transformation to transform the multi-label classification problem into multiple single-label problems. Its structure is simple but the shortcomings are also prominent, that is, the correlation between the tags is not mined, which makes the classification efficiency low. Since then, Jesse Read et al. proposed the Classifier Chain (CC) [15] against this drawback. The model links all the classifiers in a chain, so that a single trainer trains the input space and the previous classifiers in the chain. Although the correlation between the labels is considered to a certain extent, the essence is still to transform the problem into multiple Single label classification problem. The Label Powerset (LP) algorithm proposed by Boutell et al. [16] is a multi-class classifier that converts all different class label subsets into different classes for training in the training data, so as to solve the label correlation. However, as the training data increases, the number of label categories increases too fast, which increases the complexity of the model and reduces the accuracy. The above-mentioned methods are based on traditional machine learning, and not only have the cumbersome feature engineering that requires manual participation, but are also not suitable for large-scale text and extremely multi-labels. With the advent of deep learning, not only the end-to-end model is realized, but also the machine can perform feature engineering autonomously, and the performance has also been greatly improved.

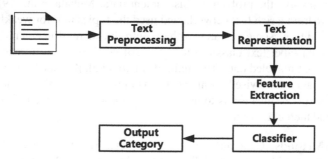

Fig. 2. Classification process.

Compared with traditional machine learning, deep learning can extract richer and deeper semantic information. From Word2vec to BERT, researchers have invested a lot of energy in feature extraction. Since then, scientific researchers have continuously improved the entire classification process, and the outstanding models that have emerged have been continuously refreshed to obtain SOAT.

3   Method

At present, related technologies such as text preprocessing in multi-label text classification are quite mature. The research content of the researchers mainly focuses on reducing dependence on the original data set, feature extraction, mining the correlation between tags, and improving the interpretability of the model. On a question. Therefore, this section will also summarize the excellent research results in recent years based on this.

3.1   Research to Reduce Dependence on Original Datasets

As one of the three major elements of the current development of artificial intelligence, the importance of data sets is self-evident. However, for the field of multi-label text classification, high-quality data sets are scarce resources, and most data sets have problems such as uneven data distribution, incorrect labeling or missing. In response to such problems, in recent years, scientific researchers have used limited supervision, joining a generative confrontation network, and strengthening data sets to solve them.

Limited Supervised. The limited supervised model has less dependence on the data set than supervised learning. Because it is very difficult to label multi-label data, a larger label space brings higher labeling costs. As the problems we face become more and more complex, sample dimensions, data volume, and label dimensions will all affect the cost of labeling. Therefore, another trend of multi-label in recent years is to pay attention to how to build better learning models under limited supervision.

Meta-learning [17] is one of the commonly used methods to solve small sample problems, and many researchers also apply it in the field of text classification. Deng et al. [18] proposed the MTM model, which uses a combination of meta-learning and unsupervised to solve the problem of insufficient data. Mekala et al. [19] fused meta data and text to train a rich text network, and used the topics in it for weakly supervised learning. In addition, some researchers have introduced reinforcement learning into the field of multi-label text classification. Ye [20] et al. used reinforcement learning to effectively use unlabeled data. The main idea Kim et al. [21] merged self-supervised learning and weakly-supervised learning to form multiple pre-training models to improve the effect of text classification is to use the label name to generate the corresponding vocabulary and then classify it.

GAN-based Methods. Generative Adversarial Network [22] is a machine learning architecture proposed by Ian Goodfellow of the University of Montreal in 2014. Generating a confrontation network is to learn by letting two neural networks play games with each other, which can generate new fake data based on the original data set. Based on GAN, there has been extensive research in the field of CV [23], and it is a good method to use GAN to solve the problem of insufficient dataset samples in multi-label text classification tasks.

Wu et al. [24] proposed a dual-adversarial collaborative learning method applied to multi-domain text classification (MDTC) to simultaneously align features in different domains and between labeled and unlabeled data to improve the generalization ability of the model. Jin et al. [25] proposed a new TextFooLER model based on generative adversarial network to efficiently generate adversarial text. Croce et al. [26] respectively proposed methods for text classification based on BERT generated adversarial examples.

Enhancing the Dataset. In view of the low quality of the data set itself, such as the long tail, one of the most direct strategies is to strengthen the data set. Of course, in addition to remanufacturing or perfecting the data set in a purely manual way, some researchers have also provided other ideas.

Yang et al. [27] proposed a hybrid CNN network to solve the problem of extreme imbalance of samples in multi-label text classification. Tepper et al. [28] proposed a BalaGen framework to expand the data set to obtain a more balanced data set. Lee et al. [29] proposed a SALNet model based on semi-supervised learning to stably expand the training data set. Mekala et al. [30] proposed a ConWea model based on weakly supervised learning to strengthen the corpus from the perspective of context.

3.2 Feature Extraction

Since computers cannot directly process text information, a method of expressing text with vectors is generally used for the computer to interpret the text. However, the vector obtained by text vectorization is not suitable for direct text classification due to its high dimensionality and sparse representation. Forcibly using text to represent the resulting vector will only lead to a huge amount of calculation and low precision. Therefore, it is necessary to remove irrelevant features from the initially obtained vector to obtain a dense vector, and it can even strengthen the favorable features for text classification.

Improve Feature Vector Representation Capabilities. Improving the characterization ability of eigenvectors is the most direct study of eigenvectors. Qin et al. [31] proposed a feature projection method, which projects existing features into the orthogonal space of common features to obtain a feature vector that is easier to classify and distinguish. He et al. [32] proposed the MSD model to improve the accuracy of uncertainty scores by reducing the overconfidence effect of winning scores and simultaneously considering the impact of different categories of uncertainty. There are also researchers who focus on proposing new term weighting schemes. Chen et al. proposed the TF-MDFS model to increase the weight of related terms in the feature vector [33]. Ibrahim et al. designed the pooling layer of CNN as a co-party pooling layer to extract feature vectors that are more suitable for classification [34].

Multi-feature Fusion. Feature fusion has many mature studies in the field of CV [35], and it is also a very valuable research direction in the field of NLP. When it is difficult for a feature vector to express the text in a deeper level, multiple vectors extracted from different features can be selected for characterization, so as to improve the accuracy of text classification.

Guo et al. combined the multi-scale structure with the self-attention mechanism so that the model can extract features from different scales [36]. Liu et al. constructed a text graph tensor, using semantic information, syntax and order constraints to describe context information [37]. Li et al. proposed an ACT model, which draws on the advantages of CNN and Transformer, combines global semantic features and local semantic features and retains order information [38]. Li et al. proposed the AGN model, which combines the statistical information of the text and the feature information of the text through a control gate mechanism to improve the text classification effect [39]. Tao et al. designed a radical feature for Chinese characters, and then combined it with text features [40]. Ali et al. combined OLDA and Bi-LSTM models for text feature extraction [41]. Ren et al. proposed the BG-TCA model, which uses an attention mechanism to replace the maximum pooling process to maximize the retention of text features in the feature fusion stage while distinguishing different features [42].

3.3 Mining Label Relevance

Compared with single-label text classification, multi-label text classification introduces a new point worth studying, that is, mining the correlation between labels.

Hierarchical Multi-label Text Classification. Compared with single-label text classification, the main challenge of hierarchical multi-label text classification lies in the exploration of the relationship between text feature expression and label structure.

Zhou et al. [43] proposed a HiAGM model that learns hierarchical perceptual label embedding through a hierarchical encoder to make full use of the interaction between the text feature space and the label space. Chen et al. introduced the joint embedding loss and matching learning loss to learn the semantic matching relationship of text labels in a hierarchical-aware manner [44]. Wang et al. proposed a new concept-based label embedding method that can express concepts explicitly and model the inter-class sharing mechanism of hierarchical text classification [45]. Huang et al. proposed a new framework, called Hierarchical Attention-Based Recurrent Neural Network (HARNN), which classifies documents into the most relevant category level by level by integrating text and hierarchical category structure [46].

Serialization Label. In 2014, the google team proposed a sequence-to-sequence model (seq2seq) [47], which simulates the way of thinking of people and designs an encoder and a decoder, which can map a sequence to another sequence. The framework of the Seq2seq model is shown in Fig. 3. At first, the seq2seq model was applied in the field of machine translation. Later, researchers discovered that if multiple tags associated with the text are regarded as a sequence, the seq2seq model can be used. Chen et al. [48] proposed the CNN-RNN model, which first extracts the text feature vector from the text through CNN, and then sends the vector to the RNN network to output the label. Yang [49] et al. introduced the attention mechanism into the seq2seq model and proposed the SGM model and used it in multi-label text classification. Later, Yang et al. [50] made improvements to SGM and added a Set Decoder module to reduce the impact of incorrect labels. Qin [51] et al. proposed an adaptive RNN sequence model to provide a new training target so that the RNN model can find the best label sequence.

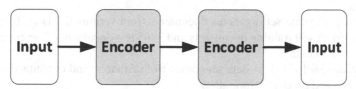

Fig. 3. seq2seq model.

3.4 Interpretability

The emergence of deep learning has greatly benefited multi-label text classification, and outstanding models that emerge continue to obtain SOAT on various data sets. However, the current deep learning model is more like a black box for humans, and it is impossible to know exactly how this box works. This also makes it difficult for researchers to predict the results of deep learning models, which requires a lot of computing resources to constantly test.

Arous et al. proposed a method of combining artificial and artificial intelligence to incorporate human classification reasons into the attention-based text classification model, thereby improving the interpretability of the classification results [52]. Sun et al. discussed the factors that may affect the attention score under the neural classification model [53]. Chrysostomou et al. proposed a series of new task scaling mechanisms to improve the credibility of the interpretation of text classification based on the attention mechanism [54]. Bhardwaj et al. conducted in-depth theoretical analysis and empirical observation on the identifiability of attention weights, and found that it is easier to identify attention weights by revealing the hidden effects of key vectors [55]. Moradi et al. proposed the BioCie method to obtain a model for electronic document classification from the post-interpretation of the backup box [56]. Chen et al. proposed a multi-label text classification framework with uncertainty quantification to better understand and evaluate the uncertainty in multi-label text classification tasks [57].

4 Dataset and Evaluation

4.1 Datasets

We have summarized 9 mainstream datasets in the field of multi-label text classification, covering Chinese and English, long text and short text, extreme multi-label and ordinary multi-label. We briefly elaborated these datasets in order of the number of tags from the least to the most, and showed the relevant data in Table 1:

- AAPD [58]: This dataset is a collection of abstracts and corresponding discipline categories of 55,840 papers collected by Yang and others from the Internet.
- Reuter-21578 [59]: The dataset contains 22 documents, a total of 21587 news articles from Reuters, and a total of 90 tags.
- RCV1 [60]: This data set is also from a Reuters news column report, collated and collected by Lewis and others.
- ToutiaoNews [61]: This data set is a Chinese data set that counts the news from today's headlines.
- Eurlex [62]: The data set organizes documents from various EU laws, treaties, etc., and contains 15,449 training documents and 3865 test documents. The entire data set has a total of 3956 tags.
- AmazonCat-13K [63]: This data set comes from Amazon and contains data such as user reviews and product information.
- Wiki0-31K [64]: The data set contains 18011 articles on Wikipedia, but the number of tags has reached 30,928.
- Wiki-500K [65]: The data is also included from Wikipedia, but compared to the Wiki10-31K data set, the number of samples is larger and the number of tags is larger.
- Amazon-670K [66]: This data set comes from Amazon's user reviews, product information and other data like AmazonCat-13K, but the number of tags in this data set reaches an astonishing 6,700,091.

Table 1. Datasets related information. Detailed datasets statistics. Ntrain is the number of training samples, Ntest is the number of test samples, L is the number of labels, $\bar{L}$ is the average number of labels per sample, $\hat{L}$ is the average number of samples per label, Wtrain is the average number of words per training sample and Wtest is the average number of words per testing sample.

Datasets	N_{train}	N_{test}	L	$\bar{L}$	$\hat{L}$	W_{train}	W_{test}
AAPD	54,840	1,000	54	2.41	2,444.04	163.42	171.65
Reuters-21578	7,769	3,019	90	–	–	–	–
RCV1	781,265	23,149	103	3.18	729.67	259.47	269.23
ToutiaoNews	23,677	5,261	1,070	–	–	–	–
Eurlex	15,499	3,865	3,956	5.30	20.79	1,248.58	1,230.40
AmazonCat-13K	1,186,239	306,782	13,330	5.04	448.57	246.61	245.98
Wiki10-31K	14,146	6,616	30,938	18.64	8.52	2,484.30	2,425.45
Wiki-500K	1,779,881	769,421	501,008	4.75	16.86	808.66	808.56
Amazon-670K	490,449	153,025	670,091	5.45	3.99	247.23	241.22

4.2 Evaluation

In multi-label text classification, commonly used evaluation indicators usually include Hamming Loss (HL) and Micro-F1.

Hamming Loss. Schapire et al. [67] proposed the Hamming loss in 1999. Simply put, it is a measure of the proportion of misclassified labels. The proportion of labels whose correct labels are not predicted correctly and the proportion of labels whose wrong labels are predicted are two. The percentage of difference in the label set, the smaller the value of Hamming loss, the better the prediction result. Calculated as follows:

$$HL = \frac{1}{|D|} \sum_{i=1}^{|D|} \frac{XOR(x_i, y_i)}{|L|} \tag{1}$$

Among them, $|D|$ is the number of samples, $|L|$ is the total number of labels, x_i represents the label, y_i represents the real label, and XOR is the exclusive or operation.

Micro-precision, Micro-recall and Micro-F1. For single-label text classification, the precision rate (Precision) is based on the prediction result, indicating how many of the samples whose predictions are positive are real samples. One is to predict the positive class as a positive class (TP), and the other One is to predict the negative class as a positive class (FP), which reflects the precision of the model. The recall rate (Recall) is for the sample, indicating how many positive samples in the sample are predicted correctly. One is to predict the original positive sample as a positive class (TP), and the other is to predict the original positive sample. It is a negative class (FN), which reflects the recall rate of the model. See Table 2 for details.

Table 2. Confusion matrix.

Confusion matrix		Predictive value	
		Positive	Negative
Actual value	Positive	TP	FN
	Negative	FP	TN

Multi-label text classification assigns text to multiple labels, and the number of labels is not fixed. Micro-precision and Micro-recall are usually used, considering the overall accuracy and recall rate of all labels. Ideally, the higher the two, the better, but the actual situation often produces contradictions. Therefore, in the field of multi-label text classification, Micro-F1 is used for evaluation. Micro-F1 is the harmonic average of Micro-precision and Micro-recall, and its calculation formula is as follows (where L represents the total number of category labels) [68]:

$$Micro - precision = \frac{\sum_{j=1}^{L} TP_j}{\sum_{j=1}^{L} (TP_j + FP_j)} \tag{2}$$

$$Micro - recall = \frac{\sum_{j=1}^{L} TP_j}{\sum_{j=1}^{L} (TP_j + FN_j)} \tag{3}$$

$$Micro - F1 = \frac{\sum_{j=1}^{L} 2TP_j}{\sum_{j=1}^{L} (2TP_j + FP_j + FN_j)} \tag{4}$$

5 Summary and Outlook

Text classification is an important basic task in the field of natural language processing, and multi-label text classification is an important branch of text classification. The research on multi-label text classification has achieved fruitful results with the advent of deep learning, especially after the advent of BERT, it has greatly improved the accuracy of related research. Although there are already quite mature and practical technologies in this field, there are still some thorny issues that are worth exploring together by researchers:

- The lack of data sets and low quality problems. Multi-label text classification is much more expensive than single-label text classification, so the lack of data set resources greatly limits the development of models by researchers. Secondly, because the current data set in this field generally has uneven data distribution, it is mainly manifested as a long-tail problem, that is, most documents in the same data set are only related to one or a very small number of tags. Therefore, creating more high-quality data sets or studying how to deal with low-quality data sets or even deep learning models without data sets is a problem worthy of long-term discussion.
- The problem of dynamic division of text-related labels. At present, multi-label text classification mainly relies on supervised learning, which means that once the label changes, the existing model needs to be retrained to adapt to this change. But this requires high costs for both relabeling the data set or training the model. Therefore, how to make the trained model adapt to the change of the label at low cost and quickly is a problem worthy of consideration.

6 Conclusion

We explained the multi-label text classification and briefly described its development. Then we summarized the excellent research results in recent years. Then it summarizes the data sets that are currently popular in the field of multi-label text classification, and introduces the evaluation indicators commonly used in this field. Finally, this article is summarized and the future development of multi-label text classification is prospected.

Acknowledgement. This work was supported by National Natural Science Foundation of China (Grant No. 62162024 and 62162022), Key Projects in Hainan Province (Grant ZDYF2021GXJS003 and Grant ZDYF2020040), the Major science and technology project of Hainan Province(Grant No. ZDKJ2020012).

References

1. Cheng, J., Liu, J., Xu, X., Xia, D., Liu, L., Sheng, V.: A review of Chinese named entity recognition. KSII Trans. Internet Inf. Syst. **15**(6), 2012–2030 (2021)
2. Ras, A., Cc, B., Rgr, C., Rn, D., Sor, A.: Knowledge-enhanced document embeddings for text classification. Knowl.-Based Syst. **163**, 955–971 (2019)

3. Min, Y.A., Wei, Z.B., Lei, C.A., Qiang, Q.A., Zhou, Z.C., Ying, S.: Investigating the transferring capability of capsule networks for text classification. Neural Netw. **118**, 247–261 (2019)
4. Chen, Y., Qi, X.L., Zhang, P.: Replica wormhole and information retrieval in the syk model coupled to majorana chains. J. High Energy Phys. **6**, 1–26 (2020)
5. Chen, J., Li, H., Ma, L., Bo, H.: Improving emotion analysis for speech-induced EEGs through EEMD-HHT-based feature extraction and electrode selection. Int. J. Multim. Data Eng. Manag. **12**(2), 1–18 (2021)
6. Ray, S.K., Shaalan, K.: A review and future perspectives of Arabic question answering systems. IEEE Trans. Knowl. Data Eng. **28**(12), 3169–3190 (2016)
7. Shah, A.A., Ravana, S.D., Hamid, S., Ismail, M.A.: Accuracy evaluation of methods and techniques in web-based question answering systems: a survey. Knowl. Inf. Syst. **58**(3), 611–650 (2018)
8. Shaheen, M., Ezzeldin, A.M.: Arabic question answering: systems, resources, tools, and future trends. Arab. J. Sci. Eng. **39**(6), 4541–4564 (2014)
9. Huang, M., et al.: Supervised representation learning for multi-label classification. Mach. Learn. **108**(5), 747–763 (2019)
10. Ruan, Q., Wu, Q., Wang, Y., Liu, X., Miao, F.: Effective learning model of user classification based on ensemble learning algorithms. Computing **101**(6), 531–545 (2018)
11. Yang, Y., Ren, G.: HanLP-based technology function matrix construction on Chinese process patents. Int. J. Mob. Comput. Multim. Commun. **11**(3), 48–64 (2020)
12. Mikolov, T., Chen, K., Corrado, G., Dean, J.: Efficient estimation of word representations in vector space. arXiv preprint arXiv:1301.3781 (2013)
13. Devlin, J., Chang, M.W., Lee, K., Toutanova, K.: Bert: pre-training of deep bidirectional transformers for language understanding. arXiv preprint arXiv:1810.04805 (2018)
14. Boutell, M.R., Luo, J., Shen, X., Brown, C.M.: Learning multi-label scene classification. Pattern Recogn. **37**(9), 1757–1771 (2004)
15. Read, J., Pfahringer, B., Holmes, G., Frank, E.: Classifier chains for multi-label classification. Mach. Learn. **85**(3), 333–359 (2011)
16. Tsoumakas, G., Katakis, I.: Multi-label classification: an overview. Int. J. Data Warehous. Min. **3**(3), 1–13 (2009)
17. Arjmand, A., Samizadeh, R., Dehghani Saryazdi, M.: Meta-learning in multivariate load demand forecasting with exogenous meta-features. Energy Efficiency **13**(5), 871–887 (2020)
18. Deng, S., Zhang, N., Sun, Z., Chen, J., Chen, H.: When low resource NLP meets unsupervised language model: meta-pretraining then meta-learning for few-shot text classification (student abstract). In: Proceedings of the AAAI Conference on Artificial Intelligence, vol. 34, no. 10, pp. 13773–13774 (2020)
19. Mekala, D., Zhang, X., Shang, J.: Meta: metadata-empowered weak supervision for text classification. In: Proceedings of the 2020 Conference on Empirical Methods in Natural Language Processing (EMNLP) (2020)
20. Ye, Z., et al.: Zero-shot text classification via reinforced self-training. In: Proceedings of the 58th Annual Meeting of the Association for Computational Linguistics. pp. 3014–3024 (2020)
21. Kim, K.M., Hyeon, B., Kim, Y., Park, J.H., Lee, S.: Multi-pretraining for largescale text classification. In: Proceedings of the 2020 Conference on Empirical Methods in Natural Language Processing: Findings, pp. 2041–2050 (2020)
22. Cheng, J., Yang, Y., Tang, X., Xiong, N., Zhang, Y., Lei, F.: Generative adversarial networks: a literature review. KSII Trans. Internet Inf. Syst. **14**(12), 4625–4647 (2020)
23. Lei, F., Cheng, J., Yang, Y., Tang, X., Sheng, V.S., Huang, C.: Improving heterogeneous network knowledge transfer based on the principle of generative adversarial. Electronics **10**(13), 1525 (2021)

24. Wu, Y., Guo, Y.: Dual adversarial co-learning for multi-domain text classification. In: Proceedings of the AAAI Conference on Artificial Intelligence, vol. 34, pp. 6438–6445 (2020)
25. Jin, D., Jin, Z., Zhou, J.T., Szolovits, P.: Is bert really robust? A strong baseline for natural language attack on text classification and entailment. In: Proceedings of the AAAI Conference on Artificial Intelligence, vol. 34, pp. 8018–8025 (2020)
26. Croce, D., Castellucci, G., Basili, R.: Gan-bert: generative adversarial learning for robust text classification with a bunch of labeled examples. In: Proceedings of the 58th Annual Meeting of the Association for Computational Linguistics, pp. 2114–2119 (2020)
27. Yang, W., Li, J., Fukumoto, F., Ye, Y.: MSCNN: a monomeric-siamese convolutional neural network for extremely imbalanced multi-label text classification. In: Proceedings of the 2020 Conference on Empirical Methods in Natural Language Processing (EMNLP), pp. 6716–6722 (2020)
28. Tepper, N., Goldbraich, E., Zwerdling, N., Kour, G., Tavor, A.A., Carmeli, B.: Balancing via generation for multi-class text classification improvement. In: Proceedings of the 2020 Conference on Empirical Methods in Natural Language Processing: Findings, pp. 1440–1452 (2020)
29. Lee, J.H., Ko, S.K., Han, Y.S.: Salnet: semi-supervised few-shot text classification with attention-based lexicon construction. In: Proceedings of the AAAI Conference on Artificial Intelligence, vol. 35, pp. 13189–13197 (2021)
30. Mekala, D., Shang, J.: Contextualized weak supervision for text classification. In: Proceedings of the 58th Annual Meeting of the Association for Computational Linguistics, pp. 323–333 (2020)
31. Qin, Q., Hu, W., Liu, B.: Feature projection for improved text classification. In: Proceedings of the 58th Annual Meeting of the Association for Computational Linguistics, pp. 8161–8171 (2020)
32. He, J., et al.: Towards more accurate uncertainty estimation in text classification. In: Proceedings of the 2020 Conference on Empirical Methods in Natural Language Processing (EMNLP), pp. 8362–8372 (2020)
33. Chen, L., Jiang, L., Li, C.: Modified DFS-based term weighting scheme for text classification. Expert Syst. Appl. **168**, 114438 (2021)
34. Ibrahim, M., Shaawat, A., Torki, M.: Covariance pooling layer for text classification. Proc. Comput. Sci. **189**, 61–66 (2021)
35. Tang, X., Tu, W., Li, K., Cheng, J.: DFFNet: an IoT-perceptive dual feature fusion network for general real-time semantic segmentation. Inf. Sci. **565**, 326–343 (2021)
36. Guo, Q., Qiu, X., Liu, P., Xue, X., Zhang, Z.: Multi-scale self-attention for text classification. In: Proceedings of the AAAI Conference on Artificial Intelligence, vol. 34, pp. 7847–7854 (2020)
37. Liu, X., You, X., Zhang, X., Wu, J., Lv, P.: Tensor graph convolutional networks for text classification. In: Proceedings of the AAAI Conference on Artificial Intelligence, vol. 34, pp. 8409–8416 (2020)
38. Li, P., et al.: Act: an attentive convolutional transformer for efficient text classification. In: Proceedings of the AAAI Conference on Artificial Intelligence, vol. 35, pp. 13261–13269 (2021)
39. Li, X., Li, Z., Xie, H., Li, Q.: Merging statistical feature via adaptive gate for improved text classification. In: Proceedings of the AAAI Conference on Artificial Intelligence, vol. 35, pp. 13288–13296 (2021)
40. Tao, H., et al.: Ideography leads us to the field of cognition: a radical-guided associative model for Chinese text classification. In: Proceedings of the AAAI Conference on Artificial Intelligence, vol. 35, pp. 13898–13906 (2021)
41. Ali, F., Ali, A., Imran, M., Naqvi, R.A., Siddiqi, M.H., Kwak, K.S.: Traffic accident detection and condition analysis based on social networking data. Accid. Anal. Prev. **151**, 105973 (2021)

42. Ren, J., Wu, W., Liu, G., Chen, Z., Wang, R.: Bidirectional gated temporal convolution with attention for text classification. Neurocomputing **455**, 265–273 (2021)
43. Zhou, J., et al.: Hierarchy-aware global model for hierarchical text classification. In: Proceedings of the 58th Annual Meeting of the Association for Computational Linguistics, pp. 1106–1117 (2020)
44. Chen, H., Ma, Q., Lin, Z., Yan, J.: Hierarchy-aware label semantics matching network for hierarchical text classification. In: Proceedings of the 59th Annual Meeting of the Association for Computational Linguistics and the 11th International Joint Conference on Natural Language Processing, vol. 1, pp. 4370–4379 (2021)
45. Wang, X., Zhao, L., Liu, B., Chen, T., Zhang, F., Wang, D.: Concept-based label embedding via dynamic routing for hierarchical text classification. In: Proceedings of the 59th Annual Meeting of the Association for Computational Linguistics and the 11th International Joint Conference on Natural Language Processing, vol. 1, pp. 5010–5019 (2021)
46. Huang, W., et al.: Hierarchical multi-label text classification: an attention-based recurrent network approach. In: Proceedings of the 28th ACM International Conference on Information and Knowledge Management, pp. 1051–1060 (2019)
47. Cho, K., et al.: Learning phrase representations using RNN encoder decoder for statistical machine translation. arXiv preprint arXiv:1406.1078 (2014)
48. Chen, G., Ye, D., Xing, Z., Chen, J., Cambria, E.: Ensemble application of convolutional and recurrent neural networks for multi-label text categorization. In: 2017 International Joint Conference on Neural Networks (IJCNN), pp. 2377–2383. IEEE (2017)
49. Yang, P., Sun, X., Li, W., Ma, S., Wu, W., Wang, H.: SGM: sequence generation model for multi-label classification. arXiv preprint arXiv:1806.04822 (2018)
50. Yang, P., Luo, F., Ma, S., Lin, J., Sun, X.: A deep reinforced sequence-to-set model for multi-label classification. In: Proceedings of the 57th Annual Meeting of the Association for Computational Linguistics, pp. 5252–5258 (2019)
51. Qin, K., Li, C., Pavlu, V., Aslam, J.A.: Adapting RNN sequence prediction model to multi-label set prediction. arXiv preprint arXiv:1904.05829 (2019)
52. Arous, I., Dolamic, L., Yang, J., Bhardwaj, A., Cuccu, G., Cudré-Mauroux, P.: Marta: leveraging human rationales for explainable text classification. In: Proceedings of the AAAI Conference on Artificial Intelligence, vol. 35, pp. 5868–5876 (2021)
53. Sun, X., Lu, W.: Understanding attention for text classification. In: Proceedings of the 58th Annual Meeting of the Association for Computational Linguistics, pp. 3418–3428 (2020)
54. Chrysostomou, G., Aletras, N.: Improving the faithfulness of attention-based explanations with task-specific information for text classification. arXiv preprint arXiv:2105.02657 (2021)
55. Bhardwaj, R., Majumder, N., Poria, S., Hovy, E.: More identifiable yet equally performant transformers for text classification. arXiv preprint arXiv:2106.01269 (2021)
56. Moradi, M., Samwald, M.: Explaining black-box models for biomedical text classification. IEEE J. Biomed. Health Inform. **25**(8), 3112–3120 (2021)
57. Chen, W., Zhang, B., Lu, M.: Uncertainty quantification for multilabel text classification. Wiley Interdiscip. Rev. Data Min. Knowl. Discov. **10**(6), e1384 (2020)
58. Pal, A., Selvakumar, M., Sankarasubbu, M.: Magnet: multi-label text classification using attention-based graph neural network. In: ICAART, vol. 2, pp. 494–505 (2020)
59. Reuters Corpus. https://martin-thoma.com/nlp-reuters (2017)
60. Lewis, D.D., Yang, Y., Russell-Rose, T., Li, F.: Rcv1: a new benchmark collection for text categorization research. J. Mach. Learn. Res. **5**, 361–397 (2004)
61. Toutiao News (2018). https://github.com/fateleak/toutiao-text-classfication-dataset
62. EUR-Lex Corpus (2019). http://www.ke.tu-darmstadt.de/resources/eurlex/eurlex.html

63. Mencía, E.L., Fürnkranz, J.: Efficient pairwise multilabel classification for large-scale problems in the legal domain. In: Daelemans, W., Goethals, B., Morik, K. (eds.) ECML PKDD 2008. LNCS (LNAI), vol. 5212, pp. 50–65. Springer, Heidelberg (2008). https://doi.org/10.1007/978-3-540-87481-2_4

64. Zubiaga, A.: Enhancing navigation on Wikipedia with social tags. ArXiv preprint arXiv:1202.5469 (2012)

65. McAuley, J., Leskovec, J.: Hidden factors and hidden topics: understanding rating dimensions with review text. In: Proceedings of the 7th ACM Conference on Recommender Systems, pp. 165–172 (2013)

66. Amazon670K Corpus (2016). http://manikvarma.org/downloads/XC/XMLRepository.html

67. Schapire, R.E., Singer, Y.: Improved boosting algorithms using confidence-rated predictions. Mach. Learn. **37**(3), 297–336 (1999)

68. Schütze, H., Manning, C.D., Raghavan, P.: Introduction to information retrieval. Camb. Univ. Press **39**, 234–265 (2008)

Interpreting Convolutional Neural Networks via Layer-Wise Relevance Propagation

Wohuan Jia, Shaoshuai Zhang, Yue Jiang, and Li Xu[✉]

College of Computer Science and Technology, Harbin Engineering University,
Harbin 150001, China
xuli@hrbeu.edu.cn

Abstract. Black box characteristics of machine learning algorithms seriously hamper their application in the certain fields, such as medicine, military, finance and so on. So far, the interpretability of machine learning remains as a challenge. In this paper, we use Layer-wise Relevance Propagation (LRP) to calculate the relevance of the Convolutional Neural Network (CNN) on the input data, and visualize it as a heat map, so as to intuitively understand which features the Convolutional Neural Network are based on to make prediction, and then improve the model by analyzing the heat maps. In this article, by using the control variable method, the LRP algorithm is applied to the improved convolution neural network to obtain a new heat map. The difference between the two heat maps is analyzed to verify that the interpretable algorithm conforms to the objective facts. In this way, the interpretability of different network structures is compared and improved.

Keywords: Convolutional neural network · Layer-wise relevance propagation · Deconvolution · Heat map

1 Introduction

With the rapid development of computer science and technology, computers have been able to replace people to do some tedious and repetitive tasks, bringing great convenience to people's lives. Thanks to the rapid development of machine learning, advanced artificial intelligence systems have successfully simulated or even surpassed human performance in many decision-making games, such as Alpha GO [1] defeating human top chess player Shishi Li in 2016. The difference from traditional modeling ideas is that neural networks are not entirely dependent on physical features, but are driven by data, and features are extracted from data through a complex network structure. CNN [2] is a feedforward neural network that includes convolution calculations and has a deep structure. It is one of the representative algorithms of deep learning. On the one hand, with the development of graphics processing unit GPU and the improvement of computer computing power, neural networks are used in autonomous driving [3], visual problem solving [4–7] image classification, natural language processing, human behavior recognition [8], medical diagnosis even weapons of mass destruction [9] and other fields. But on the other hand, it has also been used to "do bad things" or even harm humans. For

© The Author(s), under exclusive license to Springer Nature Switzerland AG 2022
X. Sun et al. (Eds.): ICAIS 2022, LNCS 13338, pp. 457–467, 2022.
https://doi.org/10.1007/978-3-031-06794-5_37

example, certain websites use artificial intelligence algorithms to perform big data kills. In 2015, Volkswagen in Germany even had a robot "killing incident". In this regard, the European Union has required all algorithms to explain their output principles [10, 11].

Neural networks perform very well in practical applications. Due to the nonlinear nested structure of neural networks, it is difficult for people to explain [12] on which features the neural network makes corresponding predictions, so it is also regarded as a black box model. In some fields that only value results, neural networks are understandable as black box models. For example, Alpha GO only needs to win the game; but in many fields, the inexplicability of neural networks is a shortcoming that cannot be ignored, such as in the field of medical diagnosis that emphasizes the decision-making process. People often don't trust the prediction results of the black box model, and they trust experts who can give a reasonable explanation. For example, in autonomous driving technology, small misjudgments may bring serious consequences, so safety must be guaranteed.

From another perspective, Explainable AI (or XAI for short) will also open up many new ways of cooperation between humans and machines. For example, many fields will try to introduce machine learning [13] technology in the absence of sufficient data and use its ability to quickly process large amounts of data. At this time, explainable artificial intelligence helps humans to determine when to let the machine process and when to intervene. For example, in the financial field such as venture capital: In the financial scenario, the interpretability of the model is particularly emphasized, so that people's risk control experience and intuitive feelings can be correlated with the results of data performance. It is precisely the interpretability of neural networks that plays an important role in more and more occasional applications. Many scholars are dedicated to studying the interpretability of neural networks. The theoretical analysis and visualization of neural network interpretability have gradually become an important subject of deep learning. The theoretical analysis and visualization of neural network interpretability have gradually become an important subject of deep learning.

The interpretability of neural networks can be used to improve the model. The improvement of the model is first to discover the shortcomings of the model. Compared with the incomprehensible black box model, the interpretable neural network is easier to find the cause of the decision error, so as to make improvements based on the error. Interpretability can also be used to verify neural network models. Neural networks must undergo rigorous verification from training to actual application. People often verify neural networks through existing data sets, so the accuracy of new sample prediction results, or data sets, cannot be guaranteed. There are systematic deviations, even if it performs well on existing data sets, it cannot be applied in practice.

The interpretability of neural networks can be used. Interpretability can be used to compare the pros and cons of different models. It can be seen from the literatures [14, 15] that although different models are similar in classification performance, they make decisions based on completely different characteristics. The interpretability can be selected from the three models that is most consistent with the actual situation from the three models.

Interpretability can bring many new discoveries. With human capabilities, the observation of data is usually very limited, but millions or more of samples are used as training sets by neural networks. And in the training process, the neural network can learn all the features that people cannot perceive. Through feature visualization, you can intuitively see the features learned by the neural network to explore new possibilities.

2 Background

2.1 Convolutional Neural Network

As a kind of deep neural network [16], convolutional neural network is used for visual image analysis in most cases. One of their main applications is image classification [17], which is the process of taking images as input and outputting image categories. When the image is input to the model, the model treats it as an array of pixel values according to the size and resolution of the image.

2.2 Explanatory Algorithm

The research and interpretation of machine learning models. Artificial intelligence has been carried out in the early stage of artificial intelligence research, but it has not been included in the research field until recent years. Although the research scope of explainable artificial intelligence focuses on deep learning, it covers artificial intelligence technology and other machine learning models.

Moritz Böhle discussed an interpretability method called Layer-wise Relevance Propagation [18] (Layer-wise Relevance Propagation, LRP), which is a general method for interpreting AI predictions. The mathematical explanation is the deep Taylor decomposition of the neural network. It was originally proposed by Bach et al. in the 2015 paper "On the Pixel-Level Explanation of Nonlinear Classifier Decisions by Hierarchical Correlation Propagation".

2.3 LRP

Deep neural networks are some of the most powerful learning algorithms ever developed. Unfortunately, they are also the most complicated. The hierarchical nonlinear transformation of neural networks applied to data is almost impossible to understand. This problem is exacerbated by the uncertainty of neural network training mechanisms. To solve this problem, deep learning researchers use a variety of tools and techniques to monitor the learning process of neural networks. Even just visualizing the weight matrices or histograms of gradients for each layer can help researchers spot problems. After training the network, it is often helpful for researchers to try to understand how the network forms predictions. For example, in this paper, we use deconvolution techniques to visualize how each layer in a convolutional neural network processes an input image by essentially reversing the hierarchical image encoding process.

LRP is a technique used to determine which features in a particular input vector contribute the most to the output of a neural network. LRP can produce some very useful and nice-looking visualizations of how neural networks interpret images.

3 Convolutional Neural Network Structure

3.1 Convolution

Convolution [19] is a mathematical operator that combines two functions f and g to produce a third function. Here, perform operations on the convolution kernel and the input to obtain a new output.

Assuming that three $5 \times 5 \times 3$ filters [20] are used, the output of the first convolutional layer will be an array of $28 \times 28 \times 3$, and the three filters represent three features. When entering the next convolutional layer, the output of the previous convolutional layer is the input of the next convolutional layer. Assuming that the previous convolution layer is the first layer, its input is the original image, and the input of the next layer of convolution is the activation map output by the previous layer. The second level of input usually depicts the location of low-level functions in the picture. Based on this, a set of filters will be used (pass it through the second convolutional layer), and the output will be an activation map that represents more advanced functions. Such features can be semicircles (combination of curves and straight lines) or quadrilaterals (combination of several straight lines). As we go deeper into the network and go through more convolutional layers, we will obtain activation maps of more complex functions. The deeper the network, the better the feel of the filter, which means that they can handle a larger range of raw input.

3.2 Pooling

The pooling layer is usually located after the convolutional layer. Its main function is to reduce the spatial size (width × height) of the input volume of the next convolutional layer, but the pooling operation does not affect the depth size of the volume. The pooling layer is very similar to the convolutional layer. It uses a sliding window or a specific area that moves across the input stride, and then converts these values into the values to be represented. The conversion is performed by taking the maximum value from the observable values in the window (called the "max pool") or taking the average of these values.

Overfitting is a characteristic considered when creating an overly complex model. Again, this is an abstract explanation of the concept of pooling, and does not delve into the mathematical and technical aspects of pooling. Here, the human brain can be used for comparison. The human brain performs the merging step. The input image received by the human eye is then extracted multiple times until the most relevant information is retained as much as possible. After completing the first two steps, you should now have a pooled feature map. What happens after the flattening step is that you finally get a long input data vector, which is then processed further through the artificial neural network.

3.3 Fully Connected

In the process of adding artificial neural networks and convolutional neural networks to the latter, the process of creating convolutional neural networks began to become more complicated. In the context of convolution, the "fully connected layer" is used. The input layer contains the data vector created in the flattening step. The functions extracted in all previous steps are encoded in this vector. At this point, they are enough to accurately identify the category to a certain extent. Now, people hope to take it to a new level in terms of complexity and accuracy.

After a series of convolution, pooling, and flattening operations, the neural network will predict it. For example, suppose that the probability that the task in the network prediction is a dog is 80%, but in fact the image is indeed a cat. In this case, an error-loss function must be calculated. In order to achieve this goal, the cross-entropy function is used, but it is only necessary to know that the function of the loss function is to tell people the accuracy of the network, and then use it to optimize the network to improve its effectiveness. This requires some changes in the network, including weights (blue lines connecting neurons) and feature detectors, because the network often proves to be looking for the wrong features and must be checked multiple times for optimization. Then the information is transmitted in the opposite direction. In the process of optimizing the network, the information continues to flow back and forth until the network reaches the desired state.

4 Interpretability of Deep Learning

In 2016, when AlphaGo and Lee Sedol played WuFan chess, AlphaGo made many moves that human Go experts had never thought of. Fan Hui [21], who was watching the game at the time, once commented: This is not a move that humans will make. I have never seen a human moves. I've never seen a human plays this move. People may have research on AlphaGo's chess ability out of curiosity and competition needs, but if artificial intelligence related technologies are to be extended to more fields, such as assisting in sentencing in courts [22] and assisting in medical diagnosis [23]. Judging the pros and cons of an investment strategy in insurance and finance [24], or dominating the allocation of resources in social welfare policies, people will more urgently need to know how the model draws conclusions.

LRP was first published in Bach et al. (2015). Generally used in the model interpretation of image recognition [25], LRP can calculate the relevance of each pixel in the input image data to the recognition result.

In fact, there have been several ways to show the importance of each dimension of input data with heat maps. Samek et al. [26] have compared the differences between LRP, sensitivity analysis, and deconvolution. The general conclusion is that LRP has better explanatory power than sensitivity analysis and deconvolution, and the amount of data in the heat map is relatively small, and the degree of disorder is relatively low. However, sensitivity analysis is mainly to calculate the norm of the gradient vector of the classification function in each dimension of the input data, so it shows which dimension changes can change the prediction results most, which is a little different from the importance.

The calculation of these heat maps is done through a certain backpropagation algorithm [27], and the output results are used to derive the importance of the input data. The algorithm used by LRP is relatively intuitive. In principle, it depends on how much the neuron of the previous layer contributes to the next layer in the prediction process. According to this ratio, the back propagation is all relevance of one layer is allocated to the previous layer and pushed back to the input layer.

5 Experiments

5.1 Applying LRP to Different Convolutional Neural Networks

We mainly use the controlled variable method to compare the heat map obtained by the LRP algorithm. First, by using different types of data sets, and then by using the same LRP algorithm to visualize different types of heat maps, the types of data sets used here are: MNIST handwritten data set and ImageNet.

For the MNIST handwritten data set, we use the transformation of the ordinary convolutional neural network and the convolutional neural network AlexNet for comparison. It is called the modified AlexNet because the data set used is MNIST, and the size and number of convolution kernels need to be changed, but the order of convolution, pooling, and full connection is exactly the same as that of the classic convolutional neural network AlexNet.

For the imagenet data set, here is a comparison between VGG16 and VGG19. Through comparison, it can be found that the network structure of VGG16 and VGG19 is basically similar, but starting from the third block, each block of VGG19 has one more convolutional layer than VGG16. Combined with "the more layers, the better the effect", you can boldly guess here: the heat map effect generated by VGG19 will definitely be better than VGG16, and this is indeed the case.

5.2 Heat Map Result Display

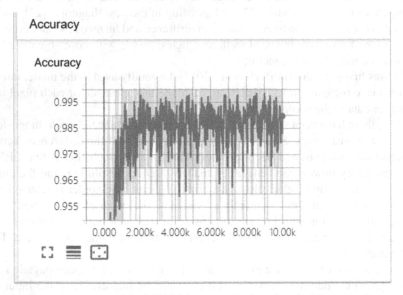

Fig. 1. The accuracy rate of the MNIST dataset trained on the AlexNet network structure.

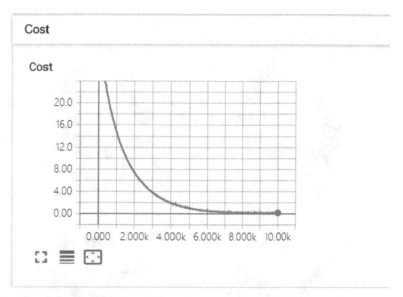

Fig. 2. The loss function trained by the MNIST dataset in the AlexNet network structure.

First of all, Figs. 1 and 2 are the accuracy and loss function trained by the MNIST data set in the AlexNet network structure. From the images, it can be clearly seen that the accuracy of the first point is extremely high, which has reached 99.5%, and the second point is the loss. As the number of iterations of the function increases, the loss becomes lower and lower, and finally approaches 0. Through these two images, it can be determined that the training is still very good.

After the training is over, start to use the LRP algorithm to get a visual heat map:

The numbers 0 and 8 on the left and on the right in the above Fig. 3 are heat maps generated by using the same LRP algorithm under the ordinary convolutional neural network and the AlexNet classic convolutional neural network, respectively.

Through the comparison of the same number, you will find that the more layers of the convolutional neural network, the darker the heat map generated. The following is the heat map generated by the VGG16 and VGG19 network structures in the same LRP algorithm:

The left side of the Fig. 4 is the heat map generated by the LRP algorithm under the VGG16 network structure, and the right side is the heat map generated under the VGG19 network structure. Through the heat map, it can be clearly compared that the heat map of VGG19 has a darker color and VGG16 has a slightly lighter color, which also confirms that the deeper the network structure mentioned above, the greater the number of layers, the darker the color of the generated heat map. The image at the Fig. 4 predicts that the image is Chihuahua, and the number 0.96 on the right represents the probability that the image is Chihuahua. Obviously, the prediction is completely correct [28, 29].

As we all know, the heat map generated under the LRP algorithm is not to let people recognize objects, but to make the recognition of the convolutional neural network interpretable through the heat map, and it is intuitive to tell people which pixels the

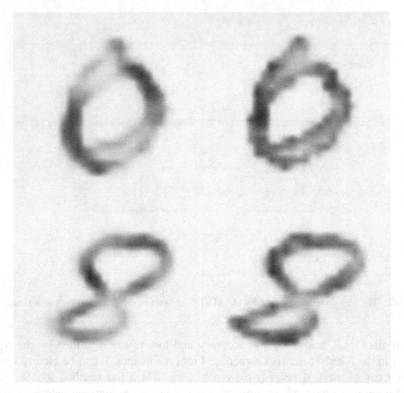

Fig. 3. MNIST data set (left picture) and AlexNet data set (right picture).

('n02085620', 'Chihuahua', 0.9698033)   ('n02085620', 'Chihuahua', 0.96787125)

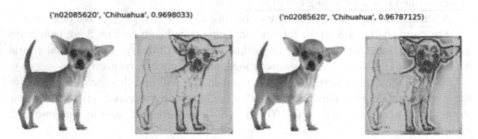

Fig. 4. Chihuahua heat map.

convolutional neural network uses to judge. What kind of image does the image belong to. Therefore, when you carefully observe the heat map of the Chihuahua above, you will find that the red pixels of the heat map are mainly concentrated on the head and footsteps, especially the mouth and eyes of the head, and the overall outline of the Chihuahua's head is clearly displayed. Out. According to the principle of the LRP algorithm-the red points in the heat map indicate the points with high correlation, that is, the main basis for the convolutional neural network to make classification decisions, and then compare the results in the heat map with the objective facts to explain the convolutional neural network model. Therefore, it can be concluded that the convolutional neural network VGG16 and VGG19 recognizes that the output picture is a Chihuahua based on the Chihuahua's head contour, ear shape, and characteristics of the foot.

This paper has visualized the LRP algorithm through a variety of data sets, and verified its feasibility, but found that the heat maps visualized by using VGG16 and VGG19 convolutional neural networks at the same time are not very different, but one color is darker and slightly lighter. This conclusion is not sufficient and does not have any substance. So continue to observe the heatmap of Fig. 5:

('n07768694', 'pomegranate', 0.20975766)　　　　　('n07873807', 'pizza', 0.2837111)

Fig. 5. Pizza heat map.

The pizza image is a heat map visualized by the same LRP algorithm in VGG16 (left image) and VGG19 (right image). VGG16 is predicted to be pomegranate, which is wrong, but VGG19 is correct. Therefore, it can be concluded that the more layers of the network structure, the higher the accuracy of the prediction.

6 Conclusion

This paper uses the LRP algorithm to calculate the trained convolutional neural network and displays the results in the form of heat maps. Through the heat map, people can intuitively see which features the convolutional neural network recognizes the image according to, and judge whether it conforms to the objective facts. This provides a basis for comparing and improving various convolutional neural networks. Through the method of controlling variables, we compare different CNNs on different types of data sets, and observe the comparison of results by improving the network structure. By using the LRP algorithm in different network structures and observing the heat map, it is confirmed that the interpretable algorithm conforms to the objective facts, and the number of network structure layers is positively correlated with the prediction accuracy.

References

1. Silver, D., Huang, A., Maddison, C.J., Guez, A.: Mastering the game of Go with deep neural networks and tree search. Nature **529**(7587), 484–489 (2016)
2. Chand, H.V., Karthikeyan, J.: CNN based driver drowsiness detection system using emotion analysis. Intell. Autom. Soft Comput. **31**(2), 717–728 (2022)

3. Jin, L.L., Liang, H., Yang, C.S.: Sonar image recognition of underwater target based on convolutional neural network. J. Northwestern Polytech. Univ. **39**(2), 285–291 (2021)

4. Cannizzaro, D., Aliberti, A., Bottaccioli, L., Macii, E.: solar radiation forecasting based on convolutional neural network and ensemble learning. Exp. Syst. Appl. **181**, 115167 (2021)

5. Lee, C.C., Gao, Z.: Sign language recognition using two-stream convolutional neural networks with wi-fi signals. Appl. Sci. **10**(24), 9005 (2020)

6. Hyun, J., Seong, H., Kim, E.: Universal pooling–a new pooling method for convolutional neural networks. Exp. Syst. Appl. **180**, 115084 (2021)

7. Zhang, Z.Z., Zhou, W.X.: Image dehazing algorithm based on deep learning. J. South China Norm. Univ. (Nat. Sci. Edn.) **53**(3), 123–128 (2019)

8. Miao, P., Srimahachota, T.: Cost-effective system for detection and quantification of concrete surface cracks by combination of convolutional neural network and image processing techniques. Constr. Build. Mater. **293**, 123549 (2021)

9. Chen, P.: Research on the knowledge based of ship collision avoidance based on HSSVM and convolutional neural networks. Dalian Maritime University (2021)

10. Acevedo, A., Merino, A., Boldú, L., Molina, A.: A new convolutional neural network predictive model for the automatic recognition of hypogranulated neutrophils in myelodysplastic syndromes. Comput. Biol. Med. **134**, 104479 (2021)

11. Khalili, E., Asl, B.M.: Automatic sleep stage classification using temporal convolutional neural network and new data augmentation technique from raw single-channel EEG. Comput. Methods Prog. Biomed. **204**, 106063 (2021)

12. Yang, B., Cao, J.-M., Jiang, D.-P., Lv, J.-D.: Facial expression recognition based on dual-feature fusion and improved random forest classifier. Multim. Tools Appl. **77**(16), 20477–20499 (2017)

13. Abu-Alhaija, M., Turab, N.M.: Automated learning of ecg streaming data through machine learning internet of things. Intell. Autom. Soft Comput. **32**(1), 45–53 (2022)

14. Maheshwari, D., Ghosh, S.K., Tripathy, R.K., Sharma, M.: Automated accurate emotion recognition system using rhythm-specific deep convolutional neural network technique with multi-channel EEG signals. Comput. Biol. Med. **134**, 104428 (2021)

15. Ding, G., et al.: Fish recognition using convolutional neural network. In: OCEANS 2017-Anchorage, pp. 1–4. IEEE (2017)

16. Shukla, A.K., Das, S.: Deep neural network and pseudo relevance feedback based query expansion. Comput. Mater. Continua **71**(2), 3557–3570 (2022)

17. Zhu, Y.H., Jiang, Y.Z.: Optimization of face recognition algorithm based on deep learning multi feature fusion driven by big data. Image Vis. Comput. **104**, 104023 (2020)

18. Böhle, M., Eitel, F., Weygandt, M., Ritter, K.: Layer-wise relevance propagation for explaining deep neural network decisions in MRI-based Alzheimer's disease classification. Front. Aging Neurosci. **11**, 194 (2020)

19. Leonid, T.T., Jayaparvathy, R.: Classification of elephant sounds using parallel convolutional neural network. Intell. Autom. Soft Comput. **32**(3), 1415–1426 (2022)

20. Venkateswaran, N., Umadevi, K.: Hybridized wrapper filter using deep neural network for intrusion detection. Comput. Syst. Sci. Eng. **42**(1), 1–14 (2022)

21. Jiang, Q.: It will take time for AI to win the highest level of human Go. Internet Weekly **4**(6) (2016)

22. Zhen, H.: Artificial intelligence intervention in sentencing mechanism: dilemma, orientation and deconstruction. J. Chongqing Univ. (Soc. Sci. Edn.) (2020)

23. Zhao, P.: Application and development of artificial intelligence technology in clinical medical diagnosis. China New Telecommun. **21**(22), 90–91 (2019)

24. Qiao, X., Xi, Y.: Artificial intelligence and the construction of modern economic system. Econ. Aspects **06**, 81–91 (2018)

25. Zhu, M., Hou, J., Sun, S.: Domestic research progress of remote sensing image recognition based on deep learning. Surv. Geospat. Inf. **44**(5), 67–73 (2021)
26. Samek, W., Binder, A., Montavon, G., Lapuschkin, S.: Evaluating the visualization of what a deep neural network has learned. IEEE Trans. Neural Netw. Learn. Syst. **28**(11), 2660–2673 (2016)
27. Guan, C., Yang, Y.: Research on the application of back propagation neural network in social development. Comput. Times **5**, 46–48 (2021)
28. Ke, Y., Lu, Y.: Pet recognition method based on vgg16. Electron. Prod. **21**, 42–45 (2020)
29. Song, F.: Research on animal facial recognition algorithm based on deep learning. Hangzhou Dianzi University (2019)

Classification and Application of Teaching Evaluation Text Based on CNN and Stacked Bidirectional LSTM

Youlin Liang⬛, Shiying Wang$^{(\boxtimes)}$ ⬛, Lu Wang⬛, Zhiqiang Liu⬛, Xianhao Song⬛, and Jiening Yuan⬛

Qinghai University, Xining 810016, China
1152658413@qq.com

Abstract. To thoroughly mine the vertical information contained in the unstructured data (text evaluation) in the teaching evaluation data and to make sure that the effective content contained in it can be used and the teaching quality will be improved completely, considering that the traditional text sentiment analysis method cannot adapt to the complexity and change. The language context has certain limitations. Taking objective data from the Department of Computing of Qinghai University as an example, this paper proposes two efficient classification methods, Convolutional Neural Network (CNN) and Stacked Bidirectional Long Short Term Memory (LSTM), and performs sentiment value calculation, descriptive analysis, and characteristic analysis based on classification, and further Excavated the essential information contained in the text teaching evaluation. The experimental results show that the average classification accuracy of the proposed method can reach 98%, which effectively solves the problem of text classification and application for teaching evaluation. This method has been applied in the actual teaching improvement link of the Computer Department of Qinghai University, and its effectiveness further demonstrates the advanced nature of the method and provides an important reference for the fundamental improvement of the teaching level.

Keywords: Text classification · Teaching text · Convolutional neural network · Stacked bidirectional long short term memory

1 Introduction

Students' Evaluation of Teaching, S.E.T. is currently an important way to supervise and guarantee the teaching quality of colleges and universities at home and abroad. It refers to the behavior of students' evaluation of teachers' teaching and their learning process by certain teaching requirements and evaluation standards [1]. Teaching evaluation is an important part of the construction of classroom quality in colleges and universities. It plays a pivotal role in promoting talent training and improving the quality of education. In the existing teaching evaluation link, only the teaching evaluation mechanism directly feeds back the subjective ideas of students. With the development of information

© The Author(s), under exclusive license to Springer Nature Switzerland AG 2022
X. Sun et al. (Eds.): ICAIS 2022, LNCS 13338, pp. 468–484, 2022.
https://doi.org/10.1007/978-3-031-06794-5_38

technology, more and more colleges and universities have adopted the mode of online teaching evaluation and accumulated a lot of data.

Students are the most direct participants in classroom activities, and the feedback information can objectively and clearly reflect the development of the classroom to the greatest extent, and the analysis of teaching evaluation data can effectively improve the teaching level. The evaluation methods used in teaching evaluation are generally objective evaluation and subjective evaluation. Since the first " Perdue Teaching Rating Scale" (the grade scale for student evaluation of teaching information) was published for teaching evaluation in the 1920s, [2] has formed several diversified index-type evaluations and Subjective evaluation with strong viewpoints, in which the form of subjective evaluation is text comment. Based on the subjective feelings of students in the learning process, the content conveys students' attitudes and thoughts on teaching work, relative to fixed indicators the type of evaluation contains a wider range of information and greater value. It is an important way for students to express their specific demands. It contains information about the nature of the process in the teaching process, which is conducive to the targeted investigation of omissions and vacancies.

Therefore, text evaluation is undoubtedly a "gold mine" of great value for teaching evaluation data mining. By analyzing the content of the text obtained from teaching evaluation, on the one hand, you can intuitively understand the situation in the classroom, help teachers improve the quality of teaching, and enhance the overall teaching level of learning. On the other hand, the subjective text data not only contains feedback on the teacher's teaching but also includes suggestions from multiple angles such as course setting and equipment arrangement, it has greater value for mining. Therefore, how to research teaching evaluation text data is particularly important.

However, most of the research focus nowadays tends to the meaning and value behind objective evaluation such as indicator setting and teaching evaluation effectiveness analysis, ignoring the deep meaning of subjective evaluation. But analyzing the subjective text also means that how to analyze the text with strong subjectivity, how to analyze the deep-level information contained in the text, and how to truly explore its potential value has become an important link that restricts the true use of the value of the text.

2 Current Status of Domestic and Foreign Research

Processing unstructured text evaluation data is currently mostly focused on sentiment analysis. The commonly used methods are mainly dictionary-based analysis methods and machine learning-based algorithms. For example, Luo Yuping [3] et al. The dictionary database gives the calculation method of the sentiment analysis of the comment evaluation. Yan Zhongping [4] et al. took the sentence pattern as the starting point to assign different levels of weight to the conjunctions, degree words, and negative words of the evaluation sentence to construct the calculation method of sentiment value. Li Yijie [5] and others constructed a new complex sentence model based on the structural characteristics of Chinese complex sentence patterns and Word2vec and combined it with SVM training to complete the emotional classification of complex sentence patterns. Bollegala [6] and others used PMI to calculate the similarity between the dictionary elements unigram and bigram and constructed a distributed sentiment dictionary, that is, for any sentiment word, there is a corresponding sentiment word list. Their research makes cross-domain sentiment analysis possible. Feng [7] et al. added the analysis of Weibo emoticons in the sentiment map and used a random walk algorithm to extract sentiment words that meet certain conditions, but the disadvantage of this method is that it ignores some low-frequency sentiment words. Yan Xia and Zhang Kun [8] based on the inconspicuous emotional characteristics of the teaching texts and the characteristics of complex sentence patterns, proposed an emotional analysis method based on the emotional dictionary, combined the characteristics of complex sentence patterns and calculated the text quantitatively. Emotional intensity. Sun Hongxia [9] and others used latent semantic analysis to reduce the dimensionality of text vectors and used the SVM classification method to classify the teaching texts. Turney et al. [10] scholars use point mutual information value (PMI) to calculate the polarity of emotional words. The basic idea is that if the co-occurrence frequency and similarity between candidate words and seed words are positively correlated.

Among them, the dictionary-based emotion discrimination method needs to construct an emotion dictionary in related fields, and the quality of the emotion dictionary determines the accuracy rate, which has certain limitations. Traditional machine learning text representation often uses the word bag model or vector space model. The biggest disadvantage is that it ignores the relationship between the text context. Each word is independent of the other and cannot represent semantic information, and the vector represented by the text is usually high. The dimensionality and sparseness require manual construction of a large number of feature projects, which is time-consuming, and the processing effect on a large amount of text is not obvious.

3   Analysis on the Processing Method of Teaching Evaluation Text

Before the emergence of deep learning methods, the mainstream text representation methods were the word bag model BOW, topic models, etc.; classification methods include SVM, LR, etc. Shweta Rana [11] and others used Naive Bayes and Linear SVM methods to classify users' film review texts respectively, and the Linear SVM method has higher accuracy on the data set of their literature. However, the above text sentiment classification model still has certain shortcomings and cannot adapt to the complex and changeable language context, so it cannot be widely promoted and applied. Take BOW as an example here. For a piece of text, BOW indicates that the word order, grammar, and syntax are ignored, and the text is only regarded as a set of words, so the BOW method cannot fully express the semantic information of the text. For example, the sentences "The class taught by the teacher is terrible" and "The content of the course is boring, empty, and without connotation" have high semantic similarity in sentiment analysis, but their BOW indicates a similarity of 0. For another example, the BOW of the sentence "The course is empty and has no connotation" and "A course that is not empty and has the connotation" is very similar, but in fact, they have opposite meanings. At present, there are still the following problems in the field of text sentiment analysis:

- The dictionary method is widely used regardless of whether it is a supervised learning method or an unsupervised learning mode. However, it only uses opinion words and phrases in the text to distinguish the polarity of words and phrases and does not regard the change of context as an influencing factor. Ignore the different meanings of the same word in different contexts.

- In daily conversations and Internet communication, texts with subjective meanings tend to be colloquial, and there may even be non-standard Internet language. There is no grammatical constraint when choosing words and sentences, and they are very random. Therefore, it is not possible to judge and study subjective colloquial texts only from the perspective of grammar. A large number of network non-standardized languages on the Internet gives the sentiment analysis model more room for improvement.
- In addition to vocabulary that clearly expresses emotions, some neutral words such as "decrease", "disappear", "increase" and so on can also affect the emotional tendency of sentences. In addition, the phenomenon of "derogation and derogation" and "derogation and compliment" has gradually appeared on the Internet. Some compliment words seem to be commendatory on the surface, but in fact, they are ridiculous. All these put forward higher requirements for the research work of text sentiment analysis.

Deep learning has become a very active research field. A Deep Learning (DL) based detection model is used due to its high detection accuracy and extensive data handling capability. By learning the characteristics of data, it has produced relatively ideal prediction results in image recognition and other fields. This strong generalization ability of deep learning currently makes it stand out from the other machine learning techniques. With the success of deep learning in many other application fields, deep learning has also been widely used in sentiment analysis in recent years. The deep learning [14] model overcomes the above shortcomings of BOW representation. It maps the text to a low-dimensional semantic space based on the word order and performs text representation and classification in an end-to-end manner. Compared with traditional methods, its performance is significantly improved. The method based on machine learning is essentially the application of automatic classification theory to realize emotional labeling. This method completes the training of the praise and criticism classifier through training samples and then uses the classifier to automatically determine the emotional tendency. Compared with the previous text analysis methods, it has the characteristics of high efficiency, accuracy, and certain innovation.

4 Deep Learning Text Classification Method

4.1 Convolutional Neural Networks

CNN is a type of feed-forward neural network that includes convolution calculations and has a deep structure. CNNs are usually utilized in image classification with high accuracy over many datasets compared to features engineering methods. This is due to the deep learning of features from raw data in the training process. It is one of the representative algorithms of deep learning. It consists of the input layer, convolution layer, pooling layer, the fully connected layer is composed of 4 parts [16, 17], and has achieved extraordinary effects in the field of image processing. There is also applicability in text information processing. Figure 1 shows the text classification model of the convolutional neural network (take 4 convolution kernels as an example). Among them, the main function of the convolutional layer is feature extraction, convolution operation on the data with the help of a specific convolution kernel, the result is added to the offset value, and the activation function is passed through, and the data is finally output. It should be noted that convolution can only extract features layer by layer. It can only extract part of the edge information in the first layer. As the number of layers increases, the dimensions of the extracted features gradually increase; because of the data after convolution Matrix feature dimensions are still not easy to calculate directly, so the pooling function is used to reduce dimensionality without distortion, that is, the main function of the pooling layer is to downsampling, which greatly improves the computational efficiency of the convolutional neural network; the fully connected layer is It is used to merge abstract features, and then use activation functions to deal with classification problems or regression problems. After a process, the data processing, extraction, and selection are completed, which can simplify the integration of large amounts of data [18].

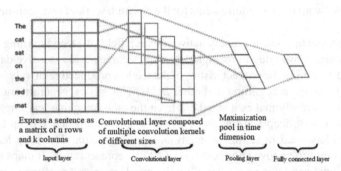

Fig. 1. Convolutional neural network text classification model.

In the text processing model, the convolutional neural network is applied. The specific process is as follows: First, the input layer processes the word vector sequence after the input text processing through the convolution kernel to generate a feature map and then adopts the largest time dimension for the feature map. The pooling operation obtains the whole sentence features corresponding to the convolution kernel, finally concatenates all the features obtained by the convolution kernel to obtain the fixed-length vector representation of the text, and finally connects the Softmax function to output a complete classification model.

The characteristics and advantages of convolutional neural networks are as follows:

• Weight sharing, that is, the same neuron shares a set of neuron parameters when extracting different regions of the same text and different texts, and multiple neurons can extract different features of the text. Compared with the traditional artificial neural network, each neural unit needs to be connected to the entire image. The convolution operation of the convolutional neural network is only locally connected to the surrounding neighborhood. Each neuron only needs to extract the features of the local area in the text, and then pass. The deep network structure integrates all local features layer by layer to obtain global information at a higher level. On the premise of fully extracting features, the strategy of local connection and parameter sharing greatly reduces the required parameter scale and greatly improves the learning efficiency. It also reduces the complexity of the model to a certain extent and prevents over-fitting in the job.

- Downsampling means that the pooling layer reduces the dimensionality of image data based on preserving the effective information of the image as much as possible, greatly reducing the number of subsequent calculations, and effectively improving the calculation efficiency.
- Local area perception, the convolution kernel perceives the local text, and gradually extracts high-dimensional features from shallow to deep. Different convolution kernels can extract different features of the text, which makes the model have generalization ability.
- Parallelism. Compared with other models, the convolutional neural network has not only improved on the algorithm level but also realized the parallel processing operation of multiple GPUs, which greatly improved the prediction accuracy of the model.

It is precise because of the above advantages that the convolutional neural network can perform higher-level and more specific analysis of the original text, to analyze the semantic meaning of the specific expression of the sentence and classify it.

4.2 Stacked Bidirectional Long Short Term Memory

Long Short Term Memory [19] was first proposed by Hochreiter and Schmidhuber in 1997. It is used to solve the problem of gradient explosion and gradient disappearance. It is an improved time loop neural network. LSTM is capable of learning long-term dependencies in data. LSTM, as the name implies, is most commonly used for processing sequence data. The text of commentary is a type of sequence data. The distinctive feature of sequence data is that the context of the sequence is strongly correlated, and the special internal structure of LSTM can store the context information of the sequence. The basic structure of the LSTM involves the memory-based RNN cell. This memory cell is beneficial for storing information and retrieving past information. This memory cell aids in the transmission of prior information to the next level. The model selects previous information based on its training requirements. Remembering useful information over a long period is regular exercise. Memorize and apply the stored information to subsequent operations compared with ordinary recurrent neural networks. The gated cell can be divided into Input Gate, Output Gate, and Forget Gate according to functional classification, collectively referred to as long and short-term memory cells. Because the memory unit in the network can save the state that changes over time, LSTM greatly improves the ability of the recurrent neural network to process long sequences of data (Fig. 2).

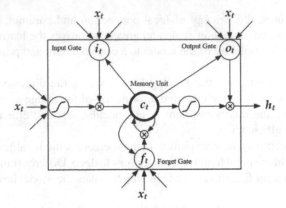

Fig. 2. LSTM at time t.

For a cyclic neural network in normal order, ht contains the input information before time t, that is, the above information in the sentence. To obtain the following information, a cyclic neural network in the reverse direction (input in reverse order) is used.

The traditional LSTM-based neural network model cannot fully extract the contextual feature-dependent information contained in other aspects of the word, especially the part of speech of the word. Part of speech plays an important role in feature selection and feature extraction. It has certain drawbacks and limits the process of text classification. And the special structure of LSTM makes it support a stacked structure design. Stacked LSTM is a variant of the LSTM model, that is, multiple LSTMs are stacked. There are two kinds of forwarding LSTM and backward LSTM. The forward LSTM is used to capture the past. Features and backward LSTM are used to obtain future features. The specific process is shown in the figure below. There are two bidirectional LSTM layers in this network structure. The input of the upper bidirectional LSTM layer is the output of the lower bidirectional LSTM layer. Each bidirectional LSTM layer consists of two LSTM layers in different directions. The input of two LSTM layers with different directions in the same bidirectional layer is the same, except that the connection direction of each LSTM cell unit is different.

In other words, compared to the traditional LSTM model, in the stacked LSTM model, text information is input from two directions, which helps to more accurately recognize the text information and greatly improves the accuracy of the traditional LSTM model in processing data. In summary, this paper combines the method of the deep recurrent neural network to build a more powerful LSTM-based stacked bidirectional LSTM (Stacked Bidirectional LSTM) [22] to model teaching texts. As shown in Fig. 3 (take three layers as an example), the odd-numbered LSTM is forward and the even-numbered LSTM is reverse. The higher LSTM uses the information of the lower LSTM and all previous layers as input, and the highest LSTM sequence is used the maximum pooling in the time dimension can obtain the fixed-length vector representation of the text. This process fully integrates the contextual information of the text and deep-level abstraction of the text. Finally, the text representation is connected to Softmax to construct a classification model.

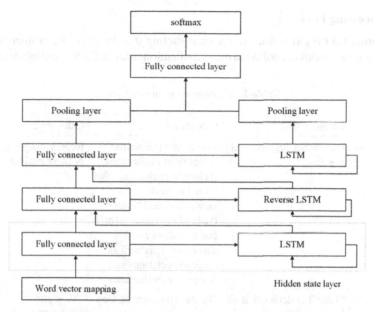

Fig. 3. Stacked Bidirectional LSTM text classification model.

5   Case Study

5.1   Data Sources

The data is selected from Qinghai University's 2019–2020 spring semester from a total of 61,161 text evaluation data from the Department of Computer Technology and Application, the School of Chemical Engineering, the School of Civil Engineering, and the School of Finance and Economics. After removing some useless data, 61,098 valid evaluations were obtained. The experimental data is shown in Table 1.

Table 1. Evaluation data set.

Serial number	Comment content
1	The teacher is very easygoing
2	The teacher lectures very well
3	Teachers can be clean and self-disciplined and strict in self-discipline
4	Thank you very much teacher, we love this course very much
5	I didn't take this course, I don't know
…	…
61098	The teacher treats his work carefully and disciplines himself strictly. He can speak completely in every class, and he treats students with due diligence and kindness

5.2   Processing Flow

Environmental Preparation. Before constructing the classifier, the evaluation data is divided into categories according to the classification rules in Table 2 and labeled (Fig. 4):

Table 2. Classification rule definition.

Item	Category 0	Category 1	Category 2
Explanation	Represents negative and negative	Represents the neutral category of evaluations, including evaluations that do not indicate viewpoints and "under" types of evaluations (both commendatory and derogatory), as well as some expectations and suggestive evaluations	Represents positive and positive evaluation
Example	"I don't understand at all in class" "Class is boring" "Teacher is stupid in class"	"None" (no point of view expressed) "The teacher didn't teach me." (no point of view) "The content is interesting, but Mandarin is not standard." (first increase and then decrease) "I hope the teacher can be a little creative." (Express expectations)	"Very good." "Teacher is serious in class, I especially like it." "The teacher is fun and responsible"

After the labeling, the proportion of each category in the statistics is Category 2:Category 1:Category 0 = 54781:5633:684 ≈ 80:8:1, before feeding the model training, the data is randomly divided into 3 parts: 60% The training set of is used for model training, 20% of the validation set is used to verify the accuracy of the model, and 20% of the test set is used to predict the effect of the model.

Data Preprocessing. Deep learning framework: paddle v1.7.2

Implementation language: Python3.7.1

Computing environment: Intel(R) Core(TM) i7-8550U CPU @ 1.80 GHz 1.99 GHz, CPU training.

Model Building. Build a CNN network and a Stacked Bidirectional LSTM network for text classification respectively, and the loss function uses cross-entropy loss.

Model Training and Verification. In each round of model training, the average loss and accuracy of the training set and the validation set are recorded, and the validation set checks whether the training model is normal.

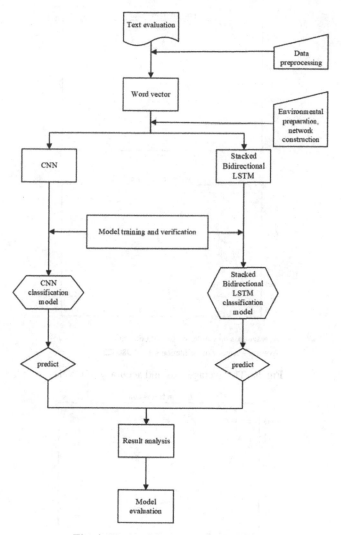

Fig. 4. Evaluation text-processing flow.

5.3 Experimental Results

Experimental Results of the Training Set and Validation Set
The average accuracy of the two types of models in the training phase and the verification phase can reach 98% (Figs. 5 and 6).

Verification Results of the Test Set
To obtain a scientific and accurate prediction effect, 20% of the test set was predicted 10 times in the CNN model and the Stacked Bidirectional LSTM model, and the average value was taken as the final result. At the same time, to understand the accuracy and

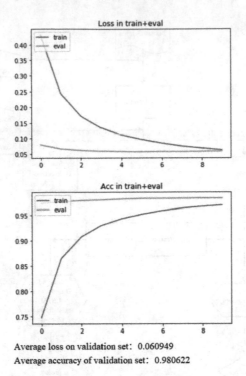

Average loss on validation set: 0.060949
Average accuracy of validation set: 0.980622

Fig. 5. The average loss and accuracy of CNN.

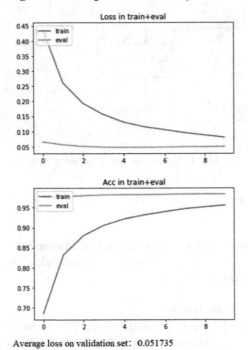

Average loss on validation set: 0.051735
Average accuracy of validation set: 0.981055

Fig. 6. Average loss and accuracy of Stacked Bidirectional LSTM.

errors of each category in the prediction stage The data are tested separately during prediction, and the data results are shown in Figs. 7 and 8.

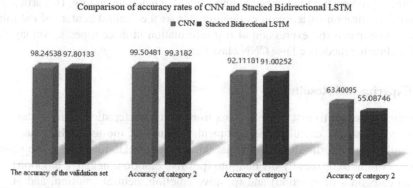

Fig. 7. Accuracy of each category predicted by CNN and Stacked Bidirectional LSTM in the test phase.

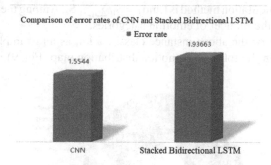

Fig. 8. Error rate predicted by CNN and Stacked Bidirectional LSTM in the test phase.

Results Analysis and Model Evaluation. Both types of models have achieved very good results in prediction, and the overall accuracy rate can reach 97%. In the comparison of the accuracy and error rates of each category, CNN is slightly better. The accuracy of category 0 is relative to category 2, 1 is low, between 55% and 64%. The reason is that the ratio of each category in the original data set is 80:8:1, and the original data is unbalanced. This is also based on the characteristics of the actual data itself, which makes the learning and representation ability of the model in the category with more data is stronger than the category with fewer data. In addition, from the perspective of lower error rates, both types of models have achieved good classification results.

6 Classification Application

In natural language processing, sentiment analysis is a typical text classification problem, but any text information mining cannot stop at the classification of text, but should further condense the essence of text information based on classification. Taking teaching evaluation as an example, the mining of teaching evaluation data should reflect the gains and losses in the teaching process, and reflect the advantages and disadvantages of teaching, to promote the fundamental improvement of teaching quality. This article takes the text classification of teaching evaluation data as the 'neural center' of the mining system and expands the expression of text information in three aspects. Among them, the classification models all use CNN classifiers.

6.1 Experimental Results

Dictionary-based sentiment analysis starts from the characteristics of the sentence pattern to quantitatively calculate the sentiment tendency of the text, which has certain applicability, but the disadvantage is that the sentiment classification in the sentence pattern is often fixed, usually divided into (positive emotion, negative emotion) There are two categories of emotion) and (positive emotion, neutral emotion, and negative emotion). Generally speaking, human emotions are divided into 7 types, and it is more difficult to construct a corresponding dictionary. From the perspective of classification, a variety of emotional categories can be customized.

The emotion calculation method is $Emo\, i = S_i / \sum_{i=1}^{n} S_i$. Among them, i is the emotion category and S_i is the number of emotion categories.

Take the result of the above instance classification as an example to calculate the emotion, and obtain the following emotion distribution map (Fig. 9).

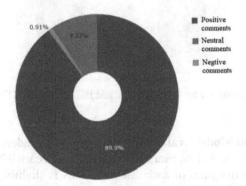

Fig. 9. The three-category sentiment distribution of the instance.

6.2 Focus Analysis

Focus analysis is mainly aimed at the subject objects in the comments. The essence of the difference in emotion categories lies in the different emotion polarities caused by the combination of words and words. Therefore, exploring the essence of emotion categories can be displayed utilizing words. Here, the nouns in each category are selected as the embodiment, as shown in the figure below (Figs. 10, 11, and 12):

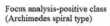

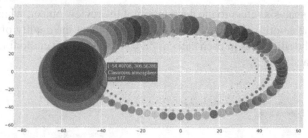

Fig. 10. Focus analysis-bubble chart of the positive category.

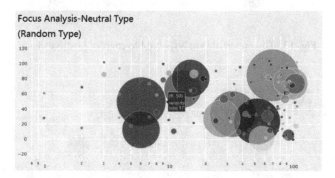

Fig. 11. Focus analysis-bubble chart of neutral class.

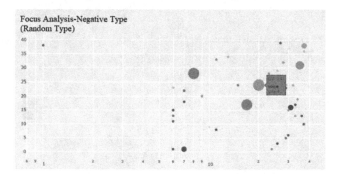

Fig. 12. Focus analysis-negative bubble chart.

6.3 Characteristic Analysis

Characteristic analysis refers to the description of the review object, which is a concrete reflection of the emotional tendency and can better reflect the quality of the evaluation object. Here, the adjectives in each category are selected as the embodiment, as follows (Figs. 13, 14, and 15):

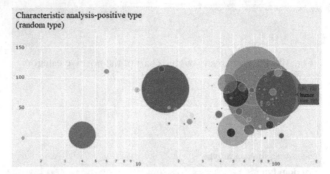

Fig. 13. Characteristic analysis-bubble chart of positive class.

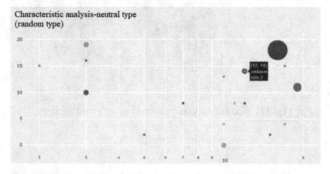

Fig. 14. Characteristic analysis-neutral bubble chart.

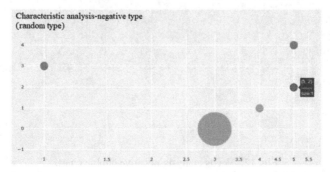

Fig. 15. Characteristic analysis-negative bubble chart.

Based on the classification of categories, show the reasons why focus words and descriptive words can specifically reflect the polarity of emotional categories, such as:

In the positive evaluation, the focus analysis reflects that the students are most concerned about the "class atmosphere", "curriculum", "content", "method", "discipline", "influence", etc., indicating that these aspects have been gained in the teaching process. Students' unanimous recognition; the descriptive words in the characteristic analysis include words such as "humor", "rigorous", "patient", "very good", "interesting" and other words that reflect the characteristics and effects of teachers' teaching. From the above words, we can understand the positive evaluation the specific embodiment of the teacher.

The previously defined content of neutral evaluations are evaluations that do not indicate opinions, evaluations of the "under" type, and evaluations of the expected suggestion type, indicating that certain aspects of the teaching process are flawed in the beauty of the situation. From the focus analysis and characteristic analysis, it can also be learned that "focus", "speed", "method", "organization", "knowledge structure", "chaos", "patience", "rigorous" and other related aspects have certain shortcomings.

The number of words related to the negative evaluation is relatively small, but this is the most critical part of the teaching evaluation because only knowing the shortcomings can prescribe the right medicine. From the perspective of the vocabulary embodied in the two types of analysis, words such as "communication", "voice", "too small", "delay class", "difficulty", "boring", "banal", and "heavy" are the main components. It is known that the reasons for the negative evaluation may include problems in the communication between teachers and students, the teacher's voice being too small, the teacher's existence being dragged in the classroom, and the class being relatively dull. If you want to improve the teaching level, you can carry out targeted work based on the above questions.

7 Conclusions

This article uses deep learning to analyze and apply texts through two methods: Convolutional Neural Network and Stacked Bidirectional LSTM. Compared with traditional text analysis methods, this method has the advantages of high accuracy and efficiency. The analysis of the results shows that the above methods can efficiently classify teaching texts with an average accuracy rate of up to 98%, and have high accuracy. And further targeted the essential information reflected in the evaluation of teaching texts, including the calculation of sentiment value, descriptive analysis, and characteristic analysis, which provides a useful reference for improving teaching methods and improving teaching quality. However, there are still some shortcomings: due to the complexity of the text itself, the mining in the classification foundation is not perfect. For example, the highly extracted text representation is not yet in place, and future research still needs further improvement. Moreover, this article only analyzes the teaching evaluation data of the Computer Department of Qinghai University, which has certain limitations. In the future, more comprehensive data sets will be used to continuously improve the method.

References

1. Zhang, J.: Research on Fine-Grained Sentiment Analysis Based on Texts of Students' Evaluation of Teaching. South China University of Technology (2020)
2. Wang, H.: Research on Data Mining and Teaching Quality Analysis System Based on Student Evaluation of Teaching. Xi'an Shiyou University (2010)
3. Luo, Y., Pan, Q., Liu, L., Zhang, L.: Design and application of student evaluation system based on emotion mining. China Audio-Vis. Educ. **2018**(04), 91–95 (2018)
4. Yan, Z., Wang, X., Gu, L.: Research on postgraduate evaluation of teaching quality verification based on sentiment analysis and data mining. High. Educ. Forum **2020**(05), 80–86 (2020)
5. Li, Y., Duan, L., Li, A.: Research on sentiment classification of short texts based on complex sentence patterns. Mod. Electron. Technol. **41**(22), 182–186 (2018)
6. Bollegala, D., Weir, D., Carroll, J.: Cross-domain sentiment classification using a sentiment sensitive thesaurus. IEEE Trans. Knowl. Data Eng. **25**(8), 1719–1731 (2013)
7. Feng, S., Song, K., Wang, D., Ge, Y.: A word-emoticon mutual reinforcement ranking model for building sentiment lexicon from massive collection of microblogs. World Wide Web **18**(4), 949–967 (2014)
8. Xia, Y., Kun, Z.: Application of sentiment analysis technology in postgraduate evaluation texts. Comput. Times **2019**, 51–54 (2019)
9. Tan, Z., Sun, H., Wang, L., Pan, Q.: Research on the classification model of Chinese teaching evaluation texts. J. Yantai Univ. (Nat. Sci. Eng. Edn.) **25**(02), 122–126 (2012)
10. Turney, P.D., Littman, M.L.: Measuring praise and criticism: inference of semantic orientation from association. ACM Trans. Inf. Syst. **21**(4), 315–346 (2003)
11. Rana, S., Singh, A.: Comparative analysis of sentiment orientation using SVM and Naïve Bayes techniques. In: International Conference on Next Generation Computing Technologies (2017)
12. Rajendar, S., Kaliappan, V.K.: Sensor data-based anomaly detection in autonomous vehicles using modified convolutional neural network. Intell. Autom. Soft Comput. **32**(2), 859–875 (2022)
13. Yu, D., Wang, J.: A survey on machine learning in chemical spectral analysis. J. Inf. Hiding Privacy Protect. **2**(4), 165–174 (2020)
14. Kim, Y.: Convolutional neural networks for sentence classification. arXiv preprint arXiv: 1408.5882 (2014)
15. Alharbi, H.A.A.H., Alghamdi, N.S.: Time-efficient fire detection convolutional neural network coupled with transfer learning. Intell. Autom. Soft Comput. **31**(3), 1393–1403 (2022)
16. Goodfellow, I., Bengio, Y., Courville, A.: Deep Learning, vol. 1. MIT Press, Cambridge (2016)
17. Gu, J., et al.: Recent advances in convolutional neural networks. arXiv preprint arXiv:1512. 07108 (2015)
18. Zhang, Z., Xing, F., Su, H., et al: Recent advances in the applications of convolutional neural networks to medical image contour detection. arXiv preprint arXiv:1708.07281 (2017)
19. Bengio, Y., Simard, P., Frasconi, P.: Learning long-term dependencies with gradient descent is difficult. IEEE Trans. Neural Netw. **5**, 157–166 (1994)
20. Kalaivani, K., Chinnadurai, M.: A hybrid deep learning intrusion detection model for a fog computing environment. Intell. Autom. Soft Comput. **30**(1), 1–15 (2021)
21. Ketu, S., Mishra, P.K.: A hybrid deep learning model for covid-19 prediction and current status of clinical trials worldwide. Comput. Mater. Continua **66**(2), 1896–1919 (2021)
22. Zhou, J., Xu, W.: End-to-end learning of semantic role labeling using. In: Proceedings of the Annual Meeting of the Association for Computational Linguistics (2015)

Research on Classroom Teaching Behavior Under the Influence of Information Technology

Weijie Yuan[1]($\boxtimes$) (iD), Yanpeng Wu[1] (iD), Chenxue Zhu[1], Changling Peng[1], and Zhichen Gao[2]

[1] Department of Information Science and Engineering, Hunan First Normal University, Changsha 410205, Hunan, China
xjzxweijieyuan@hnfnu.edu.cn
[2] Department of Applied Mathematics and Statistics, College of Engineering and Applied Sciences, Stony Brook University, Stony Brook, NY 11794, USA

Abstract. How to make information-based teaching more efficient in the digital age and provide a better reference for the integration of information technology and curriculum is a proposition that needs urgent research. The article analyzes the differences in classroom teaching behaviors in the differentiated information technology environment, and uses video analysis method to quantify the teaching records. By combining the improved Flanders interaction analysis method, the data representation of teaching behavior is discussed. Finally, combined with the characteristics of the teaching process, the improvement measures for effective teaching using information technology are proposed, which provides a useful reference for the quality assurance and promotion of the integration of information technology and curriculum.

Keywords: Informationized teaching ability · Classroom teaching behavior · ITIAS

1 Introduction

Information technology has a revolutionary impact on the development of education, and it will also cause unprecedented changes in classroom teaching. The "Horizon Report 2020 (Teaching and Learning Edition)" mentions that instructional design and learning design are the key factors for the value of educational informatization [1]. Therefore, teachers' information literacy, information technology and curriculum integration capabilities, and the ability to design information-based teaching have become important "Soft power."

But at present, the iterative speed and frequency of educational technology have been far higher than the progress of informatization teaching strategies, which indicates that more observation experiments are needed, and the purpose is to explore more efficient teaching strategies in an informatization environment. On the other hand, a certain amount of information-based teaching does not have a scientific methodological

© The Author(s), under exclusive license to Springer Nature Switzerland AG 2022
X. Sun et al. (Eds.): ICAIS 2022, LNCS 13338, pp. 485–499, 2022.
https://doi.org/10.1007/978-3-031-06794-5_39

reference, or there are doubts about the efficiency and benefit of information-based teaching. In order to ensure the success rate of teaching implementation, teachers often rely more on traditional education technology and implement the "downward compatibility" technical thinking in lesson preparation.

In fact, in the process of the penetration of information technology into the education field, the role of teachers is still a key factor. The teacher's application of information technology is directly proportional to the completion of classroom teaching [2, 17]. Many early research results related to teachers' teaching behavior contained a large amount of information and the analysis process was complicated. Although these studies have scientific research value, it is difficult to help teachers find problems in actual teaching activities. However, the emergence of experimental methods represented by the Flanders interactive analysis system has gradually inspired the work of educational data mining in the past 60 years, and has brought new opportunities for the research in the field of teachers' classroom teaching behavior. To a certain extent, it reduces the threshold and difficulty of research in this field, and makes the results more obvious. To sum up, these changes make the analysis of teachers' teaching behavior in the information classroom environment once again become a research hotspot.

2   Literature Review

2.1   Teaching Behavior Research

The research needs of teaching behavior originally originated from the needs of teaching reflection, which is a means to improve teachers' professional skills and evaluate teaching effectiveness. Early researchers conducted a large number of empirical studies on teaching effectiveness, interaction behavior, and role behavior. Among them, the study of teacher characteristics completed by Kratz is considered the beginning of the study of teachers' behavior [3], but the study of teachers' teaching behavior at this time has not been clearly defined. Since the 1920s, scholars represented by Elliott (1913) and Charters (1929) have carried out special research on teaching behavior, which confirmed the deep influence of teachers' behavior on the classroom, and clarified the value of research on teacher's teaching behavior [4, 5]. In the 1960s, researchers began to pay extensive attention to the internal connection between various factors and effects in the classroom, including teachers' teaching behavior [6, 18].

With the emergence of the above research, it can be considered that the vertical research of teacher's teaching behavior is gradually established in the long exploration, and it is still subdivided into deeper research content. Such as teaching effectiveness, interaction behavior, role behavior, teaching strategies, teaching procedures and methods, teaching models, etc.

2.2   Teaching Behavior Observation and Analysis Method

Observation tools for teaching behavior began to develop rapidly after entering the information age, and are currently showing a diversified trend. The main observation tools involved are: eye movement data, facial video, posture tilt, movement changes, pressure sensing, and even emergence The application of medical tools such as ECG, EEG, and skin conductance in the analysis of teaching behavior. When these techniques are used as observation tools, video recordings often accompany them in the form of backups. Researchers often tend to retrieve video backups to verify the reliability of the results. Because, video recording is considered to be the earliest and most mature observation method [7].

As for teaching behavior research tools, Flanders Interaction Analysis System (FIAS) [8], a coding system for teaching behavior analysis, is often mentioned as an analysis tool for classroom videos. The process is to use a fixed time interval method to encode the behavior in each time interval. However, in subsequent experiments, researchers gradually discovered the differences between regions, subjects, and classroom equipment, which would make FIAS unable to form results that meet the research objectives. Therefore, many studies have evolved modified versions on the basis of FIAS according to requirements.

Li et al. [9] believed that FIAS had defects in distinguishing traditional education technology from modern education technology, and then developed FIAS (improved) for the practical application of detection technology in the classroom on this basis effect. For the study of specific subjects, Ye and Luo [10] combined Chinese context and improved some items under "indirect influence" in FIAS, so that the whole system can have a better performance in the processing of language situations. In response to the changes in the information environment in the classroom, Gu and Wang [11] analyzed the coding system ITIAS for the interactive analysis of teaching behavior in the information environment. Then Fang et al. [12] set up specific features for the problems in the use of ITIAS. The revised version is called iFIAS. Up to now, iFIAS is still used as an effective analysis system for subject education and teaching, teaching application research, development research and other fields.

Due to its strong descriptibility and maneuverability, FIAS, as a research tool, has been widely used in the graduation thesis of masters and doctors, and the number has shown an increasing trend yearly.

3 Research Design

3.1 Object of Study

Select the teaching record of the teaching theory of Chinese language courses at the undergraduate level of higher education as the research material. A total of 2 valid samples were selected (hereinafter referred to as "Class A" and "Class B"). The teachers all have the title of associate professor or above, and are responsible for the course teaching in the video for more than 5 years. In order to ensure the quality of teaching, the selected materials are all winning works of the teaching competition.

3.2 Conditions of Study

In order to make the characterization of the results more obvious, the site for conducting research is set on a reconstructed multimedia classroom. In addition to having traditional teaching tools, a recording and broadcasting system is also set up to meet the conditions for classroom teaching video collection.

In order to try to eliminate the influence of environmental factors on the experimental results, the recording of the material belongs to the same classroom before and after the renovation, but at different times. Among them, only the display equipment in the classroom was replaced. Group A uses a reflective ultra-short throw projector with touch whiteboard for display and writing; Group B is equipped with modern educational technology equipment, using five large-scale tablet computers. These five terminals can be used for information exchange.

3.3 Methodologies

Information Technology-Based Interaction Analysis System (ITIAS) is an improved version proposed by the R&D team led by Professor Gu Xiaoqing of East China Normal University on the basis of long-term practice. It is based on Flanders Interaction Analysis System (FIAS). Gu and others believe that it solves the problem that FIAS cannot define some new teaching behaviors in modern informatization teaching. It is currently a relatively complete analysis system in the field of teaching behavior analysis in my country, with a total of 18 codes. It is divided into four categories: "teacher language", "student language", "silence", "technology and practice".

3.4 Definition of Teaching Behavior

A certain number of experiments using FIAS and its derivatives have pointed out in their conclusions that the experimental method will have definition errors in the coding process, due to the inaccurate description of some behaviors.

In order to avoid judgment errors in the encoding process, combining the definition given by academic experts, the concept of "teaching behavior" is summarized as the research scope: teaching behavior is considered to be a role behavior that occurs between teachers and students based on a certain teaching purpose, including teacher teaching and students learning, two kinds of behaviors [13, 19]. Teachers and students are the composite subjects of teaching behavior [14, 20]. But teaching behavior is usually a comprehensive behavior shown under the guidance of teacher preset content [15, 21]. Therefore, active behaviors caused by non-above subjects in the teaching are not in the scope of research. For example, automated behaviors that are not preset by teachers or students, or behaviors caused by characters other than teachers or students. (e. g. characters appearing in video content or virtual technologies).

3.5 Research Process

According to ITIAS, the classroom teaching behavior in the video has been coded at the corresponding time. Sampling is performed every 3 s, and the main actions that occur during the three-second period are recorded. According to this process, group A and group B collected 879 and 978 valid codes, respectively. (As shown in Table 1).

Table 1. Basic information of course recording video.

	Effective teaching time	Effective coding	Ordered pair
Group A	43 min 57 s	879	878
Group B	48 min 54 s	978	977

Fill in the collected data into the corresponding position of the FIAS code table (shown in Table 2), take group A as an example, intercept the first 9 min.

Table 2. FIAS code table (part of group A).

MIN\SEC	3	6	9	12	15	18	21	24	27	30	33	36	39	42	45	48	51	54	57	60
0	7	16	16	16	6	6	6	6	6	6	6	6	5	6	6	4	4	14	14	7
1	10	10	10	10	3	3	10	10	3	3	6	6	6	6	6	6	6	6	16	16
2	6	6	6	6	6	6	6	6	4	16	16	16	6	6	6	6	6	5	9	3
3	3	3	6	6	6	6	6	6	5	5	9	6	5	9	6	6	6	6	6	9
4	6	6	6	5	9	6	6	6	6	6	5	9	3	6	4	13	6	6	6	6
5	6	6	5	9	6	6	6	6	6	6	5	9	6	6	6	6	6	6	6	6
6	6	4	4	14	14	14	14	14	14	14	9	9	2	2	9	9	9	9	9	9
7	3	3	3	3	4	9	9	9	9	9	9	9	3	3	2	6	6	6	16	16
8	16	16	6	6	6	6	6	6	6	6	6	6	6	16	16	16	6	6	6	6
9	6	16	6	6	6	6	6	6	6	6	16	6	6	6	6	6	4	9	6	6

In order to form a more intuitive representation, the data in the FIAS coding table will be migrated to the interactive classification matrix. The migration rule is as follows: Suppose there are n sample data x_i $(i = 1, 2, \cdots, n)$ in the code x, and then use adjacent sample data to form an ordered pair (x_n, x_{n+1}). Taking the five data recorded in the FIAS code table (group A) from 0 min 3 s to 0 min 15 s as an example, the ordered pairs formed are $(7,16)$, $(16,16)$, $(16,16)$, $(16,6)$. Use the above method to organize all the sample data xi of group A and group B to form 878 and 977 ordered pairs, respectively.

Next, treat the ordered pair as the coordinates of a point, and fill in the rectangular coordinate system. Then count the number of ordered pairs in the corresponding coordinates in the rectangular coordinate system. Finally, the interactive classification matrix is presented (as shown in Tables 3 and 4).

Table 3. Interactive classification matrix (group A).

	1	2	3	4	5	6	7	8	9	10	11	12	13	14	15	16	17	18	F	R
1	8			1	3	3				3									18	2.05%
2		4	1						1	5									11	1.25%
3	1	2	19						7	5									34	3.87%
4			4	7		13	1		2									1	28	3.19%
5	3		1		7	21			5							4		1	42	4.78%
6	5	3	7	3	4	335			17	2			1	1		21		1	400	45.56%
7						4	2		1			1		1		1			10	1.14%
8																			0	0.00%
9		1		3	26		2	1	16					2					51	5.81%
10		1	1	3			2	3	1	89			1	2				1	104	11.85%
11																			0	0.00%
12				1		1						60							62	7.06%
13			1																1	0.11%
14			6											7					13	1.48%
15																			0	0.00%
16	1		1	3	1	20	2		1							34			63	7.18%
17																			0	0.00%
18						1										3	37		41	4.67%

For ease of expression, the research uses *cell(a, b)* to express the number of rows and columns in the interactive classification matrix *(a = 1,2, ···,18) (b = 1,2, ···,18)*. The sum of row *b* is the frequency F_b, and its calculation formula is:

$$F_b = \sum_{a=1}^{18} cell(a, b) \tag{1}$$

The calculation formula for the proportion R_b of row *b* is:

$$R_b = \frac{\sum_{a=1}^{18} cell(a, b)}{\sum_{b=1}^{18} F_b} \tag{2}$$

Table 4. Interactive classification matrix (group B).

	1	2	3	4	5	6	7	8	9	10	11	12	13	14	15	16	17	18	F	R
1	2									3							1		6	0.61%
2										1									1	0.10%
3			15	2	1				5	4						1			28	2.87%
4			3	22	2	4	2		5				1	4		1			44	4.50%
5			1		1	7			1						5		1		16	1.64%
6			3	2	5	180	1		3			1	1	1		9		1	207	21.19%
7			2		1	3	15		1			1		1					24	2.46%
8								1											1	0.10%
9			2	7	5		2		29								1		46	4.71%
10	3	1	1	1		1		1		26				1					35	3.58%
11																			0	0.00%
12			1									154			1				156	15.97%
13	1					1													2	0.20%
14				7									5						12	1.23%
15						1										78			79	8.09%
16			1	2	1	10		2								114	1	1	132	13.51%
17						2											141		143	14.64%
18						1	1									2	1	40	45	4.61%

4 Research Results and Analysis

4.1 Main Teaching Behavior Analysis

By observing the interactive analysis matrix (Tables 3 and 4), the main teaching behaviors in the classroom under different information environments are revealed. The frequency of main teaching behaviors is higher than the arithmetic mean, and the frequency of general teaching behaviors is lower than the arithmetic mean.

The calculation formula of the arithmetic means $\overline{F}$ and variance S is:

$$\overline{F} = \frac{\sum_{b=1}^{18} F_b}{18} \tag{3}$$

And:

$$S = \frac{\sum_{b=1}^{18} \left(F_b - \overline{F}\right)^2}{17} \tag{4}$$

The main teaching behaviors of group A are: teaching (45.56%), student-led ability to respond (11.85%), teacher operation skills (7.18%), discussion with peers (7.06%), and students' passive response (5.81%). By sorting out the main teaching behaviors, it can be seen that in the traditional multimedia environment, Group A still uses "transmit-receive" as the main teaching procedure, and teachers use multimedia to cooperate with speech to complete the delivery of teaching content. Among them, questions accounted for 7.97%, with 70 ordered pairs, occupying 3 min and 30 s of class time. It can be seen that teachers use questioning as the main interactive method. This method will stimulate students to think and activate the classroom atmosphere.

The main teaching behaviors of group B are: teaching (21.19%), discussion with peers (15.97%), students' independent practice (14.64%), teacher's operating skills (13.51%), and doing exercises (8.09%). By observing the main teaching behaviors, it can be concluded that compared with group A, group B has greater changes in the teaching style and teaching procedures. One is that the time spent on lectures has been drastically reduced. The second is that teaching behaviors are presented in a more diverse form, which is mainly manifested in the variance of the proportion of the main teaching behaviors of group A and group B. The teaching behavior in group B has a diversified trend, and "teaching" in group A is dominant. Third, in teaching design, Group B is more inclined to use group collaboration and practice as the main means to replace large-scale questioning and other behaviors to maintain the atmosphere and complete the teaching content.

Through the above comparison, it can be found that the emergence of interactive display terminals has changed the original course design to a certain extent. One is to break the traditional way of carrying out collaborative teaching in teaching. Traditional teaching relies on the division in the sense of physical space, and the teaching supported by information technology uses interactive devices to interact between students. The second is that the change in the way of interaction is conducive to rebalancing the discourse power of teachers and students, which has a symbolic significance for weakening teacher-led teaching.

4.2 Ratio Analysis

Ratio analysis is common in FIAS-based research, and it can provide macroscopic data conclusions for research. Classify each code in each ITIAS and calculate the ratio, and finally draw a comparison of classroom teaching behavior structure under the influence of information technology (as shown in Table 5).

Calculation formulas for the ratio of behaviors appearing in Table 5 are as follows:

$$T_L = \sum_{b=1}^{8} F \div \sum_{b=1}^{18} F_b \qquad (5)$$

$$T_{L1} = \sum_{b=1}^{5} F_b \div \sum_{b=1}^{18} F_b \qquad (6)$$

$$T_{L2} = \sum_{b=6}^{8} F_b \div \sum_{b=1}^{18} F_b \qquad (7)$$

$$S_L = \sum_{b=9}^{12} F_b \div \sum_{b=1}^{18} F_b \qquad (8)$$

Table 5. Comparison of teaching behavior structure under the influence of information technology.

	Group A	Group B
Teacher language (T$_L$)	**61.85%**	**33.47%**
Indirect effects (T$_{L1}$)	15.15%	9.72%
Direct effects (T$_{L2}$)	46.7%	23.75%
Student language (S$_L$)	**24.72%**	**24.26%**
Answer (S$_{L1}$)	17.65%	8.29%
Questions and discussions (S$_{L2}$)	7.06%	15.97%
Silence (Q)	**1.59%**	**9.52%**
Chaos that doesn't help teaching (Q$_1$)	0.11%	0.2%
Think about the problem (Q$_2$)	1.48%	1.23%
Do exercises (Q$_3$)	–	8.09%
Technology and operation (T$_{p1}$)	**11.85%**	**32.75%**
Teacher operation technology (T$_{p1}$)	7.18%	13.51%
Students try to operate (T$_{p2}$)	–	14.64%
Technology works on students (T$_{p3}$)	4.67%	4.61%

$$S_{L1} = \left[\sum_{a=1}^{18} cell(a, 9) + \sum_{a=1}^{18} cell(a, 10)\right] \div \sum_{b=1}^{18} F_b \qquad (9)$$

$$S_{L2} = \left[\sum_{a=1}^{18} cell(a, 10) + \sum_{a=1}^{18} cell(a, 11)\right] \div \sum_{b=1}^{18} F_b \qquad (10)$$

$$Q = \sum_{b=13}^{15} F_b \div \sum_{b=1}^{18} F_b \qquad (11)$$

$$Q_1 = \sum_{a=1}^{18} cell(a, 13) \div \sum_{b=1}^{18} F_b \qquad (12)$$

$$Q_2 = \sum_{a=1}^{18} cell(a, 14) \div \sum_{b=1}^{18} F_b \qquad (13)$$

$$Q_3 = \sum_{a=1}^{18} cell(a, 15) \div \sum_{b=1}^{18} F_b \qquad (14)$$

$$T_p = \sum_{b=16}^{18} F_b \div \sum_{b=1}^{18} F_b \qquad (15)$$

$$T_{p1} = \sum_{a=1}^{18} cell(a, 16) \div \sum_{b=1}^{18} F_b \qquad (16)$$

$$T_{p2} = \sum_{a=1}^{18} cell(a, 17) \div \sum_{b=1}^{18} F_b \qquad (17)$$

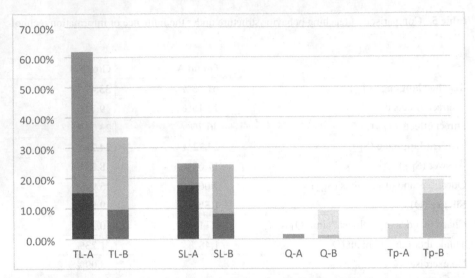

Fig. 1. Comparison of teaching behavior structure under the influence of information technology.

$$T_{p3} = \sum_{a=1}^{18} cell(a, 18) \div \sum_{b=1}^{18} F_b \qquad (18)$$

Population Ratio Distribution. Comparison of the overall structure of the two groups of classroom teaching behaviors under the influence of information technology (as shown in Fig. 1). The teacher language ratio of Group A is 61.85%, which exceeds the sum of other columns. The various languages of group B are in a more balanced state. It is worth noting that in group B, "doing exercises " accounted for 84.97% of the "silent" part and 8.09% of the total. While "students try to operate" accounted for 44.7% of the "technology and practice" and 14.64% of the total. The lack of this type of student behavior in the group A classroom affects the ratio of teachers and students participating in the classroom to a certain extent.

There are two preliminary conclusions that can be drawn from the above analysis: First, from the perspective of students, the use of information technology can strengthen students' participation in the classroom in the "Silence" part and the "Technology and Practice" part, so as to achieve a student-oriented teaching atmosphere. Second, from the perspective of teachers, the use of information technology will greatly reduce the rate of teaching using teacher language, which has caused some teaching content in the original teaching plan to be redesigned. Teachers need to think about how to re-establish interaction and evaluation mechanisms with students.

Teacher Language Ratio Distribution. Teacher language is a collection of direct effects such as teaching and Indirect effects such as questioning, which indicates the teacher's participation in leading the classroom behavior. As shown in Fig. 2, the teacher language ratio of group A is significantly higher than that of group B, and the behavior of "teaching" (code 6) of both groups is dominant in direct influence. The difference

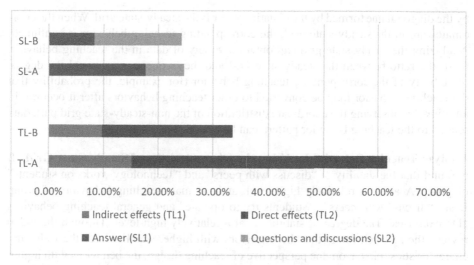

Fig. 2. The comparison of teacher's language and student's language behavior structure.

is that the ratio distribution within Indirect effects is differentiated. What is more obvi-ous is that feedback behavior (codes 1–3) is basically missing in the data of group B. Through video review, it is found that teaching is implemented in different technical environments. Not only will it affect teachers to adopt different teaching strategies. And it will lead to changes in teacher information feedback. The feedback behaviors in group A (codes 1–3) are mainly derived from real-time feedback from teachers after students answer the questions, but group B adopts more online interactive behaviors (collecting answers online, online multiple-choice questions, etc.). The results show that teachers use less time to feedback the results of such behaviors, and they also omit accurate information feedback to some students.

Students Language Ratio Distribution. Student language is the part that represents students' participation in the classroom. There are four codes for their behavior, which can be divided into two categories ("answer", "questions and discussions") by observing Table 5, it can be found that the proportions of "answer" and "questions and discussions" are opposite. Through behavioral frequency analysis, it is found that the differences in the two sets of data are derived from the differences in teaching strategies in the technical environment. In Group a, where teaching and questioning are the main teaching behav-iors, the ratio of "Answer" (17.65%) is higher than that of "Questions and discussions" (7.06%) in Group B where practice and discussion are the main teaching behaviors, the rate of "Questions and discussions" (15.97%) is higher than that of "Answer" (8.29%).

4.3 Steady State and Behavioral Frequency Analysis

Flanders (1970) described a method of behavioral analysis using the stability of observa-tion data in his research [16]. In the interactive analysis matrix, the coordinate traversed by the diagonal line formed by the equation $y = x$ is the steady-state grid. When the coordinates are in the steady-state grid, the corresponding teaching behavior is continued. Analyzing the steady-state grid can obtain a variety of data in the teaching behavior: First, the ratio between the steady-state grid and the frequency can reveal the degree of stability of the corresponding teaching behavior (for example, the probability that the teaching behavior may be converted to other teaching behaviors after it occurs). In addition, by observing the coordinate distribution of the non-steady-state grid part, data related to the teaching behavior pattern can be obtained.

Analyze Teaching Behavior by Using the Characteristics of Steady-State Grid. It is found that the stability of "discuss with peers" and "Technology works on students" of group A are at a relatively high level, and the main teaching behaviors of group B are "discuss with peers", "Students try to operate" and general teaching behaviors "Do exercises" The degree of stability is at a relatively high level. Through the video review, the research found that the behaviors with higher stability have the following characteristics: First, from the perspective of teaching design, the behaviors with higher stability usually have a strong purpose. They occur intensively in a certain period of time in order to achieve the purpose of teaching. Second, from the perspective of the object. Typically, the behavior subject of highly stable behaviors is the student. The reason for this phenomenon is that teachers take the initiative to set aside time for student activities through guidance.

By comparing the highly stable behaviors in group A and group B, the research can learn the main ways teachers and students interact in classroom teaching. Group A tends to allow students to gain experience through efficient display (long-term observation of pictures, videos). Group B tends to let students conduct discussions through group collaboration, and at the same time use the Internet to complete inter-group interaction and teacher-student interaction. The source of experience is mainly peers.

Obtain Classroom Information by Analyzing Non-steady-State Grid. For example, "indirect effects" generally show a low degree of stability, where the areas corresponding to codes 1 to 3 represent the teacher's feedback on student behavior, and the areas corresponding to codes 4 and 5 are the teacher's questioning behavior. By observing the interactive classification matrix, it can be concluded that Group A and Group B both show a relatively low level of stability in the above-mentioned areas. among them, 60% of the coordinates of $cell(a,5)$ in the interactive classification matrix of group A fall in the position of $cell(6,5)$. 61.9% of the non-steady state coordinates of $cell(a,4)$ fall in the position of $cell(6,4)$, which means that 60% of open problems and 61.9% of closed problems occur in the "teaching" behavior after the end.

Therefore, it can be known that the group A used the way of frequently asking various questions to attract the students' attention and maintain the degree of concentration when teaching content. In group B, the value of this area is relatively small, indicating that this type of questioning is not the main teaching method of group B.

5   Conclusion

First of all, it is discovered through research that the application of information technology in the classroom will further deepen the integration of information technology and courses. This study found through comparative analysis that the addition of new terminals and new functions has changed the way teachers teach to a certain extent. In the group B class, the use of digital devices to communicate has become a part of the class. For example, teachers use teaching software to post classroom tasks; students use touch screens to write and display the content of group discussions. Such classroom activities require more teaching preparation. In a sense, it can be said that the impact of technology on the classroom is extending from inside the class to outside the class. In the teaching design stage, the teacher combined the teaching content of the course and the function of the equipment in the classroom to redesign the teaching process, which will determine the degree of completion of the classroom activities. Therefore, the emergence of new technologies is conducive to the integration of information technology and curriculum to a certain extent, and guides teachers to rethink.

Secondly, the application of information technology in the classroom will further balance the discourse power of teachers and students in the classroom. In traditional classrooms, teacher language usually dominates. However, due to the emergence of new interactive channels in the classroom, the medium of dissemination of information has changed, and the teacher's characteristic of occupying the classroom will be weakened. It can be found by comparing the two groups of classrooms through ratio analysis. On the one hand, in Group B, the terminal tablet computer not only displays classroom information, but also provides an equivalent interaction space for teachers and students. On the other hand, the "quick sharing of screens" function can be used to emphasize information. This new type of function is used extensively in the classroom of Group B, and replaces the traditional way of emphasizing information such as "stand up and answer questions". These changes have further revealed the traces of balancing the discourse power of teachers and students.

However, the use of information technology will also cause the lack of some classroom teaching behaviors, which affects teaching activities to a certain extent. Through the analysis of teacher's language ratio and non-steady state, it is found that the emotional interaction between teachers and students in the classroom that uses information technology to interact is weak. This phenomenon is intuitively reflected in the classroom as two points. One is that it is difficult for teachers to participate when student complete online tasks. It is difficult for teachers to make effective teaching behaviors within the time when students complete the tasks. Normally, the teacher will intervene after the student has completed most of the tasks. Second, there is a lack of accurate feedback on the content posted by students. Although the method of collecting answers widely can improve efficiency, it also leads to the loss of emotional interaction in the classroom. In contrast, traditional classrooms use the "stand up to answer questions" method. Teachers usually make full evaluations and feedback on the results, which forms the main part of the teacher-student emotional interaction in the classroom.

6 Epilogue

This study uses ITIAS to quantitatively analyze two classrooms in different technical environments. Use data analysis as a means to mine the generated classroom behavior data. From the perspective of classroom teaching behavior, it is proved that different technologies will have an impact on teaching design and classroom behavior of teachers and students. Then, sort out the reasons behind the phenomenon, and provide experience for the development of informatization teaching level. However, it needs to be pointed out that due to the limitation of the analysis method, the metadata of this research is the result of human judgment. If the follow-up research uses AI for analysis, it can be both objective and efficient. In addition, the use of the ITIAS code sheet to analyze different lesson types is prone to data deviation, and the control experiment is still only suitable for the samples under the same lesson type. The later stage of research should also be in line with the student-centered concept, and need to pay more attention to the learning experience, starting from the student's perspective.

References

1. Brown, M., et al.: 2020 Educause Horizon Report Teaching and Learning Edition. EDU-CAUSE, 2–58 (2020)
2. Luo, H.Y.: Teachers' Classroom Teaching Behavior in the Information Environment. Central China Normal University, Wuhan (2017)
3. Kratz, H.E.: Characteristics of the best teacher as recognized by children. Pedagog. Semin. **3**(3), 413–460 (1896)
4. Medley, D.M.: Early history of research on teacher behavior. Int. Rev. Educ. **18**(1), 430–439 (1972)
5. Cadima, J., Leal, T., Burchinal, M.: The quality of teacher–student interactions: associations with first graders' academic and behavioral outcomes. J. Sch. Psychol. **48**(6), 457–482 (2010)
6. Yang, H.: The study of the knowledge services model of teachers' online communities of practice. e-Educ. Res. **37**(4), 99–106 (2016)
7. Ball, D.L., Cohen, D.K.: Developing practice, developing practitioners: toward a practice-based theory of professional education. Teach. Learn. Profess. Handb. Policy Pract. **1**, 3–22 (1999)
8. Flanders, N.A.: Analyzing Teaching Behavior. MA. Addision-Wesley Publishing, New York (1970)
9. Li, H.W., Shen, R.M., Yang, Y., Zhang, J.P.: On Flanders interaction analysis system in information teaching context. J. Southwest China Norm. Univ. (Nat. Sci. Edn.) **44**(9), 161–166 (2019)
10. Ye, J., Luo, Y.: Discussion and improvement of Flanders interaction analysis system—taking classroom teaching evaluation of two teachers' "lens in life" as an example. Res. Teach. **42**(5), 115–119 (2019)
11. Gu, X.Q., Wang, W.: New exploration of classroom analysis techniques supporting teachers' professional development. China Educ. Technol. **7**, 18–21 (2004)
12. Fang, H.G., Gao, C.Z., Chen, J.: Improved Flanders interactive analysis system and its application. China Educ. Technol. **10**, 109–133 (2012)
13. Cheng, Y.: Analytical Methods Research of Teaching and Learning Behaviors in Classroom Based on Video. Central China Normal University, Wuhan (2015)

14. Ye, L.: The re-exploration of classroom instruction process: efforts beyond opinions. Curricul. Teach. Mater. Method **33**(5), 3–13 (2013)
15. Lin, Z.F., Xu, L.H.: Recognition of the research on teachers' behavior. Teacher Educ. Res. **2**, 23–26 (2006)
16. Flanders, N.A.: Intent, action and feedback: a preparation for teaching. J. Teach. Educ. **14**(3), 251–260 (1963)
17. Xue, Y., Jiao, X., Wang, C., Chen, H., Aloqaily, M.: Analysis and design of university teaching equipment management information system. J. Cyber Secur. **3**(3), 177–185 (2021)
18. Wu, H., Nagaraj, B.: Research on college english teaching model based on decision trees. Intell. Autom. Soft Comput. **30**(1), 81–95 (2021)
19. Muhammad, A., Abdullah, S., Sani, S.: Optimization of sentiment analysis using teaching-learning based algorithm. Comput. Mater. Continua **69**(2), 1783–1799 (2021)
20. Abhirami, K., Kavitha Devi, M.K.: Student behavior modeling for an e-learning system offering personalized learning experiences. Comput. Syst. Sci. Eng. **40**(3), 1127–1144 (2022)
21. Xue, Y., Qin, S., Su, S., Slowik, A.: Brain storm optimization based clustering for learning behavior analysis. Comput. Syst. Sci. Eng. **39**(2), 211–219 (2021)

Research on Kinematics Analysis and Trajectory Planning of Loading Robot

Da Xu, Zhaoyang Wang, Hua Li[✉], Xiaochuang Wang, and Zhendi Cao

Army Academy of Armored Forces, Beijing 100071, China
iuanne@163.com

Abstract. In order to realize object loading and improve loading efficiency, a six-degree-of-freedom robot is taken as the research object, and its kinematics analysis and trajectory planning research are carried out. Establish a kinematic model for the loading robot, and perform forward and inverse kinematics analysis; use Monte Carlo method to solve the robot's workspace, and obtain a point cloud image of the workspace at the end of the robot; perform a trajectory planning simulation on the loading robot to obtain The position, velocity and acceleration curve of each joint during the movement. The results show that the robot moves continuously and smoothly, the scope of the working space is appropriate, and the loading work can be completed.

Keywords: Loading robot · Kinematics analysis · Workspace · Trajectory planning · Six degrees of freedom

1 Preface

In recent years, robots have developed very rapidly and have become an indispensable part of our daily lives. For example, in response to COVID-19, intelligent factories, etc. [1–3]. For the factory, the wide application of industrial robots helps manufacturers reduce production costs, improve production efficiency and product quality, and adapt to the changes of market demand faster. Among them, the loading robot is mainly used in the field of logistics automation to replace manual transfer and assembly of goods [4]. There are many kinds of existing robots, but there is a lack of a loading robot with a high degree of intelligence, a compact overall structure and strong load capacity [5–9]. It is necessary to develop a small, heavy-duty and high-precision robot. For this, we have Research on related basic theories and key technologies such as design, trajectory planning, dynamic simulation, motion control of small, heavy-duty and high-precision robots.

This paper takes the six-degree-of-freedom loading robot as the research object, based on the D-H parameter method to model and analyze the kinematics of the robot, analyze the workspace by Monte Carlo method, and perform the robot trajectory planning and simulation by Matlab.

© The Author(s), under exclusive license to Springer Nature Switzerland AG 2022
X. Sun et al. (Eds.): ICAIS 2022, LNCS 13338, pp. 500–512, 2022.
https://doi.org/10.1007/978-3-031-06794-5_40

2   Coordinate System Establishment

The D-H parameter method was proposed by Denavit and Hartenberg [10]. Based on the D-H parameter method, we established a coordinate system on each joint of the six-degree-of-freedom loading robot, and described the end effector pose of the loading robot through the relationship between the coordinate systems. The kinematic equation of the loading robot, the coordinate system is shown in Fig. 1, and Table 1 is the D-H parameter table of the six-degree-of-freedom loading robot.

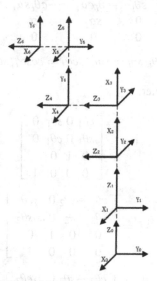

Fig. 1. Link coordinate system.

Table 1. D-H parameter table.

Link i	d_i/(mm)	α_i/(mm)	a_i/(°)	θ_i
1	201	0	$\pi/2$	θ_1
2	0	−480	0	θ_2
3	0	−360	0	θ_3
4	180	0	$\pi/2$	θ_4
5	120	0	$-\pi/2$	θ_5
6	137	0	0	θ_6

3 Forward Kinematics

The forward kinematics analysis of the loading robot is carried out, and the position and posture of the end effector of the robot relative to the reference coordinate system are obtained through its link parameters and joint variables [11].

The homogeneous transformation matrix between the adjacent joint coordinate systems of the loading robot is:

$$
{}^{i-1}_{i}T = \begin{bmatrix} c\theta_i & -s\theta_i c\alpha_i & s\theta_i s\alpha_i & a_i c\theta_i \\ s\theta_i & c\theta_i c\alpha_i & -c\theta_i s\alpha_i & a_i s\theta_i \\ 0 & s\alpha_i & c\alpha_i & d_i \\ 0 & 0 & 0 & 1 \end{bmatrix} \tag{1}
$$

$$
c\theta_i = cos\theta_i, \; s\theta_i = sin\theta_i, \; c\alpha_i = cos\alpha_i, \; s\alpha_i = sin\alpha_i \tag{2}
$$

Bring in the D-H parameter,

$$
{}^{0}_{1}T = \begin{bmatrix} c\theta_1 & 0 & s\theta_1 & 0 \\ s\theta_1 & 0 & c\theta_1 & 0 \\ 0 & 1 & 0 & d_1 \\ 0 & 0 & 0 & 1 \end{bmatrix} \tag{3}
$$

$$
{}^{1}_{2}T = \begin{bmatrix} c\theta_2 & -s\theta_2 & 0 & a_2 c\theta_2 \\ s\theta_2 & c\theta_2 & 0 & a_2 s\theta_2 \\ 0 & 0 & 1 & 0 \\ 0 & 0 & 0 & 1 \end{bmatrix} \tag{4}
$$

$$
{}^{2}_{3}T = \begin{bmatrix} c\theta_3 & -s\theta_3 & 0 & a_3 c\theta_3 \\ s\theta_3 & c\theta_3 & 0 & a_3 s\theta_3 \\ 0 & 0 & 1 & 0 \\ 0 & 0 & 0 & 1 \end{bmatrix} \tag{5}
$$

$$
{}^{3}_{4}T = \begin{bmatrix} c\theta_4 & 0 & s\theta_4 & 0 \\ s\theta_4 & 0 & -c\theta_4 & 0 \\ 0 & 1 & 0 & d_4 \\ 0 & 0 & 0 & 1 \end{bmatrix} \tag{6}
$$

$$
{}^{4}_{5}T = \begin{bmatrix} c\theta_5 & 0 & -s\theta_5 & 0 \\ s\theta_5 & 0 & c\theta_5 & 0 \\ 0 & -1 & 0 & d_5 \\ 0 & 0 & 0 & 1 \end{bmatrix} \tag{7}
$$

$$
{}^{5}_{6}T = \begin{bmatrix} c\theta_6 & -s\theta_6 & 0 & 0 \\ s\theta_6 & c\theta_6 & 0 & 0 \\ 0 & -1 & 0 & d_6 \\ 0 & 0 & 0 & 1 \end{bmatrix} \tag{8}
$$

Set the reference coordinate system to the base of the robot and bring in the D-H parameters, in there, $c\theta_i = \cos\theta_i$; $s\theta_i = \sin\theta_i$; $c\alpha_i = \cos\alpha_i$; $s\alpha_i = \sin\alpha_o$ where the above matrix is multiplied by the right to get the relationship between the end of the robot and the base:

$$_6^0T = {}_1^0T \cdot {}_2^1T \cdot {}_3^2T \cdot {}_4^3T \cdot {}_5^4T \cdot {}_6^5T = \begin{bmatrix} n_x & o_x & a_x & p_x \\ n_y & o_y & a_y & p_y \\ n_z & o_z & a_z & p_z \\ 0 & 0 & 0 & 1 \end{bmatrix} \tag{9}$$

Among:

$$\begin{cases}
n_x = c_1\left[c_{23}(c_4c_5c_6 - s_4s_5) - s_{23}s_5\,c_5\right] + s_1(c_4c_5c_6 - c_4s_6) \\
n_y = s_1\left[c_{23}(c_4c_5c_6 - s_4s_6) - s_{23}s_5\,c_6\right] - c_1(s_4c_5c_6 + c_4s_6) \\
n_z = -s_{23}(c_4c_5c_6 - s_4c_6) - c_{23}s_5c_6 \\
o_x = c_1\left[c_{23}(-c_4c_5c_6 - s_4c_6) + s_{23}s_5\,s_6\right] - c_1(-s_4c_5s_6 + c_4s_6) \\
o_y = s_1\left[c_{23}(-c_4c_5s_6 - s_4c_6) + s_{23}s_5\,s_6\right] - c_1(-s_4c_5s_6 + c_4s_6) \\
o_z = -s_{23}(-c_4c_5s_6 - s_4c_6) + c_{23}c_5s_6 \\
a_x = -c_1(c_{23}c_4s_5 + s_{23}c_5) - s_1s_4s_5 \\
a_y = -s_1(c_{23}c_4s_5 + s_{23}c_5) + c_1s_4s_5 \\
a_z = s_{23}s_4s_5 - c_{23}c_5 \\
p_x = c_1[a_2c_2 + a_3c_{23} - s_{23}d_4] - d_3s_1 \\
p_y = s_1[a_2c_2 + a_3c_{23} - s_{23}d_4] + d_3c_1 \\
p_z = -a_3c_1 - a_2s_2 - d_4c_{23}
\end{cases} \tag{10}$$

In the above formula:

$$c_{23} = \cos(\theta_2 + \theta_3) = c_2c_3 - s_2s_3, \; s_{23} = \sin(\theta_2 + \theta_3) = s_2c_3 + c_2s_3 \tag{11}$$

4 Inverse Kinematics

The inverse kinematics analysis of the loading robot is carried out, and the joint variables are reversed through the connecting rod parameters and the expected position and posture of the robot end relative to the reference coordinate system [12]. There are many solutions to robot inverse kinematics, such as geometric solution, algebraic solution, etc. [13], this paper uses algebraic method to solve the six-degree-of-freedom robot.

4.1 Solve $\theta_1, \theta_5, \theta_6$

$$_6^0T = {}_1^0T \cdot {}_2^1T \cdot {}_3^2T \cdot {}_4^3T \cdot {}_5^4T \cdot {}_6^5T = \begin{bmatrix} n_x & o_x & a_x & p_x \\ n_y & o_y & a_y & p_y \\ n_z & o_z & a_z & p_z \\ 0 & 0 & 0 & 1 \end{bmatrix} \tag{12}$$

Further available:

$$\substack{0\\1}T^{-1} \cdot \substack{0\\6}T = \substack{1\\6}T \tag{13}$$

$$\substack{0\\1}T^{-1} \cdot \substack{0\\6}T \cdot \substack{5\\6}T^{-1} = \substack{1\\2}T \cdot \substack{2\\3}T \cdot \substack{3\\4}T \cdot \substack{4\\5}T = \substack{1\\5}T \tag{14}$$

$$\substack{0\\1}T^{-1} = \begin{bmatrix} c_1 & s_1 & 0 & 0 \\ 0 & 0 & 1 & -d_1 \\ s_1 & -c_1 & 0 & 0 \\ 0 & 0 & 0 & 1 \end{bmatrix} \tag{15}$$

$$\substack{5\\6}T^{-1} = \begin{bmatrix} c_6 & s_6 & 0 & 0 \\ s_6 & -c_6 & 0 & 0 \\ 0 & 0 & 1 & -d_6 \\ 0 & 0 & 0 & 1 \end{bmatrix} \tag{16}$$

Left side of equation:

$$\substack{0\\1}T^{-1} \cdot \substack{0\\6}T \cdot \substack{5\\6}T^{-1}$$

$$= \begin{bmatrix} c_6(n_xc_1 + n_ys_1) - s_6(o_xc_1 + o_ys_1) & c_6(n_xc_1 + n_ys_1) - s_6(o_xc_1 + o_ys_1) \\ n_xc_6 - o_zs_6 & o_zc_6 + n_zs_6 \\ s_6(o_yc_1 - o_xs_1) - c_6(n_yc_1 - n_xs_1) & -s_6(n_xc_1 + n_ys_1) - s_6(o_xc_1 + o_ys_1) \\ 0 & 0 \end{bmatrix}$$

$$\begin{matrix} a_xc_1 + a_ys_1 & p_xc_1 - d_6(a_xc_1 + a_ys_1) + p_ys_1 \\ a_z & p_z - d_1 - a_zc_1 \\ a_xs_1 - a_yc_1 & -p_xc_1 + d_6(a_yc_1 - a_xs_1) + p_xs_1 \\ 0 & 1 \end{matrix} \Bigg] \tag{17}$$

From the equal sign left and right are equal, we know that the elements in the 3rd row and 4th column of the matrices on both sides of the equation are correspondingly equal.

$$-p_yc_1 + d_6(a_yc_1 - a_xs_1) + p_xs_1 = d_4 \tag{18}$$

Assume:

$$d_6a_y - p_y = m \tag{19}$$

$$a_xd_6 - p_x = n \tag{20}$$

Then:

$$mc_1 - ns_1 = d_4 \tag{21}$$

So:

$$\theta_1 = A \tan 2(m, n) - A \tan 2\left(d_4, \pm\sqrt{m^2 + n^2 - d_4^2}\right) \qquad (22)$$

$$A \tan 2(m, n) = 2\tan(m + n)/\left[1 - \tan^2(m + n)\right] \qquad (23)$$

From the 3rd row and 3rd column on the left and right are equal, we get:

$$a_x s_1 - a_y c_1 = c_5 \qquad (24)$$

$$\theta_5 = \pm \arccos\left(a_x s_1 - a_y c_1\right) \qquad (25)$$

From the left and right third row and the first column are equal, we get:

$$s_6\left(o_y c_1 - o_x s_1\right) - c_6\left(n_y c_1 - n_x s_1\right) = s_5 \qquad (26)$$

Assume: $n_x s_1 - n_y c_1 = m$, $o_x s_1 - o_y c_1 = n$
Then:

$$m c_6 - n s_6 = s_5 \qquad (27)$$

Obtained by simplification: $m^2 + n^2 = s_5{}^2$, get:

$$\theta_6 = A \tan 2(m, n) - A \tan 2(s_5, 0) = A \tan 2(m/s_5, n/s_5), (s_5 \neq 0) \qquad (28)$$

4.2 Solve $\theta_2, \theta_3, \theta_4$

$$^0_1 T^{-1} \cdot {^0_6} T \cdot {^5_6} T^{-1} \cdot {^4_5} T^{-1} = {^1_2} T \cdot {^2_3} T \cdot {^3_4} T = {^1_4} T \qquad (29)$$

Among:

$$^4_5 T^{-1} = \begin{bmatrix} c_5 & s_5 & 0 & 0 \\ 0 & 0 & -1 & d_5 \\ -s_5 & c_5 & 0 & 0 \\ 0 & 0 & 0 & 1 \end{bmatrix} \qquad (30)$$

$$^1_2 T \cdot {^2_3} T \cdot {^3_4} T = {^1_4} T = \begin{bmatrix} c_{234} & 0 & s_{234} & a_3 c_{23} + a_2 c_2 \\ s_{234} & 0 & -c_{234} & a_3 s_{23} + a_2 s_2 \\ 0 & 1 & 0 & d_4 \\ 0 & 0 & 0 & 1 \end{bmatrix} \qquad (31)$$

Calculate joint angle θ_3, because the first row and the fourth column of equations on both sides are equal, and the second row and the fourth column of equations on both sides are equal.

$$d_5\left[s_6\left(n_x c_1 + n_y s_1\right) + c_6\left(o_x c_1 + o_y s_1\right)\right] - d_6\left(a_x c_1 + a_y s_1\right) + p_x c_1 + p_y s_1 = m \qquad (32)$$

$$p_z - d_1 - a_z d_6 + d_5(o_z c_6 + n_z s_6) = n \tag{33}$$

Then:

$$m = a_3 c_{23} + a_2 c_2 \tag{34}$$

$$n = a_3 s_{23} + a_2 s_2 \tag{35}$$

Taking the sum of squares, we get:

$$a_2{}^2 + a_3{}^2 + 2a_2 a_3 (s_{23} s_2 + c_{23} c_2) = m^2 + n^2, s_{23} s_2 + c_{23} c_2 = c_3 \tag{36}$$

Therefore:

$$\theta_3 = \pm \arccos\left(\frac{m^2 + n^2 - a_2{}^2 - a_3{}^2}{2a_2 a_3}\right), m^2 + n^2 \le (a_2 + a_3)^2 \tag{37}$$

The same can be obtained:

$$\theta_2 = A\tan2(s_2, c_2) \tag{38}$$

Finally, we calculate θ_4:

$$\begin{cases} s_{234} = -s_6\left(n_x c_1 + n_y s_1\right) - c_6\left(o_x c_1 + o_y s_1\right) \\ c_{234} = o_z c_6 + n_z s_6 \\ \theta_2 + \theta_3 + \theta_4 = A\tan2(-s_6(n_x c_1 + n_y s_1) - c_6\left(o_x c_1 + o_y s_1\right), o_z c_6 + n_z s_6) \end{cases} \tag{39}$$

So:

$$\theta_4 = A\tan2\left(-s_6\left(n_x c_1 + n_y s_1\right) - c_6\left(o_x c_1 + o_y s_1\right), o_z c_6 + n_z s_6\right) - \theta_2 - \theta_3 \tag{40}$$

5 Working Space

The workspace is composed of all the points that can be reached by the robot end effector in the reference coordinate system. It is an important index to measure the performance of the robot. In this paper, Monte Carlo method is used to solve the problem, which is fast and easy to display.

First, determine the variation range of each joint variable of the robot, and generate N 0–1 random points through a random function to obtain the random value of each joint variable as the step length. Through positive kinematics the function fkine generates a working space, which is composed of all the points that can be reached by the end effector of the loading robot in the reference coordinate system, taking N = 100000, and the result is shown in the figure:

It can be seen from Fig. 2, Fig. 3, Fig. 4, and Fig. 5 that the working space of the filling robot is approximately a sphere with a radius of 1 m, and there is no obvious cavity, indicating that the robot can work at any point in the working space, and the working space of the robot can Effectively cover the task space and can adapt to various working environments.

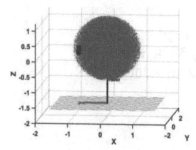

Fig. 2. Cloud map of workspace.

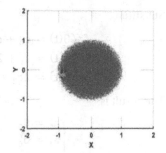

Fig. 3. XY plane projection.

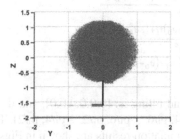

Fig. 4. YZ plane projection.

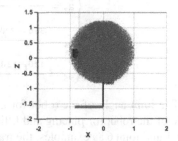

Fig. 5. XZ plane projection.

6 Trajectory Planning

Trajectory planning belongs to the robot bottom planning, which calculates the expected motion trajectory according to the requirements of the task. The so-called planning refers to the displacement, velocity and acceleration of the robot in the process of motion. The trajectory planning of the loading robot can be carried out in joint space or Cartesian space, but the trajectory is required to be smooth and continuous to make the robot move smoothly. Since trajectory planning in Cartesian space needs to be transformed through a large number of calculations [14], this paper performs trajectory planning in joint space. Polynomial interpolation is commonly used in joint trajectory interpolation, because cubic polynomial interpolation can not meet many constraints, so quintic polynomial interpolation is needed. The constraints of the loading robot are:

$$
\begin{cases}
\theta(t_0) = \theta_0 = a_0 \\
\theta(t_f) = \theta_f = a_0 + a_1 t_f + a_2 t_f^2 + a_3 t_f^3 + a_4 t_f^4 + a_5 t_f^5 \\
\dot{\theta}(t_0) = \dot{\theta}_0 = a_1 \\
\dot{\theta}(t_f) = a_1 + 2a_2 t_f + 3a_3 t_f^2 + 4a_4 t_f^3 + 5a_5 t_f^4 \\
\ddot{\theta}(t_0) = \ddot{\theta}_0 = 2a_2 \\
\ddot{\theta}(t_f) = \ddot{\theta}_f = 2a_2 + 6a_3 t_f + 12a_4 t_f^2 + 20a_5 t_f^3
\end{cases}
\tag{41}
$$

Substitute:

$$\begin{cases} \theta(t) = c_0 + c_1 t + c_2 t^2 + c_3 t^3 + c_4 t^4 + c_5 t^5 \\ \dot{\theta}(t) = c_1 + 2c_2 t + 3c_3 t^2 + 4c_4 t^3 + 5c_5 t^4 \\ \ddot{\theta}(t) = 2c_2 + 6c_3 t + 12c_4 t^2 + 20c_5 t^3 \end{cases} \tag{42}$$

The result is:

$$\begin{cases} a_0 = \theta_0 \\ a_1 = \theta_0' \\ a_2 = \dfrac{\theta_0''}{2} \\ a_3 = \dfrac{20\theta_f - 20\theta_0 - (8\theta_f' + 12\theta_0')t_f - (3\theta_0'' - \theta_f'')t_f^2}{2t_f^3} \\ a_4 = \dfrac{30\theta_0 - 30\theta_f + (14\theta_f' + 16\theta_0')t_f + (3\theta_0'' - 2\theta_f'')t_f^2}{2t_f^4} \\ a_5 = \dfrac{12\theta_f - 12\theta_0 - (6\theta_f' + 6\theta_0')t_f - (\theta_0'' - \theta_f'')t_f^2}{2t_f^5} \end{cases} \tag{43}$$

The joint angle of the robot for grabbing and filling is: [0,0,0,0,0,0], and the joint angle of the robot for placing and filling is: [pi/4, pi/6, −pi/6, pi/2, −pi/4, pi/2]. Taking joint 1 and joint 6 as examples, the trajectory simulation results are shown in Figs. 6, 7, 8, 9, 10, 11, 12, 13, 14, 15, 16, 17, 18, 19, 20, 21, 22, 23 and 24.

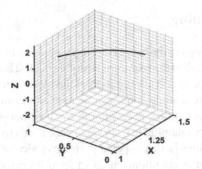

Fig. 6. Robot end trajectory.

From Figs. 6, 7, 8, 9, 10, 11, 12, 13, 14, 15, 16, 17, 18, 19, 20, 21, 22, 23 and 24, it can be seen that during the loading work, After quintic polynomial programming, the angular displacement, angular velocity and angular acceleration curves of the six joints of the robot meet the constraints, the route from the grasping position of the loading robot to the placement position is fast and smooth. There are no interruptions and jumps. The rationality of the structural design is further verified. The curves of the angular displacement, angular velocity, and angular acceleration of the loading robot joints are smooth and continuous without sudden changes, and there is no excessive acceleration, which can meet the requirements of the loading work, which meets the stability requirements during movement.

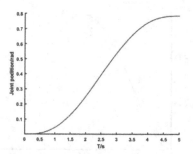

Fig. 7. Joint angle 1 displacement

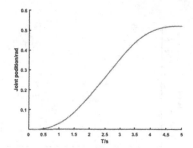

Fig. 8. Joint angle 2 displacement

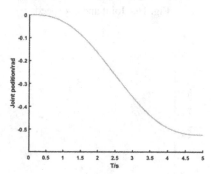

Fig. 9. Joint angle 3 displacement

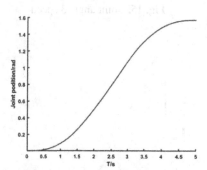

Fig. 10. Joint angle 4 displacement

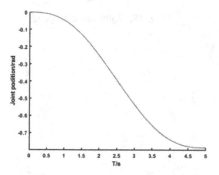

Fig. 11. Joint angle 5 displacement

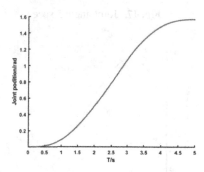

Fig. 12. Joint angle 6 displacement

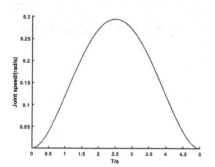

Fig. 13. Joint angle 1 speed

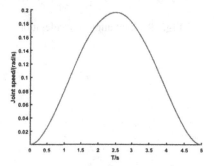

Fig. 14. Joint angle 2 speed

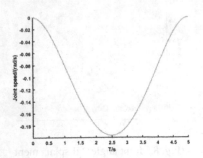

Fig. 15. Joint angle 3 speed

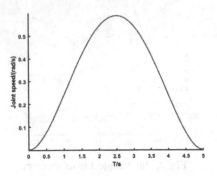

Fig. 16. Joint angle 4 speed

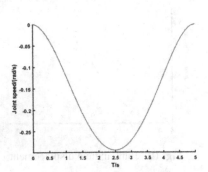

Fig. 17. Joint angle 5 speed

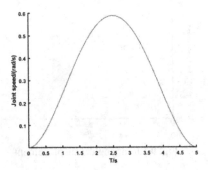

Fig. 18. Joint angle 6 speed

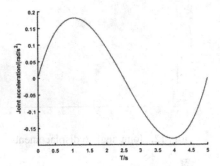

Fig. 19. Joint angle 1 acceleration

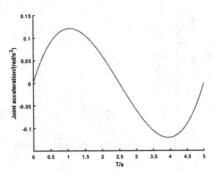

Fig. 20. Joint angle 2 acceleration

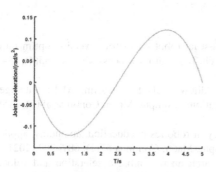

Fig. 21. Joint angle 3 acceleration

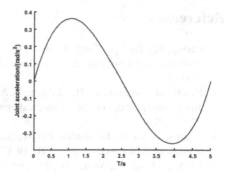

Fig. 22. Joint angle 4 acceleration

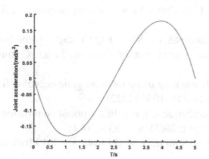

Fig. 23. Joint angle 5 acceleration

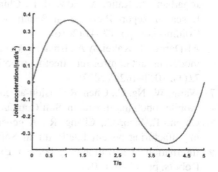

Fig. 24. Joint angle 6 acceleration

7 Conclusion

This paper aims at the loading problem of 6-DOF robot, the D-H modeling of the loading robot is carried out, and the relationship between the joint angle and the end pose of the robot is obtained through the analysis of forward kinematics and inverse kinematics; the cloud image of the working space of the loading robot is established by the Monte Carlo method, and the simulation experiment is carried out by quintic polynomial trajectory. The trajectory curve and joint displacement, velocity and acceleration of the loading robot from the grasping position to the placement are obtained. The results show that the loading robot has a simple working route, runs smoothly, the rationality of the loading robot design and geometric parameter design of the manipulator is verified, and exhibits good working performance. It lays an application foundation for the mobile robot equipped with loading robot to complete the autonomous recognition and grasping of the target object, we can get help from it for follow-up research.

References

1. Cheng, H., Zhu, X., Feng, J., et al.: 6R industrial robot geometric inversion optimization algorithm and simulation analysis. Modul. Mach. Tool Autom. Process. Technol. **63**(4), 75–79 (2021)
2. Farkh, R., Marouani, H., Jaloud, K.A., Alhuwaimel, S., Quasim, M.T.: Intelligent autonomous-robot control for medical applications. Comput. Mater. Continua **68**(2), 2189–2203 (2021)
3. Younis, H.A.S.A., Jamaludin, R.N.M.: Survey of robotics in education, taxonomy, applications, and platforms during COVID-19. Comput. Mater. Continua **67**(1), 687–707 (2021)
4. Li, K., Zhang, Z., Wang, W., Ma, Y.: Research on the initial acceleration and velocity continuous motion planning of the loading manipulator. Mod. Manuf. Eng. **44**(4), 41–47 (2021)
5. Jonathan, R., Katie, A., Edward, F.: China's industrial and military robotics development. Research Report Prepared on Behalf of the U.S.-China Economic and Security Review Commission, pp. 17–41 (2016)
6. Al-Darraji, I., Kakei, A.A., Ismaeel, A.G., Tsaramirsis, G., Khan, F.Q.: Takagi-sugeno fuzzy modeling and control for effective robotic manipulator motion. Comput. Mater. Continua **71**(1), 1011–1024 (2022)
7. Wang, W., Ng, C., Chen, R.: Vision-aided path planning using low-cost gene encoding for a mobile robot. Intell. Autom. Soft Comput. **32**(2), 991–1006 (2022)
8. Chien, T., Siao, C., Chang, R.: A general technique for real-time robotic simulation in manufacturing system. Intell. Autom. Soft Comput. **29**(3), 827–838 (2021)
9. International Federation of Robotics I, Executive Summary World Robotics 2019 Industrial Robots, pp. 13–16 (2019)
10. Ye, S., Yin, F., Wang, X., Chen, Z., Xiao, F.: Kinematics and workspace analysis of a six-degree-of-freedom manipulator. Mach. Tool Hydraul. **43**, 76–81 (2015)
11. Chen, J.: Modular robot configuration optimization based on genetic algorithm. Master's Theses, Yanshan University, China (2017)
12. Zhao, Z.: Research on kinematics and motion planning of line-driven continuous manipulator. Doctoral thesis, University of Chinese Academy of Sciences, China (2019)
13. Gu, W.: Study on control and simulation technology of six-DOF robot. Doctoral thesis, Shandong University, China (2017)
14. Shi, L.: Analysis and simulation of 6-DOF serial robot. Doctoral thesis, Shenyang University of Aeronautics and Astronautics, China (2011)

Text Sentiment Analysis Based on Improved Naive Bayes Algorithm

Xinfei Li[2], Xiaolan Xie[1,2(✉)], Jiaming Wang[2], and Yigang Tang[2]

[1] Guangxi Key Laboratory of Embedded Technology and Intelligent System, Guilin 541006, Guangxi, China
237290696@qq.com

[2] School of Information Science and Engineering, Guilin University of Technology, Guilin 541006, Guangxi, China

Abstract. Aiming at the lack of specific domain corpus in text sentiment polarity analysis, the inaccurate classification accuracy of the naive Bayes algorithm due to the independence assumption and the sparse word vector matrix, a text sentiment analysis method based on the improved naive Bayes algorithm is proposed. Combining machine learning methods with domain sentiment dictionary weighting methods. The improved word frequency inverse file frequency algorithm is used to extract the feature word vector of hotel review text, and the weight of the feature word vector of the domain dictionary after regression test is introduced to weaken the influence of the independence assumption. The singular value decomposition algorithm realizes the dimensionality reduction of the word vector sparse matrix and eliminates redundancy. The remaining features are used to construct a polynomial model of Naive Bayes. The results of simulation research show that this method can effectively improve the effect of text sentiment classification.

Keywords: Singular value decomposition · Emotion analysis · Domain dictionary · Naive Bayes

1 Introduction

With the development of social software and e-commerce platforms, various online applications are flooding our daily lives, and the acceleration of the pace of life has caused users to rely heavily on these applications. At the same time, it has produced evaluation information rich in emotional value. It will resonate with other consumers and affect their subjective intentions. The products of these online products, including textual data on consumer sentimental tendencies, have great value that can be mined. At the same time, the amount of data generated by the application is also very large [1], if you rely solely on manual identification, the amount of tasks will be very large and heavy. Therefore, it is necessary to propose a text sentiment analysis technology based on machine learning. As a text value mining process in the field of natural language processing, text sentiment analysis is the study of processing, analyzing, and mining information data in different forms of natural language. The main research here is sentiment analysis and mining of

© The Author(s), under exclusive license to Springer Nature Switzerland AG 2022
X. Sun et al. (Eds.): ICAIS 2022, LNCS 13338, pp. 513–523, 2022.
https://doi.org/10.1007/978-3-031-06794-5_41

text information. For example, in the field of hotel reviews, the user's living experience contains complex and emotional information, and the evaluation of hotel services and facilities is polar, with high-profile praise and negative rebuke. With the development of technology, the field of humanistic sentiment analysis is not only limited to word-level issues, but also extended to article-level research. Through the development of existing machine learning and data mining technology, it provides the field of text sentiment conditions for development.

This paper mainly studies the two classification problems of sentiment orientation polarity of Chinese text, combined with the more versatile machine learning methods and domain dictionary methods, and analyzes the sentiment polarity of consumers' subjective texts based on machine learning methods, such as Naive Bayes, KNN Traditional methods such as SVM, SVM, and algorithms for different problems in the research field are combined and improved. The analysis method based on the domain dictionary calculates the overall emotional strength of the text by analyzing the polar words.

2 Related Work

Scholars at home and abroad have done a lot of research on sentiment feature analysis. Literature [2] constructed a domain sentiment dictionary method based on word vectors, trained the word2vec model to obtain the seed word set vector and mapped it to the high-dimensional vector space, and realized the sentiment word The feature vector representation makes the extracted emotion word vector more domain characteristics. Literature [3] constructs a sentiment dictionary covering different parts of speech information in the field of Weibo, and introduces a combination of semantic rule sets between texts and multi-faceted sentiment dictionaries to enhance the accuracy of analysis. Literature [4] studies sentiment analysis in the homestay domain, uses an improved SO-PMI algorithm to construct a domain dictionary for homestay evaluation, and uses the LDA topic model for analysis, and finally visualizes homestay reviews. Based on the extended domain dictionary, better decision-making effects are made. Considering the low accuracy of the model prediction by the word frequency and part of speech of the sentiment dictionary, more and more researches combine the sentiment dictionary with machine learning methods to increase the learning ability of the model in addition to overcoming the shortcomings of the sentiment dictionary. It is widely used in the field of sentiment analysis. Literature [5] integrates the extended emotional dictionary into the Chi-square feature selection model (CHI) to eliminate the influence of negative words changing part of speech and feature selection on the effect of the polarity value on the result of emotion prediction during emotion prediction. Improved classification accuracy. The literature [6, 7] uses the method of integrating multiple machine learning algorithms combined with the emotional dictionary, and uses the integrated learning of Word2Vec feature extraction and support vector machine (SVM) classification method to solve the problem of machine learning methods lacking a specific corpus, and the use of multiple classifiers The fuzzy calculation of the integrated and quantified dictionary improves the accuracy of model prediction. Literature [8–10] uses convolutional neural network (CNN) and recurrent neural network (RNN) to solve the problem of high-dimensional explosion and gradient disappearance of data. The literature [11] has a large number of language constraints on utterance and polarity structure to enhance DNN and apply it to sentence sentiment analysis, using less training data to significantly improve performance. The literature [12] proposed a hierarchical Twitter sentiment model (HTSM), there are two main features: short texts without predefined levels of depth and width build important aspects of the hierarchical tree, and through the application of price perception Dictionary to discover these important aspects of emotional polarity emotional reasoner. The literature [13] developed a new fast sentiment analysis method (FAST-BiLSTM), which can strike a balance between performance and speed. The literature [14] use rough set theory (RST) and teaching-based optimization (TLBO) methods, combining natural language processing with text processing, and the effect of sentiment analysis has been improved. The literature [15] is aimed at a specific field and conducts a polar sentiment analysis of Arabic social media news. Reference [16] constructed a Bayesian network model for extracting sentiment variables with OCC model generation rules for sentiment SD symbols in text data, and realized sentence-level sentiment classification under the influence of weakening of the lack of information, and solved the category of sentiment sentences. Automatically determine the problem. Literature [17] combines parent nodes with dependent relationships and improved word frequency inverse file frequency algorithm to construct a hidden Naive Bayes model to improve classification accuracy. Literature [18] constructed a weighted naive Bayes algorithm based on the contribution rate of sentiment words, which considers the overall feature on the basis of improving its posterior probability, which is an effective analysis method. Reference [19] aimed at the assumption of conditional independence among attributes of the naive Bayes model, and studied the independence and dependence between text attributes, combined with the hidden naive Bayes model as an sentiment classification model in the field of product reviews.

Based on the research results in the field of sentiment analysis at home and abroad, it is found that the Naive Bayes algorithm has a huge space in mining the value of sentiment information. It is simple and easy to operate, but the classification effect is very good, and it has a high level of performance for special fields lacking a corpus. Conditional independence [20] hypothesis and high-dimensional word vector matrix sparse problem, select the emotional feature words in the wrong sample after the test to give a linear weight, and build an artificial label based on the frequency of the wrong sample after the regression test for the original sentiment dictionary. The sentiment dictionary enables the improved word frequency inverse file frequency algorithm to make the tested sentiment features have high-category features when extracting features, and the artificially labeled sentiment dictionary is returned to the original sentiment dictionary to construct a corpus of specific fields. While weakening the influence of the assumption of independence, the singular value decomposition algorithm is applied to the word vector sparse matrix to reduce the dimensionality to eliminate redundant features, construct a naive Bayesian polynomial model.

3 Text Sentiment Analysis Model

3.1 Data Preprocessing

Remove stop words: Stop words provide noise during the training of the model, which is detrimental to the training of the model. When the model is trained, useless symbols can be added to it through a custom stop vocabulary list, or the custom stop vocabulary can be combined with a standardized stop vocabulary widely used on the Internet. In the training process of the model, the adverse effect of stop words on the accuracy of the model is solved, and the efficiency of the model is improved.

Stuttering participle: The smallest unit of Chinese expression semantics is words, so the basis of preprocessing is the segmentation of text data. The result of word segmentation is very important for processing Chinese information. Stuttering word segmentation is the most commonly used Chinese natural language processing word segmentation method. The processed text file is the key to feature extraction and text word vector generation.

3.2 Improved TF-IDF Algorithm

1) In the process of data processing, the extraction of text feature word vectors plays a vital role, the word frequency inverse frequency algorithm, was produced in 1988, which realizes the calculation and normalization of text data to improve the classification effect of features. Feature words represent document attributes to a certain extent. Its quantitative characteristics and attribute characteristics also provide a reference for mathematical modeling for the article. Tf represents the importance of the frequency of the feature in the text, that is, the word frequency. Idf represents the distinguishing ability of features in terms of categories, that is, the frequency of feature words in the sample is very high, and the frequency of appearance in other samples is very low. The basic TFIDF algorithm formula is as follows:

$$\text{tfidf} = tf_{ij} * idf_j = tf_{ij} * \log(N/n_j) \tag{1}$$

tf_{ij} refers to the frequency of the feature t in each sample in the text d_i, that is, the word frequency, idf_j refers to the reciprocal of the text where the feature word vector t appears. The total number is N, number of texts containing feature word vectors is n_j.

2) Text data in a specific field has an impact on the accuracy of model predictions. In order to solve the above problems, it is necessary to regress the problem of inaccurate prediction of feature word vectors in the sentiment dictionary, and then construct a weighted representation of domain sentiment. Therefore, it is necessary to improve the TFIDF algorithm formula. The weight formula of improved TFIDF is:

$$\text{tfidf} = tfidf^{(1-tfidf)}, t_j \in D_{senti} \tag{2}$$

t_j is the feature word vector in the wrong matching data set, and D_{senti} is the sentiment dictionary, where the weighted tfidf value is a proportional linear weight that is adaptive compared to the original weight value [21].

3.3 Singular Value Decomposition

Due to Chinese text sentiment analysis, the text information data is huge and the extracted feature word vector is always 103, which will always cause the dimensional disaster of high-dimensional data and the generation of sparse matrix, and the linearly related features will also cause redundancy, sparse matrix It will reduce the accuracy of classification, so data dimensionality reduction is necessary. This article combines the weights of feature word vectors after data dimensionality reduction into the naive Bayes model. Singular values can be used as the criteria for selecting features of the data matrix. The hidden category information in text data [22] may be hidden in the singular values, and the obvious features, that is, the features represented by high singular values, are used as important category features for sentiment model analysis.

The text sample and word vector matrix are non-square:

$$A_{m*n} = USV^T = tfidf_{m*n} \qquad (3)$$

A_{m*n} is text samples m, and n is a feature word vector. U is the m*m matrix for the correlation between the text and the topic, V is the n*n matrix for the correlation between the feature vector and the topic, and S is the m*n matrix with singular values on the main diagonal the degree of relevance between different topics. The three matrices of U, S, V and the singular values are obtained by eigenvalues and eigenvectors.

The original data matrix can be described by the largest k singular values and the corresponding left and right singular vectors, and the largest k singular values can be obtained by the proportion threshold to solve the reduced dimensionality data matrix:

$$A_{m*n} = U_{m*k}S_{k*k}V_{k*n}^T, k < n \qquad (4)$$

The threshold is set to represent the sum of all its singular values, and k is the maximum number of singular values obtained by the proportion threshold, that is the number of final decomposed matrices.

Since the final Naive Bayes model is a polynomial model, it cannot be modeled when the word vector is negative. The value is the feature word vector of the n feature words in the text m. After verification and discarding the negative value, compared with the absolute value, the classification accuracy can be improved.

The word vector value can be improved:

$$A_{m*n}^i = \left| A_{m*n}^i \right| \qquad (5)$$

3.4 Improved Naive Bayes Model

Improve the naive Bayes model: Naive Bayesian classification is to solve the probability value $P(p_1, p_2, \ldots, p_j)$ of each word vector $X(x_1, x_2, \ldots, x_j)$ in the text belonging to the category $Y(y_1, y_2, \ldots, y_n)$, and its solving formula:

$$P(Y_j|x_1, x_2, \ldots, x_n) = \frac{P(x_1, x_2, \ldots, x_n|Y_j)}{P(Y_1, Y_2, \ldots, Y_n)} \qquad (6)$$

That is to say, under the condition that the text belongs to the category Y_j, the probability $P(x_1, x_2, \ldots, x_n | Y_j)$ of the feature word vector $x_1, x_2, \ldots, x_n$ contained in the text is the category joint probability $P(Y_1, Y_2, \ldots, Y_n)$ of all documents. The maximum value solution formula is defined as a constant during the training process. All can be expressed as:

$$Y_{nb} = \arg\max_{Y_j=Y} P(x_1, x_2, \ldots, x_n | Y_j) P(Y_j) \tag{7}$$

Due to the independence of their attributes, that is, there is no dependency relationship between the feature word vectors of the text, based on this independence assumptions:

$$P(x_1, x_2, \ldots, x_n | Y_j) = \Pi P(x_i | Y_j) \tag{8}$$

According to Eq. 8 for the preprocessed text vector $x_1, x_2, \ldots, x_n$ of unknown category, the limit value category of the probability $P(X|Y_j)P(Y_j)$ that X belongs to each category can be obtained, and then:

$$Y_{nb} = \arg\max_{C_j \in C} P(Y_j) \Pi P(x_i | Y_j) \tag{9}$$

The feature word vector here has been converted to the vector value after dimensionality reduction of the SVD algorithm:

$$X(x_1, x_2, \ldots, x_n) = SVD$$
$$(tfidf (tfidf_1, tfidf_2, \ldots, tfidf_n)) \tag{10}$$

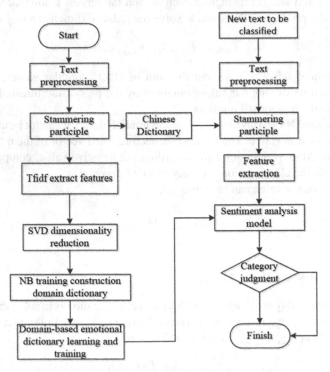

Fig. 1. Algorithm flowchart.

3) Improve the algorithm flow

Flow chart of text sentiment analysis method based on improved naive Bayes algorithm (Fig. 1).

4   Experiment and Result Analysis

4.1   Experimental Data

The experimental data in this article comes from the public data set of Dr. Tan Songbo's hotel review corpus, which mainly contains two kinds of emotional reviews, such as negative reviews "The room conditions are too bad. Perhaps the positioning is to serve those tourists who visit here. All conditions are met. Quite poor, at best the level of a guest house", positively commented, "Fortunately, a beautiful manager named Angela at the front desk took care of it in time. I am quite satisfied, and I would like to express my gratitude to him.".

4.2   Classification Evaluation Index

Text classification, natural language processing, pattern recognition, etc. in machine learning all involve a necessary task, namely evaluation, and the criteria to be considered for evaluation include Accuracy, Precision, Recall and F1 As shown in Table 1, the judgment parameter table:

Table 1. Judgment parameter table.

Accuracy parameter	Parameter description
P	Precision
R	Recall
F1	Harmonic mean of P and R

The accuracy rate is the ratio of the correct classification of the emotion model to the total number of samples in the unclassified text. Here, classification 1 is positive or positive, and classification 0 is negative or negative.

The confusion matrix is as follows (Table 2):

Table 2. Confusion matrix.

Description	Positive category	Negative category
Retrieved	TP, positive category is judged as positive	FP, the negative category is judged as positive
Not retrieved	FN, positive category is judged as negative	TN, the negative category is judged as negative

The formula of the evaluation index precision rate (Precision), recall rate (Recall) and F1:

$$P = TP/(TP + FN) \tag{11}$$

$$R = TP/(TP + FP) \tag{12}$$

$$F1 = 2PR/(P + R) \tag{13}$$

4.3 Experiment Analysis

The accuracy of the method in this paper is the average of 10 experiments to eliminate contingency.

Comparison of Classification Algorithms Based on Word2Vec. The method in this paper is compared with the classification algorithms of SVM, KNN, and random forest in the method in the literature [6], and the hotel corpus of Dr. Tan Songbo is divided in a ratio of 4/5.

It can be seen from Table 3 that the classification results of the SVM method and the method in this paper are relatively stable, while the classification effect of the random forest method under different categories is quite different. The method in this paper will be the accuracy rate, recall rate and F1 value of the active class. The indicators were increased by 3%, 5%, and 4%, compared with the maximum values of the other three methods, while the negative category was increased by 7%, 2%, and 6%, respectively. The results show that the method in this paper is better than the classification algorithms based on Word2Vec, so in terms of feature extraction, this paper chooses the improved word frequency inverse file frequency algorithm.

Table 3. Comparison of various classification methods 23 with this article.

Classification algorithm	Category	Accuracy rate	Recall rate	F1
SVM	Positive	0.83	0.80	0.82
	Negative	0.78	0.81	0.80
KNN	Positive	0.73	0.73	0.75
	Negative	0.74	0.78	0.76
Random forest	Positive	0.81	0.70	0.76
	Negative	0.74	0.84	0.78
Method of this article	Positive	0.86	0.85	0.86
	Negative	0.85	0.86	0.86

Algorithm Comparison Experiment with Literature [17]. Literature [17] combines parent nodes with dependent relationships and improved word frequency inverse file frequency algorithm to construct a hidden Naive Bayes model to improve classification accuracy. Table 4 is a comparison of the accuracy, recall and F1 value of the active class on the basis of the same experimental data set between the method in this paper and the algorithm in literature [17].

Table 4. Compared with literature 17.

Classification algorithm	Accuracy rate	Recall rate	F1
Literature 17	0.832	0.820	0.826
Method of this article	0.864	0.850	0.857

It can be seen from Table 4 that the method in this paper is better than the method in literature [17] in terms of accuracy, recall and F1 value, with an average increase of 3.2%, 3.0% and 3.1%, and the algorithm accuracy rate is above 86%. It is better than the literature [17] method.

Algorithm Comparison Experiment with Literature [7]. Literature [7] In order to solve the problem of lack of a specific corpus in machine learning and improve the accuracy of fuzzy calculation based on quantitative emotional dictionary, use hotel data set 2000 positive and negative categories. Table 5 is the algorithm of this paper and the algorithm of literature [7]. Compare the accuracy, recall and F1 value of the positive class with the average.

Table 5. Compared with literature 7.

Classification algorithm	Accuracy rate	Recall rate	F1
Literature 7	0.802	0.814	0.819
Method of this article	0.856	0.853	0.857

It can be seen in Table 5 that the performance of the method in this paper is better than that of the literature [7], and the accuracy, recall and F1 value are increased by 5.4%, 3.9% and 3.8% on average.

It can be seen from the above several comparative experiments that the method in this paper shows better performance. The reason is that when the improved word frequency inverse file frequency algorithm is introduced to extract the text feature word vector and the weight of the sentiment dictionary feature word vector after the regression test, the specific hotel sentiment dictionary corpus built is used, which has more obvious features and weakens Under the influence of the independence assumption, the singular value decomposition algorithm is used to reduce the dimension of the word vector sparse matrix and eliminate redundant features, so that the results of model training are more targeted.

The constructed polynomial model of improved naive Bayes achieves the accuracy of text classification, F1 value and performance improvement of recall rate.

5 Summary

The method in this paper is an improved text sentiment analysis method based on the naive Bayes algorithm after analyzing the text sentiment analysis method of the relevant literature. The combination of the improved naive Bayes algorithm and the SVD algorithm is based on the domain sentiment dictionary weighted On the basis of weakening the influence of the assumption of independence, on the basis of ensuring simplicity and efficiency, it effectively improves the classification effect of the macro precision rate, the macro recall rate and the macro F1 value. Although this algorithm has a certain improvement in the effect of sentiment classification based on Chinese text, there are still many shortcomings that need to be improved, and there is still room for improvement in its accuracy.

References

1. Huang, L.W., Jiang, B.T., Lu, S.Y.: A survey of research on recommendation systems based on deep learning. Chin. J. Comput. **41**(07), 1619–1647 (2018)
2. Lin, J.H., Zhou, Y.M., Yang, A.M.: The construction of domain sentiment dictionary based on word vector. J. Shandong Univ. (Eng. Technol. Ed.) **48**(03), 40–47 (2018)
3. Wu, J.S., Lu, K.: Research on sentiment analysis of Chinese Weibo based on multiple sentiment dictionaries and rule sets. Comput. Appl. Softw. **36**(09), 93–99 (2019)
4. Yang, X., Jiao, W.: Sentiment analysis of homestay reviews based on domain dictionary. Sci. Technol. Eng. **20**(07), 2794–2800 (2020)
5. Hu, S.C., Sun, J.P., Ju, S.G.: Chinese sentiment feature selection method based on extended sentiment dictionary and chi-square model. J. Sichuan Univ. (Nat. Sci. Ed.) **56**(01), 37–44 (2019)
6. Zhu, J., Liu, J.Y., Zhang, T.F.: Emotion polarity classification method based on sentiment dictionary and ensemble learning. Comput. Appl. **38**(S1), 95–98 (2018)
7. Liu, L., Li, X.Y., Huang, Y.F.: Emotional fuzzy computing classification method based on ensemble learning. Comput. Eng. Des. **39**(07), 1872–1876 (2018)
8. Cheng, Y., Yao, L.B., Zhang, G.H.: Multi-channel CNN and BiGRU based on attention mechanism text sentiment tendency analysis. Comput. Res. Dev. **57**(12), 2583–2595 (2020)
9. Chen, K., Xie, B., Zhu, X.T.: Research on sentiment analysis algorithm based on sentiment dictionary and transformer model. J. Nanjing Univ. Posts Telecommun. (Nat. Sci. Ed.) **40**(01), 55–62 (2020)
10. Shao, L.S., Zhou, Y.: Research on sentiment classification of online comments based on semantic rules and RNN model. Chin. J. Inf. **33**(06), 124–131 (2019)
11. Saraswathy, K.S., Devi, S.L.: Enhancement of sentiment analysis using clause and discourse connectives. Comput. Mater. Continua **68**(2), 1981–1999 (2021)
12. Ibrahim, A.F., Hassaballah, M., Ali, A.A.: Covid19 outbreak: a hierarchical framework for user sentiment analysis. Comput. Mater. Continua **70**(2), 2507–2524 (2022)
13. Lin, Z.L., Wang, X.C., Gu, Y.: Fast sentiment analysis algorithm based on double model fusion. Comput. Syst. Sci. Eng. **36**(1), 175–188 (2021)

14. Muhammad, A., Abdullah, S., Sani, N.S.: Optimization of sentiment analysis using teaching-learning based algorithm. Comput. Mater. Continua **69**(2), 1783–1799 (2021)
15. Hnaif, A.A., Kanan, E., Kanan, T.: Sentiment analysis for Arabic social media news polarity. Intell. Autom. Soft Comput. **28**(1), 107–119 (2021)
16. Xu, Y.Y., Chai, Y.M., Wang, L.M., et al.: Emotional sentence classification method based on OCC model and Bayesian network. Comput. Sci. **47**(03), 222–230 (2020)
17. Li, X.D., Xiao, J.Y., Zou, Y.F.: Research on sentiment classification based on improved TF-IDF and Hidden Naive Bayes. J. Nanhua Univ. (Nat. Sci. Ed.) **33**(02), 79–84 (2019)
18. Zeng, Y., Liu, P.Y., Liu, W.F., et al.: Naive Bayes sentiment classification algorithm based on feature weighted fusion. J. Northwest Norm. Univ. **53**(04), 56–60 (2017)
19. Luo, H.Q., Lu, X.Y., Zhang, X.B., et al.: Emotion classification method of product reviews based on Hidden Naive Bayes. Comput. Eng. Des. **38**(01), 203–208 (2017)
20. Qi, Y., Qiao, Y.: Text categorization based on naive Bayesian. Electron. Sci. Technol. **4**(5), 114–116 (2017)
21. Xie, X.L., Li, X.F., Chen, L.B., et al.: A method for classifying hotel reviews emotional polarity based on emotional dictionary weighting. Guangxi Zhuang Autonomous Region: CN113673239A (2021)
22. Qiu, N.J., Cong, L., Zhou, S.C., et al.: SVD-CNN barrage text classification algorithm combined with improved active learning. Comput. Appl. **39**(03), 644–650 (2019)

A Study on a Remote Sensing Image Classification Method Incorporating Multi-scale Feature Extraction and Channel Attention Mechanism

Juan Hu, Xinran Du, Hanyang Wang, Ting Jin, and Houqun Yang[✉]

Hainan University, Haikou 570228, China
yhq@hainanu.edu.cn

Abstract. With the increasing of remote sensing data sources and collection methods, its application scenarios are continuously migrating and developing. However, it is difficult to meet the demand for real-time detection due to the problems of low automation of data and poor timeliness of information extraction. After extensive research, a new method of remote sensing image classification based on the ResNet model is selected, which can shorten the training time and improve the classification accuracy. In this paper, the self-made remote sensing image dataset HN-7 and the feature classification dataset of the Shang Tang remote sensing image competition are used. Experiments were conducted on the improved network model and with a weight-shifting training method. The experimental results show that the improved network model and the robustness of the model are enhanced by the weight-shifting training method. The availability of input features is improved by combining multi-scale feature extraction and channel attention. The experimental results show that the improved network model and the weight transfer training method can improve the classification accuracy without increasing the training time.

Keywords: Remote sensing imagery · Multi-scale feature extraction · Channel attention mechanism · Feature classification methods

1 Introduction

The classification of remote sensing image is an important part of remote sensing image interpretation, and the good or bad result of the classification determines whether relevant feature information can be accurately and efficiently obtained from remote sensing image. There are two kinds of remote sensing image interpretation: one is the traditional visual interpretation method, and the other is computer interpretation. The work of visual interpretation is divided into five main stages: the collection stage of information, the preliminary interpretation and field inspection of the interpretation area, the detailed interpretation stage, the field verification, and continuous correction stage, and the mapping stage [1]. The visual interpretation method requires high geological knowledge

© The Author(s), under exclusive license to Springer Nature Switzerland AG 2022
X. Sun et al. (Eds.): ICAIS 2022, LNCS 13338, pp. 524–536, 2022.
https://doi.org/10.1007/978-3-031-06794-5_42

of the interpreter as well as a considerable amount of experience. In addition, as the amount of remote sensing image data increases, the interpreter needs to spend a lot of time interpreting, which leads to labor-intensive interpretation work and a long information acquisition cycle [2]. Moreover, the process of visual interpretation has a large role in subjective factors, which leads to a higher probability of misinterpretation, and the accuracy rate will be affected to a certain extent. Furthermore, visual interpretation cannot realize the organic combination of RS and GIS, which makes the acquired remote sensing information cannot be changed to GIS in time [3].

With the development of the computer era, machine interpretation began to show its advantages gradually. A series of human-computer interaction interpretation methods with computer interpretation as the core began to appear. In the current remote sensing applications, the technique of supervised classification is more mature and widely used. There are numerous limitations: the learning and memory of the network do not have stability, and the network convergence speed is slow and inefficient [4]. To overcome these technical shortcomings as much as possible, this paper proposes a remote sensing image classification method based on multi-scale feature extraction and channel attention mechanism, which can free human resources, reduce the subjective factors of the decoder, and improve the accuracy of classification results; on the other hand, accelerate the convergence speed of the neural network and greatly improve the efficiency of classification; in addition, the method proposed in this paper has fewer limitations and can better adapt to a variety of complex remote sensing image, and has certain generality.

The method proposed in this paper consists of three main aspects: multi-scale feature extraction, deep supervision mechanism, and channel attention mechanism.

Multi-scale Feature Extraction. Multi-scale features are obtained by analyzing remote sensing image at different scales. multi-scale features can be classified into three categories: FC features (features extracted from fully connected layers), Conv features (features extracted from convolutional layers), and combined FC and Conv features. FC features such as SPP-Net [5] spatial pyramid pooling net, SPP-Net), MOP [6] (multi-scale orderless pooling, MOP), etc. SPP-Net uses spatial pyramid pooling (SPP) to replace the average pooling or maximum pooling layer in front of the fully connected layer, where SPP can transform the feature map corresponding to an image of any size into a fixed dimensional output. That means the image is transformed into images of different sizes by scaling and other operations, and then fed into the CNN with SPP layer to obtain multi-scale features. And DAG-CNNs [7] (directed acyclic graph convolutional neural networks, DAG-CNNs) combine Conv features and Fc features to obtain better performance. The multiscale features extracted by making full use of the limited high-resolution remote sensing data truly represent the rich ground information [8] avoiding the phenomenon of overfitting, which can make the classification results do not lead to complex and diverse feature types because the feature information in high-resolution remote sensing image is highly subdivided, and avoid the phenomenon of easy to appear the same thing and different spectrum or different thing and same spectrum, which cannot achieve the expected results [9].

Implicit Deep Monitoring Mechanism. Convolutional neural networks have been continuously improved by scholars since they were first proposed by LE [10] in 1989, and have been playing a great role in areas such as image recognition. The more popular ones include DenseNet (Dense Convolutional Neural Network) proposed by GAO [11] in 2017, which absorbs the essence of ResNet (residual network) and improves on it with innovations, thus making its performance more perfect and its applications more widespread. Due to the dense connection method, DenseNet improves the backpropagation of gradients, which makes the network easier to train. Since each layer can reach the last error signal, it achieves implicit "deep supervision". Short-circuiting the connections by concat features enables feature reuse, and simplifying the model parameters reduces the computational effort of the network, which makes DenseNet more efficient and accurate than other networks [12, 13].

Channel Attention Mechanism. Convolutional neural networks are often used as the optimal choice because of their good performance, however, when processing images: at a moment in time, only the current local_neighborhood will be attended to, i.e., CNNs are characterized by focusing only on the content of the current window of attention, but cannot capture the global content.

Similar to the nature of selective visual attention mechanisms in humans, such functionally similar attention mechanisms exist in deep learning, which selects the information that is more critical and useful for the current task goal [14]. To better improve the classification of convolutional neural networks, the channel attention mechanism will be introduced in this paper. The Squeeze-and-Excitation Networks (SENet) model proposed in the paper [15] is a very important model structure in the current channel attention mechanism. SENet utilizes a rescaling method to explicitly model and thus learn the weights of each channel [16]. The above operations can make the channel attention mechanism more intuitively characterize the features that are most relevant to the task target and suppress irrelevant features, which not only speeds up the classification detection but also significantly improves the classification accuracy.

2 Related Works

2.1 Traditional Methods

The classification method of remote sensing image by visual interpretation, although the classification accuracy is guaranteed, this method requires high expertise of the interpreters, is time-consuming, and does not apply to a large number of remote sensing image. So people began to implement traditional remote sensing image classification by spectral features and texture features of images.

Texture analysis is performed by extracting texture features and thus obtaining a quantitative or qualitative description of the texture [17]. The commonly used texture analysis methods are divided into three categories: statistical analysis methods, structural analysis methods, and spectral analysis methods. The statistical analysis method became the most widely used texture feature analysis method after Haralick proposed the grayscale co-occurrence matrix method in 1973, which can well reflect the spatial grayscale distribution of the image because it is not constrained by the analysis object. The method describes the detail and randomness of the texture better and is more adaptable. The structural analysis method [17, 18] was proposed by Mandelbrot in the 1970s, which describes the macroscopic and structural nature of the texture better by selecting irregular phenomena as the description object but is much less adaptable than the statistical analysis method. The spectral analysis method mainly analyzes texture features with the help of frequency features, which can reflect the scale features of texture more comprehensively and has a good feature extraction effect, but the shortcoming is that the computational process is complex, computationally intensive, and slow.

Spectral feature extraction is the spectral analysis of a multispectral or hyperspectral image of a substance to remove redundant information and retain real and useful feature information that distinguishes it from other substances. The extraction methods are unsupervised principal component analysis (PCA), supervised support vector machine (SVM), correlation vector machine (RVM), wavelet transform (Wavelet), and linear discriminant analysis method (LDA) [19]. Spectral feature extraction has the following shortcomings: low-frequency background spectra can affect the target spectrum, changes in lighting conditions can cause multiplicative factors [20], and too much dependence on the external environment. Improving the extraction method of spectral features and choosing a suitable extraction method according to the requirements and characteristics of the research problem weaken the effects mentioned above.

2.2 Deep Learning Methods

The most used deep learning algorithm for remote sensing image classification applications is the convolutional neural network CNN, which features an image-to-image end-to-end learning model, based on which models with better results for image classification can be extended, such as deep convolutional neural network (DCNN) and full convolutional neural network (FCN) (Table 1).

Aiming at the problem that a high misclassification rate of remote sensing image occurs due to the phenomenon of "same spectrum different matter" and "same object different spectrum", DNN (deep neural networks) [21] was applied to the classification of medium-resolution remote sensing image. To solve the problems of high time complexity, small sample data, and poor recognition of small objects in separate deep learning algorithms for classification of high-resolution remote sensing image, DCNN [22] structure as well as the stitching edge effect unique to deep learning for classification of GF-1 images. Residual learning network (ResNet) [23] was used to extract depth features and low-level features of GF-2 remote sensing image. To make full use of image information to improve classification accuracy, Li et al. [24] designed a multi-scale extraction network based on residual convolution blocks (ResNet50) and pyramid pooling modules for more discriminative feature extraction of building regions. S. U. Islam [25] also showed that spatial and temporal information on urban infrastructure is essential and remote sensing image could provide valid information.

In addition, in the feature extraction stage, the Spatial Pyramid Network (SPP Net) [5] introduced the spatial pyramid pooling layer, relaxing the limitation on the input image size and improving the accuracy of feature extraction. The RCNN family [5, 27, 28] of methods provides a great improvement in accuracy, but the disadvantage is that they

Table 1. Comparison of classification methods for deep learning.

Method	Description	Advantages	Disadvantages
DBN [34]	Deep network structure and better feature extraction than traditional classifiers; better image classification when unsupervised learning of features	Prevent overfitting to some extent	The process uses stochastic gradient descent, which does not allow for effective training
CNN [35]	For hyperspectral images with a good classification effect, many branches have been developed	Shared convolutional kernel for stress-free processing of high dimensional data; feature extraction can beperformed automatically	Requires tuning, large sample size, and GPU consumption for training
DCNN [36]	Feature extraction for each candidate region using deep networks, image classification by SVM, and other methods; better for region feature classification	CNN-based algorithm for improved image classification	The process of acquiring region categoriesand training is more time-consuming
FCN [37]	Pixel-level classification of images, but upsampling results in unfine pixel segmentation and is not efficient enough	Can accept any size input image	No global contextual information is considered
RCNN [38]	A CNN network is used to extract features from candidate regions top-down, and when the size of the dataset is small, pre-trained migration learning with other auxiliary tasks are used	Significant increase in accuracy	Slow processing speed, long training time, and high memory usage for one image

cannot fully utilize the context in the whole picture information [29]. A. Asokan [30] used spatial-spectral features from each channel and fuse them with texture features, which method uses CNN to extract, solving the mixed pixel problem by considering the spatial-spectral and texture information of the input channels. S. Kim [31] proposed multi-scale feature extraction layers and feature attention layers to efficiently remove coding artifacts of compressed medical images. Y. Li [32] combined multi-scale convolution and self-attention branches to solve the problem about extracts the fine-grained features from objects of different scales difficulty. Y. Guo [33] used a cascaded network and multi-scale feature for a coarse-to-fine segmentation to improve the segmentation effect. Multi-scale feature extraction was proved to be effective.

3 Methodology

3.1 Overview

Multi-scale features can effectively improve the results of tasks such as image retrieval, image classification, and object detection. However, common network models such as SPP-Net and MOP only utilize FC features or Conv features alone, and DAG-CNNs, although combining both of them is a breakthrough, cannot obtain good performance for remote sensing image characteristics, so the addition of attention mechanism is considered. The channel attention mechanism is concatenated to the input features to let the model focus on those important channels on the input features. In this paper, we take an improved model based on ResNet pre-training and add the channel attention mechanism to extract the key channel information of remote sensing image data for selective feature addition.

Our network consists of 1 input module, 3 multi-scale feature extraction modules, 2 depth-supervised modules, a channel attention module, and a classification layer, as shown in the figure above. We first combine each RGB 3-channel remote sensing image input with the input module of the spatial attention mechanism to obtain important spatial detail features. To better fit the remotely sensed images, we use a 3×3 Adaptive Pool with a step size of 2 to lift the problem that the input images must be of the same size, unifying them into a $224 \times 224 \times 3$ outsize. then, the features are input to the 3 multi-scale feature extraction modules for expansion to obtain a more favorable combination of features for the results. Third, the expanded features are passed through 2 Denseblock as a deep supervision module to generate global contextual information. As shown in the figure below, each basic_layer of this module takes the feature outputs of all previous layers as input and the network is supervised diversely, thus improving the representativeness of the network. The features are selectively enhanced using the channel attention module after the deep supervision module. Finally, remote sensing image classification is done using global pooling, 2 fully connected layers, and softmax function (Fig. 1).

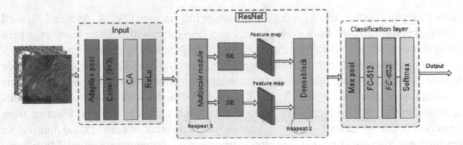

Fig. 1. Overall framework diagram of the model consisting of one input module, three multi-scale feature extraction modules, two depth-supervised modules, one channel attention module, and one classification layer.

3.2 Multiscale Feature Extraction

The input image is transformed into a feature map, and the scale change is performed at the feature map level, and different methods are used to fuse the features at different scales, and the features at lower levels are fused with the features at higher levels, and the feature extraction is performed separately at different feature layers. The scale feature extraction layer can extract features at different scales, and then fuse the features through the feature fusion layer, so that the multi-scale feature extraction network has the ability of multi-scale feature extraction with low computational complexity (Fig. 2).

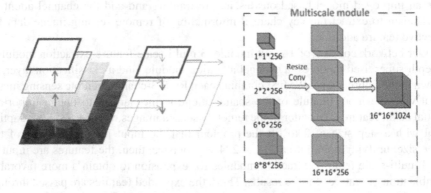

Fig. 2. The multiscale module.

3.3 Channel Attention Mechanism

The channel attention mechanism comes from SENet [15] (Squeeze-and-Excitation Networks), the winning model of the last ImageNet classification competition, with a proposed SE module that is simple in idea, easy to implement, and can easily be loaded into existing network model frameworks. SENet mainly learns the correlations between channels and filters out channel-specific attention, which slightly increases the computational effort, but is more effective.

By any given transformation F_{tr} Map the input X to the feature map U, where $U \in R^{H \times W \times C}$, H × W is the spatial dimension, C is the number of channels (Fig. 3).

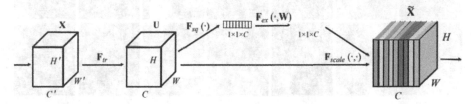

Fig. 3. Channel attention module.

3.4 Evaluation Indicators

Several commonly used evaluation metrics for remote sensing image classification are used and calculated by Confusion Matrix. The five metrics are overall classification accuracy acc (indicating the proportion of all results judged correctly by the classification model to the total observations).

$$\text{acc} = \frac{TP+TN}{TP+TN+FP+FN} \tag{1}$$

Kappa coefficient is used for consistency testing. The parameter N is the sum of the total number of images in all ground truth categories; the parameter k is the number of rows of the error matrix, such as ground coverage class; x_{ii} is the number of observation points located in the i-th row and the column; x_{i+} is the sum of the i-th row, x_{+j} is the sum of the j-th column, and N is the total number of sampling points.

$$\text{Kappa} = \frac{N \sum_{i=1}^{k} x_{ii} - \sum_{i=1}^{k} (x_{i+} \times x_{+j})}{N^2 - \sum_{i=1}^{k} (x_{i+} \times x_{+j})} \tag{2}$$

4 Experiment and Analysis

4.1 Dataset

There are 2 sources of datasets used in this paper. One dataset, HN-7, was produced from remote sensing image data provided by the Bureau of Mapping and Geographic Information of Hainan Province, which is 3.5 km long and 1.7 km wide rectangular remote sensing image of Haikou City, Hainan Province, with the data format of .tif format, with a size of 59470 KB and a resolution of 6987 × 3406. the HN-7 dataset is divided into seven categories: beach, construction site, forest, highway, industrial area, dirt road, and residential area, taking several examples as shown in Fig. 5. Each image has 256 × 256 pixels, and there are 50 remote sensing images in each category, of which 80% are divided into the training set and 20% are testing set. The dataset reflects

Fig. 4. Samples of HN-7, from left to right are seven categories: beach, construction site, forest, highway, industrial area, dirt road, and residential area.

the typical geographical characteristics of Hainan Province and is regionally specific (Fig. 4).

Since this dataset has a small sample size, the dataset is processed by borrowing the data augmentation method from small sample learning, and three strategies are adopted to convert samples from the training set, convert samples from similar datasets, and convert samples from weakly labeled or unlabeled datasets, which can expand the sample data to some extent.

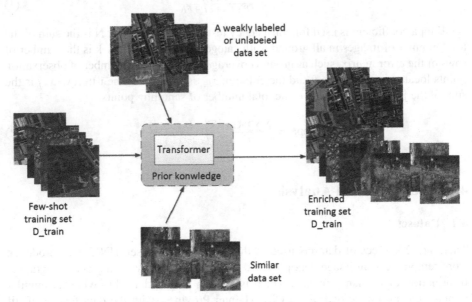

Fig. 5. Three data enhancement methods.

The other dataset is the feature classification dataset of the Shang Tang 2020 AI Remote Sensing Image Interpretation Competition, which contains 50,020 remote sensing images, also 80% of which are classified as training set and 20% as the test set. The dataset contains 8 major lasses of remote sensing image scenes (0–7): agricultural land, commercial land, industrial land, public service land, residential land, transportation land, water, and unused land. The distribution is as follows (Fig. 6).

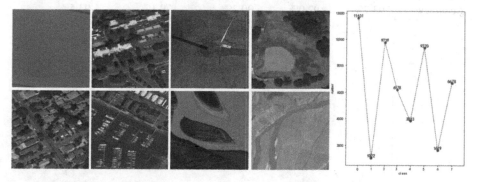

Fig. 6. Example of remote sensing image dataset for Shang Tang feature classification.

4.2 Experimental Analysis

Our model was trained on the dataset and also trained on VGG, ResNet18, and DenseNet to perform a control experiment using the same data enhancement method. The variation of accuracy and loss during the training of the model shows that the model iteration rate is fast, but the obtained loss values are not very reasonable. In addition, we also obtained average accuracy: 89.13%, and Kappa = 89.5552. The images of accuracy and loss during the training process were obtained as shown below (Figs. 7, 8 and Table 2).

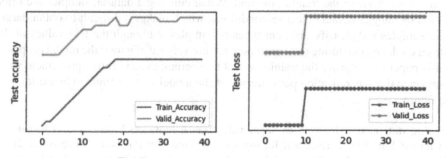

Fig. 7. Training accuracy and loss variation.

Table 2. Comparing the classification accuracy of each neural network on the test set, our model outperforms other networks.

Method	Our	VGG	ResNet18	DenseNet	HFSL [39]
Accuracy	93.7%	92.0%	90.2%	79.1%	93.5%

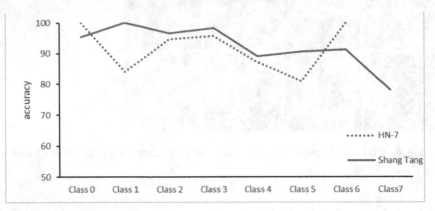

Fig. 8. The recognition accuracy of each category in the dataset, where the blue dotted line indicates the 7 classes of HN-7 and the red solid line indicates the 8 classes of the Shang Tang remote sensing image dataset. (Color figure online)

5 Conclusion

Based on the analysis of the characteristics of neural networks and remote sensing image classification, the network model is improved to shorten the training time and new attempts are made to the training method. When building a dataset, samples are often limited by subjective and objective conditions, which makes it difficult to obtain large-scale samples and classify different types of samples. Although the loss values of the dataset on the model during the experiment are not very satisfactory, the model proposed in this paper can improve the training effect to a certain extent. The improvement ways to enhance the generalization performance of the model will continue to be explored in the future.

Funding Statement.   This work was supported by Hainan Provincial Natural Science Foundation of China (620RC559), Science and Technology Plan Project of Haikou (2020-056) and (2020-051), Education Teaching Reform of Hainan University (hdjy2117), and Research Project on Education Teaching Reform in Hainan Higher Education Institutions (Hnjg2021-25).

Conflicts of Interest.   The authors declare that they have no conflicts of interest to report regarding the present study.

References

1. Ma, N.: The basic theory and method of remote sensing visual interpretation. Remote Sens. Inf. **03**, 26–29 (1987)
2. Qin, Q.: Problems faced by automatic interpretation of remote sensing images and ways to solve them. Surv. Mapp. Sci. **02**, 21–24 (2000)
3. Yang, A., Liu, X.: Research status and development trend of remote sensing image interpretation. Land Resour. Remote Sens. **02**, 7–10 (2004)
4. Zhao, L.: Research on Remote Sensing Image Classification Based on BP Neural Network. Donghua University of Technology, M.S. (2014)
5. He, K., Zhang, X., Ren, S., Sun, J.: Spatial pyramid pooling in deep convolutional networks for visual recognition. IEEE Trans. Pattern Anal. Mach. Intell. **37**(9), 1904–1916 (2015)
6. Gong, Y., Wang, L., Guo, R., Lazebnik, S.: Multi-scale orderless pooling of deep convolutional activation features. In: Fleet, D., Pajdla, T., Schiele, B., Tuytelaars, T. (eds.) ECCV 2014. LNCS, vol. 8695, pp. 392–407. Springer, Cham (2014). https://doi.org/10.1007/978-3-319-10584-0_26
7. Yang, S., Ramanan, D.: Multi-scale recognition with DAG-CNNs. In: Proceedings of the IEEE International Conference on Computer Vision, pp. 1215–1223 (2015)
8. Huang, X., Zhang, L., Li, P.: High-resolution remote sensing image classification based on multi-scale feature fusion and support vector machines. Remote Sens. J. **01**, 48–54 (2007)
9. Wang, Y., Gao, L., Chen, Z., Zhang, B.: Combining deep learning and hyperimagery for change detection in high-resolution remote sensing images. Chin. J. Graph. **25**(06), 1271–1282 (2020)
10. Lecun, Y.: Backpropagation applied to handwritten zip code recognition. Neural Comput. **1**(4), 541–551 (1989)
11. Huang, G., Liu, Z., Maaten, L.V.D., Weinberger, K.Q.: Densely connected convolutional networks. In: IEEE Conference on Computer Vision and Pattern Recognition (CVPR), pp. 2261–2269 (2017)
12. Gao, J., Wang, J.S.: Wang, H: Research on image recognition method based on DenseNet. J. Guizhou Univ. (Nat. Sci. Ed.) **36**(06), 58–62 (2019)
13. Hu, L.S., Albanie, S., Sun, G., Wu, E.: Squeeze-and-excitation networks. IEEE Trans. Pattern Anal. Mach. Intell. **42**(8), 2011–2023 (2019)
14. Zhang, H., Zhang, M.: An SSD target detection algorithm introducing a channel attention mechanism. Comput. Eng. **46**(08), 264–270 (2020)
15. Hu, J., Shen, L., Albanie, S., Sun, G., Wu, E.: Squeeze-and-excitation networks. IEEE Trans. Pattern Anal. Mach. Intell. **42**(8), 2011–2023 (2020)
16. Mou, W., Dong, M., Sun, W., Yang, X., Wang, X.: Image recognition of tea tree leaf part diseases based on SENet and deep separable convolutional capsule network. J. Shandong Agric. Univ. (Nat. Sci. Ed.) **52**(01), 23–28 (2021)
17. Liang, G., Peng, M., Wang, C.: Research on texture analysis methods of remote sensing images. Yunnan Geogr. Environ. Res. **21**(01), 93–98 (2009)
18. Sun, Y.: Application of Texture Analysis in Remote Sensing Image Recognition. Xinjiang University, M.S. (2005)
19. Li, X., Feng, C., Wang, Y., Lu, Y.: A new spectral feature extraction method. Spectrosc. Spectr. Anal. **31**(10), 2856–2860 (2011)
20. Wu, W.: Detection of red fire ant nests using spectral analysis. J. Agric. Eng. **29**(10), 175–182 (2013)
21. Lai, W.D., Wang, D., Su, A.X., Liu, W.P.: Application of deep neural networks in classification of medium resolution remote sensing image. J. Phys Conf. Ser. **1682**(1), 012014 (2020)

22. Yang, X., et al.: A fast and precise method for large-scale land-use mapping based on deep learning. In: IGARSS 2019–2019 IEEE International Geoscience and Remote Sensing Symposium, pp. 5913–5916. IEEE (2019)
23. Wang, M., et al.: Scene classification of high-resolution remotely sensed image based on ResNet. J. Geovis. Spat. Anal. 3(2), 1–9 (2019)
24. Li, J., Zhang, H., Wang, C., Wu, F., Li, L.J.R.S.: Spaceborne sar data for regional urban mapping using a robust building extractor. Remote Sens. 12(17), 2791 (2020)
25. Islam, S.U., Jan, S., Waheed, A., Mehmood, G., Zareei, M.: Land-cover classification and its impact on Peshawar's land surface temperature using remote sensing. Comput. Mater. Continua 70(2), 4123–4145 (2022)
26. Girshick, R., Donahue, J., Darrell, T., Malik, J.: Region-based convolutional networks for accurate object detection and segmentation. IEEE Trans. Pattern Anal. Mach. Intell. 38(1), 142–158 (2016)
27. Wang, W., Tian, B., Liu, Y., Liu, L., Li, J.: Research on power widget identification based on RCNN for UAV inspection images. J. Geoinform. Sci. 19(02), 256–263 (2017)
28. Ren, S., He, K., Girshick, R., Sun, J.: Faster R-CNN: towards real-time object detection with region proposal networks. IEEE Trans. Pattern Anal. Mach. Intell. 39(6), 1137–1149 (2017)
29. Xiao, X., Tian, X., Xu, M.: Research on insulator detection technology based on an end-to-end algorithm. Huadian Technol. 43(02), 28–33 (2021)
30. Asokan, A., Anitha, J., Patrut, B., Danciulescu, D., Hemanth, D.J.: Deep feature extraction and feature fusion for bi-temporal satellite image classification. Comput. Mater. Continua 66(1), 373–388 (2021)
31. Kim, S., Jun, D.: Artifacts reduction using multi-scale feature attention network in compressed medical images. Mater. Continua 70(2), 3267–3279 (2022)
32. Li, Y., Liu, J., Shang, S.J.: WMA: a multi-scale self-attention feature extraction network based on weight sharing for VQA. J. Big Data 3(3), 111–118 (2021)
33. Guo, Y., Cui, Z., Li, X., Peng, J., Hu, J.: MRI image segmentation of nasopharyngeal carcinoma using multi-scale cascaded fully convolutional network. Intell. Autom. Soft Comput. 31(3), 1771–1782 (2022)
34. Li, C., Wang, Y., Zhang, X., Gao, H., Yang, Y., Wang, J.: Deep belief network for spectralspatial classification of hyperspectral remote sensor data. Sensors 19(1), 204 (2019)
35. Yin, J., Qi, C., Chen, Q., Qu, J.: Spatial-spectral network for hyperspectral image classification: A 3-D CNN and Bi-LSTM framework. Remote Sens. 13(12), 2353 (2021)
36. Xu, B., Bin, X., Jiafei, Z., Ling, D., Wei, Z., Guoguang, C.: An improved remote sensing image classification method based on DCNN. J. Phys. 1631(1), 012041 (2020)
37. He, C.: Fully convolutional networks and a manifold graph embedding-based algorithm for polsar image classification. Remote Sens. 12(9), 1467 (2020)
38. Girshick, R., Donahue, J., Darrell, T., Malik, J.: Rich feature hierarchies for accurate object detection and semantic segmentation. In: Proceedings of the IEEE Conference on Computer Vision and Pattern Recognition, pp. 580–587 (2014)
39. Wang, Y., et al.: Heterogeneous few-shot learning for hyperspectral image classification. IEEE Geosci. Remote Sens. Lett. 19, 1–5 (2021)

Research on EVRP of Cold Chain Logistics Distribution Based on Improved Ant Colony Algorithm

Jiye Cui[1], Daqing Wu[1,2(✉)], and Romany Fouad Mansour[3]

[1] College of Economics and Management, Shanghai Ocean University, Shanghai 201306, China
dqw_1982@126.com
[2] Economic and Technological Development Zone, Nanchang Institute of Technology,
901 Yingxiong Dadao, Nanchang 330044, China
[3] Department of Mathematics, Faculty of Science, New Valley University,
El-Karaga 72511, Egypt

Abstract. The distribution of fresh products is an urgent problem to be solved. In this paper, on the basis of considering the problem of vehicle path planning in the logistics distribution process, the distribution of fresh products by electric refrigerated vehicles is added. Considering that the electricity of refrigerated trucks will be consumed by low-temperature restrictions in addition to being used for vehicle driving, the vehicle routing problem of electric refrigerated trucks is constructed with the goal of minimizing the total cost of fixed costs, power consumption costs, cargo damage costs, and penalty costs. And by improving the transition probability and pheromone update of the traditional ant colony algorithm, an improved ant colony algorithm is proposed to solve the model. Through the analysis of the improved ant colony algorithm and the traditional ant colony algorithm to solve the model, it can be seen that the improved ant colony algorithm proposed in this paper is effective and superior in solving the path planning problem of electric refrigerated vehicles.

Keywords: Fresh products · Cold chain logistics · Electric vehicle routing problem · Ant colony algorithm

1 Introduction

Fresh products such as fruits, vegetables, meat, eggs and milk are indispensable in our daily lives. Because of their perishable characteristics, they need to be transported in a low temperature environment by cold chain logistics [1]. The massive consumer demand for fresh products has also driven the vigorous development of the cold chain logistics industry. Nowadays, the combination of cold chain logistics and environmental protection has become a hot topic [2]. In September 2020, President Xi Jinping solemnly promised on behalf of the Chinese government at the 75th United Nations General Assembly that China will strive to achieve carbon peaks by 2030 and achieve carbon

© The Author(s), under exclusive license to Springer Nature Switzerland AG 2022
X. Sun et al. (Eds.): ICAIS 2022, LNCS 13338, pp. 537–548, 2022.
https://doi.org/10.1007/978-3-031-06794-5_43

neutrality by 2060. As one of the important areas of my country's carbon dioxide emissions, the transportation industry, including cold chain logistics, will gradually develop to the use of new energy transportation vehicles under the goal of carbon peaking and carbon neutrality. The traditional cold chain logistics using fuel vehicles will generate a lot of carbon emissions and cause pollution to the environment, while the use of new energy cold chain vehicles to distribute fresh products is obviously more conducive to achieving carbon peak and carbon neutral goals [3].

Vehicle Routing Problem (VRP) originated in 1959 [4]. After years of research by domestic and foreign scholars, there have been many research branches, such as Vehicle Routing Problem with Time Window (VRPTW), Electric Vehicle Routing Problem (EVRP) and so on. In VRP and its many research branches, different scholars have many different research results. Martin et al. [5] proposed a column generation method to solve the VRPTW problem, and the problem can be solved effectively through dynamic programming and branch and bound algorithms. Jose [6] used an iterative local search algorithm to solve the open vehicle routing problem with time windows, and explained the effects of the model and algorithm. Gan Junwei et al. [7] considered energy consumption and time window together, first established an energy consumption estimation model that considers vehicle speed and load, and based on this, proposed a vehicle path model that minimizes cost, and finally used a greedy algorithm to solve the problem. Sensitivity analysis. Li Juntao et al. [8] took the cold chain logistics of fresh agricultural products as the research object, and constructed a multi-vehicle route optimization model that considers carbon emissions and customer satisfaction. The adaptive genetic simulated annealing algorithm designed by them is better than other algorithms Have better performance. Ren Teng et al. [9] simultaneously considered customer satisfaction and road congestion, constructed a cold chain vehicle path optimization model that minimizes the total cost, and combined the tabu search operator and the knowledge model with the ant colony algorithm into a knowledge-based ant colony algorithm, And finally verify the effectiveness of the model and algorithm through an example. Li Qian et al. [10] conducted research on the fresh cold chain industry, constructed a multi-objective distribution route model considering satisfaction and fuzzy time windows, and designed a non-dominated sorting genetic algorithm to optimize the solution. Bac et al. [11] proposed an electric vehicle path optimization problem with time windows that considers multiple parking lots and multiple vehicle types at the same time, and proposed a neighborhood operator that can perform local search to verify the problem. Kancharla et al. [12] innovatively used an adaptive large neighborhood search algorithm to solve the problem of electric vehicle path planning considering linear charging and load power consumption, and pointed out that the key to EVRP is to consider load power consumption.

In the existing papers, compared with the research on the path planning of traditional vehicles, there are fewer researches on the path planning of electric vehicles, and most of these papers are aimed at the transportation of ordinary goods. Research on refrigerated trucks. This has the following problems: (1) In addition to the power of the electric refrigerated vehicle for normal vehicle driving, part of the power is used for low-temperature maintenance in the refrigerating room, which means that the vehicle is not driving during the delivery process. It also consumes power in the state. The consumption of electricity by the refrigerating device will definitely affect the charging time and frequency of the electric vehicle, and then affect the vehicle path planning. (2) There is no need to consider the loss cost of the goods when transporting ordinary goods, while fresh products are prone to corruption and deterioration due to their easy-to-wear characteristics, which will increase the cost of the entire logistics distribution process. From the perspective of cost, it is necessary to deliver the goods as soon as possible to reduce the loss of fresh products as much as possible, which will also affect the route planning of electric vehicle distribution.

Based on the above problems, this article takes the cold chain logistics and distribution of fresh products as the research object, and considers the consumption of electric vehicles by refrigeration equipment and the cost loss caused by the decrease in freshness of fresh products, and proposes the path optimization problem of electric refrigerated vehicles with time windows., And established an electric vehicle logistics distribution model with the total cost including fixed cost, power consumption cost, cargo damage cost and penalty cost as the optimization goal.

2 Problem Description

The distribution center shall provide fresh products distribution services for customers. In order to ensure the freshness of fresh products, the distribution vehicles are all electric refrigerated vehicles. When electric refrigerated trucks provide distribution services, different vehicles carry fixed goods from the distribution center and serve different customers in turn. The service time should be within the customer's service time window as much as possible, otherwise there will be a certain cost loss. If the power is insufficient during the delivery process, it needs to be returned to the delivery center.

2.1 Assumptions

(1) A distribution center is equipped with a fixed number of electric refrigerated vehicles, which can be charged at a fixed number and location of charging stations.
(2) Each electric refrigerated truck has the same model, has the same load limit and battery capacity, and has the same charging and power consumption speeds.
(3) All electric refrigerated trucks start from the distribution center to serve certain customers. They can be charged at the charging station on the way and return to the distribution center after serving the established customers.
(4) Each customer has a certain amount of demand for goods, and has its own service time window.
(5) Each customer is only delivered by an electric refrigerated truck, and no other fees are required for delivery within its service time window, and certain penalty fees are required for delivery within its service time window.
(6) The transportation volume of each electric refrigerated truck cannot exceed the load limit, and the demand of each customer is within the load limit of the vehicle.
(7) Only one car is allowed to depart and arrive at each customer point, and the customer's demand needs to be met at one time.
(8) At the same speed, the power consumption of all electric refrigerated trucks is only related to time, and has nothing to do with their own load and environment.

(9)   During the vehicle delivery process, the speed remains constant, and other special situations such as traffic jams are not considered.

(10)   The electric refrigerated truck is fully charged when it departs from the distribution center. When it reaches a certain point, it needs to return to the distribution center if the battery is insufficient.

2.2 Parameters and Symbols

N: The number of customers that need to be served;

K: The number of electric refrigerated trucks equipped in the distribution center;

c_k: The maximum load capacity of the electric refrigerated truck;

W: The maximum battery capacity of the electric refrigerated truck;

d_{ij}:   The distance between customer point i and customer point j;

q_i: Customer demand for products at point i;

t_{0k}:   The time point when the distribution vehicle k departs from the distribution center;

t_{ik1}:   The time point when the delivery vehicle k arrives at the customer point i;

t_{ik2}:   The time point when the delivery vehicle k arrives at the customer point i;

w_{ik1}:   The point in time when the delivery vehicle k leaves the customer point i;

w_{ik2}:   The electric quantity of the delivery vehicle k when it reaches the customer point i;

t_{ijk} :   The time of delivery vehicle k from point i to point j;

s_i :   The service time of the delivery vehicle at the customer point i;

wt_{ik}:   The waiting time of the delivery vehicle at the customer point i;

e_i: The upper limit of the delivery time window for customer point i;

l_i: The lower limit of the delivery time window for customer point i;

3   Build the Model

3.1   Cost Analysis

Fixed Costs. Electric refrigerated trucks have a certain cost for each delivery service, including driver wages, vehicle maintenance fees, vehicle depreciation costs, etc., which are called fixed costs. This article assumes that the fixed costs of all delivery vehicles are the same, so the total fixed cost is only related to the number of electric refrigerated vehicles dispatched for each delivery. The total fixed cost can be expressed as:

$$C_1 = \sum_{k=1}^{K} \sum_{j=1}^{V} f_k x_{0jk} \tag{1}$$

Among them, it is the fixed cost for each use of the electric refrigerated truck.

Power Consumption Cost. Electric refrigerated trucks consume a certain amount of electricity each time they perform distribution services, including the electricity consumed for normal vehicle driving and the electricity consumed by refrigerating devices. The cost of all consumed electricity is called electricity cost. This article assumes that the vehicle starts to consume electricity when it leaves the distribution center. During normal driving, both the vehicle driving and the refrigerating device consume electricity. When the vehicle is not running (such as charging and serving customers), only the refrigerating device consumes electricity, and the total power consumption is The cost can be expressed as:

$$C_2 = \gamma \sum_{k=1}^{K} \sum_{i=1}^{V} \sum_{j=1}^{V} [a_1 t_{ijk} + a_2 (wt_{ik} + s_i)] x_{ijk} \qquad (2)$$

Among them, is the power consumption per unit time when the vehicle is running normally, is the power consumption per unit time when the vehicle is not running, and is the unit price of electricity.

Cargo Damage Cost. Every time an electric refrigerated truck provides a fresh product distribution service, the fresh product will deteriorate even if it is in the refrigerated truck. The cost due to the corruption and deterioration of the fresh product is called the cost of cargo damage. Electric refrigerated trucks do not open the refrigerating compartment during normal driving or charging, and the temperature in the refrigerating compartment remains constant, and the rate of spoilage and deterioration of fresh products is relatively slow; when performing customer service, the refrigerating compartment door needs to be opened, which causes the temperature in the refrigerating compartment to change. The rate of product spoilage and deterioration increases, and the cost of damage to goods will also increase. From this, the total cost of damage to goods can be expressed as:

$$C_3 = \sum_{k=1}^{K} \sum_{i=1}^{V} \sum_{j=1}^{V} [b_1 (t_{ijk} + wt_{ik}) + b_2 s_i] x_{ijk} \qquad (3)$$

Among them, is the cost of damage per unit time when customer service is not performed, is the cost of damage per unit time when performing customer service, and is the waiting time.

Penalty Costs. Electric refrigerated trucks must arrive within the customer's service time window every time they perform distribution services. Failure to provide services to customers within the customer's time window requires payment of a certain fee, which is called penalty cost. Each customer has a service time window, including the earliest arrival time and the latest arrival time. Delivery vehicles arriving before the earliest arrival time and arriving after the latest arrival time need to pay penalty costs. The total penalty cost can be expressed as:

$$C_4 = u_1 \sum_{i=1}^{N} max\{e_i - t_{ik1}, 0\} + u_2 \sum_{i=1}^{N} max\{t_{ik1} - l_i, 0\} \qquad (4)$$

Among them, is the penalty cost per unit time for the vehicle to arrive before the earliest arrival time, and is the penalty cost per unit time for the vehicle to arrive after the latest arrival time.

3.2 Model

$$minz = C_1 + C_2 + C_3 + C_4 \tag{5}$$

$$\sum_{k=1}^{K}\sum_{j=1}^{V} x_{0jk} \leq K \tag{6}$$

$$\sum_{k=1}^{K}\sum_{j=1}^{V} x_{ijk}q_i \leq Q, \forall k \in K \tag{7}$$

$$\sum_{k=1}^{K}\sum_{i=1}^{V} x_{ijk} = 1, \forall j \in N \tag{8}$$

$$\sum_{k=1}^{K}\sum_{j=1}^{V} x_{ijk} = 1, \forall i \in N \tag{9}$$

$$0 < w_{ik1} \leq W, \forall i \in V, \forall k \in K \tag{10}$$

$$t_{ik2} - t_{ik1} = wt_{ik}, \forall i \in F, \forall k \in K \tag{11}$$

$$x_{ijk} = \begin{cases} 1, & \text{vehicle k drives directly from customer point i toj} \\ 0, & \text{otherwise} \end{cases} \tag{12}$$

(5) Means that the objective function is the minimization of the total distribution cost with the sum of fixed cost, power consumption cost, cargo damage cost and penalty cost; (6) Means that the number of electric refrigerated vehicles starting from the distribution center does not exceed the number of vehicles equipped in the distribution center; (7) Means that the sum of demand of all customers served by the same electric refrigerated truck is less than the specified vehicle load; (8) Means that only one electric refrigerated truck arrives at each customer point; (9) Means each customer There is only one electric refrigerated truck leaving at all points; (8) and (9) indicate that each customer is served and only served once; (10) indicates that any electric refrigerated truck has remaining power when it arrives at any node; (11) means that the entire stay time of any electric refrigerated truck at any customer point is equal to waiting time plus customer service time; (12) means 0–1 decision variable.

4   Improved Ant Colony Algorithm Design

4.1   Introduction to Ant Colony Algorithm

Ant Colony Optimization (ACO) was proposed in the 1990s: After research, it was found that there are always two behaviors of pheromone tracking and pheromone remaining when ants foraging, and the ants will leave information in the places they pass by. In this way, the ants will have a certain probability to track and forage according to the pheromone on the road, and the pheromone is also left in the tracking process. This process with positive feedback characteristics is improved into an algorithm and widely used [13]. The vehicle routing optimization problem is NP-hard, and it is difficult to obtain the optimal solution within an acceptable time using accurate algorithms [14], and the electric vehicle routing problem with time windows studied in this paper is an extension of the traditional vehicle routing optimization problem, and the calculation is more Complex, so it is more suitable to use heuristic algorithms such as ant colony algorithm to solve. The traditional ant colony algorithm has a long search time and is prone to local optimization. This article improves it from two aspects: transition probability and pheromone update strategy.

4.2 Dynamic Transition Probability Design

In the ant colony algorithm, the transition probability is composed of pheromone, expected value and their respective heuristic factors. The size of the pheromone heuristic factor reflects the strength of the ant colony's role of random factors in the path search, and the size of the expected value heuristic factor reflects the strength of the ant colony's role of deterministic factors in the path search. This paper constructs a path planning model with the goal of minimizing the total cost. In order to obtain the optimal solution faster and better, the expected value is defined as the reciprocal of the total cost. In such an ant system, when the total cost on a path is smaller, The greater the transition probability on this path.

In order to avoid the algorithm falling into the local optimum as much as possible, a random number is introduced to make the transition probability dynamic, and a constant is specified to compare with the random number, so that the transition probability can be calculated in two different ways, as shown in Eq. (13). When it is greater than or equal, the vehicle will give priority to the customer with the largest transfer factor for delivery; when it is less, the roulette method is used to select the next customer point.

$$
j = \begin{cases} \arg\max_{l \in N_i^k}\left[\tau_{il}^{\alpha}\eta_{il}^{\beta}\right], r \geq r_0; \\ \text{Use roulette to choose j according to probability} P_{ij}^k: \\ P_{ij}^k = \dfrac{\tau_{ij}^{\alpha}\eta_{ij}^{\beta}}{\sum\limits_{l \in N_i^k}\tau_{il}^{\alpha}\eta_{il}^{\beta}}, r < r_0. \end{cases} \tag{13}
$$

Among them, τ is the pheromone concentration, η is the reciprocal of the total cost, α is the pheromone heuristic factor, β is the expected value heuristic factor, and N_i^k is the set of optional customers.

4.3 Adaptive Information Update Strategy

In ant colony algorithm, the movement of ants will leave pheromone. As time goes by, the pheromone left before will gradually disappear. Pheromone disappearance factor is used to reflect the degree of disappearance of pheromone. The size of the pheromone extinction factor is directly related to the algorithm's global search ability and convergence speed.

If there are too few pheromones on the path that has never been searched, it will reduce the algorithm's global search ability. In the ant week model, the pheromone increment is related to the total pheromone and the total distance. For example, the total pheromone amount is the total amount of pheromone released on the path passed by the ant when it circulates for a week. Larger, the faster the accumulation of pheromone left by the ant on the path, the more conducive to the rapid convergence of the algorithm.

$$\Delta \tau_{ij}^k(t) = \begin{cases} \frac{Q}{L_k}, & \text{Ant k goes through the path } (i,j) \\ 0, & \text{otherwise} \end{cases} \tag{14}$$

Among them, is the pheromone update constant, and is the total distance to reach the optimal goal. When pheromone update is performed, the pheromone change amount on the optimal path is added after the disappearance of the pheromone. Other paths that are not the optimal path only perform the disappearance of pheromone without adding other forms of pheromone supplementation, as shown in Eq. (15) and (16). In order to avoid that the pheromone on the path that has never been searched is too small to reduce the global search ability of the algorithm, the volatilization of pheromone on other paths that is not the optimal path is given an adaptive pheromone extinction factor, as shown in Eq. (17).

$$\tau_{ij}(t+n) = (1-\rho)\tau_{ij}(t) + \sum_{k=1}^{K} \Delta \tau_{ij}^k(t) \tag{15}$$

$$\tau_{ij}(t+n) = (1-\rho*)\tau_{ij}(t) \tag{16}$$

$$\rho* = \rho \frac{\max iter - iter}{\max iter} \tag{17}$$

Among them, ρ is the pheromone disappearance factor, $iter$ is the number of iterations, and max $iter$ is the maximum number of iterations.

4.4 The Process of Improving the Algorithm

Step 1. Initialize the data of the distribution center, the customer's information, and the maximum number of iterations.

Step 2. Place the ants at the distribution center and let them choose the next transfer point based on the transfer probability. The transition probability is dynamically changing and is affected by the pheromone concentration and the total cost.

Step 3. After transferring to a point, add the point to the taboo table, and then select the next point by the transition probability, until all points are added to the taboo table, and the ant returns to the distribution center.

Step 4. After one ant traverses all the points and returns to the distribution center, put another ant in the main center of Pei, and traverse all the points in the same way until all the ants have completed the traversal.

Step 5. After each ant traverses all the points, calculate the total cost of this traversal, and compare the route of the optimal ant.

Step 6. Update the pheromone concentration according to the actual pheromone update strategy.

Step 7. At this point, a round of iteration is completed, the number of iterations is increased by one, and the number of iterations is increased again from step 2, until the specified maximum number of iterations is reached, the iteration is terminated and the corresponding delivery route is output.

5   Case Analysis

In order to verify the effectiveness of the model and algorithm, this paper selects 21 data in the example as the initial data of the case experiment. The specific data such as the location, time window, and service brief of the distribution center and customer points are shown in Table 1. The location coordinates are shown in Table 1. The unit is kilometers, the demand is in tons, and the time window and service time are in minutes. For the convenience of calculation, the specific parameters of the case experiment are set as follows: the maximum load of the vehicle is 50 tons, the driving speed of the vehicle is 40 km/h, the fixed cost of each electric refrigerated vehicle is 150 yuan, and the cost of cargo damage when no customer service is performed. 10 yuan/h, the cost of cargo damage during customer service is 12 yuan/h, the penalty cost for vehicles arriving before the earliest arrival time is 30 yuan/h, and the unit time penalty cost for vehicles arriving after the latest arrival time is 50 yuan/h Hours, the power consumption of the vehicle is 600 units/h when the vehicle is driving normally, the power consumption of the vehicle is 120 units/h when the vehicle is not driving, the total power of each vehicle is 5000 units, and the cost of each unit of electricity is 0.03 yuan.

Use the improved ant colony algorithm and traditional ant colony algorithm in this article to program the model and target respectively and use MATLAB to calculate it. The number of ants is 10, the pheromone heuristic factor is 1, the expected value heuristic factor is 3, and the transition probability is medium The constant of is 0.5, the pheromone update constant is 5, the pheromone disappearance factor is 0.75, and the maximum number of iterations is 30. Use MATLAB to run the programs of the two algorithms 10 times and compare the best results. The minimum cost comparison diagram of each generation is shown in Fig. 1, the path comparison diagram is shown in Fig. 2, and the result comparison table is shown in Table 2.

It can be seen from Fig. 1 and Fig. 2 that using the improved ant colony algorithm proposed in this paper and the traditional ant colony algorithm to solve the model will have different vehicle path planning results. The improved ant colony algorithm gradually converges to 2190 after three minimum cost reductions. However, the traditional ant colony algorithm gradually converges to 2272 after two costs. From the point of view of the minimum cost convergence process, the improved ant colony algorithm in this paper is superior to the traditional ant colony algorithm. It can be seen from Table 2 that the total cost, total distance, and various costs of the vehicle path planning results obtained by the improved ant colony algorithm are reduced compared with the results obtained by the traditional ant colony algorithm: the total cost is reduced by 3.6%, and the total cost is reduced by 3.6%. Distance has been reduced by 3.7%, and power consumption costs, cargo damage costs, and penalty costs have been reduced by 3.4%, 3%, and 13.4%,

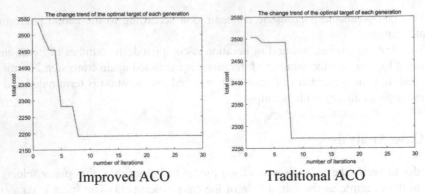

Improved ACO   Traditional ACO

Fig. 1. Comparison of the minimum cost of each generation.

Table 1. Distribution data sheet.

Number	Abscissa	Ordinate	Demand	Left time window	Right time window	Service hours
0	56	56	0	0	480	0
1	56	78	17	0	120	102
2	88	27	8	210	300	48
3	50	72	4	270	450	24
4	30	38	6	270	360	36
5	16	80	13	90	330	78
6	88	69	5	120	390	30
7	48	96	5	240	330	30
8	48	96	3	90	390	18
9	32	104	13	150	300	78
10	68	48	10	0	60	60
11	24	16	11	180	420	66
12	16	32	4	210	300	24
13	8	48	3	180	330	18
14	32	64	4	60	450	24
15	24	96	9	180	270	54
16	72	104	13	150	240	78
17	72	32	16	30	120	96
18	72	16	8	120	390	48
19	88	25	8	90	450	48
20	104	56	5	270	390	30

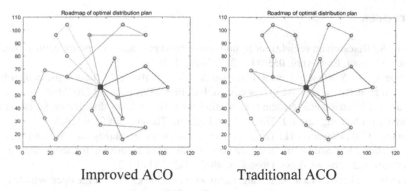

Improved ACO   Traditional ACO

Fig. 2. Path comparison chart.

Table 2. Results comparison table.

	Improved ACO	Traditional ACO
Total cost	2190	2272
Fixed cost	900	900
Electricity cost	452	468
Cargo damage cost	516	532
Penalty cost	322	372
Total distance	783	813

respectively. In summary, the improved ant colony algorithm proposed in this paper is effective and superior in solving the route optimization problem of electric refrigerated trucks for fresh products.

6 Conclusion

In this paper, on the basis of considering the problem of vehicle path planning in the logistics distribution process, the distribution of fresh products by electric refrigerated vehicles is added. Considering that the electricity of refrigerated trucks will be consumed by low-temperature restrictions in addition to being used for vehicle driving, the vehicle routing problem of electric refrigerated trucks is constructed with the goal of minimizing the total cost of fixed costs, power consumption costs, cargo damage costs, and penalty costs. And by improving the transition probability and pheromone update of the traditional ant colony algorithm, an improved ant colony algorithm is proposed to solve the model. Through the analysis of the improved ant colony algorithm and the traditional ant colony algorithm to solve the model, it can be seen that the improved ant colony algorithm proposed in this paper is effective and superior in solving the path planning problem of electric refrigerated vehicles.

References

1. Feng, S.: Research on vehicle routing problem of fresh products with pure electric refrigerator truck. Comput. Eng. Appl. **055**(009), 237–242 (2019)
2. Zhang, C., Li, Y.: Research on optimization decision of urban cold chain logistics distribution system from the perspective of low carbon. Ind. Eng. Manag., 1–17 (2021)
3. Zhao, L.: Electric vehicle route optimization for fresh logistics distribution based on time-varying traffic congestion. J. Transp. Syst. Eng. Inf. Technol. **20**(5), 9 (2020)
4. Dantzig, G.B., Ramser, J.H.: The truck dispatching problem. Manag. Sci. **6**(1), 80–91 (1959)
5. Desrochers, M., Solomon, D.M.: A new optimization algorithm for the vehicle routing problem with time windows. Oper. Res. **40**(2), 342–354 (1992)
6. Brandao, J.: Iterated local search algorithm with ejection chains for the open vehicle routing problem with time windows. Comput. Ind. Eng. **120**, 146–159 (2018)
7. Gan, Z.: Electric refrigerated vehicle routing optimization with time windows and energy consumption. Ind. Eng. Manag. **27**(01), 204–210 (2022)
8. Li, L.: Route optimization of multi-vehicle cold chain logistics for fresh agricultural products. J. Chain Agric. Univ. **26**(07), 115–123 (2021)
9. Ren, L.: Knowledge based ant colony algorithm for cold chain logistics distribution path optimization. Control Decis. **37**(03), 545–554 (2022)
10. Li, J.: Multi-objective cold chain distribution optimization based on fuzzy time window. Comput. Eng. Appl. **57**(23), 255–262 (2021)
11. Bac, U., Erdem, M.: Optimization of electric vehicle recharge schedule and routing problem with time windows and partial recharge: A comparative study for an urban logistics fleet. Sustain. Cities Soc. **70**, 102883 (2021)
12. Kancharla, S.R., Ramadurai, G.: Electric vehicle routing problem with non-linear charging and load-dependent discharging. Expert Syst. Appl. **160**, 113714 (2020)
13. Dorigo, M., Maniezzo, V., Colorni, A.: Ant system: optimization by a colony of cooperative agents. IEEE Trans. Syst. Man Cybern. **26**(1), 29–41 (1996)
14. Kallehauge, B.: Formulations and exact algorithms for the vehicle routing problem with time windows. Comput. Oper. Res. **35**(7), 2307–2330 (2008)
15. Zhang, L.: Research on dynamic distribution vehicle route optimization under the influence of carbon emission. Chin. J. Manag. Sci., 1–13 (2021). https://doi.org/10.16381/j.cnki.iss n1003-207x.2019.0816

A Spatial-Temporal Integration Analysis to Classify Dynamic Functional Connectivity for Brain Disease Diagnosis

Gaoxu Xu[1], Yin Liang[1(✉)], Shanshan Tu[1], and Sadaqat ur Rehman[2]

[1] Beijing University of Technology, Beijing 100124, China
yinliang@bjut.edu.cn

[2] Department of Natural and Computing Science, University of Aberdeen, Aberdeen, UK

Abstract. The analysis of functional connectivity (FC) has become the major method in recent functional magnetic resonance imaging (fMRI) research for brain disease diagnosis. Most of the present FC classification methods were established based on the static FC patterns. However, an increasing number of studies have shown that dynamic FC (DFC) patterns contain abundant spatial and temporal information, which may further promote the classification. In this study, we constructed the DFC patterns and proposed a novel DFC spatial-temporal integration analysis (DFC-ST) to classify DFC patterns for the brain disease diagnosis. This model extracted the abstract spatial FC features and retained the time dependence of DFC by adopting a two-stage configuration, which separately centered on the spatial and temporal property. In the spatial analysis stage, we designed multiple feature extractors based on autoencoders to extract the abstract feature representations for the FC patterns at each time point. In the temporal analysis stage, the learnt abstract features were gathered chronologically, and a separate deep neural network (DNN) was trained to classify the fused features and obtain the prediction labels. To validate the model performance, we conducted experiments on the Autism Brain Imaging Data Exchange (ABIDE) dataset. Results demonstrate that the proposed model can more accurately distinguish the autism groups from healthy controls and the fused DFC features contain more decoding information. Our study provides an effective approach to analyze and classify the DFC patterns and further promote the classification performance for the FC-based brain diseases diagnosis.

Keywords: Dynamic functional connectivity (DFC) · Resting-state functional magnetic resonance imaging (rs-fMRI) · Spatial-temporal integration analysis · Deep learning · Brain disease diagnosis

1 Introduction

In 21st century, brain disease diagnosis has become the hot spot in the interdisciplinary research of artificial intelligence and life science [1, 2]. With the rapid development of neuroimaging technologies, the functional magnetic resonance imaging (fMRI) has

© The Author(s), under exclusive license to Springer Nature Switzerland AG 2022
X. Sun et al. (Eds.): ICAIS 2022, LNCS 13338, pp. 549–558, 2022.
https://doi.org/10.1007/978-3-031-06794-5_44

been widely applied in the studies of brain diseases. The fMRI is a non-invasive imaging technique, which unveiling the functional properties of brain regions by measuring the changes of blood oxygen level-dependent (BOLD) signals. Recently, functional connectivity (FC) has become the major method to analyze the fMRI data. Employing machine learning (ML) methods to classify the brain FC patterns is considered as a promising means to investigate the mechanism of various brain diseases as well as detect the potential diagnostic biomarkers [3, 4].

The FC networks, which refer to the quantitative measurement of the brain functional interactions, are commonly generated by calculating the correlations between pair-wise brain regions. It has been proved that the FC features are informative which could be benefit to classify the brain diseases [5, 6]. Most of previous studies were focusing on constructing static FC (SFC) networks and employing ML models, such as support vector machine (SVM) and random forest (RF) to classify the SFC patterns for the brain disease discrimination [7, 8]. However, the SFC pattern was generated based on the assumption of time stationarity, which may ignore the dynamic changes in the FC patterns. Recent studies have shown that the dynamics in the FC patterns are hierarchically organized in time and the transition of the FC states are more likely to occur preceding or following others [9–11]. Accordingly, compared with traditional SFC patterns, studies on the dynamic FC (DFC) patterns may provide additional biomarkers and further improve the performance for brain disease classification.

To capture the dynamic changes in the FC patterns, the sliding-window approach is widely adopted in the DFC networks construction [12, 13]. Due to the continuous changes in the FC patterns, the dimensionality of features from the DFC is much higher than that from the SFC, which leads to challenges in developing robust ML-based model to effectively learn and classify DFC patterns. Most of existing studies mainly employed statistical methods for the DFC feature dimensionality reduction and employed SVM for the classification. For instance, Reference [14] reduced the DFC features by root-mean-square statistics and employed SVM to classify the mild cognitive impairment (MCI) patients and healthy controls. Reference [15] trained a least absolute shrinkage and selection operation (LASSO) model to extract DFC features and used SVM as classifier for the MCI patients and healthy controls classification. Reference [16] directly applied SVM on the constructed SFC and DFC patterns to predict the major depressive disorder (MDD). Compare to the traditional statistical analysis and ML methods, deep learning methods can automatically learn multi-level abstract feature representations from the initial high dimensional features. Considering the promising performance achieved by deep neural networks (DNN) in recent computer science [17] and fMRI studies [18], the exploration of DNN in learning and classifying DFC patterns is meaningful.

In this paper, we constructed DFC patterns for each subject and proposed a novel DFC spatial-temporal integration (DFC-ST) analysis based on DNN for brain disease classification. Our model contained two parts, which separately focused on the spatial and temporal property of the DFC patterns. In the spatial analysis stage, we designed DNN models as spatial feature extractors to obtain the low dimensional abstract feature representations for the FC patterns at each time point. In the temporal analysis stage, we gathered the learnt abstract features chronologically and trained a separate DNN on the fused features for classification. To evaluate the effectiveness of our model, we conducted experiments on the large-scale Autism Brain Imaging Data Exchange (ABIDE) dataset [19, 20] to discriminate autism patients from healthy controls. The main contributions of this paper are summarized as follows:

(1) We constructed DFC patterns for autism patients and healthy controls from the fMRI data and proposed a novel DFC-ST analysis framework based on DNN for brain disease classification.

(2) Our model employed a two-stage design, which separately centered on the spatial and temporal property of the DFC patterns. Firstly, multiple DNN extractors were built to learn abstract feature representations for the FC patterns at each time point. Then the learnt features were gathered chronologically and a separate DNN was trained on the fused dynamic features for classification.

(3) Experimental results on ABIDE dataset indicate the effectiveness of our model. Our study provides a promising approach for DFC classification, which extends previous SFC studies and further improve the performance for the FC-based brain disease classification.

2   Materials and Methods

2.1   Data Acquisition and Preprocessing

In this study, the ABIDE data were downloaded from the Preprocessed Connectomes Project (PCP) website. The preprocessing for rs-fMRI was according to the Configurable Pipeline for the Analysis of Connectomes (CPAC), which mainly included slice-timing correction, motion correction, normalization to the standard MNI152 template, nuisance signal regression (except global signal), and band-pass filtering with 0.01–0.1 Hz. Subsequently, the CC200 brain parcellation atlas [21] was used to divide the whole brain into 200 regions of interest (ROIs) to extract the regional fMRI time series. Due to the different scanning times across acquisition sites, we discarded the subjects who contained less than 110 time points. Table 1 summarized the data used in the following analysis.

Table 1. The summary of subjects used from ABIDE.

Type	Number	Avg Age (±SD)	Gender(M/F)
ASD	468	16.7 (±8.2)	410/58
HC	495	16.8 (±7.3)	404/91

ASD: Autism spectrum disorder; HC: Healthy control; Avg Age: Average age of the subjects in each group; SD: Standard deviation; M: Male; F: Female.

2.2   Dynamic Functional Connectivity (DFC) Patterns Construction

We adopted the widely used sliding-window approach to construct the DFC patterns. Figure 1 shows the main steps for the DFC generation. Firstly, for the total T time points, the mean time series of 200 ROIs were obtained by averaging the time series of all voxels within each ROI, which could be represented as a matrix of $200 \times T$. Then, a sliding window with a length of W slid on the whole time series in the step of s. This analysis generated N consecutive dynamic windows, where $N = \lfloor (T - W)/s \rfloor + 1$. Within each sliding window, a FC matrix was estimated by computing the Pearson correlation for each ROI pair. The Pearson correlation coefficients of the ith and j^{th} ROIs can be defined as:

$$r_{ij} = \frac{\sum\limits_{w=1}^{W} \left[(x_i(w) - \overline{x}_i) \cdot (x_j(w) - \overline{x}_j) \right]}{\sqrt{\sum\limits_{w=1}^{W} (x_i(w) - \overline{x}_i)^2} \cdot \sqrt{\sum\limits_{w=1}^{W} (x_j(w) - \overline{x}_j)^2}} \tag{1}$$

where $x_i(w)$ and $x_j(w)$ represent the average fMRI signals for the ith and j^{th} ROIs at the time point $w(w = 1, 2, \ldots, W)$, $\overline{x}_i$ and $\overline{x}_j$ respectively denote the means of $x_i(w)$ and $x_j(w)$. By computing Pearson correlation, a FC Matrix $M_n(n = 1, 2, \ldots, N)$ with 200×200 elements was obtained for each sliding window. To improve the normality of the FC matrices, we transformed the Pearson correlation coefficients into z-scores by Fisher's r-to-z transformation. At last, we flatten the upper triangle elements of symmetric matrix M_n to generate the FC vector V_n for the nth sliding window. For each subject, we obtained the DFC patterns with $N \times 19900$ elements, which contained temporal features of N sliding windows and spatial features of 19900 pairs of ROI correlations. In this study, the sliding window length W was set as 30 time points and step s was set as 1 time point. In this way, we obtained 81 sliding windows. Thus, the DFC patterns contained 81 vectors (i.e. $N = 81$) with each length of 19900.

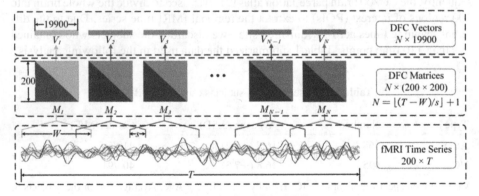

Fig. 1. The construction of the DFC patterns.

2.3 DFC Spatial-Temporal Integration Analysis Framework (DFC-ST)

The overview of the proposed DFC-ST framework is shown in Fig. 2. In the spatial analysis stage, we built multiple feature extractors to learn the abstract feature representations for the FC patterns at each sliding window. Then in the temporal analysis stage, we gathered the learnt features chronologically and trained a separate DNN to classify the fused dynamic features and obtained the prediction labels. Details for each stage will be introduced in the subsections.

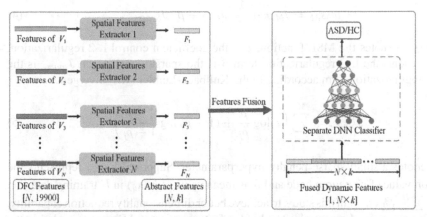

Fig. 2. The overview of the proposed DFC-ST analysis framework. In the spatial analysis stage, DFC patterns $[V_1, V_2, V_3, \ldots, V_n]$ $\left(V_n \in \mathbb{R}^{1 \times 19900}\right)$ from N sliding windows were entered in the spatial feature extractors to obtain the abstract feature representations $[F_1, F_2, F_3, \ldots, F_N]$ $\left(F_n \in \mathbb{R}^{1 \times k}\right)$. In the temporal analysis stage, the learnt abstract features were gathered chronologically, then the fused dynamic features were used to train a separate DNN for classification.

2.4 Spatial Feature Extractor

To effectively reduce the dimensionality of DFC features, we combined the unsupervised learning model stacked autoencoders (SAE) and supervised learning model multilayer perceptron (MLP) to build the spatial feature extractor.

The AE is a classical deep learning model that tries to reconstruct the input vectors as exactly as possible. Given the input data x, AE first encodes it into a lower dimensional representation h_{enc}:

$$h_{enc} = f_{enc}(x) = Tanh(W_{enc} \cdot x + b_{enc}) \tag{2}$$

where $Tanh$ is Tanh activation function, W_{enc} and b_{enc} respectively represent the weights and biases in the encoding stage. Similarly, h_{enc} will be reconstructed to the output x' in the decoding stage:

$$x' = f_{dec}(h_{enc}) = Tanh(W_{dec} \cdot h_{enc} + b_{dec}) \tag{3}$$

W_{dec} and b_{dec} respectively represent the weights and biases in the decoding stage. In the training phase of AE, we used back-propagation algorithm to optimize the parameters by minimizing the loss function in Eq. (4). Mean square error (MSE) function was employed to measure the difference between the initial input and reconstructed output. We also added sparse constraint and L-2 regularization to the loss function to further avoid over-fitting.

$$loss_{AE} = J_{MSE} + \frac{\lambda}{2} \cdot J_{L-2} + \beta \cdot J_{Sparse} \tag{4}$$

where J_{MSE} denotes the MSE function, λ is the coefficient control L-2 regularization, J_{L-2} represents the L-2 regularization term, β is the sparsity coefficient, J_{sparse} is the sparsity regularization term according to the Kullback-Leibler (KL) divergence.

$$J_{Sparse} = \sum_{j=1}^{M} \left(\rho \log \frac{\rho}{\hat{\rho}_j} + (1 - \rho) \log \frac{1 - \rho}{1 - \hat{\rho}_j} \right) \tag{5}$$

the ρ denotes a small sparse penalty hyperparameter. Supposed $h_j(x_u)$ represents the activation value of jth neuron node and $\hat{\rho}_j$ is mean value of $h_j(x_u)$ in U training data (i.e. $\hat{\rho}_j = \frac{1}{U} \sum_{u=1}^{U} h_j(x_u)$). In this study, to achieve better dimensionality reduction capability, four AEs were trained separately. The hidden features of prior AE were regarded as the input for the next AE training.

To further improve the robustness of feature learning, a supervised MLP was built to fine-tune the parameters further. The MLP has the same structure as previous Stacked AEs and the pre-trained parameters were used to initialize the corresponding layers of MLP. In the top of MLP, the softmax function was used to normalize the output as prediction probability. The cross-entropy loss was used to fine-tune the overall parameters, which is defined as:

$$loss_{MLP} = -\frac{1}{U} \sum_{u=1}^{U} \sum_{c=1}^{2} y_c^{(u)} \cdot \log \hat{y}_c^{(u)} \tag{6}$$

where $y_c^{(u)}$ denotes the true label of the uth subject belongs, $\hat{y}_c^{(u)}$ denotes the probability of predicting the uth subject into the cth category ($c = 1, 2$ in this study), and U denote the total number of training data. When the fine-tuning step was finished, we removed the label layer and obtained the abstract features F_n for the nth sliding window. The process of extracting and learning the spatial features in all time windows for one subject is illustrated in Algorithm 1. In this study, the dimension of the learned abstract features F_n was set as 60.

Algorithm 1: The process of extracting the spatial features in all time windows

---

Input: The training subject (V, y), where $V \in R^{N \times l}$, $V = [V_1, V_2, V_3, ..., V_N]$ is FC features of all sliding windows and y is true label of subject, N and l respectively represents the number of sliding windows and the length of each FC features.

Output: The abstract spatial features $F = [F_1, F_2, F_3, ..., F_N]$, where $F \in R^{N \times k}$ and k is the length of each abstract features F_n.

1 **for** n *in* N **do**

2   **Step 1:** Unsupervised training phase of SAE

3   **for** AE *in* $\{AE1, AE2, AE3, AE4\}$ **do**

4   **Initialization:**Randomly initialize parameters$\{W_{enc}, b_{enc}, W_{dec}, b_{dec}\}$ of AE;

5   **Forward propagation:** Encoding the encoded features from $(l-1)^{th}$ as $h_{enc}^{(l)}$ $(l \geq 2)$;Decoding the $h_{enc}^{(l)}$ as reconstruction data;

6   **Computation of the loss:** Computing the value of AE loss function on training set by equation (4);

7   **Back propagation and parameters updating:** Adopting the gradient descent-based algorithm Adam to update parameters of AE;

8   **end**

9   **Return:** The optimized parameters of SAE

10   **Step 2:** Supervised training phase of MLP

11   **Initialization:**Adopting the encoding weights and biases of SAE to initialize the corresponding layers of MLP;

12   **Forward propagation:** Taking the FC features V_n of nth sliding window as input and obtaining the abstract spatial FC features F_n and predicted label $\hat{y}$;

13   **Computation of the loss:** Computing the value of MLP loss function by equation (6);

14   **Back propagation and parameters updating:** Adopting the gradient descent-based algorithm Adam to update parameters of MLP;

15   **Return:** The abstract spatial FC features F_n of nth sliding window

16 **end**

17 **Return:** The abstract spatial features $F = [F_1, F_2, F_3, ..., F_N]$ of all sliding window

---

2.5 The Classification of Fused Dynamic Features

After the learning of spatial feature extractor, we obtained the abstract FC features at each time window. In the temporal analysis stage, we gathered the learnt features chronologically and trained a separate DNN to classify the fused dynamic features and obtained the prediction labels. The abstract features $F_n (F_n \in \mathbb{R}^{1 \times k})$ for total N sliding windows were connected in time order to generate the fused dynamic feature vector (contained $N \times k$ elements). In this study, the total number of sliding window was 81 and the feature dimension for each F_n was 60, thus the dimension of the fused dynamic feature was $81 \times 60 = 4860$. A separate DNN classifier was trained on the fused dynamic features for classification. In this section, the DNN structure and training process was similar as that was implemented in the spatial feature extractor, which also contained both unsupervised and supervised training steps. The detailed configuration for DNN classifier is summarized in Table 2.

Table 2. The configuration of the DNN classifier.

Model	Learning rate	Network structure	Epochs	Mini-batch
AE1	0.0001	4860-2000-4860	120	128
AE2	0.0001	2000-600-2000	300	128
AE3	0.0001	600-60-600	300	128
AE4	0.0001	60-2-60	1200	128
MLP	0.00001	4860-2000-600-60-2	150	128

3 Experimental Results

To evaluate the performance of our DFC-ST framework, we conducted experiments on the large aggregate ABIDE dataset. We compared our model with classical SFC classification methods, including the widely used SVM and the SAEs recently proposed by Reference [18]. In addition, we conducted a comparative experiment by replacing the DNN classifier in the temporal analysis stage with a simple SVM classifier to further validate the effectiveness of the learned dynamic features. To maximize the available data, 5-folds cross-validation approach was adopted to evaluate the overall classification performance on the whole dataset. Briefly, the dataset was randomly partitioned into 5 equal sized subsets, one subset was used as the testing set and the remaining 4 subsets were used as the training data. The same process repeated for 5 times until each subset was used as testing set once. The classification performance was evaluated by accuracy (ACC), specificity (SPE), sensitivity (SEN), precision (PRE) and F-score (F1) based on the mean results of 5 folds. The evaluation metrics are defined as follows:

$$ACC = \frac{TP + TN}{TP + TN + FP + FN}$$
$$SPE = \frac{TN}{FP + TN}$$
$$SEN = \frac{TP}{TP + FN}$$
$$PRE = \frac{TP}{TP + FP}$$
$$F1 = \frac{2TP}{2TP + FP + FN}$$

(7)

where, TP, TN, FP, and FN denote the true positive, true negative, false positive, and false negative, respectively.

The classification performances of different methods are summarized in Table 3. In general, the DFC classification results are higher than those from SFC. In detail, when the SVM is employed to classify the fused dynamic features, the accuracy is improved by 2.1%, 0.2% than that of SFC-SVM and SFC-SAEs and when DNN model is embedded in the SFC-ST framework, the accuracy is significantly improved by 4.6%, 2.7% than that of SFC-SVM and SFC-SAEs. In addition, our DFC-ST shows more robust results than other methods with the lower SEMs. Together, our results suggest that the fused DFC features contain more decoding information than the SFC patterns and demonstrate the effectiveness of the proposed DFC-ST model.

Table 3. Classification performances of different models.

Model	ACC (%)	SPE (%)	SEN (%)	PRE (%)	F1 (%)
SFC-SVM	63.1 ± 1.4	62.3 ± 1.8	69.5 ± 2.5	66.2 ± 1.2	67.6 ± 1.5
SFC-SAEs	65.0 ± 1.3	61.3 ± 1.8	68.5 ± 2.5	65.2 ± 1.2	66.6 ± 1.5
DFC-SVM	65.2 ± 1.1	60.8 ± 1.4	69.0 ± 1.6	65.3 ± 1.0	67.1 ± 1.4
DFC-ST	**67.7 ± 1.2**	**62.3 ± 1.1**	**70.2 ± 1.3**	**67.2 ± 1.2**	**68.5 ± 1.1**

All ± values are mean ± standard error of mean (SEM).

4 Conclusion

In this study, we proposed a novel DFC-ST analysis framework based on DNN to classify DFC patterns for the brain disease diagnosis. Our model contained two parts, which separately focused on the spatial and temporal property of the DFC patterns. In the spatial analysis stage, multiple DNN extractors were built to learn abstract feature representations for the FC patterns at each time point. In the temporal analysis stage, the learnt features were gathered chronologically and a separate DNN was trained on the fused dynamic features for classification. Experiments were conducted on the large-scale ABIDE dataset. The results demonstrate that the proposed model can more accurately distinguish the autism groups from healthy controls and the fused DFC features contain more decoding information. In the future work, we will further try other DNN structures to further improve the performance for DFC-based brain disease classification.

Acknowledgement. Multi-sites fMRI data of autism spectrum disorder patients and healthy controls were downloaded from the Autism Brain Imaging Data Exchange (ABIDE) dataset. We sincerely thank ABIDE for the publicly access and download of data for further research.

Funding Statement. This work was supported by the Beijing Natural Science Foundation (No. 4204089), and the National Natural Science Foundation of China (No. 61906006).

Conflicts of Interest. We declare that we have no actual or potential conflict of interest including any financial, personal or other relationships with other people or organizations that can inappropriately influence our work.

References

1. Langen, M., Durston, S., Staal, W., Palmen, S., Engeland, H.: Caudate nucleus is enlarged in high-functioning medication naive subjects with autism. Biol. Psychiatry **62**(3), 262–266 (2007)

2. Yk, A., Jg, A., Yx, A.: Classification of autism spectrum disorder by combining brain connectivity and deep neural network classifier. Neurocomputing 324(Jan. 9), 63–68 (2019)

3. Nielsen, J.B., Zielinski, F., Alexander, A., Nicholas, L., Bigler, E.: Multisite functional connectivity MRI classification of autism: ABIDE results. Front. Hum. Neurosci. 20137(1), 599 (2013)

4. Abraham, A., Milham, M., Martino, A., Craddock, R.: Deriving reproducible biomarkers from multi-site resting-state data: an Autism-based example. NeuroImage 147–736 (2016)

5. Liang, M., Zhou, Y., Jiang, T.: Widespread functional disconnectivity in schizophrenia with resting-state functional magnetic resonance imaging. NeuroReport 17(2), 209–213 (2006)

6. Yong, L., Meng, L., Yuan, Z.: Disrupted small-world networks in schizophrenia. Brain 131(4), 945–961 (2008)

7. Du, W., Calhoun, V.D., Li, H.: High classification accuracy for schizophrenia with rest and task fMRI data. Front. Hum. Neurosci. 6, 145 (2012)

8. Rosa, M.J., Portugal, L., Shawe-Taylor, J.: Sparse network-based models for patient classification using fMRI. Neuroimage 105(3), 66–69 (2013)

9. Vidaurre, D., Smith, S.M., Woolrich, M.: Brain network dynamics are hierarchically organized in time. Proc. Natl. Acad. Sci. 114(48), 12827–12832 (2017)

10. Shakil, S., Lee, C., Keilholz, S.: Evaluation of sliding window correlation performance for characterizing dynamic functional connectivity and brain states. Neuroimage 111–128 (2016)

11. Ashikh, V., Deshpande, G., Rangaprakash, D., Dutt, D.N.: Clustering of dynamic functional connectivity features obtained from functional magnetic resonance imaging data. In: International Conference on Advances in Computing, pp. 308–312. IEEE (2015)

12. Calhoun, V., Miller, R., Pearlson, G.: The chronnectome: time-varying connectivity networks as the next frontier in fMRI data discovery. Neuron 84(2), 262–274 (2014)

13. Allen, E., Damaraju, E., Plis, S.: Tracking whole-brain connectivity dynamics in the resting state. Cereb. Cortex 24(3), 663–676 (2014)

14. Chen, X., Han, Z., Zhang, L.: Extraction of dynamic functional connectivity from brain grey matter and white matter for MCI classification. Hum. Brain Mapp. 38(10), 5019–5034 (2017)

15. Lei, B., et al.: Diagnosis of early Alzheimer's disease based on dynamic high order networks. Brain Imaging Behav. 15(1), 276–287 (2020). https://doi.org/10.1007/s11682-019-00255-9

16. Sen, B., Cullen, K., Parhi, K.: Classification of adolescent major depressive disorder via static and dynamic connectivity. IEEE J. Biomed. Health Inform. 99, 1 (2020)

17. Tu, S., Waqas, M., et al.: Social phenomena and fog computing networks: a novel perspective for future networks. IEEE Trans. Comput. Soc. Syst. (2021). http://doi.org/10.1109/TCSS.2021.3082022

18. Heinsfeld, A.: Identification of autism spectrum disorder using deep learning and the ABIDE dataset. Neuroimage-Clin 324(Jan 9),16–23 (2018)

19. Martino, A., Yan, C., Li, Q.: The autism brain imaging data exchange: towards a large-scale evaluation of the intrinsic brain architecture in autism. Mol. Psychiatry 19(6), 659–667 (2014)

20. Epalle, T., Song, Y., Liu, Z.: Multi-atlas classification of autism spectrum disorder with hinge loss trained deep architectures: ABIDE I results. Appl. Soft Comput. 2021(3), 107375 (2021)

21. Craddock, R., James, G., Iii, P.: A whole brain fMRI atlas generated via spatially constrained spectral clustering. Hum. Brain Mapp. 33(8), 1914–1928 (2012)

5G Message Cooperative Content Caching Scheme for Blockchain-Enabled Mobile Edge Networks Using Reinforcement Learning

Mei Du[1(⊠)], Siyuan Sun[1,2], Ligang Ren[2], Dong Tian[2], and and Yifei Wei[1]

[1] Beijing University of Posts and Telecommunications, Beijing 100876, China
dmxy54210383@163.com
[2] China Unitied Network Communications Co, Ltd. Beijing Branch, Beijing 100052, China

Abstract. In order to meet the rapid growth of rich media message service demands of mobile users in 5G environment, content caching in mobile edge network is an effective solution. In this paper, deep reinforcement learning and blockchain technology are used to solve the problem of Content Cooperative Caching and routing requests between base stations. A 5G Message Cooperative Content Caching Scheme for blockchain-enabled is proposed. aiming to minimize the average transmission delay of user requests on the premise of satisfying quality of service for the user. Deep reinforcement learning is used to train the optimal cache decision, and blockchain is used to publish the cache file directories and record the query cache log, while gathering global information for decision makers. Simulation results show that the performance of the proposed algorithm in reducing system response delay and improving cache hit rate is significantly better than the traditional LRU and FIFO algorithms.

Keywords: 5G message · Content caching · Blockchain · Mobile edge computing · Deep reinforcement learning

1 Introduction

With the rapid development of the Internet of Things (IoT) and 5G communication technology, mobile devices and 5G data traffic have grown rapidly. In 2020, the number of mobile terminal devices has reached tens of billions. At the 5G Emerging Service Trade Development Forum held on September 5, 2020, the communication management department announced data that More than 480,000 5G base stations have been built in China, and the number of 5G terminals has exceeded 100 million. According to the forecast of International Data Corporation (IDC), the global data volume will increase from 33ZB in 2018 to 175ZB in 2025. At the same time, new applications such as virtual reality, ultra-high definition video and autonomous driving with ultra-low latency, high reliability and low power requirements are emerging[1]. Massive terminals, massive data and performance requirements of emerging applications pose great challenges to existing cloud computing framework. In this context, Mobile Edge Computing (MEC) came into being. Mobile edge computing is a new architecture mode that descends computing,

© The Author(s), under exclusive license to Springer Nature Switzerland AG 2022
X. Sun et al. (Eds.): ICAIS 2022, LNCS 13338, pp. 559–572, 2022.
https://doi.org/10.1007/978-3-031-06794-5_45

storage and processing functions from centralized cloud platform to the edge of wireless network. Mobile edge computing can effectively reduce service response delay, reduce bandwidth pressure of return link and improve user experience by extending computing, storage and other resources to the edge of the network [2].

There is a broad consensus among operators around the world that traditional SMS services need to be upgraded to rich media messaging, or 5G messaging. According to the 5g messaging white paper, 5G messaging supports a variety of media formats, including text, pictures, audio and video. The audio and video part of rich media message has the characteristics of large volume and high repetition rate. According to [3], 59% of the global mobile data traffic is generated by the demand for videos in 2017. In addition, a 9-fold increase in video data traffic is predicted by 2022, making the mobile video traffic to account for 79% of total mobile traffic. Studies [4, 5] revealed that a large amount of the raised video data traffic is due to the duplicate downloads of popular video files. Using mobile content distribution techniques, popular video files can be cached in intermediate servers or proxies (e.g., gateways, routers) so that the requests for the same video file can be available without duplicate transmissions from remote servers. Since the base station and other edge servers in mobile edge computing network have the ability of data processing and content caching, which can be exploited to deploy applications and 5G multimedia services as well as to cache rich media audio and video data with high repetitive access [1]. At the same time, in order to improve the degree of information sharing between edge servers and record data access, blockchain technology can be combined. As a decentralized digital technology, the characteristics of block chain are very consistent with the development direction of edge computing network, which emphasizes decentralization, autonomy and intelligence. It can help edge computing network better cooperate to allocate resources, record and share important information.

Up to now, deep reinforcement learning has been applied in communication, biology, medicine and other fields. [6] formulated the energy-efficiency oriented user scheduling and resource allocation problem with modelfree reinforcement learning framework, in order to maximize energy efficiency of the overall network. [7] proposed a sustainable deep learning-based heartbeat classification system, called BeatClass. Simulation results show that rather than using one classification model to classify the five-class heartbeats, BeatClass uses two classification models to improve the classification results step-by-step. [8] proposed a dual reinforcement learning (DRL)-based cooperative DCA (DRL-CDCA) mechanism. DRL-CDCA jointly optimizes the decision-making behaviors of both the channel selection and back-off adaptation based on a multi-agent dual reinforcement learning framework. [9] proposed a Q-learning-based approach to help the drone fly with minimum handover cost along with robust connectivity.

At present, there has been some progress in the research of content caching strategy at the edge of mobile network. [10] used the DQN algorithm in reinforcement learning to explore the cache strategy in the mobile edge network. [11–13] discussed the potentials of employing caching technique in mobile networks. [14] presented a decentralized optimization method for the design of caching strategies that aimed at minimizing the energy consumption of the network. [15] proposed a decentralized framework for proactive caching is proposed based on blockchains considering a game-theoretic point of view. [16, 17] proposed strategies of collaborative caching in BSs to improve the QoS of users especially on access delay. However, these studies have been conducted on finding an optimal/suboptimal solution via traditional optimization techniques, which are often lack of the self-adaption in dynamic environments and need nearly global information that is hard to achieve in the real-world systems. Deep reinforcement learning (DRL) combines high dimensional perception ability of deep learning and dynamic decision ability of reinforcement learning, which can perceive dynamic network topology and time-varying wireless channel environment, and solve complex optimization problems with dynamic and time-varying characteristics [18]. A deep actor-critic framework for content caching at the base station is proposed in [19]. In [20], researchers formulate the cooperative content caching problem as a multi-agent multi-armed bandit problem and propose a MARL-based algorithm to solve the problem. In [21], researchers studies the content caching problem that maximizing the use of the cache capacity of the base stations to minimize the average transmission delay of the user request and the energy loss of the network. Deep Deterministic Policy Gradient (DDPG) algorithm is used to interact with the environment to learn the optimal cache strategy.

Inspired by [15] and [21], in this paper, we put forward a DDPG reinforcement learning-based framework for 5G message cooperative content caching and request routing among BSs in mobile edge network, aiming to minimize the average transmission delay of user requests on the premise of satisfying quality of service for user. In addition, we use blockchain technology to cache the record of resource catalog publication and access. The main contributions of this article are summarized as follows:

- We consider cooperative content caching and request routing in mobile edge networks. In the three-layer network architecture, mobile terminal devices request 5G message content from the edge server layer, and the result is directly returned if the cache is matched, while the edge server requests original data from the core network and caches it locally. All edge servers join the blockchain shared network to publish cache decision information and record cache access logs through the blockchain network.
- We propose a cooperative content caching and routing request scheme with user quality of service constraints in order to minimize the average transmission delay of user requests. All edge servers participating in the blockchain 5G message caching shared network are regarded as an intelligent whole, and DDPG algorithm is used to solve the optimal caching scheme.
- Simulation results show that compared with the existing LRU and FIFO schemes, the proposed solution based on DDPG algorithm and block chain has better performance in reducing system response delay and improving cache hit ratio.

2   System Model

In this section, we introduce the general cooperative edge caching architecture including network model, communication model, time delay model and caching model.

2.1 Network Model

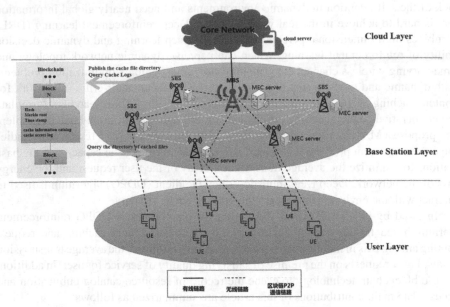

Fig. 1. System model.

Figure 1 shows a three-layer heterogeneous network with edge caching capability, which consists of the user layer composed of U users, the base station layer composed of one MBS and K SBSs, and the cloud layer where the core network is located. In the base station layer, all BS are connected to each other to form a blockchain network. Each BS, as a blockchain node, shares information such as cache information catalog and cache access log, and maintains logistically unique and immutable ledger records. In the decision-making process, MBS performs the cache decision of specific request files, and then publishes the decision results to the blockchain network for sharing and storage. The MBS requests data through a wired backhaul link from the core network, which is connected with the content server. The set of SBSs is denoted as $\mathcal{K} = \{1, \cdots, K\}$, and the set of UEs is denoted as $\mathcal{U} = \{1, \cdots, U\}$. Core network has abundant storage capacity, which store all available contents. We assume the MBS is the central controller in the architecture, which determines the connection between the UEs and the BS, the cache of the requested files and etc.

We denote $\mathcal{F} = \{1, \cdots, F\}$ as the set of F files in the content library. Each file is identified by three features, which can be described as $f = \{s_f, \rho_f, \zeta_f\}$, s_f, ρ_f and ζ_f denote the size, the popularity and the maximal content delivery latency of file f. Denote P_f is the probability of files follows the Zipf distribution [23].

$$\mathrm{P}_f = \frac{\rho_f^{-\beta}}{\sum_{i=1}^{F} \rho_i^{-\beta}} \tag{1}$$

where β is the file request coefficient.

2.2 Communication Model

We assume that each user equipment only sends one request for a period of time, and whole transmission process is divided into T time slots discretely. Similar to [24], there are M wireless orthogonal subchannels in each SBS and each subchannel is only used to serve one user equipment. So, there is no co-channel interference between all users served by the same SBS. We denote $\mathcal{M} = \{1, \cdots, M\}$ as the set of subchannels, $\vartheta_i \in \mathcal{M}$ as the channel allocation decision of the SBS to UE i. At time t, the signal to noise ratio between SBS k and UE u can be formulated as

$$SNR_{u,k}(t) = \frac{p_u(t)g_{u,k}(t)d_{u,k}^{-\alpha}(t)}{\sigma^2 + \sum_{u' \in \mathcal{U}/\{u\}} \sum_{k' \in \mathcal{K}/\{k\}} p'(t)g_{u',k'}(t)d_{u',k'}^{-\alpha}(t)} \qquad (2)$$

where $p_u(t)$ indicates transmission power of UE u, $g_{u,k}(t)$ indicates the channel gain between SBS k and UE u, $d_{u,k}^{-\alpha}(t)$ indicates the distance between SBS k and UE u, σ^2 is the power of Gaussian noise. $\sum_{u' \in \mathcal{U}/\{u\}} \sum_{k' \in \mathcal{K}/\{k\}} p'(t)g_{u',k'}(t)d_{u',k'}^{-\alpha}(t)$ indicates the interference between SBSs. The SBS chooses a wireless subchannel ϑ_u to communicate to UE u with bandwidth B, the transmission rate from SBS k to UE u can be expressed as

$$r_{u,k}(t) = Blog_2(1 + SNR_{u,k}(t)) \qquad (3)$$

Each user is served by the local SBS via cellular links. If the requested file is not cached in the local SBS, the local SBS will get it from its cooperative SBS or directly download it from core network through backhaul links. Furthermore, the local SBS communicate with each other via the MBS. So, in the network architecture, each request file can be transmitted via 4 types of links, link1: SBS-UE, link2: MBS-SBS-UE, link3: SBS-MBS-SBS-UE, link4: core network-MBS-SBS-UE.

We assume the SBSs in Base Station Layer are connected by fiber and the distance is short, the transmission time is very short. So, the transmission time of a request file in Base Station Layer can be seen as a fixed value denoted as t_b, and the transmission time of link2 and link3 is the same. Furthermore, we assume that the communication between cloud content server and the MBS is via fiber, the transmission time is a fixed value denoted as t_c. Define t_u as the wireless transmission time between SBS and UE, which can be expressed as

$$t_u = \frac{s_f}{r_{u,k}(t)} \qquad (4)$$

At time t, define $t1, t2, t3, t4$ as the time delay of link1, link2, link3, link4.

$$t1 = t_u \qquad (5)$$

$$t2 = t_u + t_b \qquad (6)$$

$$t3 = t_u + t_b \qquad (7)$$

$$t4 = t_u + t_b + t_c \qquad (8)$$

2.3 Caching Model

Each SBS and MBS are equipped with a content caching unit of limited storage resource, which can cache n and m files, respectively, where $n < m < F$. The base stations located in Base Station Layer form a base station group. If the file is cached in the base station group, it can be forwarded to the SBS which serves the user that requests the file. Otherwise, the file will be downloaded from cloud content server to the MBS through backhaul link, and then forwarder to the SBS that provides services. At time t, if the file requested by the user is not cached in the base station group, the MBS will decide whether to cache it and where to cache it. We define $\beta_u \in \{0, 1, 2\}$ as the caching decision. If file f requested by UE u is cached in the connecting SBS, $\beta_u = 1$, and then if it is cached in the MBS, $\beta_u = 2$. Otherwise, $\beta_u = 0$ indicates that the file is not cached. Due to limited available caching capacity, the total cache size of the files on base stations should not exceed their caching capacities.

3 Problem Formulation

In this section, we formulate the cooperative content caching and request routing problem as Markov Decision Process (MDP) to minimize the long-term content delivery delay with system state space, action space, and reward function.

3.1 State Space

At the beginning of each time slot, the MBS observes network state which includes the available caching capacity of the MBS and SBSs, all content requests of UEs, the maximal delivery delay of files, the content popularity of files, the distance between UEs and SBSs, the cache status of files, the channel information of base stations. State $s_t \in S$ at time t in our cooperative caching system is defined as

$$s_t = \{c(t), f(t), o(t), \rho(t), d(t), w(t), h(t)\} \tag{9}$$

where

$c(t) = \left[c_0^m(t), c_1^s(t), \cdots, c_K^s(t)\right]$: represents the available caching capacity of base stations at time t. $c_0^m(t)$ represents the available caching capacity of the MBS;

$f(t) = \left[f_1(t), \cdots, f_U(t)\right]$: represents the content requests of UEs at time t;

$o(t) = [o_1(t), \cdots, o_F(t)]$: represents the maximal delivery delay of all files at time t;

$\rho(t) = [\rho_1(t), \cdots, \rho_F(t)]$: represents the content popularity of all files at time t;

$d(t) = \{[d_{11}(t), \cdots, d_{1U}(t)], \cdots, [d_{K1}(t), \cdots, d_{KU}(t)]\}$: represents the distance between UEs and SBSs at time t;

$w(t) = \{[w_{01}(t), \cdots, w_{0F}(t)], [w_{11}(t), \cdots, w_{1F}(t)], \cdots, [w_{K1}(t), \cdots, w_{KF}(t)]\}$: represents the cache status of F files at time t. $[w_{01}(t), \cdots, w_{0F}(t)]$ represents the state that the MBS caches files;

$h(t) = \{[h_{01}(t), \cdots, h_{0M}(t)], [h_{11}(t), \cdots, h_{1M}(t)], \cdots, [h_{K1}(t), \cdots, h_{KM}(t)]\}$: represents the channel information of all base stations at time t. $[h_{01}(t), \cdots, h_{0M}(t)]$ represents the channel information of the MBS. Denote $h_{ij}(t) \in \{0, 1\}$ to describe the subchannel j occupancy information of BS i. $h_{ij}(t) = 0$ means that the subchannel j is not occupied, otherwise $h_{ij}(t) = 1$.

3.2 Action Space

After receiving the content requests, the MBS selects SBS to serve and decides which contents should be cached to which cache nodes in order to minimize transmission delay under the premise of guaranteeing the hit rate of the request. Action $a_t \in \mathcal{A}$ at time t is defined as

$$a_t = \{\alpha(t), \beta(t), \vartheta(t)\} \tag{10}$$

where

$\alpha(t) = [\alpha_1(t), \cdots, \alpha_U(t)]$: represents the connection between SBSs and UEs at time t. $\alpha_i(t) \in \mathcal{K}$ represents the number of SBSs which serve UE i;

$\beta(t) = [\beta_1(t), \cdots, \beta_U(t)]$: represents the decision where to cache the request file at time t. $\beta_i(t) \in \{0, 1, 2\}$, if $\beta_i(t) = 1$ or 2, cache the file in the connecting SBS or the MBS. Otherwise, if $\beta_i(t) = 0$, not to cache it;

$\vartheta(t) = [\vartheta_1(t), \cdots, \vartheta_U(t)]$: represents the subchannel allocation of UEs at time t. $\vartheta_i(t) \in \mathcal{M}$ represents the subchannel number of SBSs which serve UE i;

3.3 Reward Function

After an action a_t is taken, the system will compute immediate reward and then update system state. The objective of edge caching problem is to minimize the long-term average content transmission delay. Thus, the immediate reward function at time t can be defined as

$$\Upsilon(s_t, a_t) = -\mathbb{E}\left[\sum_{i=1}^{U} P_f T_{if}(t)\right] \tag{11}$$

where $T_{if}(t)$ represents the transmission delay for UE i requesting file f at time t. Since UE i can obtain the request file from the local SBS, other BS that cooperate with the local BS, the MBS, and core network, the transmission delay $T_{if}(t)$ can be expressed as

$$T_{if}(t) = \begin{cases} t_u, & \text{the local SBS responds to UE } i \\ t_u + t_b, & \text{other BS or MBS in Base Station Layer responds to UE } i \\ t_u + t_b + t_c, & \text{download file from the core network} \end{cases} \tag{12}$$

4   DDPG Reinforcement Learning

Reinforcement learning is an important branch of machine learning that can make a smart agent learn from a set of optimal policies in a dynamic environment by minimizing/maximizing the expected cumulative cost/reward. There are two major categories of RL algorithms: (1) the modelbased approach and (2) the model-free approach. The former is mainly used in the automatic control field. Generally, the Gaussian process or the

Bayesian network is used to model this type of problems. The model-free framework can be regraded as a data-driven approach to obtain an optimal policy by estimating value function or policy function. In this article, we focus on the model-free learning approach in order to provide a training guidelines based on a large number of historical experiences. The model-free approach can be divided into three types: (1) critic-model (value-based approach); (2) actor-model (policy-based approach); and (3) actor-critic learning approach. Critic-model, such as Q-learning, is a classical RL learning algorithm that obtains optimal policies based on the estimated action-value function $Q(s, a)$. Actor-model can learn a stochastic policy function $\pi_\theta(s|a)$ with network parameter θ. Konda and Tsitsiklis [24] combined the actor-model and the criticmodel in order to address the individual disadvantages of policy gradient and value predication scheme. The actor-critic approach exhibits good convergence properties with continuous action spaces. However, the good performance is based on a large amount of training samples. In order to solve the challenge, Silver et al. [25] developed a deterministic policy gradient approach that can directly learn deterministic policy $\mu(s)$. Based on the deterministic actor-critic model, we leverage deep neural networks to provide accurate estimation of deterministic policy function $\mu(s)$ and value function $Q(s, a)$.

4.1 Value Function and Bellman Equation

The reward is an instant grant that reflects the current action that is good or not. The state value is a measure of the quality of the current agent's environment and is a long-term indicator. We define the policy function $\pi(s|a) = P(a_t = a, s_t = s)$ which is mapping the probability of taking action set a in the state s. The value of a states is worth the average reward under state s, i.e.,

$$v_\pi(s) = E_\pi(r_{t+1} + \gamma r_{t+2} + \gamma^2 r_{t+3} + \cdots |s_t = s) \tag{13}$$

r_t is the reward obtained after taking action at time t, $\gamma \in [0, 1]$ is a discount factor, the value is only determined by the delay bonus of the current state, and the weight of the current delayed reward is greater than the subsequent weight. According to the expression of the value function, we can deduce the recursive relationship of the adjacent state of the value function, which is the Bellman equation, i.e.,

$$v_\pi(s) = E_\pi(r_{t+1} + \gamma v_\pi(s_{t+1})|s_t = s) \tag{14}$$

Meanwhile, the action value function is defined in the same way to measure the degree of the current action, i.e.,

$$q_\pi(s, a) = E_\pi(R_{t+1} + \gamma q_\pi(s_{t+1}, a_{t+1})|s_t = s, a_t = a) \tag{15}$$

According to the definition of the action value function $q_\pi(s, a)$ and the state value function $v_\pi(s)$, we can easily get the conversion relationship formula between them:

$$v_\pi(s) = \sum_{a \in A} \pi(s|a) q_\pi(s, a) \tag{16}$$

The comparison strategy is generally compared by the corresponding value function. That is to say, finding a better strategy can be accomplished by finding a better value function, i.e.,

$$v_*(s) = \max_a (R_s^a + \gamma \sum_{s' \in S} P_{ss'}^a v_*(s')) \tag{17}$$

$$q_*(s, a) = R_s^a + \gamma \sum_{s' \in S} P_{ss'}^a \max_{a'} q_*(s', a') \tag{18}$$

$P_{ss'}^a$ denotes the probability of action a transitioning to the s' state in the s state. So we need to find the max q value during every step. In the real problem, because the state and motion space is very complicated, it is difficult to calculate by ordinary methods, so we can use the neural network method to fit the q value in each state.

4.2 DDPG Algorithm

The DDPG (Deep Deterministic Policy Gradient) algorithm is also model free, off-policy, and also uses deep neural networks for function approximation. DDPG is an actor-critic method, which has both a value function network (critic) and a policy network (actor). DDPG adopts the method of offline update. Both the actor and the critic have two identical networks, and the delay is updated to reduce the correlation. The actor part generates the deterministic action a through the current state, and the critic part obtains TD-error by calculating the state value to evaluate the pros and cons of the current strategy and determine the direction and speed for updating the policy network.

In this process, the action value function selected by the action policy $\pi(s; \theta^\pi)$ will be used as the basis for critc $Q(s, a|\theta^Q)$ evaluation, where θ^π and θ^Q are parameters of the actor network and the critic network respectively. The critic network is updated by minimizing the loss function (19):

$$Loss(\theta^Q) = \frac{1}{N} \sum_t [y_t - Q(s_t, a_t|\theta^Q)]^2 \tag{19}$$

where

$$y_t = r_t + \gamma Q'(s_{t+1}, \pi'(s_{t+1}; \theta^{\pi'})|\theta^{Q'}) \tag{20}$$

$\pi'(s; \theta^{\pi'})$ and $Q'(s, a|\theta^{Q'})$ are the target networks of actor and critic.

The actor-network is used to output the determined action type. We need to have an optimization goal called policy objective function, denoted as $J(\theta)$. We want to find the best θ to maximize the $J(\theta)$. The partial derivative $\nabla_\theta J(\theta)$ of $J(\theta)$ to θ is the policy gradient. Intuitively, we should update the parameter θ^π of the policy in the direction that makes the value function Q increase.

$$\nabla_{\theta^\pi} = \mathbb{E}[\nabla_{\theta^\pi} Q(s, a|\theta^Q)|_{s=s_t, a=\pi(s_t)} \nabla_{\theta^\pi} \pi(s; \theta^\pi)|s = s_t] \tag{21}$$

We can train the actor network by minimizing the loss of the actor:

$$Loss(\theta^\pi) = \frac{1}{N} \sum_t -Q(s_t, \pi(s_t; \theta^\pi)|\theta^Q) \qquad (22)$$

The detailed DDPG pseudocode is shown in Algorithm 1:

Algorithm1 DDPG-based Cooperative Caching Algorithm	
1	Initialize the experience replay buffer $\mathcal{B}$
2.	Initialize the networks which including actor network $\pi(s; \theta^\pi)$ with weights θ^π and the critic network $Q(s, a|\theta^Q)$ with weights θ^Q
3.	Initialize the target actor and critic network with weights $\theta^{\pi'} = \theta^\pi$ and $\theta^{Q'} = \theta^Q$
4.	**for** each episode1 **do**
5	on-line training
6	**for** each episode2 **do**
7.	Initialize the caching capacity of the MBS and SBSs, all content requests of UEs, the maximal delivery delay of files, the content popularity of files
8	Receive the initial state s_1
9.	**for** each time slot t **do**
10.	Select action $a_t = \pi(s_t; \theta^\pi) + \mathcal{N}$
11.	var $\leftarrow$ var $\times$ 0.995
12.	All of agents take the action a_t
18.	Update the state s_{t+1} and obtain the reward
19.	Store $\{s_t, a_t, r_t, s_{t+1}\}$ in experience replay buffer $\mathcal{B}$
20.	**end for**
21.	Sample M random minibatches $\{s_t, a_t, r_t, s_{t+1}\} \in \mathcal{B}$
22.	Set target critic to (20)
23.	Update the critic network weights θ^Q by minimizing loss in (19)
24.	Update the actor network weights θ^π by minimizing loss in (22)
25.	Update two target network weights:
26.	$\theta^{Q'} \leftarrow \tau\theta^Q + (1-\tau)\theta^{Q'}$
27.	$\theta^{\pi'} \leftarrow \tau\theta^\pi + (1-\tau)\theta^{\pi'}$
28.	**end for**

5   Simulations

In this section, we investigate the proposed algorithm and analyze the simulation results. We implemented the simulation using Python 3.6 and TensorFlow 1.1.2.

In the simulation environment, there is one MBS with the capacity 100 of caching contents, and there is K = 4 SBSs with the same capacity 20 of caching contents and U = 10 users. The default cache storage at MBS maintains totally F = 100 contents, and size of each content is L = 1. The bandwidth of every subchannel is set as B = 1 Hz. Set $t_b = 0.1$, $t_c = 0.3$.

In DDPG algorithm, the size of the mini-batch and replay memory are set as 32 and 2000 respectively. The maximum number of episodes is 3000 and the maximum number of steps in each episode is set to 300. To verify the performance of our proposed algorithm, we introduce the following two baseline solutions:

(1) LRU: Replace the least recently used content first.
(2) FIFO: Replace the first-in content first.

As the learning curve in Fig. 2 shows, as the number of training steps increases, the cumulative expected reward increases and converges at about 800 sets, with the average total reward per 100 sets eventually stabilizing at about −4.5. The more rewards earned in each episode, the better the transmission delay and power consumption control in the current episode. Therefore, the algorithm proposed in this paper achieves good performance.

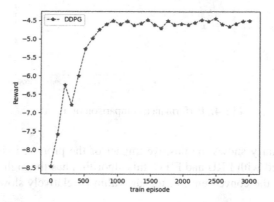

Fig. 2. The convergence performance of DDPG algorithm.

The effectiveness of the proposed algorithm can be attributed to that the reward function is designed for reducing the user delay, which make the DRL agent march toward minimizing the average delay. Figure 3 shows the time delay comparison between the proposed algorithm and the traditional LRU algorithm and FIFO algorithm. By comparison, it can be found that the average time delay of the proposed algorithm after convergence is much lower than that of LRU and FIFO algorithm. However, because the intelligent algorithm proposed in this paper needs a lot of learning to gradually converge, the convergence speed is slower than LRU and FIFO algorithms.

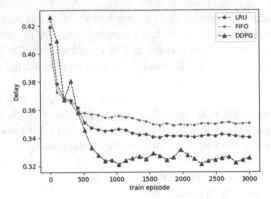

Fig. 3. Performance comparison of average delay.

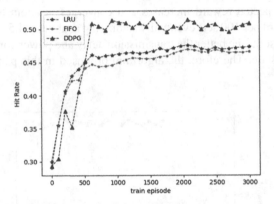

Fig. 4. Performance comparison of hit rate.

Figure 4 similarly shows the positive impact of the proposed algorithm on cache hit ratio. Compared with LRU and FIFO, this algorithm has the highest cache hit ratio. At the same time, the convergence of the algorithm is relatively slow due to the above reasons.

6 Conclusions

In this paper, we consider cooperative content caching and request routing in mobile edge networks. A 5G Message Cooperative Content Caching Scheme for blockchain-enabled using DDPG algorithm is proposed in order to minimize the average transmission delay of user requests on the premise of satisfying quality of service for user. Numerical results show that compared with LRU and FIFO, the proposed framework can achieve excellent performance in terms of the average delay and the hit rate.

Acknowledgement. This work was supported by the research project of China Unicom: Research on the Core Technology of SMS Capability Platform Based on "5G Message + Blockchain".

References

1. Abbas, N., Zhang, Y., Taherkordi, A., Skeie, T.: Mobile edge computing: a survey. IEEE Internet Things J **5**(1), 450–465 (2018)
2. Mach, P., Becvar, Z.: Mobile edge computing: a survey on architecture and computation offloading. IEEE Commun. Surv. Tut. **19**(3), 1628–1656 (2017)
3. Cisco Visual Networking Index, Global Mobile Data Traffic Forecast Update, 2017–2022 White Paper. (2019) https://www.cisco.com/c/en/us/solutions/collateral/service-provider/vis ual-networking-index-vni/white-paper-c11-738429.html
4. Qiu, L., Cao, G.: Popularity-aware caching increases the capacity of wireless networks. In: Proceedings of IEEE INFOCOM, pp. 1–9 (2017)
5. Zhou, Y., Chen, L., Yang, C., Chiu, D.M.: Video popularity dynamics and its implication for replication. IEEE Trans. Multimedia **17**(8), 1273–1285 (2015)
6. Wei, Y., Yu, F.R., Song, M., Han, Z.: User scheduling and resource allocation in het- nets with hybrid energy supply: an actor-critic reinforcement learning approach. IEEE Trans. Wirel. Commun. **17**(1), 680–692 (2018)
7. Sun, L., Wang, Y.L., Qu, Z.G., Xiong, N.N.: BeatClass: a sustainable ECG classification system in IoT-based eHealth (2021)
8. Duan, X., Zhao, Y., Zheng, K., Tian, D., Zhou, J.: Cooperative channel assignment for VANETS based on dual reinforcement learning. Comput. Mater. Cont. **66**(2), 2127–2140 (2021)
9. Tanveer, J., Haider, A., Ali, R., Kim, A.: Reinforcement learning-based optimization for drone mobility in 5g and beyond ultra-dense networks. Comput. Mater. Cont. **68**(3), 3807–3823 (2021)
10. Sun, S., Zhou, J., Wen, J., Wei, Y., Wang, X.: A DQN-based cache strategy for mobile edge networks. Comput. Mater. Cont. **71**(2), 3277–3291 (2022)
11. Wang, X., Chen, M., Taleb, T.: Cache in the air: Exploiting content caching and delivery techniques for 5G systems. IEEE Commun. Mag **52**(2), 131–139 (2014)
12. Sheng, M., Xu, C., Liu, J., Song, J., Ma, X., Li, J.: Enhancement for content delivery with prox-imity communications in caching enabled wireless networks: Architecture and challenges. IEEE Commun. Mag. **54**(8), 70–76 (2016)
13. Zeydan, E.: Big data caching for networking: moving from cloud to edge. IEEE Commun. Mag. **54**(9), 36–42 (2016)
14. Kvaternik, K., Llorca, J., Kilper, D., Pavel, L.: A methodology for the design of self- opti-mizing, decentralized content-caching strategies. IEEE/ACM Trans. Netw. **24**(5), 2634–2647 (2016)
15. Wang, W., Niyato, D., Wang, P., Leshem, A.: Decentralized caching for content delivery based on blockchain: a game theoretic perspective. arXiv:1801.07604 (2018)
16. Li, X., Wang, X., S, X., Leung, V.C.M.: Delay performance analysis of cooperative cell caching in future mobile networks. In: Proceedings of IEEE ICC, pp. 5652–5657 (2015)
17. Chae, S.H., Ryu, J.Y., Quek, T.Q.S., Choi, W.: Cooperative transmission via caching helpers. In: Proceedings of IEEE GLOBECOM, pp. 1–6 (2015)
18. Tan, L.T., Hu, R.Q., Qian, Y.: D2D communications in heterogeneous networks with full-duplex replays and edge caching. IEEE Trans. Ind. Inform. **14**(10), 4557–4567 (2018)
19. Zhong, C., Gursoy, M.C., Velipasalar, S.: A deep reinforcement learning-based framework for content caching. In: 52nd Annual Conference on Information Sciences and Systems (CISS), pp. 1–6 (2018)
20. Jiang, W., Feng, G., Qin, S., Liu, Y.: Multi-agent reinforcement learning based cooperative content caching for mobile edge networks. IEEE Access **7**, 61856–61867 (2019)

21. Li, Q., Sun, Y., Wang, Q., Meng, L., Zhang, Y.: A green DDPG reinforcement learning- based framework for content caching. In: 2020 12th International Conference on Communication Software and Networks (ICCSN), pp. 223–227 (2020)
22. Breslau, L., Cao, P., Fan, L., Phillips, G., Shenker, S.: Web caching and Zipf-like distribution: evidence and implications. In: Proceedings of IEEE Computer and Communication Societies (INFOCOM), pp. 126–134 (2014)
23. Chen, X., Jiao, L., Li, W., Fu, X.: Efficient multi-user computation offloading for mobile-edge cloud computing. IEEE Trans. Netw. **24**(5), 2795–2808 (2016)
24. Konda, V.R., Tsitsiklis, J.N.: Actor-critic algorithm. In: Proceedings of NIPS **13**, 1008–1014 (1999)
25. Silver, D., Lever, G., Heess, N., Degris, T., Wierstr, D., Riedmiller, M.: Determinstic policy gradient algorithms. In: Proceedings of 31st International Conference on Machine Learning (ICML), pp. 387–395 (2014)

A Survey of Deep Learning for Named Entity Recognition in Chinese Social Media

Jingxin Liu[1], Jieren Cheng[1,2]([✉]), Ziyan Wang[1], Congqiang Lou[1], Chenli Shen[1], and Victor S. Sheng[3]

[1] School of Computer Science and Technology, Hainan University, Haikou 570228, China
cjr22@163.com
[2] Hainan Blockchain Technology Engineering Research Center, Hainan University, Haikou 570228, China
[3] Department of Computer Science, Texas Tech University, Lubbock, TX 79409, USA

Abstract. Named Entity Recognition is the research foundation of many Natural Language Processing sub-tasks. Named Entity Recognition for Chinese social media is to identify entity nouns such as person names, place names, and organization names in Chinese Social Media corpus. Due to the non-standardization of Chinese Social Media texts and the small size of the corpus, the accuracy of entity recognition will be affected. In this review, aiming at the above issues, we first introduce the historical development and research background of Chinese named entity recognition. Then, we investigate the latest improvement methods of Chinese named entity recognition for social media, and divide these improvement methods into methods to improve model recognition performance with external knowledge and methods to enhance internal knowledge to improve model performance. Finally, we summarize the challenges Chinese named entity recognition in social media based on deep learning, and propose the future development direction for these challenges.

Keywords: Named Entity Recognition · Natural Language Processing · Chinese social media

1 Introduction

Named Entity Recognition (NER) [1] refers to the identification of entity nouns with actual meaning in unstructured text, such as: names of persons, names of places, names of organizations, dates and times, numbers, currencies, etc. At present, NER technology has extremely wide application in natural language processing tasks [2–5], and it is also the research foundation of many natural language processing sub-tasks. For example, the construction of knowledge graph [6, 7], knowledge base construction [8–10], network information retrieval [11], machine translation [12, 13], automatic question answer system [14–16], etc. The function of social media-oriented named entity recognition is to provide conditions and foundations for solving Internet information clutter, redundancy, noise interference and irregularity, and it can also provide technical means for processing and analyzing unstructured text information.

© The Author(s), under exclusive license to Springer Nature Switzerland AG 2022
X. Sun et al. (Eds.): ICAIS 2022, LNCS 13338, pp. 573–582, 2022.
https://doi.org/10.1007/978-3-031-06794-5_46

The development history of Chinese social media NER. Research on NER in foreign countries started relatively early in China. In the 7th IEEE Conference on Artificial Intelligence Applications (1991), Rau et al. [17] creatively realized the extraction and recognition of company names by using heuristic algorithms and manual rule writing methods. In MUC-6, DANIEL M. BIKEL et al. [18] applied the hidden Markov model to English text NER for the first time, and the test results were better than the previous methods. Since then, NER has been applied to various evaluation tasks as sub-tasks, such as MUC-7 [19], CoNLL-2002 [20] and so on. However, most of these tasks are aiming at the research of English data sets. Because each word in English text has a natural space separator, and two adjacent words are naturally divided into words. Compared with other languages, the work of English ner is relatively simple. The performance of the model proposed by the scientists has also been improved. In the Bakeoff-2006 conference [21], the NER method for Chinese text became the main research object. Since then, many Chinese NER researchers have proposed various methods for the progress of Chinese NER. Mao Xinnian et al. [22] used conditional random fields with different functions for Chinese word segmentation and part-of-speech tagging to improve Chinese vocabulary processing performance. Li Lishuang et al. [23] used statistical methods and support vector machines (SVM) in different situations to identify Chinese location names and Chinese names. For a long time, the research of named entity recognition work has focused on formal texts. It was not until 2005 that it gradually turned to the field of Chinese social media [24–26]. In the study of Chinese social media texts, Liu Xiaohua et al. [24] combined The K-nearest neighbor (KNN) classifier and linear conditional random field (CRF) model to solve the problems of insufficient annotation data and unavailability of training data when establishing NER in a specific field for tweets. Ling Wang et al. [25] proposed a method of extracting parallel data to obtain a large amount of parallel data in some social media for free. Peng Nanyun et al. [26] proposed the Weibo corpus for the first time, which contains names of people, places, organizations, and geopolitical names. They combined neural embedding and joint training objectives to improve the Chinese social media named entity recognition model.

The motivation for this review. In recent years, with the rapid development of artificial intelligence and Internet technology [27–32], more and more important Chinese information can be obtained from social media through deep learning methods, which makes NER technology for Chinese social media attract much attention. Although Liu Jingxin et al. [33] analyzed the Chinese NER method in detail from the traditional method and the deep learning method for the Chinese NER method, they didn't make a systematic summary of the Chinese NER method for social media. At the same time, Chinese social media based on deep learning still faces many challenges. Based on the above issues, it becomes extremely important to systematically summarize the challenges faced by Chinese social media NER method and classify Chinese social media NER method based on in-depth learning.

2 Background

2.1 NER Resources:Datasets

The data sets for Chinese social media NER include several shared data sets of Sighan in Chinese NER, Weibo NER, etc. Several of Sighan's shared data sets in Chinese NER are mainly used for official Chinese texts like news [34, 35], and it is not suitable for informal texts on the Internet. However, weibo NER was built by Peng Nanyun et al. [26] who collected Sina Weibo information in 2015. It has many problems that the informality of Chinese social media brings to natural language, such as such as non-standard sentence grammar, random construction of new words, lack of punctuation, etc. The emergence of Weibo NER fills in the gaps in the text of informal Chinese social networks. As shown in Table 1, it contains four types of entities: person name (PER), place name (LOC), organization name (ORG), and political geopolitical information (GPE). It contains a total of 1890 sentences, 102729 characters, and 7000 marked characters. Among them, there are 1350 sentences, 773378 characters, and 4951 marked characters in the training set; the test set contains 270 sentences, 14842 characters, and 1078 marked characters; The verification set contains 270 sentences, 14,509 characters, and 971 marked characters.

Table 1. Weibo NER dataset.

Weibo NER	Train dataset	Test dataset	Dev dataset	Total
Sentences	1350	270	270	1890
Mark Characters	4951	1078	971	7000
Characters	773378	14842	14509	102,729
Entity Types	4	4	4	4

2.2 NER Labeling Method and Evaluation Mechanism

NER annotation annotation methods for Chinese social media mainly include IO, bio, bmoes, etc. [36]. Among them, BIO labeling method and BMOES are the most common methods. In the BIO labeling method, B represents the starting position of an entity noun, I represents the remaining position of an entity noun except the first word, and O represents an intangible noun. The BMOES annotation method is an extension of the BIO annotation method. Compared with BIO labeling method, it has more perfect labeling rules and is also the labeling method used in weibo NER corpus at present. In the BMOES labeling method, B represents the start position of an entity noun, M represents the internal position of an entity noun, E represents the end position of an entity noun, S represents a separate entity noun, and O represents an intangible noun.

$$PRECISION = \frac{TP}{FP + TP} \times 100\% \tag{1}$$

$$RECALL = \frac{TP}{FN + TP} \times 100\% \qquad (2)$$

$$F_1 = \frac{2PR}{P + R} \times 100\% \qquad (3)$$

The NER labeling system for Chinese social media is mainly to correctly evaluate the recognition results. The three evaluation indexes are [36]: accuracy rate, recall rate and F1 value. The accuracy rate represents the ratio of the correct number of classified samples to the total number of samples in a given data set; The recall rate represents the ratio of the true number to the total number of samples; F1 value represents the comprehensive index of reconciliation, balance precision rate and recall rate; TP refers to the sample with correct prediction and correct reality; FP refers to the sample whose prediction is correct and the actual is wrong; FN indicates that the prediction is wrong and the actual is correct.

Table 2. Comparison of Chinese NER deep learning methods for Chinese social media.

Work	Method	Network coding layer	Label decoding layer	Performance (F1)
Peng Nanyun [35]	Jointly Train LSTM + Emb	LSTM	CRF	Weibo NER:46.85%
He Huangfeng [36]	F-Score driven	LSTM	CRF	Weibo NER:50.60%
He Huangfeng [37]	Unified model for cross-domain and semi-supervised	LSTM	MMNN	Weibo NER:54.50%
Wang Binhui [38]	Attention-based recurrent neural model	LSTM	Attention + softmax	Weibo NER:54.87%
Nie Yuyang [39]	Attentive semantic augmentation	/	CRF	Weibo NER:69.80%
Gong Zhaoheng [40]	Integrate a boundary assembling method with the state-of-the-art deep neural network model	LSTM	CRF	Weibo NER:56.82%
Dong Chuanhai [41]	Multichannel (S + T, 1random, 2CRF)	LSTM	CRF	Weibo NER:60.68%

3 Research Progress of Deep Learning

With the emergence of BiLSTM-CRF, the prologue of Chinese NER based on deep learning is unveiled. The common BiLSTM-CRF model based on character vector embedding is shown in Fig. 1. The existing Chinese NER deep learning methods for Chinese social media are mainly divided into two solutions. The first is to use external knowledge (dictionary information, joint training models, transfer learning based methods, etc.) to improve model recognition performance; The second is to enhance internal knowledge (attention mechanism enhances semantics, boundary assembly, etc.). We counted the performance of work based on deep learning in Weibo NER in recent years, as shown in Table 2.

Borrowing external knowledge to improve model recognition performance. Peng Nanyun et al. [37] improved the performance of NER in specific applications of Chinese social media through joint training of the NER model and Chinese word segmentation. He Hangfeng et al. [38] used semi-supervised learning methods combined with neural networks to better solve the problem of rarely labeled or unlabeled text in Chinese social media. He Hangfeng et al. [39] used a combination of semi-supervised learning and cross-domain learning methods to learn more effectively the unlabeled information and extra-domain information in order to solve the problem of difficult named entity recognition in informal Chinese text with noise.

Enhance internal knowledge to improve model performance. Wang Binhui [40] et al. applied the attention mechanism to the model to improve the performance of Chinese social media NER by focusing on the correlation between the part of speech of a character in the text and the named entity of the text. Nie Yuyang et al. [41] adopted a method of enhancing semantics to solve the problem of sparse data and informal text in social media that are difficult to deal with NER tasks. Gong zhaoheng et al. [42] accurately divided the boundaries of Chinese words through the boundary assembly method to solve the problem of poor quality of named entity recognition caused by inaccurate entity boundary division. Dong Chuanhai et al. [43] proposed a multi-channel method to obtain data of different patterns in Chinese social media, which was used to solve the problem of difficult named entity recognition in informal Chinese text with noise, and found that shared embedding and randomness Initial embedding can significantly improve model performance.

4 The Challenge of Chinese NER for Social Media

At present, researchers in this field believe that the performance of Chinese-oriented social media NER has made some progress compared with previous studies, but there are still some challenging problems that are difficult to solve in many aspects. After research and analysis, we believe that Chinese NER for social media still has strong challenges in the following aspects.

4.1 The Particularity of Chinese Characters

Due to the inherent characteristics of Chinese characters, their font forms are diverse, and their sentence structure is complex, which is not similar to the prompt information such as solid spelling of special words, obvious word boundary segmentation and inherent definite articles in English texts, and it is difficult to distinguish entity nouns easily. Chinese sentences are generally composed of multiple words and characters, but there is no space distinction between words and characters. The composition of sentences is closely arranged by Chinese characters, and the special vocabulary is difficult to divide, which makes the application of NER in the Chinese field much more difficult than that in the English field. In the application of NER in different languages,the basic technical means and ideas are the same, but different models need to be selected and adjusted according to different language features to achieve better results.

4.2 Non-standardization of Chinese Social Media Texts

Informal text content in social media often contains a large number of new words and wrong words, the format of text content is not standardized, and the text usually contains noise interference such as network terms, emoticons, special symbols, etc. These ambiguous text contents and complex and changeable (or unfixed) expressions, to some extent, it makes the task of natural language understanding more difficult. There are differences in the application of Chinese named entities in different knowledge fields, different languages and different historical and cultural backgrounds. Therefore, these differences should be taken into account in the technical implementation of NER in the field of Chinese social media, so as to better realize the cross-domain application of NER. When using Chinese social media text, we should consider the problems of different knowledge strength, different confidence and no normative constraints in the text in this field. Under the condition of fully understanding the context semantic information, we can dig deep into the entity semantics and effective information through the methods such as fusion alignment and entity linking, so as to avoid the problems of ambiguous expression, unclear reference and wrong segmentation of Chinese named entities in the process of processing.

4.3 Chinese Social Media Corpus is Small in Scale

At present, the general corpus for informal Chinese social media is the Weibo NER corpus proposed by Peng Nanyun et al., and its training set is only 1/30 of that of MSRA corpus. Too few training sets in the corpus result in too few annotation data, and the corpus for Chinese social media itself has many uncertain factors, such as, more typos, nonstandard grammatical structures, ambiguous language descriptions, etc. These will lead to large training errors and low accuracy of the deep learning model due to insufficient prediction database. This is also the direct reason why the accuracy rate of using Weibo NER corpus for Chinese social media NER is only about 60% (Fig. 1).

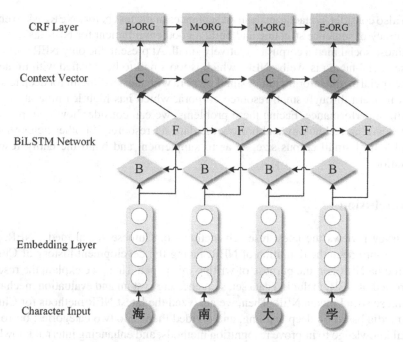

Fig. 1. Character vector-BiLSTM-CRF Model.

5 Future Development Direction

The particularity of Chinese characters. There are fundamental differences between Chinese characters and English letters in the form of construction. Chinese characters are the combination of sound, shape and meaning, developed from pictures, and are the oldest hieroglyphics. There are no marks and division symbols between each word and the expression form of each word is roughly the same. While English is phonography. English letters come from spelling, and there are obvious space separators between each word. People's names, place names, organization names and geopolitical names have different expressions in uppercase or italics. Since we can't change its basic font features, we can consider adding some radical features and English spelling features of Chinese characters in the embedded presentation layer to enhance the characteristics of Chinese characters and express their glyph features as much as possible, so as to make the model learn better.

Non-standardization of Chinese social media. Most information of Chinese social media comes from network information release. Compared with non-network information, network information is numerous and its quality is difficult to control. Nowadays, the randomness of network language is also increasing. The non-standard sentence structure and the emergence of homophonic words have exacerbated the challenge of NER technology for Chinese social media. In the face of a large number of non-normative texts, we can consider adding attention mechanism in the embedded presentation layer to express the meaning of semantic information of non-network texts. At the same time, we can also consider syntactic analysis of sentences in the text before NER task to ensure the accuracy of sentence structure and build a good environment for NER task.

Chinese social media corpus is relatively small. At present, the only NER corpus for Chinese social media is Weibo NER, which is too small to be satisfied with numerous Chinese social media information. A small corpora will make it difficult for deep learning models to learn through small resource corpora, which has high learning ability and recognition performance. Facing these problems, we can consider how to improve the transfer learning technology and borrow the data set resources in other fields to solve the problem of small corpus size, so as to supplement and build the entity resource information.

6 Conclusion

This survey reviews the latest research methods of Chinese social media NER. First of all, we introduce the definition of NER, facing the development history of Chinese social media NER and the purpose of writing this paper. Then, we explain the research background of NER, including data set, sequence tag system and evaluation mechanism for Chinese social media NER. Then, we analyzed the latest NER methods for Chinese social media based on deep learning, and divided them into two categories: borrowing external knowledge to improve recognition methods, and enhancing internal knowledge to improve recognition methods. Finally, we put forward the challenging problems in this field and the future development direction. We hope that this paper can provide a new inspiration for researchers facing Chinese social media NER.

Acknowledgments. This work was supported by National Natural Science Foundation of China (Grant No.62162024 and No. 62162022), Key Projects in Hainan Province (Grant No. ZDYF2021GXJS003 and No. ZDYF2020040), the Major science and technology project of Hainan Province(Grant No.ZDKJ2020012) and Graduate Innovation Project (Grant No.Qhys2021–187).

References

1. Nadeau, D., Sekine, S.: A survey of named entity recognition and classification. Lingvisticae Investigationes **30**, 3–26 (2007)
2. Tran, P., Ta, V., Truong, Q., Duong, Q., Nguyen, T., Phan, X.: Named entity recognition for vietnamese spoken texts and its application in smart mobile voice interaction. In: Nguyen, N.T., Trawiński, B., Fujita, H., Hong, TP. (eds.) Intelligent Information and Database Systems. ACIIDS 2016. LNCS, vol. 9621, pp. 170–180. Springer, Heidelberg (2016). https://doi.org/10.1007/978-3-662-49381-6_17
3. Yang, J., Zhang, Y., Dong, F.: Neural reranking for named entity recognition RANLP. In: Advances in Natural Language Processing Meet Deep Learning, pp. 84–92 (2017)
4. Wang, Y., Sun, Y., Ma, Z., Gao, L., Xu, Y., Sun, T.: Application of pre-training models in named entity recognition. In: 2020 12th International Conference on Intelligent Human-Machine Systems and Cybernetics (IHMSC), vol. 1, pp. 23–26. IEEE (2020)
5. Klinger, R., Friedrich, C.: User's choice of precision and. named entity recognition. In: Proceedings of the International Conference RANLP-2009, pp. 92–96 (2009)

6. Yoo, S., Jeong, O.: EP-Bot: empathetic chatbot using auto-growing knowledge graph. Comput. Mater. Cont. **67**(3), 2807–2817 (2021)
7. He, Q., Wu, L., Yin, Cai, Y., H: Knowledge-graph augmented word representations for named entity recognition. In: Proceedings of the AAAI Conference on Artificial Intelligence, vol. 34, pp. 19–26 (2020)
8. Lossio-Ventura, J., et al.: Towards an obesity-cancer knowledge base: Biomedical entity identification and relation detection. In: IEEE International Conference on Bioinformatics and Biomedicine (BIBM), pp. 81–88. IEEE (2016)
9. Loster, M. Knowledge base construction with machine learning methods. Universität Potsdam (2021)
10. He, Z., Li, W.H.: Named entity recognition and disambiguation. General Information (2013)
11. Adak, C., Chaudhuri, B., Blumenstein, M.: Named entity recognition from unstructured handwritten document. In: Images Document Analysis Systems, pp. 75–80. IEEE (2016)
12. Dandapat, S., Way, A.: Improved named entity recognition using machine translation- based cross-lingual. Information Computacion Y Sistemas **20**, 495–504 (2016)
13. Li, Z., Qu, D., Xie, C., Li, Y.: Language model pre-training method in machine translation based on named entity recognition. Int. J. Artif. Intell. Tools **29**(7n08), 2040021 (2020)
14. Al-Besher, A., Kumar, K., Sangeetha, M., Butsa, T.: Bert for conversational question answering systems using semantic similarity estimation. Comput. Mater. Cont. **70**(3), 4763–4780 (2022)
15. Wang, Z., Guan, H.: 2020 Research on named entity recognition of doctor-patient question answering community based on bilstm-crf model. In: IEEE International Conference on Bioinformatics and Biomedicine (BIBM), pp. 41–44. IEEE (2020)
16. Lamurias, A., Couto, F.: Biomedical question answering using bidirectional transformers and named entity recognition. In: Proceedings of the 18th BioNLP Workshop and Shared Task, pp. 23–27 (2019)
17. Rau, L.: Extracting company names from text. In: Proceedings of the Seventh IEEE Conference on Artificial Intelligence Application, pp. 29–32. IEEE (1991)
18. Bikel, D., Schwarta, R., Weischedel, R.: An algorithm that learns what's in a. name. Mach. Learn. **34**, 211–242 (1999)
19. Chinchor, N., Robinson, P.: MUC-7 named entity task definition. In: Proceedings of the 7th Conference on Message Understanding, vol. 29, pp. 1–21 (1997)
20. Wu, Y., Lin, Y.J., Q: Description of the NCU Chinese word segmentation and named entity recognition system for SIGHAN Bakeoff. In: Proceedings of the Fifth SIGHAN Workshop on Chinese Language Processing, pp. 209–221 (2006)
21. Sang, E.F.T.K., DeMeulder, F.: Introduction to the CoNLL-2003 shared task: language-independent named entity recognition. In: Proceedings of the Seventh Conference on Natural Language Learning at HLT-NAACL, pp. 142–147 (2003)
22. Mao, X., Dong, Y., He, S., Wang, H., Bao, S.: Chinese word segmentation and named entity recognition based on conditional random fields. In: Proceedings of the Sixth SIGHAN Workshop on Chinese Language Processing, pp. 90–93 (2008)
23. Li, L., Mao, T., Huang, D., Yang, Y.: Hybrid models for Chinese named entity recognition. In: Proceedings of the Fifth SIGHAN Workshop on Chinese Language Processing, pp. 72–78 (2006)
24. Liu, X., Zhang, S., Wei, F., Zhou, M.: Recognizing named entities in tweets. In: Proceedings of the 49th annual meeting of the association for computational linguistics: human language technologies, pp. 59–67 (2011)
25. Llng, W., Xiang, G., Dyer, C., Alan, B., Isabel, T: Microblogs as parallel corpora. In: Proceedings of the 51st Annual Meeting of the Association for Computational Linguistics, vol. 1, pp. 76–86 (2013)

26. Peng, N., Dredze, M.: Named entity recognition for Chinese social media with jointly trained embeddings. In: Proceedings of the 2015 Conference on Empirical Methods in Natural Language Processing, pp. 48–54 (2015)
27. Cheng, J., Yang, Y., Tang, X., Xiong, N., Zhang, Y., Lei, F.: Generative adversarial net- works: a literature review. KSII Trans. Internet Inf. Syst. **14**(12), 4625–4647 (2020)
28. Lei, F., Cheng, J., Yang, Y., Tang, X., Sheng, V., Huang, C.: Improving heterogeneous network knowledge transfer based on the principle of generative adversarial. Electronics **10**(13), 1525 (2021)
29. Tang, X., Tu, W., Li, K., Cheng, J.: DFFNet: an IoT-perceptive dual feature fusion network for general real-time semantic segmentation. Inf. Sci. **565**, 326–343 (2021)
30. Cheng, J., Peng, X., Tang, W., Tu, W., Xu: MIFNet: a lightweight multiscale information fusion network. Int. J. Intell. Syst. 1–26 (2021)
31. Li, T., Hu, Y., Ju, A., Hu, Z.: Adversarial active learning for named entity recognition in cybersecurity. Comput. Mater. Cont. **66**(1), 407–420 (2021)
32. Zhao, S., Hu, M., Cai, Z., Zhang, Z., Zhou, T., Liu, F.: Enhancing Chinese character representation with lattice-aligned attention. IEEE Trans. Neural Netw. Learn. Syst. (2021). https://doi.org/10.1109/TNNLS.2021.3114378
33. Cheng, J., Liu, J., Xu, X.: A review of Chinese named entity recognition. KSII Trans. Internet Inf. Syst. (TIIS) **15**(6), 2012–2030 (2021)
34. He, J., Wang, H.: Chinese named entity recognition and word segmentation based on character. In: Proceedings of the Sixth SIGHAN Workshop on Chinese Language Processing, pp. 28–32 (2008)
35. He, Z., Li, W.H., S: The task 2 of CIPS-SIGHAN 2012 named entity recognition and disambiguation. In. Chinese Bakeoff Proceedings of the Second CIPS-SIGHAN Joint Conference on Chinese Language Processing, pp. 108–122 (2012)
36. Li, J., Sun, A., Han, J., Li, C.: A survey on deep learning for named entity recognition. IEEE Trans. Knowl. Data Eng. (2020). https://doi.org/10.1109/TKDE.2020.2981314
37. Peng, N., Dredze, M.: Improving named entity recognition for Chinese social media with word segmentation representation learning. In: Proceedings of the 54th Annual Meeting of the Association for Computational Linguistics, vol. 2, pp. 49–55 (2016)
38. He, H., Sun, X.: Score driven max margin neural network for named entity recognition in Chinese social media. In: Proceedings of the 15th Conference of the European, chap. 2, pp. 713–731 (2017)
39. He, H., Sun, X.: A unified model for cross-domain and semi-supervised named entity recognition in Chinese social media. In: Proceedings of the AAAI Conference on Artificial Intelligence, vol. 31 (2017)
40. Wang, B., Chai, Y., Xing, S.: Attention-based recurrent neural model for named entity recognition in. Chinese social media. In: Proceedings of the 2019 2nd International Conference on Algorithms, Computing and Artificial Intelligence, pp. 91–96 (2019)
41. Nie, Y., Tian, Y., Wan, X., Song, Y., Dai, B.: Named entity recognition for social media texts with semantic augmentation. In: Proceedings of the 2020 Conference on Empirical Methods in Natural Language Processing (EMNLP), pp. 83–91 (2020)
42. Gong, Z., Chen, P., Zhou, J.: integrating boundary assembling into a DNN framework for named entity recognition in Chinese social media text. arXiv:2002.11910 (2020)
43. Dong, C., Wu, H., Zhang, J., Zong, C.: Multichannel LSTM-CRF for named entity recognition in Chinese social media. In: Sun, M., Wang, X., Chang, B., Xiong, D. (eds.) NLP-NABD CCL 2017. LNCS, vol. 10565, pp. 197–208. Springer, Cham (2017). https://doi.org/10.1007/978-3-319-69005-6_17

A Survey on IPv6 Security Threats and Defense Mechanisms

Ning Liu[1], Jing Xia[1(✉)], Zhiping Cai[1], Tao Yang[1], Bingnan Hou[1], and Zhilin Wang[2]

[1] College of Computer, National University of Defense Technology, Changsha 410073, China
jingxia@nudt.edu.cn
[2] Technical Service Center for Vocational Education, National University of Defense Technology, Changsha 410073, China

Abstract. Compared with IPv4 network, IPv6 network has some new characteristics, such as larger address space and more simplified message header structure. These new characteristics in IPv6 network may introduce both security enhancement opportunities and new security challenges. At present, there are mainly two threats in IPv6 network during its wide deployment. On one hand, during the transition from IPv4 to IPv6, "dual stack", "traffic tunneling" and "translation" are three building blocks, all of which may introduce new security threats. On the other hand, IPv6 networking internal caused by new characteristics of IPv6 can also incur vulnerability. In view of these new forms of threats, network managers will generally adopt some defense mechanisms based on the characteristics of IPv6. This paper introduces and classifies the security threats in IPv6 network, then analyzed the defense mechanisms against different security threats in detail. Finally, we present some thoughts and future research directions in the field of IPv6 security.

Keywords: Ipv6 · Security · Threat · Defense mechanism

1 Introduction

With IPv4 address allocation exhausted, the next generation Internet Protocol IPv6 is beginning to accelerate the promotion and deployment all over the world. The system of IPv6 protocol is first constructed in 1995 [1, 2], with a series of RFC documents on the definition and specification of IPv6 published. The large-scale commercial deployment of IPv6 has been carried out rapidly. In recent years, the global IPv6 deployment has shown a trend of rapid progress. Since 2012, many well-known websites such as Facebook and Google have begun to permanently support IPv6. According to the statistics of APNIC labs [3], by July 2020, the IPv6 deployment rate of 16 countries has exceeded 40%, 23 countries has exceeded 30%, and 39 countries has exceeded 20%. On November 10, according to the real-time data of the website, these three numbers became 14, 28, 43. By June 2020, the top five countries/regions in the number of IPv6 users in the world are India (358 million), the United States (143 million), China (120 million), Brazil (50 million) and Japan (40 million).

© The Author(s), under exclusive license to Springer Nature Switzerland AG 2022
X. Sun et al. (Eds.): ICAIS 2022, LNCS 13338, pp. 583–598, 2022.
https://doi.org/10.1007/978-3-031-06794-5_47

However, with the rapid development of IPv6 in recent years, the security threats [4, 5] and challenges of IPv6 network have become important research issues. Meanwhile, the security threats of Mobile IPv6 [6, 7] and the IPv6 security in IoT [8, 9] also become research hot spots. Li, Xiang, et al. [10] used XMap to present the large-scale measurement study on the IPv6 network and found that IPv6 faces potential security threats. Thanks to the significant increase in address space (the address space of IPv6 is 2^{96} times that of IPv4) and the addition of security features in the protocol cluster, IPv6 has certain enhancement in ensuring Internet security. The enhancement of security is reflected in the following aspects: IPv6 improves anti hacker sniffing and scanning capabilities, improves the traceability of network information, strengthens the security capability of the protocol itself and some common attack risks in IPv4 are avoided or mitigated. But there are still security risks in IPv6 networks.

At present, The Internet is in the stage of coexistence of IPv4 and IPv6 network. Compared with IPv4 protocol, IPv6 has some new features which may have an impact on the security policy and bring new security challenges of the Internet. As a result, there are mainly two types of security challenges. One security issue comes from the transmission of information in IPv4 and IPv6 networks [11], but with the full deployment of IPv6 and the discontinuation of IPv4, this challenge will disappear. The other is from IPv6 network internal, e.g., host tracking, packet filtering policies, extension headers security, and IID generation mechanism, which is caused by the new characteristics of IPv6 protocol.

In order to deal with these security threats, IPv6 protocol takes some defensive measures to ensure the security of the network. In the early IPv6 network, researchers mainly relied on the security characteristics of IPv6 protocol to ensure Internet security. IPv6 protocol requires mandatory support for Internet Protocol Security (IPSec) [12] which is not necessarily supported in the IPv4 network and relies on IPSec to realize data security at the network layer, including data encryption and data authenticity. Then researchers took some other measures to deal with the security threats caused by the new characteristics of IPv6. IPv6 protocol uses MAC address to generate interface IP (last 64 bits), which increases the risk of privacy related attack. The current mechanism to protect privacy is frequently modifying interface IP. IPv6 use Duplicate address detection (DAD) to ensure the availability and uniqueness of the address, but DAD mechanism can cause Denial-of-Service (Dos) attacks. As a result, researchers use hash algorithm to encrypt the address to prevent DoS attacks. Different from IPv4 protocol, IPv6 supports Neighbor Discovery Protocol (NDP) [13] which provides for stateless address auto configuration of nodes (SLAAC) [14], neighbor unreachability detection and resolution of link layer addresses. But attackers can disguise as legitimate users to launch DoS attacks [15] and Man-in-the-Middle (MiTM) attacks in IPv6 network [16, 17]. Researchers adopt a mechanism called Intrusion Detection System (IDS) [18] which uses an active probing mechanism to detect NDP related attacks. Recently researchers designed an active defense approach based on web honeypot [19]. Threats can be cleverly identified by deploying honeypot and network managers can modify the current security policy to ensure network security.

In this paper, we first introduce the new features of IPv6 protocol and their impact on network security. With these preliminary knowledge, we then analyze the security threats with deliberate classification and introduce the defense mechanisms against the security threats in IPv6 networks. Finally, this paper introduces the summary and prospect for the research towards of IPv6 security.

2 New Features of IPv6

As the next generation IP protocol, IPv6 has new characteristics and security mechanism. Among them, the core change is the expansion of address space. Unlike IPv4 address composed of 32 bits, IPv6 is composed of 128 bits, which can assign an IP address to every grain of sand on earth. In general, there are mainly five new features in IPv6 protocol.

2.1 Huge Address Space and Hierarchical Address Structure

IPv6 is composed of 128 bits, which can provide a real address for each network node. The huge address space overcomes the limitation of the number of network address resources. At the same time, IPv6 supports more levels of address hierarchy. The designers of IPv6 divide the IPv6 address space according to different address prefixes, and adopt a hierarchical address structure which IP address consists of a 64 bit subnet prefix and a 64 bit interface ID (as shown is Fig. 1) to facilitate the fast forwarding of data packets by backbone routers.

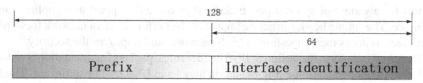

Fig. 1. The composition of IPv6 address.

Thanks to the huge address space resources of IPv6, The IPv6 network security has been significantly improved. In IPv4 network, due to the limitation of address space, Network Address Translation (NAT) [20] has been widely deployed by network developers, and most network communication is realized through NAT. In IPv6 network, every equipment can get a real and unique IP address, therefore end-to-end communication can be truly realized. IPv6 has rich address resources which ensuring that each packet forwarded by the router has a real source address. True network address of each equipment can solve the problems of network real name system and user identity traceability through the established address verification mechanism.

In general, huge address space and sparse address distribution effectively improve the security and transparency of the IPv6 network, although it may cause trouble to researchers who conduct network asset analysis and network scanning (researchers need to take strategies to improve the scan efficiency, e.g. 6Forest [21], 6Hit [22]and 6Graph [23]).

2.2 More Compact Header Structure and Stronger Scalability

The format of IPv6 datagram is composed of IP header and data (called payload in IPv6). The data part of IPv6 datagram can also include 0 or more IPv6 extension headers which is different from that of IPv4. Figure 2 shows the structure of IPv6 packet. The IPv6 basic header part is fixed to 40 bytes in length. The total length of IPv6 basic header is greatly reduced by cutting some fields in IPv4 header or moving some fields into extended header.

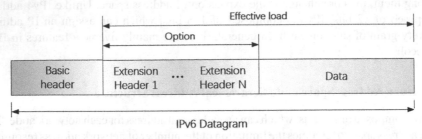

Fig. 2. The structure of IPv6 packet.

The IPv4 header length is specified by the IHL domain, while the IPv6 base header is fixed at 40 bytes in contrast. As a result, it simplifies the processing of IPv6 messages by forwarding equipment and improves the forwarding efficiency in IPv6 network. IPv6 also defines a variety of extended headers, which makes IPv6 flexible and can provide support for a variety of applications, making it possible to support new applications in the future. The simple header structure improves the performance of network forwarding equipment, reduces the congestion in IPv6 network, and improves the security.

Moreover, thanks to the design of IPv6 header rules, packets fragmentation is reduced in IPv6 network and common fragmentation attacks in IPv4 will be mitigated. The link layer has the characteristic of maximum transmission unit (MTU), which limits the maximum length of data frames. In IPv4 protocol, if the length of the data message is greater than the MTU of current link, the packets start fragmentation. After reaching the destination host, it is reorganized at the IP layer. IPv6 prohibits intermediate node equipment from slicing IP messages. Packets fragmentation only occur at the start point, and fragment information is stored in the extension header of IPv6 packets. As a result, the times of data message fragmentation reduce reduces fragment attacks reduce.

2.3 Neighbor Discovery Protocol in Place of ARP Function

Neighbor discovery protocol (NDP) is a new protocol proposed in IPv6, which is mainly responsible for the communication between nodes. The packets of NDP are based on efficient multicast and unicast instead of the broadcast mechanism in Address Resolution Protocol (ARP). Therefore, NDP can eliminate the risk of "broadcast storm" in IPv4 network. Compared with ARP, NDP has more functions, such as router discovery through sending RS packet, address resolution (replace ARP) and duplicate address detection (DAD). NDP uses the following five ICMPv6 protocol version messages to perform its functions:

- Router solicitation (RS) type (133): Make a request to the router.
- Router advertisement (RA) type (134): In response to RS message or claim the existence of router.
- Neighbor solicitation (NS) type (135): Get the link layer address of the neighbor, check the reachability of hosts and verify the address uniqueness.
- Neighbor advertisement (NA) type (136): In response to a NS message.
- Redirect Message (RM) type (137): Redirect the traffic of a host from one path to another path.

However, nodes in IPv6 can not only use DHCPv6 [24] to obtain the address in a stateful way, but also use NDP to realize stateless address automatic configuration. In the stateless address automatic configuration, hosts generate a global unicast address by receiving the RA message sent by routers on the link (subnet prefix) and combining the interface ID (IID). IPv6 adopts NDP, which solves the transmission security problems such as broadcast storm and ARP spoofing [25] caused by ARP adopted in IPv4.

Moreover, the existing IP layer encryption authentication mechanism such as IPSec and Security Neighbor discovery protocol (SeND) [26] can protect the NDP and ensure the security of transmission.

2.4 IPSec Support in IPv6

Internet Engineering Task Force (IETF) issued the IPSec in November 1998 [27], which is a group of secure communication protocol family based on network layer and applied cryptography. IPSec is optional in IPv4 but must be supported in IPv6. Therefore, IPv6 network effectively improves the safety performance. The design goal of IPSec is to provide flexible security services for network layer traffic in IPv4 and IPv6 environments. IPSec provides services for data integrity, data confidentiality and data source reliability. Figure 3 shows the message of normal network layer and the message with IPSec transmission mode. When the IPSec transmission mode is enabled, Authentication Headers (AH) [28] or Encapsulating Security Payload (ESP) [29] is insert between the IP header and Transport datagrams to protect the message.

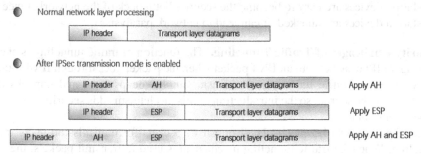

Fig. 3. Messages in normal network and IPSec transmission mode.

IPSec architecture is mainly composed of AH, ESP and Internet Key Exchange (IKE) [30]. AH is a message header verification protocol, which mainly provides the functions of data source verification, data integrity verification and message replay prevention. But AH cannot provide confidentiality because it cannot encrypt the content carried by packets. ESP is an encapsulated payload protocol. In addition to providing all the functions of ah protocol, it can also provide the encryption function of IP messages. AH and ESP can be used alone or nested. IKE protocol is used to automatically negotiate the cryptographic algorithms used by AH and ESP. In general, thanks to IPSec supported in IPv6 network, the security ability effectively improves. IPSec guarantees the integrity and confidentiality of data in IPv6 network.

3 Security Threats in IPv6 Network

Although new features of IPv6 improve network security, they also have limitations and weaknesses [31]. There are mainly two types of threat in IPv6. One threat is in IPv4 and IPv6 coexisting networks, the other is in IPv6 only networks. At present, almost all networks cannot turn off their IPv4 functionality although the IPv6 is being widely deployed. As a result, IPv6 networks will run in parallel with IPv4 based networks, which may last for a long time. "Dual stack", "traffic tunneling" and "translation" are three mechanism used for the transition from IPv4 to IPv6. Moreover, many new features and protocols have been introduced in IPv6 only networks, which may cause security challenges.

3.1 Security Challenges in IPv4/IPv6 Transition Networks

Security Challenges of the Transition Mechanism. First mechanism is called translation mechanism (protocol translation). This mechanism uses a protocol and address translation gateway to convert IPv4 packets to IPv6 packets or convert IPv6 packets to IPv4 packets. However, translation mechanism has its own disadvantages, which significantly slow down packet flow and do not allow the network to take advantage of the specific functions of any protocol. Translation mechanism can also cause serious security challenges when the network is attacked. Translation devices are the key equipment in the whole network when used as IPv6 and IPv4 interconnection nodes. As a result, translation devices are easy to become the security bottleneck of the network. Once the translation devices are attacked, it can lead to network paralysis.

Security Challenges of Traffic Tunneling. The function of traffic tunneling is encapsulating an IPv6 packet into an IPv4 packet when the packet goes through IPv4 routers, and vice versa. Traffic tunneling mechanism simply encapsulates and unpacks data packets from the source, so the introduction of this mechanism adds security risks to the network environment.

IPv6 packets can be encapsulated into IPv4 packets for transmission using traffic tunneling. When the traffic tunneling mechanism is used to transmit packets, the relationship between IPv4 and IPv6 addresses is not checked. Moreover, the IPv4 network cannot verify the authenticity of the source address due to the use of NAT mechanism. As a result, attackers can forge tunnel packets and inject them into the destination network resulting in network security challenges.

The traffic tunneling does not check the contents of the packets. As a result, attackers can encapsulate attack packets through traffic tunneling. For instance, if network managers deploy an IPv6-unaware firewall at an endpoint, firewall rules will allow IPv4 packets to pass without checking encapsulated IPv6 packets. However, the malicious packets can also be encapsulated in IPv4 traffic and cause the security challenges.

Security Challenges of Dual Stack. During the transition period, IPv4 and IPv6 logical channels are running simultaneously in the dual stack deployed network. But dual stack mechanism increases the exposure of equipment, which also means that protective equipment needs to be configured with dual stack strategy at the same time, resulting in more complex policy management and more security risks.

Moreover, in the IPv4 network, some operation systems start the IPv6 automatic address configuration function by default, so that there are hidden IPv6 channels in the IPv4 network. However, IPv6 channel is not configured with protection mechanism, and attackers can use IPv6 channel to attack.

3.2 Security Challenges in IPv6-Only Networks

The new features of IPv6 bring security mechanism, but also increase the security challenges. New fields introduced in IPv6 packets structure (such as flow label, routing header, etc.) and new protocols may have vulnerabilities and attackers can use these vulnerabilities to launch sniffing attacks, dos attacks.

Host Auto Configuration Related Attacks. Compared with IPv4, nodes in IPv6 networks can automatically generate the address of each network interface using NDP. As a result, network administrators do not have to manually configure addresses for hosts or maintain DHCPv6 servers. However, when the nodes use NDP to generate the address, it can cause malicious attacks by attackers.

In IPv6 networks, nodes obtain the network prefix from the routers located in the network segment after receiving the RA packets. And the nodes generate interface ID (IID) using media access control (MAC) address. Then nodes combine two pieces of IP address. Before the IP can be used, the nodes need to use duplicate address detection (DAD) to check if the address is unique. In DAD, nodes send NS packets containing the tentative IP address in order to get the response from the nodes which have generated the same IP address. If there is no reply, the nodes consider the generated IP to be unique and use it.

However, the generation mechanism of IID is based on the MAC address of the node, which can lead to privacy related attacks. Extended Unique Identifier (EUI-64) is the standard used in the generation of IID which is generated by the concatenation of an Organizationally Unique Identifier (OUI) with the Extension Identifier assigned by the hardware manufacturer. If both the OUI and the extension identifier are 24 bits, a hexadecimal value 0xFFEE will be inserted between the two values. Then the leftmost bits 7 and 8 of EUI are set to 1 in order to generate the IID. When a node joins a new network, its MAC address is constant. This IID generation mechanism makes it vulnerable to privacy related attacks. As a result, attackers can track the location of a node based on its IP address. Moreover, attackers can track the node in multiple networks and have enough time to collect the confidential information of the node.

Further, it can cause dos attacks during the period of DAD. If the node receives a NA packet meaning that the generated IP has been used, it needs to generate the interface ID again which may last a long time. As a result, attackers in the same network can send NA packets to the source node informing that the address is being used, although the IP address of attackers is different from the generated IP address in NS packets. Then the node needs to generate the interface ID again, and repeats the DAD process, but the generated address cannot be checked as the unique address due to the NA packets from attackers. Then the nodes continue to generate address automatically which results in resource consumption. In the end, the node gives up without configuring its address.

In IPv6 network, NDP is used to replace ARP function used in IPv4 networks. However, it can cause MiTM attacks. Different from IPv4, nodes obtain the MAC address of other nodes in IPv6 network through NDP (NS packets and NA packets). When a node A needs to obtain the MAC address of another node B in the same network, it sends NS packets to the all-nodes multicast address. Only node B send a NA packet containing its MAC address to node A. But attackers on the same link can also get NS packet, and send NA packets containing false MAC address to node A. Therefore, both A and B are connected to this attack node, and the traffic flow between A and B must be passed through the attackers. Attackers peek at the packets from node A and forward the modified packets to launch MiTM attacks.

Attackers can also implant bogus router to prevent the nodes in IPv6 from accessing the desired network. As mentioned earlier, nodes in IPv6 network can use NDP to discover the prefix information. However, nodes do not validate RA packets from the routers. If a malicious node impersonates a network default gateway, attackers can advertise RA packets containing fake address prefix. As a result, nodes in this subnet update their address prefix after receiving RA packets. Eventually, attackers can reroute legitimate traffic and nodes cannot access the desired network.

Routing Headers Related Attacks. IPv6 source route can specify the intermediate node to be accessed on the way to the destination node. Attackers can generate specific packets with routing options that specify the same intermediate nodes, then there will be a large amount of traffic on the same link, resulting in network paralysis. Further, if the intermediate nodes accept these headers and follow the routing instructions, the designated routers may receive toxic packets.

Multicast-Based Attacks. Compared with IPv4 networks, IPv6 networks cancel the broadcast mechanism and makes extensive use of multicast mechanism. Attackers constantly send packets to the multicast group address notifying members of the group to leave, resulting in DoS attacks. In addition, because the IPv6 network configures standard multicast addresses for key devices, attackers can modify the messages pointing to these addresses on the network and intercept the packets sent by the target node to these key devices.

4 Security Mechanisms in IPv6 Networks

In order to deal with the possible security threats in IPv6 network and improve its security and stability, researchers have taken corresponding measures against different security threats, and gradually improved these measures with the development of the IPv6 networks.

4.1 Algorithms for Protecting User Privacy

The generation method based on MAC address is vulnerable to privacy related attacks. In order to prevent privacy related problems, researchers have made many attempts.

According to RFC 4941 [32], IID has two new generation methods, one of which makes use of available stable storage. First, nodes select the last IID from the history of stable storage. If the history is empty or no stable storage is available, nodes selects a random value. Then the retrieved IID or random value is concatenated with the EUI generated as explained in RFC 4941. Then nodes perform MD5 algorithm on the resulting value and take the leftmost 64 bits in the MD5 summary. Then nodes compare the data with the IIDs in stable storage. If no matches are found, the data will be used as the IID. Otherwise, nodes repeat the above steps. But this mechanism also has defects. If the address of nodes in the network does not reach the maximum lifetime, it will keep using this IID without generating a new IID. Moreover, this mechanism has high requirements for hardware, which a stable storage area is required.

Then researchers tried to generate IID using Cryptographically Generated Address (CGA) [33], which is an important part of Secure-Neighbor Discovery (SeND). CGA makes use of one way hashing to generate IID which is not based on the MAC address. First, nodes use CGA to generate a random number called modifier. Then the modifier is connected with the real subnet prefix, the public key, and the collision count. Then nodes use the public key to implement SHA1 algorithm on the connected data and take the leftmost 64 bits of SHA1 summary and set the seventh bit and the eighth bit to 1. Before generating IID, nodes need to connect the modifier with other parameters for a hash operation to ensure its security in dealing with brute force cracking. Therefore, the drawback of CGA is the huge calculation. It is unrealistic to deploy this strategy in the future IPv6 network. Researchers proposed some other strategies, but these strategies either have too much computational overhead or lack the ability to protect privacy.

Rafiee et al. proposed a new strategy [34]. This strategy first generates a 16 bytes random number called modifier. Then the modifier is connected with router prefix and the timestamp of current time. Then the strategy hashes the generated random number using SHA2 algorithm to generate a summary and take the left 64 bits of the summary as the IID. The IID generation method is shown in Fig. 4. Moreover, the lifetime of IID is related to application layer which ensures the normal connection of the network layer during the operation of the upper application. If the current application using the existing address is active, nodes can still use the expired IID although maximum lifetime of that address has been reached.

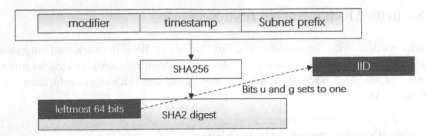

Fig. 4. Random generation Of IID.

As a result, this strategy for generating IID is not only highly randomized, but also ensures the network layer connection in order to support the application layer life cycle. This mechanism is suitable for large-scale deployment in the future IPv6 network.

4.2 Algorithms for Securing the DAD Process

DAD is used to judge the uniqueness of the newly generated address in current IPv6 network. DAD process is based on NDP utilizing NS and NA messages. Nodes generate the IID called temporary IP address. The temporary IP address needs to go through the DAD process. Only after the DAD process, the temporary address can be connected with the subnet prefix and become the unicast address of the node. During the DAD process, the node multicasts NS packets containing temporary IP to solicit-node multicast address (SNMA). All nodes joining in the same SNMA will receive the NS packet. If a node has the same temporary IP as that in NS packet, it will reply NA packets to the source node. Other nodes discard the NS packet. Moreover, If the source node does not receive the NA message after three seconds, it will consider IID to be unique and connect it with the subnet prefix to configure its unicast address.

However, DAD process is vulnerable to Dos attacks. Attackers joining in the same SNMA can send NA packets to the source host as a response, although its IID is different from that in NS messages. Then the source node needs to generate temporary again and repeat the DAD process. After three attempts, the node will stop generating IID and gives up address configuration due to the failure of DAD process. Figure 5 shows a Dos attacks during DAD process in IPv6 local-link network. The source node sends NS packets containing temporary IP to SNMA, and all nodes in local-link network will receive the NS packet and check it. If the temporary IP of Host A, B, C does not match with that in NS packet, they will discard it. However, attacker in the local-link network also received the NS packet, it will send NA packets in response to NS packets without checking the temporary IP in the NS packet. Then the source node receives the NA packet and generates temporary again and repeat the DAD process. In the end, the source node initialization failed.

In order to protect DAD process, researchers have proposed different mechanisms. SeND is proposed to ensure the safety of NDP packets which contains new security options such as CGA, RSA and time stamp. But previous studies showed the limit of SeND for protecting NDP packets. First, CGA cannot identify the characteristics of a legitimate node. Therefore, attackers can abuse the target nodes by modifying CGA

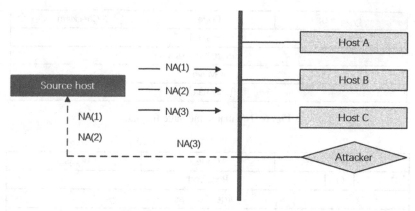

Fig. 5. Dos attack on DAD process.

parameters. Moreover, the use of SeND increases the process overhead resulting in a long processing time. As a result, SeND is not suitable for large-scale deployment in IPv6 link-local network.

Then, researchers proposed Trust-Neighbor Discovery (Trust-ND) [35] to protect DAD process. Trust-ND uses a new security option called Trust-Option to extend the NDP header in order to ensure each packet to contain NS and NA messages. Trust-ND is based on SHA-1 hash algorithm to protect NDP with less complexity. But SHA-1 algorithm is vulnerable to hash collision attacks [36, 37]. Attackers can carefully construct packets to create hash collision attacks. Therefore, Trust-ND is vulnerable to collision attacks, resulting in Dos attacks during DAD process.

In 2016, Song and Ji [38] proposed a new security mechanism called Duplicate Address Detection–Hash (DAD-h) to protect DAD process. DAD-h is based on MD5 hash algorithm which is defined in RFC1321 [39]. DAD-h mechanism uses MD5 algorithm to hide IID during DAD process in order to prevent attackers to identify the IID to be used by the node. However, MD5 in IPv6 networks requires higher delay costs which is vulnerable to Dos attacks. Furthermore, MD5 is vulnerable to hash collision attacks [40]. As a result, DAD-h mechanism is not recommended for protecting DAD process.

Then Ahmed K. et al. proposed a mechanism called DAD-match [41]. The main idea of DAD-match mechanism is protecting IID by hash algorithm during transmission. DAD-match is based on SHA3 algorithm which uses a quick sponge construct to generate hash values. Thanks to the fast hash process and availability, SHA3 hash function is considered as the most suitable algorithm for this technology. DAD-match redesigns NS and NA messages which introduce DAD-match option to preserve the hash value of the target address. Figures 6 and 7 illustrate the NS match and NA match message formats respectively.

The workflow of DAD-match mechanism is that nodes generate IID using the privacy extension method, hash the first 40 bits of the IID and insert the hash value into the DAD-match option. Then the node multicasts NS packets to the SNMA based on the last 24 bits of IID. Then the receiving nodes check the DAD-match option of NS packets, and match the hash value generated by the first 40 bits of the IID. If the hash value is equal to that in

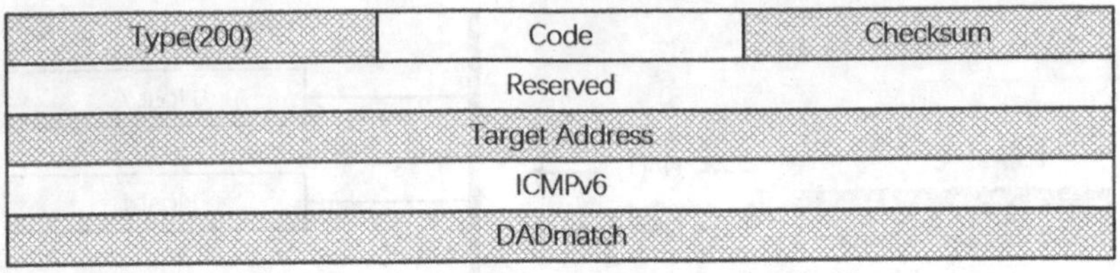

Type(200)	Code	Checksum
Reserved		
Target Address		
ICMPv6		
DADmatch		

Fig. 6. NS-match message format.

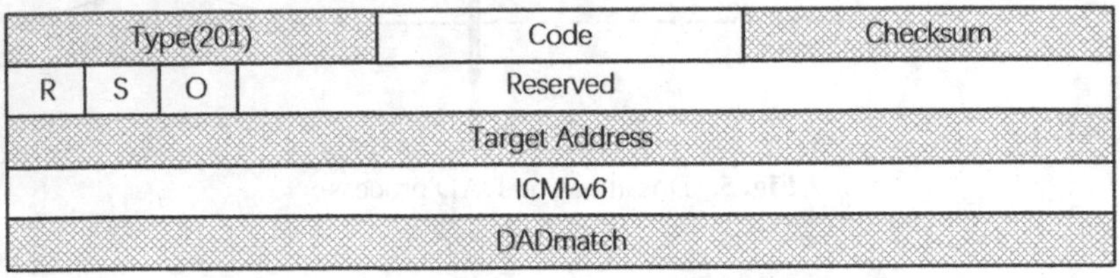

Type(201)			Code	Checksum
R	S	O	Reserved	
Target Address				
ICMPv6				
DADmatch				

Fig. 7. NA-match message format.

DAD-match option, the receiving node will hash the IID and insert it into DAD-match option in the NA packet. Then NA packets will be sent to the SNMA as a response to the NS packet. Otherwise, receiving nodes discard the NS packet. The source node receives the NA packet and match the hash value generated by the 64 bits of the IID. If the hash value is equal to that in DAD-match option which means that the generated IID is not unique, the source node will generate an IID again and repeat DAD process. By contrast, if a match is not detected or there are no NA packets received within 3 s, the source node will consider IID as unique and connect it with subnet prefix to generate the unicast address. DAD-match mechanism hides the IID during the DAD process which prevent malicious nodes from launching Dos attacks. As a result, DAD-match mechanism can effectively protect the DAD process.

4.3 Attack Detection for NDP

In IPv6 networks, NDP can be used to find MAC address which replaces the function of ARP in IPv4 networks. ARP is stateless and many attacks like request spoofing, response spoofing, MiTM, Dos attacks etc. are incident. NDP is also stateless and suffers from attacks which are similar to ARP. There are various attack detections available for ARP attacks, but not implemented for NDP. As a result, researchers proposed an active detection mechanism for NDP related attacks.

As mentioned earlier, NDP is stateless and considers that all nodes joining the same link are legal. Therefore, it does not authenticate the messages by default which can cause neighbor solicitation spoofing, neighbor advertisement spoofing neighbor unreachability detection attacks etc. As mentioned in Sect. 3.2, IPv6 uses NDP to obtain MAC address of other nodes joining in the same SNMA. The IP-MAC pairing information from NS and NA messages is not verified. As a result, attackers can disguise as legitimate nodes to launch neighbor solicitation spoofing and neighbor advertisement spoofing.

Researchers has proposed some mechanisms to detect NS/NA spoofing. IPSec AH can be used to protect NS/NA messages and verify the accuracy of NS/NA messages. SA can only be created through IKE, which requires an effective IP stack. But IP stack can cause a bootstrapping problem. As a result, SA can only be configured by manually which is not suitable for deployment in large-scale IPv6 networks. Then, researchers proposed SeND to detect NA/NS spoofing, but key management in a LAN is cumbersome for a medium scale organization. Researchers also proposed to use CGA, whose overhead associated can cause Dos attacks.

Then, Barbhuiya et al. proposed an active attack detection mechanism called Intrusion Detection System (IDS) for neighbor solicitation spoofing and neighbor advertisement spoofing. Network managers can install the IDS in just one system in the IPv6 network, without requiring changes in the standard NDP. Moreover, the IDS can detect MiTM and Dos attacks generated by NA/NS spoofing. IDS is a trusted machine with a static IP-MAC binding, which has two network interfaces with different functions. One is responsible for collecting network data in the LAN through port mirroring, the other is used to handle NS/NA probe requests/replies. IDS mechanism uses an active verification mechanism to ensure the authenticity of IP-MAC pairing.

IDS mechanism uses the first interface to connect with the switch through port mirroring in order to intercept all traffic while using the second interface to send and receive probe packets in the network. When IDS intercepts a NA packet from the switch, it will check the authenticity of IP-MAC pair in Authenticated bindings table (AUTH) in which IP-MAC bindings have been found to be authentic by the verification mechanism of IDS. If a match is found, which means that IP-MAC pair has been already recorded in the Authenticated bindings table, the IP-MAC pair will be verified to be genuine. If the MAC address does not match, which means that the NA packets is a spoofed packet, the IDS will record the details of this spoofing message in the log table. If the IP does not find any match in AUTH, which means the IP address in the NA packet has never been verified by IDS, IDS will send out probe packets to verify the genuineness of the packet through the second interface.

An example to explain neighbor advertisement verification mechanism for normal and spoofing packets in the network is shown in Fig. 8. The network has 6 hosts called A, B, C, D, E, F. Node F is a router and node E is a monitor machine running IDS. The first interface of IDS is connected to switch through port mirroring while the second interface is responsible for sending and receiving probe packets. Node D is the attacker. If node A responds a NA packet 1 to node B. Node E will intercept the NA packet and match the IP-MAC pair in AUTH. No matches are found in AUTH, so that node E will send a NS packet 2 to verify the authenticity of source MAC address. If node E receives only one NA packet 3 and the IP-MAC pair in the packet is the same as the packet 1, then packet 1 will be considered as genuine and the AUTH table will be updated with the addition of IP-MAC pair of node A. If attacker D sends a NA packet 4 containing the IP address of node C and the MAC address of D, node E will intercept it and match the IP (C)-MAC (D) pair in AUTH table. No matches are found in AUTH, so that node E will send a NS packet 5 to verify the authenticity of source MAC address. Then node C will reply a NA packet containing IP(C)-MAC(C) pair. However, attacker will also respond with a NA packet containing IP(C)-MAC(D) pair in response to NS packet in order to make its original deceptive advertising package appear genuine. As a result, node E receives two NA packets with different MAC addresses of the same IP (C), so that the IDE considers there is an attempt of spoofing against IP of C and record the details of this spoofing message in the log table.

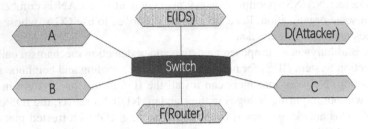

Fig. 8. Topology of IPv6 LAN

IDS is an active probing mechanism without any change in NDP. This mechanism can also detect MiTM and Dos attacks generated by NA/NS spoofing. Moreover, IDS is an approach based on software without requiring any additional hardware which makes it easy to deploy IDS on a large scale in IPv6 networks.

5 Conclusion

In this paper, we described the security characteristics of IPv6 protocol. Huge address space improves security which makes IPv6 networks overcome the dependence on NAT mechanism. More compact header structure reduces fragment attack and improves network performance. SeND and IPSec can effectively protect IPv6 network. Then we introduced two types of security threat in IPv6 networks. One security threat exists in IPv4 and IPv6 coexisting networks, the other security threat exists in only IPv6 networks. Next, we introduced some mechanisms for different security threats in IPv6 network. In the future, researchers should find solutions to the security problems in the network where IPv4 and IPv6 coexist.

References

1. Deering, S., Hinden, R.: Internet protocol, version 6 (ipv6) specification. RFC 1883 (Proposed Standard) (1995)
2. Aura, T.: Neighbor discovery for IP version 6 (ipv6). RFC2461, Internet Engineering Task Force (1998)
3. APNIC. Measuring IPv6 (2020). https://labs.apnic.net/?p=1335
4. Carlos, E., Caicedo, J., Joshi, B.D.: IPv6 security challenges. Computer **42**, 36–42 (2009)
5. Hosnieh, R., Christoph, M.: Privacy and security in ipv6 networks: challenges and possible solutions. In: SIN (2013)
6. Praptodiyono, S., et al.: Mobile IPv6 vertical handover specifications, threats, and mitigation methods: a survey. Secur. Commun. Netw. **2020**, 5429630 (2020)

7. Praptodiyono, S., et al.: Improving the security of mobile IPV6 signalling using KECCAK/SHA-3. J. Eng. Sci. Technol. **16**(3), 2312–2325 (2021)
8. Ubiedo, L., et al.: Current State of IPv6 Security in IoT. arXiv:2105.02710 (2021)
9. Liu, R., et al.: Addressless: enhancing IoT server security using IPv6. IEEE Access **8**, 90294–90315 (2020)
10. Li, X.: Fast IPv6 network periphery discovery and security implications. In: 51st Annual IEEE/IFIP International Conference on Dependable Systems and Networks (DSN) (2021)
11. Al-Azzawi, A., Lencse, G.: Towards the identification of the possible security issues of the 464xlat ipv6 transition technology. In: 2020 43rd International Conference on Telecommunications and Signal Processing (2020)
12. Narten, T., Nordmark, E., Simpson, W.: Security features in IPv6. Whitepaper, SANS Institute (2002)
13. Narten, W.A.S.T., Nordmark, E., Soliman, H.: Neighbor discovery for IP version 6 (IPv6). RFC 4861 (2007)
14. Tayal, P.: IPV6 SLAAC related security issues and removal of those security issues. Int. J. Eng. Comput. Sci. **3**(9), 4 (2014)
15. Ferdous, A.B., Santosh, B., Sukumar, N.: Detection of neighbor solicitation and advertisement spoofing in ipv6 neighbor discovery protocol. In: SIN (2011)
16. Rehman, S.U., Manickam, S.: Improved mechanism to prevent denial of service attack in IPv6 duplicate address detection process. Int. J. Adv. Comput. Sci. Appl **8**(2), 63–70 (2017)
17. Trabelsi, Z., Shuaib, K.: Man in the middle intrusion detection. In: Globecom, pp. 1–6 (2006)
18. Barbhuiya, F.A., Biswas, S., Nandi, S.: Detection of neighbor solicitation and advertisement spoofing in IPv6 neighbor discovery protocol. In: Proceedings of the 4th International Conference on Security of Information and Networks, SIN, pp. 111–118 (2011)
19. Wang, K.: A web-based honeypot in IPv6 to enhance security. Information **11**(9), 440 (2020)
20. Audet, F., Jennings, C.: Network address translation (NAT) behavioral requirements for unicast UDP. IETF (2007)
21. Yang, T., Cai, Z., Zhou, T.: 6Forest: an ensemble learning-based approach to target generation for internet-wide IPv6 scanning. In: Proceedings of INFOCOM (2022)
22. Hou, B.: 6Hit: a reinforcement learning-based approach to target generation for internet- wide IPv6 scanning. In: IEEE INFOCOM 2021-IEEE Conference on Computer Communications (2021)
23. Yang, T., Hou, B., Cai, Z., Wu, K., Zhou, T., Wang, C.: 6Graph: a graph-theoretic approach to address pattern mining for Internet-wide IPv6 scanning. Comput. Netw. (2021). https://doi.org/10.1016/j.comnet.2021.108666
24. Droms, R., Bound, J., Volz, B., Lemon, T., Perkins, C., Carney, M.: Dynamic host configuration protocol for IPv6 (DHCPv6). IETF (2003)
25. Abad, C.L., Bonilla, R.I.: An analysis on the schemes for detecting and preventing ARP cache poisoning attacks. In: International Conference on Distributed Computing Systems Workshops, pp. 60–67 (2007)
26. Arkko, E.J., Kempf, J., Zill, B., Nikander, P.: Secure neighbor discovery (SEND). RFC 3971, Internet Engineering Task Force (2005)
27. Deering, S., Hinden, R.: Internet Protocol, version 6 (IPv6) specification. IETF (1998)
28. Kent, S.: IP authentication header. RFC 4302 (2005)
29. Kent, S.: IP encapsulating security payload (ESP). RFC 4303 (2005)
30. Kaufman, C., Hoffman, P., Nir, Y., Eronen, P.: Internet key exchange protocol version 2 (ikev2). RFC5996 (2010)
31. Arkko, J., Nikander, P.: Limitations of IPSec policy mechanisms. In: Christianson, B., Crispo, B., Malcolm, J.A., Roe, M. (eds.) Security Protocols 2003. LNCS, vol. 3364, pp. 241–251. Springer, Heidelberg (2005). https://doi.org/10.1007/11542322_29

32. Narten, T., Draves, R., Krishnan, S.: Privacy extensions for stateless address autoconfiguration in IPv6. IETF (2007)
33. Aura, T.: Cryptographically generated addresses (CGA). RFC3972 (2005)
34. Hosnieh, R., Christoph, M.: Privacy and security in IPv6 networks: challenges and possible solutions. In: SIN (2011)
35. Praptodiyono, S., Hasbullah, I.H., Kadhum, M.M., Wey, C.Y., Murugesan, R.K., Osman, A.: Securing duplicate address detection on IPv6 using distributed trust mechanism. Int. J. Simul. Syst. Sci. Technol. **17**(26) (2016)
36. Andreeva, E., Mennink, B., Preneel, B.: Open problems in hash function security. Des. Codes Crypt. **77**(2–3), 611–631 (2015). https://doi.org/10.1007/s10623-015-0096-0
37. Polk, T., Chen, L., Turner, S., Hoffman, P.: Security considerations for the sha-0 and sha-1 message-digest algorithms (2011)
38. Song, G., Ji, Z.: Novel duplicate address detection with hash function. PLoS ONE **11**(3), 151612 (2016)
39. Rivest, R.: The MD5 message-digest algorithm (1992)
40. Butler, K., Farley, T.R., Mcdaniel, P., Rexford, J.: A survey of BGP security issues and solutions. Proc. IEEE **98**(1), 100–122 (2010)
41. Al-Ani, A.K., Anbar, M., Manickam, S., Al-Ani, A., Leau, Y.B.: Proposed dad-match security technique based on Hash Function to secure duplicate address detection in IPv6 Link-local Network. In: ICIT (2017)

Research on the Detection of Causality for Textual Emotion-Cause Pair Based on BERT

Qian Cao[1,2], Charles Jnr.Asiedu[1], and Xiulan Hao[1,2(✉)]

[1] School of Information Engineering, Huzhou University, Huzhou 313000, China
hxl2221_cn@zjhu.edu.cn
[2] Zhejiang Key Laboratory of Smart Management and Application of Modern Agricultural Resources, Huzhou 313000, China

Abstract. The detection of textual Emotion-Cause Pair causality is very helpful for improving the accuracy of emotion-cause extraction and understanding the causes behind specific events. To solve the polysemy problem of static word vector representation in word2vec, an Emotion-Cause Pair causality discrimination model based on Bidirectional Encoder Representation from Transformers (BERT) is proposed. Firstly, each independent clause in the document is transformed into a word vector sequence by pretraining BERT, and the semantic representation of each independent clause is obtained by pooling. Secondly, the generated independent clause vector is used as the input of Bidirectional Long Short-Term Memory (BiLSTM) or SelfAttention, and then the deep semantic representation of the relevant independent clause context is obtained. Finally, the feature vectors extracted in the previous two stages are subjected to multi-target weighted fusion correction and input to the fully connected layer, and the maximum probability label sequence is calculated by the Softmax function to achieve causality detection. The experimental results show that compared with the baseline model, the Recall value of the proposed method is increased by 9.01%, and the F1 value is increased by 2.71%.

Keywords: Emotion-cause pair · Causality detection · BERT · Bilstm

1 Introduction

With the proliferation of subjective texts, sentiment analysis [1–3] has been studied extensively. In recent years, people have done a lot of research work on emotion classification [4–7]. In January 2020 "COVID-19 outbreak" began fermentation and incurred millions of Weibo posts, further forwarded by tens of millions of WeChat in China. Many provinces have launched major public health emergency response, and the majority of netizens express their concerns for the COVID-19 outbreak. Weibo emotional map shows that the "fear" mood dominates the emotion of netizens, and becomes an important public opinion. The text emotion analysis of netizen posts and the study of emotion causes have great value and practical significance for strengthening the information content governance and purifying the network ecology. At the same time, Emotion Cause

© The Author(s), under exclusive license to Springer Nature Switzerland AG 2022
X. Sun et al. (Eds.): ICAIS 2022, LNCS 13338, pp. 599–613, 2022.
https://doi.org/10.1007/978-3-031-06794-5_48

analysis can constructively guide future works, for example, in public opinion monitoring and government decision-making, it is helpful to better understand the reasons for the formation of public opinions.

Emotion-Cause Extraction (ECE) task was originally defined by Lee et al. [8], to discover the potential word-level causes in emotionally expressive news texts. Early researchers were primarily working to identify linguistic cues related to textual emotional causes and to manually construct relevant rules, then the rules were used to extract the causes of emotional changes [9–11]. However, emotional causes usually appear at the clause level. In order to make up for inadequate expression of emotional reasons at the character level, Gui et al. [12] constructed a new Chinese ECE benchmark corpus and formally defined the task as a binary clause classification task. They use event-based 7-tuple to define a multi-core Support Vector Machine (SVM) algorithm to extract the reason. With the rise of deep learning, many related methods are applied to emotion-cause analysis [13–16].

ECE requires emotional labels, but emotional labeling is time-consuming and laborious, which greatly hinders the application scenario of the tasks. To solve this problem, Xia and Ding [17] designed a challenging new task called Emotion-Cause Pair Extraction (ECPE) based on ECE in 2019, to extract potential emotions and their corresponding reasons in the text at the same time.

Although ECE and ECPE are becoming more and more popular, the two tasks are only for extracting clauses containing causality, and ignore the influence of context clauses in the text on whether the extracted Emotion-Cause Pair have effective causality. Chen et al. [18] elaborated on the importance of context in the problem of causality identification in the analysis of emotional causes, and studied this special causality in the proposed text data set.

Inspired by the excellent performance of the BERT model in many difficult tasks, this paper attempts to introduce the pre-training vector in Chinese BERT into the task of the detection of causality for Emotion-Cause Pair. On this basis, an end-to-end BERT-BiLSTM/SelfAttention model is proposed. The model first obtains the semantic representation of the input sentence through BERT based on transfer learning; then input the sentence vector sequence into BiLSTM or SelfAttention for further semantic coding; finally, it jointly models the front and posterior stages to calculate whether the Emotion-Cause Pair has an effective causal relationship in a specific context by the Softmax function. Compared with the baseline, the proposed method was able to overcome the defect that word2vec cannot capture enough semantic and emotional information and the performance of the model was tested with 10428 pieces of data in the benchmark, achieving satisfactory results.

2   Related Work

Understanding causal relationships between events is an important topic that has been applied in many domains, such as event prediction, risk analysis, or decision support [19]. Recognizing the "causal relationship" between these natural language events remains a challenge and due to natural language flexibility, even if causality is unambiguous, there are a variety of expressions. The model must be able to identify various grammatical structures implying causality.

Earlier approaches focused on manually formulated rules and various cues between events. The measure of event pair "causal potential" was estimated using the distribution information [20], verb pair [21], or utterance relationship marker [22]. For instance, Hashimoto et al. [23] proposed a supervised method for extracting causality that utilize some specific binary semantic relation features, grammatical context features, and association features. In recent years, the recognition of causality has been expressed as a classification problem based on machine learning [24, 25]. For example, de Silva et al. [26] used convolutional neural networks to identify event causality. However, the above methods have three main shortcomings: (1) pay less attention to implicit causality in the text; (2) failure to incorporate document-level structural information into the model; (3) not taking full advantage of external knowledge, which is very useful for detecting causality importance.

Some studies have begun to explore the causality of implicit events. For example, Liang et al. [27] used a multi-level neural network to detect implicit and ambiguous expressions of causality. Gao et al. [28] modeled document-level graph reasoning mechanism for causality recognition. On the other hand, researchers use richer data sets that include temporal relationships [29], event types [30], or coreference relationships [31] to identify causal relationships. However, these methods rely heavily on supervised learning and are limited by data labels. For the above problems in the event causality task, Zuo et al. [32] designed a long-distance supervised data augmentation method based on knowledge enhanced in 2020. The next year, Zuo et al. [33] again designed a learnable data enhancement method based on knowledge base that can generate task-relevant sentences for event causality identification through dual learning.

To summarize, researches prefer traditional methods (such as NB, KNN, etc.) to deep learning to realize text causality detection. In particular, pre-training-based deep learning methods have achieved significant improvements in many text analysis tasks. In our work, BERT is used as a word encoder, followed by BiLSTM or SelfAttention to construct a discriminant model. Compared with the traditional methods and the typical deep learning methods that employ BERT to provide dynamic word vectors, the causal detection effect of this method is significantly improved.

3   The Proposed Detection Algorithm

3.1   Problem Definition

(1)   Document: a document $d = (e_i, C_i, con_i)$, where e_i represents an emotional clause, C_i represents a set of reason clauses, and con_i represents a context clause. They are composed of Chinese characters and punctuation sequences.
(2)   Classification goal: a set of causality (denoted as $Y = \{1, 0\}$), that is, a binary label y that determines whether the input pair (e_i, C_i) has a causal relationship in a specific context con_i.
(3)   Classification model: It is a function f that maps document d to a causal relationship y, that is, $y = f(d)$.

The goal is to construct a discriminant function f, which can predict the causality of the Emotion-Cause Pair of the document d with unknown causality. In the specific implementation, the classification function f will be constructed based on the BERT deep pre-training model.

3.2 Overall Model Architecture

No Multi-Objective Optimization Module. This paper combines three models: BERT, BiLSTM and SelfAttention to build a unified model BERT-BiLSTM/SelfAttention and predict the causal relationship of Emotion-Cause Pair in a specific context. The structure is shown in Fig. 1.

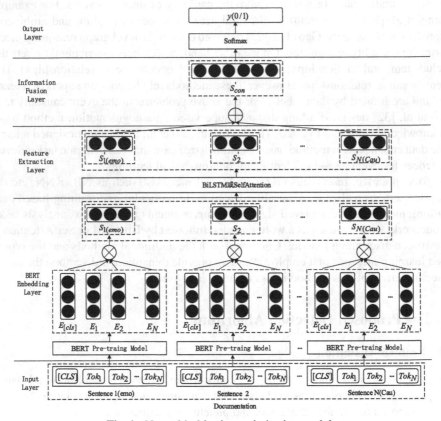

Fig. 1. No multi-objective optimization module.

The model first provides word vectors combined with context information by pre-training BERT, and embeds real semantic information into the model pool to obtain sentence vectors; then uses BiLSTM or SelfAttention mechanism to extract the context-related features of different sentences in the document for deep learning to obtain the final result Semantic expression.

More specifically, this model uses BERT to obtain prior general information to enhance semantic representation, and obtains word level semantic representation in pre-training. At the same time, in order to consider the information of context between document sentences, solve the semantic connection between long-distance contexts between sentences and the problem of gradient disappearance and explosion in the process of causal discrimination of Recurrent Neural Network (RNN) model, the deep learning model BiLSTM or SelfAttention is introduced. Therefore, BERT-BiLSTM/SelfAttention has the ability to distinguish whether the Emotion-Cause Pair in a specific context has an effective causal relationship.

Add Multi-Objective Optimization Module (MOO). Chen et al. [18] proposed a Predictive Aggregation Module (PAM), which divides the causality judgment of Emotion-Cause Pair into two optimization objectives for joint training, namely, the prediction y' before the context clause coding and the prediction y'' after the context clause coding. First, without coding the context clause, PAM directly predicts the causal relationship y' according to the original embedding vector of the input pair (emotion clause $S'_{(emo)}$ and cause clause set $S'_{N(Cau)}$). When $P(y' = 1) > P(y'' = 0)$, that is, the input pair has a causal relationship, according to intuition, it can be considered that the emotion-cause pair is more likely to produce a valid causality in any different context, so the final result should be biased towards predicting y' before the context clause encoding; on the contrary, when $P(y' = 1) < P(y' = 0)$, the final result should give more weight to the prediction y'' after the context clause is encoded. This can be formalized as:

$$P(y) = weight \cdot P(y') + (1 - weight) \cdot P(y'') \tag{1}$$

$$weight = P(y' = 1) \tag{2}$$

As shown in Fig. 2 below, by constructing this multi-objective module, a trade-off can be made between the two components, and the causality of the input pair in a specific context can be better predicted. This trade-off is crucial, because in some cases, the document context clause should cover the background knowledge of the Emotion-Cause Pair, while in other cases the opposite is true.

3.3 BERT Pre-trained Language Model

BERT [34] is a Transformer architecture [35]. In order to better capture word-level and sentence-level information, two training targets are used for joint pre-training on large-scale corpus Wikipedia and Bookcorpus [36]: (1) Masked Language Model, Which helps it learn the context in the sentence; (2) Next Sentence Prediction, from which it can learn the relationship between two sentences. In fact, the core idea of the pre-training BERT is to use the complex structure of the deep learning model and the powerful nonlinear representation learning ability to learn the essential knowledge existing in massive text data, store this knowledge in the form of vectors or parameters, and transfer it into other related fields.

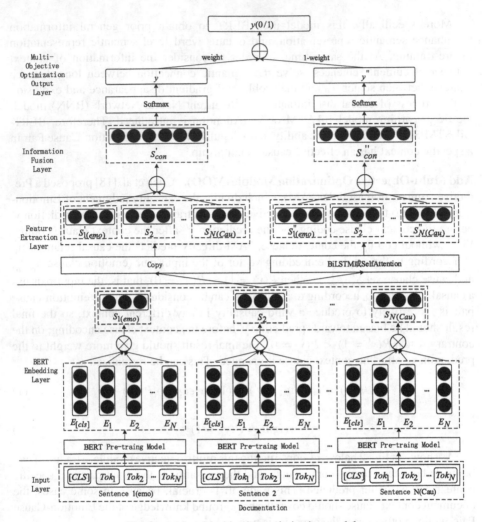

Fig. 2. Add multi-objective optimization module.

BERT decomposes the input sentence into chunks by training the word segmenter on the training corpus [37]. The use of word chunks allows BERT to reduce the vocabulary, and at the same time it can be more robust to the external vocabulary that appears. As shown in Fig. 3, BERT uses three vectors to represent each word block respectively, namely word embedding, position embedding and section embedding. These embeddings are aggregated together, and the output representation is generated by the main body of the model (Transformer coding layer) and provided to the downstream task. The Transformer layer has multiple stacked encoder units, and each encoder unit mainly has two sub-units: Multi-Head SelfAttention and FeedForward network. In addition, there are two special steps in Multi-Head SelfAttention in Tranformer, which are residual connection and normalization. Residual connection refers to summing the output of the shallow layer and the deep layer as the input of the next stage, which can simplify the learning process and solve the problem of network degradation. Normalization refers to the mapping of the input information to the interval [0,1]. By losing some unimportant information, it reduces the difficulty of fitting and the risk of overfitting, thereby accelerating the convergence of the model. Avoid the problem of gradient disappearance due to input data falling in the saturation region of the activation function. Its purpose is to stabilize the data distribution.

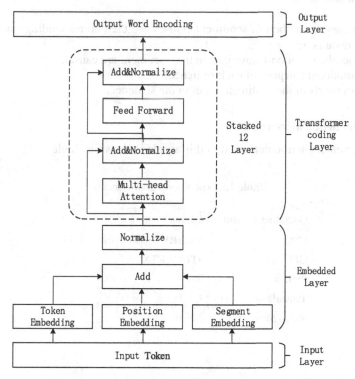

Fig. 3. BERT model.

BERT had more advantages than earlier word2vec. (1) Word vector representation: static to dynamic. BERT uses the context information of words for feature extraction, dynamically adjusts the word vector according to the different context information, and solves the phenomenon that word2vec cannot model polysemy. (2) Semantic information: simple to rich. BERT can learn surface, parase, syntactic and semantic level information from shallow level to high level, which is naturally more reasonable than word2vec.

4 Experiments

4.1 Data Set

The data set used in this experiment is Chen et al. [18] after sorting and merging the data set from the ECPE [17] following the negative sampling procedure [38], it is an open benchmark data set.

The data set has a total of 10428 pieces of data, and each document has the following information annotated:

(1) The sequence numbers of sentiment clauses and their corresponding cause clauses in the document;
(2) Whether the Emotion-Cause Pair in the document are causal;
(3) The emotional category of each sentence;
(4) The keywords of the sentiment label in the sentence.

4.2 Experiment Environment

The experimental environment used in this article is shown in Table 1.

Table 1. Experiment Environment.

Operating System	Centos7
CPU	Intel(R) Xeon(R) Silver 4214
GPU	TITAN RTX
Python	3.6
Tensorflow	1.4.0
Video Memory	24GB

4.3 Evaluation Metrics

The evaluation indicators of the experiment are precision (P), recall (R) and F1-measure (F1) and are defined as:

$$P = \frac{TP}{TP + FP} \tag{3}$$

$$R = \frac{TP}{TP + FN} \tag{4}$$

$$F1 = \frac{2 \cdot P \cdot R}{P + R} \tag{5}$$

In the formula, Precision calculates the probability of the actual positive sample among all the predicted positive samples, Recall calculates the probability of samples predicted to be positive in the actually positive samples, and F1-score is a comprehensive index that fuses Precision and Recall.

4.4 Parameter Settings

The experiment uses Adam as the optimizer, logarithmic loss function, and the model parameters are randomly sampled in uniform distribution U(−0.01, 0.01) during initialization. We randomly divided the training and test set in a ratio of 9:1. The corpus is used to fine-tune the parameters of the BERT, LSTM or SelfAttention model. The hyperparameter selection of the experiment is shown in Table 2.

Table 2. Hyperparameter selection.

Hyperparameter	Quantity	Explanation
learning_rate	4e-6	Learning rate
batch_size	3	Minimum training batch
epoch	30	Number of iterations
l2-norm	1e-6	L2 regularization
max_doc_len	75	Maximum number of sentences per document
max_cau_num	3	Maximum number of reason sentences per document
max_sen_len_bert	60	BERT handles the maximum number of tokens in a single sentence
num_hidden_layers	12	Transformer network layers
hidden_size	768	BERT vectorized dimensions
hidden_dropout_prob	0.1	Probability of BERT hidden layer dropout
vocab_size	21128	Vocabulary size
n_hidden	100	The number of neurons in the hidden layer of the BiLSTM module
num_heads	2	The number of self-attention heads in the SelfAttention module

4.5 Experimental Results and Analysis

Experiment Results. The proposed method is compared with the baseline model [18], and the experimental datas are shown in Table 3. We calculate the precision, recall and F1 score of causality detection, and use F1 as the overall criterion. In order to obtain statistically credible results, a ten-fold cross-validation is performed. To ensure fairness, rerun all baseline methods with the same settings. However, the actual results of the baseline method are slightly different from the original paper, and the values in parentheses are the original paper results of the baseline model.

It can be seen from Table 3:

(1) Among all the baseline methods, the BiLSTM + BiLSTM model achieved the best overall performance with F1 score 69.83%. The performance of the BERT + BiLSTM + MOO model is 2.71% better than the BiLSTM + BiLSTM baseline model, which can initially prove the effectiveness of the proposed method;

(2) In addition to the BERT + BiLSTM model, the experimental results of the other proposed models have an increment 3% in F1 compared with the baseline method, which shows that the BERT character embedding vector can dynamically generate character vectors based on context-related information, learn more hidden knowledge, and accurately understand semantics and alleviate the ambiguity of word2vec;

(3) The performance of the BiLSTM + BiLSTM and BiLSTM + BiLSTM + PAM baseline models is little different. This seems to go against common sense. Intuitively, the baseline model with the PAM auxiliary module should be better than the model without PAM under the same conditions. This phenomenon may result from the bottleneck of the semantic understanding capability of the BiLSTM + BiLSTM model, which makes the improvement brought by the PAM module appear to be minimal, and may even cause the information conflict between the two, resulting in a slight performance degradation;

(4) BiLSTM + BiLSTM is 3.5% higher than BiLSTM + SelfAttention model, BERT + BiLSTM is 2.4% lower than BERT + SelfAttention model, and BiLSTM + BiLSTM is 2.7% higher than BERT + BiLSTM model. From these results, we can infer because BiLSTM, SelfAttention, and BERT have different architectures, and SelfAttention is the core module of BERT, therefore, the semantic representation generated by BiLSTM cannot well integrate with the semantic information generated by SelfAttention or BERT, resulting in information loss and underutilization. However, the semantic representation generated by BERT can be compatible with the semantic information generated by SelfAttention and blend well with each other.

Table 3. Performance comparison of different algorithms.

Model	P	R	F1
Baseline model			
1 BiLSTM + Concatenation	54.08(54.12)	70.91(71.19)	61.25(61.27)
2 BiLSTM + Concatenation + PAM	58.83(60.24)	74.35(75.91)	65.47(67.10)
3 BiLSTM + BiLSTM	**66.94**(66.06)	73.06(74.00)	69.83(69.76)
4 BiLSTM + BiLSTM + PAM	64.31(65.11)	74.75(78.30)	69.12(71.10)
5 BiLSTM + Self-Attention	59.67(57.66)	75.08(77.70)	66.36(66.05)
6 BiLSTM + Self-Attention + PAM	61.26(61.95)	76.93(78.65)	68.20(69.29)
Proposed model			
1 BERT + BiLSTM	60.27	76.16	67.11
2 BERT + BiLSTM + MOO	65.03	**82.07**	**72.54**
3 BERT + SelfAttention	64.40	75.76	69.57
4 BERT + SelfAttention + MOO	64.53	79.72	71.30

Epoch Comparison. We further compares the convergence speed of the model. As shown in Fig. 4, the proposed model obtains good results around epoch = 10, which shows that BERT integrates general language knowledge in advance and can fine-tune and converge in a smaller epoch, and its robustness is good. Considering classification performance and training time complexity, we use epoch = 20 for the next two experiments.

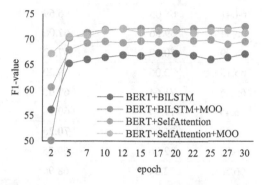

Fig. 4. F1 value of different models with different epochs.

Comparison of BERT Coding Layers with Different Numbers of Transformer Blocks. Ganesh Jawahar et al. [39] showed that BERT captures a rich level of language information, in which the shallow features are in the lower layer, the linguistic information are in the middle layer, and the semantic information are in the higher layer.

It can be seen from Table 4 that the proposed model can reach a higher F1 value when there are 6 to 8 Transformer blocks.

We increase the Transformer block layer by layer to 12 layers, which basically does not bring additional performance improvements, indicating that the task has not changed the capability of BERT to capture semantic features. On the contrary, it only needs to model syntactic information to get good results. Based on this, a graph neural network will be constructed in the follow-up research to model the syntactic relationship between clauses in order to seek better experimental results.

Comparison of Different Sentence Representations in BERT Coding Layer. In order to test whether different sentence vector combinations have a great influence on the prediction results, the sentence vectors obtained by three pooling strategies (CLS, MEAN, and MAX) are evaluated. CLS pooling: the start tag vector in BERT is used as the sentence vector of the whole sentence; MEAN pooling: the word vector in the sentence is averaged by element, which is equivalent to considering the information of each word; MAX pooling: the word in the sentence taking the maximum value for each dimension of the vector is used, equivalent to considering the most significant information, and other irrelevant or unimportant information is ignored.

The experimental datas are shown in Fig. 5. The overall performance is: CLS pooling > MEAN pooling > MAX pooling.

Table 4. Comparison of BERT coding layers with different numbers of Transformer blocks.

Transformer Layers	BERT + BiLSTM	BERT + BiLSTM + MOO	BERT + SelfAttention	BERT + SelfAttention + MOO
1	61.98	64.17	64.49	65.23
2	62.68	67.38	65.53	67.42
3	64.41	68.05	66.69	69.26
4	63.94	69.56	67.06	69.37
5	64.09	70.69	67.82	70.01
6	65.15	72.06	68.20	71.01
7	65.86	71.64	69.02	70.94
8	66.45	71.94	69.78	71.33
9	66.90	71.92	**70.23**	71.31
10	66.02	72.06	69.75	**71.88**
11	66.56	**72.34**	68.96	71.48
12	**67.22**	72.04	69.84	71.82

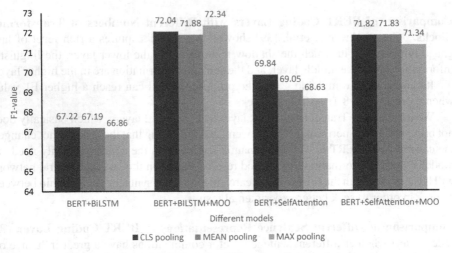

Fig. 5. Model performance analysis under different pooling modes of sentence vectors.

It can be inferred from Fig. 5 that CLS pooling is more suitable than maximum pooling and average pooling, but the difference is not obvious. The possible reason is that BERT needs a larger data set for training to highlight the differences between the three strategies. The small dependence of the task on the semantic level of the sentence vector leads to little difference in the experimental performance brought by different pooling strategies, which just verifies the conclusions drawn in Table 4.

5   Conclusion

This paper improves the baseline model and proposes a causality detection model for text Emotion-Cause Pair. In the experiment, the BERT model was used to replace the commonly used word2vec baseline model. The BERT pre-training language model uses a bidirectional Transformer structure to dynamically generate the contextual semantic representation of characters, which can represent the character level, syntactic structure and semantics of the context better than traditional word embedding vectors. The characteristics of information, and the modeling of polysemous words are realized through pre-training and fine-tuning. The proposed method improves the performance of text Emotion-Cause Pair for causality detection.

However, compared with the baseline model, the proposed model has high time and space complexity. In the future, further improvements to the model will be considered: (1) Interaction modeling of structural information between document sentences, such as using graph attention network that fuses syntactic information to build a new causality discrimination model for Emotion-Cause Pair; (2) Data augmentation is performed on the corpus to further improve causal detection. (3) Compare the impact of the embedding of different pre-training word vectors on the causality detection; (4) Add a lot of external knowledge to the model to improve performance.

Acknowledgement. This research was supported by General Project of Graduate Research and Innovation of Huzhou University (2020KYCX24).

References

1. Zhang, L., Wang, S., Liu, B.: Deep learning for sentiment analysis: a survey. Wiley Interdiscipl. Rev. Data Min. Knowl. Discov. **8**(4), 1253 (2018)
2. Guo, L.: Social network rumor recognition based on enhanced naive bayes. J. NewMedia **3**(3), 99–107 (2021)
3. Alsukayti, I., Singh, A.: Cross intelligence evaluation for effective emotional intelligence estimation. Comput. Mater. Continua **70**(2), 2489–2505 (2022)
4. Singla, C., Al-Wesabi, F.N., Pathania, Y.S., Alfurhood, B.S., M. A.: An optimized deep learning model for emotion classification in tweets. Comput. Mater. Continua **70**(3), 6365–6380 (2022)
5. Abas, A.R., Elhenawy, I., Zidan, M., Othman, M.: Bert-cnn: a deep learning model for detecting emotions from text. Comput. Mater. Continua **71**(2), 2943–2961 (2022)
6. Van, L.T., Nguyen, Q.H., Dao, T.: Emotion recognition with capsule neural network. Comput. Syst. Sci. Eng. **41**(3), 1083–1098 (2022)
7. Howard, J., Ruder, S.: Universal language model fine-tuning for text classification. In: Proceedings of the 56th Annual Meeting of the Association for Computational Linguistics, vol. 1 (2018). https://doi.org/10.18653/v1/P18-1031
8. Lee, S.Y.M., Chen, Y., Huang, C.R.: A text-driven rule-based system for emotion cause detection. In: Proceedings of the NAACL HLT 2010 Workshop on Computational Approaches to Analysis and Generation of Emotion in Text, pp. 45–53 (2010)
9. Neviarouskaya, A., Aono, M.: Extracting causes of emotions from text. In: Proceedings of the Sixth International Joint Conference on Natural Language Processing, pp. 932–936 (2013)

10. Gui, L., Yuan, L., Xu, R.: Emotion cause detection with linguistic construction in Chinese weibo text. In: CCF International Conference on Natural Language Processing and Chinese Computing, pp. 457–464 (2014)
11. Li, W., Xu, H.: Text-based emotion classification using emotion cause extraction. Expert Syst. Appl. **41**(4), 1742–1749 (2014)
12. Gui, L., Xu, R., Wu, D.: Event-driven emotion cause extraction with corpus construction. M. Social Media Content Analysis: Natural Language Processing and Beyond, pp. 145–160 (2018)
13. Gui, L., Hu, J., He, Y.: A question answering approach for emotion cause extraction. In: Proceedings of the 2017 Conference on Empirical Methods in Natural Language Processing (2018)
14. Xia, R., Zhang, M., Ding, Z.: RTHN: a rnn-transformer hierarchical network for emotion cause extraction. In: Eighth International Joint Conference on Artificial Intelligence (2019). https://doi.org/10.24963/ijcai.2019/734
15. Yu, X., Rong, W., Zhang, Z.: Multiple level hierarchical network-based clause selection for emotion cause extraction. J. IEEE Access **7**, 9071–9079 (2019)
16. Hu, G., Lu, G., Zhao, Y.: FSS-GCN: a graph convolutional networks with fusion of semantic and structure for emotion cause analysis. Knowl.-Based Syst. **212**(1), 106584 (2021)
17. Xia, R., Ding, Z.: Emotion-cause pair extraction: a new task to emotion analysis in texts. In: Proceedings of the 57th Annual Meeting of the Association for Computational Linguistics (2019). https://doi.org/10.18653/v1/P19-1096
18. Chen, X., Li, Q., Wang, J.: Conditional causal relationships between emotions and causes in texts. C. In: Proceedings of the 2020 Conference on Empirical Methods in Natural Language Processing (EMNLP), pp. 3111–3121 (2020)
19. Ackerman, E.J.M.: Extracting a causal network of news topics. In: OTM Confederated International Conferences, pp. 33–42 (2012). https://doi.org/10.1007/978-3-642-33618-8_5
20. Beamer, B., Girju, R.: Using a bigram event model to predict causal potential. In: Gelbukh, A. (ed.) CICLing 2009. LNCS, vol. 5449, pp. 430–441. Springer, Heidelberg (2009). https://doi.org/10.1007/978-3-642-00382-0_35
21. Riaz, M., Girju, R.: Toward a better understanding of causality between verbal events: extraction and analysis of the causal power of verb-verb associations. In: Proceedings of the SIGDIAL 2013 Conference, pp. 21–30 (2013)
22. Do, Q., Chan, Y.S., Roth, D.: Minimally supervised event causality identification. In: Proceedings of the 2011 Conference on Empirical Methods in Natural Language Processing, pp. 294–303 (2011)
23. Hashimoto, C., Torisawa, K., Kloetzer, J.: Toward future scenario generation: Extracting event causality exploiting semantic relation, context, and association features. In: Proceedings of the 52nd Annual Meeting of the Association for Computational Linguistics, vol. 1, pp. 987–997 (2014)
24. Hu, Z., Rahimtoroghi, E., Walker, M.: Inference of fine-grained event causality from blogs and films. In: Proceedings of the Events and Stories in the News Workshop (2017). https://doi.org/10.18653/v1/W17-2708
25. Hu, Z., Walker, M.: Inferring narrative causality between event pairs in films. In: Proceedings of the 18th Annual SIGdial Meeting on Discourse and Dialogue (2017). https://doi.org/10.18653/v1/W17-5540
26. Silva, T.N., Zhibo, X., Rui, Z.: Causal relation identification using convolutional neural networks and knowledge based features. Int. J. Comput. Syst. Eng. **11**(6), 696–701 (2017)
27. Liang, S., Zuo, W., Shi, Z., et al.: A multi-level neural network for implicit causality detection in web texts. arXiv:1908.07822 (2019)

28. Gao, L., Choubey, P.K., Huang, R.: Modeling document-level causal structures for event causal relation identification. In: Proceedings of the 2019 Conference of the North American Chapter of the Association for Computational Linguistics: Human Language Technologies, pp. 1808–1817 (2019)
29. Mostafazadeh, N., Grealish, A., Chambers, N.: CaTeRS: causal and temporal relation scheme for semantic annotation of event structures. In: Proceedings of the Fourth Workshop on Events, pp. 51–61 (2016)
30. Caselli, T., Vossen, P.: The event storyline corpus: a new benchmark for causal and temporal relation extraction. In: Proceedings of the Events and Stories in the News Workshop, pp. 77–86 (2017)
31. Ning, Q., Wu, H., Roth, D.: A multi-axis annotation scheme for event temporal relations. In: Proceedings of the 56th Annual Meeting of the Association for Computational Linguistics, pp. 1318–1328 (2018)
32. Zuo, X., Chen, Y., Liu, K.: KnowDis: knowledge enhanced data augmentation for event causality detection via distant supervision. In: Proceedings of the 28th International Conference on Computational Linguistics, pp. 1544–1550 (2020)
33. Zuo, X., Cao, P., Chen, Y.: LearnDA: Learnable knowledge-guided data augmentation for event causality identification. In: Proceedings of the 59th Annual Meeting of the Association for Computational Linguistics and the 11th International Joint Conference on Natural Language Processing, pp. 3558–3571 (2021)
34. Devlin, J., Chang, M.W., Lee, K.: Bert: pre-training of deep bidirectional transformers for language understanding. In: Proceedings of the 2019 Conference of the North American Chapter of the Association for Computational Linguistics: Human Language Technologies, pp. 4171–4186 (2019)
35. Vaswani, A., Shazeer, N., Parmar, N.: Attention is all you need. In: Advances in Neural Information Processing Systems, pp. 5998–6008 (2017)
36. Zhu, Y., Kiros, R., Zemel, R.: Aligning books and movies: towards story-like visual explanations by watching movies and reading books. In: Proceedings of the IEEE International Conference On Computer Vision, pp. 19–27 (2015)
37. Yonghui, W., Schuster, M., Chen, Z., et al.: Bridging the gap between human and machine translation. arXiv:1609.08144 (2016)
38. Mikolov, T., Sutskever, I., Chen, K.: Distributed representations of words and phrases and their compositionality. In: Advances in neural information processing systems, pp. 3111–3119 (2013)
39. Jawahar, G., Sagot, B., Seddah, D.: What does BERT learn about the structure of language. In: Proceedings of the 57th Annual Meeting of the Association for Computational Linguistics, pp. 3651–3657 (2019)

Cigarette Packaging Quality Inspection Based on Convolutional Neural Network

Zhijun Xu[1], Shuxi Guo[1], Yuefeng Li[2], Jianchao Wang[2(✉)], Yinuo Ma[2], and Lee Henna[3]

[1] Hebei Baisha Tobacco Co., Ltd., Shijiazhuang 050000, Hebei, China
[2] School of Information Science and Engineering, Hebei University of Science and Technology, Shijiazhuang 050000, Hebei, China
Wjc107960@163.com
[3] University of Nevada:Reno, Reno, USA

Abstract. In recent years, in the process of cigarette production, there is the quality problem of cigarette package, which has become a very important factor restricting manufacturers to comprehensively improve the quality level. In order to improve the production quality of cigarettes, the quality inspection of cigarette package is very important. In this paper, an improved Bilinear-VGG16 model is proposed for cigarette carton quality detection. Firstly, images of qualified cigarette pack and defective cigarette pack are collected and enhanced to establish a data set of cigarette pack images. Secondly, the original convolutional neural network model is analyzed and improved, and a lot of training is carried out. Then, the trained model is used in the quality inspection of cigarette pack, and the defective cigarette pack is removed, and the inspection is continued if there is no defect. The final experimental results show that the improved network model in this paper has a high accuracy process for the quality detection of collected cigarette packs, reaching 96.3%, and the average detection time has also been improved. Compared with the original method, this method is more efficient than the traditional cigarette packaging quality detection method.

Keywords: Convolutional neural network · Cigarette packaging quality inspection · Improved Bilinear-VGG16 model

1 Introduction

In the process of cigarette packaging in many cigarette factories, there are often problems such as package damage, side ear opening of the package and blemishes in the printing process. This phenomenon accounts for a certain proportion in the quality of cigarette packaging, seriously affecting the quality of cigarette production, so it is very important to detect the quality of cigarette packaging. The traditional detection method is slow and inefficient. Convolutional neural network is an important deep learning model, which can extract features from image data and is widely used in image recognition. In this paper, a cigarette pack quality detection method based on the improved Bilinear-VGG16 model can accurately eliminate cigarette packs with defects and improve the production quality of cigarettes.

© The Author(s), under exclusive license to Springer Nature Switzerland AG 2022
X. Sun et al. (Eds.): ICAIS 2022, LNCS 13338, pp. 614–626, 2022.
https://doi.org/10.1007/978-3-031-06794-5_49

2 Data Acquisition and Processing

2.1 Image Acquisition of Cigarette Packaging

Cigarette packaging appearance quality detection equipment to collect cigarette case image through visual imaging system, the effect of imaging system greatly influence the performance of the whole detection system, the core components of the image imaging system mainly include image acquisition card, camera, light sources, etc. The role of the image acquisition card in the imaging system is to control the camera and digitize the image. The camera is used to realize the rapid acquisition of images, and then the electrical signal is saved as a picture signal in a certain form, forming the final digital image signal. The light source is used to illuminate and highlight the cigarette case object [3].

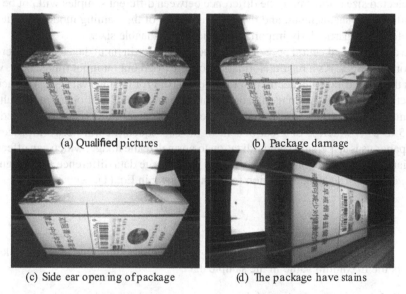

(a) Qualified pictures   (b) Package damage

(c) Side ear opening of package   (d) The package have stains

Fig. 1. Common cigarette packaging defect images.

In the collection process of cigarette packaging testing equipment, first of all, product packaging to be tested is imaged on the conveyor belt by multiple cameras, the camera is triggered to take pictures in a position-triggered way, that is, the position trigger is set. After reaching this position, the camera triggers imaging to realize real-time acquisition of the cigarette package, and then the image acquisition card collects the signal. Finally, the image is transmitted to the computer memory to complete the whole image acquisition process.

To train an accurate neural network model, the establishment of data set is a key step. Therefore, we first need to establish a relatively complete data set, and select qualified pictures of cigarette packaging and relatively typical defect images, such as damaged packaging boxes, side ear openings of the packaging boxes, and stains on the packaging boxes. Part of the defect samples and qualified samples are shown in Fig. 1(a) is the qualified picture, (b), (c), (d) are the defect pictures.

2.2   Establishment of Data Set on Cigarette Packaging

Picture Cutting and Normalization of Cigarette Case. The size normalization of the collected image data can make the training process smoother, and the training model will not be affected. If the selected size is too large when the size is normalized, the effective feature information of images may not be extracted in the training process. If the selected size is too small, the difference between different samples will not be obvious after data enhancement, and the learning ability of the training model may decline. Therefore, it is particularly important to select a reasonable size.

In convolutional neural network, too much difference in input data leads to decreased network accuracy. As a result, Normalization is carried out on input image data, which maps the input data to the decimal of the interval $(0, 1)$ or the interval $(-1, 1)$ to facilitate extraction. The original image is consistent with the normalized operation result. The information of the image itself is not changed, but the pixel value range is changed from 0–255 to 0–1, which is of great benefit to the subsequent neural network processing. This paper uses dispersion standardization to normalize the image, which can effectively alleviate the poor recognition effect caused by the large data difference and irregularity of the data set. The standardization formula is shown in Eq. (1).

$$x' = \frac{(x - X_{min})}{X_{max} - X_{min}} \tag{1}$$

where, x' is the normalized result value; X_{min} is the minimum value in the sample data; X_{max} is the maximum value in the sample data.

Data Enhancement. In the training process of neural network model, the number of training samples plays a key role in the accuracy and performance of the model. If there are fewer data sets of cigarette package defects, when the trained network model performs feature learning on the training set, it will produce fitting phenomenon which will result in the decrease of model identification accuracy, the neural network model will also easily lose the generalization ability. Therefore, in the case of a small number of data sets, it is necessary to enhance the data set to improve the generalization ability of the model and avoid the phenomenon of over-fitting. There are many ways of data enhancement [6], the more common ones are rotating, mirroring, brightness change, blurring, adding noise, etc. This project will expand image data through various data enhancement methods. As shown in Fig. 2., some data enhancement operations such as rotating, mirroring, highlighting, blurring and adding noise are performed on the images.

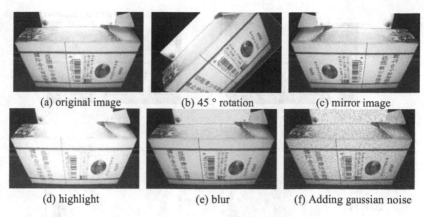

(a) original image	(b) 45 ° rotation	(c) mirror image
(d) highlight	(e) blur	(f) Adding gaussian noise

Fig. 2. Some data enhancement operations.

Data Set Establishment. After the data enhancement processing of the collected cigarette package image data, the image data set of cigarette packaging is established. The cigarette package image data set mainly includes four types of images, which are qualified pictures, damaged package boxes, open ears on the side of the package box, and stains on the package box. There are a total of 2000 cigarette package image data. In the experimental process of the convolutional neural network model, the collected data set is divided into training set and test set, with a ratio of 9:1. Therefore, there are 1800 images in the training set and 200 images in the test set.

2.3 Image Preprocessing

Different light sources of image imaging systems may lead to image defects and distortion. In practical application, low-quality images may produce deviation to training results. Therefore, in the subsequent application, the histogram equalization is carried out for low-quality images to strengthen the learning and feature extraction ability of neural network.

By observing the histogram, the brightness distribution of the image can be dynamically adjusted. In fact, histogram equalization is to improve the contrast of the image through nonlinear stretching, so that the pixels of the image of cigarette case packaging are evenly distributed, and finally the histogram of the image becomes a relatively evenly distributed histogram [8]. The effect diagram of equalization of cigarette package is shown in Fig. 3.

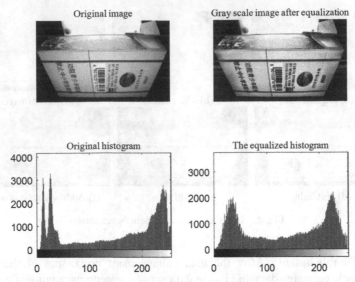

Fig. 3. Equalization renderings.

3   Model Design Based on Bilinear Convolutional Neural Network

3.1   Defects of Traditional VGGNet Network Model

VGGNet network belongs to the general classification model, so it has the disadvantage of the general image classification model, that is, fine-grained images cannot be classified well. Even if the depth of the neural network and the number of training are constantly increased, the accuracy rate will only fluctuate within a range. Therefore, to detect defects in cigarette packaging, a fine-grained classification model must be used.

Fine-grained classification is an important field in image classification, and there are two classification models based on strong supervised learning and weak supervised learning [9]. Among them, the learning classification model based on strong supervision has high classification accuracy, but at the same time, it takes a lot of time to label the image data set, which limits the application value of the model to a certain extent. Another method is based on the weakly supervised classification learning classification model, although the data set needs to be preprocessed, but the dependence is small, saving the time for preprocessing the data set. The accuracy of the best weakly-supervised classification model is about 1% –2% from that of the strong-supervised classification model, and the accuracy is also within an acceptable range. With the continuous improvement of classification accuracy, the labeling information required by the model is also decreasing, and the model is becoming more and more practical. Therefore, the classification model has a high cost performance ratio.

Common weakly supervised learning classification Models include two-level hierarchical attention networks [11] and Bilinear CNN. The former utilizes the mechanism of attention. The method of image classification can accurately locate the key parts of the image without additional information. The main idea of the latter is to extract the features of the image using dual-channel convolutional neural network, and then multiply the outer product of the two extracted features to enrich the feature information.

3.2 Overview of Bilinear Convolutional Neural Network Models

Bilinear model was proposed by Lin Equals at ICCV conference in 2015. It is used for fine-grained image classification and improves the accuracy of fine-grained image classification. The model has a simple structure and two independent feature extractors, so as to improve the accuracy of fine-grained image classification and achieve better classification effect [13]. In addition, the two networks in the bilinear convolutional neural network can be the same model or different model. The network structure of bilinear convolutional neural network is shown in Fig. 4.

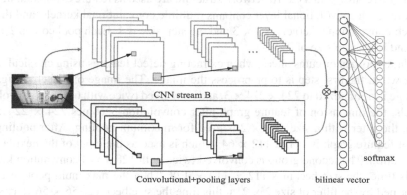

CNN stream B

Convolutional+pooling layers   bilinear vector

softmax

Fig. 4. Bilinear model structure diagram

The mathematical expression of the bilinear convolutional neural network model is shown in Eq. (2).

$$Y = (f_A, f_B, P, K) \tag{2}$$

where, f_A and f_B represent two convolution bases for extracting different features, specifically expressed as feature mapping function, P represents pooling function, K represents classification function of the full connection layer, and the function expression is shown in Eq. (3).

$$f : l \times \tau \rightarrow R^{C \times D} \tag{3}$$

where, τ represents the input image, and l represents the features of C × D dimension.

A complete bilinear convolutional neural network consists of two parallel convolutional neural networks, which are respectively used to extract different features of the image, and then calculate the outer product of the two different features at each position to obtain the bilinear features of the image. The mathematical expression is shown in Eq. (4).

$$b(l, \tau, f_A, f_B) = f_A(l, \tau)^T \cdot f_B(l, \tau) \tag{4}$$

where, $f_A(l, \tau)$ and $f_B(l, \tau)$ are the feature vectors of the two feature extractors at l.

3.3 Construction of Improved Bilinear-VGG16 Network Model

Bilinear fusion is the fusion of two features, that is, the features extracted from the network structure of two depth features. The experimental method adopted in this paper is based on the improved Bilinear-VGG16 network model. Firstly, the batch normalization layer is added, and the feature graph during training is utilized repeatedly to reduce the problem of gradient disappearance. Secondly, based on the original bilinear-CNN model, a Bilinear pooling method for single feature extraction is designed to reduce the number of parameters and computation. As for the Loss function, the auxiliary function Center Loss is added to further improve the network performance. Finally, a four-object classifier is used to identify the corresponding four cigarette packages.

Batch Normalization Layer. In the feature extraction of cigarette package defects, conv1_1 to conv5_3 in VGG16 network structure are used as feature extractors. In VGG network, each convolutional layer contains multiple convolutional kernels, and the size of each convolutional kernels is 3×3 and the step size is 1. Each pool core is 2×2 in size and has a step size of 2.

Under normal circumstances, when extracting defect features using classical VGG-16 network, the first step is to preprocess the image. The image of defective cigarette package is normalized to $224 \times 224 \times 3$, and convolved twice with 64 3×3 convolution kernels, the dimension of feature graph after convolution becomes $224 \times 224 \times 64$. Then, the filter with a size of 2×2 is used for maximum pooling. After pooling, the size of feature graph is $111 \times 112 \times 64$, which is used as the input of the next layer of convolution. The second group is convolved twice with 128 3×3 convolution kernels, at this time, the size becomes $112 \times 112 \times 128$. Then the maximum pooling is also performed by the filter of size 2×2, at this time the size becomes $56 \times 56 \times 128$. The convolution layer of the third group is different from the first two groups by adding a set of convolution. At this time, 256 3×3 convolution kernels are convolved for three times, and the size becomes $56 \times 56 \times 256$. Then the size becomes $28 \times 28 \times 256$ through the filter of size of 2×2 for maximum pooling, which serves as the input of the lower level. The fourth group is convolved three times with 512 3×3 convolution kernels, and the size becomes $28 \times 28 \times 512$, which still performs maximum pooling by a filter of size 2×2. The fifth group is similar in structure to the fourth group, with the final size of $7 \times 7 \times 512$, and 512 feature maps are obtained.

From the above content, we can know that once the network is trained, its parameters will change. Except for the sample data that has been normalized in the input layer, as the network deepens and the number of iterations increases, the input of each subsequent layer the data will be offset, so that the gradient disappears in the process of back propagation. In order to solve the situation that the data in the middle layer changes, the batch normalization layer (BN) is added after the convolutional layer of VGG16. The batch normalization layer can accelerate the convergence of the network, and the data of the upper layer can be normalized and then input to the next layer as input data, which can make the network training better. The connection diagram of single convolution block is shown in Fig. 5.

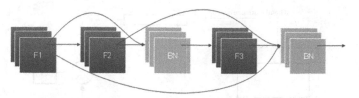

Fig. 5. Connection diagram of single convolution block.

As can be seen from Fig. 5, different colors in the figure represent feature images obtained in different forms. Blue represents feature images extracted by convolution, and gray represents feature images extracted by adding batch normalization layer. When performing the convolution extraction feature operation, the features extracted by F1 and F2 are combined as the input of the F3 layer. After the feature maps extracted by F1 and F2 are combined, the batch normalization layer is added. Then the feature maps of F1, F2 and F3 are combined as input of the next layer, and the batch normalization layer is also added after the combination for batch normalization processing. Through such operations, the feature information of each layer can be fully utilized when extracting features by convolution, and the combination with feature graph will not increase the complexity of the network. Moreover,the features of each layer are equivalent to directly connecting from the input to the output, thus effectively alleviating the phenomenon that the gradient gradually disappears due to the deepening of the network. In this paper, the batch normalization layer is added only after F1 and F2 are combined, and after F1, F2 and F3 are combined, in order to prevent over-fitting of the network.

Single Feature Path Bilinear Pooling Method. Original bilinear convolutional neural network extracts the image features through two parallel convolutional neural networks, and performs bilinear pooling operations on the extracted features. Then Gram matrix is calculated which is composed of the pairwise inner product of any key vectors. It can extract the fine-grained features of the image to the greatest extent, but the corresponding amount of calculation and parameters will also increase due to the use of two parallel convolutional neural networks. Therefore, the improvement of bilinear-CNN in this project is to design a Bilinear pooling method for single feature extraction based on the Bilinear pooling characteristics of the original model, as shown in Fig. 6. After extracting image features through a separate convolutional neural network, two pooling methods are adopted which are global average pooling and global maximum pooling respectively. While reducing the amount of calculation and the number of parameters, it fully excavates the fine-grained features of defective cigarette package images.

It can be seen from Fig. 6 that a $h \times w \times c$ feature graph is extracted by the VGG16 convolutional layer after adding the batch normalization layer. After global maximum pooling and global average pooling, the global vector describing the feature is obtained, and then taking the outer product of the two vectors to obtain the Gram matrix.

Combined Loss Function. In multi-classification problems, Softmax Loss is usually used as the Loss function of the convolutional network. However, because the characteristics of different defect types in cigarette packages are similar, in order to maximize the difference distance between classes in the model, the Center Loss function is introduced

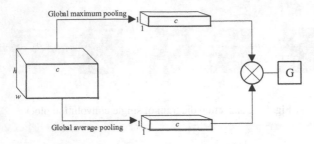

Fig. 6. Bilinear pooling method for single feature extraction.

to build a joint Loss function with Softmax Loss. Among them, Softmax Loss focuses on increasing the inter-class distance of image samples, while Center Loss focuses on reducing the intra-class distance of image samples, so as to improve the recognition rate of various cigarette packs. The formula of Softmax Loss function is shown in Eq. (5).

$$L_S = -\sum_{i=1}^{m} \log \frac{e^{w_{yi}^T x_i + b_{yi}}}{\sum_{j=1}^{n} e^{w_{yi}^T x_i + b_{yi}}} \tag{5}$$

In the formula, x_i represents the depth feature of the i-th category, y_i represents the depth feature of the j-th category, W_{yi} and W_j represent the weight value corresponding to different input feature vectors, b_{yi} and b_j represent the offset term corresponding to them, m represents the size of batch training in the training set, and n represents the training category.

The formula of Center Loss function is shown in Eq. (6).

$$L_C = \frac{1}{2} \sum_{i=1}^{m} \|f(x_i) - c_{yi}\|_2^2 \tag{6}$$

In the formula, $f(x_i)$ is the feature vector, c_{yi} represents the center of the y_i-th feature. The combination of the two loss functions is the Eq. (7).

$$L_{C-S} = L_S + \lambda L_C \tag{7}$$

In the formula, λ represents the balance parameter of the joint loss function, because the value of Center Loss is much larger than that of Softmax Loss, so parameter λ is introduced to balance the two function values.

The training process of CNN can be understood as the process of Loss function optimization, in which the value of Center Loss gradually decreases and the feature vector $f(x_i)$ gradually gathers to the Center of the y_i-th features. As the number of iterations increases, all features in the network will converge toward the center of features, so as to achieve the purpose of intra-class aggregation degree and inter-class dispersion degree.

In the improved joint Loss function structure, the specific application diagram of Softmax Loss and Center Loss in the network is shown in Fig. 7.

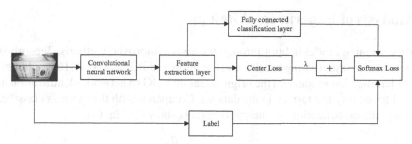

Fig. 7. The joint loss function diagram.

Improved Network Structure. VGG16 has 1000 categories in Softmax classification layer, but this paper only studies one qualified package picture and three defective package picture, the output node is changed to four nodes, that is, the classifier is changed to four target classifiers, corresponding to the four categories of cigarette package.

The overall network structure designed in this paper is shown in Fig. 8. When the feature graph is combined, the method adopted in this paper is to directly sum up the features of corresponding positions, instead of using the direct splicing method to merge the features according to the depth of the network. This summation method can better adapt to the VGG16 network structure we choose.

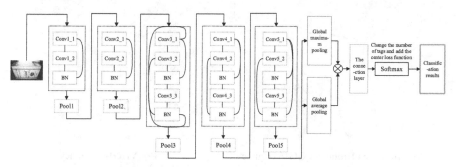

Fig. 8. Improved Bilinear-VGG16 network model.

3.4 Work Flow of Cigarette Package Quality Inspection

The process of cigarette package quality inspection mainly includes the following steps:

(1) Collect pictures of cigarette packs to be detected through the camera;
(2) The collected images are put into bilinear convolutional neural network to detect and determine whether there are defects;
(3) If there is a defect, it will be removed; if there is no defect, the inspection will continue.

4   Analysis of Experimental Results

After the training model is built through the above improved methods, Tensorboard is used to visualize the training results, and the improved Bilinear-VGG16 neural network defect identification model and the original classic VGG16 network identification model are used to identify the test set in the data set. Compared with the model's classification Accuracy, the classification Accuracy formula is shown in Eq. (8).

$$Accuracy = \frac{R_a}{R} \tag{8}$$

where, R is the number of images in the test set, and R_a is the number of correctly classified images in the test experiment.

At the same time, single image detection time T is introduced as an evaluation index, t = total test time/number of test images.

As can be seen from Fig. 9, the accuracy of the improved Bilinear-VGG16 model tends to be stable after 35 iterations, and the accuracy rate (Acc) reaches 96.3%. Due to the large number of full-connection layer-parameters of the unimproved network, the optimization time is long. After 40 iterations, the accuracy rate (Acc) stabilizes at around 94.1%. It can be seen that the improved model in this paper has significantly improved the accuracy of cigarette case defect detection.

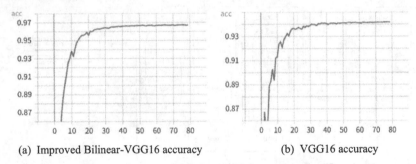

(a) Improved Bilinear-VGG16 accuracy   (b) VGG16 accuracy

Fig. 9. Comparison of accuracy between improved Bilinear-VGG16 and VGG16.

In order to verify the effectiveness of the improved single feature path Bilinear pooling method in this paper, the improved model is compared with the unimproved Bilinear-CNN model. The analysis results are shown in Table. 1.

Table 1. Improved Bilinear-VGG16 and Bilinear-CNN comparison experiment.

Model	Acc/%	Mean test time/s
Bilinear-CNN	94.8	0.558
The model of this paper	96.3	0.407

It can be seen from Table 1 that under the same experimental environment, the average accuracy of the improved Bilinear-VGG16 model reached 96.3%, which is 1.5% higher than that of the original Bilinear-CNN model. After reducing the number of parameters and computation, the average test time is also accelerated by 0.151 s.

From the above experimental results, the comprehensive performance of the cigarette package quality detection model proposed in this paper is obviously better than the original model.

5 Conclusion

This paper mainly carries on the cigarette package detection work. Firstly, the image of cigarette package is collected and the data is enhanced to establish a data set. Then the defects of the general classification model VGG network and the classic weakly supervised learning classification model Bilinear-CNN are introduced, and an improved Bilinear-VGG16 network model is established to identify the defects of cigarette package. In this model, the network part of conv1_1 to conv5_3 in VGG16 is used as feature extraction of Bilinear network, and the batch normalization layer is added. Then, on the basis of Bilinear-CNN, a Bilinear pooling method of single feature extraction is designed to reduce the calculation of parameters. At the same time, global average pooling and global maximum pooling are used to extract the fine particle features of defective cigarette package images. In addition, the combined loss function is used to further improve the performance of the network. Finally, four classifiers are used to classify cigarette package defects. The experimental results show that the accuracy rate of the improved model recognition is 96.3%, which is better than that of the popular network models before.

References

1. Zhai, J., Zhang, S., Pu, He.: Convolutional neural networks and their research progress. J. Hebei Univ. (Nat. Sci. Edition) **37**(6), 640–651 (2017)
2. Xu, J., Chen, W.: Convolutional neural network-based identity recognition using ecg at different water temperatures during bathing. Comput. Mater. Continua **71**(1), 1807–1819 (2022)
3. Sun, N.: Study on on-line inspection method of cigarette packaging appearance quality. Kunming University of Science and Technology (2020). https://doi.org/10.27200/d.cnki.gkmlu.2020.000360
4. Yuan, F., Shao, X.: Multi-scale blind image quality predictor based on pyramidal convolution. J. Big Data **2**(4), 167–176 (2020)
5. Habib, S., Khan, N.F.: An optimized approach to vehicle-type classification using a convolutional neural network". Comput. Mater. Continua **69**(3), 3321–3335 (2021)
6. Liang, D., Hu, F.: Theory and method analysis of image enhancement. Electron. World **2021**(08), 59–60 (2021)
7. Yang, H., et al.: Image preprocessing method for Wire Rope defect detection. Fujian Comput. **2021**(01), 23–25 (2021)
8. Mohineet, K., Sarkar, R., Krishna, D.M.: Kumar: Investigation on quality enhancement of old and fragile artworks using non-linear filter and histogram equalization techniques. Optik **249**, 168252 (2022)

9. Ge, Z.Y., Bewley, A., Mccool, C., et al.: Fine-grained classification via mixture of deep convolutional neural networks. In: Applications of Computer Vision, pp. 1–6. IEEE (2016)

10. Sun, W., Zhang, G., Zhang, X., Zhang, X., Ge, N.: Fine-grained vehicle type classification using lightweight convolutional neural network with feature optimization and joint learning strategy. Multimedia Tools Applicat. **80**(20), 30803–30816 (2020). https://doi.org/10.1007/s11042-020-09171-3

11. Xiao, T., Xu, Y., Yang, K., et al.: The application of two-level attention models in deep convolutional neural network for fine-grained image classification. IEEE (2014)

12. Lin, T.Y., Roychowdhury, A., Maji, S.: Bilinear cnn models for fine-grained visual recognition. In: Proceedings of the IEEE International Conference on Computer Vision, pp. 1449–1457 (2015)

13. Wang, Z.: Research on fine-grained image classification based on bilinear convolutional Neural Network. Dissertation of Beijing Jiaotong University, Beijing, China (2020)

14. Qin, X., Song, G.: Pig face recognition algorithm based on bilinear convolutional neural network. J. Hangzhou Dianzi Univ. (Nat. Sci. Edition) **2019**(02), 12–17 (2019)

15. Ahmad, G., Alanazi, S., Alruwaili, M., Ahmad, F., Khan, M.A.: Intelligent ammunition detection and classification system using convolutional neural network. Comput. Mater. Continua **67**(2), 2585–2600 (2021)

Research on Pear Tree Flowering Period Prediction Method Based on Neural Network

Qi Gao[1], JinMeng Du[2], JingFang Su[2(✉)], and Annan Gilmore[3]

[1] Ecological and Agricultural Meteorological Center, Hebei 050000, China
[2] School of Information Science and Engineering, Hebei University of Science and Technology, Hebei 050000, China
Sujingfang1980@hebust.edu.cn
[3] Civil and Infrastructure Engineering Discipline, School of Engineering, Royal Melbourne Institute of Technology (RMIT), Victoria 3001, Australia

Abstract. Plant phenotype is all physical, physiological, biochemical characteristics and traits that reflect the entire process of plant structural composition, growth and development. Timely phenotypic observation of plants is of great significance in terms of crop safety and environmental sustainability. Aiming at the problems of inaccurate flowering time prediction, time-consuming and waste of energy prediction in traditional pear tree phenotype observation, this paper studies the flowering prediction method of pear tree plants based on PCA-BP neural network. Taking pear tree as the research object, the meteorological observation data of Shijiazhuang Meteorological Station was analyzed by principal component analysis method, then three principal components with large correlation with pear flowering period were obtained. BP neural network model was introduced into the pear tree flowering period prediction and the error was reduced to one day, then.

Keywords: Plant phenotype · PCA-BP neural network · Principal component analysis

1 Introduction

The inflorescence and flowering period of the pear tree are the basis of the fruit and are one of the specific in phenotype of the fruit tree plant. Since fruit tree plants bloom only once a year, so too many or too few flowers will have an effect on yield. In addition, the flowering period data of pear trees is an important support for the development of tourism activities, which can not only provide a scientific basis for fruit trees to prevent frost damage, provide reference for relevant scenic spots to plan flower viewing activities, but also provide guidance for tourists to formulate flower-viewing tourism plans, and also provide reference for surrounding community businesses to participate in tourism-related operations. Therefore, it is particularly important to accurately understand the flowering period and manage the flowering period. By introducing a pear tree flowering prediction method based on PCA-BP neural network, this essay obtains a flowering prediction result that is superior to the traditional method, and also verifies the correlation with meteorological factors.

© The Author(s), under exclusive license to Springer Nature Switzerland AG 2022
X. Sun et al. (Eds.): ICAIS 2022, LNCS 13338, pp. 627–638, 2022.
https://doi.org/10.1007/978-3-031-06794-5_50

2 Research Status at Home and Abroad

Foreign scholars have produced many research results on the flowering period of plants and their relationship with climate and climate change, as well as the prediction of the flowering period of ornamental plants. In 2013, Gonsamo and others used phenological records from PlantWatch Canada to study the relationship between flowering phenology changes and climate in 19 Canadian plant species [1]. Hoffmann and others used regional climatic and phenological models to predict future flowering and flowering frost risk of apples [2]. In 2015, Aono and others studied cherry blossom phenology data since the 17th century in Edo, Japan, and their application to the estimation of temperature in March, using observational data on the time of cherry blossom bloom and the time of viewing [3]. Hur and others used physics-based dynamic models to generate mesh data with high spatial (3 km) and temporal (day) resolution, and made predictions of surface temperature and early flowering seasons in Korea [4]. In 2020, Kozlov and others collected about 300 phenological data from Vigna radiata and developed a new model that describes the dynamic control of flowering time by the maximum and minimum temperatures, precipitation, day length, and solar radiation values for predicting flowering time [5].

3 Principal Component Analysis

3.1 Basic Ideas

Principal component analysis (PCA) is a data representation method used to highlight similarities and differences between raw data [6, 7], Its basic idea is dimensionality reduction, in the actual measurement data, different variables will have a certain correlation, resulting in overlapping information, resulting in greater difficulty in data processing, and because the data is complex and large, it will increase the complexity of the calculation amount and analysis problems, so when processing data, it is necessary to organize and simplify, less redundant information, reduce the complexity of the problem, find the correlation, choose from the relevant variables, one of the two, get more effective information in a small number of data variables [8]. It has been widely used in many fields such as data analysis and data pre-processing [9].

3.2 Calculation Process

Step 1: Standardize on the raw data. Suppose that in the original data of the principal component analysis, there are m indicator variables:$x_1, x_2 \ldots, x_m$, the evaluation object is n, and the Jth index value of the ith evaluation object is set as x_{ij}. The standardization process is to each index value x_{ij} into a standardized index $\tilde{x}_{ij}$, shown in Eq. (1).

$$\tilde{x}_{ij} = \frac{x_{ij} - \bar{x}_j}{s_j}, (i = 1, 2, \cdots, n; j = 1, 2, \cdots, m) \tag{1}$$

where, $\bar{x}_j$ is the sample mean of the JTH indicator, and s_j is the standard deviation of the JTH indicator, shown in Eqs. (2) and (3).

$$\bar{x}_j = \frac{1}{n} \sum_{i=1}^{n} x_{ij} \tag{2}$$

$$s_j = \sqrt{\frac{1}{n-1} \sum_{n-1}^{n} (x_{ij} - \bar{x}_j)^2}, (j = 1, 2, \cdots, m) \tag{3}$$

where is the standardized indicator variable, the calculation formula is shown in Eq. (4).

$$\tilde{x}_i = \frac{x_i - \bar{x}_i}{s_i}, (i = 1, 2, \cdots, m) \tag{4}$$

Step 2: Calculate the correlation coefficient matrix R. The calculation formula is shown in Eqs. (5).

$$R = (r_{ij})_{m \times n} \tag{5}$$

where, r_{ij} represents the correlation coefficient between the ith index and the JTH index, shown in Eq. (6).

$$r_{ij} = \frac{\sum_{k=1}^{n} \tilde{x}_{ki} \cdot \tilde{x}_{kj}}{n-1}, (i, j = 1, 2, \cdots, m) \tag{6}$$

$r_{ij} = 1, r_{ij} = r_{ji}$.

Step 3: Calculate the eigenvalues and eigenvectors in the correlation coefficient matrix.The eigenvalue of the correlation coefficient matrix R is λ, $\lambda_1 \geq \lambda_2 \geq \cdots \geq \lambda_m \geq 0$, the corresponding eigenvector $u_1, u_2, \cdots u_m$, where,

$$u_j = (u_{1j}, u_{2j}, \cdots, u_{nj})^{\mathrm{T}} \tag{7}$$

At this point, m new indicator variables are composed of eigenvectors, shown in Eq. (8).

$$\begin{cases} y_1 = u_{11}\tilde{x}_1 + u_{21}\tilde{x}_2 + \cdots + u_{n1}\tilde{x}_n \\ y_2 = u_{12}\tilde{x}_1 + u_{22}\tilde{x}_2 + \cdots + u_{n2}\tilde{x}_n \\ \qquad \cdots\cdots\cdots\cdots \\ y_m = u_{1m}\tilde{x}_1 + u_{2m}\tilde{x}_2 + \cdots + u_{nm}\tilde{x}_n \end{cases} \tag{8}$$

where in, y_1 represents the first principal component after principal component analysis, y_2 represents the second principal component, and so on, y_m represents the mth principal component.

Step 4: Calculate the comprehensive evaluation value. Select the $p(p \leq m)$ principal components, calculate the information contribution rate and cumulative contribution rate of eigenvalue $\lambda_j (j = 1, 2, \cdots m)$ are calculated, and the information contribution rate of the jth principal component is as shown in Eq. (9).

$$b_j = \frac{\lambda_j}{\sum_{k=1}^{m} \lambda_k} (j = 1, 2, \ldots, m) \tag{9}$$

The cumulative contribution rate of principal component $y_1, y_2, \cdots y_p$ is shown in Eq. (10).

$$\alpha_p = \frac{\sum_{k=1}^{p} \lambda_k}{\sum_{k=1}^{m} \lambda_k} \tag{10}$$

When the value α_p is close to 1 (the general selection range is 85%–95%), the first p indicator variable $y_1, y_2, \cdots y_p$ can be selected as the p principal components, replacing the m indicator variables in the original data, so that the p principal components after dimensionality reduction can be comprehensively analyzed.

Step 5: Calculate the overall score. The calculation of the composite score value is shown in Eq. (11).

$$Z = \sum_{j=1}^{p} b_j y_j \tag{11}$$

where b_j is the information contribution rate of the j principal component, it can be evaluated according to the calculated comprehensive score value.

4 Data Sources and Criteria

4.1 Sources of Data

The flowering data are derived from the phenological observation data of the pear blossom period provided by the pear tree planting area of Shijiazhuang City and the Shijiazhuang Meteorological Bureau from 1995 to 2020, The observed plant varieties are medium-growing and representative snowflake pears.

4.2 Data Standards

The observation basis and observation standards for the flowering period of pear trees in this chapter are the observation standards of the "China Phenological Observation Network" and the "Agricultural Meteorological Observation Specifications" of the China Meteorological Administration [10].

By analyzing the phenological data of the positioning observation of the pear tree planting area and the Shijiazhuang Meteorological Bureau from 1995 to 2020 and the meteorological data of parallel observations, the flowering period of the pear tree planting area was statistically calculated.

According to the statistical results, it is concluded that the average flowering period of pear blossoms in the observation area is April 3, of which the earliest date is March 20 and the latest date is April 16; The average blooming period of pear blossoms is April 10, of which the earliest is March 28 and the latest is April 24; The average pear blossom flowering ends on April 20, with the earliest being April 8 and the latest being May 4. According to the analysis of observational data for many years, it is found that the entire flowering period of pear trees lasts for about 20 days, and when the flowering rate is 50 to 80%, it enters the full flowering period of pear blossoms. In addition, the full flowering period of pear trees is also the best viewing period, it is recommended that tourists travel during this period to watch, and at the same time, they should make good use of the full flowering period, timely flower thinning and artificial pollination, and improve the fruit set rate and fruit quality.

5 Data Analysis

5.1 Sample Correlation Coefficient Matrix Eigenvalues

Using the meteorological observation data of Shijiazhuang Meteorological Station from 1995 to 2020, the data is standardized according to the calculation process of principal component analysis method, and the relevant coefficient matrix characteristic values and contribution rates of meteorological station samples are found, and the results are shown in Table1.

Table 1. Eigenvalues of sample correlation coefficient matrix of Shijiazhuang meteorological station from 1995 to 2020.

Ingredients	Feature root	Contribution rate /%	Cumulative contribution rate
1	3.8978	48.75	48.75
2	2.8867	30.65	79.40
3	1.5892	12.54	91.94
4	0.5093	4.09	96.03
…	…	…	…

From the calculation process, it can be seen that when selecting principal components, p principal components with feature roots greater than 1 and cumulative contribution rates ranging from 85% to 95% are generally selected, and in the experiments in this chapter, we select p principal components with a cumulative contribution rate greater than 90%. By analyzing Table 1, it can be seen that the eigento roots of the first 3 principal components are 3.8978, 2.8867, and 1.5892, the values of the eigen root are greater than 1, and the cumulative contribution rate reaches 91.94%, so we believe that the first 3 principal components can basically reflect most of the information in the original meteorological indicators, reduce the complexity of the data, and achieve the purpose of using this method to reduce dimensionality.

5.2 Principal Component Characteristic Vectors

The principal component analysis of the original meteorological data obtained, the characteristic vectors of the three principal component factors in the meteorological factors are obtained, shown in Table 2. From the analysis of Table 2, it can be seen that in the eigenvectors of the 1st principal component, the values of the meteorological factors x_1,

x_2, and x_3 eigenvectors are large and positive, and these three meteorological factors are related to temperature, so the principal component 1 can be classified as a temperature factor. In the principal component 2 eigenvector, it can be seen that the meteorological factor x_5 eigenvalue is large and positive, and it can be seen that the principal component 2 has the greatest correlation with insolation, so it is classified as a sunshine factor. In the principal component 3 eigenvector, the meteorological factors with large eigenvalues and positive values are x_4 and x_6, which are mainly related to precipitation and are therefore classified as humidity factors.

Table 2. Characteristic vectors of principal components of meteorological data of Shijiazhuang Meteorological Station from 1995 to 2020.

Meteorological factors	Principal component 1	Principal component 2	Principal component 3
x_1: Average daily minimum temperature in winter	0.4123	0.3198	0.0011
x_2: Average daily maximum temperature in winter	0.3923	−0.0301	−0.1027
x_3: The average daily temperature in winter	0.3911	0.1500	0.0776
x_4: Average daily precipitation in winter	0.2011	−0.3298	0.3423
x_5: Average sunshine hours in winter	−0.0889	0.4788	0.1199
x_6: Average daily relative humidity in winter	0.2153	−0.5064	0.4019

5.3 Meteorological Conditions from the Beginning of Flowering to the Peak of Flowering

According to the statistics of Shijiazhuang meteorological data over the years, after the correlation analysis of the initial flowering period and the full flowering period of the pear tree, the analysis results show that the correlation coefficient is high, reaching 0.995, so it can be explained that the earlier the pear tree first flowering period, the earlier the blooming period.

Statistics show that among the many meteorological factors, the influence of temperature on the flowering process of plants is the largest, and the effective accumulated temperature above 3 °C, 5 °C and 7 °C at the beginning flowering period - full flowering period is the most significant, and the correlation is tested by the significance level of 0.01. The correlation coefficient between the initial flowering period to the full flowering period and the accumulated temperature of the pear tree is shown in Table 3.

It can be seen from Table 3 that in the effective accumulated temperature of 3 °C, 5 °C and 7 °C above the initial flowering period to the full flowering stage, the effective accumulated temperature correlation coefficient of ≥7 °C is 0.812, which has the most significant impact on the full flowering period of pear trees, so we select the effective

Table 3. Correlation coefficient between the initial flowering period and the accumulation temperature of pear trees from the beginning of flowering to the full flowering period.

	Effective accumulated temperature at 3 °C	Effective accumulated temperature at 5 °C	Effective accumulated temperature at 7 °C
Correlation coefficient	0.653	0.726	0.812

accumulated temperature of ≥ 7 °C from the beginning of flowering to the full flowering period of pear trees for the prediction of the full flowering period.

6 Experimental Results and Analysis

6.1 Experimental Environment

The predictive model built in this chapter is programmed using Python, and the experimental environment is shown in Table 4.

Table 4. Experimental environment.

name	Experimental environment
operating system	Windows 10
processor	I5–8600
GPU	GTX-2080Ti
memory	16GB
programming language	Python3.9
Compilation tools	Pycharm2019

6.2 Model Evaluation Indicators

In order to visually compare the applicability and accuracy of the PCA-BP neural network prediction model to the pear blossom period prediction in Shijiazhuang City, some indicators need to be used to measure the performance of the mode [11]l. This chapter evaluates models using Mean Squared Error (MSE), Root Mean Squared Error (RMSE), Mean Absolute Error (MAE), and R2 (R-Squared).

6.3 Experimental Parameter Design

In this study, a three-layer BP neural network model is selected, the number of input nodes is the number of predictors[12], the number of factors at the beginning of flowering is to obtain 3 principal component factors by principal component analysis method, and the number of factors in the flowering period plus the number of daily ordinals of the first flowering period and the accumulated temperature of more than 7 °C since the beginning of flowering. The pear tree flowering period is used as the output vector, from which the number of output layer nodes is determined to be 1. There is no specific specification for the number of neurons in the implicit layer, which generally needs to be associated with the actual problem solved, and the optimal number of neurons is determined by formula[13], shown in Eq. (12).

$$m = \sqrt{n + q} + \alpha \tag{12}$$

where in: n is the number of neurons in the input layer, q is the number of neurons in the output layer, the α is the integer in [1, 10], m is the number of neurons in the implicit layer, and the number of hidden layers plays a role in the accuracy of the model. In the case of the same sample test, this paper evaluates the performance of the model by comparing the training errors under different numbers of hidden layers, and uses mean squared errors, and obtains the results through 6 experiments, see Table 5. It can be seen from the experimental results that when the number of hidden layers is 6, the MSE is 0.1466 at this time, and the training results are the best.

Table 5. Network training errors for different number of hidden layer nodes.

Number of nodes	4	5	6	7	8	9	10
Training error	0.2123	0.1647	0.1466	0.1698	0.2211	0.2451	0.2767

The activation function uses the Sigmoid function [14], the learning rate is set to 0.01, dropout is set to 0.1, and the Adam optimization algorithm is used. In the process of training the determined network structure, in order to prevent overtraining, the following convergence rules are set: the number of samples with an absolute error of less than 2 is statistically less than 2, if it reaches 85% of the total sample, the training is stopped, if it is not satisfied, the maximum number of training is specified, set to 5000 times, and the training is stopped after the training meets the requirements, and the trained network is verified with samples.

6.4 Model Training and Analysis of Results

In order to intuitively express the prediction effect of this model, the trained PCA-BP neural network prediction model and the traditional law of effective accumulated temperature and stepwise regression method were used to predict the pear blossom period data from 2015 to 2019, and the results were compared and verified, and the three verification results are shown in Table 6.

Table 6. Comparison of results of different prediction models.

Year	Actual flowering period	PCA-BP model	Law of effective accumulated temperature	Stepwise regression method
2015	April 4	April 2	April 1	April 1
2016	April 6	April 5	April 5	April 5
2017	April 3	April 3	April 5	March 29
2018	April 7	April 5	April 8	April 4
2019	March 29	March 29	April 2	March 31

It can be seen from Table 6 that from 2015 to 2019, the flowering prediction error based on the PCA-BP neural network model was 1 day, the law of effective accumulated temperature was 2.2 days, and the stepwise regression prediction method was 2.8 days, and the flowering date of the predicted model in this paper was closer to the actual flowering date. It can be seen that the prediction method based on PCA-BP neural network improves the accuracy of flowering prediction and effectively reduces the forecast error.

In order to further measure the performance of the prediction model, the evaluation performance index parameters and their results of several prediction flowering models are compared and analyzed, and the results are shown in Table 7.

Table 7. Model performance indicators.

Model	R^2 R2	MAE	RMSE
PCA-BP model	0.83	1.892	1.54
Law of effective accumulated temperature	0.71	2.643	2.12
Stepwise regression method	0.68	2.982	2.98

As can be seen from Table 7, in the error indicators of the three prediction models, The root mean square error (RMSE) of the PCA-BP neural network prediction model used in this chapter is 1.54d, which is significantly lower than the traditional law of effective accumulated temperature and the stepwise regression method, and the value of the mean absolute error (MAE) is also smaller than that of the traditional prediction method, in addition, the R2 (R-Squared) based on the PCA-BP neural network prediction model is 0.83, and the correlation is higher than the effective accumulation temperature method (0.71) and the stepwise regression method (0.68), so it can be said that the PCA-BP neural network flowering prediction model used in this chapter is better than the traditional prediction model.

7 Actual Forecast of the Flowering Period of Pear Trees

After the training is completed, the trained model is used to predict the initial flowering period of the pear tree, and then the blooming period is predicted, the neural network topology is readjusted, the number of nodes in the input layer is the 3 main component factors obtained by the main component analysis, plus the number of day sequences in the initial flowering period and the effective accumulated temperature of $\geq 7\ °C$ after the first flowering period, and the number of nodes in the output layer is the number of forecast objects (the output result is 1/0 to indicate whether the next day reaches the peak flowering period), which can complete the peak flowering period forecast of the pear tree. The blooming period forecast flow chart is shown in Fig. 1.

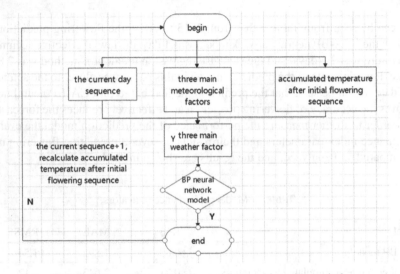

Fig. 1. Forecast flow chart of pear blossom blooming period.

Using the flowering prediction model constructed in this paper, the flowering period of pear trees in 2020 in Shijiazhuang area is predicted, and after the initial flowering period prediction is completed using the PCA-BP network prediction model, the prediction of the full flowering period is continued, and only the full flowering period is predicted after the initial flowering period.

First predict the flowering period, the principal component analysis of the 3 main component factors input model, predict the beginning of the flowering period in 2020 is March 28 (error 0 days), and then carry out the flowering period prediction, that is, the flow chart 3–4 began to cycle, the first cycle indicates that March 28 predicts whether March 29 is the full flowering period, the output result is 0, at this time into the second cycle, predict whether March 30 is the peak flowering period, at this time the result is still 0, continue the cycle, the cycle to the 7th time when the result appears 1, The prediction result is that the flowers bloom on April 4 (the error is 1 day), and the prediction model has a better effect. The specific forecast results are shown in Table 8.

Table 8. Actual prediction effect of pear blossom period in Shijiazhuang City in 2020.

Year	The actual flowering period	Predict the beginning of flowering	Error	Actual flowering period	Predict the blooming period	Error
2020	March 28	March 28	0 days	April 5	April 4	1 days

8 Summary of This Chapter

This essay mainly implements the work of predicting the flowering period of pear trees based on the PCA-BP neural network prediction model. First of all, the basic idea, geometric significance and calculation process of the principal component analysis method are introduced, and the pear trees planting area of Shijiazhuang City is selected as the target area for prediction, then the three main component factors affecting the flowering period of the pear blossom are analyzed by the principal component analysis method, they respectively are temperature factor, weather factor and humidity factor. Introduction of PCA-BP-based neural network models into pear tree flowering prediction applications. The experimental results show that the error of flowering prediction using the prediction model used in this project is 1 day, the law of effective accumulated temperature is 2.2 days, and the stepwise regression prediction method is 2.8 days. It can be seen that through the PCA-BP neural network prediction model based on the pear tree flowering prediction results that not only better than the traditional method, but also verified the correlation with meteorological factors. Relevant departments in the flowering forecast service, can be combined with this method, so that the prediction results and the actual flowering period of the year is more consistent, for the later fruit yield to do a good job of flower thinning work, and for the citizens to go out to visit the arrangement to provide a reasonable reference. The result is effectively improve the viewing quality of scenic spots.

References

1. Gonsamo, A., Chen, J.M., Wu, C.: Citizen science: linking the recent rapid advances of plant flowering in Canada with climate variability. Sci. Rep. 3(1), 2239 (2013)
2. Hoffmann, H., Rath, T.: Future bloom and blossom frost risk for malus domestica considering climate model and impact model uncertainties. PLoS ONE 8(10), 75033 (2013)
3. Aono, Y.: Cherry blossom phenological data since the seventeenth century for Edo (Tokyo), Japan, and their application to estimation of march temperatures. Int. J. Biometeorol. 59(4), 427–434 (2015)
4. Hur, J., Ahn, J.B.: Seasonal prediction of regional surface air temperature and first flowering date over South Korea. Int. J. Climatol. 35(15), 4791–4801 (2015)
5. Kozlov, K., Sokolkova, A., Lee, C.R.: Dynamical climatic model for time to flowering in vigna radiate. BMC Plant Biol. 2020(S1), 20 (2020)
6. Jolliffe, I.T.: Principal component analysis. J. Mark. Res. 87(4), 513 (2002)
7. Jolliffe, I.T.: Principal Component Analysis. Springer, Cham (2005). https://doi.org/10.1007/b98835

8. Shu, X., Liu, J.: Some problems of multicollinearity are treated by principal component regression. Statist. Decis. **2004**(10), 25–26 (2004)
9. Dubey, R.: J: An improved genetic algorithm for automated convolutional neural network design. Intell. Automat. Soft Comput. **32**(2), 747–763 (2022)
10. Huang, J., Cheng, X.: Norms for Agrometeorological Observations. China Meteorological Press, Beijing (1993)
11. Haq, M.A.: Cdlstm: a novel model for climate change forecasting. Comput. Mater. Continua **71**(2), 2363–2381 (2022)
12. Wang, Q., Wang, X.: Parameters optimization of the heating furnace control systems based on BP neural network improved by genetic algorithm. J. Internet Things **2**(2), 75–80 (2020)
13. Xia, P.P., Xu, A.H., Lian, T.: Analysis and prediction of regional electricity consumption based on BP neural network. J. Quant. Comput. **2**(1), 25–32 (2020)
14. Yuan, S., Wang, G.Z., Chen, J.B., Guo, W.: Assessing the forecasting of comprehensive loss incurred by typhoons: a combined PCA and BP neural network model. J. Artif. Intell. **1**(2), 69–88 (2019)

Research on Environmental Assessment Method of Meteorological Observation Station Detection Based on Panoramic Image Processing

Haichuan Li[1], Lijing Xu[1], Zhaoyang Shi[2], Xiang Wang[2(✉)], Jiashuo Li[2], and Gunase Manogaran[3]

[1] Meteorological Observation Center of Cangzhou Meteorological Administration, Cangzhou 061001, China
[2] School of Information Science and Engineering, Hebei University of Science and Technology, Shijiazhuang 050018, China
wangxiang@hebust.edu.cn
[3] Department of Computer Science, Faculty of Computers and Artificial Intelligence, Benha University, Benha 13511, Egypt

Abstract. At present, the meteorological observation station detection environment evaluation is completed by manual method, which is not only inefficient, but also lack of objective factors in the results. In order to solve this problem, this paper proposes a meteorological station detection environment assessment method based on panoramic image processing. SIFT (scale invariant feature transform) algorithm combined with fast (features from accelerated segment test) algorithm is used to extract and process the corresponding information of some overlapping images in adjacent areas. According to the pixel coordinates of the highest obstacle in the image, binocular ranging algorithm is used to build the detection environment model. The experimental results show that this method not only saves manpower, but also meets the needs of ground weather station to detect the environment of meteorological observation station, and can improve the efficiency of meteorological evaluation process.

Keywords: Meteorological observation station · SIFT · FAST · Panoramic image

1 Introduction

At present, the evaluation of the detection environment of meteorological observation stations at home and abroad mainly relies on manual work [1], which not only consumes a lot of manpower and material resources, but also results are not objective. However, with the rapid development of computer network and technology, it has become possible to design an automatic evaluation system for detecting the environment. The panoramic image or panorama is an image with a wide-angle of view [2]. In order to ensure the accuracy, authenticity and efficiency of meteorological monitoring data. In this paper,

© The Author(s), under exclusive license to Springer Nature Switzerland AG 2022
X. Sun et al. (Eds.): ICAIS 2022, LNCS 13338, pp. 639–649, 2022.
https://doi.org/10.1007/978-3-031-06794-5_51

an environmental evaluation method for meteorological observation station based on panoramic image processing is proposed.

The meteorological observation station of panoramic image mainly contains two core technologies: one is feature point extraction of the collected panoramic image [3], the other is image matching and image fusion technology [4]. In this paper, based on the classical panoramic image observation station, SIFT algorithm and FAST algorithm are used to achieve real-time extraction of image feature points and SURF algorithm is used to generate a complete panoramic image. At the same time, the shadowing Angle in the panoramic image is obtained by binocular distance measurement. This method not only ensures the authenticity and validity of the image but also improves the efficiency and reduces the time and space complexity of the algorithm.

2 Plan Design

This meteorological environment assessment algorithm mainly includes the following aspects:

(1) Image acquisition: Through the eight-eye camera, the triangular bracket, The PTZ captures multiple overlapping images of the surrounding adjacent areas of the meteorological observation station detection environment.

(2) Image Mosaic and fusion: The cylinder panoramic mosaic method is used to generate the panoramic image of the detection environment of the meteorological observation station. For the generated image, the improved scale invariant feature transform (SIFT) [5] algorithm and fast algorithm [6, 7] are used to extract the corresponding features. Because the feature vector matching method is based on geometric constraints, the overlapping areas are stitched and fused by the "progressive fading" algorithm, so that the complete panoramic image of the meteorological detection environment can be obtained.

(3) Measure shielding angle: The panoramic image is preprocessed by image processing technology and the occlusion angle is obtained by binocular ranging algorithm.

(4) Test evaluation: Analyze the evaluation indexes of meteorological observation stations and display the evaluation results in real time.

3 Image Mosaic Fusion Algorithm

Mosaic fusion of panoramic images is the key to the design of this method. The system mosaic panoramic images generate a panoramic image of the detection environment of the meteorological observatory. As shown in Fig. 1, method for generating cylindrical panorama, multiple images are obtained from one or more images by an eight- eye camera. Triangular support and cradle head. The resulting image is converted into a cylindrical projection to realize the mosaic of multiple images. Extracting processed images from feature points, adapt, transform and integrate into feature points to generate panoramic images.

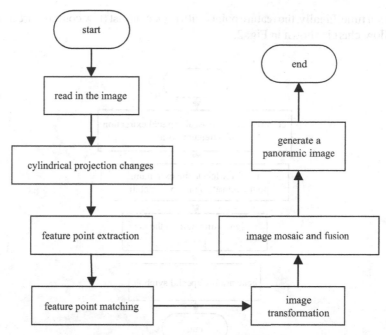

Fig. 1. Flow chart of panoramic cylinder.

3.1 Feature Point Extraction

When the monocular camera takes pictures, the angle and orientation of the image will change with the rotation of the camera. In this paper, the eight-eye camera is used for shooting and the angle of each camera is fixed, so the collected image will not produce geometric deformation and the overlapping part between images can be directly used to realize image matching. The traditional SIFT algorithm needs to extract feature points in the same scale and direction. Although the algorithm has high accuracy, it also improves the time complexity and reduces the extraction efficiency of the algorithm. In order to solve this problem, the feature points are extracted from the key points of the image based on SIFT algorithm and FAST algorithm. Select multiple points. By comparing the difference of pixel values between pixels, feature points are extracted quickly, so as to improve the efficiency of the classical single SIFT algorithm.

SIFT algorithm extracts the feature points of the image. Firstly, the scale space is constructed and its scale space transformation is defined as follows:

$$L(x, y, \sigma) = G(x, y, \sigma) \times I(x, y) \tag{1}$$

(x, y) is Spatial coordinates, $I(x, y)$ represents the two-dimensional image where the coordinate is located. The Gaussian kernel is

$$G(x, y, \sigma) = \frac{1}{2\pi\sigma^2} e^{\frac{-(x^2+y^2)}{2\sigma^2}} \tag{2}$$

The next step of SIFT algorithm is to scan the scale space to obtain the corresponding extreme points. LoG [8] is used, which can build the space quickly and reduce the calculation time. Finally, the feature points with poor contrast (low contrast) are discarded and its flow chart is shown in Fig. 2.

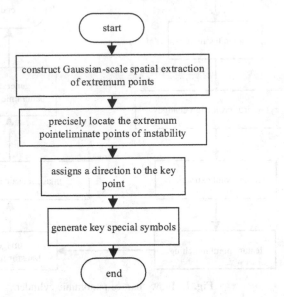

Fig. 2. Flow chart of Improved SIFT algorithm.

For FAST, first select the image pixel, then set the threshold, take the pixel selected in advance as the center of the circle, get the surrounding 16 pixels with a radius of 3 and divide them into three categories, as shown in the following formula:

$$S_{o\to x} = \begin{cases} a, & I_{o\to x} \le I_o - n \\ b, & I_o - n < I_{o\to x} < I_o + n \\ c, & I_o + n \le I \end{cases} \tag{3}$$

By traversing and calculating 16 pixels, classify and judge whether o is a corner, there is a gray difference between the pixel value of point o and the points on the circumference around point o. Therefore, firstly, the gray difference between point o and these points is calculated and compared with the threshold n. If the gray difference between the circumference and point o is greater than the threshold n and the number of points greater than is greater than 3/4 of the total number of selected points or the gray difference is less than the opposite number of threshold n, then o point is the candidate feature point. The brightness represented by a,b and c increases gradually. b is similar to o,if the results of 12 consecutive points are a and c, then the pixel point o is a corner.

Set the maximum parallax radius di for the feature point t_1 extracted by SIFT algorithm and the feature point t_2 extracted by FAST algorithm, and set the distance between t_1 and t_2 as $d(t_1, t_2)$. When $d(t_1, t_2) < di$, the unified image is judged.

The feature point sets S_{sift} (number is N_{sift}) and S_{fast} (number is N_{fast}) obtained by referring to the images SIFT and FAST, the feature point sets obtained by SIFT and

FAST of the images to be spliced $S_{de-sift}$ − (the number is $N_{de-sift}$) and $S_{de-fast}$ − (the number is $N_{de-fast}$).

Reference image each feature point $t_i (i = 1, 2, \cdots, N_{sift})$ in the S_{sift} and each feature point $t_j (j = 1, 2, \cdots, N_{fast})$ in $S_{de-fast}$ calculate the euclidean distance, The feature points satisfying the parallax constraint condition $d(t_1, t_2) < di$ is determined as common feature points as the common feature point set S_r of the reference image

$$S_r = \{S_{sift} \cap S_{fast}\} \tag{4}$$

Similarly, the common feature point set S_d to be spliced

$$S_d = \{S_{de-sift} \cap S_{de-fast}\} \tag{5}$$

3.2 Image Matching and Fusion

Traditional images are captured by monocular or binocular cameras. When matching feature points, there will be insufficient image feature points and deformation. The eight-eye camera is used for shooting, each camera presents a fixed angle, and the image has overlapping parts, which greatly improves the efficiency of image matching. The above feature point sets and are matched by geometric constraints [9].

In order to obtain a complete panoramic image, we must first obtain the overlapping part of the image, and then obtain the panoramic image. The overlapping area of the image is the transformation model calculated by the feature points in the image and then fused into a complete image [10–12]. The image can be properly shifted and corrected to ensure the integrity of splicing. Generally, the overlapping area of the image can be completely matched by offsetting the image in the horizontal and vertical directions.

The fusion of mosaic panoramic images is to eliminate the obvious cracks in the mosaic panorama. In order to preserve the image feature information and realize image fusion at the same time, the fusion algorithm used in this paper is the "gradual out" image fusion method. This improved algorithm based on weighted average image fusion can better solve the problem of large picture gap. The expression based on the weighted average image fusion algorithm [13] is:

$$\begin{cases} F(x, y) = W_A * A(x, y) + W_B * B(x, y) \\ \qquad\qquad W_A + W_B = 1 \end{cases} \tag{6}$$

In Eq. (6), $F(x, y)$ represents the fused image result, $A(x, y)$ and $B(x, y)$ respectively represent the two images to be fused. W_A and W_B are the weights of image $A(x, y)$ and image $B(x, y)$ respectively. Because the weighted average method first needs to know the weight values W_A and W_B, so the image fusion will lead to unsatisfactory image effect. In order to solve this problem, the weight can be changed adaptively. Let x be the horizontal coordinate direction of the fused image pixels, then the initial point coordinate of the overlapping area in the horizontal direction is X_{min} and the final end point coordinate is X_{max}. In this way, W_A and W_B are changed in a progressive adaptive way, and then the following expression can be obtained:

$$\begin{cases} F(x,y) = W_A(x,y) * A(x,y) + W_B(x,y) * B(x,y) \\ W_A = 1 - \frac{x - X_{min}}{X_{max} - X_{min}} \\ W_B = 1 - W_A \end{cases} \quad (7)$$

4 Measurement Method of Shielding Angle Based on Binocular Ranging

In the actual meteorological observation, it is usually necessary to measure the data information of the shielding angle of the obstacles in the captured pictures. Combined with wind speed, geographical location, etc., all meteorological information of the whole region can be obtained. At present, the existing ranging methods [14] include ultrasonic ranging [15], radar ranging, laser ranging, etc. How-ever, ultrasonic ranging is affected by wavelength and atmosphere, which restricts the range of ranging. Radar ranging and laser ranging need to send and receive signals through radar, so the cost of this method is relatively high. This paper uses binocular camera to measure the distance. This method does not need the measured object to transmit signals, and different obstacles in the image will not produce interference. In addition, using the camera to capture images not only greatly saves time, but also has low cost.

The technology of binocular ranging [16] is based on the fact that when human eyes obtain the information of the surrounding scene, there will be a certain parallax, so as to measure the distance between different objects and human body in the same scene. Place the two cameras in parallel on the same horizontal line and get the left and right pictures. Figure 3 shows the geometric model of binocular ranging are the optical centers of the two cameras respectively. After imaging, the two cameras meet at a point and are the phase points of the two cameras respectively.

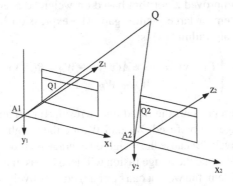

Fig. 3. Geometric model of binocular rang.

Figure 4 shows the principle model of binocular parallax. In the figure S is the real distance between the obstacle and the camera, H is the actual height of the obstacle, Q_1

and Q_2 are the coordinate origin of the two coordinate systems respectively and f is the focal length of the camera. According to the geometric knowledge, it can be concluded that $\triangle PQ_1Q_2$ is similar to $\triangle PA_1A_2$, so there is the following formula:

$$d = B_1 - B_2 \tag{8}$$

$$\frac{S-d}{S} = \frac{H-f}{H} \tag{9}$$

$$\frac{S-d}{S} = \frac{f}{H} \tag{10}$$

After simplification, the actual height can be obtained:

$$H = \frac{fS}{d} \tag{11}$$

Similarly, the actual distance of the building can be measured by this principle:

$$S = \frac{Hd}{f} \tag{12}$$

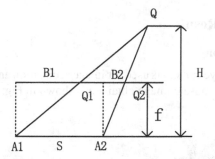

Fig. 4. Principle model of binocular parallax.

Based on the above principles, image preprocessing, image correction, image projection and other steps are carried out and the distance between the image and the camera is obtained by combining geometric coordinates, camera parameters and so on.

The height of two points in space is calculated as

$$\alpha = arctan\frac{h_2-h_1}{\sqrt{(x_2-x_1)^2+(y_2-y_1)^2}} \tag{13}$$

The size of the shielding angle depends on the horizontal distance and height difference, where x_1, y_1 and h_1 are the coordinates and height of the camera, and x_2, y_2 and h_2 are the coordinates and height of the shelter. The horizontal distance is calculated by binocular ranging method, and then the shielding angle is calculated.

Firstly, the image is grayed to facilitate binocular image stereo matching. In this paper, the above methods are used for feature extraction and matching. Then filter the grayed image and finally complete the visual ranging and masking angle calculation of the actual distance between the image target and the equipment. Among them, the median

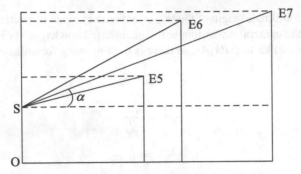

Fig. 5. Measurement chart of shielding angle.

filtering method is used for image preprocessing [17]. In order to make the gray image more reasonable, the filter can suppress noise and eliminate image distortion. We will use the weighted average method to remove the color of the image. In order to better display the image contour, make the image simple and small, this paper uses the maximum deviation method to classify the gray panoramic image [18]. This image processing helps to further process the image and minimize the possibility of misclassification.

5 Experimental Result

5.1 Image Acquisition

In this paper, an eight-eye camera is used for image acquisition and the instrument setting is shown in Fig. 6. The mosaic image obtained is shown in Fig. 7.

Fig. 6. Instrument installation drawing.

5.2 Image Mosaic and Fusion

The method of cylinder panoramic mosaic and fusion is adopted, the mosaic image is obtained by assembling the data collected in Fig. 7. The panoramic image of the meteorological observation station is shown in Fig. 8.

5.3   Information Extraction

When the panorama is grayed, three different color bases are weighted to generate grayscale images with different depths. This method is also called weighted average method, as shown in Fig. 9(a). In order to reduce the amount of image processing and highlight the outer contour, the image after graying in the previous step is binarized by the maximum interclass variance method. As shown in Fig. 9(b). When performing morphological processing on the binarized panoramic image, open operation and closed operation are used, as shown in Fig. 9(c). For better edge detection and denoising, Canny algorithm is used to detect the edge of the image after morphological processing, as shown in Fig. 9(d).

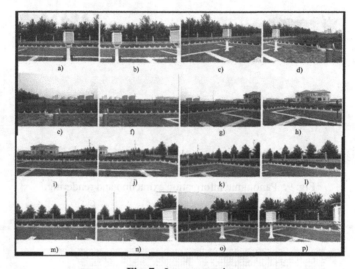

Fig. 7. Image mosaic.

Fig. 8. Panoramic view of meteorological observation station.

The schematic diagram of the occlusion area depends on the horizontal direction of the separation wall in the observation area and its maximum elevation at the center of the observation area. The pixel z coordinate of the obstacle in the image is obtained through the data after edge extraction, so as to calculate the actual area and azimuth angle. The final result is shown in Fig. 10.

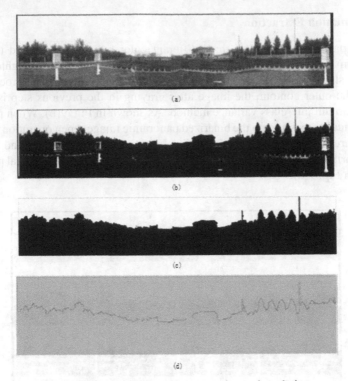

Fig. 9. Panoramic information extraction and rendering.

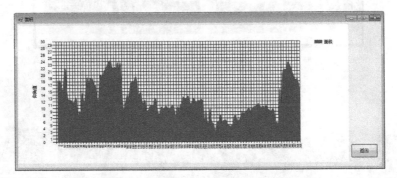

Fig. 10. Schematic diagram of obstruction area.

6 Conclusion

Based on the panoramic image processing, the measurement method of the detection environment of the meteorological observation station is to complete the image preprocessing through the mosaic fusion of multiple images of the meteorological observation station and the extraction of panoramic image information and obtain the shielding position of unqualified obstacles around the observation field and the shielding area of unqualified obstacles around the observation field according to the extracted edge pixel coordinates. Thus, the evaluation results of meteorological observation stations are obtained. The experimental results show that this method saves time and labor, the evaluation results meet the requirements of the ground meteorological base station for the observation environment of the meteorological observation station.

References

1. Guo, J.: A study on image-based cylinder panoramic image generation technology. Xi'an University of Science and Technology, Xi'an, China (2010)
2. Han, S.W., Suh, D.Y.: A 360-degree panoramic image inpainting network using a cube map. Comput. Mater. Continua **66**(1), 213–228 (2021)
3. Yang, T., Jia, S., Yang, B., Kan, C.: Research on tracking and registration algorithm based on natural feature point. Intell. Automat. Soft Comput. **28**(3), 683–692 (2021)
4. Yan, P., Zou, J., Li, Z., Yang, X.: Infrared and visible image fusion based on NSST and RDN. Intell. Automat. Soft Comput. **28**(1), 213–225 (2021)
5. Zhang, Z., Feng, J., Yan, J., Wang, X., Shu, X.: Ground-based cloud recognition based on dense sift features. J. New Media **1**(1), 1–9 (2019)
6. Rosten, E., Porter, R., Drummond, T.: FASTER and better: a machine learning approach to corner detection. IEEE Trans. Softw. Eng. **32**(1), 105–119 (2010)
7. Liu, H., Gong, T., Zhang, Q.: Improvement of the algorithm of dbscan of image matching based on fast and brief. Geomat. Spat. Inf. Tech. **43**(03), 54–57 (2020)
8. Lindeberg, T.: Scale-space for discrete signals. IEEE Trans. Pattern Anal. Mach. Intell. **12**(3), 234–254 (1990)
9. Yi, Y., Lu, Y., Xiao, Y.: Improved SURF algorithm based on geometric constraints. Comput. Eng. Des. **41**(10), 2855–2861 (2020)
10. Ebtsam, A., Elmogy, M., Elbakry, H.M.: Image stitching system based on orb feature-based technique and compensation blending. Int. J. Adv. Comput. Sci. Appl. **6**(9), 55–62 (2015)
11. Du, Y.: Research on Key Technologies of Image Stitching. University of Electronic Science and Technology of China, Chengdu (2020)
12. Szeliski, R.: Video mosaics for virtual environments. IEEE Comput. Graphics Appl. **16**(2), 22–30 (1996)
13. Brown, M., Lowe, D.G.: Automatic panoramic image stitching using invariant features. Int. J. Comput. Vision **74**(1), 59–73 (2007)
14. Yang, M., Yang, J.: Feature selection based on distance measurement. J. New Media **3**(1), 19–27 (2021)
15. Yang, L., Zhou, W., Tang, W.: Research and hardware design of ultrasonic ranging system. Instrum. Tech. Sensor **2018**(02), 41–47 (2018)
16. Gao, M., Xiang, M., Yang, Y., et al.: A traffic avoidance system based on binocular ranging. In: 2017 12th IEEE Conference on Industrial Electronics and Applications (ICIEA). IEEE (2017)
17. Hsu, C.T., Tsan, Y.C.: Mosaics of video sequences with moving objects. In: International Conference on Image Processing. IEEE (2002)
18. Zhao, M.: Study of Algorithm in Generating Image-Based Cylinder Panoramic Image. Guizhou University, Guizhou (2006)

An Alphapose-Based Pedestrian Fall Detection Algorithm

Xiaodong Zhao[1], Fanxing Hou[1(✉)], Jingfang Su[1], and Lane Davis[2]

[1] Hebei University of Science and Technology, Shijiazhuang 050000, China
2508932605@qq.com
[2] University of East London, London 999020, England

Abstract. In order to identify the falling behavior quickly and accurately from the surveillance video, an optimized model of alphapose is proposed here. First, the pedestrian target detection model and pose estimation model are accelerated by the lightweight YOLOv4-tiny model that we adopted. Then, the human pose joint point coordinate data obtained by the alphapose model is used to judge the occurrence of a falling action by the proposed judging algorithm. We use relationship between the head joint point line velocity and the crotch joint line velocity at the moment of a human fall and the change of angle between the perpendicular bisector and the x-axis of the image to judge the occurrence of the fall action. The algorithm proposed in this paper was compared with the main human posture-based fall detection algorithms for comparative analysis, with an image resolution of 320 × 240. The results show that the model proposed in this paper can timely and accurately detect the occurrence of pedestrian fall behavior.

Keywords: Object detection · Fall behavior · Alphapose · Yolov4

1 Introduction

With a breakthrough of 230 million in the elderly population aged over 60 years (including 60 years old) in China by 2020, it is the world's largest elderly population [1], and data from China's disease surveillance system show that falls have become the leading cause of death from injury among the elderly over 65 years old in China [2]. Medical investigations have shown that if treated promptly after a fall, it can reduce the risk of death by 80% and significantly improve the survival rate of the elderly, therefore, rapid detection of the occurrence of a fall event is of great significance [3]. At present, there are three main kinds of common fall detection methods: the detection method based on environmental equipment, which detects falls based on the environmental noise formed when a human falls, [4]such as the change of perceived pressure and sound of objects to detect falls, has a high rate of false positives, and is rarely adopted [5]. Detection methods based on wearable sensors, using accelerometers and gyres to detect falls, and wearing sensors for a long period of time affects the life comfort of people, will increase the body burden of the elderly, and the false positive rate is higher when engaged in complex activities. Visual recognition-based detection methods can be divided into two

© The Author(s), under exclusive license to Springer Nature Switzerland AG 2022

X. Sun et al. (Eds.): ICAIS 2022, LNCS 13338, pp. 650–660, 2022.
https://doi.org/10.1007/978-3-031-06794-5_52

categories: one is the traditional machine vision method to extract effective fall characteristics, which has low hardware requirements, but is susceptible to environmental factors such as background and light change, and has poor robustness [6].

One class is artificial intelligence methods that use camera image data for training and inference of convolutional neural networks, and although identification accuracy is high, efficient performance is often accompanied by high hardware costs, greatly limiting floor to floor applications. Mobile terminals and small embedded devices also have favoured computational power in recent years and are inexpensive, offering the possibility of migratory deployment of AI algorithms. It put human 3D pose data into the convolutional neural network with training to obtain a fall detection model and achieved a high accuracy rate, but the average recognition time was 0.178 s and the real-time performance was low.proposed an embedded machine learning algorithm to extract image features using sliding windows, In the computer side, support vector machine (SVM) is utilized to classify the features with high accuracy, but limited by lack of memory and parallel computation in low-power embedded devices, this method cannot be transplanted into low-cost embedded controller in the literature [7–9].

A lightweight structural build depth convolutional network with attention mechanism is used to extract the coordinates of human joint points, trace pedestrians and detect fall behaviors using the variation of inter frame joint points, The frame rate reached 16.74 FPs in the jetsontx2 (hardware cost about 4 times that of jetsonnano) embedded platform [10]. Literature [11] utilized the deep learning algorithm acquires skeletal map data of the human body and determines whether a fall occurs by calculating the rate of descent of the human center of mass points, whether the ordinate value of the cervical joint points after a fall is greater than the threshold value, and the relative positional relationship of the shoulder and lumbar joint points, achieving an average detection accuracy of 92.8% on a home-made dataset [12]. proposed an optical anonymous image sensing system using convolutional neural networks and auto encoders for feature extraction and classification, detecting abnormal behaviors of old people, which protected the privacy of old people to some extent.[13]utilized two-dimensional image data, which were analyzed by the frame difference method Kalman filtering and so on extract effective image background as the input of KNN (k-nearest neighbor) classifier, which achieves a 96% accuracy rate, vulnerable to variable environmental factors, a large amount of work in the preprocessing stage.

According to the literature [14], using YOLOv3 (you only look once) to detect the human target to get rectangular boxes in the human region, the human motion characteristics during the fall process are compared with the convolutional neural network (convolutional neural networks, CNN) extracted deep feature fusion for human fall detection discrimination, in both environmental adaptability and fall detection accuracy rates are higher than traditional human fall detection methods [15]. Literature [16] used two-dimensional image data to calculate optical flow information, and fed into VGG (visual geometry group) performed feature extraction and classification for optical flow information, detecting fall phenomenon. Literature [17] put feature information extracted by CNN convolutional layer and full connectivity layer into LSTM (long-short term memory), which is trained to extract the temporal correlation of human spatial actions and identify human behaviors.

The occurrence of falls is random and unpredictable, and the external environmental influences at different times and places may lead to the occurrence of falls [18]. If the person who falls lives alone at home, it is difficult to be found and treated in time. Moreover, falls will certainly cause harm to the parties to a certain extent. This will put a great burden on many families and families [19]. If we can send out the alarm for help in time at the first time of falling, so that the fallen person can get help in time, then we can greatly reduce the occurrence of disability and even death caused by falling behavior [20].

On the one hand, necessary anti-skid measures should be installed to prevent the occurrence of falls [21], such as placing fewer obstacles in the home. Even so, it is difficult to ensure that the fall event does not occur, so the research on the fall detection algorithm is extremely meaningful [22]. On the one hand, if the fall detection algorithm can be better applied to the actual environment, it will have very important practical significance for the prevention of human falls. On the other hand, as falling is only one form of many human movements, if the fall detection algorithm can be better studied, it will also be of great value to the theoretical study of human posture.

Therefore Pedestrian target detection model and pose estimation model for accelerated optimization, the occurrence of fall occurrence was judged by quickly acquiring human pose joint point image coordinates through the optimized pose estimation model, combining the human fall process instantaneous pose change characteristics and the fallen state characteristics that remain constant for a short time, and the algorithm was transplanted into an embedded development board, A comparative analysis was performed with the main human posture based fall detection algorithms.

2   Analysis of Human Body Pose Estimation Models

There are two main detection methods for human posture joints: top-down and bottom-up.

The bottom-up method, represented by OpenPose, is a bottom-up human pose estimation algorithm using Part Affinity Fields (PAFs). Firstly, the position of the key bone points of human body is detected, and the detection result is obtained by predicting the hot spot map of the key bone points of human body. It can be seen that there is a Gaussian peak on each key bone point of human body, representing the neural network believes that there is a key bone point of human body. Do the same with other key bone points in the body, such as the right elbow, and get another result. After all the test results are obtained, the key point test results are connected. For this step, OpenPose's approach is to speculate from a new feature, a vector field called the human Key Bone point affinity field (PAFs). Then repeat this step to speculate on the connections between the remaining key bone points, again through the human key affinity field, and repeat this step until you get all the bone information of all human bodies (in the multi-player scenario). So it is easy to introduce interference from non-human objects, resulting in low detection accuracy.

The top-down method, represented by Alphapose, is a phased detection model. Firstly, target detection is carried out to identify human targets in the image, and rectangular boxes of each human area are marked to exclude interference from non-human objects. This method has a high accuracy. Table1 shows the performance comparison of mainstream human pose detection models on COCO data set. It can be seen that AlphaPose is superior to the comparison algorithm in major accuracy indexes. Based on the high accuracy of AlphaPose, the algorithm designs the human pose model inference acceleration and fall algorithm.

Table 1. Performance comparison of mainstream human pose detection models

Model	AP@0.5:0.95	AP@0.5	AP@0.75
OpenPose	61.8	84.9	67.5
Detectron	67.0	88.0	73.1
AlphaPose	73.3	89.2	79.1

3   The Proposed Fall Detection Model

The main related work of this paper includes: accelerate the inference speed of the pose estimation model, which includes speeding up the human target detection and pose node inference speed, providing low delay and high throughput deployment inference for the embedded platform transplantation application of the algorithm; Based on the coordinate data of human body posture node image, a human fall judgment algorithm was established to judge the occurrence of human fall phenomenon by combining the characteristics of instantaneous posture change and the short duration of fallen state.

3.1   Inference Acceleration Optimization of the Human Pose Estimation Model

Alphapose is a phased pose estimation model, so the inference acceleration work is mainly divided into the optimization of target detection model and the optimization of posture node detection model. After accelerating the inference of human target detection model, the human target image is serialized to improve the data exchange efficiency between target detection model and posture node detection model.

The original Alphapose human target detection adopts YOLOv3. In recent years, the emergence of YOLOv4 has obviously surpassed YOLOv3 in detection accuracy and detection speed, and can cope with more complex detection environment (such as complex light and occlusion), reaching a new level in the field of target detection. In this paper, the human target detection model uses the lightweight model YOLOv4-Tiny-416 (parameter number: 24.3 m) in the YOLOv4 series so as to achieve a balance between detection accuracy and detection speed. The output dimensions of the YOLOv4 network model are initialized, where the network layer '030_convolutional' = [C, H //32, W //32], '037_convolutional' = [C, H //16, W //16], where C represents the number of input image channels, H represents the input image's height, W represents the input image's width, // represents exact divisible operation; Onnx network nodes are created in pedestrian target detection model after dimension initialization, and Route and YOLO nodes in dummy network layer are removed. If the input layer is "convolutional", the convolutional weight parameter is loaded; if the input layer is "up-sample", the up-sampling parameter is loaded. The calculation diagram of pedestrian target detection model after dimension initialization was created, and the model conversion optimizer was loaded. After transformation, the optimized target detection model YOLOv4-tiny-416 was obtained, and the number of model parameters was 32.7 m.

3.2 The Human Fall Determination Algorithm

The fall process in life is generally as follows: walking (standing) → falling process → fallen state, and the fall process is often very sudden and rapid, and can be completed in a moment. Due to the short time of falling process, it is not easy to obtain the fall characteristics of this process. However, the fallen state will generally remain for a period of time, especially the fallen state that will last longer after the fall of the elderly, and its fall characteristics are easier to obtain. Therefore, in the process of falling, the reliable and rapid detection of fallen state is more practical (Fig. 1).

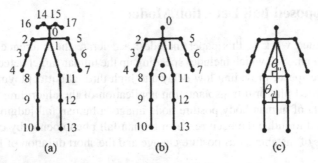

Fig. 1. Human posture and fall characteristics

Based on the data of human body posture nodes, a human fall determination algorithm was established to detect human fall events by combining the characteristics of instantaneous posture change during fall process with the characteristics of short-term persistence of fallen state. It includes:

1) The characteristics of instantaneous fall: the mathematical relationship between the linear velocity of head joint and the linear velocity of crotch joint at the moment of human fall; when the human body falls it moves around the ankle as the center of the circle in a certain direction, so the line speed of the point far from the center of the circle is larger.
2) The characteristics of fallen state: The characteristics of fallen state make use of the characteristics of human body's natural standing balance. When the Angle between the body and horizontal plane reaches a certain Angle, there is a great possibility of falling.

Step1: calculate the linear velocity V_O of human head junction 0 and V_O of gravity center of chest o. The position of gravity center of the human chest is calculated from the coordinates of human body junction 1, 8 and 11. Calculate the line speed of human ankle $V_{10\text{-}13}$, $V_{10\text{-}13}$ is the average line speed of human body's key points 11 and 13. The above linear velocity is the average linear velocity calculated by frames at each N interval in continuous M frames of images.

Step2: If V_o, V_O and $V_{10\text{-}13}$ satisfy the formula (1), the suspected fall is judged.

$$\begin{cases} \dfrac{V_0}{V_O} > \chi \\ V_{10-13} \in [\alpha, \beta] \end{cases} \tag{1}$$

According to the characteristics of human standing balance, when the Angle between the perpendicular bisector of upper part of human trunk and horizontal plane less than a certain value, the human body will lose balance and falls, but this isn't a sufficient condition. For example, bent down to pick up things, tie his shoes and so on. After falling, it generally keeps falling for a period of time before posture changes occur, such as hand support, sitting up, bowing and bending up, etc., so time threshold filtering is needed.

Hence, combining with step2, detection the angle between perpendicular bisector of lower part of human torso and the horizontal, and at the same time the time-threshold filtering to determine the fall of the body is objective and comprehensive.

Step1: calculate the Angle Θ_u between the middle vertical line and the horizontal line of the upper part of the body. If $\Theta_u < \varepsilon_1$ and keep $\Theta_u < \varepsilon_1$ within the time threshold T1, it is judged as falling. Otherwise, go to step2.

Step2: calculate the Angle Θ_d between the vertical line and the horizontal line in the lower part of the body. If $\Theta_d < \varepsilon_1$ and $\Theta_d < \varepsilon_1$ is maintained within the time threshold T2, it is judged as falling.

4 Experimental Process and Result Analysis

The software environment used in the experiment relying on major tools including opencv4.1.1, torch1.6.0, torchvision0.7.0, tensorRT7.1.3. Experimental data: 104 human fall videos were selected from the public dataset UR Fall Dataset [19]. Each video contained a complete fall process (from standing posture to falling state) with a resolution of 320 × 240, and the scene included three types, namely home, office and teahouse. The home environment is a living room scene, including sofas, dining tables, stairs, chairs, lamps and other accessories, including a variety of lighting conditions. The office scene includes tables and chairs, and the lighting is normal and evenly distributed. The scene of the tea room includes sofa, table, tea set, etc., and the light is normal and evenly distributed. Each video contains 1 person, and a total of 7 people participated in the video collection, including 1 woman and 6 men, including a variety of falling posture, including walking, bending and sitting posture interference posture.

4.1 Human Body Detection

We evaluate our proposed YOLOv4-tiny-416 model with the other two popular object detection algorithms, namely NanoDet-m and YOLOv3-spp. The average accuracy and frame rate of YOLOv4-Tiny-416 are significantly better than nanodet-m, As can be seen from Table 2, the detection frame rate of YOLOv4-Tiny-416 reaches 9.6, which is 2.8 times that of the original YOLOv3-spp, and the average accuracy difference is very small, which is superior to other comparison methods. Therefore, from the comprehensive consideration of detection accuracy and detection speed, YOLOv4-Tiny-416 is the optimal target detection method among the comparison algorithms. The average accuracy and frame rate of YOLOv4-tiny-416 are obviously better than nanodet-m.

Table 2. Performance comparison of target detection models

Target detection model	Frame rate	Average accuracy	Image resolution
YOLOv4-tiny-416	9.6	88.6	320 × 240
NanoDet-m	7.62	49.4	320 × 240
YOLOv3-spp	3.43	85	320 × 240

4.2 Fall Behavior Detection

Figure 2 (a) and (b) represents two frames of standing and falling state in the video we used in our experiment

(a)   (b)

Fig. 2. (a) a frame of standing state in the test video, (b) a frame of fallen state in the test video

The above figure shows the result of YOLOv4-tiny-416+alphaPose check algorithm. In the similar scene, with good lighting conditions and uniform distribution of light, the method in this paper can successfully detect the action of falling in side lying posture, leaning posture and lying posture, and can completely detect the key points of the human body, which is close to the real posture. YOLOv3-spp+alphaPose detected the state of human falling, but the attitude estimation of the upper body of human body was poor, and the connection between nodes was chaotic.

In the image, the human body falls, and a part of the human body is already in the blind area of the camera, so the whole human body is not detected, but the target is detected and the fall of the target is judged. Meanwhile, the label fall appears on the outer rectangular frame, which has a good detection effect. Both of them are walking in the video and the two targets can be well detected and their heads can also be detected. If one of them falls, it can be accurately detected, which proves that the target has fallen. Another person walking normally can also be well detected. Experiments prove that the detection result of this algorithm is very good.

Table 3. Performance comparison of pose detection models

Pose estimation model	Frame rate	Average accuracy	Image resolution
AlphaPose	7.12	73	320 × 240
OpenPose	4.38	55	320 × 240
trt_Pose	6.38	55.1	320 × 240

As can be seen from Table 3, the frame detection rate of alphaPose model is 1.1 times that of openPose, and the frame rate reaches 7.12 frames, while maintaining the same accuracy rate and possessing certain real-time performance. The frame rate and evenness accuracy of alphaPose are both better than that of OpenPose, and the average accuracy of OpenPose is higher than that of trt_Pose, and the frame rate of alphaPose is nearly 1 times lower than that of trt_Pose. Therefore, alphaPose is optimal in the comparative pose estimation model.

To verify the timeliness and accuracy of the proposed algorithm, the proposed algorithm YOLOv4-Tiny-416+alphaPose was compared with YOLOv3-spp+alphaPose and trt_pose algorithms. The evaluation criteria mainly include detection frame rate and detection accuracy. The accuracy rate is the ratio of the number of fall detection videos to the total number of fall test videos. The number of missed and false detections of test videos was counted, and the effectiveness of instantaneous fall feature and fall state feature on detection of fall events was analyzed. The missed detection refers to the number of videos in the fall test that fail to detect falls, and the false detection refers to the number of videos in the fall test that detect non-fall behaviors as falls.

Table 4. Uses the fall videos in the public dataset LE2i Fall Dataset for comparative analysis

Compare the algorithm	Mistakenly identified	Instantaneous fall feature	Characteristics of fallen state	Accuracy	Frame rate
YOLOv3-spp + alphaPose	9	6	78	0.759	3.05
YOLOv4-tiny-416 + alphaPose	3	7	93	0.894	4.38
trt_pose	10	3	77	0.634	4.31

The performance of the comparison algorithm is shown in Table 4. It can be seen from Table 4 that the frame rate and accuracy of YOLOv4-Tiny-416+alphaPose detection are significantly higher than other comparison algorithms, and the number of Mistaken detection is the least, and the accuracy is nearly 90%, which is the most accurate method among the above three. Trt_pose adopts the bottom-up method to detect the human body posture node, and its detection effect is not ideal.

After comparative analysis, the shortcomings of the proposed fall detection algorithm are as follows: The detection effect is not ideal in the case of uneven light distribution; he low height of the monitoring camera leads to obvious image malformations after human falls in the images taken, and the algorithm cannot detect falls effectively; When the human fall direction is parallel to the image Y axis, the fall position is close to the image X axis midpoint, and the head image coordinates of human fall are larger than the ankle image coordinates, the fall posture is very close to the normal standing posture, so the fall discrimination cannot be carried out. In order to improve the accuracy of the algorithm, the following research work will be carried out in the next stage: 1) The illumination adaptive reinforcement algorithm will be integrated into the fall detection system to increase the anti-illumination variation ability of the system; 2) Research on multi-camera joint detection method, try to use multiple cameras to detect falls from multiple angles, and solve local occlusion phenomenon to a certain extent; 3) Fall detection specifically for the elderly. Since there is no public abnormal behavior data set for the elderly, hence, collecting abnormal behavior data of the elderly and establishing the data set is also the work that we will try in the future.

5 Conclusion

In order to speed up the practical process of human fall detection using computer vision method, this paper put forward a kind of fall behavior detection model based on alphapose platform, which includes the acceleration optimization of human objective detection model and the determination algorithm of occurrence of falling action based on the body posture data. We also carried out a large number of experiments to verify this model, and compared it with many similar algorithms. The results show that the model proposed in this paper can achieve higher recognition accuracy.

References

1. Yin, J., Yang, Q.: Sensor-based abnormal human-activity detection. IEEE Trans. Knowl. Data Eng. **20**(8), 1092–1099 (2008)
2. Khan, A.M., Lee, Y.K., Lee, S.Y., Kim, T.S.: A Triaxial accelerometer-based physical- activity recognition via augmented-signal features and a hierarchical recognizer. Inf. Technol. Biomed. IEEE Trans. **14**(5), 1166–1172 (2010)
3. Sigg, S., Scholz, M., Shi, S., Ji, Y.: RF-sensing of activities from non-cooperative subjects in device-free recognition systems using ambient and local signals. IEEE Trans. Mob. Comput. **13**(4), 907–920 (2014)
4. Wang, X., Gao, L., Wang, P., Sun, X., Liu, X.: Two-stream 3-d convnet fusion for action recognition in videos with arbitrary size and length. IEEE Trans. Multimed. **20**(3), 634–644 (2017)
5. Arif, S., Wang, J., Ul Hassan, T., Fei, Z.: 3D-CNN-based fused feature maps with LSTM applied to action recognition. Future Int. **11**(2), 42 (2019)

6. Kong, Y., Huang, J., Huang, S., Wei, Z., Wang, S.: Learing spatiotemporal representations for human fall detection in surveillance video. J. Vis. Commun. Image Represent. **59**, 215–230 (2019)
7. Espinosa, R., Ponce, H., Gutiérrez, S., Martínez-Villaseñor, L., Brieva, J., Moya-Albor, E.: A vision-based approach for fall detection using multiple cameras and convolutional neural networks: a case study using the UP-Fall detection dataset. Computer. Biol. Med. **115**, 103520 (2019)
8. Xu, T., Zhou, Y.: Elders' fall detection based on biomechanical features using depth camera. Int. J. Wavelets, Multires. Inf. Process. **16**(02), 1840005 (2018)
9. Kaihoko, Y., Tan, P.X., Kamioka, E.: Prevention of unintended appearance in photos based on human behavior analysis. Information **11**(10), 468 (2020)
10. Thacker, C.B., Makwana, R.M.: Human behavior analysis through facial expression recognition in images using deep learning. Int. J. Innov. Technol. Exp. Eng. **9**(2), 391–397 (2019)
11. Xu, Q., Zheng, W., Song, Y., Zhang, C., Yuan, X., Li, Y.: Scene image and human skeleton-based dual-stream human action recognition. Pattern Recogn. Lett. **148**, 136–145 (2021)
12. Athavale, V.A., Gupta, S.C.: Human action recognition using CNN-SVM model. Adv. Sci. Technol. **6258**, 282–290 (2021)
13. Bulbul, M.F., Ali, H.: Gradient local auto-correlation features for depth human action recognition. SN Appl. Sci. **3**(5), 1–13 (2021)
14. Saifuddin, S.F.M., Shaahriar, K.A.: Silhouette pose feature-based human action classification using capsule network. J. Inf. Technol. Res. **14**(12), 106–124 (2021)
15. Zhdanova, M.M., Balabaeva, O.S.: Improvement of the human action recognition algorithm by the pre-processing of input data. In: IOP Conference Series: Materials Science and Engineering vol. 1029, no. 1, pp. 12119–12119 (2021)
16. Suresh, K.B., Viswanadha, R.S.: Human action recognition using a novel deep learning approach. In: IOP Conference Series: Materials Science and Engineering. Vol. 1042, no. 1, p. 012031 (2021)
17. Hao, X., Li, J., Jiang, T., Yu, M.: Hypergraph neural network for skeleton-based action recognition. IEEE Trans. Image Process. **30**, 2263–2275 (2021)
18. Xu, J. and Luo, Q.: Human action recognition based on mixed gaussian hidden markov model. In: MATEC Web of Conferences, vol. 336, p. 06004. EDP Sciences (2021)
19. Sargano, A.B., Gu, X., Angelov, P., Habib, Z.: Human action recognition using deep rule-based classifier. Multimedia Tools Appl. **79**(41), 30653–30667 (2020)
20. Ramya, P., Rajeswari, R.: Human action recognition using distance transform and entropy based features. Multimedia Tools Appl. **80**(6), 8147–8173 (2020)
21. Latha, B., Latha, B.M., Manjula, B.K., Sumana, V., Hemalatha, C.H.: Human action recognition using stip evaluation techniques. IOP Conf. Series: Mater. Sci. Eng. **925**(1), 12026–12026 (2020)
22. Abdelbaky, A., Aly, S.: Two-stream spatiotemporal feature fusion for human action recognition. Vis. Comput. **37**(7), 1821–1835 (2021)
23. Berlin, S.J., John, M.: R-STDP based spiking neural network for human action recognition. Appl. Artifi. Intell. **34**(9), 656–673 (2020)
24. Mishra, S.R., Mishra, T.K., Sanyal, G., Sarkar, A., Satapathy, S.C.: Real time human action recognition using triggered frame extraction and a typical CNN heuristic. Pattern Recogn. Lett. **135**, 329–336 (2020)
25. Khan, K., Ali, J., Ahmad, K., Gul, A., Sarwar, G.: 3d head pose estimation through facial features and deep convolutional neural networks. Comput. Mater. Continua **66**(2), 1757–1770 (2021)

26. Rehman, M.U., Ahmed, F., Khan, M.A., Tariq, U., Alfouzan, F.A.: Dynamic hand gesture recognition using 3d-cnn and lstm networks. Comput. Mater. Continua **70**(3), 4675–4690 (2022)
27. Anitha, G., Priya, S.B.: Vision based real time monitoring system for elderly fall event detection using deep learning. Comput. Syst. Sci. Eng. **42**(1), 87–103 (2022)
28. Zou, J., Zhu, N., Ge, B., Hong, D.: Elderly fall detection based on improved SSD algorithm. J. New Media **3**(1), 1–10 (2021)
29. Wang, J., Feng, S., Cheng, Y., Al-Nabhan, N.: Survey on the loss function of deep learning in face recognition. J. Inf. Hiding Privacy Protect. **3**(1), 29–45 (2021)

Application of MEA Optimized Wavelet Neural Network Model in Traffic Flow Prediction

Qian Yu and Haibo Wang[✉]

Department of Vehicle Engineering, Hunan Automotive Engineering Vocational College,
Zhuzhou 412000, China
yuqian_hn@163.com

Abstract. In order to improve the prediction mode accuracy of wavelet neural network, a prediction model of optimized wavelet neural network based on mind evolutionary algorithm (MEA) is proposed. Firstly, using MEA with extremely strong global search ability to train and optimize the connection weight and the extension scale of the wavelet neural network. Secondly, establish the wavelet neural network using the optimized connection weight and the extension scale. After comparative study of the prediction mode of MEA optimized wavelet neural network, genetic algorithm (GA) optimized wavelet neural network (GAWNN) and not optimized wavelet neural network (WNN) on the prediction for short-term traffic flow, the results show that MEAWNN method has higher prediction accuracy than other two methods.

Keywords: Wavelet neural network · Mind evolutionary algorithm · Genetic algorithm · Traffic flow prediction · Prediction accuracy

1 Introduction

Forecasting based on time series is one of the problems that humans often encounter in daily life. In recent years, a large number of scholars have conducted in-depth studies on various time series forecasting issues, such as traffic flow, stock market trends, and weather forecasts [1–3]. At present, prediction models mainly include: Historical Average method, Regression Analysis method, Kalman Filter method [4], neural network method and so on. Neural Networks have good nonlinear quality, self-adaptation and self-learning capabilities, they have shown great advantages in Time Series Forecasting l Various Forecasting Techniques [5]. Wavelet neural network is a coupling model of BP neural network and Wavelet Analysis [6]. The transfer function of the hidden layer in BP neural network is replaced by Wavelet Function. Therefore, wavelet neural network not only has the learning ability, nonlinear ability and generalization ability of neural network, but also has the multi-scale time-frequency local characteristics of wavelet transform and good approximation characteristics, which can improve the approximation ability of neural network to non-stationary signals. More accurate forecasts for time

© The Author(s), under exclusive license to Springer Nature Switzerland AG 2022
X. Sun et al. (Eds.): ICAIS 2022, LNCS 13338, pp. 661–671, 2022.
https://doi.org/10.1007/978-3-031-06794-5_53

series. However, wavelet neural networks also have shortcomings. It performs initial network parameters such as the connection weight between the input layer and the hidden layer, the expansion factor and translation factor of the wavelet basis function, and the connection weight between the hidden layer and the output layer. Values are more sensitive. If the initial values of these parameters are set unreasonably, it is easy to cause the wavelet neural network to converge slowly and fall into a local optimum.

In this paper, the mind evolutionary algorithm (MEA) and wavelet neural network (WNN) are combined to establish MEAWNN, and the thought evolution algorithm is used to optimize the connection weights and expansion and translation factors of the wavelet neural network, thereby improving the convergence speed of the wavelet neural network and reducing its falling into the local optimum. possibility. In order to verify the effectiveness of MEAWNN, the measured short-term traffic flow was predicted simultaneously with GAWNN and WNN, and the prediction performance of the three models was compared. Experimental results show that MEAWNN has the highest prediction accuracy.

2   Optimization of WNN with MEA (MEAWNN)

2.1   Wavelet Neural Network (WNN)

In 1992, Zhang Qinghua and other scholars of IRLSA, a famous French information science institution, first proposed wavelet neural networks [7, 8]. It is based on the BP neural network structure and uses wavelet basis functions to replace hidden layer transfer functions. It organically combines neural network and wavelet transform, fully inheriting the advantages of both [9, 10]. The use of related mathematical theories has proved that a three-layer neural network can solve any complex nonlinear mapping problem [11–13]. Therefore, this article only studies wavelet neural networks with a single hidden layer. Its topology is shown in Fig. 1:

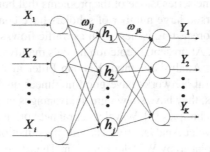

Fig. 1. Topology of wavelet neural network.

In Fig. 1, X_1, X_2, $\cdots$, X_i are the input parameter of the wavelet neural network, Y_1, Y_2, $\cdots$, X_k are the predicted output of the wavelet neural network, and ω_{ij} and ω_{jk} are the connection weights of the wavelet neural network. h_j is the transfer function of the hidden layer neuron. In this paper, the transfer function of the hidden layer neuron takes the Morlet wavelet basis function, and its mathematical expression is:

$$h_j(x) = cos(1.75x)e^{-\frac{x^2}{2}}$$ (1)

The output formula of the hidden layer is:

$$h(j) = h_j\left[\frac{\sum_{i=1}^{k}\omega_{ij}x_i - b_j}{a_j}\right] j = 1, 2, \cdots, l$$ (2)

Among it, $h(j)$ is the output value of the j-th node in the hidden layer; ω_{ij} is the connection weight from the input layer to the hidden layer; b_j and a_j are the translation factor and the expansion factor of the wavelet basis function hj respectively.

The output formula of the output layer is:

$$Y(k) = \sum_{j=1}^{l}\omega_{jk}h(j) \, k = 1, 2 \cdots, N$$ (3)

Among it, ω_{jk} is the connection weight of the hidden layer to the output layer, $h(j)$ is the node output of the j-th hidden layer, l is the number of nodes in the hidden layer, and N is the number of nodes in the output layer.

The wavelet neural network uses the gradient descent method to modify the weight of the network and the parameters of the wavelet basis function [14], so that the actual output value of the wavelet neural network prediction model is constantly approaching the expected output value. The correction process is as follows.

(1) Calculate the prediction error of the network:

$$E = \frac{1}{2}\sum_{p=1}^{P}\sum_{k=1}^{N}\left(d_k^p - y_k^p\right)^2$$ (4)

Among it, d_k^p is the expected output of the k-th node of the wavelet neural network output layer corresponding to the p-th training sample; y_k^p is the actual output of the k-th node of the wavelet neural network output layer corresponding to the p-th training sample, and p is The number of training samples.

(2) Correct the wavelet neural network weights and wavelet basis function parameters according to the prediction error E:

$$\omega_{ij}(t+1) = \omega_{ij}(t) - \mu \frac{\partial E}{\partial \omega_{ij}} \tag{5}$$

$$\omega_{jk}(t+1) = \omega_{jk}(t) - \mu \frac{\partial E}{\partial \omega_{jk}} \tag{6}$$

$$a_j(t+1) = a_j(t) - \mu \frac{\partial E}{\partial a_j} \tag{7}$$

$$b_j(t+1) = b_j(t) - \mu \frac{\partial E}{\partial b_j} \tag{8}$$

Among them, μ is the learning rate, and the calculation formulas of $\frac{\partial E}{\partial \omega_{ij}}$, $\frac{\partial E}{\partial \omega_{jk}}$, $\frac{\partial E}{\partial a_j}$, $\frac{\partial E}{\partial b_j}$ are as follows:

$$\frac{\partial E}{\partial \omega_{ij}} = -\sum_{p=1}^{P} \sum_{k=1}^{N} \left(d_k^p - y_k^p\right) \frac{\partial y_k^p}{\partial \omega_{ij}}$$

$$= -\sum_{p=1}^{P} \sum_{k=1}^{N} \left(d_k^p - y_k^p\right) \omega_{jk} \frac{\partial h(j)}{\partial \omega_{ij}} \tag{9}$$

$$= -\sum_{p=1}^{P} \sum_{k=1}^{N} \left(d_k^p - y_k^p\right) \omega_{jk} h'(j) \frac{x_{ij}}{a_j}$$

$$\frac{\partial E}{\partial \omega_{jk}} = -\sum_{p=1}^{P} \sum_{k=1}^{N} \left(d_k^p - y_k^p\right) \frac{\partial y_k^p}{\partial \omega_{jk}} \tag{10}$$

$$= -\sum_{p=1}^{P} \sum_{k=1}^{N} \left(d_k^p - y_k^p\right) h(j)$$

$$\frac{\partial E}{\partial a_j} = -\sum_{p=1}^{P} \sum_{k=1}^{N} \left(d_k^p - y_k^p\right) \frac{\partial y_k^p}{\partial a_j} \tag{11}$$

$$= \sum_{p=1}^{P} \sum_{k=1}^{N} \left(d_k^p - y_k^p\right) \omega_{jk} h'(j) \left(\sum_{i=1}^{M} \omega_{ij} x_i - b_j\right) \frac{1}{a_j^2}$$

$$\frac{\partial E}{\partial b_j} = -\sum_{p=1}^{P} \sum_{k=1}^{N} \left(d_k^p - y_k^p\right) \frac{\partial y_k^p}{\partial b_j}$$

$$= -\sum_{p=1}^{P} \sum_{k=1}^{N} \left(d_k^p - y_k^p\right) \omega_{jk} \frac{\partial h(j)}{\partial b_j} \tag{12}$$

$$= \sum_{p=1}^{P} \sum_{k=1}^{N} \left(d_k^p - y_k^p\right) \omega_{jk} h'(j) \frac{1}{a_j}$$

2.2   MEA Optimized Wavelet Neural Network Algorithm Flow

This paper uses the MEA algorithm to train and optimize the weights of the wavelet neural network and the parameters of the wavelet basis function, and then use the optimized initial weights and the parameters of the optimal initial wavelet basis function to initialize the wavelet neural network, and then use the wavelet The neural network makes predictions. The specific process is as follows:

(1) The samples are divided into training samples and test samples. The training samples are used for network training, and the test samples are used for network prediction accuracy testing.

(2) The MEA algorithm is used to obtain the wavelet basis function expansion factor a_j and the translation factor b_j in the wavelet neural network, as well as the optimal initial values of the network connection weights ω_{ij} and ω_{jk}.

(3) Determine the maximum number of iterations and learning rate μ.

(4) Normalize the training samples.

(5) Input the training sample, calculate the network output value according to formula (1), (2), (3), and calculate the network prediction error E by formula (4).

(6) Calculate $\frac{\partial E}{\partial \omega_{ij}}$、$\frac{\partial E}{\partial \omega_{jk}}$、$\frac{\partial E}{\partial a_j}$、$\frac{\partial E}{\partial b_j}$ from Eqs. (9), (10), (11), (12).

(7) According to formulas (5), (6), (7), (8), the network connection weights ω_{ij}, ω_{jk} and wavelet basis function parameters a_j, b_j are adjusted.

(8) If $E < E_{max}$ (E_{max} max is the maximum allowable error), or the maximum number of iterations is reached, the training ends, otherwise it returns to step (5).

(9) Input the normalized test samples, and then calculate the prediction accuracy of the wavelet neural network after training.

3 Design and Analysis of Experimental Results

3.1 Design of Experiments

In order to verify the effectiveness of the method proposed in this paper, MEAWNN, GAWNN, WNN three prediction methods are used to predict the actual short-term traffic flow.

The experimental data in this article comes from University of Minnesota Duluth (http://www.d.umn.edu/tdrl/index.htm). The data includes traffic data on the highways around the University of Minnesota Twin Cities. More than 4,000 loop coil detectors are collected throughout the year and compressed in a proprietary format. The traffic flow data recorded by any detector at several time intervals can be obtained as needed [15].

According to formula (14), the traffic flow data in the experiment becomes a normalized time series with a mean value of 0 and an amplitude of 1, and the normalized time series are reconstructed in phase space. The experiment uses a three-layer wavelet neural network with input layer nodes m, hidden layer nodes 2m + 1, and output layer nodes 1. m is the embedding dimension of the phase space reconstruction of the traffic flow time series. In this paper Take m = 5. The parameter settings of the wavelet neural network are: the number of training times is 100, the learning rate is 0.01; the parameters of the thinking evolution algorithm are: the population size is 100, the number of winning subpopulations is 5, the number of temporary subpopulations is 5, and the number of iterations is 20.

$$y_i = \frac{x_i - \frac{1}{n}\sum_{i=1}^{n} x_i}{\max(x_i) - \min(x_i)} \tag{13}$$

Among it, $\{x_i\}$ is the original traffic flow sequence, and $\{y_i\}$ is the normalized traffic flow sequence.

The evaluation system of the experiment uses absolute error err, average absolute error MAE and relative error perr, as follows:

$$err = |x_i - \hat{x}_i| \tag{14}$$

$$MAE = \frac{1}{N_p}\sum_{i=1}^{N_p} |x_i - \hat{x}_i| \tag{15}$$

$$perr = \frac{\sum_{i=1}^{N_p} (x_i - \hat{x}_i)^2}{\sum_{i=1}^{N_p} x_i^2} \tag{16}$$

Among them, x_i and $\hat{x}_i$ are the actual and predicted values of traffic flow; N_p is the number of predicted samples.

3.2 Analysis of Experimental Results

This article uses the data detected by the No. 10 detector to output the traffic flow data for the four days from January 16 to January 19, 2015, with a total of 1152 data at five-minute intervals.

This experiment takes the first 1052 of the traffic flow data as training samples, and the last 100 data as prediction test samples. In order to verify the effectiveness of the method proposed in this paper, this paper conducts comparative experiments on different numbers of training samples, repeats each experiment 1000 times, and then takes the statistical average of the average absolute error MAE and relative error perr.

Figure 2, Fig. 3, and Fig. 4 respectively show the prediction results of an experiment when the training sample is 1052 and the prediction sample is 100. Table 1 shows the three prediction models for 100 models under different numbers of training samples. The statistical average of the predicted average absolute error MAE and relative error perr of the predicted sample.

It can be seen from Fig. 2, Fig. 3, and Fig. 4 that the three prediction models can predict the traffic flow trend better, but MEAWNN has the best prediction effect, and GAWNN has a better prediction effect than WNN.

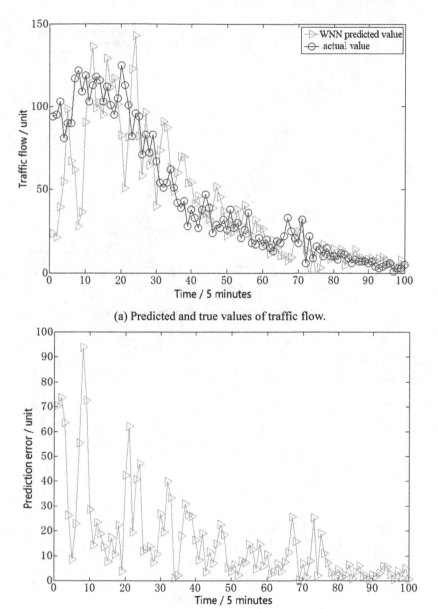

(a) Predicted and true values of traffic flow.

(b) Absolute error of prediction

Fig. 2. Predicted results of WNN model.

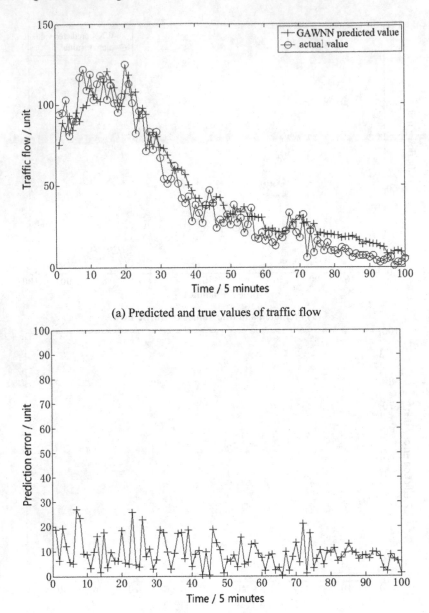

(a) Predicted and true values of traffic flow

(b) Absolute error of prediction

Fig. 3. Predicted results of GAWNN model.

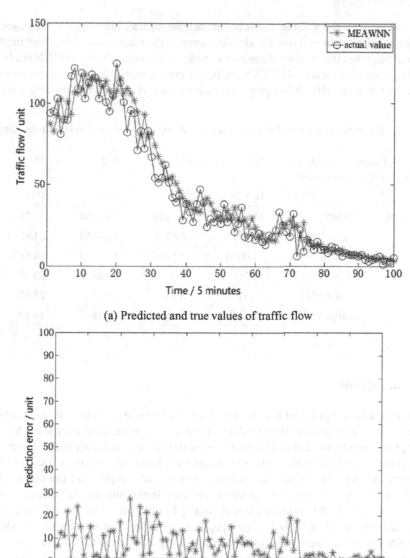

(a) Predicted and true values of traffic flow

(b) Absolute error of prediction

Fig. 4. Predicted results of MEAWNN model.

It can be seen from Table 1 that as the number of training samples decreases, the average absolute error and relative absolute error of the prediction of the three methods increase, but when the number of training samples is the same, the MEAWNN prediction error is the smallest, and the GAWNN prediction error less than WNN prediction error. It can be seen that the MEAWNN proposed in this article is an effective predictive model.

Table 1. The prediction error of the measured traffic sequence with different training sample.

Number of training samples/unit Forecast sample number/unit		1052	952	852	752
		100	100	100	100
MAE/unit	WNN	15.8079	17.4156	20.1654	33.7132
	GAWNN	9.1173	10.0716	15.6164	23.4283
	MEAWNN	7.0084	7.5496	10.2426	14.8176
Perr/%	WNN	16.75	23.42	29.88	40.56
	GAWNN	3.37	3.85	8.71	25.97
	MEAWNN	2.61	3.19	7.18	16.10

4 Conclusion

In order to solve the problem that the wavelet neural network is sensitive to the network connection weights and the initial values of the wavelet basis function parameters, this paper proposes a prediction model based on the thought evolution algorithm to optimize the wavelet neural network. First, the thought evolution algorithm is used to obtain the optimized wavelet the neural network connects the weights and the initial values of the wavelet basis function parameters, and then builds the wavelet neural network model according to the optimized initial values. In order to verify the effectiveness of the prediction model proposed in this paper, three prediction models of MEAWNN, GAWNN and WNN were used to predict the actual measured traffic flow data at the same time, and the prediction errors of the three models were compared. The results show that the prediction error of the MEAWNN model proposed in this article is smaller than the other two prediction models, so MEAWNN is an effective prediction model.

Funding Statement. The author(s) disclosed receipt of the following financial support for the research, authorship, and/or publication of this article: his work was supported by the scientific research project of Hunan provincial department of education (18c1462).

Conflicts of Interest. The author(s) declared no potential conflicts of interest with respect to the research, authorship, and/or publication of this article.

Acknowledgement. The author(s) thank colleagues who have provided the process data.

References

1. Thamizhazhagan, P., et al.: Ai based traffic flow prediction model for connected and autonomous electric vehicles. Comput. Material. Continua **70**(2), 3333–3347 (2022)
2. Kulaglic, A., Ustundag, B.B.: Stock price prediction using predictive error compensation wavelet neural networks. Comput. Mater. Continua **68**(3), 3577–3593 (2021)
3. Pandu, S.B., et al.: Artificial intelligence based solar radiation predictive model using weather forecasts. Comput. Mater. Continua **71**(2), 109–124 (2022)
4. Jwo, D., Lee, J.: Kernel entropy based extended kalman filter for GPS navigation processing. Comput. Mater. Continua **68**(1), 857–876 (2021)
5. Assiri, A.S.: Efficient training of multi-layer neural networks to achieve faster validation. Comput. Syst. Sci. Eng. **36**(3), 435–450 (2021)
6. Zhou, H., Chen, Y.J., Zhang, S.M.: Ship trajectory prediction based on BP neural network. J. Artif. Intell. **1**(1), 29–36 (2019)
7. Zhang Q.: Regressor selection and wavelet network construction. IEEE (1993)
8. Zhang, Q.H., Qiang, F.: Performance evaluation model of engineering project management based on improved wavelet neural network. J. Service Sci. Manag. **2**(1), 10–14 (2009)
9. Zhou, F.Y., Jin, L.P., Dong, J.: Review of convolutional neural network. Chin. J. Comput. **40**(7), 1229–1251 (2017)
10. Yu, C., et al.: Short-term traffic state prediction based on wavelet neural network. Mob. Commun. **42**(5), 91–96 (2018)
11. Jie, C., et al.: Short-term traffic flow forecasting based on BP neural network with wavelet and multidimensional reconstruction. Comput. Appl. Softw. **35**(12), 61–65 (2018)
12. Liu, J., et al.: Simulation research on predictive wavelet neural network intelligent control system. J. Syst. Simulat. **30**(10), 3770–3780 (2018)
13. Wang, S., et al.: Multi-mapping convolution neural network for the image super-resolution algorithm. Xi'an Dianzi Keji Daxue Xuebao/J. Xidian University **45**(4), 155–160 (2018)
14. Jin, R., Zhou, X., Wang, Y.: An efficient energy routing protocol based on gradient descent method in WSNS. J. Inf. Hiding Privacy Protect. **2**(3), 115–123 (2020)
15. Rota, B.C.R., Simic, M.: Traffic flow optimization on freeways. Proc. Comput. Sci. **96**, 1637–1646 (2016)

Energy Reduction Method by Compiler Optimization

Sheng Xiao[1,2]([✉]), Jing Selena He[3], Jingwen Yang[1], Xiaomeng Hong[1], and Jinke Luo[1]

[1] Computer School, Hunan First Normal University, 1015 Fenglin Third Road, Yuelu, Changsha 410205, China
sxiao@hnfnu.edu.cn
[2] Computer School, Wuhan University, 299 Bayi Road, Wuchang, Wuhan 430072, China
[3] Department of Computer Science, Kennesaw State University, Kennesaw 30144-5588, USA

Abstract. As nanoscale processing becomes the mainstream in IC manufacturing, the crosstalk problem rises as a serious challenge, not only for energy-efficiency and performance but also for security requirements. In this paper, we propose a register reallocation algorithm called Nearby Access based Register Reallocation (NARR) to reduce the crosstalk between instruction buses. The method includes construction of the software Nearby Access Aware Interference Graph (NAIG), using data flow analysis at assembly level, and reallocation of the registers to the software. Experimental results show that the crosstalk could be dramatically minimized, especially for 4C crosstalk, with a reduction of 80.84% in average, and up to 99.99% at most.

Keywords: Crosstalk · Energy efficiency · Register reallocation · Green compilation

1 Introduction

Energy efficiency is a hot topic in computer system [1–4].With the progress of technological development, the size of embedded devices becomes smaller and smaller, so the bus lines lay out more and more intensively, making the crosstalk a more and more serious challenge for the circuit design. The increments of crosstalk not only influence the scalability and performance of the embedded system, but also consume more power, making the device more vulnerable to overheat and to malicious attacker. The additional power consumption of crosstalk can particularly be used by attackers through the Differential Power Analysis to get the security and hidden information of the system, such as revealing hidden hardware faults on integrated circuits, accessing cryptographic keys, and getting the actual executing codes of the microprocessors [5]. Furthermore, the extra power needed increases noise and decreases the lifetime of the embedded device, therefore compromising the current "green compilation" pursuit.

© The Author(s), under exclusive license to Springer Nature Switzerland AG 2022
X. Sun et al. (Eds.): ICAIS 2022, LNCS 13338, pp. 672–683, 2022.
https://doi.org/10.1007/978-3-031-06794-5_54

Crosstalk is a traditional problem for circuit design and many efforts have been done for it. Circuit designers proposed sorts of methods to reduce the crosstalk between couple buses, such as Codec [6], buffer insertion [7], Shielding [8], gate sizing [9], and so on. Some scholars evaluated different crosstalk fault tolerant approaches for Networks-on-chip (NoCs) links such that the network can maintain the original network performance even in the presence of errors. Their results demonstrated that the use of CRC coding at each link should be preferred if minimal area and power overhead were the main goals [10]. Some scholars proposed an enhanced code based on the Fibonacci number system (FNS) to suppress the crosstalk noise below 6C level, in which both the redundancy of numbers and the non-uniqueness of Fibonacci-based binary codeword were utilized to search the proper codeword. Experimental results showed that the proposed technique decreased about 22% latency of TSVs comparing with the worst crosstalk cases [11]. Some scholars propose DR coding mechanism, which uses a novel numerical system in generating code words that minimizes overheads of codec and is applicable for any arbitrary width of wires. Experimental results show that worst crosstalk-induced transition patterns are completely avoided in wires using DR coding mechanism. Some scholars proposed a crosstalk-noise-aware bus coding scheme with ground gated repeaters. This approach minimized the routing overhead as well as power consumption of data bus systems. The routing overhead was reduced by 12.31% with the new bus coding scheme compared to the conventional data bus with shielding wires. Furthermore, the power leakage and worst-case active power consumptions were reduced by 12.5% and 18.26%, respectively, with the new crosstalk-noise-aware data bus system compared to the previously published bus coding system in an industrial 40 nm CMOS technology [12]. Some scholars proposed a selection method of adjacent lines for assigning signal transitions in test pattern generation. The selection method could reduce the number of adjacent lines used in test pattern generation without degrading the quality of test pattern that could excite the fault effect. Some scholars presented a 3D CAC method which was based on an intelligent fixed mapping of the bits of existing 2D CACs onto rectangular or hexagonal TSV arrangements. Their method required less hardware and reduced the maximum crosstalk of modern TSV and metal wire buses by 37.8% and 47.6%, respectively, while leaving their power consumption almost unaffected. However, these methods either need extra hardware unit support or must increase the area of chip, making them unfavorable for the development of advanced embedded devices requiring portability and minimized cost [13].

With the existing Selective Shielding method, some scholars proposed a co-hardware/software register relabeling combination to reduce the crosstalk of instruction bus [14]. Some scholars adapted also a combination approach with instruction rescheduling, register renaming, NOP instruction padding, and instruction opcode assignment. They proposed the software method to eliminate the 4C crosstalk. These methods are either based on current hardware support or having limitations, illustrated in the next section, to reduce the crosstalk [15].

Register allocation is also an important component of compilers, many techniques have been proposed, such as Graph-base register allocation [16, 17], Linear scan register allocation [18, 19], tree-based register allocation, and others [20–22]. Some scholars propose a new register renaming technique that leverages physical register sharing by introducing minor changes in the register map table and the issue queue. Experimental results show that it provides 6% speedup on average for the SPEC2006 benchmarks in modern out-of-order processor [23]. Some scholars propose a new class of register allocation and code generation algorithms that can be performed in linear time. These algorithms are based on the mathematical foundations of abstract interpretation and the computation of the level of abstraction. They have been implemented in a specialized library for just-in-time compilation. The specialization of this library involves the execution of common intermediate language (CIL) and low level virtual machine (LLVM) with a focus on embedded systems. But most of these proposed methods were aiming at increasing the performance with litter spill codes, while the crosstalk between instructions was seldom considered [24].

We propose here a software method Nearby Access based Register Reallocation (NARR) to reduce the crosstalk. Though similar to the graph color register allocation method, it is distinguished by combining the frequency of near neighbor access to assign the registers. Our register reallocation approach is not only a software-only method requiring no modifications in hardware, but also improves performance in reducing the instruction bus crosstalk since it deeply analyzes the data flow.

2   Methods and Materials

2.1   Crosstalk Overview

Crosstalk is the noise signal for one circuit or channel of a transmission system caused by the other circuits or channels that are usually parallel to the effected one. The strength of crosstalk is often subject to the following factors: wire length, wire width, switching pattern of nearby wires, and so on. For better evaluating the delay and energy caused by crosstalk, researchers have established the crosstalk delay model and energy model [25].

According to the effective capacitance of different switching patter of nearby wires in continuous cycles, the crosstalk is classified into six classes shown in Table 1. (The symbols -, ↑, ↓, x stand for no, positive and negative, any transitions, respectively.)

Table 1. Classification of crosstalk.

Class	Transition Patterns $\Delta_{j-1}\Delta_j\Delta_{j+1}$
0	$x-x$
0C	↑↑↑, ↓↓↓
1C	$-$ ↑↑, $-$ ↓↓, ↑↑ $-$, ↓↓ $-$
2C	↓↑↑, ↑↓↓, ↑↑↓, ↓↓↑, $-$ ↑ $-$, $-$ ↓ $-$
3C	$-$ ↑↓, $-$ ↓↑, ↓↑ $-$, ↓↑ $-$
4C	↓↑↓, ↑↓↑

Currently, research work focuses on how to eliminate the 3C and 4C classes of crosstalk and also to reduce those of other classes. But the established techniques are more or less based on to modification of the integrated circuit that could increase the overhead of the system and therefore can't be used for some cost-constraint embedded systems. There are some software researches attempting to reduce the crosstalk between instruction data buses. Some approaches need to insert extra "NOP" instructions. Others can't make use of the full power of changing register because insufficient amount of program information such as data flow is analyzed. In the next section, we will illustrate the limitations of register renaming techniques, as well as how to overcome these limitations by using register reallocation, with a example.

2.2 Crosstalk Case Study

In t Register renaming is used as software-only or software/hardware combined technique for reducing the crosstalk. Since the lifetime of registers is not analyzed and the results of register allocation are not used, Register renaming alone can't alleviate the limitation of register allocation which aims to use a minimal number of registers to generate a good program performance, therefore losing potential improvement in crosstalk reduction.

Considering the example instruction lists in [26], as illustrated in Fig. 1(a), we can see that the instruction scheduling fail to reduce the crosstalk of instruction buses between $I1 \rightarrow I2 \rightarrow I3$. From the $I2$ and $I3$ lines, we can see that $R5$ is lastly used of its previous definition in $I2$. And for saving registers, register allocator assigns $R5$ for saving the results of $I3$ which causes the $4C$ crosstalk between $I2$ and $I3$.

From this piece of codes, $R6$ is not used and we assume that $R6$ is available too. If the register allocator uses the $R6$ to replace $R5$ for saving the results of $I3$, the crosstalk will be eliminated (shown in Fig. 1(b)). However, if we use the register renaming to rename $R5$ with $R6$, the crosstalk between $I2$ and $I3$ will be eliminated, but the new $3C$ crosstalk will occur between $I1, I2$ and $I2, I3$ (see Fig. 1(b)).

This example allows us to see the potentially better capability of register allocation in crosstalk reduction, compared to register renaming and to other software techniques.

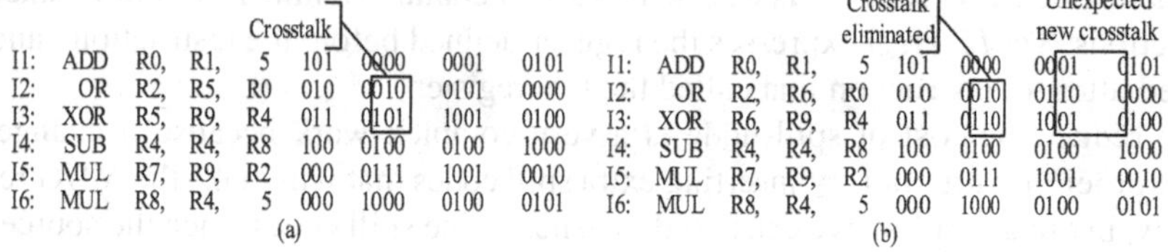

```
                  Crosstalk                              Crosstalk          Unexpected
                                                         eliminated         new crosstalk
I1:  ADD  R0,  R1,  5   101  0000  0001  0101   I1:  ADD  R0,  R1,  5   101  0000  0001  0101
I2:  OR   R2,  R5,  R0  010  0010  0101  0000   I2:  OR   R2,  R6,  R0  010  0010  0110  0000
I3:  XOR  R5,  R9,  R4  011  0101  1001  0100   I3:  XOR  R6,  R9,  R4  011  0110  1001  0100
I4:  SUB  R4,  R4,  R8  100  0100  0100  1000   I4:  SUB  R4,  R4,  R8  100  0100  0100  1000
I5:  MUL  R7,  R9,  R2  000  0111  1001  0010   I5:  MUL  R7,  R9,  R2  000  0111  1001  0010
I6:  MUL  R8,  R4,  5   000  1000  0100  0101   I6:  MUL  R8,  R4,  5   000  1000  0100  0101
                   (a)                                              (b)
```

Fig. 1. Register assignments example

2.3 Crosstalk Aware Register Allocation, Optimization Process Outline

In order to get an effective optimization for the total program such as the library of system, our optimization process utilizes the disassemble codes and the profiling results as inputs. Then *NAIG* constructor is used to build the *NAIG* from the disassemble codes and set the weight of it. Finally, the *NARR* processor analysis the *NAIG* to reallocation the register and generate the optimized code. In our methods, *NAIG* construction and *NARR* process are the most important processes, which will be presented in the following two subsections in detail.

2.4 NAIG Construction

The goal of this work is to reduce the crosstalk on instruction data bus. So the more frequently access patterns of registers pairs are, the more important the registers are. For better illustrating the nearby accesses frequency feature combining with the register allocation, we enhanced the original Interference graph that was widely used for register allocation and constructed the new nearby access aware interference graph, called *NAIG*.

NAIG is a weighted undirected graph that can be represented by a four tuple $G = (V, E_I, E_N, W_E)$. Where $v \in V$ represents a variable or constant of the program, $e(u, v) \in E_I$ expresses that the node u and node v can't share the same register, $e'(u', v') \in E_N$ expresses that the node u and node v may be nearby access and the weight $w(e) \in W_E$ represents the frequency of such access pattern $e(u, v)$.

For building the *NAIG*, we get the disassemble code as input and suppose that there are unlimited registers, the same as the registers called virtual registers in many compilers. Firstly, we change the disassemble codes to the SSA form for each basic block that makes sure the registers are defined only once (Algorithm 1, line 1–4). Then, we use the methods described in to construct the data flow of each basic block and get the lifetime of each register in each instruction (line 5–6). The interference graph can be constructed of analysis the live register in each instruction (line 7–15). After getting the interference graph, we can use the profiling results to add the weight of edges (line 16–21). And then we return the constructed *NAIG* at last (line 22). The detailed construction algorithm is expressed in Algorithm 1. In this program, the *CFG* is control flow graph for the program and each node $v \in V'$ represents a basic block that contains number of in order executed instructions. The *Liveregi* expresses the register defined before the instruction i and will be used after the instruction that called the live register.

To reduce the cost of spill node is a very complex work because it changes the source order of instruction by inserting extra spill codes that will make the *NAIG* rebuilt. Luckily, in our algorithm, we can avoid to generate the spill codes since the source code is allocated successfully and we can always eliminate the spill code by assigning the spill node with its original one. The detailed reallocation algorithm is presented in next section.

Algorithm 1 *NAIG* construction algorithm.
_____
Input:
    source disassemble codes, S;
    The profiling results, $P:V_p \rightarrow V_p \rightarrow W_E$;
Output:
    $NAIG(V,E_I,E_N,W_E)$;
1: $CFG(V',E') := ConstructCFG(S)$
2: **for** each $v \in V'$ **do**
3:    Translate v to SSA form
4: **end for**
5: $DS = DateFlowAnalysis(CFG)$
6: $Livereg_i = GetLivereg_i(DS)$based on methods in[1]
7: **for** each $v \in V'$ **do**
8:    **for** each $i \in v$ **do**
9:     **for** each $j \in Livereg_i$ && $i \neq j$ **do**
10:      $NAIG.V.add(i)$
11:      $NAIG.V.add(j)$
12:      $NAIG.E_I.add(i,j)$
13:     **end for**
14:    **end for**
15: **end for**
16: **for** each$pair < r_i,r_j,w_{i,j} > \in P$**do**
17:    $NAIG.V.add(i)$
18:    $NAIG.V.add(j)$
19:    $NAIG.E_N.add(i,j)$
20:    $NAIG.W_E.add(w_{i,j})$
21: **end for**
22: **return** *NBTI*;
_____

2.5 NARR Algorithm

Based on the above *NAIG*, we implement our new *NARR* algorithm as follow: firstly, we construct the *NAIG* for each function of the program; then, we sort the edge of *NAIG* by the decreased weight order (Algorithm 2, line 1). Since the heavily weighted edge represents that the nodes own the edge are more frequently nearby access in instruction date buses, we expect it in the same register or the least crosstalk registers. At the same time, we expect the lowest spill code which will not only lose the performance of the system, but also increase the undetected crosstalk by this algorithm, so we make sure that no additional new spill codes will be emerged in our algorithm.

Then, we analyze the ordered edges one by one to finish the register allocation for each node (line 2–36). For each edge $e(u, v) \in E_I$, we first check whether a node is assigned. If any one of nodes u is assigned for register r_i, we will choose the register other than r_i but with minimal crosstalk to assign it for v (line 5–7). If both nodes are not assigned, we first assign any of them to one register and then find the other suitable register as the previous case for the other one (line 15–19). If the two nodes are assigned with the same register, we will try to change one assigning into another register (line 6–14). For the edge not in E_I, we first try to assign the two nodes in the same register. If it is not reasonable, we can handle it as the edge in EI (line 22–34). The program detail is shown in Algorithm 2.

Algorithm 2 *NARR* algorithm.

Input:
    the $NAIG(V,E_I,E_N,W_E)$ for each function of program;
    the available registers $R=\{r_0,r_1,\cdots,r_n\}$

Output:
    The allocation map M: $V \to R$ for each node V in *NAIG*;

1: $E' := sortE_N$ by decreased order in W_E
2: **while** $E' \neq \varnothing$ **do**
3:   $e(u,v):=$pop the first element of E'
4:   **if** $e \in E_I$ **then**
5:     **if** only one node (assuming for u) is assigned for register r_i **then**
6:       get the register $r_j \neq r_i$ with minimal cost *crosstalk(r_i,r_j)*
7:       $M.add(v,r_j)$
8:     **else if** both u, v are assigned for the same register r_i **then**
9:       **if** one of this two node (assuming for u) can be changed to other register
        Set R' without violating the *IG* of current analysis **then**
10:         $r_j := r_k$ where $r_k \in R'$, $e(n,u) \in E_N$ and satisfy
          $\min \sum \omega_{n,u} \cdot crosstalk(M(n),r_k)$
11:         $M(u):=r_k$
12:       **else**
13:         assign the two nodes for original regisers.
14:       **end if**
15:     **else if** both u, v are not assigned for any register **then**
16:       $r_i :=$ get the random register that node v can be used.
17:       $M.add(v,r_i)$
18:       get the register $r_j \neq r_i$ with minimal cost *crosstalk (r_i,r_j)*
19:       $M.add(u,r_j)$
20:   **end if**
21: **else**
22:   **if** only one node (assuming for u)is assigned for register r_i **then**
23:     **if** r_i without violate the conflict of the other assignments till now **then**
24:       $M.add(v,r_i)$
25:     **else**
26:       assign as line $5-7$
27:     **end if**
28:   **else if** none of node is assigned **then**
29:     **if** exist an register r_k can be used for both node without violate the
        conflict of the other assignments till now **then**
30:       $M.add(v,r_k), M.add(u,r_k)$
31:     **else**
32:       assign as line $15-19$
33:     **end if**
34:   **end if**
35: **end if**
36: **end while**
37: **return** M

2.6 Experimental Setup for Performance Evaluation

The experiment is built up in Fedora 12 combined with Windows 7 home basic version. The test cases are selected from the MIBench [27].

The compiler tools are arm-linux-gcc 4.4.3, and combined with objdump 2.19.51 to get the disassemble codes. The sim-profile tool for arm is used as profile tool to get the access frequency of instructions. Specifically, we use the arm-linux-gcc to compile the source code to binary codes in Fedora 12 environment, firstly. Then, we disassemble and get profile information for the binary codes respectively. After getting the disassemble codes and profile information, we use them as input for the *NARR* processor to get the crosstalk aware optimized binary codes. Finally, we compare the source binary codes to the optimized binary codes to evaluate the performance of *NARR,* and analyze the improvement details in crosstalk reduction, especially for *3C* and *4C* ones.

3 Results and Discussions

3.1 Performance of NARR

Figure 2 presents the decreased percentage of 4C and 3C+4C crosstalk for *NARR,* compared with the results of GCC. From this benchmark, we can see that the 4C crosstalk has been significantly reduced. In the cases such as *stringsearch_large, stringsearch_small, dijkstra,* and *crc,* the reduction percentage of 4C crosstalk is higher than 95%, eliminating almost all 4C crosstalk of the program. And the average decrease rate is about 81%. And for 3C+4C crosstalk, we can see that most of them are also significantly reduced except *dijkstra* since the *dijkstra* has many conflicts between the 3C and 4C crosstalk. We force a crosstalk avoid priority for 4C, so the *dijkstra* benchmark result is not so good in 3C+4C condition. However, we still get an excellent reduction rate under the major benchmark tests for 3C+4C and the average reduction rate of all tested benchmarks is about 44%.

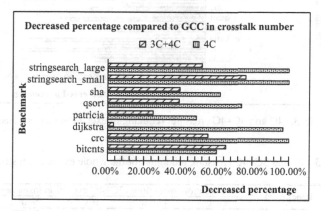

Fig. 2. 4C and 3C+4C crosstalk reducing in crosstalk number

For better understanding the crosstalk avoid in instruction level, we also analyze the 4C and 3C+4C crosstalk in dynamic execution with profile recorded in Fig. 3. From this result, we can see that the 4C crosstalk shows again a good reduction and the average decreased percentage is 80.87%. The highest reduction rate is 99.99% for the *crc* test under that only two 4C crosstalk appeared in the program after optimization (shown in Table 2). And for 3C+4C crosstalk, the average reduction percentage is also 37.01%, similar to the results shown in Fig. 2. Special cases are, however, again a smaller reduction rate recorded in 3C+4C crosstalk condition for *stringsearch_large, patricia* and *dijjkstra* tests. The main reason could be that in an instruction, there may be some crosstalk in the same class such as 3C. So if the instruction frequently executes, the crosstalk data at instruction level will be less than those at crosstalk number level. However, getting crosstalk statistics at instruction level is reasonable since the program is executed at instruction level and the possible attackers might also try to work in the instruction level to get the most detailed information of the system.

Table 2. Crosstalk comparison of *GCC* and *NARR*

Benchmark	3C Crosstalk			4C Crosstalk		
	GCC	*NARR*	*NARR/GCC*	*GCC*	*NARR*	*NARR/GCC*
bitcnts	87750075	5625002	0.06410	33750073	2250001	0.0667
crc	159667218	26611206	0.1667	79833611	2	0
dijkstra	76644109	7562503	0.0987	63344776	86222	0.0014
patricia	590383	38600	0.0654	466640	19041	0.0408
qsort	1250019	400005	0.3199	1050022	100003	0.0952
sha	69017038	11570830	0.1677	39583124	4264487	0.1077
stringsearch_small	16563	15185	0.9168	15509	57	0.0037
stringsearch_small	381159	352483	0.9247	705765	1334	0.0019

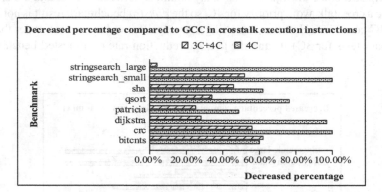

Fig. 3. 4C and 3C+4C crosstalk reducing in execution instructions

Table 3. 4C and 3C+4C crosstalk reducing for the whole execution instructions

Benchmark	4C execution instuctions		3C+4C execution instuctions	
	GCC	NARR	GCC	NARR
bitcnts	0.78%	0.31%	13.01%	5.02%
crc	7.69%	0.00%	53.85%	23.08%
dijkstra	3.08%	0.04%	34.33%	25.86%
patricia	1.51%	0.74%	24.61%	19.00%
qsort	11.27%	2.82%	46.48%	32.39%
sha	8.20%	3.02%	57.10%	31.07%
stringsearch_small	23.10%	0.09%	48.29%	23.68%
stringsearch_large	23.29%	0.09%	48.48%	46.73%
Average	9.87%	0.89%	40.77%	25.85%

Table 3 shows the evaluation results of adapting *NARR* to reduce the 4C and 3C+4C crosstalk in the aspect of the whole executed instructions. We can see that after *NARR*, the crosstalk percentage is significantly reduced for almost every benchmark tested, in both 4C and 3C+4C cases, in comparison with GCC. The average percentage of 4C crosstalk is reduced to a level of 0.89%, compared with the initially compiled result of 9.89% with GCC (with a relative reduction rate of 91% based on the GCC value). Furthermore, under specific tests such as *crc*, *dijkstra*, etc., we get nearly 0 crosstalk in 4C situation after NARR. And the 3C+4C crosstalk is also reduced from 40.77% for

GCC to 25.85% after NARR, in average. So the *NARR* method is good for reducing the crosstalk, especially for the 4C case.

Table 4 shows all types of crosstalk decreased percentage compared to GCC by NARR. We can see that the overall crosstalk is also decreased largely. For the bitcnts and qsort, the reduction rate is up to more than 44%. The average reduction rate is also achieved to 24.24%. So our NARR method is not can get good performance for crosstalk.

Table 4. All types crosstalk reducing in execution instructions.

Benchmark	GCC	NARR	decreased rate
bitcnts	2781573971	1553071408	44.17%
crc	2261952341	1809561893	20.00%
dijkstra	1606207102	1384640962	13.79%
patricia	12692958	11624053	8.42%
qsort	270214	150181	44.42%
sha	1168409001	935588937	19.93%
search_small_pro	451658	325107	28.02%
search_large_pro	10470186	8885138	15.14%
Average	980253428.9	712980959.9	24.24%

4 Conclusions

Crosstalk is a challenge not only for acquiring power-efficiency and performance, but also for satisfying the security and green requirements of an IC design since the nanoscale manufacturing has become the mainstream now. The new method we proposed here in crosstalk aware register reallocation is to reduce the influence of crosstalk for the couple instruction buses. The method is a software-only technique without any needs to modify the traditional hardware. Our NARR method can result in a reduction of 80.87% for 4C crosstalk in average and up to 99.99% at most. The percentage of 4C and 4C+3C crosstalk at instruction level is also reduced from the control GCC average value, by 9% and 15% in crosstalk rate difference, respectively. It confirms so that our *NARR* algorithm is effective in reducing the crosstalk especially for the 4C class. Of course, we can combine in the future with the methods proposed in such as instruction scheduling [28], NOP padding to reduce further the crosstalk interference.

Funding Statement. This work was supported by the Foundation Project of Philosophy and Social Science of Hunan (17YBA115, Sheng Xiao, 2018); Project of Hunan Social Science Achievement Evaluation Committee (XSP20YBZ090, Sheng Xiao, 2020).

References

1. Hemalatha, P., Dhanalakshmi, K.: Cellular automata based energy efficient approach for improving security in IoT. Intell. Autom. Soft Comput. **32**(2), 811–825 (2022)
2. Mahmoud, S., Salman, A.: Cost estimate and input energy of floor systems in low seismic regions. Comput. Mater. Continua **71**(2), 2159–2173 (2022)

3. Maharajan, M., Abirami, T.: Energy efficient QoS aware cluster based multihop routing protocol for WSN. Comput. Syst. Sci. Eng. **41**(3), 1173–1189 (2022)
4. Zaini, H.G.: Forecasting of appliances house in a low-energy depend on grey wolf optimizer. Comput. Mater. Continua **71**(2), 2303–2314 (2022)
5. Bamberg, L., Najafi, A., Garciaortiz, A.: Edge effect aware low-power crosstalk avoidance technique for 3D integration. Integration **69**(1), 98–110 (2019)
6. Chen, W., Lueh, G., Ashar, P.J., Chen, K., Cheng, B.: Register allocation for Intel processor graphics. In: Symposium on Code Generation and Optimization, pp. 352–364 (2018)
7. Cui, X., Ni, Y., Miao, M., Yufeng, J.: An enhancement of crosstalk avoidance code based on fibonacci numeral system for through silicon vias. IEEE Trans. Very Large Scale Integr. (VLSI) Syst. **25**(5), 1601–1610 (2017)
8. Duan, C., Calle, V.H.C., Khatri, S.P.: Efficient on-chip crosstalk avoidance codec design. IEEE Trans. Very Large Scale Integr. (VLSI) Syst. **17**(4), 551–560 (2009)
9. Florea, A., Geliert, A.: E-learning approach of the graph coloring problem applied to register allocation in embedded systems. In: The Sixth International Conference on Innovative Computing Technology (INTECH 2016), pp. 173–178 (2016)
10. Gupta, U., Ranganathan, N.: A utilitarian approach to variation aware delay, power, and crosstalk noise optimization. IEEE Educ. Activities Dept. **19**(9), 1723–1726 (2011)
11. Guthaus, M.R., Ringenberg, J., Ernst, D.J., Austin, T., Mudge, T., et al.: MiBench: a free, commercially representative embedded benchmark suite. In: The 4th Annual IEEE International Workshop on Workload Characterization (WWC 2001), pp. 3–14 (2001)
12. Halak, B., Yakovlev, A.: Throughput optimization for area-constrained links with crosstalk avoidance methods. IEEE Trans. Very Large Scale Integr. (VLSI) Syst. **18**(6), 1016–1019 (2010)
13. Jiao, H., Wang, R.R., He, Y.: Crosstalk-noise-aware bus coding with low-power ground-gated repeaters. Int. J. Circuit Theory Appl. **46**(2), 280–289 (2018)
14. Kananizadeh, S., Kononenko, K.: Improving on linear scan register allocation. Int. J. Autom. Comput. **15**(2), 228–238 (2018). https://doi.org/10.1007/s11633-017-1100-0
15. Kuo, W.A., Chiang, Y.L., Hwang, T.T., Wu, A.C.H.: Performance-driven crosstalk elimination at postcompiler level-the case of low-crosstalk op-code assignment. IEEE Trans. Comput. Aided Des. Integr. Circuits Syst. **26**(3), 564–573 (2007)
16. Liu, F., Yarom, Y., Ge, Q., Heiser, G., Lee, R.B.: Last-level cache side-channel attacks are practical. In: IEEE Symposium on Security and Privacy (SP), pp. 605–622 (2015)
17. Lozano, R.C., Carlsson, M., Blindell, G.H., Schulte, C.: Combinatorial register allocation and instruction scheduling. arXiv:1804.02452 (2018)
18. Lucas, A.H., Moraes, F.: Crosstalk fault tolerant NOC: design and evaluation. In: IFIP IEEE International Conference on Very Large Scale Integration, pp. 81–93 (2009)
19. Mangard, S., Oswald, E., Standaert, F.X.: One for all-all for one: unifying standard differential power analysis attacks. IET Inf. Secur. **5**(2), 100–110 (2011)
20. Moll, F., Roca, M., Isern, E.: Analysis of dissipation energy of switching digital CMOS gates with coupled outputs. Microelectron. J. **34**(9), 833–842 (2003)
21. Mutyam, M.: Selective shielding technique to eliminate crosstalk transitions. ACM Trans. Des. Autom. Electron. Syst. (TODAES) **14**(3), 1–43 (2009)
22. Odaira, R., Nakaike, T., Inagaki, T., Komatsu, H., Nakatani, T.: Coloring-based coalescing for graph coloring register allocation. In: IEEE/ACM International Symposium on Code Generation & Optimization, pp. 160–169 (2010)
23. Ohama, Y., Yotsuyanagi, H., Hashizume, M., Higami, Y., Takahashi, H.: On selection of adjacent lines in test pattern generation for delay faults considering crosstalk effects. In: International Symposium on Communications and Information Technologies, pp. 1–5 (2017)

24. Park, J., Xu, X., Jin, Y., Forte, D., Tehranipoor, M.: Power-based side-channel instruction-level disassembler. In: IEEE 2018 55th ACM/ESDA/IEEE Design Automation Conference (DAC), pp. 1–6 (2018)
25. Poletto, M., Sarkar, A.V.: Linear scan register allocation. ACM Trans. Program. Lang. Syst. (TOPLAS) 21(5), 895–913 (1999)
26. Shirmohammadi, Z., Mozafari, F., Miremadi, S.G.: An efficient numerical-based crosstalk avoidance codec design for NoCs. Microprocess. Microsyst. 50(1), 127–137 (2017)
27. Shirmohammadi, Z., Sabzi, H.Z.: DR: overhead efficient RLC crosstalk avoidance code. In: International Conference on Computer and Knowledge Engineering, pp. 1–6 (2018)
28. Su, X., Wu, H., Xue, J.: An efficient WCET-aware instruction scheduling and register Allocation approach for clustered VLIW processors. ACM Trans. Embed. Comput. Syst. 16(5), 1–21 (2017)

Review on Intelligent Processing Technologies of Legal Documents

Guolong Zhao[1], Yuling Liu[1(✉)], and E. Erdun[2]

[1] College of Computer Science and Electronic Engineering, Hunan University,
Changsha 410082, China
yuling_liu@126.com
[2] Amazon Services LLC, Seattle, USA

Abstract. Due to the imbalance between a large number of litigation cases and the number of judicial personnel, many legal documents to be processed greatly increase the burden of legal practitioners. So the intelligent processing of legal documents is especially important. At present, machine learning and deep learning have made great achievements in the intelligent processing of legal documents, including the elements extraction of legal documents, classification of legal documents, generation of legal documents, abstract extraction of legal documents etc. The main aim of this paper is to present a review of legal documents intelligent processing based on deep learning from legal documents representation, elements extraction of legal documents, classification of legal documents, automatic generation of legal documents.

Keywords: Deep learning · Intelligent justice · Legal documents representation · Elements extraction of legal documents · Classification of legal documents · Automatic generation of legal documents

1 Introduction

Legal documents are composed of litigation documents, arbitration documents, judgment documents and other legal contents related to law. Intelligent processing technology of legal documents refers to that the processing of legal documents can be completed efficiently with the support of natural language processing(NLP), deep learning and other technologies. At present, the research on legal documents processing has made some achievements in the extraction of elements of legal documents, the classification of legal documents etc., which can reduce legal practitioners participation and improve legal documents processing efficiency.

Lucien put forward an automatic retrieval model of legal documents and a judge discretion model in 1958, which was the first to apply information processing technology to the law domain. Buchanan published "Some Speculation About Artificial Intelligence and Legal Reasoning", which marked the birth of artificial intelligence and law as a research branch in 1970 [1]. Thorne applied rule-based reasoning to corporate tax text analysis. Carole Hafner proposed a method of legal text retrieval based on legal concepts

© The Author(s), under exclusive license to Springer Nature Switzerland AG 2022
X. Sun et al. (Eds.): ICAIS 2022, LNCS 13338, pp. 684–695, 2022.
https://doi.org/10.1007/978-3-031-06794-5_55

and relevance. From 1980s to 1990s, expert system began to be applied in the judicial field to help legal practitioners complete legal work by means of legal provisions-based method, case-based method and knowledge-based method [2–4]. However, these expert systems have many shortcomings, such as only suitable for limited fields and requiring a large number of expert handwriting rules. With the vigorous development of AI+ Law, the expert system disappear from the scene gradually. In recent years, the development of artificial intelligence in judicature is amazing. In order to accurately understand the information expressed in legal documents and make full use of the potential value in legal documents, research on legal documents intelligent processing has been emerging.

This paper introduces the legal documents representation which is the basis of legal documents intelligent processing in Sect. 2. Section 3 describes the elements extraction of elements of legal documents. Section 4 presents the classification of legal documents and Sect. 5 describes the automatic generation of legal documents. Finally, Sect. 6 presents conclusion and future research directions (Fig. 1).

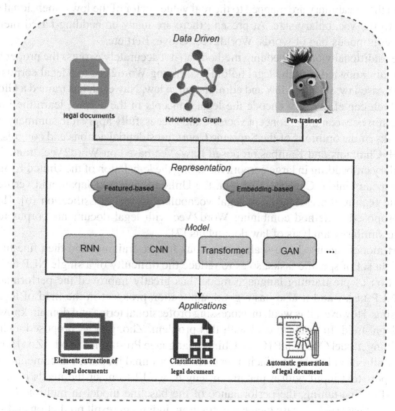

Fig. 1. An overview of intelligent processing technologies of legal documents.

2 Legal Documents Representation

The task of legal documents representation is to map unstructured legal documents data into low dimensional vector space, and then legal documents can be calculated and processed by mathematical methods. Compared with general domain texts, legal documents have the characteristics of strong domain, intensive information and relatively obvious structure. More effective legal documents representation technology can significantly improve the performance of downstream tasks, such as elements extraction of legal documents, classification of legal documents and automatic generation of legal documents etc. This section mainly introduces legal documents representation from embedding-based method and feature-based method.

2.1 Embedding-Based Method

Word embedding is a common method in text representation, which refers to that the words in the vocabulary are mapped to the real value vector of the low dimensional space related to the vocabulary size. At present, there are many embedding-based methods, such as continuous bag of words, World2vec, Glove, Bert etc.

The traditional word embedding method can not accurately express the proper nouns and domain knowledge in the legal field. By applying Word2Vec to a legal corpus composed of case law, statutory law and administrative law, Nay et al. has trained a Glo2Vec tool, which can effectively encode the legal concepts in the corpus, learn the implicit relationship between these concept vectors, and successfully apply it to summary generation tasks of the opinions of the Supreme Court, presidential actions and congressional bills [5]. Chalkidis and Kampas proposed Law2Vec based on Word2Vec, trained legal vocabulary embedding in large corpora including the legislation of the United Kingdom, the European Union, Canada, Australia, the United States and Japan, and verified the semantic feature representation of legal vocabulary in text classification [6]. He, Xia et al. proposed a method combining Word2Vec with legal documents corpus to deal with the similarity analysis of law documents [7].

Bert model can use large-scale text corpus for pre-training, and then fine tune the small data set of specific tasks, so as to reduce the difficulty of a single NLP task. The application of pre-training language model has greatly improved the performance of many NLP tasks, and it also has a good application prospect in the field of legal text processing. However, it is weak in expressing professional terms and domain knowledge in the legal field. In order to deal with this problem, Zhong et al. proposed a Chinese pre-training model OpenClaP (Open Chinese language Pre-trained Model Zoo) based on tens of millions of legal texts (including civil and criminal judgment documents), which can support text input with a maximum length of 512 to meet the needs of multiple tasks. After fine-tuning, the performance of the baseline model in multiple legal text processing tasks such as case element extraction, judgment result prediction and similar case matching is effectively improved [8]. Chalkidis et al. applied BERT to the processing of legal text and release LEGAL-BERT which is trained by specialized legal domain corpora. Besides, they proposed a broader hyper-parameter search space when fine-tuning for downstream legal tasks. LEGAL-BERT has better performance on legal task than normal BERT [9].

2.2 Feature-based Method

With neural network, embedding-based method can well mine the potential semantics in legal documents, however, the text vector generated by this method is often difficult to explain. Traditional feature engineering methods need manual annotation, which is obviously impractical for large-scale legal corpus processing. Feature-based method combine the two methods mentioned above, which uses a certain amount of domain knowledge to define the feature pattern of legal text representation, and then uses neural network model to learn and represent these features.

According to the definition of theft in China's criminal law, Li et al. summed up 9 dimensional characteristics related to conviction and sentencing (including suspect's basic information, whether recidivism, whether to carry weapons, value of goods involved), and encoded the legal texts by using long short-term memory network. Then, according to the generated vector representation, the classification algorithm was used to judge whether it conforms to a feature, and then the 9-dimensional vector representation for the legal text was obtained. While reducing the dimension of the feature, the feature had good interpretability under the framework of legal knowledge [10]. Li et al. proposed a legal text representation model based on attention mechanism to deal with the prediction of judgment results. Through training in the corpus of judgment documents involving 10 types of criminal charges, they generated latent semantic feature representation vectors based on case facts, defendant information and relevant criminal law provisions, which could represent people and events. This method greatly improved the performance of prediction tasks such as crime, legal provisions and sentence and the interpretability of prediction results [11].

3   Elements Extraction of Legal Documents

Legal documents contain important information such as plaintiff, defendant, litigation content, defense content, legal parties and date. Correctly extracting the element information in legal documents is conducive to the research of legal documents processing. At present, the element extraction of legal documents is mainly the extraction of entities in legal documents, which is often processed by named entity recognition. Deep learning model represented by neural network can effectively model context information and improve the model's ability to understand text. This section mainly introduces elements extraction of legal documents based on deep learning.

Bi-LSTM-CRF is a model commonly used in named entity recognition and many researcher applied this model to elements extraction of legal documents. For example, Zou used Bi-LSTM combined with CRF to identify legal entities and build a map of legal knowledge [12]. Xie combined gating network structure with LSTM to identify segment level legal entities [13]. Chalkidis used Bi-LSTM model to complete the task of contract element extraction without relying on manual annotation [14]. Li et al. competed a task of event extraction for Chinese criminal legal text with the help of Bi-LSTM-CRF and BERT. They firstly used BERT to pre-train word vectors which is the input of the Bi-LSTM-CRF model to extract even information of larceny case, and then visualized the result of the first step in chronological order [15]. Wang et al. used LSTM to recognize entities in legal documents. In addition, a global objective function was defined to obtain the recognition results and globally optimize through constraints, i.e., label transition, entity length, label consistency and domain-specific regulation constrains. The experimental results showed that this method can obtain better entity recognition results in text level legal documents [16].

Wang divided legal elements into three categories: basic elements, characteristic elements and core elements. Different algorithms were used to extract different legal elements. Iterative rules were used to extract basic elements with relatively stable location and quantity, and conditional random fields were used to extract feature elements with uncertain location and description. The combination of semantic feature classification model and linear annotation model was used to extract the core elements of strong semantic information [17].

Jiang introduced ensemble learning to named entity recognition. Through this method, model performance was improved to some extent, which contributed to that the problems of limited training corpus and high recognition performance requirements were solved effectively in the process of building property knowledge base of criminal cases [18]. Besides, there are some Hybrid methods to extract elements of legal documents, for example, Samarawickrama used Co-reference Resolution and Named Entity Recognition to identify legal parties [19]. Almeida et al. combined existing annotators with sequence to sequence learning to extract legal parties in legal documents which can make good outcome in experiment [20].

4 Classification of Legal Documents

The classification of legal documents is an important task in the research of legal documents processing. At present, the classification of legal documents mainly solves the following three classification problems. The first is a two classification problem to judge whether the defendant has surrendered. The second is a multi classification problem that the defendant's main crime is determined by the case description. The third is multi-label classification problem, which is to analyze the litigation and defense contents in the judgment documents, and identify the focus of controversy (identified on the basis of manually generated dispute focus system).

The existing text classification methods include rule-based classification, machine learning based text classification and deep learning model based text classification. Rule-based classification method is that experts in a certain field write classification rules according to their actual experience to help the classifier complete the classification task. This method only has certain advantages in a specific field, and thus the classification effect and the scope of use is seriously limited. From 1960s to 2010, the text classification models based on machine learning were dominated, which is composed of text prepossessing, feature extraction, text representation and classifier. The traditional machine learning methods generate high latitude and sparse text representation, and the ability of text feature expression is weak. Since the 1990s, text classification has gradually changed from machine learning model to deep learning model. The deep learning model represented by neural network has strong feature learning ability, and does not need manual intervention and prior knowledge, which can automatically extract important features of text [21]. Wu et al. summarized the current text classification methods based on deep learning and showed the powerful classification performance of deep learning [22]. The development of deep learning model in text classification is shown in Fig. 2. According to the model architecture, classification of legal documents model can be divided into the four categories: RNN-Based Models, CNN-Based Models, Models with Bert and Hybrid Models.

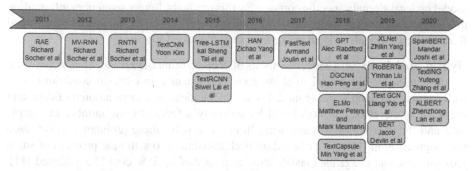

Fig. 2. Development of text classification based on deep learning.

RNN-Based Models. Benjamin et al. proposed LegalLMFiT, an LSTM-Based model, which can reach excellent performance on classification of short legal text and need less computational costs and pre-training data than transformer-based model [23]. Li et al. proposed a method for Chinese legal documents classification which combines Graph LSTM and domain Knowledge extraction. This method can not only capture legal background knowledge, but also understand the special structure of legal documents with the help of experts in legal field [24].

CNN-Based Models. CNN-Based Models firstly map the text into a vector, then uses multiple filters to capture the local semantic information of the text, and then uses max-pooling or average-pooling to capture the most important features. These features are input into the full connection layer to obtain the probability distribution of the label. Wu et al. used TextCNN and deep convolution neural network model to extract high-dimensional features, and used pooling for dimension reduction, which not only reduced the amount of calculation, but also ensured higher classification accuracy compared with the traditional relative entropy classification algorithms [25]. Wei et al. used CNN to predict predictive coding which has been widely used in legal affairs to find relevant or privileged files in large electronic storage information sets. They proved that compared with SVM, CNN has better performance on legal data through legal documents classification experiments [26]. French legal texts are rich in morphology and flexible word order. The current CNN model have trained on English or Chinese legal documents, but it is difficult to capture the hidden semantics in French legal texts. So Hammami et al. proposed a dynamic convolutional neural network which allows the input length for French legal to be variable. Compared with the original model with a fixed input length, dynamic convolutional neural network had a higher classification accuracy of legal text [27].

Models with Bert. The emergence of Bert [28] has become an important turning point in the development of NLP. Ashutosh et al. used Bert model to fine tune the text classification task, and achieved better classification effect than previous models in text classification prediction [29]. Although Bert based model has good performance in text classification task, these model fails to deal with longer legal documents. Purbid et al. proposed a new model which combines "long" attention with DistilBERT, and pre-train model on legal-domain specific corpora. By this methods, longer sequences information in legal documents can be captured which makes the proposed model overtake fine-tuned Bert and other models in legal documents classification [30].

Hybrid Models. Hybrid Models consists of deep learning model and other technology, which can enable the model to show good performance in extreme conditions. It is well-known that deep learning model is very dependent on a large amount of data, and the training effect of the model will be seriously affected by the number of sample data and the distribution of categories. In order to solve these problems, Ni etc. used text augmentation technology based on back translation to settle the problem of small judicial data, and the crime classification accuracy of 90.35% could be achieved [31]. Yin et al. used Relation Network and Induction Network algorithms based on few-shot learning to handle controversial issues classification in legal documents. In multi-label classification tasks, it is very challenging to classify datasets with thousands of labels [32]. Zein et al. combined transformer-based model with generative pre-training and discriminative learning rates etc., which can make good results of 0.661(F1) for JRC-Acquis and 0.754 for EURLEX57K, even with the lack of labeled data [33].

Table 1. Comparison between classification models on EURLEX57X and JRC-ACQUIS.

Model	EURLEX57k		JRC-ACQUIS	
	nDCG@5	Micro-F1	nDCG@5	Micro-F1
LegalLMFiT	0.729	N/A	N/A	N/A
DistilBERT	**0.833**	**0.754**	0.75	0.652
BERT	0.828	0.751	0.750	**0.661**
AWD-LSTM	N/A	N/A	0.594	0.493

We compared the performance of existing classification models in JRC-ACQUIS [34] and EURLEX57X [35] datasets (see Table 1), and used two evaluation metrics: nDCG@K and Micro-F1. nDCG@ is normalized discounted cumulative gain which aims to measure ranking quality for the list of top K ranked labels.

$$nDCG@K = \frac{1}{N}\sum_{n=1}^{N} Z_{k_n}\sum_{k=1}^{K} \frac{2^{Rel(n,k)} - 1}{log_2(1 + k)} \qquad (1)$$

Micro F1 is the F1 value obtained from the total precision and recall of all categories.

$$Precision = \frac{True\ Postives}{True\ Postives + False\ Postives} \qquad (2)$$

$$Recall = \frac{True\ Positives}{True\ Postives + False\ Negatives} \tag{3}$$

$$F1 = 2 * \frac{Precision * Recall}{Precision + Recall} \tag{4}$$

5 Automatic Generation of Legal Documents

At present, the shortage of human resources in the legal service industry has greatly affected the efficiency of judicial services. Automatic generation of legal documents is an important research direction in the field of legal documents intelligent processing. The generation model based on deep learning has gradually become the preferred tool for text generation research. Text generation models are mainly divided into the following three categories:

RNN-Based Models. In text sequence processing, RNN models are prone to gradient disappearance and gradient explosion. Hochreiter et al. proposed the LSTM model which is a variant of RNN model. It can effectively solve the problem of long-term dependence in text sequences [36]. Alschner and Skougarevskiy proposed an novel framework for RNN-Based text generation that prior knowledge were introduced into the model during the training phase and then q-gram distance and GloVe were used as filters to draw the generated legal text closer to target. By this way, they successfully generated a legal text in the field of international investment law [37].

Transformer-Based Models. With the popularity of transformer model, natural language generation (NLG) model has gradually turned to Transformer. At present, the output of many NLG models has good readability. In a broad sense, NLG tasks belong to sequence to sequence, in which the standard architecture is the encoder decoder mode. Tran et al. proposed an encoder decoder framework to deal with the generation of sequence to sequence [38]. Park et al. proposed an encoder decoder model based on LSTM, which improved the generation effect from sequence to sequence [39]. Hai et al. used charge labels to promote the generation of charge-discriminative rationales in court views and proposed a label-conditioned Seq2Seq model with attention. A large number of experiments had proved the effectiveness of the model [40]. Peric et al. applied Transformer-XL [42] to generate judicial opinions automatically. Legal documents are much longer than normal text and involve multiple documents. Transformer-XL consists of a segment-level recurrence mechanism and a relative positional encoding scheme, which is very suitable for generation of legal documents and performs better in generation of judicial opinions than GPT-2 [41]. Legal documents have higher requirements for logical rationality than ordinary texts, so Huang Weijing et al. proposed CoLMQA which can generate reasonable legal documents. It consists of Language Modeling and Transformer-based Key-Value Memory Networks. They used Language Modeling to generate texts with slots which is divided into 7 categories: [NAME], [DATE], [MONEY], [ADDRESS], [NUMBER], [LAW], [ARTICLE_NUMBER] and then used Transformer-based Key-Value Memory Networks to fill the slots with the support of

Legal Knowledge Base. Experiments showed that this method can generate correct and reasonable legal documents [43]. Besides the standard encoder decoder mode, GPT structure [44] and UniLM structure [45] can be used for NLG tasks. GPT training is divided into two stages: unsupervised pre-training language model and fine-tuning of each task. The GPT model uses transformer network instead of LSTM as language model to better capture long-distance language structure.

GAN-Based Models. The Generative Adversarial Network (GAN) consists of two modules: generative model and discriminant model. Its goal is to train a generation model to perfectly fit the real data distribution, so that the discrimination model cannot be distinguished [46]. GAN originally used for image generation is applied to text generation, which can effectively solve the problem of cumbersome parameter training [47, 48]. However, there are many problems in applying GAN to text, such as convergence and discrete data processing. In order to solve these problems, Zhang et al. introduced an approach for text generation with GAN, TextGAN, which had better performance of text generation than existing methods [49]. Guo proposed a LeakGAN model. The discriminator can leak some extracted features to the generator in the middle time step. The generator used this additional information to guide the generation of sequences and effectively solve the problem of long text generation [50].

6 Conclusions

Aiming at legal documents intelligent processing, this paper mainly introduced the research progress and achievements of four parts: legal documents representation, the elements extraction of legal documents, classification of legal documents and automatic generation of legal documents. Besides, there are many other tasks like abstract extraction of legal documents and legal question-answering. Although great progress has been made in the research of legal documents intelligent processing, there are many challenges to be addressed in the legal domain.

In the future, we can apply few-shot or zero-shot method to intelligent processing technologies of legal documents for lack of datasets or no datasets. There are many forms of legal problems, such as audio, text, image, etc. we can also introduce multi-modal methods like Katamesh et al. [51]. Furthermore, we need to attach much weight to the ethical issues like gender bias and racial discrimination. The results produced by intelligent processing technologies of legal documents should be ethical. It is difficult to avoid ethical issues only by relying on intelligent processing technologies. To note that, the model plays an auxiliary role in legal documents processing. Besides, there are relatively few studies on automatic generation of legal documents. There is still a lot of research space on the rationality and correctness of the legal documents generated by generation models.

References

1. Buchanan, B.G., Headrick, T.E.: Some speculation about artificial intelligence and legal reasoning. Stanford Law Rev. **23**(1), 40–62 (1970)

2. Deedman, C., Smith, J.C.: The nervous shock adviser: a legal expert system in case- based law. In: Operational Expert Systems Applications in Canada, pp. 56–71 (1991)

3. Bench-Capon, T.: Knowledge based systems applied to law: a framework for discussion. In: Knowledge Based Systems and Legal Applications, pp. 329–342 (1991)

4. Hafner, C.D., Berman, D.H.: The role of context in case-based legal reasoning: teleological, temporal, and procedural. In: Artificial Intelligence and Law, vol. 10, pp. 19–64 (2002)

5. Nay, J.J.: Gov2vec: learning distributed representations of institutions and their legal texts. arXiv:1609.06616 (2016)

6. Chalkidis, I., Kampas, D.: Deep learning in law: early adaptation and legal word embeddings trained on large corpora. Artif. Intel. Law **27**(2), 171–198 (2018)

7. Xia, C., He, T., Li, W.: Similarity analysis of law documents based on Word2vec. In: 2019 IEEE 19th International Conference on Software Quality, Reliability and Security Companion (QRS-C), pp. 354–357 (2019)

8. Zhong, H., Zhang, Z., Liu, Z., et al.: Open Chinese language pre-trained model zoo. In: Technical report (2019)

9. Chalkidis, I., Fergadiotis, M., Malakasiotis, P., et al.: LEGAL-BERT: The muppets straight out of law school. arXiv:2010.02559 (2020)

10. Li, S., Zhang, H., Ye, L.: Evaluating the rationality of judicial decision with LSTM-based case modeling. In: 2018 IEEE Third International Conference on Data Science in Cyberspace (DSC), pp. 392–397 (2018)

11. Li, S., Zhang, H., Ye, L.: MANN: a multichannel attentive neural network for legal judgment prediction. IEEE Access **7**, 151144–151155 (2019)

12. Zou, A.: Construction of knowledge graph based on law. In: University of Electronic Science and Technology of China (2019)

13. Xie, Y.: Research on named entity recognition for Chinese legal texts. In: Nanjing Normal University (2018)

14. Chalkidis, I., Androutsopoulos, I.: A deep learning approach to contract element extraction. JURIX **2017**, 155–164 (2017)

15. Li, Q., Zhang, Q., Yao, J.: Event extraction for criminal legal text. In: 2020 IEEE International Conference on Knowledge Graph (ICKG), pp. 573–580 (2020)

16. Wang, L.: Research on Chinese named entity recognition for legal documents. Soochow University (2018)

17. Wang, L.: Study and implementation of extraction of legal elements in judicial documents. In: Southeast University (2018)

18. Jiang, Z.: The application of ensemble learning on named entity recognition for legal knowledgebase of properties involved in criminal cases. In: 2020 IEEE International Conference on Advances in Electrical Engineering and Computer Applications (AEECA), pp. 701–705 (2020)

19. Samarawickrama, C., Almeida, M.D., Silva, D.N.: Party identification of legal documents using co-reference resolution and named entity recognition. In: 2020 IEEE 15th International Conference on Industrial and Information Systems (ICIIS), pp. 494–499 (2020)

20. Almeida, M.D., Samarawickrama, C., Silva, N.D.: Legal party extraction from legal opinion text with sequence to sequence learning. In: 2020 20th International Conference on Advances in ICT for Emerging Regions (ICTer), pp. 143–148 (2020)

21. Mustajar, H., Ge, S.A., Haider, M., Irshad, S.M.: Noman: a quantum spatial graph convolutional network for text classification. Comput. Syst. Sci. Eng. **36**(2), 369–382 (2021)

22. Wu, H.P., Liu, Y.L., Wang, J.W.: Review of text classification methods on deep learning. Comput. Mater. Continua **63**(3), 1309–1321 (2020)

23. Clavié, B., Gheewala, A., Briton, P., et al.: LegaLMFiT: efficient short legal text classification with LSTM language model pre-training. arXiv:2109.00993 (2021)

24. Li, G., Wang, Z., Ma, Y.: Combining domain knowledge extraction with graph long short-term memory for learning classification of Chinese legal documents. IEEE Access **7**, 139616–139627 (2017)
25. Suyan, W., Entong, S., Binyang, L.: TextCNN-based Text Classification for E-government. In: 2019 6th International Conference on Information Science and Control Engineering (ICISCE), pp. 929–934 (2019)
26. Wei, F., Qin, H., Ye, S.: Empirical study of deep learning for text classification in legal document review. In: 2018 IEEE International Conference on Big Data (Big Data), pp. 3317–3320 (2018)
27. Hammami, E., Faiz, R., Akermi, I.: A dynamic convolutional neural network approach for legal text classification. In: Saad, I., Rosenthal-Sabroux, C., Gargouri, F., Arduin, P.-E. (eds.) ICIKS 2021. LNBIP, vol. 425, pp. 71–84. Springer, Cham (2021). https://doi.org/10.1007/978-3-030-85977-0_6
28. Devlin, J., Chang, M.W., Lee, K.: Bert: pre-training of deep bidirectional transformers for language understanding. arXiv:1810.04805 (2018)
29. Adhikari, A., Ram, A., Tang, R., et al.: Docbert: bert for document classification. arXiv:1904.08398 (2019)
30. Bambroo, P., Awasthi, A.: LegalDB: long distilbert for legal document classification. In: 2021 International Conference on Advances in Electrical, Computing, Communication and Sustainable Technologies (ICAECT), vol. **2021**, pp. 1–4 (2021)
31. Qing N., Cong, Y., Dong, Z.: Research on small sample text classification based on attribute extraction and data augmentation. In: 2021 IEEE 6th International Conference on Cloud Computing and Big Data Analytics (ICCCBDA), pp. 53–57. IEEE (2021)
32. Fang, Y., Tian, X., Wu, H., et al.: Few-shot learning for Chinese legal controversial issues classification. IEEE Access **8**, 75022–75034 (2020)
33. Shaheen, Z., Wohlgenannt, G., Filtz, E.: Large scale legal text classification using transformer models. arXiv:2010.12871 (2020)
34. JRC-Acquis (2020). https://ec.europa.eu/jrc/en/language-technologies/jrc-acquis
35. EURLEX57K dataset (2020). http://nlp.cs.aueb.gr/softwareanddatasets/EURLEX57K/
36. Hochreiter, S., Schmidhuber, J.: Long short-term memory. Neural Comput. **9**, 1735–1780 (1997)
37. Alschner, W., Skougarevskiy, D.: Towards an automated production of legal texts using recurrent neural networks. In: Proceedings of the 16th Edition of the International Conference on Articial Intelligence and Law, pp. 229–232 (2017)
38. Tran, V.K., Nguyen, L.M.: Natural language generation for spoken dialogue system using RNN encoder-decoder networks. arXiv:1706.00139 (2017)
39. Park, S.H., Kim, B.D., Kang, C.M.: Sequence-to-sequence prediction of vehicle trajectory via LSTM encoder-decoder architecture. In: 2018 IEEE Intelligent Vehicles Symposium (IV), pp. 1672–1678. IEEE (2018)
40. Ye, H., Jiang, X., Luo, Z., et al.: Interpretable charge predictions for criminal cases: learning to generate court views from fact descriptions. arXiv:1802.08504 (2018)
41. Peric, L., Mijic, S., Stammbach, D.: Legal language modeling with transformers. CEUR Workshop Proc. CEUR-WS **2020**, 2764 (2020)
42. Dai, Z., Yang, Z., Yang, Y.: Transformer-xl: Attentive language models beyond a fixed-length context. arXiv:1901.02860 (2019)
43. Huang, W., Liao, X., Xie, Z.: Generating reasonable legal text through the combination of language modeling and question answering. In: Proceedings of the Twenty-Ninth International Conference on International Joint Conferences on Artificial Intelligence, vol. 2021, pp. 3687–3693 (2021)
44. Radford, A., Narasimhan, K., Salimans, T., et al.: Improving language understanding by generative pre-training (2018)

45. Dong, L., Yang, N., Wang, W., et al.: Unified language model pre-training for natural language understanding and generation. arXiv:1905.03197 (2019)
46. Goodfellow, I., Pouget-Abadie, J., Mirza, M., et al.: Generative adversarial nets. In: Advances in Neural Information Processing Systems (2014)
47. Wang, C.L., Liu, Y.L., Tong, Y.J., Wang, J.W.: GAN-GLS: generative lyric steganography based on generative adversarial network. Comput. Mater. Continua **69**(1), 1375–1390 (2021)
48. Cheng, J., Yang, Y., Tang, X., Xiong, N., Zhang, Y., Lei, F.: Generative adversarial networks: a literature review. KSII Trans. Internet Inf. Syst. **14**(12), 4625–4647 (2020)
49. Zhang, Y., Gan, Z., Fan, K.: Adversarial feature matching for text generation. In: International Conference on Machine Learning, pp. 4006–4015. PMLR (2017)
50. Guo, J., Lu, S., Cai, H.: Long text generation via adversarial training with leaked information. In: Proceedings of the AAAI Conference on Artificial Intelligence (2018)
51. Katamesh, O., Abu-Elnasr, S.: Elmougy: deep learning multimodal for unstructured and semi-structured textual documents classification. Comput. Mater. Continua **68**, 589–606 (2021)

Author Index

Printed in the United States
by Baker & Taylor Publisher Services